Solaris 9: Sun Certified Systen
Study Guide

MW00844690

Exam CX-310-015

SYBEX

OBJECTIVE	CHAPTER

Set Up Naming Services (*continued*)

Explain the purpose, features and functions of NIS namespace information, domains and daemons.	15
Explain how to configure the name service switch for different lookups and configure a NIS domain using the required maps, files, commands and scripts.	15
Explain how to build custom NIS maps.	15

Perform Advanced Installation Procedures

Explain the purpose, features and functionality of Jumpstart, including boot services, identification services, configuration services and installation services.	16
Given a scenario, explain the procedures, scripts and commands to implement a Jumpstart server.	16
Given a scenario describing Jumpstart configuration alternatives, explain how to establish a boot-only server, identification service alternatives, configuration service alternatives and installation service alternatives.	16
Given scenarios involving Jumpstart problems with booting, identification, configuration, install or begin/finish scripts, analyze and select a course of action to resolve the problem.	16
Explain how to use the Flash installation feature and describe requirements and limitations of this feature.	16
Explain how to create and use a Flash archive and how to use a Flash archive for installation with Webstart, interactive install and Jumpstart.	16

Exam objectives are subject to change at any time without prior notice and at Sun's sole discretion. Please visit Sun's website (http://training.sun.com/US/certification/solaris/certification_details.html#0E9) for the most current listing of exam objectives.

SYBEX

Solaris 9:
Sun Certified System Administrator
Study Guide

Solaris 9™:
Sun® Certified System Administrator
Study Guide

Quentin Docter

San Francisco • London

Associate Publisher: Neil Edde
Acquisitions Editor: Elizabeth Hurley Peterson
Developmental Editor: Colleen Wheeler Strand
Editor: Sharon Wilkey
Production Editor: Elizabeth Campbell
Technical Editor: Patrick Born
Book Designer: Bill Gibson
Graphic Illustrator: Tony Jonick
Electronic Publishing Specialist: Interactive Composition Corporation
Proofreaders: Emily Hsuan, Eric Lach, Nancy Riddiough, Sarah Tannehill, Monique van den Berg
Indexer: Nancy Guenther
CD Coordinator: Dan Mummert
CD Technician: Kevin Ly
Cover Designer: Archer Design
Cover Photographer: John Wang, PhotoDisc

Library of Congress Card Number: 2002113842

ISBN: 0-7821-4181-1

SYBEX

To Our Valued Readers:

Thank you for looking to Sybex for your Solaris 9 exam prep needs. We at Sybex are proud of the reputation we've established for providing certification candidates with the practical knowledge and skills they need to succeed in the highly competitive IT marketplace.

Sun developed the Sun Certified System Administrator for the Solaris 9 Operating Environment certification for administrators tasked with performing essential procedures on the Solaris OE and technical support staff responsible for administering a networked server running on the Solaris OE. CertCities.com recently included this certification in its list of the "10 Hottest Certifications for 2003."

This *Solaris 9: Sun Certified System Administrator Study Guide* was developed to help you optimize learning and retention of topics you can expect to be tested on, both in the exams and in real life. It has always been Sybex's mission to teach individuals how to utilize technologies in the real world, not to simply feed them answers to test questions. Just as Sun is committed to establishing measurable standards for professionals who work with the Solaris operating environment, Sybex is committed to providing those professionals with the means of acquiring the skills and knowledge they need to meet those standards.

The Sybex team of authors, editors, and technical reviewers has worked hard to ensure that this Study Guide is comprehensive, in-depth, and pedagogically sound. We're confident that this book, along with the collection of cutting-edge software study tools included on the CD, will meet and exceed the demanding standards of the certification marketplace and help you, the Solaris 9 SCSA exam candidate, succeed in your endeavors.

Good luck in pursuit of your Solaris 9 certification!

Neil Edde
Associate Publisher—Certification
Sybex, Inc.

To Kara, Abbie, and Lauren.

Acknowledgments

Ask anyone who's written a book, and they'll tell you that it's a huge undertaking. I agree. I wouldn't have gotten through this process without the unconditional and unwavering love and support from my wife Kara. So, deservedly, she gets first billing.

The crew at Sybex, as always, has been great to work with. Neil Edde, Elizabeth Hurley Peterson, Colleen Strand, Heather O'Connor, Study Guide Expert Elizabeth Campbell, Sharon Wilkey, Patrick Born, and Gareth Bromley all contributed a great deal toward making this book a success. Thanks also to the proofreaders Emily Hsuan, Eric Lach, Nancy Riddiough, Sarah Tannehill, and Monique van den Berg.

On the personal side, I want to thank Doc and Sue and Mike and Marsha for being wonderfully supportive grandparents to Abbie and Lauren, as well as being there for us. Joe Hohlfled, thank you for helping cultivate my interest in computers, golf, and chess, as well as teaching me so many important lessons about life. To my friends, Rob and Amy, Scott and Robyn, and Eron and Lisa, thanks for providing sanity or helping detract from my sanity at just the right times. To all of my students, both past and present, thanks for asking the tough questions and making me think. And finally, to Lee Rittenour, thank you for sharing your incredible talents and passion for music with the rest of us.

Contents at a Glance

Contents

Part II   **Solaris 9 Sun Certified System Administrator**   **295**

Chapter 10   **The Solaris Networking Environment**   **297**

Chapter 11   **Virtual File Systems and NFS**   **325**

Introduction

There is high demand for professionals in the information technology (IT) industry, and because Solaris is the most widely used UNIX implementation in the world, Solaris certifications are very worthwhile to obtain. You have made the right decision to pursue certification, because being Solaris certified will give you a distinct advantage in this highly competitive market.

Solaris 9 is Sun Microsystems' latest version of their popular UNIX-based operating environment. Sun's first operating system was released as SunOS in 1983, based on BSD UNIX. Throughout the years, SunOS went through many transformations, most recently with the release of Solaris 9 in 2002.

Sun Microsystems is known for their innovative and reliable hardware (namely the SPARC processor) as well as their Solaris operating environment. Because of their large and loyal user base, and their willingness to take calculated chances to remain on top, Sun is poised to remain an industry leader for years to come.

This book is intended to help you on your exciting path toward becoming a Sun Certified System Administrator for the Solaris 9 Operating Environment. Basic knowledge of Solaris is an advantage when reading this book but is not mandatory. Using this book and the Solaris operating environment, you can start learning Solaris and pass the CX-310-014: Sun Certified System Administrator for the Solaris 9 Operating Environment, Part I, and the CX-310-015: Sun Certified System Administrator for the Solaris 9 Operating Environment, Part II, exams.

Why Become a Sun Certified System Administrator?

The number one reason to become an SCSA is to gain more visibility and greater access to some of the industry's most challenging opportunities. Solaris certification is the best way to demonstrate your knowledge and skills in the Solaris operating environment. The certification tests are a combination of multiple choice, matching, and fill-in-the-blank questions. They test your knowledge of Solaris commands and components, as well as your understanding of system administration principles.

Certification is proof of your knowledge and shows that you have the skills required to support Solaris. Sun Microsystems' certification program can help a company to identify proven performers who have demonstrated their skills and who can support the company's investment in both Sun Microsystems' hardware and software. It demonstrates that you have a solid understanding of your job role and the Sun products used in that role.

SCSAs are highly respected and well paid in the IT industry. Although there might be a significant number of IT professionals certified in other network operating systems, Solaris-certified and other UNIX-certified professionals are still in very high demand.

So, whether you are beginning a career, changing careers, securing your present position, or seeking to refine and promote your position, this book is for you!

Sun Microsystems Certifications

Sun Microsystems offers a variety of certifications to help you demonstrate your expertise in several functional areas. There are currently four certification areas: Solaris Operating Environment, Java Technology, Sun ONE Middleware, and Network Storage. Representatives from Sun Microsystems have announced plans for a security certification to be released in 2003.

For the latest certification information, visit the Sun certification page at `http://suned.sun.com/US/certification/`.

Solaris Operating Environment

The Solaris operating environment is the premier UNIX-based network operating environment available in the world today. Many companies swear by Sun hardware and software, because of their high reliability, availability, security, and scalability. Sun is committed to meeting today's networking demands, while anticipating tomorrow's innovations.

Sun offers two certification tracks for the Solaris operating environment: Sun Certified System Administrator and Sun Certified Network Administrator. Both of these tracks are currently offered for the Solaris 7, Solaris 8, and Solaris 9 Operating Environments. Because this book focuses on Solaris 9, detailed information will be provided for only this track. Attaining certifications in Solaris 7 and Solaris 8 is a very similar process to that of Solaris 9.

The Sun Certified System Administrator certification is for system administrators who perform system administration functions on Solaris client and server computers. In order to become certified as a Sun Certified System Administrator in Solaris 9, you must pass two exams:

- Sun Certified System Administrator for the Solaris 9 Operating Environment, Part I (CX-310-014)

- Sun Certified System Administrator for the Solaris 9 Operating Environment, Part II (CX-310-015)

Most people find the Part II exam to be more difficult, and it's possible to see questions from Part I objectives on the Part II test. If you are already certified as a system administrator for a previous version of the Solaris operating environment, you can take an upgrade exam instead of the two exams:

- Sun Certified System Administrator for the Solaris 9 Operating Environment Upgrade Exam (CX-310-016)

The Sun Certified Network Administrator exam is for individuals who are or will be responsible for managing Sun computers in a networked environment. To become a Sun Certified Network Administrator, you must first become a Sun Certified System Administrator. After you have attained that status, you need only one more exam to become a Network Administrator:

- Sun Certified Network Administrator for the Solaris 9 Operating Environment (CX-310-044)

At the `http://suned.sun.com/US/certification/solaris/sysadmin.html` website, there are free sample exams, as well as full-length practice exams available for purchase.

Java Technology

Java technology has taken the computer industry by storm and appears poised to remain a force for quite some time. If you're a Java developer, you should consider obtaining a Java certification. Sun offers four Java certifications:

- Sun Certified Programmer for the Java 2 Platform
- Sun Certified Developer for the Java 2 Platform
- Sun Certified Web Component Developer for the Java 2 Platform, Enterprise Edition (J2EE)
- Sun Certified Enterprise Architect for J2EE Technology.

For more information, go to `http://suned.sun.com/US/certification/java/index.html` and choose the certification you are interested in.

Sun ONE Middleware

Sun Open Net Environment (ONE) is Sun's software for building and deploying Services on Demand. Because of its scalability and reliability, it has a place in current traditional software settings as well as advanced web-based applications.

Sun provides both developer and engineer certifications for Sun ONE:

- Sun Certified Developer for Sun ONE Application Server 6.0
- Sun Certified Engineer for Sun ONE Directory Server 5.x

For more information, see `http://suned.sun.com/US/certification/middleware/index.html` and choose the certification you are interested in.

Network Storage

For IT professionals who have extensive storage management needs, such as those who use VERITAS Volume Manager, VERITAS Backup, Solstice DiskSuite, or Solstice Backup, Sun offers three storage technology certifications:

- Sun Certified Data Management Engineer
- Sun Certified Backup and Recovery Engineer
- Sun Certified Storage Architect

For more information, go to `http://suned.sun.com/US/certification/storage/index.html` and choose the certification you are interested in.

More Information

The most current information about Sun certifications can be found at `http://suned.sun.com/US/certification/`. Follow the Certification link and choose the certification path that you are interested in. Test objectives are available on the website, and keep in mind that they can change at any time without notice.

Skills Required for SCSA Certification

To pass the Part I certification exam, you need to master the following skill areas:

- Managing file systems
- Installing software

- Performing system boot procedures
- Performing user and security administration
- Managing network printers and system processes
- Performing system backups and restores

To pass the Part II certification exam, you need to master the following skill areas:

- Describing network basics
- Managing virtual file systems and core dumps
- Managing storage volumes
- Controlling access and configuring system messaging
- Setting up naming services
- Performing advanced installation procedures

The complete list of specific objectives is on the tear-out card included at the front of this book. At the beginning of each chapter, you'll also see a list of which objectives will be covered. It's quite a laundry list of things to know. But this book is here to help you.

NOTE   Exam objectives are subject to change at any time and without prior notice at Sun's discretion, so be sure to check the website (`http://suned.sun.com/US/ certification/objectives/index.html`) for the most up-to-date objective list.

Sun Certified System Administr

Tips for Taking the SCSA Exams

Use the following tips to help you prepare for and pass each exam.

- You do not need to complete both tests in one sitting. Even if you are prepared to take both exams, it's usually best to take them on separate days so you are fresh for each exam.
- The Part I exam has 57 questions, and the Part II exam has 58 questions. You will have 105 minutes to complete each test. Plan accordingly so that you do not run out of time.
- Many questions on the exam have answer choices that at first glance look identical. Read the questions carefully. Do not just jump to conclusions. Make sure that you clearly understand exactly what each question asks.
- You need to be able to identify what's important and what's not important in a test question. Question writers will include extraneous information in the question to throw you off. If some of the information presented doesn't seem to fit with the other information, it might not be relevant.
- Some of the questions will require fill-in-the-blank answers. Remember that case-sensitivity is important when typing directory paths, commands, and command options.
- Do not leave any questions unanswered. There is no negative scoring. After selecting an answer, you can mark a difficult question or one that you're unsure of and come back to it later.

- When answering questions that you are not sure about, use a process of elimination to get rid of the obviously incorrect answers first. Doing this greatly improves your odds if you need to make an educated guess.

- If you're not sure of your answer, mark it for review and then look for other questions that may help you eliminate any incorrect answers. At the end of the test, you can go back and review the questions that you marked for review.

Where Do You Take the Exam?

You can take Solaris exams at any of the more than 800 Thompson Prometric Authorized Testing Centers around the world. For the location of a testing center near you, call 1-800-891-3926. Outside the United States and Canada, contact your local Thompson Prometric Registration Center.

In order to register with Thompson Prometric, you must first purchase an exam voucher from Sun. To do this, call Sun Training at 1-800-422-8020. Exam vouchers are nonrefundable, must be used within one year of the purchase date, and can be used only once. After you have your exam voucher number, you can register for the test with Thompson Prometric.

To register for a proctored Sun Certified System Administrator exam at a Thompson Prometric test center:

- Determine the number of the exam you want to take.

- Register with Thompson Prometric online at `http://www.2test.com` or in North America, by calling 1-800-891-EXAM (800-891-3926). At this point, you will be asked for your exam voucher number.

- When you schedule the exam, you'll get instructions regarding all appointment and cancellation procedures, the ID requirements, and information about the testing-center location.

You can schedule exams up to six weeks in advance or as soon as one working day before the day you wish to take it. If something comes up and you need to cancel or reschedule your exam appointment, contact Thompson Prometric at least 24 hours in advance.

What Does This Book Cover?

This book provides details to help you learn about the Solaris 9 Operating Environment and to help you pass two exams: Sun Certified System Administrator for the Solaris 9 Operating Environment, Part I (CX-310-014), and Sun Certified System Administrator for the Solaris 9 Operating Environment, Part II (CX-310-015). After passing both exams, you will be a Sun Certified System Administrator for the Solaris 9 Operating Environment. This book starts with the basics of Solaris and dives into detail very quickly. Because there are two exams, this book has two parts. Chapters 1 through 9 cover the Part I exam, and Chapters 10 through 16 cover the Part II exam. Each chapter begins with a list of exam objectives.

Chapter 1   Starts with the basic fundamentals and concepts central to the Solaris 9 Operating Environment.

Chapter 2   Covers installations, including installing the entire operating system, software packages, and software patches.

Chapter 3 Describes how to properly boot and shut down a Solaris computer, including using the OpenBoot PROM.

Chapter 4 Explains how to manage user accounts and groups.

Chapter 5 Explores file and directory structure, as well as Solaris file system security.

Chapter 6 Examines the management of system devices and hard disks.

Chapter 7 Provides details on file system management, including the types of file systems available in Solaris.

Chapter 8 Discusses the management of printers and processes.

Chapter 9 Explains the processes for creating system backups and restoring those backups.

Chapter 10 This begins the second part of the book, covering the second exam, and discusses the Solaris networking environment.

Chapter 11 Examines details about virtual file systems, NFS, and core dumps.

Chapter 12 Covers storage volumes, including RAID and the Solaris Volume Manager.

Chapter 13 Introduces advanced security concepts such as Access Control Lists and role-based access control.

Chapter 14 Explores auditing and system messaging.

Chapter 15 Describes naming services such as local files, NIS, NIS+, DNS, and LDAP.

Chapter 16 Explains the custom JumpStart and Web Start Flash installation methods.

Each chapter ends with Review Questions that are specifically designed to help you see what you remember and to retain the knowledge presented. To ensure that you understand the material, read and answer each question carefully.

How to Use This Book

This book can provide a solid foundation for the serious effort of preparing for the SCSA certification. To best benefit from this book, use the following study method:

1. Take the Assessment Test immediately following this introduction. (The answers are at the end of the test.) Carefully read over the explanations for any questions you get wrong and note which chapters the material comes from. This information should help you plan your study strategy.

2. Study each chapter carefully, making sure that you fully understand the information and the test objectives listed at the beginning of each chapter. Pay extra close attention to any chapter related to questions you missed in the Assessment Test.

3. Work through all procedures detailed in the chapter, referring to the chapter so that you understand the reason for each step you take. If you do not have a Solaris 9 installation available, you will be at a disadvantage, so be sure to study all procedures and screen output carefully. Answer the Review Questions related to that chapter. (The answers appear at the end of each chapter, after the "Review Questions" section.)

4. Note the questions that confuse or trick you, and study those sections of the book again.

5. Before taking the exam, try your hand at the two Bonus Exams that are included on the CD that comes with this book. There are two Bonus Exams for both Part I and Part II. The questions on these exams appear only on the CD. This will give you a complete overview of what you can expect to see on the real test.

6. Remember to use the products on the CD included with this book. The electronic flashcards exam preparation software has been specifically designed to help you study for and pass your exam. The electronic flashcards can be used on your Windows computer or on your Palm device.

To learn all the material covered in this book, you'll need to apply yourself regularly and with discipline. Try to set aside the same time period every day to study, and select a comfortable and quiet place to do so. If you work hard, you will be surprised at how quickly you learn this material. All the best!

What's on the CD?

We have worked hard to provide some really great tools to help you with your certification process. All of the following tools should be loaded on your workstation when you're studying for the test.

Interactive Testing Software with Hundreds of Sample Questions

You will find all of the questions from the book, plus two Bonus Exams that appear exclusively on the CD. You can take the Assessment Test, test yourself by chapter, take one or both of the Bonus Exams, or take an exam randomly generated from all of the questions.

Electronic Flashcards for PC and Palm Devices

After you read the *Solaris 9: Sun Certified System Administrator Study Guide*, read the Review Questions at the end of each chapter and study the Bonus Exams included on the CD. But wait, there's more! Test yourself with the flashcards included on the CD. If you can get through these difficult questions and understand the answers, you'll know that you're ready for the exam.

The flashcards include 150 questions specifically written to hit you hard and make sure you are ready for the exam. There are separate flashcards for the Part I and Part II exams. Between the Review Questions, Bonus Exams, and flashcards, you should be more than prepared for the exam.

Solaris 9: Sun Certified System Administrator Study Guide in PDF

Sybex is now offering this Solaris certification book on the CD so you can read the book on your PC or laptop. It is in Adobe Acrobat format. Acrobat Reader 5 is also included on the CD. This will be extremely helpful to readers who fly or commute on a bus or train and don't want to carry a book, as well as to readers who find it more comfortable reading from their computer.

How to Contact the Author

You can reach Quentin Docter by e-mailing him at `qdocter@yahoo.com`.

Assessment Test

1. What is the core of the Solaris operating system is called?

   A. Shell

   B. Kernel

   C. Core

   D. Daemon

2. Which of the following file systems does Solaris 9 support? (Choose all that apply.)

   A. UFS

   B. UDF

   C. PCFS

   D. NFS

   E. HFS

3. If you want to get help on a specific Solaris command, what command do you use?

   A. man

   B. help

   C. !

   D. ?

4. You are adding a patch to your Solaris server. Which of the following commands do you execute if you want to save disk space and not create a backout directory when you install the patch?

   A. patchadd -d

   B. patchadd -r

   C. patchadd -n

   D. patchadd -nobackout

5. On which hardware platforms can you install Solaris 9? (Choose all that apply.)

   A. sun4d

   B. sun4m

   C. sun4u

   D. i86pc

6. You have just upgraded your Solaris 8 server to Solaris 9. Which file contains a list of local modifications that the upgrade could not preserve?

A. `/a/var/sadm/data/upgrade`

B. `/a/var/sadm/system/data/upgrade_cleanup`

C. `/var/sadm/install/contents`

D. `/var/sadm/install/upgrade_cleanup`

7. In the Boot PROM, which command is used to create permanent device aliases?

A. `devalias`

B. `nvalias`

C. `tdalias`

D. `alias`

8. From the Forth Monitor prompt, which of the following commands displays the computer's Ethernet address?

A. `banner`

B. `addr`

C. `enetaddr`

D. `ethernet`

9. In the OpenBoot PROM, which of the following commands enables you to run a diagnostic test on the floppy disk drive?

A. `test,floppy`

B. `test /floppy`

C. `test-floppy`

D. `test floppy`

10. Which of the built-in user accounts has the User ID of 1?

A. `root`

B. `bin`

C. `daemon`

D. `lp`

11. Which of the following commands creates a user named `abradley` with a primary group of `mdte` and a UID of 1068?

A. `useradd -G mdte -U 1068`

B. `useradd -G mdte -u 1068`

C. `useradd -g mdte -U 1068`

D. `useradd -g mdte -u 1068`

12. Which of the following files contains a user account's encrypted password?

   A. /etc/passwd

   B. /etc/shadow

   C. /etc/encrypt

   D. /etc/users

13. Consider the following directory output:

```
lrw-r--r--   1 root        other       4105 Aug  1 12:21 abc123
```

   What type of file is abc123?

   A. A locked file

   B. A regular file

   C. A symbolic link

   D. A hard link

14. What is the result of the following command?

```
# chmod 640 file1
```

   A. On file1, the user will have Read access, the group will have Read and Write access, and other will have Limited access.

   B. On file1, the user will have Read, Write, and Execute access; the group will have Read and Write access; and other will have no access.

   C. On file1, the user will have Read, Write, and Execute access; the group will have Read-only access; and other will have no access.

   D. On file1, the user will have Read and Write access, the group will have Read-only access, and other will have no access.

15. You have just installed Solaris 9 by using all default options. What is the default umask on this computer?

   A. 000

   B. 022

   C. 755

   D. 644

   E. Unable to determine

16. Which of the following commands displays system configuration information, including the hardware platform, memory, and device configuration?

   A. sysdef

   B. prtconf

   C. dmesg

   D. config

17. Which hard disk slice is typically reserved for the /home or /export/home file systems?

   A. 0

   B. 1

   C. 4

   D. 7

18. You are presented with the following menu:

```
MENU:
        disk       - select a disk
        type       - select (define) a disk type
        partition  - select (define) a partition table
        current    - describe the current disk
        format     - format and analyze the disk
        repair     - repair a defective sector
        show       - translate a disk address
        label      - write label to the disk
        analyze    - surface analysis
        defect     - defect list management
        backup     - search for backup labels
        verify     - read and display labels
        save       - save new disk/partition definitions
        volname    - set 8-character volume name
        !<cmd>     - execute <cmd>, then return
```

Which command did you type to display this menu?

   A. fdisk

   B. partition

   C. format

   D. analyze

19. Which of the following is the correct function of an inode?

   A. It contains enough information to begin the system's boot process.

   B. It contains file system information, including the size of the file system and the disk label.

   C. It contains information about a file except for the file's filename.

   D. It contains a listing of all directories in the file system.

20. Which of the following are not pseudo file systems? (Choose all that apply.)

A. PROCFS

B. NFS

C. TMPFS

D. LOFS

E. HSFS

21. During system maintenance, you have unmounted all file systems. You want to remount the file systems listed in the local /etc/vfstab file. Which command should you execute to accomplish this?

A. mount

B. mountall

C. umount

D. umountall

22. Which of the following directories is the default print spooling directory?

A. /var/spool/lp

B. /var/spool/print

C. /etc/lp/spool

D. /var/lp/spool

23. Which of the following Solaris print commands prevents the printer from receiving print requests from print clients?

A. stop

B. cancel

C. disable

D. reject

24. You want to stop a misbehaving process named proc1, but your attempt to stop the process has failed. Therefore, you want to stop the process unconditionally. Which of the following commands should you use?

A. kill -9 proc1

B. kill proc1

C. pkill -9 proc1

D. pkill proc1

25. Which file maintains a list of the dates, times, and levels of system backups made with ufsdump?

A. /etc/dump.log

B. /etc/ufsdump.log

C. /etc/dump

D. /etc/dumpdates

26. You make a level 0 backup on Sunday, a level 5 backup on Tuesday, and a level 6 backup on Thursday. If you make a level 5 backup on Friday, from how far back will the files be backed up?

   A. Files that have changed since Sunday.

   B. Files that have changed since Tuesday.

   C. Files that have changed since Thursday.

   D. More information is needed.

27. You perform a level 0 backup on a Wednesday evening. What files are backed up?

   A. All files that have been modified that day.

   B. All files on the root file system (/) that have been modified that day.

   C. All files on the root file system (/) only.

   D. All files on the computer.

28. Which of the following is layer 5 in the OSI networking model?

   A. Data Link

   B. Network

   C. Session

   D. Transport

29. Which of the following files contains the domain name of the computer you are logged into?

   A. /etc/domain

   B. /etc/defaultdomain

   C. /etc/hosts

   D. /etc/domainname

30. Which of the following protocols are used to boot diskless client computers over the network? (Choose all that apply.)

   A. RARP

   B. TFTP

   C. DHCP

   D. RPC

31. Which one of the following file systems enables you to create a new virtual root file system (/) within an existing file system?

   A. CacheFS

   B. LOFS

   C. TMPFS

   D. VFS

32. Which of the following daemons must be running on an NFS server for it to function properly? (Choose all that apply.)

   A. `nfsd`

   B. `mountd`

   C. `nfslogd`

   D. `automountd`

   E. `statd`

   F. `lockd`

33. Which of the following is an automount point that contains associations between a mount point on a client and a directory on a server?

   A. Automount map

   B. Indirect map

   C. Direct map

   D. Master map

34. Which of the following storage volume types provides fault tolerance with the greatest increase in disk read speed?

   A. Transactional volume

   B. RAID 0

   C. RAID 1

   D. RAID 5

35. Which of the following are read policies on a RAID 1 volume? (Choose all that apply.)

   A. Parallel

   B. Serial

   C. Round robin

   D. Geometric

   E. First

36. What is the primary advantage of using a RAID 0 volume?

   A. Increased storage capacity

   B. Increased disk I/O performance

   C. Provides fault tolerance

   D. Allows more than eight volumes per hard disk

37. You have just created a role named backupadm on your Solaris computer. You are going to assign the role to a user named cmalcolm. Which of the following commands do you use to perform this task?

A. rolemod -R backupadm cmalcolm

B. rolemod -R cmalcolm backupadm

C. usermod -R backupadm cmalcolm

D. usermod -R cmalcolm backupadm

38. Which of the following commands is used to create Access Control Lists on files and directories?

A. setacl

B. setfacl

C. chmod

D. mkacl

39. Consider the following information:

root::::auths=solaris.*,solaris.grant;profiles=All

Which RBAC file is this information from?

A. /etc/user_attr

B. /etc/security/auth_attr

C. /etc/security/prof_attr

D. /etc/security/exec_attr

40. You run the last command on your Solaris workstation. From which database does the last command pull its data?

A. /var/adm/utmpx

B. /var/adm/wtmpx

C. /var/adm/messages

D. /var/log/syslog

41. You want to manually add an entry into the system log after you force a reboot of your Solaris server. Which command should you use?

A. syslog

B. syslogedit

C. logedit

D. logger

42. Which of the following daemons is responsible for listening for and responding to all incoming TCP connections?

    A. `inetd`

    B. `syslogd`

    C. `listend`

    D. `tcpd`

43. Your NIS server is responsible for a domain named `flyingsquid.com`. Which of the following directories, by default, stores the maps for the NIS server?

    A. `/var/yp/flyingsquid.com`

    B. `/var/nis/flyingsquid.com`

    C. `/var/flyingsquid.com`

    D. `/var/nisplus/flyingsquid.com`

44. You are configuring a NIS server for your domain. What is the default directory that contains the source files for the NIS maps?

    A. `/var/maps`

    B. `/var/nis`

    C. `/var/yp`

    D. `/etc`

45. You are attempting to connect to a server on your network by using your Solaris client computer. Which of the following files on your computer tells it which name service to use to resolve the name of the server?

    A. `/etc/hosts`

    B. `/etc/nsswitch.conf`

    C. `/etc/nameservice`

    D. `/etc/defaultdomain`

46. Which of the following installation programs can be used to install from a Web Start Flash archive? (Choose all that apply.)

    A. Solaris Live Upgrade

    B. Web Start

    C. Custom JumpStart

    D. `suninstall`

47. You are beginning a custom JumpStart installation. Which of the following files is used by custom JumpStart to match a computer to an installation profile?

 A. A begin script

 B. `rules`

 C. `rules.ok`

 D. Web Start Flash archive

48. Which of the following are legal values for the `install_type` variable in a custom JumpStart profile? (Choose all that apply.)

 A. `install`

 B. `initial_install`

 C. `upgrade`

 D. `flash_install`

Answers to Assessment Test

1. B.   The core of Solaris is called the kernel. The shell is the user interface, where users enter commands. A daemon is a background process running in Solaris. See Chapter 1 for more information.

2. A, B, C, D.   Solaris 9 supports the UNIX File System (UFS), Universal Disk Format (UDF), Personal Computer File System (PCFS), and Network File System (NFS), as well as many others. HFS is not a valid file system. See Chapter 1 for more information.

3. A.   The man command, used as man *name*, will give you the manual page for that command. See Chapter 1 for more information.

4. A.   The patchadd -d command will not create a backout directory. This saves hard disk space, but prevents you from uninstalling the patch in the future. None of the other switches are valid. See Chapter 2 for more information.

5. B, C, D.   Solaris 9 can be installed on the sun4m, sun4u, and i86pc platforms. Although sun4d is a valid Sun hardware platform, it is not supported by Solaris 9. See Chapter 2 for more information.

6. B.   To see whether any local modifications were not kept during the upgrade process, check the /a/var/sadm/system/data/upgrade_cleanup file. The /var/sadm/install/contents file is the installed software database. The other two files are fictional. See Chapter 2 for more information.

7. B.   The devalias and nvalias commands are used to create device aliases. Only the nvalias command is used to create permanent aliases in NVRAMRC. See Chapter 3 for more information.

8. A.   The banner and the .enet-addr commands display the computer's Ethernet address. Only banner is correct among the answer options. See Chapter 3 for more information.

9. D.   The test floppy command will run a diagnostic test on the floppy disk drive. All of the other commands use the wrong syntax. See Chapter 3 for more information.

10. C.   The daemon account has the UID of 1. The root account is UID 0, bin is UID 2, and lp is UID 71. See Chapter 4 for more information.

11. D.   The correct syntax to create the user with the specified options is useradd -g mdte -u 1068. An uppercase -G switch is used for secondary groups, and the -U switch is not valid with the useradd command. See Chapter 4 for more information.

12. B.   The user's encrypted password is located in the /etc/shadow file. The /etc/passwd file contains usernames and a placeholder for the password. See Chapter 4 for more information.

13. C.   Symbolic links are preceded with an l as the first character, before the permissions. Locked files, "regular" files, and hard links do not have a designation. Their permission block would look like -rw-r--r--. See Chapter 5 for more information.

14. D.   The chmod command changes permissions. The permissions on file1 are being changed by using absolute mode. The first number is for the user (6 means Read and Write), the second number is for group (4 is Read-only), and the third number is for other (0 is no access). See Chapter 5 for more information.

15. B.   The default umask in Solaris is 022. See Chapter 5 for more information.

16. B.   The prtconf command displays all of the listed configurations. See Chapter 6 for more information.

17. D.   Slice 7 is usually reserved for /home or /export/home. Slice 0 is for the root file system (/), 1 is typically swap space, and 4 is usually free for whatever the user wants to use it as. See Chapter 6 for more information.

18. C.   The displayed menu is the format menu, from which you can manage hard disks. See Chapter 6 for more information.

19. C.   Inodes are responsible for containing all the information about a file except for the file's filename. The boot process information is stored in the boot block, and the superblock contains file system information. See Chapter 7 for more information.

20. B, E.   The Process File System (PROCFS), Temporary File System (TMPFS), and Loopback File System (LOFS) are all pseudo, or virtual, file systems. The Network File System (NFS) is a network-based file system, and the High Sierra File System (HSFS) is a disk-based file system. See Chapter 7 for more information.

21. B.   The mountall command mounts all file systems listed in the /etc/vfstab file. The mount command mounts one specific file system. The umount command unmounts a file system, whereas umountall unmounts all file systems listed in /etc/vfstab. See Chapter 7 for more information.

22. A.   The /var/spool/lp directory is the default directory for print spooling jobs. The /var/spool/print directory is the client-side print job staging area. The /etc/lp/spool and /var/lp/spool directories do not exist by default. See Chapter 8 for more information.

23. D.   The reject command is used to keep print queues from accepting new print jobs. The disable command keeps the printer from printing, but new jobs can still enter the queue. The cancel command will cancel a specific print job. See Chapter 8 for more information.

24. C.   The pkill -9 proc1 command will send a KILL signal to the process proc1. You cannot use the process name, only the process ID number, with the kill command. Not specifying a signal number sends a SIGTERM signal (signal 15), which is not an unconditional kill. See Chapter 8 for more information.

25. D.   The /etc/dumpdates file tracks backups made with ufsdump. The log includes backup dates, times, and levels. See Chapter 9 for more information.

26. A.   A level 5 backup is an incremental backup. Incremental backups back up files that have changed since the last lower-level backup. In this case, that was on Sunday. See Chapter 9 for more information.

27. D.   A level 0 backup is a full backup, which backs up all files on the computer. See Chapter 9 for more information.

28. C.   The Session layer is layer 5. In order, the layers (from bottom up) are Physical, Data Link, Network, Transport, Session, Presentation, and Application. See Chapter 10 for more details.

29. B.   The /etc/defaultdomain file contains the name of the domain that the computer belongs to. There is no /etc/domain file or /etc/domainname file. The /etc/hosts file is for host name resolution. See Chapter 10 for more information.

30. A, B.   Reverse Address Resolution Protocol (RARP) and Trivial File Transfer Protocol (TFTP) are used to boot computers over the network. Dynamic Host Configuration Protocol (DHCP) is for assigning IP addresses and other network-related information to computers, and Remote Procedure Call (RPC) is a protocol to initiate processes on remote computers that are already operational. See Chapter 10 for more information.

31. B.   The Loopback File System (LOFS) enables you to create a new virtual root file system (/) within an existing file system. The Cache File System (CacheFS) is for speeding up access to slow devices, such as remote volumes or CD-ROM drives, and the Temporary File System (TMPFS) is for temporary files. VFS typically stands for Virtual File System, but all of the examples listed are virtual file systems (there is no specific VFS in Solaris). See Chapter 11 for more information.

32. A, B.   All of the listed daemons are part of the NFS service. The only two that are required to be running for NFS to work are nfsd and mountd. See Chapter 11 for more information.

33. C.   The direct map contains mappings between a mount point and a directory. All of the maps listed are automount maps. See Chapter 11 for more information.

34. D.   A RAID 5 volume, also known as a disk stripe with parity, provides built-in fault tolerance as well as increased disk read speed. Transactional volumes are for logging and are being phased out. RAID 0 volumes do not provide fault tolerance. RAID 1 volumes (mirrored volumes) provide fault tolerance but aren't noted for their speed. See Chapter 12 for more information.

35. C, D, E.   The RAID 1 read policies are round robin, geometric, and first. Parallel and serial are RAID 1 write policies. See Chapter 12 for more information.

36. B.   RAID 0 volumes are used for speed. They increase hard disk I/O performance. They do not increase storage capacity, nor do they provide fault tolerance. Soft partitions allow for more than eight volumes per hard disk. See Chapter 12 for more information.

37. C.   Users are associated with roles with the usermod command, not the rolemod command. The proper syntax is usermod -R *rolename username*. See Chapter 13 for more information.

38. B.   The setfacl command is used to create Access Control Lists. The setacl and mkacl commands do not exist. The chmod command is used to modify standard file and directory permissions. See Chapter 13 for more information.

39. A.   The entry is a user entry from the /etc/user_attr file, which grants access to profiles and authorizations. The four files listed are all role-based access control (RBAC) database files. See Chapter 13 for more information.

40. B.   The last command gets its information from the /var/adm/wtmpx file. The who command gets its information from the /var/adm/utpmx file. See Chapter 14 for more information.

41. D.   The logger command is used to manually edit the system log. The syslog command is shorthand for the system log, and the syslogedit and logedit commands do not exist. See Chapter 14 for more information

42. A.   The Internet services daemon, inetd, is responsible for listening for and responding to all incoming TCP and UDP connection requests. The syslogd daemon is responsible for logging syslog activity. The listend and tcpd daemons do not exist. See Chapter 14 for more information.

43. A.   The maps for a domain are stored in the /var/yp/*domainname* directory. In this case, that would be /var/yp/flyingsquid.com. See Chapter 15 for more information.

44. D.   The /etc directory is the default directory for the source files. This can be changed by editing /var/yp/makefile. By default, the /var/maps and /var/nis directories do not exist. The /var/yp directory contains NIS information and files. See Chapter 15 for more information.

45. B.   The name service switch file, /etc/nsswitch.conf, tells the local computer which name service (NIS, NIS+, DNS, LDAP, or files) to use to resolve host names, as well as to obtain other critical network information. The /etc/hosts file resolves IP addresses to host names, and the /etc/defaultdomain file contains the computer's domain name. See Chapter 15 for more information.

46. A, B, C, D.   All of the Solaris installation programs can be used to install from a Web Start Flash archive. See Chapter 16 for more information.

47. C.   The rules.ok file is used to match a client computer to an installation profile. As the administrator, you create the rules file and validate it. The validated version, rules.ok, is used by custom JumpStart. See Chapter 16 for more information.

48. B, C, D.   You have three options for an installation type when using custom JumpStart. You can choose an initial installation (initial_install), an upgrade (upgrade), or an installation from a Web Start Flash archive (flash_install). See Chapter 16 for more information.

Solaris 9 Sun Certified System Administrator

Chapter 1

Introduction to Solaris 9

Welcome to Solaris 9, the latest and greatest operating environment (OE) offering from Sun Microsystems. This book is designed to help you get ready to take and pass the two exams required to become a Sun Certified System Administrator (SCSA) on Solaris 9.

This first chapter provides a bit of history about the Solaris family of operating environments and gives you information on critical system concepts. Although Chapter 1 does not specifically map to any exam objectives, the information herein is essential base knowledge before proceeding with the rest of the book. The concepts presented in this chapter appear repeatedly throughout this volume, and it will be assumed that you understand them. So without any further delay, let's take a look at how Solaris has evolved into what it is today.

A Brief History of Solaris

Solaris is based upon UNIX, an operating system that was originally developed in 1969 and became widely available in 1975. UNIX was (and still is) very popular among universities and governmental research facilities. By the time UNIX was released in 1975, it was written in the C programming language, which made it useable by a variety of hardware platforms. The operating system was becoming popular because of its portability as well as its ease of maintenance as opposed to previous lower-level, assembly-language-based operating systems. Even though UNIX is more than 30 years old, it still enjoys considerable usage and it is continually evolving.

The original Sun operating system, released in 1983, was called SunOS and was based on the *Berkeley Software Distribution (BSD)* version of UNIX. The name was changed to Solaris when Sun first bundled OpenWindows with SunOS version 4.1.2 in 1991. The package was known as Solaris 1.0.

Possibly the most confusing part about Solaris is keeping track of the naming conventions. Like many other operating systems, Solaris has gone through a number of revisions and therefore quite a few titles. The most current versions are the second generation of Solaris (Solaris 2) and are based on UNIX *System V Release 4 (SVR4)*. Solaris 2 was first released in 1992. Solaris 9 is part of the second generation of Solaris and is also referred to as SunOS 5.9. The recent release history for Solaris has been 2.5.1, 2.6, 7, 8, and now 9. Since Sun shifted to the single-number naming scheme, they name their operating system on the minor revision number. In other words, Solaris 7 is SunOS 5.7, and Solaris 8 is SunOS 5.8. So, although it might seem that Solaris 2.6 is ancient (after all, we are on version 9 now), it's really not that far back in history. Now that you know that Solaris is numbered based on the "minor" revision number, it should come as no surprise that the core architecture of Solaris 9 is in many ways similar to that of Solaris 7. There are just a lot of new bells and whistles.

To make matters even more confusing, the Solaris 7 operating system is occasionally referred to as Solaris 2.7. This is because it belongs to the second family generation of Solaris (which is also known as SunOS 5.*x*).

Scalable Processor Architecture (SPARC) chips are based on Reduced Instruction Set Computers (RISC) chip technology, which makes them very quick. SPARC was developed at Sun Microsystems and released in 1986. (As an aside, RISC is basically the alternative to CISC, or Complex Instruction Set Computers, which is what Intel and all Intel clones are.)

Features of Solaris 7 and 8

The key features of every version of Solaris are too many to list. However, knowing some key features of recent releases of Solaris might help give you perspective as to where this operating system has come from and, possibly, where it's going.

Here are some key features introduced with Solaris 7, which was released in 1998:

For the SPARC platform, 64-bit computing supported   This feature was added primarily because of consumer demand. It provided for a more powerful operating platform.

UNIX File System (UFS) logging added   This was done to improve file system consistency.

Lightweight Directory Access Protocol (LDAP) included   LDAP is an industry-standard protocol. Because it's lightweight (read: quick) and reliable, it can be used to manage name databases.

Remote Procedure Call (RPC) security enhanced   Increasing security over networks is never a bad thing.

Domain Name Service (DNS) Berkeley Internet Name Domain (BIND) upgraded to version 8.1.2
At the time, this was the most current BIND version of DNS. BIND 8.1.2 included features such as Dynamic DNS (DDNS), improved zone transfers, and increased security.

Common Desktop Environment (CDE) version 1.3 introduced   CDE greatly simplified end-user access. CDE was originally introduced with Solaris 2.6, and this version provided new features.

Netscape Communicator included   Communicator provided an all-in-one online communications tool, including web browser and e-mail capabilities.

Improved access to AnswerBook2   This made getting answers to questions about Solaris easier.

Solaris 8, released in 2000, had a considerable list of innovations as well. Some of the more notable ones include:

Support for Internet Protocol version 6 (IPv6), the next-generation Internet protocol   This was more of a preemptive upgrade. Eventually, the current IP addressing scheme (IPv4) will be converted to IPv6 worldwide.

Role-based access control (RBAC)   RBAC allows users some administrative privileges without granting them superuser power.

Graphical Dynamic Host Configuration Protocol (DHCP) manager   This graphical manager greatly eased DHCP administration.

Product Registry   Created as an all-in-one software management interface, this feature enabled administrators to easily manage and delete installed software packages.

Support for the Universal Disk Format (UDF) file system   UDF is used with CD-ROMs, DVDs, and other optical media.

Improved device configuration, through the `devfsadm` command   This eases administration and provides for automatic device configuration.

Smart Card support, based on the Open Card Framework (OCF) 1.1 standard   OCF 1.1 provides for greater security by requiring users to validate with a Smart Card rather than a standard username and password.

SunScreen   Not only is it a catchy name, but it's a dynamic packet-filtering firewall designed to protect your Solaris servers from would-be hackers.

As you can see, the previous two versions of Solaris have brought about many changes, and the ones listed barely begin to scratch the surface of all the new operating system enhancements.

Features of Solaris 9

Sun realized that their existing operating environments, Solaris 7 and 8, were solid. Although they added new features to Solaris 9, they didn't try to reinvent the wheel. As with all versions of Solaris, new features have been added for developers, system administrators, and end users. Because this book focuses on achieving system administrator certification, the following list of Solaris 9 features concentrates on system administrator and end-user enhancements. Here are some of the new features of Solaris 9:

Solaris 9 Resource Manager   This allows for detailed control and allocation of system resources, such as processor and memory.

Integrated iPlanet Directory Server   This makes use of the LDAP protocol and provides a distributed directory server capable of managing an enterprise-wide network of users and resources.

Internet Protocol Security (IPsec)   This is now supported in IPv6, as is IPv6 over Asynchronous Transfer Mode (ATM).

Solaris Volume Manager   This enables administrators to create and manage RAID 0, RAID 1, and RAID 5 volumes, transactional devices, soft partitions, and hot spare pools.

Patch Manager   This provides for easy location, installation, tracking, and administration of software patches.

Enhanced installation features   These include updates to Solaris Live Upgrade and Web Start Flash installation, and a new Minimal Installation feature.

Integrated Secure Shell (SSH)   This supports the SSHv1 and SSHv2 protocol versions.

Enhanced CD features   These changes include the ability to record to Compact Disc-Recordable (CD-R) and Compact Disc-Rewritable (CD-RW) devices with the `cdrw` command.

GNOME 2.0 desktop   This is a popular graphical user interface that runs across multiple UNIX platforms and integrates seamlessly with the Internet.

For a complete listing of new features for a variety of Solaris versions, please visit the Sun documentation website at `http://docs.sun.com`.

Key System Concepts

Understanding the elements listed in this section is the first critical step to understanding how Solaris 9 works. Sun assumes that its certification candidates have a firm grasp of basic system and networking concepts, and doesn't directly test on such cursory information. But only after you understand the basics can you master more difficult and tested concepts.

These concepts are by no means unique to Solaris, or even UNIX for that matter. However, this section is primarily concerned with how these concepts relate to the Solaris operating environment. If you have solid computer experience, you are probably already familiar with most of these ideas, but you might not be sure how they fit into the Solaris world. By reading this section, you will be able to impress your techno-friends with your vast, detailed knowledge of often ambiguous computer concepts.

Operating System

An *operating system* should be easy to define, right? After all, we use them every day. The operating system is the under-appreciated workhorse of the software side of your computer. It's always there, always running (at least in theory), and usually ignored (unless it's not running).

Operating systems are programs in their own right, with a few express functions. First, they provide an interface between the computer hardware and software. In a sense, they are the translator that makes the hardware and software play nice together. Second, based on the first function, they enable users to run applications. So, operating systems are applications that let you run other applications.

Sun makes a differentiation between an operating system and an *operating environment*. Technically, Solaris 9 is the name of the operating environment built around the SunOS 5.9 operating system. The operating environment consists of the core operating system and all bundled features, such as management programs and software. Even though delineation is made, no one at Sun is likely to get mad at someone calling Solaris an "operating system." At least I hope not, because I will certainly do it a lot in this book.

Kernel and Processes

The *kernel* is the brain of the operating system. Although kernels vary among operating systems, they all have some common characteristics. In the case of UNIX-based operating systems, kernels are written in the C programming language. Kernels are responsible mainly for managing computer input/output (I/O), allocating system resources, and managing processes.

Processes are the running parts of an application. A common misconception is that an application is a process. That's not true, because many applications (especially newer games) will be running as multiple processes at one time. Such applications are known as multithreaded applications. Multithreading speeds up the application and allows for smoother execution. System tasks other than applications, such as daemons (which we'll discuss in just a bit), run as processes as well. In UNIX, all processes have a process identifier (PID), which is used by the kernel to identify and manipulate the process as needed.

Shells

In UNIX, the *shell* enables users to input information to be interpreted by the operating system. Consider the operating system to be the interface between the computer hardware and software, and the shell to be the interface between the user and the operating system. Shells also enable users to program commonly used or frequently used lists of applications to run with the execution of one command. These are called scripts, macros, or batch files.

Solaris 9 provides multiple shells, and each one has different features. The three most common shells are the Bourne shell (`sh`), the C shell (`csh`), and the Korn shell (`ksh`).

 The Bourne shell is the default shell for Solaris 9. Shells will be discussed in greater detail in Chapter 4, "User and Group Administration."

Although Sun provides a graphical user interface (GUI) for Solaris 9, the shell itself is command-prompt-based. For example, if you are using the Bourne shell, your prompt will be $—unless you are the all-powerful superuser, in which case your prompt will be #. Some other operating systems do use GUI shells, such as Windows Explorer. Keep in mind that even though Solaris 9 runs the *Common Desktop Environment (CDE)* GUI by default, CDE is not a shell.

Daemons

Depending on where you look, you can find two common definitions for daemons. The first one describes a *daemon* as a program that runs automatically in the background without the need for user intervention. The second definition is that a daemon provides a service. The service can be administrative, such as cleaning up temporary files, or the service can be one that provides meaningful interaction to clients, such as a print daemon, DHCP server, or DNS server. Daemons run as processes, and can either start automatically when the operating system starts, or be started manually.

File Systems

Like *daemon*, the term *file system* also has various definitions. There are two common ways to look at file systems.

One way to see a file system is as a collection of files that have a similar purpose on one logical section of the hard drive. Solaris provides many such file systems, including the root (/), /etc, /usr, /opt, /var, and others. These file systems will be further organized by using directories.

Another way to think of a file system is the specific method in which data is stored and organized on the hard drive. All data is written in bits (0s and 1s) in some way or another, but file systems logically make sense of the 0s and 1s. Here are some file systems supported within Solaris 9:

- UNIX File System (UFS) for local hard disks

- High Sierra File System (HSFS) for CD-ROMs

- Universal Disk Format (UDF) for optical media, such as DVDs

- Personal Computer File System (PCFS) for floppy disks

- Network File System (NFS) for networked volumes

We will focus on file systems in greater detail in Chapter 7, "File System Management."

Clients and Servers

On networks, computers can be divided into two broad categories: clients and servers. Some operating systems, such as Novell NetWare, are designed to be a server only. Others, such as Microsoft Windows 98, are to be clients only. Solaris 9 is a versatile operating system that can be used as either a client or a server.

As a rule of thumb, end users sit at client machines and perform daily tasks. Clients will often request information (files and applications) from centralized servers, which are located in some sort of server room. Servers should be secured away from prying (or hacking) hands, because they often hold critical and sensitive information.

Clients make requests of servers, and servers fulfill client requests. A computer with the right operating system can function as both a client and a server at the same time. Solaris, and UNIX in general, is a powerful enough operating system to function as a client and a server at the same time.

Where to Get Help

As much as you might already know about the Solaris operating environment, you will never know everything there is to know about Solaris. Although my last statement might sound harsh, it's true. There is so much to know, including commands (and all related switches), concepts, and creative ways to fix problems you might encounter. Even if you know a considerable amount, it's unlikely that you will have every switch of every command memorized.

Fortunately, there are a number of resources that you can use when you get stuck or simply need a quick refresher. This section highlights the most common resource spots.

man Pages

The man command displays reference manual pages about Solaris commands and concepts. The syntax is man *arguments name*, where *name* is the command or file that you want to know about. For example, you could type **man -a passwd**, which would display all man pages that match the word passwd. You can even type **man man** to get information on the man command itself. Table 1.1 lists a few of the most common man switches.

TABLE 1.1   *man* Command Arguments

Argument	Function
-a	Shows all manual pages matching name within the search path and displays them in order found
-f *file*	Attempts to locate manual pages related to the specified files
-k *keyword*	Prints one-line summaries from the table of contents that contain any of the given keywords
-1	Lists all manual pages found within the search path
-s *section*	Specifies which section number of the reference manual to search

When using the man command, the output indicates which section of the reference manual the query was located in. The reference manual is divided into nine sections, which are listed in Table 1.2.

TABLE 1.2   Reference Manual Sections

Section	Description
1	User commands
1M	System administration commands

TABLE 1.2 Reference Manual Sections *(continued)*

Section	Description
2	System calls
3	Programming library functions
4	File formats
5	Standards, environments, and macros
6	Demos and games
7	Device and network interfaces
9	Device Driver Interface (DDI) and Driver/Kernel Interface (DKI) specifications

Some words have more than one `man` page. For example, if you type **man passwd**, you will find `passwd(1)` and `passwd(4)`. The `passwd(1)` page describes the `passwd` command, and the `passwd(4)` page describes the `passwd` file. The Solaris 9 Reference Manual is also available for purchase in printed format. Solaris 9 also comes with the AnswerBook2, which contains a great deal of helpful information.

Online Resources

The `docs.sun.com` website is an excellent resource if you need to know anything about a multitude of Sun's products. The entire reference manual is available online, and there is a link specifically for `man` pages. If the information you're looking for isn't on this page, just follow one of the links and you're likely to find it.

Solaris newsgroups can also provide helpful information. The `comp.unix.solaris` group is popular; you can either just look at it for information, or post a question if you are looking for an answer. If you don't already have a newsgroup server that you frequent, you can find `comp.unix.solaris` at `www.Google.com` under the Groups section.

A lot of administrators also like to install a local copy of AnswerBook2. It contains much of the same information as `docs.sun.com` and finding the information you need is a lot quicker.

This Book

Is this just a shameless plug? Not at all. Not only can this book help you pass your SCSA exams, but it can also serve as a useful reference book. Throughout the book, many commands and their commonly used arguments are listed. If you get stuck, you can flip to the section containing the command you want and likely find some help.

Summary

In this chapter, you began your Solaris certification journey by looking at a bit of UNIX history. Solaris has gone through many revisions, and Solaris 9 (SunOS 5.9) is based on the UNIX SVR4 standard. You then looked at some key new features of Solaris 9, which include Resource Manager, Volume Manager, Patch Manager, integrated iPlanet Directory Server, integrated Secure Shell, and installation features.

The middle part of this chapter presented some key concepts in Solaris. You looked at Sun's differentiation between an operating system and an operating environment. Kernels and processes, shells, daemons, file systems, and clients and servers were explored briefly.

Finally, this chapter indicated places where you can get help. No one will ever know everything, so it's important to be able to find useful information quickly. Besides, your main goal should be to understand the concepts, not remember esoteric commands. Some options for Solaris help include man pages, AnswerBook2, docs.sun.com, and this book.

Exam Essentials

Know which UNIX standard Solaris is based upon.   Solaris 9 is based upon the UNIX System V Release 4 (SVR4) standard.

Know what the default shell is in Solaris 9.   The default shell is the Bourne shell (sh).

Understand the difference between a shell and a GUI.   A shell processes commands and acts as the interface between the user and the operating system. Although some shells are graphical in nature, there are GUIs (such as CDE and GNOME) that are not shells.

Know which file systems are supported in Solaris 9.   Solaris 9 supports UFS, HSFS, UDF, PCFS, NFS, and other file systems.

Know where to get help if you need it.   Many help resources are available. Some important ones are man pages, AnswerBook2, docs.sun.com, and this book.

Key Terms

Before you take the exam, be certain you are familiar with the following terms:

Berkeley Software Distribution (BSD)	operating system
Common Desktop Environment (CDE)	processes
daemon	Scalable Processor Architecture (SPARC)
file system	shell
kernel	System V Release 4 (SVR4)
operating environment (OE)	

Commands Used in This Chapter

The following list contains a summary of all the commands introduced in this chapter:

Command	Description
man	Displays online help in the form of reference manual pages.

Review Questions

1. You are the manager of the in-house Solaris 9 computers for your company. One of your developers is creating a new program to be deployed on one of your servers and is asking about library functions. Which section of the Solaris 9 Reference Manual should you refer her to?

    A. Section 1

    B. Section 3

    C. Section 4

    D. Section 8

2. You are the systems administrator for your company. You were just told to set up five Solaris 9 workstations for new employees. As you are installing Solaris 9, one of the employees asks which file system will be installed on the hard drives. What is your answer?

    A. UFS

    B. UDF

    C. HSFS

    D. Solaris 9 does not use file systems.

3. You are installing a new Solaris 9 workstation for an employee. During the installation, the employee, who is somewhat familiar with UNIX, asks what the default shell for Solaris 9 is. What do you tell him?

    A. Korn

    B. Bourne

    C. C

    D. Bash

4. You are running five applications at once on your Solaris 9 computer. Which part of the operating system is responsible for scheduling and managing all your running applications?

    A. Shell

    B. Daemon

    C. Process Manager

    D. Kernel

5. One of your Solaris users calls, wondering how to change his password. You tell him to use the `passwd` command. He's not sure how to use it and wants additional information. You tell him to type `man passwd`, which produces multiple outputs, confusing him even more. Which `man` page do you tell him to look at?

   A. `passwd(1M)`

   B. `passwd(4)`

   C. `passwd(1)`

   D. `passwd(u)`

6. Which of the following are file systems supported in Solaris 9? (Choose all that apply.)

   A. HSFS

   B. PCFS

   C. UFS

   D. UDS

   E. HPFS

   F. FAT

   G. NTFS

   H. NFS

7. Which of the following are shells supported in Solaris 9? (Choose all that apply.)

   A. C

   B. Born

   C. Corn

   D. GNOME

8. One of your network users tells you that she formatted a floppy disk on her Solaris 9 computer and copied some files to that disk. She wonders whether those files can be copied to a Windows-based machine. You tell her that it will work. Why is this?

   A. Because the floppy disk was formatted with FDFS, which is also used by Windows-based computers

   B. Because the floppy disk was formatted with PCFS, which is also used by Windows-based computers

   C. Because the floppy disk was formatted with HSFS, which is also used by Windows-based computers

   D. Because the floppy disk was formatted with HPFS, which is also used by Windows-based computers

9. You are delivering a proposal to management regarding operating systems within your company. You are recommending that the company should switch to Solaris 9. One of the managers asks you what operating system Solaris 9 is based on. Which core operating system is it?

A. UNIX BSD

B. UNIX SVR2

C. UNIX SVR4

D. VMS

10. You are delivering a proposal to management regarding operating systems within your company. You are recommending that the company should switch to Solaris 9. One of the managers asks you what UNIX standard Solaris 9 is based upon. What do you tell her?

A. BSD

B. SVR4

C. SVR2

D. SCO

Answers to Review Questions

1. B.   Section 3 of the reference manual contains information on programming library functions. Section 1 has user commands, and Section 4 has file formats. Section 8 does not exist.

2. A.   For local hard disks, Solaris 9 uses the UFS file system. UDF is used for optical media, and HSFS is for CD-ROMs. And of course, Solaris does indeed use file systems.

3. B.   In Solaris 9, the Bourne shell is the default shell. Korn, C, and Bash are also supported shells.

4. D.   The kernel schedules and manages processes and resources. The shell is an interface between the user and operating system, and a daemon is a process that runs in the background. Process Manager enables you to display running processes and kill them if necessary. However, it is not responsible for scheduling applications.

5. C.   The `man` page for `passwd(1)` will contain information on using the `passwd` command. `passwd(4)` will contain information on the `passwd` file.

6. A, B, C, H.   Solaris 9 supports the HSFS, PCFS, UFS, and NFS file systems, among others. UDS does not exist as a file system. HPFS, FAT, and NTFS are file systems supported by other operating systems.

7. A.   The C shell is supported in Solaris 9. Some of the other supported shells include Bourne and Korn, but not spelled as in the options. GNOME is a graphical user interface, not a shell.

8. B.   Floppy disks formatted on Solaris 9 computers use the PCFS file system. HSFS is used for CD-ROMs. FDFS does not exist, and HPFS is not supported by Solaris 9 (or Windows for that matter).

9. C.   Solaris 9 has the SunOS 5.9 operating system at its core, which is based on the UNIX SVR4 standard.

10. B.   Solaris 9 is based upon UNIX System V Release 4 (SVR4).

Chapter

2

Installation

SOLARIS 9 EXAM OBJECTIVES COVERED IN THIS CHAPTER:

✓ Explain how to install the Solaris operating system from CD/DVD, including installation and upgrade options, hardware requirements, Solaris OS software components (software packages, clusters, and groups).

✓ Explain the purpose of the /var/sadm/install/contents file, and how to administer packages (how to display, add, check, and remove a package, and add a package into the spool directory) using the command-line interface.

✓ Explain how to obtain, install, and remove patches and patch clusters using either the command-line interface or the Solaris Management Console.

Many people find installing an operating system to be incredibly boring. In fact, installations often rank on the excitement meter somewhere between watching paint dry and watching grass grow. Although no one is going to confuse a Solaris 9 installation with weekend entertainment, Sun has made improvements to the Solaris 9 installation process.

Even though installations might not be the most exciting things to administer, knowing how to properly install an operating system is a critical task. You might know everything there is to know about managing users and security, but if you can't put the operating system on the machine, there won't be any users or security to control.

Sun's exam objectives classify installations into three categories: operating system, packages (software), and patches. This chapter starts by examining how to install Solaris 9, continues with installing and managing software packages, and finishes by showing how to obtain, install, and manage software patches.

Installing Solaris 9

You can make all the jokes you want about how unexciting installing an operating system is, but the fact remains that you need to know how to do it. Everything that will happen on your computer depends on the initial installation process. Installing Solaris 9 might seem easy, but if the installation goes poorly, one of two things will happen: either you will have to deal with a system that isn't optimally configured, which could cause performance issues, or you will have to reinstall the operating system. Neither alternative is pleasant. The first step to ensuring a good installation is proper planning.

Planning the Installation

The planning phase of installation is one of the most overlooked tasks in all of computing. This is really unfortunate, because good planning *before* you install can save you a lot of headaches *after* you install.

Obviously, if you are installing only one computer, your planning will not be as detailed as if you were installing a large network. But there are still some important things to consider, such as whether it will be a new installation or an upgrade, whether your computer meets system requirements, where you will be installing from, and planning details such as host name, IP address, superuser password, and disk space allocation.

Choose Initial Installation or Upgrade

This decision should be pretty easy. If your system is running Solaris 2.6, 7, or 8, you can upgrade it to Solaris 9. If your system has any other operating system installed, or no operating system at all, you must choose an initial installation.

There might be times when you are running Solaris version 2.6, 7, or 8 but want to do a clean installation. That's fine too, as long as you understand the logistical differences between upgrading and installing. If you upgrade, Solaris will migrate as many system configuration options as possible, but if you do a clean installation, you will need to reconfigure everything after the installation is complete.

Whether you choose to perform an initial installation or an upgrade, you can use any of the four installation methods listed in the "Choose an Installation Method" section later in this chapter.

Review System Requirements

You need to make sure your system meets the requirements for Solaris 9. At a minimum, you need at least 96MB of RAM, although 128MB is recommended. If you use the CD-ROM to install, you will also need a slice (or partition) on your hard disk that's at least 512MB in size and is not already used to store files. Using the swap slice is recommended.

Your hardware platform must also support the Solaris 9 operating system. If your computer belongs to the sun4m, sun4u, or i86pc platform groups, you should be okay. The sun4m computers will be able to run Solaris 9 only in 32-bit mode (instead of 64-bit mode), and some sun4u platform machines will need an OpenBoot upgrade to run Solaris 9 in 64-bit mode. The sun4u computers that might need the OpenBoot upgrade are Ultra 1, Ultra 2, Ultra 450, Enterprise 450, and Enterprise 3000, 4000, 5000, and 6000.

 The sun4d platform group is not supported in Solaris 9.

Unless your Sun computer is very old, you shouldn't have to worry about whether Solaris 9 will install. SPARCstation 4 and newer, Ultra, Blade, and Fire systems should all run Solaris 9 with no difficulties, save for a possible OpenBoot upgrade to support 64-bit mode. To determine your system's platform group, type **uname -m** from a command prompt.

Plan and Allocate Disk Space

Most modern computers have ample disk space for the installation of Solaris 9 and any software that the user could desire. If you have an older machine with a smaller hard disk, you could run into problems. Of course, you can add another disk, if needed, to provide additional space.

When you install Solaris, it will set up your disk space automatically based on a profile for the size of your hard disk. There are times, though, that you will want to customize disk allocation. Here are some pointers to keep in mind when planning your disk usage:

- Servers require more disk space than clients. If this machine is going to be a server, you might need to allocate extra space for user home directories, which are located in the /export file system by default.

- If this computer is going to be a print or mail server, provide extra disk space for the /var file system.

- Allocate at least 512MB for swap space.

- If you are planning on using the crash dump feature savecore, make the /var file system at least twice as big as the amount of physical memory in your computer.

- If you are going to be installing additional languages, make sure to provide enough disk space for each additional language.

- Allocate the proper amount of space for the software group you plan on installing, as well as space for third-party applications.

One other good planning tip regarding disk space is to plan for future expansions and upgrades of Solaris. Sun recommends creating disk slices at least 30 percent larger than required. In other words, if you determine that your /var file system needs 1GB of space, make it at least 1.3GB. It's estimated that each new Solaris release needs about 10 percent more space than the previous release, so if you give your file systems room to grow, you won't have to reallocate your disk space for quite some time. Disk space is cheap, so don't skimp on it when planning file systems.

Pick a Software Group

There are more than 650 software packages listed on the Solaris 9 Operating Environment Package List. Fortunately, Solaris 9 has assembled them into five software groups for ease of installation. A *software group* is a collection of Solaris packages. Each group has a different intended function and requires a different amount of disk space. Obviously, the more software you install, the more hard drive space is used. Pick one of the following five clusters based on your needs (all disk space recommendations include swap space):

Core Solaris Software Group   The Core software group is the smallest and contains the minimum number of files required to boot Solaris. It also includes some network software and the drivers needed to run the OpenWindows environment. For the Core software group, allocate a minimum of 1GB of disk space. For frame of reference, this group contains only about one-quarter of all available packages.

End User Solaris Software Group   The End User software group contains enough files to run a networked Solaris computer, as well as the Common Desktop Environment (CDE). The recommended disk space for this group is 2GB.

Developer Solaris Software Group   This group contains everything in the End User group and adds files needed for software development. These files include programming libraries, man pages, and programming tools, but no compilers. The recommended disk space for the Developer group is 2.4GB.

Entire Solaris Software Group   Based on its name, you would think that this group contains all 650-plus packages. It doesn't, but it's missing only a few. Close enough. This package contains everything that's in the Developer group, plus software that is needed for servers. For this package, allocate 2.7GB of disk space.

Entire Solaris Software Group Plus OEM Support   Finally, the package that has it all. It contains all software packages, which according to Sun include "drivers for hardware that is not on the system at the time of installation." Allocate 2.9GB of disk space for this package.

Generally speaking, the End User software group is appropriate for client computers, and the Entire software group (plus OEM support, if you want) is recommended for servers.

During installation, you can add or remove software packages from the group you select. However, be careful when doing so. Some packages are dependent upon others, and removing the wrong package can have drastic consequences. If you are going to customize your software group installation, be sure to first understand the interdependencies of the software you are adding or removing.

 Memorizing exact disk requirements for software packages isn't the point of this section. Simply become familiar with the software packages available and the general disk requirements of each one. Also know some basic features of each group—for example, the Core group does not come with CDE.

Choose an Installation Method

There are four ways to install the Solaris 9 operating environment. They are suninstall, Web Start, JumpStart, and Live Upgrade.

suninstall

The *suninstall* program is located on the Solaris 9 Software 1 of 2 CD. It is an installation program run from the *command-line interface (CLI)* only, which makes it a good choice if you have a system with only 96MB of RAM. Of all the installation methods, suninstall is the most basic and it installs only Solaris operating environment software. To install third-party software, you must either use a different installation method or wait until Solaris 9 is operational.

If you use suninstall, you will be asked to enter system configuration information manually. Therefore, suninstall is not recommended if you have a large number of machines to install. Instead, use Web Start Flash or a custom JumpStart installation. The suninstall program is run from the CD-ROM, but can be executed either locally or remotely.

Web Start and Web Start Flash

The *Web Start* installation program is included on both the Solaris 9 Installation CD and the Solaris 9 DVD. You can run Web Start with either a CLI or a user-friendly graphical user interface

(GUI). Web Start enables you to install the Solaris 9 operating environment, as well as any additional software. Essentially, Web Start creates an installation profile that is used by JumpStart to install the required software.

 Web Start does require you to enter some system configuration information. Consequently, it is not recommended for use if you need to install Solaris on a large number of systems.

Web Start Flash enables you to install multiple systems, based on an original configuration. First you need to install a *master system*, which is simply a Solaris 9 computer with the configuration you wish to duplicate. Then you create a Web Start Flash archive from the master system, which can be used to install other machines quickly and without intervention.

Each of the installation methods enables you to use a Web Start Flash archive. If you have multiple configurations, you can create as many archives as necessary. Be aware, however, that archives are very large and can quickly eat up chunks of disk space. Also, after an archive is created, it cannot be modified. If you require modifications to a Web Start Flash archive, you must create a new one.

 Understanding how to use Web Start Flash is an objective for Exam II and is covered in more detail in Chapter 16, "Advanced Installation Procedures."

JumpStart

There are two types of *JumpStart* installations available in Solaris 9: factory JumpStart and custom JumpStart.

Factory JumpStart automatically installs Solaris on a SPARC computer when you insert either the Solaris 9 DVD or Solaris Software 1 of 2 CD and turn on the system. It installs Solaris based on a default profile, which is determined by your system model and disk size. The best thing about JumpStart is that you are not prompted for configuration information. JumpStart is the recommended method for installing multiple machines.

JumpStart requires a boot image, which is pre-installed on all new SPARC-based computers. If you have an older SPARC-based machine, you can add the JumpStart installation method to the computer by using the `re-preinstall` command.

Custom JumpStart enables you to install one or more machines automatically based on profiles that you have created. Custom JumpStart provides the greatest flexibility in installation options and is recommended if you have a large number of machines to install. With custom JumpStart, you can define specific software installation requirements, pre-installation tasks, and post-installation tasks.

 Using JumpStart is an objective for Exam II and is covered in more detail in Chapter 16.

Live Upgrade

Solaris *Live Upgrade* is new to the Solaris 9 operating environment and is an efficient, incredibly cool installation method.

With Live Upgrade, you create a duplicate boot environment on your existing Solaris installation. After the duplicate boot environment is created, you use a Web Start Flash archive to upgrade or perform a fresh installation on the inactive boot environment. The computer stays running the whole time. After the upgrade or installation is complete, you activate the inactive boot environment. The next time you reboot the system, the inactive boot environment is switched to active. If you have problems, you can reactivate the old boot environment, reboot the computer, and be back to your original configuration.

Live Upgrade can significantly reduce downtime associated with server upgrades. There is one negative, however. Because you are creating multiple boot environments, you need the disk space to support essentially two operating systems. It's a trade-off of time versus hardware, but it's a trade-off that can easily pay large dividends in production environments.

Gather Information about Your System

If you are using `suninstall` or the Web Start installation program, you will be prompted to enter system configuration information during the installation. Writing down the information you need before you begin the installation will make the whole process much smoother. Now the question becomes, "What information do I need?" Sun created an installation worksheet to help you gather information about your system; it is posted on Sun's website, at `http://docs.sun.com/?p=/doc/806-5205/6je7vd5r3&a=view`. Here are some questions that you'll want to have answers to before installing:

- What is your computer's name (hostname)?
- What time zone are you in, and will you need to install additional languages?
- Which software group do you want to install?
- Are you on a network? If so:
  - What is your domain name?
  - What is your IP address, subnet mask, and default gateway (router), or are you using DHCP?
  - What is the name and address of your name server, if you have one?
  - Are there any additional network configuration requirements, such as a Kerberos server or Proxy server? If so, you will need their configuration information.
- Do you want Solaris to wipe out your hard disks and reconfigure them automatically, or do you want to save existing data?

Using Sun's worksheet or answering these questions before installing might seem like a lot of work, but planning ahead and having your configuration information readily available can save you time and future headaches. Configuration worksheets are especially helpful when you have many computers to install. Consider worksheets critical if you are the one planning the network configuration and someone else is doing the actual installation.

You can use the worksheet on Sun's website (or make your own) for either installing or upgrading. As listed, the worksheet is designed for an initial installation. If you are upgrading, there are only a few minor differences. As an example, instead of asking whether you want to allocate disk space, it will ask whether you want to reallocate disk space. Also, upgrades will preserve data automatically, without prompting you.

Perform Optional Tasks

Depending on the type of installation that you want to perform, you might want to complete one or both of the optional tasks covered in this section.

Preconfigure System Information

You can preconfigure system information if you are installing fresh or upgrading. One of the annoyances of installing an operating system is responding to the prompts asking for system configuration information. JumpStart, Web Start Flash, and suninstall enable you to circumvent these prompts through preconfiguration.

There are two ways to preconfigure system information. The first is to use a *sysidcfg* file on a remote system or floppy disk, and the second is to use an available Network Information Service (NIS) or NIS+ database.

Of the two choices, the sysidcfg file allows for more preconfiguration options. However, information in sysidcfg is machine specific. So, if you want to use sysidcfg to configure the IP address and host name, you will need a unique sysidcfg file for each machine. For parameters that all machines will share, such as time zone, domain name, and name server, sysidcfg can save you a lot of time.

For detailed information on how to create a sysidcfg file, please use the *Solaris 9 Installation Guide* from Sun Microsystems, available at http://docs.sun.com/?p=/doc/806-5205.

The only item that neither sysidcfg nor NIS/NIS+ can preconfigure is power management. If you wish to preconfigure power management, you have to use a custom JumpStart installation and create a finish script to create an /autoshutdown or /noautoshutdown file on the computer. The /autoshutdown file enables power management, whereas /noautoshutdown disables it.

Prepare to Install from the Network

If you are going to be installing your computers over the network instead of from a local CD-ROM or DVD drive, you need to prepare your local area network servers for the installation. You can install from a remote server that either has the installation media copied to its local hard disk or has its CD-ROM or DVD drive mounted and available for remote use.

Installing over the network is a three-step process:

1. Create an installation server. Use the setup_install_server command to copy the Solaris 9 Software 1 of 2 CD to the server's hard disk, and the add_to_install_server command to copy the Solaris 9 Software 2 of 2 CD to the server's hard disk. If you want to add the Solaris Web Start user interface software to the installation image, you can use the modify_install_server command.

2. Create a boot server if needed. You need a boot server only if you are installing computers that are not on the same subnet as your installation server and you are not running DHCP.

3. Add systems to be installed from the network. From the server, use the `add_install_ client` command for each system you want to install from the network. Each client computer will need to be able to find the install server, boot server (if necessary), `sysidcfg` file or name server for preconfiguration information (if necessary), and JumpStart profile if you are using a custom JumpStart installation.

Performing the Initial Installation

After you've taken care of your planning activities, it's time to begin the actual installation. You will need to perform an initial installation if your hard disk does not have an operating system on it, or if it has an operating system other than Solaris 2.6, 7, or 8. You can still choose to do an initial installation even if you do have an upgradeable operating system. The specific steps required to install Solaris 9 on your computer will depend upon which installation method you choose.

 Because they are included in objectives from Exam II, Web Start Flash and JumpStart will be covered in Chapter 16.

suninstall

Of the installation options, `suninstall` is the most rudimentary. It runs only through a command-line interface and comes on the Solaris 9 Software 1 of 2 CD, not the Solaris 9 DVD. This program also does not allow you to install any additional software, just the Solaris operating environment. To use `suninstall`, you will need both Solaris 9 Software CDs, as well as the Solaris 9 Languages CD if you are supporting additional languages besides English.

Here are the steps to install Solaris 9 by using `suninstall`:

1. Choose to install from the CD-ROM drive or from the network.

    - If you choose the CD-ROM drive, insert the Solaris 9 Software 1 of 2 CD.

    - If you are installing from the network, change to the directory where the installation media is located to make sure the files are available.

2. Boot the system by using one of the following methods.

    - If the system is new out of the box, turn it on.

    - To boot from the CD-ROM, type **boot cdrom** at the ok prompt.

    - To boot from the network, type **boot net** at the ok prompt.

3. Provide answers to the system configuration questions. It's best to use your installation worksheet that you completed earlier. If you have complete preconfigured system information, you will not be prompted for answers.

4. Follow the on-screen prompts to install Solaris 9. When the installation is completed, `suninstall` will prompt you to reboot or will reboot automatically after a brief delay.

5. Examine your installation logs for any errors. The installation logs will be located in the `/var/sadm/system/logs` and `/var/sadm/install/logs` directories.

6. Install any additional software as needed.

The list of steps to use suninstall might seem a bit simplistic. Realize, though, that the installation program is designed to walk you through the whole process. If you have your installation worksheet, you will find the installation process very straightforward. The hardest part is usually the planning.

Web Start

Solaris Web Start can be used to install Solaris 9 from a local or remote CD-ROM, DVD drive, or over the network. Like suninstall, Web Start can use a command-line interface, but Web Start also features a user-friendly graphical interface for installing Solaris.

 Web Start can be used to install Solaris 9 from a CD-ROM or DVD drive that is not attached to the local machine. For information on how to do this, please see the *Solaris 9 Installation Guide*, Appendix B, "Installing or Upgrading Remotely."

Most people prefer Web Start to suninstall simply because of the graphical interface. Also, Web Start will enable you to install additional software (suninstall does not) and Web Start can be run from a DVD. Here are the steps to install Solaris 9 by using Web Start:

1. Choose to install from the CD-ROM or DVD-ROM drive or from a network image.

    - If you are installing from the CD-ROM or DVD-ROM drive, insert the Solaris 9 Installation CD or Solaris 9 DVD.

    - If you are installing from a net installation image, change to the directory where the installation media is located to verify that the files are available.

2. Boot the system by using one of the following methods.

    - If the system is new out of the box, turn it on.

    - To boot from the CD-ROM or DVD-ROM, type **boot cdrom** at the ok prompt.

    - To boot from the network, type **boot net** at the ok prompt.

 If you wish to run Web Start in CLI mode instead of GUI mode, use the boot cdrom nowin or boot net nowin commands to boot without the windows interface.

3. Answer the system configuration questions. Use your installation worksheet that you completed earlier. If you have preconfigured system information, you will not be prompted for answers. After you answer the system configuration questions, the Solaris Web Start Kiosk and Welcome to Solaris dialog box appears if you are using the GUI.

4. On the Installer Questions screen, decide whether you want to reboot the system automatically and whether you want to eject the disc after installation. Click Next.

5. On the Specify Media screen, choose the media type that you will be installing from. Click Next.

6. Choose an initial installation or upgrade installation.

7. Follow the on-screen instructions to complete the installation.

8. Check your installation logs for any errors. The installation logs will be located in the /var/sadm/system/logs and /var/sadm/install/logs directories.

Like the suninstall process, Web Start is easy to use and doesn't require a great deal of thought. Most of your time during a Web Start installation will be spent watching the blue progress bar creep along your screen as software packages are installed.

Upgrading from Previous Versions

If you want to upgrade from your current installation of Solaris 2.6, 7, or 8, you can use the same tools you used to perform an initial installation. In fact, the steps listed in the "Performing the Initial Installation" section will work. Just be sure to choose an upgrade installation instead of an initial installation when prompted.

 To see which version of Solaris you are running, type **uname –a** or **uname –r** at a command prompt.

One of the useful features available for upgrading Solaris is the disk space *reallocation* feature (also called *auto-layout*) provided with suninstall, Web Start, and custom JumpStart. If during the upgrade the installation program determines that the existing file systems do not have enough space for the upgrade, the auto-layout feature will attempt to alleviate the situation by reallocating disk space. It's important to know that the auto-layout feature can't actually grow existing file systems. It works by backing up the existing data, deleting the file system, re-creating a larger file system, and restoring the data. If auto-layout cannot reallocate space the way it wants to because of insufficient available disk space, you will have to manually reallocate enough space for the upgrade. The suninstall program enables you to manually reallocate disk space, but Web Start Flash archive extraction does not.

When performing an upgrade as opposed to an initial installation, there are some additional pre- and post-upgrade tasks you need to complete.

Pre-Upgrade Tasks

There are a series of pre-upgrade tasks that you will need to perform before you begin your upgrade. However, the actual upgrade process should be as simple as installing a fresh copy.

One of the first things to be aware of before you attempt an upgrade is that you cannot upgrade your system to a software group that is not installed on your system. In other words, if your current Solaris 8 installation has the End User Software Group installed, you cannot upgrade to the Entire Software Group. If you now want the Entire Software Group, you will need to perform an initial installation.

If you already have Solaris 9 installed on your computer and you want to upgrade to a Solaris 9 Update release, you need to be aware of changes to installed patches. If the patch is part of the Solaris 9 Update release, it will be reapplied to your system. However, if the patch is not part of the Update release, it will be removed from your system. Using Sun's Patch Analyzer (which appears automatically in Solaris Web Start and `suninstall`) can help determine which patches will be affected by the upgrade.

The most important thing you can do before beginning an upgrade is to back up your existing system. In fact, it's so important that I'm going to mention it here in the text as well as in a warning. Obviously, if you don't care about the data on the system, then backups can be ignored. However, many people who care about their data forget about this crucial task. If you don't have your data backed up and something goes wrong during the upgrade, you might lose all your original data. It's a mistake you'll only make once.

Always back up critical data before beginning an upgrade!

The last thing to check before beginning an upgrade is to see whether there are any existing problems on the computer. Check `docs.sun.com` for potential problems or release notes regarding upgrade conflicts. Also, if your current machine is having particular problems, you will want to fix them before upgrading.

Post-Upgrade Tasks

When you perform an upgrade, both the `suninstall` and Web Start programs attempt to merge existing local software settings with the new Solaris software. Most of the time, no problems arise. However, if there are problems, they could be serious enough to make your system not boot. After you upgrade, follow these three steps to ensure proper operation:

1. Review the `/a/var/sadm/system/data/upgrade_cleanup` file to determine whether you need to correct any local settings that the installation program could not preserve.

You must review the `/a/var/sadm/system/data/upgrade_cleanup` file before you perform your initial reboot, or it will be erased.

2. Correct any local modifications that were not preserved.

3. Reboot your system by typing **reboot** at a command prompt.

Installing and Managing Software Packages

Applications are the lifeblood of any computer system. Some applications, such as StarOffice, enable you to be productive. Other applications, such as Netscape Navigator and various games, might have questionable productivity value but provide considerable entertainment.

Regardless of your productivity or entertainment goals, you need to know how to install and manage software on Solaris 9 computers.

In many cases, an application needs more than one file to run. Sure, one file, the executable, actually opens the application, but additional support files might be needed as well. When you install an application, you need to install the required files, directories, and paths in addition to the executable.

In Solaris, applications are bundled as software packages. A *software package* is the collection of files and directories needed to run a particular program. Packages might be provided by Sun or a third party, but are always identified by a unique name. Sun packages will always start with the SUNW moniker, whereas other companies' programs will start with their company ticker symbol. As an example, Sun's audio drivers are installed as the SUNWaudd package, whereas Netscape Communicator is the NSCPcom package.

Solaris 9 has multiple options for installing, managing, and removing software. Graphical options include Admintool and the Solaris Product Registry 3.0. Command-line options include `pkgadd`, `pkginfo`, `pkgchk`, `pkgask`, and `pkgrm`. To add or remove software packages from Solaris 9, you must have superuser privileges or be able to assume an equivalent role.

Managing Software Graphically

The three options for managing software through a graphical interface in Solaris 9 are Web Start, Admintool (`admintool`), and the Solaris Product Registry (`prodreg`). There are both positive and negative aspects to managing your software through graphical interfaces in Solaris 9. On the positive side, if you are unsure of the program's package name but you need to remove it, the list of packages is more manageable with the graphical interfaces. The negative aspect is that the graphical interfaces do not afford you the flexibility of their command-line counterparts.

All three graphical installation programs enable you to add and remove software packages from stand-alone or networked systems, view currently installed software, and choose software from an installation media.

 None of the graphical software management tools enable you to add packages to a spool directory or to use an administration file to eliminate user interaction.

Of the three, Web Start is the least useful after Solaris 9 is installed and running. Web Start is used to install Solaris (as you read about earlier in this chapter), and although it can install software groups, it cannot be used to install individual software packages.

Admintool was a popular administrative tool in Solaris 8 for managing users and groups, in addition to software. Although Admintool is still available in Solaris 9, Sun is phasing it out in favor of the Solaris Management Console. To manage software by using Admintool, launch Admintool by choosing Workspace Menu ➤ Tools from Application Manager, or by typing **admintool** from a command prompt. From the Browse menu, choose Software. The Admintool Software screen is shown in Figure 2.1.

FIGURE 2.1   Admintool Software management

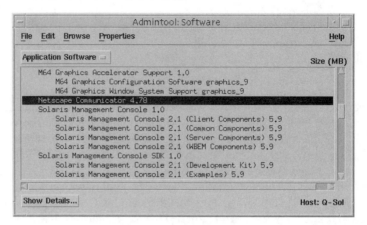

 When you open Admintool in Solaris 9, it warns you that Admintool has been declared obsolete and might not be present in Solaris releases after May 2002. If it's one of your preferred management tools, you might want to find an alternative.

As you can see in Figure 2.1, Admintool lists the various packages that are installed on your machine. To find out detailed information about a package, simply double-click it, or highlight it and click the Show Details button. Software details are shown in Figure 2.2. Packages are added, modified, and removed in Admintool by using the Edit ➢ Add, Modify, and Delete menu options.

FIGURE 2.2   Admintool software details

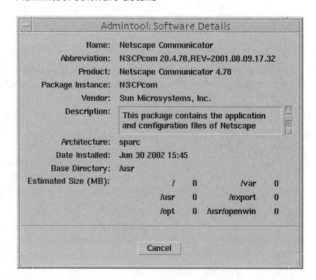

The Solaris Product Registry 3.0 is new to Solaris 9. Like Admintool, the Product Registry provides an easy-to-use graphical interface to manage your software. It also categorizes your software and tracks all software installed on the system. The Product Registry displays all software listed in the /var/sadm/install/contents file, otherwise known as the software installation database.

To launch the Solaris Product Registry, use the icon in Application Manager or type **prodreg** from a command line. Figure 2.3 shows the Solaris Product Registry.

FIGURE 2.3   Solaris Product Registry

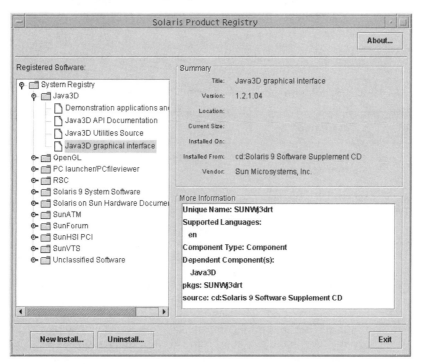

To add or remove software, use the New Install or Uninstall buttons at the bottom of the console. As always, when removing packages, be mindful of software dependencies. If you remove a package that is required for an application to function, your action will obviously cause problems. The Product Registry conveniently displays dependent components to help avoid potential conflicts.

Managing Software via Command Line

Although the command-line interface (CLI) does not offer pretty pictures, it does have one distinct advantage: flexibility. Managing software through the CLI is the only way to use many options, including installing a package into a spool directory and using an administration file to abolish the need for user interaction.

Installing Software

The primary command to install software in Solaris 9 is pkgadd. This command enables you to install software from an installation medium (CD, DVD, or other hard disk) and copy installation files to a spool directory for future installation. By default, pkgadd will look in the default spool directory, /var/spool/pkg, for the installation files. The syntax for pkgadd is as follows:

pkgadd *arguments package_name*

If you wanted to install a package called SUNWexp from the files directory on a CD-ROM named CDR1, you would type the following:

pkgadd -d /cdrom/CDR1/files SUNWexp

Table 2.1 lists some of the common command-line arguments for pkgadd.

TABLE 2.1   *pkgadd* Command-Line Arguments

Argument	Description
-a *admin*	Defines an installation administration file to be used instead of the default administration file.
-d *device*	Instructs pkgadd to install or copy a package from a specified directory instead of the default (/var/spool/pkg).
-r *response*	Identifies a file or directory that contains output from a previous pkgask session. Using this option can eliminate user interaction during the installation.
-s *spool*	Copies the package into a specified spool directory instead of installing the application.
-Y *category*	Installs packages based on their category (as defined by the CATEGORY parameter in the packages' pkginfo file), not package name.

When you install a package, pkgadd checks the current directory for an administration file. Administration files provide information as to how the installation should proceed, such as installing without asking the user for confirmation. If there is no administration file in the current directory, pkgadd checks the /var/sadm/install/admin directory or the directory specified by the -a switch.

On a network, perhaps the most useful pkgadd switch is -s. This enables an administrator to set up a network installation server and copy frequently installed packages into a spool directory. The administrator can then mount the remote directory on the local machine (we'll look at how to do that in Chapter 7, "File System Management") and use pkgadd -d to install the package.

After you've installed software, it's a good idea to check the integrity of the installation with the *pkgchk* command. The syntax for pkgchk is as follows:

pkgchk *arguments package_name*

Some popular command-line arguments for pkgchk are listed in Table 2.2.

TABLE 2.2 *pkgchk* Command-Line Arguments

Argument	Description
-a	Checks only file attributes, not attributes and contents. Checking attributes and contents is the default action.
-c	Checks only file contents, not contents and attributes.
-d *device*	Specifies the device to check as the spool directory.
-f	Fixes file attributes, if possible.
-n	Does not check editable or volatile files. For any application that has been modified since installation, this is a good option.
-q	Indicates quiet mode, which does not give information about missing files.
-v	Indicates verbose mode, which lists all files as they are checked.

If you do not supply a specific package to check, pkgchk will look at all installed packages on your system. This operation could take a while. If pkgchk does not discover any error messages, it will return you to a command prompt. Any errors will be listed on-screen.

Response Files

If you want to minimize user interaction when installing packages, you can create a response file that provides answers to questions asked by the installation program. First, you need to make the package an *interactive package* by creating a request script. After the request script is created, you use the pkgask command to create the response file. When installing a package, use pkgadd -r to invoke a response file.

Package Information

To find information about all packages installed on your system or to gain information about a specific package, use the pkginfo command.

If you type **pkginfo** at the command line, you will receive brief information about all software packages installed on your system. To get information on a specific package, type **pkginfo *package_name***. For more detailed information, use **pkginfo -l *package_name***, as shown in Figure 2.4.

FIGURE 2.4 pkginfo -l output

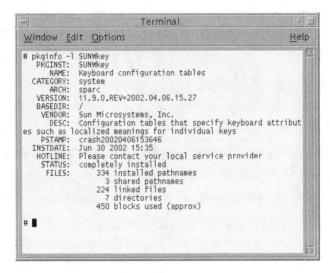

Removing Software

To remove installed packages in Solaris 9, use the pkgrm command. The syntax of pkgrm is as follows:

```
# pkgrm arguments package_name
```

Many of the same arguments that are used for pkgadd are also used for pkgrm. For example, the -s switch is used to remove spooled packages. The one major exception is the -A switch, which will remove the package from the computer regardless of any shared files. When removing software on a Solaris machine, keep in mind the following points:

- By default, files shared with other applications (besides the one you are removing) are not deleted.

- Be aware of package dependencies. Don't remove a package if a program you need to use requires it.

- Although you can use the rm command to remove files, don't use it to remove software packages. It will corrupt the software database.

- The removef command can be used to remove an individual file and it will update the software database. However, it's not recommended for removing packages, which contain many files. Removing one file can cause packages to fail.

It's important to know how to both add and remove software properly. If you add software that corrupts your system, you could have to reinstall your operating system. The same goes for removing software. Doing so improperly could have you performing an installation.

Last but not least, don't forget that to remove software packages, you must have superuser privileges or be able to assume an equivalent role.

Real World Scenario

Problems Installing Software

You have recently been promoted to systems administrator for your small service field office, and the former systems administrator has moved on to greener pastures. You know that the previous administrator set up one of your two Solaris 9 servers as an installation server so she could install software on clients without having to carry the installation media around with her.

One of your users has just received a promotion and needs to have some new software packages installed on his machine. So, you go to the client machine and mount the directory on the server that you know contains the installation files. When you try to use the pkgadd command to install the ACCTwksp package, you get the following error message: WARNING: ACCTwksp <not present on Read Only file system>. What could be the problem?

Behind the scenes, what has happened is that the files necessary to install the ACCTwksp package were for some reason not installed on the server by the first administrator. If you get this warning message, you must first install the package on the server, as opposed to just copying it to a spool directory. After that, the installation should proceed normally. When using installation servers, make sure the software installation packages are current.

Installing and Managing Patches

A *patch* is a collection of files and directories designed to improve the performance of a program or operating system. To put it in a more un-politically correct way, patches fix problems. Patches can fix simple things, such as misbehaving utilities, as well as serious security flaws. In Solaris 9, Sun provides the graphical Patches Tool and the patchadd and patchrm commands for patch management. To see whether your system needs a patch, go to http://sunsolve.sun.com/patches.

Sun distributes patches in three ways. You can obtain them from Sun's web page (http://sunsolve.sun.com/patches), anonymous FTP site (ftp://sunsolve.sun.com), or by CD-ROM if you have a SunSpectrum service contract.

A six-digit number followed by a hyphen and a two-digit extension identifies all Sun patches. Valid examples of patch numbers are 109715-05 and 110927-01. The first six numbers are referred to as the base code, and the last two numbers are the revision number of the patch. To add or remove patches, you must be the superuser or be able to assume an equivalent role.

If you want to, you can even sign up on Sun's support website to have new patch advisories e-mailed to you directly.

Managing Patches Graphically

The Solaris Management Console includes a Patch Tool that enables you to view installed patches, add new patches, and add new patches to multiple systems at once. When you install Solaris 9 and open Patch Tool, it informs you that in order to achieve full functionality, you must download and install the PatchPro application from www.sun.com/PatchPro. If you download PatchPro, the Patch Tool can also analyze your system for patch needs and download them from the Internet for you. Sun insists that the process is secure and that no information about your computer is transmitted to Sun. Patch Tool is shown in Figure 2.5.

FIGURE 2.5   Solaris Management Console's Patch Tool

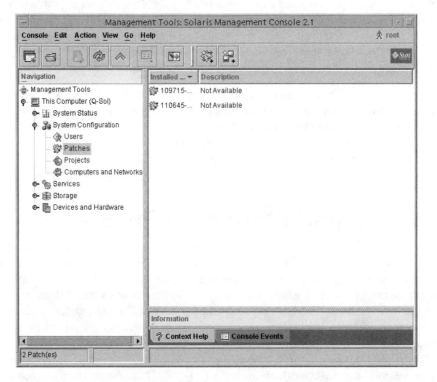

In Patch Tool, all patch management functions are performed through the Action menu.

Managing Patches via Command Line

Patches are added in Solaris 9 through the `patchadd` command. The syntax for `patchadd` is as follows:

```
# patchadd arguments patch_id
```

in which *patch_id* is the number of the patch you wish to install. Multiple patches can be added at once by separating the patch numbers with spaces.

When you use patchadd, the patch installation is logged in the /var/sadm/patch/*patch_id*/log file. If for some reason the patch installation fails, or you want to later remove the patch, the log file is used to restore the patched files to their original state. If you use patchadd -d, the files to be patched will not be backed up and you will not be able to subsequently delete the patch. The -d option will save hard disk space. The following items will cause patch installation to fail:

- The patch requires another patch that is not installed.
- The patch is for a different hardware architecture.
- There is already an installed patch with the same base code but higher revision.
- The patch is incompatible with a currently installed patch.

To see what patches are installed on your computer, you have two options: patchadd -p and showrev -p. You can use either option to see installed patches on local and remote systems.

To remove a patch, use the patchrm command. There are three cases in which patchrm will fail:

- The patch you are trying to remove is required by another patch.
- The patch has been made obsolete by another patch.
- The patch was installed with the patchadd -d command.

Although the graphical management interfaces are easier to use, you are more likely to be tested on the CLI commands and associated switches.

Summary

In this chapter, you looked at the first critical step to ensuring proper operation of your Solaris 9 computer, the installation. Good installations generally result from good planning. Be sure to know your goals of the installation before you begin the process. Solaris 9 can be installed locally from CD-ROM or DVD-ROM, or over the network from an installation server. The installation programs are suninstall, Web Start, JumpStart, and Live Upgrade.

You then looked at installing software on Solaris 9. Solaris programs are distributed as software packages. Packages can be added during installation or after the system is operational. The graphical Admintool and Product Registry, as well as the command-line pkgadd, pkgchk, and pkgrm utilities, can be used to manage software.

Finally, you explored software patches. If bugs are found in an existing application, or a potential security breach is discovered, Sun will create and issue a patch to eliminate the problem. Patches can be managed with the graphical Patch Tool in the Solaris Management Console, or with the patchadd and patchrm utilities at the command line.

Exam Essentials

Understand how the suninstall program works. suninstall is a CLI installation utility for the Solaris 9 operating environment.

Know the four installation methods for Solaris 9. The four installation options are suninstall, Web Start, JumpStart, and Live Upgrade.

Know the five software groups available in Solaris 9. The five software groups are Core, End User, Developer, Entire, and Entire plus OEM.

Understand the two options available for preconfiguring a system for installation. You can preconfigure an installation with a sysidcfg file, or by supplying necessary information to a NIS or NIS+ name server. Preconfiguration can be used with suninstall, Web Start, and custom JumpStart.

Know the commands to add and remove software packages in Solaris 9. To add a software package, use the pkgadd command. To remove a package, use the pkgrm command.

Know the commands to add and remove patches in Solaris 9. To add a patch, use the patchadd command. Patches are removed with the patchrm command.

Key Terms

Before you take the exam, be certain you are familiar with the following terms:

auto-layout	pkgchk
command-line interface (CLI)	pkginfo
interactive package	pkgrm
JumpStart	reallocation
Live Upgrade	response file
master system	software group
patch	software package
patchadd	suninstall
patchrm	sysidcfg
pkgadd	Web Start

Commands Used in This Chapter

The following list contains a summary of all the commands introduced in this chapter:

Command	Description
boot	Boots the computer
patchadd	Adds patches
patchrm	Removes patches
pkgadd	Adds software packages
pkgask	Creates a response file for automated installation
pkgchk	Checks the integrity of installed packages
pkginfo	Provides information about software packages
pkgrm	Removes software packages
reboot	Reboots the computer
showrev	Displays installed patches
uname	Displays system name information including operating system and platform version

Review Questions

1. You are beginning a Solaris 9 installation on a group of computers for your company's network. Two of the computers have only 96MB of RAM, and the others all have at least 128MB of RAM. For the computers with 96MB of RAM, which installation method should you choose?

    A. Web Start

    B. JumpStart

    C. `suninstall`

    D. Solaris 9 cannot be installed on a computer with only 96MB RAM.

2. The Sun workstation that you are currently using is running Solaris 2.5.1. You just received your copy of Solaris 9 and want to perform an upgrade that will preserve your system's settings. What is the likely result of your upgrade attempt?

    A. The upgrade will succeed, but you will be able to install only the software group level currently installed on your computer.

    B. The upgrade will succeed, and you will be able to install any software group you choose.

    C. The upgrade will fail because your computer does not have sufficient RAM to run Solaris 9.

    D. The upgrade will fail because you cannot directly upgrade Solaris 2.5.1 to Solaris 9.

3. From a command prompt on your Solaris 9 workstation, you want a complete listing of all software packages installed on your system. Which command should you execute?

    A. `pkginfo -s`

    B. `pkginfo`

    C. `pkginfo -e`

    D. `pkgchk -s`

    E. `pkgparam -s`

4. You are the in-house Solaris 9 administrator for your company. Recently, you purchased a software package that is a newer version of a software package you are currently running. The manufacturer of the package recommends deleting the current software before installing the new version. The name of both packages is ACMEexec. The current version is installed in the /opt/acme directory. What command should you execute to remove this software?

    A. `pkgrm -s /opt/acme ACMEexec`

    B. `pkgrm ACMEexec -d /opt/acme`

    C. `pkgrm -R /opt/acme ACMEexec`

    D. `rm /opt/acme ACMEexec`

5. You are preparing to install Solaris 9 from a CD-ROM on a new computer for your supervisor. What are some requirements for the installation to be successful? (Choose all that apply.)

   A. 96MB of RAM

   B. 128MB of RAM

   C. 512MB of unused disk slice

   D. SPARC platform

6. You are in charge of managing your company's Solaris 9 servers. You need to see which patches are currently installed on your servers in order to determine whether new patches are needed. What commands can you issue to see which patches are currently installed? (Choose all that apply.)

   A. patchadd -p

   B. patchchk -p

   C. patchinfo -p

   D. showrev -p

7. You are the network administrator for your company. Your network consists of two Sun servers and forty Sun Ultra 450 client machines. You are concerned that your computers will not be able to support an upgrade to Solaris 9. What can you do to find out the platform group of your computers?

   A. Issue the uname -m command.

   B. Issue the uname -r command.

   C. Check the system's sysidcfg file.

   D. Issue the sysver -m command.

   E. Issue the sysver -a command.

8. You are installing Solaris 9 onto a new production server for your network. You plan to use the crash dump feature on this server. To do so, which of the following requirements must be met?

   A. The /opt file system must be at least twice the size of physical memory.

   B. The /var file system must be at least twice the size of physical memory.

   C. The /temp file system must be at least twice the size of physical memory.

   D. The /var file system must be at least three times the size of physical memory.

9. You are the network administrator for your company. Employees at your company work around the clock and require constant access to your company's two Solaris production servers. You are going to upgrade your servers from Solaris 8 to Solaris 9. Which option should you choose to perform the upgrade while minimizing downtime?

   A. Web Start Flash

   B. Custom JumpStart

   C. suninstall

   D. Live Upgrade

10. You are performing an initial installation of Solaris 9 on your Sun workstation. Because disk space is limited, you want to install the least amount of software possible. However, you still want to install the Common Desktop Environment (CDE) without having to add the package for it manually. Which software group should you choose during installation?

A. Core

B. End User

C. Developer

D. Entire

11. You are the network administrator for your company. You've been asked to explore adding software packages to your Solaris 9 server. Which of the following tasks can you accomplish by using the Solaris Product Registry? (Choose all that apply.)

A. Install packages into a spool directory

B. Install packages onto multiple systems

C. View currently installed software packages

D. Choose packages from different installation media

12. As the network administrator, you approach one of your users in the engineering department about upgrading his computer to Solaris 9. He says that the upgrade is fine with him, but he's not sure whether the version he has is upgradeable. When you ask him what version he has, he says that he's not sure because he's deleted and reinstalled many versions multiple times. What command can you use to find the version of Solaris he is currently running? (Choose all that apply.)

A. name -a

B. uname -m

C. uname -r

D. uname -v

13. You just completed an installation of a new software package called SUNWgspt on one of your Solaris 9 servers. As the network administrator, you now want to verify that the package installed properly. During verification, you want to check file attributes, repair file attributes if possible, and list all files as they are being checked. Your working directory is the directory that the application is installed in. What command should you execute?

A. pkgchk -f -v SUNWgspt

B. pkgchk -c -f -v SUNWgspt

C. pkgchk -f -l SUNWgspt

D. pkgchk -c -f -l SUNWgspt

14. You are the in-house Solaris manager for your company. You have 20 identical Sun workstations that you want to install Solaris 9 on. To save time, you want to automate the installation as much as possible. Which installation methods enable you to perform this automation? (Choose all that apply.)

    A. `suninstall`

    B. Web Start Flash

    C. Custom JumpStart

    D. Live Upgrade

15. You are the network administrator for your company and you've been asked to install Solaris 9 on all the workstations in the accounting department. Because these accounting users are not computer savvy, you want to preconfigure as much of the installation process as possible. You decide to use a `sysidcfg` file. Which of the following options cannot be preconfigured when using a `sysidcfg` file? (Choose all that apply.)

    A. Host name

    B. IP address

    C. Time zone

    D. Name server

    E. Power management

16. You are the systems administrator for your company. One of your tasks is to upgrade all Solaris 8 servers to Solaris 9. What are the recommended pre-upgrade tasks that you should complete? (Choose all that apply.)

    A. Back up the existing system

    B. Verify disk space and hardware requirements

    C. Analyze patches that will need to be replaced

    D. Create a Web Start Flash archive

17. You are the network administrator for your company. You are beginning an initial installation of Solaris 9 from the Solaris 9 DVD. Your computer boots to an `ok` prompt. What do you type to boot the computer from the DVD-ROM?

    A. `boot dvdrom`

    B. `boot cdrom`

    C. `boot`

    D. `boot dvd`

18. You are the network administrator for your company. You are going to install three patches on your Solaris 9 server. The patch numbers are 115083-01, 116552-03, and 152431-01. All three patches are located in the /tmp/patches directory. What command can you execute to install all patches at the same time?

   A. patchadd –M /tmp/patches 115083-01 116552-03 152431-01

   B. patchadd –M /tmp/patches 115083-01, 116552-03, 152431-01

   C. patchadd –M /tmp/patches 115083-01; 116552-03; 152431-01

   D. patchadd –M /tmp/patches 115083-01: 116552-03: 152431-01

19. You are the network administrator for your company. To expedite software installation, you have created interactive software packages. Now you need to create a response file for use with those packages. What command can you use to create the necessary response files?

   A. pkgparam

   B. pkgask

   C. pkginfo

   D. pkgresp

20. You are the Solaris 9 administrator for your company. Recently, you set up a Solaris 9 server to act as a network installation server for commonly installed software packages. You just received a new CD-ROM containing a package that you want to make readily available. The package is the only file on the CD-ROM, and you want to copy it to the default spool directory without installing it. What command should you issue?

   A. pkgadd –d /cdrom/cdrom0

   B. pkgadd –Y –d –s/cdrom/cdrom0

   C. pkgadd –d –s /cdrom/cdrom0

   D. pkgadd –s –d /cdrom/cdrom0

Answers to Review Questions

1.   C.   For computers with fewer than 128MB of RAM, `suninstall` is the best choice. This is because it uses only a command-line interface, whereas the other installation programs default to a graphical interface, which requires more resources.

2.   D.   The upgrade will indeed fail. To perform an upgrade, you must have Solaris 2.6 or higher. No mention was made of your computer's hardware configuration, so it cannot be assumed that you do not have enough memory for the upgrade.

3.   B.   To list all the software packages installed on your system, execute the `pkginfo` command with no arguments. The `-s` and `-e` switches are invalid for use with `pkginfo`. The `pkgchk` command will check the integrity of installed packages, and `pkgparam` displays values associated with specified parameters of a package.

4.   C.   To remove the software, use the `pkgrm` command. The -R switch should be used to specify the directory that the package is installed in. Never use the `rm` command to delete software packages because it will corrupt the software database.

5.   A, C.   Although it's recommended to use at least 128MB of RAM, Solaris 9 *requires* 96MB of RAM. Because you are installing from a CD-ROM, you need a disk slice that is at least 512MB in size and not used to store files (preferably the swap slice).

6.   A, D.   The two commands that will show you currently installed patches are `patchadd -p` and `showrev -p`. The other two commands, `patchchk` and `patchinfo`, do not exist.

7.   A.   The `uname -m` command will return information about your system's platform group, such as sun4m or sun4u. The `uname -r` command will show which version of Solaris you are currently running. The `sysidcfg` file is for automating installations, and the `sysver` command does not exist.

8.   B.   To use the `savecore` crash dump feature, the `/var` file system must be at least twice the size of the amount of physical memory installed in the computer.

9.   D.   Live Upgrade enables you to create a duplicate boot environment on a running Solaris server. You can then install Solaris 9 onto the dormant boot environment, activate it, and then reboot your server. Of all the installation methods, Live Upgrade enables you to upgrade with the least disruption to a production environment.

10.   B.   The core software group does not install CDE. The end user, developer, and entire software groups do install CDE. Of the three, the End User software group is the smallest.

11.   B, C, D.   With the graphical Solaris Product Registry, you can install packages onto one or more stand-alone or networked systems, view currently installed packages, and choose from installation media when installing packages. You cannot install packages into a spool directory. To do that, you must use the `pkgadd -s` command.

12.   A, C.   The `uname -r` or `uname -a` command is used to display the current Solaris version. The `uname -m` command will display the hardware platform of the computer.

13. A.   The `pkgchk` command is used to verify installation of packages. Checking files and attributes is default behavior, so no switches are needed. To fix files, use the `-f` switch. To list all files as they are being checked, use the `-v` switch.

14. B, C.   Web Start Flash and Custom JumpStart enable you to automate an installation of Solaris 9. The `suninstall` and Live Upgrade programs are installation options, but they do not provide for automation of installations.

15. E.   A `sysidcfg` file can be used to supply answers to most installation questions. However, it cannot be used to preconfigure power management. If you want to use `sysidcfg` to configure a host name and IP address, you will need a separate `sysidcfg` file for each computer. It might be a time-consuming option, but it is possible.

16. A, B, C.   Before upgrading a server, it is imperative that you back up existing data. That way, if something goes wrong with the upgrade, you don't lose everything. Also, you should verify that you have enough disk space and hardware to support Solaris 9, and determine which critical patches will be overwritten and need to be replaced. Although you could create a Web Start Flash archive, there is no need to do so.

17. B.   At the ok prompt, to boot the computer from the DVD-ROM, you type **boot cdrom**. Just typing **boot** does not specify the DVD-ROM device, and `boot dvdrom` and `boot dvd` are not valid commands.

18. A.   Multiple patches can be added with one command of `patchadd`. Simply separate the patch numbers with spaces.

19. B.   To create a response file to be used with interactive packages, use the `pkgask` command. The `pkgparam` command will display parameters about a package, and `pkginfo` will display information about one or more installed packages. The `pkgresp` command does not exist.

20. D.   The `-s` option tells `pkgadd` to spool the package into the default spool directory (although another can be specified) instead of installing it. The `-d` option tells `pkgadd` to look at a specific device or directory for the installation files, instead of looking in the spool directory.

Chapter

3

System Initialization and Shutdown

SOLARIS 9 EXAM OBJECTIVES COVERED IN THIS CHAPTER:

✓ Explain how to execute boot PROM commands to: identify the system's boot PROM version; boot the system; access detailed information; list, change, and restore default NVRAM parameters; display devices connected to the bus; identify the system's boot device; create and remove custom device aliases; view and change NVRAM parameters from the shell; and interrupt a hung system.

✓ Given a scenario involving a hung system, troubleshoot problems and deduce resolutions.

✓ Explain how to perform a system boot, control boot processes, and complete a system shutdown, using associated directories, scripts, and commands.

Understanding the Solaris boot process will help eliminate many potential boot problems and enable you to effectively troubleshoot any boot problems that do arise. On SPARC-based Solaris systems, the boot process is divided into two major categories: the boot PROM (Programmable Read-Only Memory) and system initialization.

The boot PROM, officially called the OpenBoot PROM, isn't directly part of Solaris. Rather, it is firmware stored on the motherboard and it runs before Solaris does. OpenBoot is in operation from the time the power is turned on and is responsible for loading the Solaris operating environment.

Intel-based Solaris computers do not have an OpenBoot PROM. Instead, Intel-based computers have a system BIOS (Basic Input/Output System) that controls the boot process. Although the BIOS performs many of the same tasks as OpenBoot, it typically lacks the complete functionality provided by OpenBoot.

After Solaris is initialized, there are many ways the boot process can unfold. The SPARC and Intel platforms use different boot files. But regardless of your platform, booting Solaris requires selecting a run level and executing the proper run control scripts, ultimately providing access to system resources. Shutting down Solaris properly also requires the use of scripts.

In this chapter, you will look at the OpenBoot PROM, including configuration, diagnostic, and boot options, followed by an overview of the Intel boot process. Then you will learn how to properly boot the Solaris operating environment, as well as how to properly shut down Solaris and troubleshoot a hung system.

Understanding the OpenBoot PROM

On *Scalable Processor Architecture (SPARC)* computers, the initial booting of the computer is controlled by the *OpenBoot PROM (OBP)*. The OBP acts as an intermediary between the hardware and the Solaris operating system, preparing the computer for the loading of an operating system during boot.

The OBP is stored in two chips on your motherboard and controls the entire boot process of your Sun computer. The two parts of the OBP are the boot PROM itself, which contains startup information regarding your system, and the *Non-Volatile Random Access Memory (NVRAM)*. The NVRAM contains built-in hardware diagnostics, device information, device aliases, the host ID, Ethernet address, and system Time of Day (TOD) clock. The most current version of OpenBoot is version 4.*x*, and the examples listed in this chapter reflect this version.

OBP is often referred to as firmware, because it's not quite classified as software or hardware but acts as a liaison between the two. Without OBP, the system would not know how to boot, and Solaris would never load.

The OBP is directly responsible for the following tasks:

- Determining the system's hardware configuration
- Testing and initializing the system's hardware
- Loading the operating system from a local storage device or the network
- Providing an interface for modification of system startup configuration parameters and NVRAM parameters
- Interpreting programs written in the Forth programming language

The boot process on a SPARC computer has four distinct phases: the boot PROM, boot programs, kernel initialization, and init. The boot process on a SPARC machine follows this order:

1. In the boot PROM phase, the boot PROM displays system information and runs the Power-On Self-Test (POST), which checks the integrity of the system's hardware and memory. The hardware check is fairly superficial and will detect only serious problems. After the POST, the boot PROM loads *bootblk (boot block)*, the primary startup program. The sole purpose of `bootblk` is to find and execute the secondary boot program, `ufsboot`, and load it into memory.

2. During the boot programs phase, `bootblk` finds and executes the secondary boot program, *ufsboot*, and loads it into memory. Then `ufsboot` loads the operating system's kernel.

3. During the kernel initialization phase, the kernel initializes and begins loading modules. After enough modules are loaded, the kernel mounts the root (/) file system. The kernel then starts the `/sbin/init` process, which reads the `/etc/inittab` file to start other processes.

4. The last phase is the init phase. Here the `/sbin/init` process loads *run control (rc) scripts*, which in turn execute other scripts to complete the operating system initialization.

Know the order of boot phases for a SPARC computer: boot PROM, boot programs, kernel initialization, and init.

The `/sbin/init` process and `/etc/inittab` files will be discussed in more depth later in this chapter. Knowing the order of the boot process can help you determine where to start troubleshooting if there is a boot problem on your computer.

OpenBoot Features

Although OpenBoot was originally designed to work on SPARC systems, it features a processor-independent design. Because of this, it is not proprietary, and its considerable functionality can be used on many platform types. Here are some notable features of OpenBoot:

Plug-in device drivers   A plug-in driver is a driver loaded from an expansion bus card located within your machine. Plug-in drivers can be used to boot the operating system, thereby avoiding the boot PROM. This feature is useful if you have devices that are not supported by your existing firmware; you can operate your system without changing your boot PROM.

FCode interpreter   Plug-in drivers are written in a language called FCode, which is machine independent. Each OBP contains an FCode interpreter. This enables the same devices and drivers to be used on machines that have differing CPU types.

Device tree   All hardware devices installed in a Sun computer are part of a hierarchical classification system called a *device tree*. The position within the device tree identifies the physical location of the device (also known as a node) within the system.

A node with children is typically a system bus (such as an IDE or SCSI bus). Child devices (physical disks, expansion cards) are identified by a unique hardware address, with their address being based on their parent node. The hardware address (also called the physical address) is based upon the unique physical location of the device in the system, such as a particular controller or slot.

Programmable user interface   The OBP is based on the Forth programming language. Users can create programs in this language to perform various tasks, including modifying some boot processes, and debugging hardware and software problems.

Accessing OpenBoot

OpenBoot is accessed through a user interface based on the Forth programming language. Consequently, you will often hear the OBP prompt referred to as a *Forth Monitor* or Forth prompt. When you are in the OBP, you will be given an ok prompt.

Some older versions of OpenBoot used a > as their prompt. This was known as the Restricted Monitor. If your machine gives you this prompt, type **n** and press Enter to switch to an ok prompt.

There are four ways to enter the OBP:

- If you are in Solaris, use the init 0 or shutdown commands to halt the operating system.
- Press the Stop and A keys at the same time (Stop+A).
- Reboot the machine. If your computer is not configured to boot automatically, it will stop at the OBP prompt. If your system is configured to boot automatically, you can stop it by pressing Stop+A on the keyboard after the display banner appears but before the operating system loads.
- When the system detects an unrecoverable hardware error (called a Watchdog Reset).

If you are at the ok prompt and need assistance, type **help**.

Devices and Device Aliases

OpenBoot deals directly with all hardware devices in the system. Each device is identified by a unique device name, which categorizes the device based on its type and location within the system. All system devices are then organized into a device tree, which is built with information gathered during system POST. The following are two examples of device names:

`/pci@1f,0/ide@d/disk@0,0`

`/pci@1f,0/usb@c,3/keyboard@4`

The full device path names shown in the examples are a series of node names separated by slashes. The slash at the beginning indicates the machine node. The machine node is the root of the device tree and does not receive an explicit name. The first device name in the example shows the first internal IDE hard disk, disk0. The second device in the example is an external Universal Serial Bus (USB) device, the keyboard. Each device listed will have the following form:

`driver-name@unit-address:device-arguments`

To gain a better understanding of what all this means, analyze the earlier example. First, the hard disk. The first part of the device name (`/pci@1f,0`) indicates that this system has a PCI architecture. The `1f,0` portion represents an address on the main PCI system bus. Another common architecture to see with Sun systems is the SBus architecture, which will generally read as `/sbus@1f,0`. The `ide@d` portion indicates that this is an IDE controller, at address d. The last portion of the first example shows the device name of the disk, which is at address `0,0`. This generally refers to the first disk on that particular IDE controller.

Now on to the second example, this time without extra commentary. The keyboard is attached to the same motherboard as the hard disk, identified as `/pci@1f,0`. There is a USB controller at address c,3 (`usb@c,3`), and the keyboard itself is at address 4 on the USB controller. The more you deal with full device names, the more sense they tend to make. To display the list of configured devices in your system, use the following command:

ok **show-devs**

A lot of the devices that you will see will make some sense. Names such as `serial`, `parallel`, `floppy`, and `cdrom` are somewhat intuitive. Others might not make any sense at all, for example, `/pci@1f,0/pmu@3/ppm@0,b3`. Unless you know what `ppm` stands for, this name might not do much for you.

None of the earlier examples had any device arguments, so here's one more example for good measure:

`/sbus@1f,0/scsi@1,2/sd@2,0:a`

This example is from a system with SBus architecture, and `1f,0` represents an address on the main board. The SCSI controller is at address 1,2. The SCSI disk (`sd`) is attached to the SCSI bus at target 2, with a logical unit number of 0. Device arguments differ in format based on the device they are attached to, but they always follow a colon (such as `:a`, seen in the code line above). In this case, the driver for the SCSI disk interprets the argument as a partition value. So, this particular example refers to partition a of this SCSI disk.

It might be a necessary evil to have long device names to keep track of all unique devices on a computer. However, always having to type in the long name when referring to a device can get a bit cumbersome. There has to be an easier way, doesn't there? There is: device aliases.

Device Aliases

The sad fact is, computers are smarter than humans. Just ask a computer. They can look at a device name such as /sbus@1f,0/scsi@1,2/sd@2,0:a and immediately know everything they need to about the device. Humans on the other hand prefer simplicity. We'd rather call the device something easy to remember, such as "disk1." Disk1 is easier to say, type, and remember.

Device aliases are for human ease. A *device alias* is an ordinary name for a configured device on a Solaris-based computer. You can also think of a device alias as a shorthand notation for a full device path. Not all devices have device aliases, but some common ones are set up during installation. You can see the device aliases and their associated devices by typing the following:

ok **devalias**

Devices that are commonly referred to, such as the floppy, hard disks, CD-ROM drives, network card, keyboard, and mouse are among the devices that have default aliases. For devices that do not have an alias, you can manually create one by using the devalias command. Options for devalias are shown in Table 3.1.

TABLE 3.1   *devalias* Usage

Command	Description
devalias	Displays all current device aliases and their associated devices.
devalias *alias*	Displays the full path name to the specified device alias.
devalias *alias devicepath*	Defines an alias for the device path provided. If the alias provided already exists, the new value overwrites the old value.

If the system is reset or loses power, all user-defined device aliases are lost. To avoid this, you have two choices. One is to save the devalias command used to create the device in a portion of NVRAM called NVRAMRC (Non-Volatile Random Access Memory Run Control). The other is to use the nvalias command to create your aliases.

Booting from the Boot PROM

By default, most systems boot to a user login screen. This is because of two NVRAM variables: auto-boot? (set to true) and boot-command (set to boot). These two variables tell the system to auto-boot and to use the boot command, respectively. These NVRAM parameters will be discussed in more detail shortly.

However, there might be cases when you don't want your system to auto-boot, or maybe you have rebooted the system into the boot PROM and want to get back to Solaris. To boot your system manually from the ok prompt, you use (ironically) the boot command. Here is the syntax for the boot command:

ok **boot** *device filename arguments flags*

The boot command offers many options and gives the user great flexibility when controlling the boot process. The various parameters of the boot command are as follows:

- *device* enables the user to specify the device that the system will boot from. The default is generally the hard disk. Some choices for this parameter are disk, net, cdrom, tape, and floppy. Full device paths and device aliases can also be specified.

Booting from the network requires a boot server on the network and one of two protocols: Dynamic Host Configuration Protocol (DHCP) or Reverse Address Resolution Protocol (RARP). RARP is the default network boot protocol in Solaris 9.

- If you want to specify an alternate kernel as opposed to the default, you could use the *filename* option as the full path to the alternate kernel's file name. This could be handy if you are testing new products.

- The boot command supports various arguments. They include: -a, which boots into interactive mode, requiring the user to specify boot details (such as kernel, system file, root file system type, and physical name of the root device); -r, which is used after the system is reconfigured; and -s, which forces Solaris into the S run level.

To boot your Solaris computer into kernel debugging mode, type **boot kadb** at the ok prompt.

- All *flags* are passed on to the file specified in the *filename* parameter and are dependent upon how the file itself interprets them.

Running Diagnostics and Displaying System Information

One of the helpful features of OpenBoot is the built-in set of diagnostic tools. Diagnostic tools incorporated into OpenBoot enable you to test various system devices, including the system clock, floppy disk drive, network interface card, SCSI devices, and memory. A list of common diagnostic commands is displayed in Table 3.2.

TABLE 3.2   OpenBoot Diagnostic Commands

Command	Description
test floppy	Tests the floppy disk drive
test net	Tests the network adapter
test scsi	Tests SCSI adapters (if applicable)

TABLE 3.2   OpenBoot Diagnostic Commands *(continued)*

Command	Description
test /memory	Tests the system's memory
probe-scsi	Displays attached SCSI devices in the system (if applicable)
watch-clock	Displays the computer's real-time clock
watch-net	Monitors the network for broadcast packets

Unfortunately, not all the tests listed in Table 3.2 are available in all versions of OpenBoot. To see which tests are valid on your computer, type **help test** or **help diag** at the ok prompt.

OpenBoot also comes with a set of commands designed to display system information. We have already looked at two such commands: show-devs to display system devices and devalias to show device aliases. Table 3.3 lists more commands used to display system information.

TABLE 3.3   OpenBoot System Information Commands

Command	Description
banner	Displays the system's power-on banner
show-sbus	Shows a list of installed and probed SBus devices (if your computer has this architecture)
.enet-addr	Displays the current Ethernet address
.id-prom or .idprom	Displays ID PROM contents
.traps	Displays a list of processor trap types
.version	Shows detailed information about the OpenBoot PROM
.speed	Displays processor and system bus speeds

As with the diagnostic commands, not all of these informational commands are available in all OpenBoot versions. As an example, .speed does not work in OpenBoot release 4.5.

The most versatile of the information commands is banner. The banner command displays the same power-on banner you see at the beginning of the boot process and contains a great deal of information, including the OpenBoot version, amount of memory installed, serial number, Ethernet address, and host ID number. Here is an example.

ok **banner**

Sun Blade 100 (UltraSPARC-IIe), Keyboard Present
Copyright 1998-2002 Sun Microsystems, Inc. All rights reserved.
OpenBoot 4.5, 256 MB memory installed, Serial #8675309.
Ethernet address 0:3:ba:15:d:18, Host ID: 84107d19.

Both the banner and .version commands display information about the OpenBoot version. However, banner displays more-general system information, whereas .version displays detailed information about just the OpenBoot PROM.

Modifying NVRAM

Most user-definable OpenBoot variables are stored in an area of the OpenBoot PROM called Non-Volatile Random Access Memory (NVRAM). With these variables, you can control everything from the boot process to system output to OpenBoot security parameters. The exact variables offered depend on the version of OpenBoot you are using. Table 3.4 lists some of the more common variables, their default values, and a brief description. These values are listed in alphabetical order and might not be listed in this exact order on your computer.

TABLE 3.4   NVRAM Configuration Variables

Variable	Default	Description
auto-boot?	true	If true, the system boots automatically after power on or reset.
boot-command	boot	Command to execute if auto-boot? is true.
boot-device	disk	Default device from which to boot.
boot-file	empty	Optional arguments for the boot program.
diag-device	net	Boot source device for diagnostic testing.
diag-file	empty	Optional arguments for the boot program in diagnostic mode.
diag-switch?	false	If set to true, the system boots into diagnostic mode.
error-reset-recovery	boot	Recovery action to take after an error reset CPU trap. Options are none, sync, or boot.
fcode-debug?	false	If true, include name fields for plug-in device FCodes.
input-device	keyboard	Console input device. Usually keyboard, ttya, or ttyb.
nvramrc	empty	Contents of NVRAMRC.

TABLE 3.4 NVRAM Configuration Variables *(continued)*

Variable	Default	Description
oem-banner	empty	If oem-banner? is true, the custom banner to use.
oem-banner?	false	If true, use a custom OEM banner.
oem-logo	empty	Byte array of the custom OEM banner, displayed in hexadecimal.
oem-logo?	false	If true, use the custom OEM logo instead of the Sun logo.
output-device	screen	Console output device. Usually screen, ttya, or ttyb.
screen-#columns	80	Number of characters per line on-screen.
screen-#rows	34	Number of on-screen rows or lines.
security-#badlogins	empty	Number of incorrect firmware security password attempts.
security-mode	none	Firmware security level. Options are none, command, or full.
security-password	empty	Firmware security password. Not displayed for obvious security reasons.
use-nvramrc?	false	If true, executes the command located in NVRAMRC during system boot.

As you can see in Table 3.4, quite a few parameters can be set in NVRAM. Some of them, such as the boot options, can be critical to system operation. Others, such as the OEM series of parameters, don't exactly affect critical system functions. However, by using oem-banner and oem-logo, you can create your own custom boot banner and logo to be displayed when the system is powered on. They might not be critical settings, but they can be fun.

With so many possible NVRAM parameters, you can't be expected to memorize them all. Besides, Solaris 9 can be installed on a variety of systems. Therefore, you won't have to know all options for OpenBoot 4.5 (or any other version) by heart. That being the case, it's still a good idea to know some of the more common options, for example, the boot series and the security series. You don't need to commit Table 3.4's contents to memory, but be able to recognize NVRAM configuration options when presented with them.

Configuration options that end in a ? always require true or false values. If the values are set to true, then another parameter needs to be configured as well.

NVRAM parameters are displayed with the `printenv` command and set by using the `setenv` command. The syntax of `setenv` is as follows:

ok **setenv** *variable value*

To make your system halt at the Forth Monitor instead of booting to a Solaris login prompt, you could type this:

ok **setenv auto-boot? false**

What if you've changed a variable, and for some reason it messes up your system? Or what if someone has changed a lot of variables (primitive hacking), trying to mess up your computer? Is there a way to fix problems like these? Yes. The `set-default` *variable* command will reset a specific variable to factory defaults. The `set-defaults` command resets all variables back to their default settings, as does pressing Stop+N (the Stop and N keys simultaneously) during boot.

Solaris 9 provides the `eeprom` command for managing NVRAM variables from within the operating environment. The `eeprom` command offers the functionality of the OpenBoot `printenv` and `setenv` commands.

NVRAMRC

The *NVRAMRC* is a customizable configuration area of NVRAM. If you use NVRAMRC, its contents (called a script) will run during the boot process. The most common use of NVRAMRC is to store permanent device aliases, although other startup options (defining startup variables, patching device drivers) are possible.

Earlier in this chapter, you learned about device aliases. If you use the `devalias` command to set up an alias, the alias will be lost when the system loses power or is rebooted. Another command, `nvalias`, creates the alias and writes the necessary information to re-create the alias upon reboot into the NVRAMRC. If you use the `nvalias` command to create an alias, the `use-nvramrc?` variable is automatically set to `true`.

The syntax for creating an alias with `nvalias` is identical to `devalias`:

ok **nvalias** *alias devicepath*

Aliases created with `nvalias` are essentially permanent. They can be deleted by using the `nvunalias` command. Just type **nvunalias** *alias* at the ok prompt to delete the alias.

To edit the NVRAMRC directly, you can use a script editor named `nvedit`. Using `nvedit` is beyond the scope of this book and beyond the scope of the Solaris 9 System Administrator exams.

Firmware Security

The OpenBoot firmware can be protected from would-be hackers through password security. The three NVRAM variables that control security are `security-mode`, `security-password`, and `security-#badlogins`. By default, `security-mode` is set to `none`, so `security-password` and `security-#badlogins` are not used either.

There are three options for the level of security: `none`, `command`, and `full`. With no security set, any user can access OpenBoot and make any changes they want. With command security enabled, the boot and go commands don't require a password, but all other commands do. If you enable full security, all commands except the go command require a password.

When using command security, the boot command by itself does not require a password. However, the boot command with any arguments does need a password to execute.

The setenv command is used to configure the vast majority of NVRAM parameters. One exception is security-password. To set the security password, use the password command. Here's what setting your password will most likely look like:

```
ok password
ok New Password (only first 8 chars are used):
ok Retype new password:
ok
```

The password will not be displayed for security reasons.

Enable your security password before you set the security mode. Also, if you enable full security mode and forget your password, you will render your computer useless. To fix your machine, you will have to contact your vendor or Sun's technical support.

Understanding the Intel Boot Process

The OBP is specific to SPARC-based computers. Most commonly, you will see the OBP on Sun-manufactured computers, although other vendors that use the SPARC platform can also use OBP. Because the OpenBoot PROM does not work with Intel-manufactured chips (or Intel clones), there needs to be a substitute for OBP. Intel-based computers use the system BIOS instead.

One of the new features of the Solaris 9 Intel Platform Edition is the support of booting from the *Preboot Execution Environment (PXE)* network booting protocol. If your computer has a network card that is PXE compliant, as well as a BIOS that supports PXE, you can boot Solaris from over the network without a boot disk.

To use PXE, you must first configure your BIOS to recognize that it can boot from the network card. Then, during the boot process, your BIOS will tell you to press a certain key (it varies, depending on the BIOS, but N is a popular choice) to boot from the network. If you've configured a network boot server, the computer will get its necessary boot information from the boot server.

Booting Solaris 9 Intel Platform Edition

During the discussion of the OpenBoot PROM, you learned that the OBP loads and configures devices, and stops at an ok prompt, waiting for you to type boot to load Solaris. If you're using a default configuration, then variables in OBP execute the boot command automatically, and you're presented with the Solaris 9 login screen.

Instead of seeing an ok prompt on Intel Architecture (IA) computers, you will be given a menu presenting the current boot parameters and asking you to make a boot decision. It will look similar to this:

```
                <<< Current Boot Parameters >>>
Boot path: /pci@0,0/pci-ide@7,1/ide@0/cmdk@0,0:a
Boot args:
Type    b [file-name] [boot-flags] <ENTER>    to boot with options
or      i <ENTER>                             to enter boot interpreter
or      <ENTER>                               to boot with defaults


                <<< timeout in 5 seconds >>>


Select (b)oot or (i)nterpreter:
```

At this screen, you have two choices. You can either boot Solaris (with or without options) or enter the boot interpreter. To boot Solaris, either press Enter, or type b and press Enter. You will then be taken to the Solaris login screen.

Booting with the defaults will take you to run level 3 (described later in this chapter). If you want to boot to an alternate run level, use the run level as an argument for the boot command. For example, to boot to run level S, you would use b -s.

Changing BIOS Configuration and Boot Parameters

During the boot phase of Solaris, the Solaris Device Configuration Assistant scans for installed devices and displays identified devices. The Device Configuration Assistant is also used to make changes to hardware configurations, as opposed to using the OBP on a SPARC computer. You can access the Device Configuration Assistant by booting from either a Solaris boot disk or the Solaris installation CD-ROM, or by interrupting the auto-boot process. If your BIOS does not support booting from CD-ROM, you will need to use the Solaris boot disk.

To create a Solaris boot disk, go to http://soldc.sun.com/support/drivers/dca_diskettes. Booting or rebooting Solaris with the installation CD-ROM or boot disk inserted will automatically activate the Device Configuration Assistant.

Upon entering the Solaris Device Configuration Assistant, you will get a menu similar to the following:

```
Solaris Device Configuration Assistant

The Solaris(TM) (Intel Platform Edition) Device Configuration Assistant scans
to identify system hardware, lists identified devices, and can boot the Solaris
software from a specified device. This program must be used to install the
Solaris operating environment, add a driver, or change the hardware on the system.

> To perform a full scan to identify all system hardware, choose Continue.
```

> To diagnose possible full scan failures, choose Specific Scan.

> To add new or updated device drivers, choose Add Driver.

About navigation...
- The mouse cannot be used.
- If the keyboard does not have function keys or they do not respond, press ESC. The legend at the bottom of the screen will change to show the ESC keys to use for navigation.
- The F2 key performs the default action.

F2_Continue   F3_Specific Scan   F4_Add Driver   F6_Help

Pressing the appropriate function key will invoke the option you want. To continue booting, press the F2 key.

Alternate Boot Scenarios

When you're at the Current Boot Parameters menu, you can either boot Solaris (with options, if you want) or enter the boot interpreter. Listed here are ways you can boot into different modes of Solaris, such as booting interactively or with the kernel debugger.

Choosing to boot interactively is necessary if you want to specify an alternate system kernel or /etc/system file. To boot interactively, type **b -a** at the Current Boot Parameters prompt. You will then be required to provide information on the directories to load modules from, the name of the system file, the file system type for the root file system (/), and the physical boot device.

If you are having kernel problems, you will want to boot by using the kernel debugger. At the Current Boot Parameters menu, type **b kadb**. After the login screen is displayed, press the F1 and A keys at the same time, and you should get a kadb[0]: prompt. You are now in the kernel debugger.

One of the reasons you might want to use the kernel debugger is to force a crash dump of system memory (for troubleshooting purposes) and a system reboot. To force a crash dump and system reboot, first boot into the kernel debugger. Then, follow this command sequence:

```
kadb[0]: vfs_syncall/W fffffff
kadb[0]: 0>eip
kadb[0]: :c
kadb[0]: :c
kadb[0]: :c
```

This will force a crash dump, and the computer will reboot. For more information on crash dumps, see Chapter 11, "Virtual File Systems and NFS."

Details about the Intel Boot Phases

By now, you should understand that the boot processes for SPARC and IA platforms are different. One of the main differences is that on an IA computer, you will be presented with a

Primary Boot Subsystem menu (also called the Boot Partition menu) if you have multiple operating systems installed on your computer. If you choose an alternate operating system, the Solaris boot process ceases. If you choose to boot into Solaris, you will be given additional options, such as to interrupt the auto-boot process and enter the Solaris Device Configuration Assistant. The final menu you will see during the boot process is the Current Boot Parameters menu. That's where you can boot Solaris with or without options, or just wait five seconds for Solaris to boot automatically.

After Solaris begins its boot process, you will see a short series of screens, such as the Scanning Devices screen and the Identified Devices screen. Solaris is merely detecting and displaying devices. If the computer appears to hang for a long time, use the reset button to restart the computer.

Like the SPARC edition of Solaris, the Intel edition has four generalized boot phases: BIOS, boot programs, kernel initialization, and `init`. Unlike the SPARC version, though, different files are used during the boot phases. Here's an overview of what happens during each phase:

1. During the BIOS phase, the system BIOS runs diagnostic tests to ensure that the system's hardware and memory are running properly. Then, the BIOS reads the first physical sector on the boot device, looking for the master boot record `mboot`. If `mboot` is not found, the boot process will stop with an error message.

2. The loading of `mboot` starts the boot programs phase. The `mboot` program looks for the Solaris boot program, `pboot`. After `pboot` loads, `pboot` looks for and loads the primary boot program, `bootblk`. If you have more than one bootable partition, `bootblk` reads the `fdisk` table and displays a menu enabling you to choose which operating system to boot into. You will have 30 seconds to make this choice. Choosing Solaris will cause `bootblk` to find the secondary boot program, `boot.bin` in the root file system (/). During this time, you will have a five-second pause in which you can choose to execute the Device Configuration Assistant. The secondary boot program will load the `/etc/bootrc` script, which displays the Current Boot Parameters menu. You will have five seconds to make a boot choice, or Solaris will load with the default options.

3. The kernel will initialize and use `boot.bin`, the secondary boot program, to load kernel modules. When enough modules are loaded to mount the root file system (/), the secondary boot program is unloaded, and the kernel continues to initialize. The kernel then loads the `/sbin/init` program, which reads the `/etc/inittab` file, and loads other processes.

4. The final phase, `init`, is when the `/sbin/init` process begins to load run control (rc) scripts, in turn loading other scripts. These scripts mount file systems, load services, and perform other miscellaneous tasks.

Overall, this four-phase process is very similar to the SPARC boot process. However, more files are needed to complete the boot process, meaning that there is more room for problems to occur.

 For test purposes, know the SPARC boot process well.

Performing Solaris Initialization and Shutdown

Earlier in this chapter, you learned about the Solaris boot process. Now is a good time to review that four-phase SPARC boot sequence and the files involved:

1. Boot PROM

2. Boot programs (`bootblk`, `ufsboot`)

3. Kernel initialization (`ufsboot`, `/sbin/init`, `/etc/inittab`)

4. Init (`/sbin/init`, `/sbin/rc*`)

   After the boot PROM is done with its initial boot sequence, it finds and loads the `bootblk` file. The `bootblk` file then loads `ufsboot`, which finds and begins to load the kernel. Although `bootblk` and `ufsboot` are critical to the Solaris boot process, they're not very exciting to talk about. Because we've already discussed the boot PROM in some depth, and `bootblk` and `ufsboot` don't merit a great deal of dialogue, it's time to take a look at what happens on the computer when loading Solaris.

System Initialization

If your SPARC system is configured to auto-boot (`auto-boot?` = `true` in OpenBoot), you don't need to worry about starting the `/sbin/init` process (also known just as the `init` process). It will happen as the system boots. However, if your system doesn't auto-boot, you'll be sitting at an ok prompt waiting for something to happen.

   Instead of sitting there waiting (computers can wait a long time), type **boot** to get the computer to start Solaris. There are various command-line arguments you can use with `boot`, and some are shown in Table 3.5.

TABLE 3.5 Common *boot* Command Options

Option	Description
-a	Performs an interactive boot
-r	Performs a reconfiguration boot
-s	Boots into run level S (regardless of what's in the `/etc/inittab` file)
-v	Boots and displays messages in a verbose mode
net	Boots from the network instead of the local disk

TABLE 3.5 Common *boot* Command Options *(continued)*

Option	Description
cdrom	Boots from the local CD-ROM or DVD-ROM
floppy	Boots from the floppy disk drive

Command options can be combined. If, for example, you wanted to boot from the CD-ROM and also wanted to boot in verbose mode, you could type **boot -v cdrom**. After initiating the boot command, Solaris will begin to load.

The first process the kernel starts is called the swapper. Swapper has the official name of sched and a process ID of 0. The swapper's responsibility is to schedule all other processes, so it makes sense that it needs to be started first.

Because /sbin/init is directly responsible for starting all other processes when Solaris boots, it's known as a parent process. Spawned processes are called children or child processes. One of the first things that /sbin/init does is to look at the /etc/inittab file to see which other processes need to be started and what order they should be started in. Here is an example /etc/inittab file:

```
ap::sysinit:/sbin/autopush -f /etc/iu.ap
ap::sysinit:/sbin/soconfig -f /etc/sock2path
fs::sysinit:/sbin/rcS sysinit >/dev/msglog 2<>/dev/msglog </dev/console
is:3:initdefault:
p3:s1234:powerfail:/usr/sbin/shutdown -y -i5 -g0 >/dev/msglog↵
    2<>/dev/msglog
sS:s:wait:/sbin/rcS          >/dev/msglog 2<>/dev/msglog </dev/console
s0:0:wait:/sbin/rc0          >/dev/msglog 2<>/dev/msglog </dev/console
s1:1:respawn:/sbin/rc1       >/dev/msglog 2<>/dev/msglog </dev/console
s2:23:wait:/sbin/rc2         >/dev/msglog 2<>/dev/msglog </dev/console
s3:3:wait:/sbin/rc3          >/dev/msglog 2<>/dev/msglog </dev/console
s5:5:wait:/sbin/rc5          >/dev/msglog 2<>/dev/msglog </dev/console
s6:6:wait:/sbin/rc6          >/dev/msglog 2<>/dev/msglog </dev/console
fw:0:wait:/sbin/uadmin 2 0   >/dev/msglog 2<>/dev/msglog </dev/console
of:5:wait:/sbin/uadmin 2 6   >/dev/msglog 2<>/dev/msglog </dev/console
rb:6:wait:/sbin/uadmin 2 1   >/dev/msglog 2<>/dev/msglog </dev/console
sc:234:respawn:/usr/lib/saf/sac -t 300
co:234:respawn:/usr/lib/saf/ttymon -g -h -p "`uname -n` console login:↵
    " -T sun -d /dev/console -l console -m ldterm,ttcompat
```

Each line in the inittab file is a separate entry, and each entry in the /etc/inittab file contains the following fields:

```
id:runlevel:action:process
```

Each entry starts with a one- to four-character identifier (id), which is just a name for the particular entry. The runlevel field specifies which run levels this entry applies to. The action field describes how the process listed in the process field is supposed to be executed. Possible values include initdefault, sysinit, boot, bootwait, wait, powerfail, and respawn. The last field, process, identifies a program or script to execute. Table 3.6 describes the action field values used in the default /etc/inittab file.

TABLE 3.6 *action* Field Values

Value	Description
initdefault	Defines the default run level for this computer.
powerfail	This process is executed when init receives a power fail signal.
respawn	If the process associated with this entry fails, restart it immediately.
sysinit	These actions are executed before the login prompt is displayed. Each entry using sysinit must be completed before the next entry can be processed.
wait	The process associated with this field must be completed before another process linked to the same run level can be started.

On the exam, you might be expected to read parts of an /etc/inittab file and to determine what actions Solaris will take based on the information presented.

Based on the /etc/inittab file presented earlier, the default run level for Solaris 9 is run level 3. This is defined by the fourth entry, which uses the initdefault variable in the action field. If you're not clear about what a run level is, don't worry just yet, because we'll cover that in the next section. For now, just accept run level 3 as the default.

If the system boots into run level 3, entries in the /etc/inittab file that have a 3 in the runlevel field will be processed. Those lines are as follows:

```
ap::sysinit:/sbin/autopush -f /etc/iu.ap
ap::sysinit:/sbin/soconfig -f /etc/sock2path
fs::sysinit:/sbin/rcS sysinit >/dev/msglog 2<>/dev/msglog </dev/console
is:3:initdefault:
p3:s1234:powerfail:/usr/sbin/shutdown -y -i5 -g0 >/dev/msglog↩
    2<>/dev/msglog
s2:23:wait:/sbin/rc2          >/dev/msglog 2<>/dev/msglog </dev/console
s3:3:wait:/sbin/rc3          >/dev/msglog 2<>/dev/msglog </dev/console
sc:234:respawn:/usr/lib/saf/sac -t 300
```

```
co:234:respawn:/usr/lib/saf/ttymon -g -h -p "`uname -n` console login: ⏎
    " -T sun -d /dev/console -l console -m ldterm,ttcompat
```

You might take a look at these lines and say, "Wait a minute. The first three lines don't have a 3 anywhere in them!" That's true, but remember that because they have `sysinit` in the `action` field, they will be processed regardless of the run level. The fourth line defines the default run level (`initdefault`) as 3.

The fifth entry, p3, tells Solaris to run the shutdown process (`/usr/sbin/shutdown`) if a power fail signal is detected. This line also applies to run levels S, 1, 2, and 4. Line 6, s2, says to run the `/sbin/rc2` script, and line 7 says to run the `/sbin/rc3` script. More on rc scripts a few sections from now.

Line 8 and 9 both start processes that need to be restarted if they ever fail. The `/usr/lib/saf/sac` process starts the port monitors, and the `/usr/lib/saf/ttymon` process monitors the console for login requests.

Run Levels

A *run level* defines the operation of Solaris, including what resources and services are available to users. You will also hear run levels called run states or init states. Although Solaris 9 has eight run levels, a system can be in only one run level at a time. Run levels and their associated scripts are not platform dependent. They will be the same whether you're running SPARC or IA. Table 3.7 describes the eight run levels and their features.

TABLE 3.7   The Eight Solaris Run Levels

Run Level	Description	Purpose
0	Stops all services, terminates all processes, and unmounts all file systems.	To shut down Solaris and return the machine to the Forth Monitor. Preparation for system shutdown.
S or s	Single-user state. Only root is allowed to log in, and all logged-in users are logged out.	For performing administrative tasks that require all users to be logged out (such as system backups).
1	Single-user state. Logged-in users are allowed to remain logged in.	For performing administrative tasks, and not allowing new users to log in.
2	Multiuser state. All file systems are mounted, but NFS is not started.	For normal operations when the sharing of file systems across a network is not required.
3	Multiuser state with NFS. All file systems are mounted, and the NFS daemon is started.	For normal operations that require resources to be shared across a network.

TABLE 3.7   The Eight Solaris Run Levels *(continued)*

Run Level	Description	Purpose
4	Alternative multiuser state.	Not currently used.
5	Power-down state.	To shut down the computer. On supported systems, run level 5 will automatically power down the computer. If not, the Forth Monitor will be presented.
6	Reboot.	To reboot the machine into the default run level.

Although init state 4 is not used, Sun still considers Solaris to have eight run levels.

Run states can be changed with the `init` command. The `init` command calls the `/etc/inittab` file and processes whatever scripts are needed to change to the run level you indicated. For example, to change to run state S, you could issue the command `init s`. Reading the `/etc/inittab` file tells the init process to run the `/sbin/rcS` script.

To determine which run state your computer is in, issue the `who -r` command. It will tell you which run state you are in and when the system was last booted into this state.

Run Control Scripts

There's one more piece to the puzzle of understanding the boot process and init states. You already know that the init process reads the `/etc/inittab` file whenever the system is booted or a run level is changed by way of the `init` command. In the example we used earlier, changing the system to run level 3 forces the execution of the `/sbin/rc2` and `/sbin/rc3` scripts. In fact, each of the run levels has an associated run control (rc) script located in the `/sbin` directory. They are named `rcS` and `rc0` through `rc6`.

For each script in the `/sbin` directory, there exists a related directory named `/etc/rc#.d` that contains scripts to run in order to affect the desired run level's characteristics. For example, if you issue the `init 1` command, you execute the `/sbin/rc1` script, which in turn executes all scripts located in the `/etc/rc1.d` directory (of which there are 40). Those scripts are designed to keep the system running, but not allow any new users to log in.

The exceptions are the `/sbin/rc5` and `/sbin/rc6` scripts, which execute the `/etc/rc0.d/K*` scripts to kill all active processes and unmount all file systems.

Each /etc/rc#.d directory contains a number of scripts designed to either stop or start services and daemons. Script names start with either an *S* or a *K*, followed by two digits and a name. Examples are S88sendmail and K21dhcp. S scripts are designed to start services, and K scripts kill services. The number after the *S* or *K* indicates the order in which to execute the script. All kill scripts are executed before start scripts, and lower-numbered scripts will be executed before higher-numbered scripts.

The combination of scripts in a directory is really the key to setting up a run level. As you might expect, the /etc/rc2.d and /etc/rc3.d directories contain a lot more S scripts than K scripts, whereas the /etc/rc0.d directory has nothing but K scripts by default.

If you want to stop an individual service without changing the run level, scripts in the /etc/init.d directory can be executed. For example, if you wanted to change the running status of the NFS server daemon without leaving run level 3, you could run the /etc/init.d/ nfs.server script with either the stop or start argument:

/etc/init.d/nfs.server stop

If there is no script that stops or starts a service that you require, you can create your own, give it an appropriate name, and place it in the directory corresponding to the run level in which you want the script to execute. To prevent a script from running, disable it by renaming it. It must not start with a K or S, or the script will be run. A good recommendation is to rename it with a preceding underscore. The script S90samba would become _S90samba. This way, if you ever want to re-enable the script, it is easy to find and rename appropriately.

System Shutdown

Solaris 9 is designed to run continuously for long periods of time. It's conceivable to run a Solaris machine for a year or longer without needing to power down or reboot. However, at times you might need to shut down the system. Perhaps you want to upgrade the memory in your Solaris server. Or the power went out in your building and your backup power supply has only about 10 minutes left. Or you have made changes to kernel parameters in the /etc/system file and need to reboot. These are all times that you need to either power cycle or kill the power completely, and it's best to shut down Solaris gracefully.

The two preferred commands to shut down Solaris are init and shutdown. To execute either command, you must be logged in as the superuser or have an equivalent role. Both init and shutdown perform a clean shutdown of Solaris, meaning they run all the necessary kill scripts to shut down services and daemons in an orderly manner.

The reboot and halt commands can also be used to stop Solaris, but they are not recommended. Neither reboot nor halt performs a clean shutdown, and using these commands can result in data loss or corrupt files.

Shutting Down a Server

The preferred command to bring down a server properly is the shutdown command. By default, this command takes the system to init state S. Before it shuts down the system (remember, all users are logged off when the system is changed to run state S), the shutdown command can send a message to all logged-in users and wait a specified amount of time before shutting down.

The shutdown command uses the following syntax:

shutdown -i *init_state* **-g** *grace_period* **-y** *"message"*

All the arguments are optional. By executing shutdown with no arguments, the system will reboot into run state S, wait 60 seconds to reboot, and ask you to confirm the reboot. To specify an alternate run state or grace period, use the -i or -g arguments, respectively. The grace period is specified in seconds. The -y argument will execute the shutdown command after the grace period without prompting you. The -y switch is not required to supply a shutdown message.

 If you have made changes to the /etc/inittab file and want it to be reread without rebooting, issue the **init q** command.

Before shutting down a server, it's recommended that you see who is logged in first. To do this, use the who command. You will see something like this:

```
# who
root          console      Aug  4 09:27
ramini        pts/0        Aug 31 13:02        (badpun)
mgantz        pts/1        Mar 17 05:44        (macuser)
```

This output shows three users logged in. The superuser is logged in locally, whereas the other two users are logged in remotely. You can see when each user logged in and the name of the computer that each user is logging in from. Although the shutdown command does warn users, you might want to send the users an e-mail or warn them personally for good measure.

Shutting Down a Workstation

Generally speaking, only one user is logged into a workstation at a time. Warnings and grace periods don't need to be issued, so you can use init to shut down the system properly. The init command requires a run level to be specified as an argument. To change a system to run level 0, type **init 0**.

 The poweroff command can also be used and is the equivalent of init 5.

Using the init 0 command will return a SPARC computer to the OpenBoot ok prompt. If you're using an IA computer, you will see the message Type any key to continue. In either case, it's safe to power off the computer. If you want to reboot, type **boot** at the ok prompt, or press any key on the IA computer to reboot.

Although the reboot and halt commands are not recommended for general use, they do have a purpose. Neither command takes as long to execute as init or shutdown, by virtue of not running kill scripts. So if you're desperate and in a hurry to save a few seconds, feel free to use reboot or halt. Also, reboot and halt might work if either init or shutdown fail.

If none of the shutdown commands work, it's possible that the system is hung. You have a few options when this happens. One is to use a Stop key sequence, such as Stop+A or L1+A, depending on your keyboard type (or the Break key if you're logged in through a terminal). Another option is to simply power the machine down. Neither option is very attractive, but they're about all you have left if nothing else works.

 **Real World Scenario**

The Pitfalls of Shutting Down a Server

Your Solaris server is in need of a memory upgrade. You decide that next Tuesday at 8 P.M. you are going to take the server down, install the memory, and perform some routine cleaning. That late at night will be a good time to perform maintenance because everyone in the office is usually gone by then. Just to be safe and to warn everyone far in advance, you send out a company-wide e-mail to alert users of the scheduled downtime.

Tuesday arrives, and 8:00 eventually does as well. You execute a `shutdown -i 0 -y "Log out now!"` command to bring down the server. No more than two minutes later, your phone starts ringing off the hook. Four angry managers want to know where their unsaved files are. What happened?

You did use the `shutdown` command, which was a good choice, but a few things could have made this scenario turn out better. First, you could have used a longer grace period; 60 seconds is not a lot of time for users to save files and log off. Besides, what if someone is away from his or her desk?

Second, you forgot the almighty rule when scheduling and performing server maintenance: some users will always, always forget about the e-mail they received (not to mention ignore the warning) and then be mad when the server does go down. To alleviate this issue, educate your users. Make sure they understand that when you say the server is coming down, you're not kidding. It would be wise for them to save their files and log off. To help them remember, you could take a brief tour of your facilities and warn users personally (although this isn't always possible).

To summarize, when bringing down a server, give the users plenty of warning, educate them about your IT department practices, and make sure to bring the server down gracefully. In the end, everyone will benefit.

Troubleshooting a Hung System

Solaris 9 is a solid operating system and rarely has serious operational problems. Occasionally, though, a process or application can hang or even cause the operating system itself to hang. If your system seems to be unresponsive, there are some steps you can take in an attempt to rectify the situation.

If your system is running in a windowed environment (such as CDE), a hung application can be terminated without affecting the rest of the system. The first thing to try is moving the mouse pointer. If it moves, then it's possible the application is frozen. If the mouse pointer does not move, it could indicate that CDE has locked up or the operating system is stuck.

If your mouse pointer works, move it over the open window that is not responding. Press Control+Q (the Control and Q keys at the same time) to attempt to unfreeze the window. (A common sequence is to use Control+Q to attempt to activate the window, followed by Control+C, and then Alt+F4.) If the window you are in is unresponsive, you can always attempt to use another window. You can also try logging into the machine remotely and using the `pgrep` utility to find the hung process and `pkill` to kill it.

On IA computers, if the keyboard and mouse are not responding, you might have to use the computer's reset button if it has one. If the reset button does not work, hold the power button in, and the computer should power itself off after about four seconds. Again, these aren't recommended ways to shut down a normally operating computer, but if it's hung, you might not have any other choice.

If the preceding actions don't help, or you are not running a windowed system, you can try the following:

1. Press Control+\ to force the running program to quit.

2. Press Control+C to interrupt the running program.

3. Log in remotely, identify the hung process, and kill it.

4. Log in remotely, become a superuser, and reboot the computer.

5. If none of the first four steps work, force a crash dump and reboot. To force a crash dump:

   A. Press Stop+A or L1+A to stop your system (or the Break key if you are logged in remotely).

   B. Type **sync** at the ok prompt.

   C. Reboot the computer and log back in.

6. If nothing else works, turn the power off, wait a minute, and turn the power back on.

Using common sense in troubleshooting can go a long way, too. For example, if your keyboard is not responding (for example, the Caps Lock and/or Num Lock keys don't toggle the lights on the keyboard), then all the key sequences designed to kill applications are not likely to work. Similarly, if your keyboard and mouse are not responsive in a windowed system, it's probable that the operating system is locked, and you will need to turn the power off and back on.

Summary

In this chapter, you looked at what happens on a SPARC computer before Solaris loads. The OpenBoot PROM loads as the system is powered on, performs diagnostic tests, and loads the Solaris operating environment. Although OpenBoot has the main responsibility of loading Solaris, it also holds hardware and boot configuration information, and provides a list of diagnostic tests.

The Solaris 9 Intel Platform Edition runs on the IA platform. Computers using Intel chips will not have the OpenBoot PROM but will have a system BIOS. The hardware configuration and boot options can be configured through the Solaris Device Configuration Assistant.

The exact functionality of Solaris 9 depends on which of the eight run levels it enters when it boots. Run levels are designed to provide flexibility for administrative tasks in addition to providing an easily configurable user environment. Run levels are exacted through a series of run control (rc) scripts.

Shutting down Solaris also uses run control scripts. Instead of starting services and daemons, the shutdown process runs scripts to properly stop all running services. The preferred commands to shut down Solaris are init and shutdown.

Finally, you examined troubleshooting procedures for a hung system. It's important to determine whether an individual application is being problematic or whether it's the operating system. Depending on the severity of your problem, you have a variety of keystrokes and troubleshooting methods at your disposal.

Exam Essentials

Know the SPARC boot phase order.   The order is the boot PROM, boot programs, kernel initialization, and init.

Know what the device tree is and where it is accessed.   The device tree lists all configured system devices. It can be accessed through the OpenBoot interface, the Forth Monitor.

Understand how devices are named.   All devices in a SPARC computer are uniquely named based on their physical location. Each name maps to the following form: *driver-name@unit-address:device-arguments*.

Know how to create a device alias and make it permanent.   Device aliases can be created with the devalias command. However, to make them permanent, use the nvalias command.

Know how to quickly display the OpenBoot version, amount of memory installed, serial number, Ethernet address, and host ID number.   All these parameters are displayed by using the banner command from the Forth Monitor.

Know how to modify NVRAM configuration variables.   NVRAM variables are modified by using the setenv command. The security password is the only exception, and it is modified by using the password command.

Understand the structure of the /etc/inittab file.   Each entry of the /etc/inittab file has the following fields: id:runlevel:action:process.

Know how to identify the default run level.   The default run level is specified in the /etc/inittab file by the initdefault option.

Know how many run levels Solaris 9 has.   Solaris 9 has eight run levels, although only seven are used.

Understand the proper way to shut down a Solaris system. To shut down Solaris, the `init` and `shutdown` commands are recommended. Use `init` for workstations, and `shutdown` for server machines.

Key Terms

Before you take the exam, be certain you are familiar with the following terms:

`bootblk` (boot block)	OpenBoot PROM (OBP)
device alias	Preboot Execution Environment (PXE)
device tree	run control (rc) scripts
Forth Monitor	run level
Non-Volatile Random Access Memory (NVRAM)	Scalable Processor Architecture (SPARC)
Non-Volatile Random Access Memory Run Control (NVRAMRC)	`ufsboot`

Commands Used in This Chapter

The following list contains a summary of all the commands introduced in this chapter:

OpenBoot Command	Description
`.enet-addr`	Displays the computer's Ethernet address
`.idprom`	Shows the contents of the computer's ID PROM
`.speed`	Displays the processor speed
`.traps`	Displays processor traps
`.version`	Shows detailed OpenBoot PROM version information
`banner`	Displays the computer's power-on banner
`boot`	Boots the computer
`devalias`	Creates and displays device aliases
`help`	Displays information on OpenBoot commands
`nvalias`	Creates permanent device aliases

OpenBoot Command	Description
nvunalias	Deletes permanent device aliases
password	Sets the firmware security password
printenv	Displays NVRAM variables and their settings
probe-scsi	Lists all detected SCSI devices
setenv	Used to modify NVRAM parameters
show-devs	Displays all system devices
show-sbus	Displays all system SBus devices
test /memory	Tests system memory
test floppy	Tests the floppy disk drive
test net	Tests the internal network adapter
test scsi	Tests the SCSI adapter
watch-clock	Displays the system Time of Day (TOD) clock
watch-net	Watches the network for broadcast packets

Solaris Command	Description
halt	Immediately halts the operating system
init	Used to change run levels or power down the system
reboot	Used to reboot the system
shutdown	Used to properly shut down a Solaris machine
sync	Synchronizes file systems
who	Displays who is currently logged in

Review Questions

1. You are the Solaris administrator for your network. One of your Solaris workstations has stopped responding while in the CDE environment. You want to return the system to the Forth Monitor. Which combination of keystrokes will accomplish this task?

    A. Control+A

    B. Stop+A

    C. Alt+A

    D. Stop+H

2. You are the Solaris network architect for your company. You are giving a briefing to senior executives regarding the flexibility of Solaris. After you mention the concept of run levels, one of the executives asks how many run levels Solaris has. What do you tell her?

    A. Six

    B. Seven

    C. Eight

    D. Indefinite

3. You are the Solaris administrator for your company. A user complains that his workstation no longer boots into Solaris automatically. He must type **boot** at the ok prompt and he no longer wants to do this. His system is running Solaris 9. You want to get to the Forth Monitor to change this setting. What is the recommended way to get to the Forth Monitor on his system?

    A. halt

    B. init 0

    C. init 3

    D. Press Stop and A at the same time.

4. You are the network administrator for your company. You are troubleshooting a Solaris 9 computer that is not booting properly. What is the name of the primary startup file in Solaris 9?

    A. ufsboot

    B. solboot

    C. bootblk

    D. init

    E. kernel

5. One of your users calls in with an error message during bootup. She reports that there is a cryptic message with the following information in it: `/pci@1f,0/ide@d/disk@2,0`. Which of the following are likely conclusions based on the information presented? (Choose all that apply.)

   A. The device is an IDE hard disk attached to the motherboard.

   B. The device is an IDE CD-ROM attached to the motherboard.

   C. The device has a device alias of `disk2`.

   D. The device has a device alias of `IDED`.

   E. The device has a device alias of `disk0`.

6. You are on the phone with Sun tech support regarding problems you are having with one of your workstations. The computer you are working on is at an OpenBoot prompt. The tech support agent asks you for the version of OpenBoot PROM in your computer. Which two commands can you use to find this? (Choose all that apply.)

   A. `banner`

   B. `.version`

   C. `.idprom`

   D. `.traps`

7. You are the Solaris server administrator for your company. Tomorrow night at 7:00, you are going to bring down the server for maintenance and an upgrade. You want to bring the server to run level 0, give the users five minutes warning, and you want the server to ask for confirmation from you before shutting down. Which command will you need to execute tomorrow evening at 6:55?

   A. `shutdown -i 0 -g 5`

   B. `shutdown -i 0 -g 5 -y`

   C. `shutdown -i 0 -g 300`

   D. `shutdown -i 0 -g 300 -y`

8. You are the server administrator for your company. Your server had two tape drives in it, and each one had its own permanent custom device alias. They were `backup1` and `backup2`. Recently, you removed one of the tape drives (`backup2`) and no longer want the alias to exist. What do you need to do to remove the alias?

   A. Use the `nvunalias backup2` command.

   B. Use the `unnvalias backup2` command.

   C. Use the `undevalias backup2` command.

   D. Nothing. The device alias will be removed automatically after the system detects that the device is no longer present.

9. You are the Solaris administrator for your company. You need to shut down a Solaris workstation after a user failed to do so during the day. Which is the best choice to properly shut down the system?

    A. Turn off the power.

    B. Issue the `halt` command.

    C. Issue the `init 5` command.

    D. Issue the `powerdown` command.

10. You are the server administrator for your company. You just added a new SCSI hard disk to your server and want to create a permanent alias for it. The path of the new device is `/sbus@1f,0/scsi@0,1/sd@0,3`, and the alias you want to use is `scsi3`. What command do you use to create the alias?

    A. `devalias scsi3 /sbus@1f,0/scsi@0,1/sd@0,3`

    B. `devalias /sbus@1f,0/scsi@0,1/sd@0,3 scsi3`

    C. `nvalias scsi3 /sbus@1f,0/scsi@0,1/sd@0,3`

    D. `nvalias /sbus@1f,0/scsi@0,1/sd@0,3 scsi3`

11. Which of the following options is required if you want your Solaris computer to boot directly to a login screen instead of a Forth prompt?

    A. `boot-command boot`

    B. `boot-login? true`

    C. `auto-boot true`

    D. `auto-boot? true`

12. You are concerned with OpenBoot security on your 50 Solaris workstations. You decide to modify the security mode to command and want to set a firmware password. Which of the following is the correct method to set your `security-password` variable to k10Wn?

    A. `password k10Wn`

    B. `password security-password k10Wn`

    C. `setenv security-password k10Wn`

    D. `setenv security-mode command password k10Wn`

13. Based on the provided `/etc/inittab` file, which of the following statements are correct? (Choose all that apply.)

    ```
    ap::sysinit:/sbin/autopush -f /etc/iu.ap
    ap::sysinit:/sbin/soconfig -f /etc/sock2path
    fs::sysinit:/sbin/rcS sysinit>/dev/msglog 2<>/dev/msglog </dev/console
    is:2:initdefault:
    p3:s1234:powerfail:/usr/sbin/shutdown -y -i5 -g0 >/dev/msglog 2<>/dev/msglog
    ```

```
sS:s:wait:/sbin/rcS            >/dev/msglog 2<>/dev/msglog </dev/console
s0:0:wait:/sbin/rc0            >/dev/msglog 2<>/dev/msglog </dev/console
s1:1:respawn:/sbin/rc1         >/dev/msglog 2<>/dev/msglog </dev/console
s2:23:wait:/sbin/rc2           >/dev/msglog 2<>/dev/msglog </dev/console
s3:3:wait:/sbin/rc3            >/dev/msglog 2<>/dev/msglog </dev/console
s5:5:wait:/sbin/rc5            >/dev/msglog 2<>/dev/msglog </dev/console
s6:6:wait:/sbin/rc6            >/dev/msglog 2<>/dev/msglog </dev/console
fw:0:wait:/sbin/uadmin 2 0     >/dev/msglog 2<>/dev/msglog </dev/console
of:5:wait:/sbin/uadmin 2 6     >/dev/msglog 2<>/dev/msglog </dev/console
rb:6:wait:/sbin/uadmin 2 1     >/dev/msglog 2<>/dev/msglog </dev/console
sc:234:respawn:/usr/lib/saf/sac -t 300
co:234:respawn:/usr/lib/saf/ttymon -g -h -p "`uname -n` console login:↵
" -T sun -d /dev/console -l console -m ldterm,ttcompat
```

    A. The default run level for this computer is init state 3.

    B. When entering into init state 3, the `rc2` script must completely execute before the `rc3` script begins.

    C. Upon receiving a power failure message, the computer will give users a five-minute warning before shutting down.

    D. `/usr/lib/saf/sac` will restart automatically if at any time it fails while the system is in run states 2 or 3.

    E. To enter init state 3, eight of the entries in the `/etc/inittab` file are processed.

14. You are the Solaris server administrator for your company. You want the server to automatically boot to a run level that enables users to log in remotely and access NFS-based resources. To which run level should you have your server boot?

    A. S

    B. 2

    C. 3

    D. 5

15. You are the Solaris administrator for your company. One of your client machines is having problems operating properly. You suspect that a user changed multiple NVRAM variables to improper settings. Which command can you issue to set the variables back to factory settings?

    A. `setenv defaults`

    B. `setenv defaults NVRAM`

    C. `set-default NVRAM`

    D. `set-defaults`

16. You are a kernel developer for your company. You have been tasked with developing an alternate kernel for network use. You want to reboot your Solaris computer and use your experimental kernel. Which command should you issue?

   A. `boot -a`

   B. `boot -v`

   C. `boot -k`

   D. `boot kadb`

17. You are the Solaris administrator for your network. You just issued an `init 6` command on one of your Solaris workstations. The scripts in which directory will be immediately executed?

   A. `/etc/rc6.d`

   B. `/etc/rc0.d`

   C. `/sbin/rc3.d`

   D. `/sbin/rc0.d`

18. You are the network administrator for your company. You are making changes on one of your Solaris servers and want to temporarily stop the `boot.server` service on that server. Which command should you execute?

   A. `/etc/init.d/boot.server stop`

   B. `stop /etc/init.d/boot.server`

   C. `pause /etc/init.d/boot.server`

   D. `/etc/init.d/boot.server pause`

   E. Individual services cannot be stopped in Solaris 9.

19. You are the Solaris administrator for your network. You want to prevent the `S75cron` script from running whenever the system boots. What is the recommended way to accomplish this?

   A. Delete the `S75cron` file.

   B. Rename `S75cron` to `K75cron`.

   C. Rename `S75cron` to `OldFile`.

   D. Rename `S75cron` to `_S75cron`.

20. You are the network administrator for your company. You believe that the floppy drive in one of your workstations is not functioning properly and decide to test it from OpenBoot. Which command do you use to test the floppy disk drive?

   A. `test /floppy`

   B. `test floppy`

   C. `test-floppy`

   D. `test.floppy`

Answers to Review Questions

1. B. The Stop+A key sequence will halt the operating system and return the computer to the OpenBoot (Forth Monitor) prompt.

2. C. Solaris 9 has eight run levels. Only seven are currently used.

3. B. The recommended way to shut down Solaris (and return to an `ok` prompt) is to issue an `init 0` command or use the `shutdown` command. Because the user is on a workstation, `shutdown` is unnecessary. The `halt` command and Stop+A will work, but they are not recommended because they do not perform a proper shutdown of Solaris.

4. C. The primary startup file in Solaris is `bootblk`. The secondary startup file is `ufsboot`, which is loaded by `bootblk`. The `solboot` file does not exist. The init process and kernel are critical to Solaris operation, but neither are the primary startup file.

5. A, C. Based on the information presented, the device is the third IDE hard disk (disks start with number 0, so the third one would be 2) connected to the motherboard. Disk 2 has the default device alias `disk2`.

6. A, B. To display the OpenBoot PROM version, the `banner` and `.version` commands can be used. The `.idprom` command will show contents of the PROM, but no version number. The `.traps` command is used to display processor traps, not OpenBoot information.

7. C. The `shutdown` command can be used to shut down a server, provide a grace period (specified in seconds), and send a message to the users warning them to log out. The proper argument for specifying an init state is `-i`, and grace period is `-g`. If you wanted the server to shut down automatically without prompting you to continue, you could use the `-y` option as well.

8. A. To remove permanent device aliases, which were likely created with the `nvalias` command, use the `nvunalias` command. The other two commands do not exist. Permanent device aliases must be deleted to be removed and are not removed automatically.

9. C. The only recommended method among the available answers is the `init 5` command. Using `init 5` will force the system into an OpenBoot prompt and shut down the computer if possible. The `halt` command should be used only in emergency situations or if other shutdown commands fail.

10. C. The correct order for creating an alias is command, alias, device path. To create a permanent alias, use the `nvalias` command. The `devalias` command would create the alias, but `devalias` does not create permanent aliases.

11. D. To make your Solaris computer auto-boot, you need to make sure the `auto-boot?` option is set to `true`. Typically, the `boot-command` parameter will be set to `boot` as well, but this is not required to automatically boot.

12. A. Most NVRAM parameters are set by using the `setenv` command. The security password is the one exception. Set the security password with the `password` command and then enable `security-mode` by using `setenv`.

13. B, D, E. The default run level for this computer is 2, as specified by the `initdefault` option in line 4. Therefore, answer A is incorrect. When entering run state 3, the `rc2` script must complete first. The `s2:` line specifies that `rc2` must complete and the init process wait before continuing, so answer B is correct. When receiving a `powerfail` message, the server will give zero grace period, as specified by the `-g0` option on the `p3:` line. Answer C is incorrect. The `respawn` variable tells init to automatically start `/usr/lib/saf/sac` if it fails, so answer D is correct. Answer E is correct. There are five lines that specifically call init state 3, and the first three lines, marked by the `sysinit` variable, always process.

14. C. Run level 3 enables users to log in and also starts the NFS server and NFS client daemons.

15. D. The `set-defaults` command will set all NVRAM parameters back to factory defaults. The `setenv` command is used to set individual parameters to specific values. The `set-default` *parameter* command will set the specified parameter back to factory defaults.

16. A. The `boot -a` command invokes an interactive boot. An interactive boot will ask for the kernel, system file, root file system type, and physical name of the root device for booting. Using the `-v` argument initiates verbose mode during boot, and `-k` is not a valid option. To boot and use the kernel debugger (for troubleshooting), use `boot kadb`.

17. B. In most cases, scripts are executed in the `/etc/rc#.d` directory that corresponds to the desired run level. As an example, `init 3` will execute the scripts in the `/etc/rc3.d` directory. However, changing to run levels 5 and 6 cause the system to run the kill scripts in the `/etc/rc0.d` directory. There is no `/etc/rc5.d` or `/etc/rc6.d` directory by default.

18. A. The correct syntax to stop a service is `/etc/init.d/`*filename* `stop`. To stop a service, you must be logged in as the superuser or have an equivalent role.

19. D. If you no longer want a script to execute, rename it. However, it's best to rename it to something that is easily identifiable in case you ever want to re-enable the script. You definitely don't want to replace the *S* with a *K*, which would indicate a kill script instead of a start script.

20. B. To test the floppy disk in OpenBoot, use the `test floppy` command. None of the test commands uses a hyphen or a period between the command and the device (although the `watch` and `probe` commands do). The forward slash (/) can be used to test memory, as in `test /memory`.

Chapter

4

User and Group Administration

SOLARIS 9 EXAM OBJECTIVES COVERED IN THIS CHAPTER:

- ✓ Identify the main components of a user account, identify the system files that store account information, and explain what information is stored in each file.

- ✓ Explain how to manage user accounts and describe system-wide initialization files.

- ✓ Identify the procedures and commands, variables, or permissions to monitor and control system access, switch users on a system, and restrict access to data in files.

Users are one of the most critical components of any Solaris system. When the system is booted, you must log in to use resources. To log in, you provide a valid username and password. Every time you attempt to access a system resource, you user account is checked for appropriate permissions. All resources in Solaris must have an owner, and without users, there are no owners. Solaris is a multiuser environment, meaning that multiple users can be created (and indeed should be created), and multiple users can be logged in to the same system at one time.

Groups are designed to make system administration easier. Groups are not used to log in to a system, as that's what users are for, but every user account belongs to at least one group. Assigning resource access to groups makes security administration easier than assigning permissions directly to users. Anything that makes administration more convenient is a good thing.

When a user logs in to Solaris, they are assigned a shell. Shells define the command environment for users. Depending on the shell you are using, commands will be processed in a different manner. Commands or variables used in one shell might or might not work in another.

In this chapter, you'll examine user and group management, including graphical and command-line options for management. Additionally, this chapter covers some features and options of different shells used in Solaris.

Managing User and Group Accounts

You have just turned on your Solaris workstation and you receive an innocent-looking message: "Welcome to Solaris, please enter your username." The friendly, blinking cursor waits patiently for your response. Enter your username and the appropriate password on the next screen, and you will soon be logged in and ready to work. But what if you don't have a username? The once-innocent message mocks you, and the friendly cursor now flashes ominously. Your heart races and you feel a cold sweat envelop you. You're not going to use Solaris.

Fortunately, logging in to Solaris usually isn't quite this dramatic. Simply type in your username and password, and you are logged in. The username and password are part of your user account. Every person who uses the computer should have his or her own unique account. User accounts have the following components:

- A unique *username* (also known as a login name) that identifies the user on the system.

- A *User ID (UID)* number that identifies the user.

- A password that enables the user to access the system. Passwords can be any length, but only the first eight characters are used by Solaris.

- A home directory that can be used to contain the user's files and serve as the default directory at login.

- Initialization files (also called shell scripts) that customize the user's environment upon login. The initialization files will vary depending on the user's choice of shell.

New to Solaris 9 is the concept of a project. A *project* identifies a workload component that can be used to allow system usage or provide a basis for resource allocation charge-back. To successfully log in to Solaris 9, users must be part of a project. By default, new users are members of the `group.staff` project.

Project information is stored in the `/etc/project` file. This file must exist if users are to log in to Solaris 9, but adds no administrative overhead if you are not actively using projects.

Groups are used to organize users who have similar resource access needs. As an example, consider an accounting department with 20 accountants. If all accountants needed access to an accounting database, you could assign permissions to each accountant individually, or place all users in an accounting group and assign permissions to the group. It might sound like the same amount of work either way, but in the long run, with users added and deleted and new accounting resources brought online, it's far easier to manage resource access through groups.

Each group in Solaris has a name and a *Group ID (GID)*. The GID for a group is analogous to a UID for a user. Users must belong to one group, their primary group, and can be a part of up to 15 other secondary groups.

Solaris 9 has a number of built-in user and group accounts.

Default User and Group Accounts

Built-in users in Solaris 9 are for administrative purposes. Each default user has a specific UID, and it's recommended that you not change the default usernames or UIDs. UIDs 0–99 are reserved for system accounts. The list of default users is shown in Table 4.1.

TABLE 4.1   Default User Accounts

Username	User ID	Comment
root	0	Superuser
daemon	1	
bin	2	
sys	3	
adm	4	Admin
uucp	5	uucp Admin
nuucp	9	uucp Admin
smmsp	25	SendMail Message Submission Program

TABLE 4.1 Default User Accounts *(continued)*

Username	User ID	Comment
listen	37	Network Admin
lp	71	Line Printer Admin
nobody	60001	Nobody
noaccess	60002	No Access User
nobody4	65534	SunOS 4.*x* Nobody

When these default user accounts attempt to perform system tasks, the program they are trying to access will look at either the UID or the username for access. In other words, some programs will want to see the superuser as UID 0, whereas others are looking for the username of root. In either case, it's not a good practice to rename the default accounts or to attempt to change their UIDs.

Some services, such as the UNIX-to-UNIX Copy Program (uucp) and its associated daemons, require two user accounts to function properly. The listen user monitors the network for service requests. The nobody and nobody4 accounts are for anonymous access, and noaccess is for non-trusted users (non-authenticated users).

Built-in groups are for administrative purposes as well. For example, if a user wants to run Admintool, one way you can allow them to do this is to place the user account in the sysadmin (GID 14) group. The list of default groups, their GID, and default members is shown in Figure 4.1.

FIGURE 4.1 Default groups

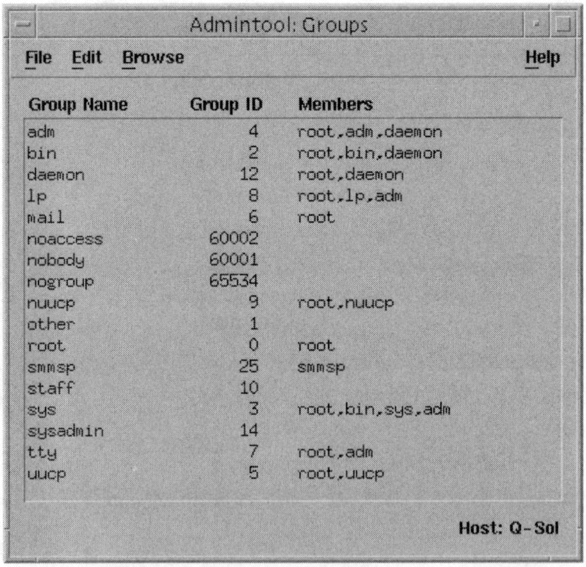

As with default users, it's not a good idea to rename or try to renumber default groups. Also, although you can add users to the default groups, don't remove any users that were placed in the built-in groups during installation.

Managing Users

User accounts are stored on the machine on which they were created. If you have 10 Solaris workstations and 10 users, then each user would need an account on each workstation they plan on using. This configuration can get quite cumbersome in a hurry. The alternative is to use a naming or directory service, such as LDAP, NIS, or NIS+. All three of these services will be discussed in more detail in Chapter 15, "Naming Services." For now, we will discuss creating users on a local machine.

Usernames and User IDs

For every account you create, you must create a username. Usernames must be unique within an organization. In fact, if you try to create a duplicate username, you will get this error message:

`Warning! This user name is already being used in the name service user map.`

To help alleviate potential naming issues, it's a good idea to use or create a company-wide user-naming standard. Some common ones are to use the user's first initial and last name, or the first five characters of the user's last name and first initial. Using the two options, the user Joe Smith would have a login of `jsmith` or `smithj`. Usernames in Solaris must be between two and eight characters, and can contain uppercase and lowercase letters, numbers, periods, hyphens, and underscores.

 Even though names can contain periods, underscores, and hyphens, the use of these characters is not recommended because they can cause problems with some software products.

Also be sure that usernames are distinct from any mail aliases known to the system. Problems can occur when a username duplicates a mail alias.

Each user account is associated with a User ID (UID). UIDs can be any integer between 0 and 2147483647, the maximum value of a signed integer. UIDs in the 0–99 range are reserved for system accounts and should not be used for regular user accounts. Although a UID can be as large as 2147483647, it is not recommended that you create users with a UID greater than 60000. UIDs 60001 and 60002 are the default users nobody and noaccess.

Users with a UID greater than 60003 might experience difficulties, including NFS and NIS usage issues, problems using the `ps -l`, `cpio`, `ar`, and `tar` commands, and compatibility problems with older Solaris versions that did not recognize UIDs of greater than 65534.

Not only does the UID identify users, but it is also used by systems to identify the owners of files and directories. In the example we used earlier with 10 users and 10 workstations, the best way to approach creating users on all machines would be to make certain that the users had the same username on each machine and the same UID. This would ensure that users wouldn't have ownership problems when transferring files between computers.

Users cannot be created with an existing UID but can be later modified to share an existing UID with another user. Although this is possible, creating duplicate UIDs can cause serious security problems, and is not recommended.

To minimize security risks, never reuse a UID from a deleted user. Solaris assigns permissions based on the UID. Re-using an old UID (that had been deleted) could inadvertently grant access to resources that the current user should not have access to.

Graphical Administration Tools

Solaris 9 has two bundled graphical utilities that can be used to manage users: Admintool and the Solaris Management Console (SMC).

Admintool is the interface that many Solaris administrators are used to. However, when you open Admintool in Solaris 9, you receive a warning: Admintool will be phased out, so you had better find another tool you like. To view users in Admintool, open the utility and choose Browse ➤ Users. Adding, modifying, and deleting users is done from the Edit menu. The Admintool: Add User window is shown in Figure 4.2.

FIGURE 4.2   Adding a user with Admintool

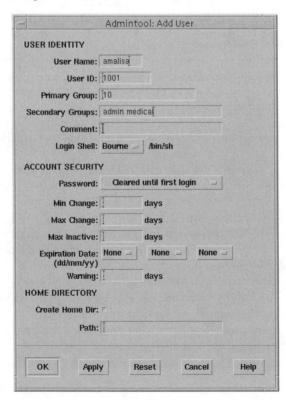

As you can see in Figure 4.2, there are three major sections to the Add User window: User Identity, Account Security, and Home Directory. Each of the fields represented in Figure 4.2 is explained in Table 4.2.

TABLE 4.2   Add User Fields

Attribute	Description
User Name	The user's login name.
User ID	The UID for this user. Admintool defaults to 1001 or the next-lowest UID available.
Primary Group	The name or number of the primary group that this user will belong to. The default is group 10 (staff).
Secondary Groups	This optional field can contain up to 15 additional groups that the user will belong to. Groups are specified by name or GID, and multiple groups can be supplied, separated by spaces.
Comment	Additional information pertaining to the user.
Login Shell	The user's shell. Choices are Bourne, C, Korn, and Other.
Password	Specifies how the user's password is handled during account creation. The default is Cleared Until First Login, which will ask the user for a password the first time they log in. Other choices are Account Is Locked, No password—Setuid Only, and Normal Password (which the administrator specifies).
Min Change	The minimum number of days that a user must wait between password changes.
Max Change	The maximum number of days that a password is valid.
Max Inactive	Maximum number of days the account can go without being used, before it is locked.
Expiration Date	Date at which the user account expires.
Warning	The number of days warning you want to give a user before their password expires.
Create Home Dir	A check box that automatically creates the home directory.
Path	The absolute path to the new user's home directory.

The new graphical user management tool of choice is the Solaris Management Console (SMC). The graphics in the SMC are much better than the ones in Admintool, and SMC gives you more options for managing users. For example, you can add multiple users with a wizard, assign rights to users, create user account templates, and set user policies.

SMC enables you to view users in various ways: large or small icons, List view, Details view, and even Web Style. Figure 4.3 displays users in Details view in SMC.

FIGURE 4.3   Solaris Management Console: User Accounts

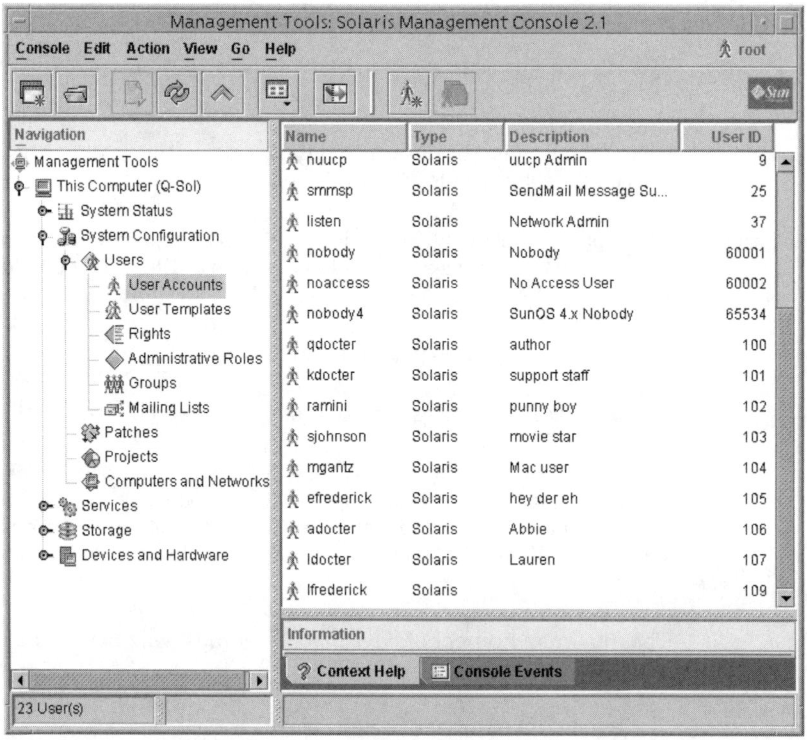

To modify a user account, highlight the user and choose Action ➢ Properties, or double-click the user. Figure 4.4 displays the User Properties window.

User Properties in SMC has nine tabs that enable you to configure various aspects of a user's account. The tabs are explained in Table 4.3.

To delete a user from SMC, highlight the user and choose Edit ➢ Delete, or right-click the user and choose Delete.

If you are going to use a graphical tool to manage your users, the SMC is more convenient and provides more flexibility than Admintool. For the certification exam, though, you will be expected to know how to add, manage, and delete users from a command prompt.

FIGURE 4.4   User Properties

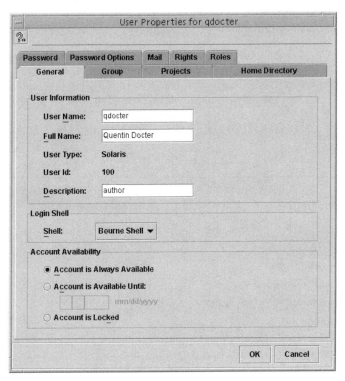

TABLE 4.3   User Properties

Tab	Description
General	Provides general information about the user, such as the username, description, login shell, and account availability
Group	Specifies the user's primary group and any secondary groups
Projects	Defines the primary project and any additional projects the user is associated with
Home Directory	Provides the home directory path, an option to automatically mount the home directory, and home directory sharing options
Password	Contains two options: User Must Set Password At Next Login, or User Must Use This Password At Next Login (the administrator supplies the password)

TABLE 4.3 User Properties *(continued)*

Tab	Description
Password Options	Contains minimum and maximum password change variables, warning time, and idle account expiration time
Mail	Sets the user's mail server and mail directory
Rights	Enables you to assign system rights to the user
Roles	Enables you to assign administrative roles to the user

Adding Users From a Command-Line Interface

The useradd command is for adding users from a command prompt. The syntax for useradd is as follows:

useradd *arguments login*

No arguments for the useradd command are required. Therefore, if you wanted to add a user named sjohnson, all you need to type is this:

useradd sjohnson

But what fun is that? You added a user with all default settings and didn't use any switches. It might have been easy to type, but it positively lacked any sort of customization or creativity. And it certainly wouldn't be any fun to write test questions about a boring command, would it?

While programming arguments for useradd, the developers at Sun nearly exhausted the alphabet. It's a good thing that Solaris is case-sensitive because that gave the developers twice as many possibilities to use. The useradd options are listed in Table 4.4.

TABLE 4.4 *useradd* Arguments

Argument	Description
-A *authorization*	Specifies one or more authorizations (separated by commas) as defined in /etc/security/auth_attr.
-b *directory*	The base directory for the user if the -d option is not specified. If -m is not used, the base directory must already exist.
-c *comment*	A comment relating to the user (such as the user's full name).
-d *dir*	The home directory of the new user.
-D	Enables the administrator to set default values for any or all of the -A, -b, -e, -f, -g, -P, -p, or -R options.

TABLE 4.4   *useradd* Arguments *(continued)*

Argument	Description
-e *date*	Expiration date for the account. Can be entered as a date format (12/25/2003) or as a text string surrounded by quotes ("December 25, 2003").
-f *days*	The maximum number of consecutive inactive days before the user account is locked.
-g *group*	The user's primary group, specified as either a group name or GID.
-G *group*	The user's secondary group(s), if any.
-k *dir*	Specifies skeleton information (such as .profile files) that can be copied into the user's home directory.
-m	Creates the user's home directory if it does not already exist.
-o	Allows for the creation of duplicate UIDs.
-P *profile*	Specifies one or more execution profiles.
-p *name*	The name of the project that the user is to be associated with.
-R *role*	One or more roles to be assigned to the user.
-s *shell*	Full path to the user's shell. The default is /bin/sh (Bourne shell).
-u *UID*	The UID of the new user. If none is specified, useradd defaults to the next available number above the highest UID currently assigned.

Table 4.4 might seem to contain a lot of options, but considering the flexibility required to create new user accounts, the arguments are necessary. Perhaps the most interesting switch is -D. It enables the administrator to set a default value for one of the supported options (-A, -b, -e, -f, -g, -P, -p, or -R). Any users subsequently added to the system will be assigned the new default value.

As an example, the default for the primary group (-g) is other (GID 1). However, consider the following command:

```
# useradd -D -g trainers
# useradd thudson
```

The new user, thudson, will have a primary group of trainers (this group must already exist, or you will receive an error message). All subsequently added users will also be assigned to this primary group, unless specified otherwise with the -g switch.

There is one potentially negative aspect to adding users through useradd. Users created with useradd have no password, and their accounts are disabled by default. To enable the user account, you must use the passwd command to set a password. If you have just created the thudson account with useradd, you would need to enable the account by using the following command:

passwd thudson

Supply a password (even if it is blank), and the account will be enabled.

Modifying and Deleting Users From a Command-Line Interface

The usermod and userdel commands are used to modify and delete users. In most cases, it's easier to use the graphical tools for user management. However, there are some tasks that you cannot complete unless you use the command-line tools. For example, changing a user's UID is done through the usermod command, and cannot be done through a graphical interface.

The usermod command supports most of the same arguments that useradd does. The exceptions are -b, -D, -k, and -p, which do not exist. The -l switch is unique to usermod and enables you to create a new login name for the user. The -m option (when used in conjunction with –d) will move the existing user's home directory to the new directory location, instead of creating a new empty home directory.

Sun recommends not changing the user's login name or UID for any reason. However, some reasons for changing the user's login name, such as marriage or a legal name change, make sense. It's still not recommended to change the user's UID for any reason.

Let's say you want to modify the user jgebelt. She has recently been promoted (necessitating a primary group change) and has long wanted to use the C shell instead of the Bourne shell. You would execute the following command to modify her account:

usermod -g cpuguru -s /bin/csh jgebelt

She will now have the cpuguru group as her primary group and the C shell as her default shell.

Deleting users is accomplished with the userdel command. There is only one switch for userdel: -r. The -r option deletes the user's home directory and any files and subdirectories. The syntax for userdel is the same as the other user* commands:

userdel -r *username*

Home Directories

A *home directory* can be provided to users as a place to store their personal files. As an administrator, you can place home directories on local machines or on a centralized server. If you have a large number of users, placing home directories on a server facilitates backups. Sun recommends that user home directories be created as /export/home/*username*, whether they are located on a server or local machine.

Regardless of where the user's home directory is located, users should access the directory through a mount point called /home/*username*. When using AutoFS to mount file systems, the /home mount point will be reserved specifically for home directories.

To use a home directory from anywhere on the network, users should always refer to the directory as $HOME. Do not refer to it as /export/home/*username* because this path is machine-specific.

Home directories can be created when the user's account is created. If the user already has an account but no home directory, create the directory manually. Then modify the user's properties to specify the location of the home directory.

Password Management

To log in to Solaris, users must provide a valid username and password. Usernames are often public knowledge or at least company-wide knowledge. In most companies, if you know a person's first and last name, you can figure out their username quite easily. Passwords should be a different story because the password is the only obstacle between the potential hacker and critical network resources.

Passwords can contain any keyboard character and should contain a combination of uppercase and lowercase letters, numbers, and special characters, such as $, %, @, or whatever the user prefers. Passwords must be at least six characters, and the first six characters must contain at least two alphabetic characters and at least one numeric or special character. Although passwords in Solaris can be more than eight characters long, only the first eight are processed during user authentication.

 If you are setting passwords from a command line, Solaris doesn't enforce the character requirements described in the preceding paragraph.

To increase network security, force users to change their passwords periodically. How often depends on how strict of a security environment you have. Once every six weeks is appropriate for many networks, although users in less-secure installations can possibly afford to change their passwords every three months.

Information that can be easily guessed should not be used for any password. Any part of the user's name, the user's significant other, children, or pets' names, and important numbers (Social Security number, driver's license number, telephone number) should be avoided at all costs. Nonsense words make the best passwords, and users should avoid any words listed in common dictionaries.

All of this might sound a bit paranoid, but when it comes to security, it's better to err on the side of safety. If a user uses his first name as his password, it's incredibly easy to figure out. More complex password-cracking programs will run a "dictionary test." If the user's password appears in a dictionary, the program will eventually find it.

Solaris 9 has a feature called *password aging*, which enables an administrator to force users to change their passwords periodically or to prevent users from changing their passwords too frequently. (When users change their passwords too frequently, they are apt to forget their password.)

The best way to secure your network and protect passwords is to educate your users. Many users don't understand the severity of security risks and they don't understand what they can do to help protect the network, their data, and the company. When educated as to proper password use, users can be security allies instead of unwitting security risks.

Managing Groups

Using groups is a great way to ease your administrative burden. The nature and scope of groups that you can create is limited only by your organization's structure. In other words, if you have an accounting department, it makes sense to have an accounting group. Or it might make even more sense to have multiple accounting groups, including accounts receivable, accounts payable, and auditors. Groups are flexible enough to accommodate nearly any company's structure.

Each group must have a name, a Group ID (GID), and a list of users who belong to the group. GIDs are analogous to UIDs for users. They can be any number between 0 and 2147483647, but it's recommended to keep them between 100 and 60000.

Users must belong to at least one group. This will be the user's *primary group*. By default, the primary group for users is `staff` (GID 10). However, you can change that to suit your needs.

In most cases, a user's primary versus secondary group memberships don't cause problems. File ownership is based on primary group membership, but file access (permissions) can be related to any of the user's groups. To see which groups you are a member of, issue the `groups` command at a command prompt. Also, a user might change his or her primary group membership to any other group in which he or she is a member. This is done with the `newgrp` command. To change your primary group to the `root` group, you would type **newgrp root**. To revert to your original group, use **newgrp** with no arguments.

Graphical Administration Tools

The Admintool and Solaris Management Console are available for managing groups as well as users. In Admintool, click Browse ➢ Groups to see a group listing. Groups can be added, modified, and deleted from the Edit menu. Even though Admintool is older and has fewer features than SMC, it does have one very useful element: it shows the members of the groups. Figure 4.5 shows the Groups node of Admintool.

Adding a group in Admintool is easy. Choose Edit ➢ Add to access the window shown in Figure 4.6. Supply a group name, GID, and group members.

FIGURE 4.5   Admintool: Groups

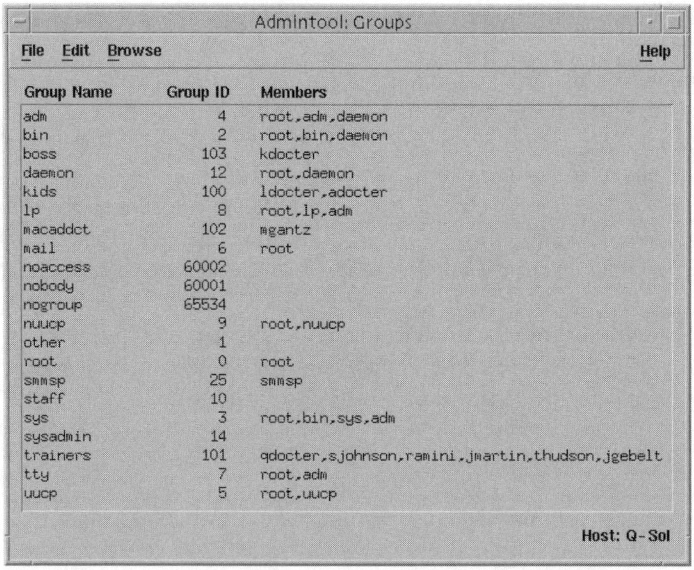

FIGURE 4.6   Adding a group in Admintool

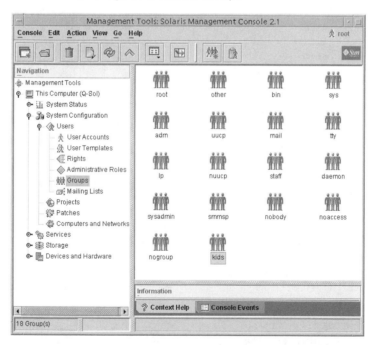

To modify or delete a group, highlight the group and choose either Edit ➢ Modify or Edit ➢ Delete.

It's true that the SMC often outperforms Admintool. However, group management in SMC has some minor inconveniences. When viewing groups in the SMC main window, you can see the group name and GID, but you can't see the group members. To view group members, you must double-click the group to view its properties. The Groups node of SMC is shown in Figure 4.7.

FIGURE 4.7   Solaris Management Console Groups

Adding groups in SMC is easier than it is in Admintool, because you can see the list of users on your system. There is one minor annoyance with adding groups in SMC though. The Group ID Number box is far too small to see the whole number (the GID in Figure 4.8 is 5150, not 50) unless you leave the help portion of the screen up when you open the Add Group box. Perhaps this and the viewing group membership issue will be fixed in a later release. Figure 4.8 shows the Add Group dialog box in SMC. To get there, click Action ➢ Add Group.

FIGURE 4.8   Adding a group in Solaris Management Console

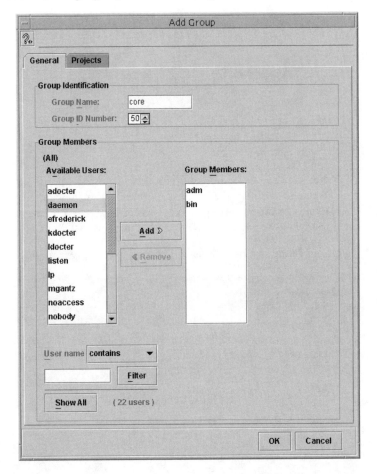

You can add users to a group or modify group properties by double-clicking the group, or by highlighting the group and choosing Action ➢ Properties. Groups are deleted by right-clicking the group and choosing Delete, or by choosing Edit ➢ Delete.

Command-Line Interface

From the command line, groups can be added, modified, and deleted with the `groupadd`, `groupmod`, and `groupdel` commands.

The syntax for the `groupadd` command is as follows:

```
# groupadd -g gid -o groupname
```

The `groupadd` command has only two possible switches: `-g` to specify a certain GID, and `-o` to enable duplicate GIDs to be created. As with duplicate UIDs, it's not a good idea to create duplicate GIDs.

To modify a group, use the `groupmod` command:

```
# groupmod -g gid -o -n name groupname
```

For example, if you wanted to rename the `techs` group to `support`, and change the GID to 1814, you would issue the following command:

```
# groupmod -g 1814 -n support techs
```

To delete a group, use the `groupdel` command. To delete the group, you must supply the group name as an argument for the `groupdel` command. You cannot supply the GID. To delete the `acctng` group, issue this command:

```
# groupdel acctng
```

To add users to groups, you must use the `usermod` command. None of the group management commands support adding users.

Account Configuration Files

User and group account information can be stored on a local machine, or in a centralized network location on an NIS or NIS+ server. If user and group information is stored locally, it will be in three separate files: `/etc/passwd`, `/etc/shadow`, and `/etc/group`. On NIS and NIS+ servers, the same information is stored in maps and tables, respectively. Regardless of the location of the user and group information, Sun refers to all three options (files, maps, and tables) simply as files to avoid confusion.

/etc/passwd

The `/etc/passwd` file holds critical user account information, such as usernames and UIDs. There are seven fields in the `/etc/passwd` file, separated by colons. Here are the seven fields:

```
username:password:UID:GID:comment:home_directory:login_shell
```

Most of the fields are self-explanatory if you have already read the section in this chapter on creating users or you are already familiar with user creation. However, the `password` field in this file needs some explanation. Every user will have an *x* in their `password` field, which serves as a placeholder for the user's real password.

Older versions of Solaris (and other UNIX-based operating systems) used to put the password, in encrypted form, right in the `/etc/passwd` file. The problem is, users need read access to `/etc/passwd` to log in. Therefore, all users had access to all passwords in the system, including that of the `root` account. Yes, the passwords were encrypted, but brute force hacking methods could still decode them. After a user had the `root` password, they could do anything they wanted, benign or otherwise.

To solve this problem, the `/etc/passwd` file contains a mere placeholder, and the encrypted password is stored in a second file, `/etc/shadow`. More on `/etc/shadow` in the next section. Here is a sample `/etc/password` file:

```
root:x:0:1:Super-User:/:/sbin/sh
daemon:x:1:1::/:
bin:x:2:2::/usr/bin:
```

```
sys:x:3:3::/:
adm:x:4:4:Admin:/var/adm:
lp:x:71:8:Line Printer Admin:/usr/spool/lp:
uucp:x:5:5:uucp Admin:/usr/lib/uucp:
nuucp:x:9:9:uucp Admin:/var/spool/uucppublic:/usr/lib/uucp/uucico
smmsp:x:25:25:SendMail Message Submission Program:/:
listen:x:37:4:Network Admin:/usr/net/nls:
nobody:x:60001:60001:Nobody:/:
noaccess:x:60002:60002:No Access User:/:
nobody4:x:65534:65534:SunOS 4.x Nobody:/:
qdocter:x:100:10:author:/export/home/qdocter:/bin/sh
```

Every user created on the system will appear in the /etc/passwd file. As you can see, every user has an *x* placeholder after their username, followed by the user's UID and the GID of the user's primary group.

Although it's possible to directly edit the /etc/passwd file to add, modify, and delete user accounts, it's not recommended. Instead, use your favorite graphical utility or the useradd, usermod, and userdel commands. Editing the /etc/passwd file directly does not modify the critical /etc/shadow directory, whereas using the user management utilities does.

 If you have to edit the /etc/passwd file manually, you can use the pwconv command to update /etc/shadow. However, editing the passwd file directly is still not recommended.

To verify the integrity of /etc/passwd, you can use the pwck command.

/etc/shadow

The /etc/shadow file holds all usernames and information regarding the user's password. The fields for /etc/shadow are as follows:

```
username:password:lastchg:min:max:warn:inactive:expire:flag
```

Table 4.5 explains the fields in /etc/shadow.

TABLE 4.5 /etc/shadow Fields

Field	Description
username	The user's login name.
password	This field will have one of three entries: a 13-character encrypted password; LK, which indicates the account is locked; or NP, which means the account has no password.
lastchg	The number of days between January 1, 1970 and the last password modification date.

TABLE 4.5 */etc/shadow* Fields *(continued)*

Field	Description
min	The minimum number of days required between password changes.
max	The maximum number of days that a password is valid.
warn	The number of days' warning the user has that their password is going to expire.
inactive	The number of days that an account can be inactive before it is automatically locked.
expire	The date at which the account expires and is no longer valid.
flag	Field reserved for future use.

Here is a sample `/etc/shadow` file:

```
root:AaSfeBzrNVeao:11920::::::
daemon:NP:6445::::::
bin:NP:6445::::::
sys:NP:6445::::::
adm:NP:6445::::::
lp:NP:6445::::::
uucp:NP:6445::::::
nuucp:NP:6445::::::
smmsp:NP:6445::::::
listen:*LK*:::::::
nobody:NP:6445::::::
noaccess:NP:6445::::::
nobody4:NP:6445::::::
qdocter:DXvo9wTm2tZmQ:11899:5:42:7:21::
```

You can see that the `qdocter` user account created on this system has a 5-day minimum and 42-day maximum password life, a 7-day warning window, a 21-day inactive grace period, and no expiration date.

If you have manually created or modified users in the `/etc/passwd` file, the `pwconv` command can be used to automatically update the `/etc/shadow` file. Again, this method is not recommended for creating or modifying users.

/etc/group

The `/etc/group` file contains—you guessed it—group information. Although users can belong to multiple groups, the user is associated only with their primary group in this file. (This is not true for built-in administrative accounts, which appear multiple times.) Listing all group member-ships could quickly become unwieldy, especially on larger networks. The /etc/group file has four fields:

```
group_name:password:GID:users
```

The password field is optional. Most groups do not require passwords, but passwords can be used for security purposes. If a group has a password, a user will be required to supply it if they try to use the newgrp command to change their primary group. Here is a sample /etc/group file:

```
root::0:root
other::1:
bin::2:root,bin,daemon
sys::3:root,bin,sys,adm
adm::4:root,adm,daemon
uucp::5:root,uucp
mail::6:root
tty::7:root,adm
lp::8:root,lp,adm
nuucp::9:root,nuucp
staff::10:
daemon::12:root,daemon
sysadmin::14:
smmsp::25:smmsp
nobody::60001:
noaccess::60002:
nogroup::65534:
kids::100:ldocter,adocter
macaddct::102:mgantz
boss::103:kdocter
author::104:qdocter
```

None of the preceding groups has a password, but then again, none of them need one. You can verify the consistency of the /etc/group file with the grpck command, which is identical in usage to pwck.

User Account Commands

This section contains information that is useful for managing users on a daily basis. In addition, the information presented here is potential certification exam material.

Seeing Who Is Logged In

There might be several reasons why you want to see who is logged in to your system. Perhaps you need to change the run level to S to perform a system backup and want to warn users. Maybe you think someone who shouldn't be logging in *is* logging in. Or you might be just curious.

Any reason is good enough. The basic command to see logged-in users is who. The who command examines the /var/adm/utmpx file to obtain information on current connections.

To see a historical listing of all logins and logouts on your system, use the last command. This command checks the /var/adm/wtmpx file for all logins and logouts. The last command can display quite a bit of information, too much to sift through in a lot of cases. To help squelch output, use the last -n *number* command, which will display only the number of lines you request.

Switching Users

If you are the administrator of your network, you probably realize that it's not a good idea to log in to your machine as root and leave the superuser account logged in all day. If you were to leave your desk for any reason, another person could use your machine to perform malicious tasks.

A good way to give yourself administrative access while protecting your network is to create a normal user account for yourself and to use the su (switch users) command to assume administrative powers when you need them. After you are done with your administrative duties, you can go back to using your regular user account.

If you use su with no arguments, Solaris assumes that you are trying to switch to the superuser account and will prompt you for the superuser password. You can, however, su to any valid user or role on your system. Instead of just typing su, you can issue the command with a username argument, such as su jdoe. Again, you will be prompted for the user account's password.

All attempts to use the su command are logged in /var/adm/sulog file. The sulog file records where, when, and who attempted to su, and the result of the attempt. Here is an example from a sulog file:

```
SU 07/26 11:43 + pts/4 qdocter-root
SU 07/29 13:20 + pts/4 qdocter-root
SU 07/29 16:11 - pts/3 jmartin-root
SU 07/29 16:12 - pts/3 jmartin-root
SU 07/29 16:13 - pts/3 jmartin-qdocter
SU 07/30 10:01 + pts/4 qdocter-root
```

All entries start with *SU* and the date and time of the su attempt. The plus indicates a successful su, whereas a minus indicates a failure. The first username listed is the account that attempted to su, and the second account name listed is the account that the user attempted to switch to.

In the example, it can be concluded that the jmartin user account does not have administrative access and is trying to hack the root password. For security purposes, it's a good idea to periodically monitor the sulog file.

After you have successfully used su, your command prompt will change from that of a regular user ($, if you use the Bourne or Korn shells) to the superuser, #. Otherwise, your environment will stay the same. To assume the environment (in addition to the identity) of the user you are changing to, you could use su - *username*. To "un-su" yourself, press Control+D on your keyboard, or type **exit** and press Enter.

Changing User Passwords

Passwords can be changed in Solaris through either a graphical user interface or the command line. The graphical tools are Admintool and the Solaris Management Console, which are described earlier in this chapter. In Admintool, passwords can be cleared but not changed. From a command line, use the `passwd` command.

If you are the superuser or have equivalent rights, you can change any user's password by using the `passwd` command. If you are a regular user, you can change only your own password.

 Real World Scenario

Catching Would-Be Hackers

You are the network administrator for a technical consulting firm. One afternoon, you receive a call from one of your users, Steve. He's frantic because he believes that one of his coworkers, Jason, has gone off the deep end. Jason has been making off-handed comments about hacking the network. Apparently this would-be hacker is disgruntled and wants to harm the company by destroying large amounts of sensitive data.

Steve says that he normally wouldn't consider it a big deal, but Jason's rhetoric has become stronger in recent weeks. That, and Jason claims to have the "ultimate hacking program" that would guarantee his success. Steve is worried and wanted to warn you.

You have a potential hacker on your hands and you need to stop him. The question is, how? You need proof that Jason is trying to behave in a malicious manner. So what do you do?

If you suspect that someone is trying to hack the superuser account, one of the first places you should check is the `/var/adm/sulog` file.

Sure enough, when you check the file, there are literally thousands of lines indicating that Jason has been trying to use the `su` command to assume administrative control. Fortunately, he hasn't had any success so far. You now have the proof you need to confront Jason's manager with your suspicions.

This time, you were lucky enough to get a tip from a concerned user that someone was trying to hack the superuser account. But is there anything you can do to help yourself, so you don't need to rely on conscientious users? There is. By editing the `/etc/default/su` file, you can set up your system to pop up a display on the console each time the `su` command is used in an attempt to gain superuser access. To activate this option, uncomment the `CONSOLE=/dev/console` line in `/etc/default/su`.

Using Shells

In Solaris, the *shell* functions both as a command interpreter and a high-level programming language. When you type a command at the command line, the shell processes the command and responds appropriately. Used as a programming language, various commands can be grouped together into what's known as a shell script. You can then run the script (which might be just multiple commands) by executing a single command. Although users can use whichever shell they prefer, only one shell can be used at a time.

The default shell for Solaris 9 is the Bourne shell (sh). Other shells supported by Solaris 9 are the Bourne Again shell (bash), C shell (csh), Korn shell (ksh), TC shell (tcsh), and Z shell (zsh). Each of these shells has unique features. Although all these shells are available, this chapter focuses mainly on three shells: Bourne, C, and Korn. These three shells are perhaps the most common and the most commonly tested.

We will examine features of the three most common shells and look at configuration files for these shells.

Bourne, C, and Korn

Because each shell is its own command interpreter, some commands work in one shell but not another. The Bourne shell is considered the most basic of all the shells and is therefore the default shell. Many other shells are described in terms of Bourne compatibility. Table 4.6 lists some basic features of the Bourne, C, and Korn shells.

T A B L E   4 . 6   Shell Features

Feature	Bourne	C	Korn
Default prompt	$	%	$
Bourne-compatible syntax	N/A	No	Yes
Job control	Yes	Yes	Yes
Command history list	No	Yes	Yes
Command line editing	No	Yes	Yes
Repeat last command	No	!!	Yes
Supports aliases	No	Yes	Yes
Single-character abbreviation for login directory	No	Yes	Yes
Protection from file overwriting	No	Yes	Yes
Supports enhanced cd	No	Yes	Yes
Initialization file separate from .profile	No	Yes	Yes
Logout file	No	Yes	No

The Korn shell is highly compatible with the Bourne shell. This makes sense, considering that the Korn shell was developed from the Bourne shell. Also, the Bourne Again shell is, as you might expect, highly Bourne-compatible. The C shell was developed separately and is based on the C programming language. Therefore, it tends to work a bit differently than Bourne. The TC and Z shells tend to act a lot like the C shell.

Initialization Files

When you log in to Solaris, the default system profile file, /etc/profile, is run. After the system profile executes, the user profile is run. Your user profile can have one or more files, known as *initialization files*, and is dependent upon the shell you are using. Table 4.7 shows the profile initialization files based on the shell.

TABLE 4.7   Profile Initialization Files

Shell	Initialization File(s)
Bourne and Korn	.profile
C	.login and .cshrc
TC	.tcshrc and .cshrc
Z	.zlogin and .zshrc
Bourne Again	.bash_profile

The initialization files are essentially a shell script. However, their primary purpose is to set up the user's work environment, including the home directory, path, and other environment variables.

Solaris 9 provides default initialization files for each profile in the /etc/skel directory. These files are local.cshrc, local.login, and local.profile. As an administrator, you can customize these files to your liking.

When a user account is created, the appropriate files in the /etc/skel directory are copied to the user's home directory. For users with the Bourne and Korn shells, the /etc/skel/local.profile file is copied as $HOME/.profile. For users using the C shell, /etc/skel/local.cshrc is copied as $HOME/.cshrc, and /etc/skel/local.login is copied as $HOME/.login. In most cases, users have read and write access to their local profile files and can adapt them as necessary.

Site Initialization Files

One way to affect all user profiles on a network is to introduce a *site initialization file*. Site initialization files must be located on a server that is accessible to all users on your network, and are called from within the user's local initialization file. Therefore, if you want to make network-wide changes, you can make the change in the site initialization file, and all users will receive the change when they log in.

Place the following variable at the beginning of a Bourne or Korn initialization file to reference a site initialization file:

```
./net/machine_name/init_file
```

The *machine_name* and *init_file* variables must point to the physical location of the site initialization file. If you are configuring the C shell initialization file (.cshrc), you will need the following variable:

```
source /net/machine_name/init_file
```

The previous two variables are a great example of the differences between the Bourne and Korn initialization files and the C shell initialization file. Both types of files can accomplish the same goals, but require different syntax.

Adding Initialization File Variables

When adding variables to initialization files, you need to know which shell your user is using.

In the Bourne and Korn shells, you use an uppercase value name and a value parameter to specify a new variable. You also have to use the export command to finish setting the environment variable. As an example, to set a user's mail directory, you could execute the following command:

```
# MAIL=/var/mail/qdocter;export MAIL
```

To set variables for C shell users, you use one of two commands. To set shell variables (local variables known only within the shell), use the set command with lowercase variable names. To set environment variables (global variables, available in subshells), use the setenv command with uppercase variable names. If you set a shell variable, the shell automatically sets the environment variable, and vice versa. To set the *MAIL* variable, you would execute the following:

```
# setenv MAIL /var/mail/qdocter
```

Both of the preceding examples set the same environment variable to the same value, but in different shells. Table 4.8 lists some of the more common variables you will set.

TABLE 4.8   Shell and Environment Variables

Variable	Description
history	Sets command history for the C shell.
HOME	Defines the path to the user's home directory.
LANG	Sets the local language for the computer.
LPDEST	The user's default printer.
MAIL	The path to the user's mailbox.

TABLE 4.8 Shell and Environment Variables *(continued)*

Variable	Description
noclobber	Prevents unintentional file overwrites when using the cp command to copy a file. Not available in the Bourne shell.
PATH	Specifies the order of the search path for the user. When the user types in a command, they either need to be in the directory the command is located in, or have the directory in their path. Although the search path is automatically configured during user creation, you can modify it as necessary.
prompt	Sets the shell prompt for the C shell.
PS1	Sets the shell prompt for the Bourne and Korn shells.
SHELL	Sets the default shell used by make, vi, and other tools.
TZ	Defines the time zone the system is located in.

Generally speaking, it's best to refer to all shell and environment variables by their upper-case names.

Summary

In this chapter, we examined many concepts critical to user administration in Solaris 9. First, we looked at how to manage user and group accounts. Users can be managed through graphical interfaces, or the useradd, usermod, and userdel commands. Groups can also be managed through graphical interfaces, or the groupadd, groupmod, and groupdel commands. Each user has a login name and a User ID (UID). Each group has a group name and a Group ID (GID). UIDs and GIDs should be unique on the system.

We then looked at vital account configuration files. The files were /etc/passwd, which contains user accounts, /etc/shadow, which contains the user's encrypted password, and /etc/group, which contains group information.

From there, we moved on to a few miscellaneous user management commands. The who and last commands can show who is or was logged in. The su command can be used to switch users or assume a role, and the passwd command is used to change passwords on the system.

Finally, we looked at shells. The three most common shells in Solaris are Bourne, C, and Korn. Each shell has different features and acts as a command interpreter as well as a programming interface. Users will have initialization files that configure their environment at login. The specific initialization file, and the variables within, will depend on the user's shell.

Exam Essentials

Know the UIDs for the built-in root, daemon, bin, nobody, and noaccess accounts.   root is UID 1, daemon is 2, bin is 3, nobody is 60001, and noaccess is 60002.

Know the recommendations for using UIDs and GIDs.   Although UIDs and GIDs can be as large as the largest value for a signed integer, 2147483647, it's recommended that you not use numbers greater than 60000. Numbers below 100 should be reserved for system accounts as well.

Know the commands used to add, modify, and delete users.   To add users, use the useradd command. Use usermod to modify users, and userdel to delete users.

Know the commands used to add, modify, and delete groups.   Groups are added with the groupadd command, modified with groupmod, and deleted with groupdel.

Know how to read an /etc/passwd file.   User account information is stored in /etc/passwd. The fields in /etc/passwd are as follows: username:password:UID:GID:comment:home_directory:login_shell.

Know how to read an /etc/shadow file.   The /etc/shadow file contains the users' encrypted passwords and is very important to protect. The fields in /etc/shadow are as follows: username:password:lastchg:min:max:warn:inactive:expire:flag.

Know how to switch users on a system.   To switch users on a system, use the su command.

Know what the default shell is in Solaris 9.   The default shell is the Bourne shell.

Know the initialization files for the Bourne, C, and Korn shells.   For the Bourne and Korn shells, the initialization file is $HOME/.profile. For the C shell, they are $HOME/.cshrc and $HOME/.login.

Key Terms

Before you take the exam, be certain you are familiar with the following terms:

Group ID (GID)

home directory

initialization files

password aging

primary group

shell

site initialization file

User ID (UID)

username

Commands Used in This Chapter

The following list contains a summary of all the commands introduced in this chapter:

Command	Description
groupadd	Adds groups
groupdel	Deletes groups
groupmod	Modifies groups
groups	Identifies group membership
grpck	Checks the consistency of the /etc/group file
last	Provides a historical list of all system logins and logouts
newgrp	Changes the user's primary group membership
passwd	Changes user passwords
pwck	Checks the consistency of the /etc/passwd file
set	Sets shell variables in the C shell
setenv	Sets environment variables in the C shell
su	Enables you to switch users or assume a role
useradd	Adds users
userdel	Deletes users
usermod	Modifies users
who	Shows who is logged in to the system

Review Questions

1. You are the network administrator for your company. You have just tried to add a user account with the `useradd` command but you received the following message:

   `UX: useradd: WARNING: uid is reserved.`

   What is the most likely cause of the message?

   A. The UID you specified is already being used by another account. Use a different UID.

   B. The UID you specified is already being used by another account. Use the `-o` option with `useradd`.

   C. The UID you specified is in the 0–99 range. Use a different UID.

   D. The UID you specified is in the 0–99 range. Use the `-o` option with `useradd`.

2. You are the Solaris administrator for your company. One of your users, who is using the C shell, wants to know the location and name of his initialization file or files. What do you tell him? (Choose all that apply.)

   A. `$HOME/.login`

   B. `$HOME/.kshrc`

   C. `$HOME/.cshrc`

   D. `$HOME/.profile`

3. You are the Solaris administrator for a major performing arts company. You want to add a user, `aamini`, to the `directors` group. This should be a secondary group membership. Which command should you execute?

   A. `usermod -G directors aamini`

   B. `usermod -g directors aamini`

   C. `usermod aamini -G directors`

   D. `usermod aamini -g directors`

4. You are the Solaris administrator for your company. Because of merging corporate divisions, you need to delete the finacct group (GID 1111) from your server. Which command should you use to accomplish this?

   A. `groupdel finacct`

   B. `groupdel 1111`

   C. `groupdel -g 1111`

   D. `delgroup finacct`

   E. `delgroup 1111`

   F. `delgroup -g 1111`

5. One of your users is attempting to run multiple shells in the same terminal window at once in Solaris 9. However, he doesn't seem to be having much luck. What advice should you give him?

   A. Configure the profile file in your home directory to support the multiple shells you wish to run concurrently.

   B. Set up a second user profile for yourself with the desired shell and then use the su command to assume your secondary identity.

   C. Execute the **shell -d** *path* command at the command line, where *path* is the absolute path to the secondary shell you wish to run (such as /bin/sh, /bin/csh, or /bin/ksh).

   D. It's not going to happen. One user can run only one shell at a time in Solaris 9.

6. You are the network administrator for your company. Because of changes in corporate structure, you are required to change your network's group structure. All 50 users in the finance group need to be members of a newly created corpfin group (instead of the finance group), which should have a GID of 1776. What is the easiest way to accomplish this goal?

   A. Create a new group called corpfin with a GID of 1776. Move all finance users into this group by using the usermod command. Delete the finance group.

   B. Create a new group called corpfin with a GID of 1776. Move all finance users into this group by using the groupmod command. Delete the finance group.

   C. Use the groupmod finance -g 1776 -n corpfin command to rename the finance group and give it the appropriate GID.

   D. Use the groupmod -g 1776 -n corpfin finance command to rename the finance group and give it the appropriate GID.

7. One of your Solaris servers has the following lines in its /etc/passwd file:

   ```
   root:x:0:1:Super-User:/:/sbin/sh
   daemon:x:1:1::/:
   bin:x:2:2::/usr/bin:
   sys:x:3:3::/:
   adm:x:4:4:Admin:/var/adm:
   lp:x:71:8:Line Printer Admin:/usr/spool/lp:
   uucp:x:5:5:uucp Admin:/usr/lib/uucp:
   nuucp:x:9:9:uucp Admin:/var/spool/uucppublic:/usr/lib/uucp/uucico
   smmsp:x:25:25:SendMail Message Submission Program:/:
   listen:x:37:4:Network Admin:/usr/net/nls:
   nobody:x:60001:60001:Nobody:/:
   noaccess:x:60002:60002:No Access User:/:
   nobody4:x:65534:65534:SunOS 4.x Nobody:/:
   qdocter:x:100:10:author:/export/home/qdocter:/bin/sh
   jsmith:x:1001:101:Jane Smith::/bin/ksh
   jdoe:x:1002:101:John Doe:/export/home/jdoe:/bin/csh
   ```

Based on the information presented, which of the following statements is true? (Choose all that apply.)

A. The `jdoe` user is using the C shell.

B. The `jsmith` user does not have a home directory configured.

C. The UID of the `root` account is 0.

D. The `qdocter` user is a member of a default group.

8. You are the Solaris server administrator for your company. You need to bring the server down for a system backup. Before you do so, you want to see the list of currently logged-in users, so you can warn them to log off. Which command can you use to accomplish this?

A. list

B. user

C. who

D. login

9. You are presented with the following information from an `/etc/shadow` file:

```
root:AaSfeBzrNVeao:11920::::::
daemon:NP:6445::::::
bin:NP:6445::::::
sys:NP:6445::::::
adm:NP:6445::::::
lp:NP:6445::::::
uucp:NP:6445::::::
nuucp:NP:6445::::::
smmsp:NP:6445::::::
listen:*LK*:::::::
nobody:NP:6445::::::
noaccess:NP:6445::::::
nobody4:NP:6445::::::
qdocter:DXvo9wTm2tZmQ:11899:5:42:7:21::
```

Based on the information, which of the following statements is true? (Choose all that apply.)

A. The `root` account has a password of AaSfeBzrNVeao.

B. The `root` account's password has been changed more recently than the `qdocter` account's password.

C. The `listen` account is locked and cannot be used.

D. The `qdocter` account expires in 21 days.

10. You are the network administrator for your company. You want to add a user, `abradley`, to your system. The user should have a UID of 3422, have the `admin` group as her primary group, the `mdte` group as her secondary group, and have her home directory created automatically. Which command should you execute?

    A. `useradd -u 3422 -d /export/home/abradley -g admin -G mdte abradley`

    B. `useradd -u 3422 -d /export/home/abradley -m -G admin -g mdte abradley`

    C. `useradd abradley -u 3422 -d /export/home/abradley -m -g admin -G mdte`

    D. `useradd -u 3422 -d /export/home/abradley -m -g admin -G mdte abradley`

11. You are the Solaris administrator for your company. You are concerned that someone is trying to hack the superuser's password. Which file can you check to see whether there have been any failed attempts to switch users?

    A. `/etc/default/su`

    B. `/etc/default/sulog`

    C. `/var/adm/sulog`

    D. `/var/adm/su`

12. You are presented with the following information from an `/etc/group` file:

    ```
    root::0:root
    other::1:
    bin::2:root,bin,daemon
    sys::3:root,bin,sys,adm
    adm::4:root,adm,daemon
    uucp::5:root,uucp
    mail::6:root
    tty::7:root,adm
    lp::8:root,lp,adm
    nuucp::9:root,nuucp
    staff::10:
    daemon::12:root,daemon
    sysadmin::14:
    smmsp::25:smmsp
    nobody::60001:
    noaccess::60002:
    nogroup::65534:
    macaddct::102:mgantz
    author::104:qdocter
    ```

Based on the information presented, which of the following statements are true? (Choose all that apply.)

A. The Group ID for the `smmsp` group is 25.

B. The password for the `macaddct` group is `mgantz`.

C. The `staff` group has no members.

D. The `sysadmin` group has a User ID of 14.

13. In Solaris 9, the shell provides which of the following functions? (Choose all that apply.)

A. Provides a graphical interface for user interaction

B. Acts as a command interpreter

C. Functions as a high-level batch programming language

D. Defines the user environment variables as specified in the `/etc/users/profiles` file

14. You are the Solaris administrator for your company. A new working division was recently formed, and you need to create a new group named nwtrade. Which command should you use to accomplish this task?

A. `addgroup -o nwtrade`

B. `addgroup nwtrade`

C. `groupadd -o nwtrade`

D. `groupadd nwtrade`

15. Which of the following are features of the Korn shell in Solaris 9? (Choose all that apply.)

A. Bourne-shell-compatible syntax

B. Job editing

C. Repeat last command

D. Supports aliases

E. Protection from overwriting files

16. Which Bourne shell environment variable allows for customization of the command prompt?

A. PS1

B. PROMPT

C. Prompt

D. Command

17. You are the Solaris 9 administrator for your company. You are using the Solaris Management Console to set up user accounts. Which of the following are requirements for user passwords when setting them up in SMC? (Choose all that apply.)

   A. Passwords must be at least six characters long.

   B. Passwords must be at least eight characters long.

   C. The first six characters must include at least two alphabetic characters and at least two numeric or special characters.

   D. The first six characters must include at least two alphabetic characters and at least one numeric or special character.

   E. Passwords cannot contain any part of the user's login name.

18. One of your network users poses a question about user shells. She occasionally needs to use the su command to switch users and assume her bosses' network credentials. She wants to know how the shell responds when she uses the su command to assume another identity. What should you tell her?

   A. She will retain her original shell.

   B. She will get the shell specified for the account identity she is assuming.

   C. She will get the default shell specified in the /etc/default/su file.

   D. She will get the default shell specified in the /etc/default/users file.

19. You are the Solaris administrator for your company. One of your users in the finance department, cmalcolm, has just left for a better job. You need to delete the user's account along with the user's home directory. Which command should you execute?

   A. userdel –h cmalcolm

   B. userdel –r cmalcolm

   C. userdel –d /export/home/cmalcolm cmalcolm

   D. userdel cmalcolm

20. You are the Solaris administrator for your network. You require users to use either the Bourne or Korn shells. You want to set up a default initialization file, so that when new users are created, the accounts have the settings you require. Which file(s) should you modify to accomplish this goal? (Choose all that apply.)

   A. /etc/skel/local.profile

   B. /etc/skel/local.login

   C. /etc/skel/local.cshrc

   D. /etc/skel/local.kshrc

Answers to Review Questions

1. C.   User IDs in the 0–99 range are reserved for system user accounts. Although it's possible to create a user with a UID in this range, it's not recommended. Use a UID in the 100–60000 range instead.

2. A, C.   For users that use the C shell, the initialization files are located in their home directory, and are named .cshrc and .login.

3. A.   To add a user to a secondary group, use usermod -G. The user's name appears after the arguments in the command. The -g argument modifies the user's primary group.

4. A.   To delete groups, use the groupdel command. When using groupdel, you must supply the group's name, not its GID.

5. D.   No matter how hard you try, one user can run only one shell at a time from the same terminal. If you use the su command, you will assume another user's identity, and possibly another shell. However, this still fits under the "one user, one shell" axiom.

6. D.   Groups can be given a new GID and new name with the groupmod command. In this case, modifying the existing group would be a lot easier than creating a new group and moving all the users. If you were to move users from one group to another, you would use the usermod command, not groupmod.

7. A, B, C, D.   All of the answers are correct. The C shell is specified for jdoe with the /bin/csh variable. The sixth field configures a user's home directory, and that field is empty for jsmith. The third field is the UID, and the root account always has the UID of 0. The qdocter account is a member of group 10, which is the built-in staff group.

8. C.   To see a list of currently logged-in users, use the who command. The list and user commands do not exist. The login command can be used to prompt for a new user login.

9. B, C.   The root account's password, when encrypted, is AaSfeBzrNVeao. However, this is not the real account password. The root account's password was changed 21 days after qdocter's password was changed. The listen account is locked, as shown by *LK* in the second field. The qdocter account has no expiration date set.

10. D.   The useradd command has a lot of switches that can be used. To specify a user's UID, use -u. The -d switch specifies the location of the home directory, but requires -m to create the directory automatically if it does not already exist. The -g switch is for primary group membership, and -G is for secondary group membership. Finally, the user login name appears after the switches.

11. C.   The /var/adm/sulog file tracks all attempts to use the su command, whether successful or not. A plus sign indicates a successful su, whereas a minus sign indicates that the attempt failed. The /etc/default/su file can be used to modify sulog behavior. The /etc/default/sulog and /var/adm/su files do not exist.

12. A, C.   The smmsp built-in group has a GID of 25 (located in the third field). mgantz is a member of the macadct group, but the group has no password. Passwords would be in the second field. The staff group has no members. The sysadmin group has a GID of 14, but groups do not have UIDs.

13. B, C.   In Solaris 9, the shell acts as both a command interpreter and a high-level batch programming language. A graphical user interface provides graphical interaction. The /etc/users/ profiles file does not exist.

14. D.   To add a group, use the groupadd command. If no specific GID is required, and the GID of the group will not duplicate another group, then the only argument needed is the group name. To specify a GID, use the -g switch. To specify a duplicate GID, use -o.

15. A, B, D, E.   The Korn shell uses Bourne-shell-compatible syntax, allows for job editing, supports aliases, and enables you to protect yourself from overwriting files. The C and Bourne shells enable you to repeat the last command entered.

16. A.   In the Bourne and Korn shells, the command prompt can be customized by using the PS1 environment variable. In the C shell, the prompt can be customized with the prompt variable.

17. A, D.   When setting up user passwords by using the Solaris Management Console, passwords must be at least six characters long, and the first six characters must include at least two alphabetic characters and at least one numeric or special character. Although it's not recommended that the password contain any part of the user's login name, it's not a requirement.

18. B.   When users use the su command, they get the shell of the account they are assuming the role of. After the user exits the su session, they are returned to their original shell. The /etc/default/su file affects the behavior of the sulog file. The /etc/default/users file has nothing to do with su behavior.

19. B.   To delete the user's home directory when removing the user's account, use userdel -r. The -d and -h options do not exist for userdel.

20. A.   The lone initialization file for users of the Bourne and Korn shells is .profile. Skeleton files (which can be used as defaults) are located in the /etc/skel directory. Users of the C shell would use the .login and .cshrc files.

Chapter 5

Files, Directories, and Security

SOLARIS 9 EXAM OBJECTIVES COVERED IN THIS CHAPTER:

- ✓ Describe the purpose, features, and functions of root subdirectories, file components, file types, and hard links in the Solaris directory hierarchy.

- ✓ Explain how to create and remove hard links in a Solaris directory.

- ✓ Identify the procedures and commands, variables, or permissions to monitor and control system access, switch users on a system, and restrict access to data in files.

Good security measures are critical to the safety of your data and your company. In Chapter 4, "User and Group Administration," you looked at setting up user accounts and learned how passwords are used to protect login access to the network. But beyond the login, additional security measures are needed to ensure that users have access only to the information that they are supposed to have access to. This is where file and directory security comes into play.

To understand how to set up and manage file and directory security, you first need to understand how files and directories are organized in Solaris. Also, some directories in Solaris are intended for specific purposes, and you need to know what they are.

This chapter starts with file and directory concepts. Some of this information might seem straightforward if you have Solaris experience. However, even if you are already comfortable with file and directory structure, you will agree that this knowledge is fundamental to understanding system security concepts. Moving from core file concepts, this chapter then covers the default directories and their intended purposes. Finally, you will explore security, the most critical concept of this chapter, and arguably one of the most important facilities in a real networking environment.

Understanding File and Directory Concepts

In Solaris, data is stored within a file system located on a hard disk. A file system is simply a logical unit of space on the disk and is divided into two basic components: files and directories. Files contain data, and a directory is a specialized file that lists filenames.

Think of a hard disk as a filing cabinet. The purpose of a filing cabinet, of course, is to store files. Filing cabinets have drawers, which are analogous to file systems. Some cabinets have more drawers than others, and the same can be true of file systems on a hard disk. Inside the drawers, there are folders. The folders play the role of directories in a file system. Inside the folders are your documents. These are files themselves.

Reviewing File Types

Solaris 9 employs eight types of files. The most common type is a "regular" text or application file. The file types supported in Solaris are shown in Table 5.1.

TABLE 5.1   Solaris File Types

Symbol	Meaning
–	Text or application
D	Door
d	Directory
b	Block special file
c	Character special file
p	Named pipe
l	Symbolic link
s	Socket

Solaris regards almost everything on your system as a file. Documents and programs are files. Commands are essentially programs and are therefore files. Directories are files that contain other files. Even devices on your computer, such as your hard drive, terminal, and printer, are considered files.

To show a listing of files in a directory, use the `ls` command. The `ls` command has 26 arguments that you can use to customize your display. The most commonly used options for `ls` are `-l` (long listing) and `-la` (long listing and including files that start with a period, which are usually hidden). For a complete listing of `ls` switches, type **man ls**. Here is a sample directory listing:

```
$ ls -l
total 7
-rw-rw-r--  1 root      other       35068 Aug  4 13:39 bookdoc
drwxr-xr-x  2 root      other         512 Aug  3 10:01 dir1
drwxr-xr-x  1 root      other         512 Aug  3 10:02 dir2
-rwxrwxrwx  1 root      other      188326 Aug  2 19:11 fungame
-rw-r--r--  1 root      other        4105 Aug  1 12:21 textfile
$
```

The long listing of a directory shows seven fields. On the left, you see the file's permissions. The *d* in front of `dir1` and `dir2` indicates that they are directories. The number after the permissions indicates the number of links to the file. After the links, you see the owner of the file (`root` in this case) and the primary group of the owner. The file size in bytes, last modification date and time, and filename end each entry.

Using the File System

Solaris file systems are organized in a hierarchical tree. The base of this tree, or the root directory, is called *root* and is represented with a slash (/). All other files and directories can be thought of in terms of their relationship to the root. Figure 5.1 illustrates this hierarchical structure.

FIGURE 5.1   Solaris hierarchical file structure

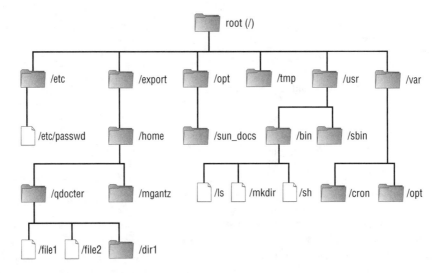

 The superuser account and the base of the directory structure are both named root. This can be confusing to new administrators. To avoid potential confusion, be sure to specify "the root directory" or "the superuser."

One of the basic tenets of file systems is that each object must have a unique *absolute pathname*. For example, consider the /etc directory. This directory named etc exists right off of the root (/). Therefore, you cannot create another directory named etc from within the root directory. However, if you were to switch to the /export directory, you could create a directory called etc. The absolute pathname of this new directory would be /export/etc. Also remember that Solaris is case sensitive; the directory /export/dir1 is different from /export/DIR1.

File System Navigation

To determine where you are in the file system, use the pwd (print working directory) command. Your *working directory* is the first directory checked by the kernel when you enter a command to execute (if you have . as your $PATH variable) or want to see a directory listing. The working directory is also known as the current directory.

 Using . in your path can compromise system security. This path designation can cause you to inadvertently execute a program you did not intend to, such as a Trojan horse.

WARNING Don't confuse the working directory with the home directory. Your *home directory* is used to store personal files, whereas the working directory is the directory you are currently working in. Your working directory might or might not be your home directory. You can change working directories easily with the cd command, but your home directory does not typically change.

To illustrate the importance of knowing your working directory, let's look at creating a directory with the mkdir command. Say you execute the following command sequence:

```
$ ls
file1 file2
$ mkdir dir1
$ ls
dir1 file1 file2
$
```

You have just created a directory called dir1. Congratulations! You log out of Solaris and go home for the day. The next day when you get to work, you can't seem to find the dir1 directory. But you created it, right? So where is it? That's a good question.

Unfortunately, you don't remember what your working directory was when you created dir1. So although you will likely be able to find dir1 eventually, it might not be where you think it is. To help, you could have (and should have) used pwd to verify that you were in the right directory before creating a new one.

Relative Pathnames

A *relative pathname* indicates the location of a file based on your current working directory. Any pathname that does not begin at the root directory, or with a tilde (~), is a relative pathname. Absolute pathnames never change, but relative pathnames do, based on where you are in the directory tree structure.

Say that you want to create a directory called /export/home/user1/files. There are a couple of ways you can go about it. One option is to create it from the root:

```
$ pwd
/
$ mkdir /export/home/user1/files
$ ls /export/home/user1
files
$
```

To create this directory, you type in the absolute pathname. But that is a lot of typing, and it's easy to make a mistake when you type that much. If you are user1, it's probable that your home directory is /export/home/user1, and just as likely that it's your default working directory as well.

```
$ pwd
/export/home/user1
```

```
$ mkdir files
$ ls
files
$
```

Both command sequences create the same directory. However, the first one uses an absolute pathname, and the second one uses a relative pathname. Although using relative pathnames can save you time, using them also increases the probability of creating a directory in the wrong place. If you're going to use relative pathnames, make sure to use pwd to verify your working directory.

The . and .. Directories

Each directory automatically has two entries: a single period and a double period. The single period represents the directory itself, and the double period represents the directory's parent directory. When you use the ls command, you typically don't see these entries, because they begin with a period, and by default ls doesn't show entries that begin with a period.

 The double period can be especially useful as a shortcut when copying or moving files, and when using utilities that require filenames or pathnames.

Useful File Commands

There are literally dozens of commands you can use to create, copy, move, rename, display, and modify files. Although listing them all here would be impractical, a quick review of some common commands doesn't hurt. Table 5.2 lists some common file-management-based commands.

TABLE 5.2 File Commands

Command	Description
cat	Concatenates and displays files. For example, **cat file1 file2 >file3** combines files file1 and file2 in a new file named file3. The command **cat file1** simply displays the contents of file1.
cd	Changes directories. For example, **cd /export/home/user1** changes the working directory to /export/home/user1. The command **cd ..** moves up one directory in the tree, and **cd /** changes to the root directory.
cp	Copies files. The command **cp file1 file2** creates a copy of file1 named file2. For copying directories, use **cp -r**, which copies the directory as well as any files or subdirectories to the desired destination.
file	Determines file type.
find	Finds files.

TABLE 5.2 File Commands *(continued)*

Command	Description
ls	Lists files in a directory. If no directory is specified, the working directory is used.
mkdir	Creates directories. The command **mkdir dir1** creates a directory called dir1 in the current working directory.
more	Filter that enables you to display one screen of information at a time. For example, to see your /etc/passwd file one page at a time, use **more /etc/passwd**.
mv	Moves or renames files. The command **mv file1 file2** renames file1 to file2. The command **mv file1 /etc/acct** moves file1 to the /etc/acct directory.
pwd	Displays the present working directory.
rm	Removes (deletes) a file. To delete file1, use **rm file1**.
rmdir	Removes empty directories. If the directory has files in it (other than . and ..), delete the files first and then use rmdir to remove the directory.

The rm -r command can be used to remove a directory and all files within the directory. This is an incredibly powerful command, and you should use care when executing it. Just think about what would happen if you ran this command from the root directory.

One other handy navigation shortcut is the tilde (~). The tilde is used as a shorthand representation of the user's home directory. To change to his home directory quickly, a user can use **cd ~**. To create a directory called myfiles in her home directory, a user could execute the **mkdir ~/myfiles** command, regardless of her working directory.

The ~ shortcut does not work in the Bourne shell. To reference the home directory in the Bourne shell, use the $HOME variable.

Modifying File Characteristics

When you use the ls -l command to display files in a directory, you see seven fields of information about the file. The fields are permissions, links, owner, group, size, modification date and time, and filename. Here is an example:

```
$ ls -l
total 3
drwxrwxr-x  2 root      other       512 Aug 10 11:23 docs
```

This section shows how to modify file characteristics other than permissions and links. Links are covered two sections from now, and security is covered in the second half of this chapter.

The owner of the example directory is root. This is very important, considering that the base set of security permissions relates specifically to the owner of the file. To change owners, use the chown command:

```
# ls -l
total 3
drwxrwxr-x  2 userx      other      512 Aug 10 11:23 docs
# chown qdocter docs
# ls -l
total 3
drwxrwxr-x  2 qdocter    other      512 Aug 10 11:23 docs
```

The ownership group can also be changed, but that is done with the chgrp command:

```
# ls -l
total 3
drwxrwxr-x  2 qdocter    other      512 Aug 10 11:23 docs
# chgrp author docs
# ls -l
total 3
drwxrwxr-x  2 qdocter    author     512 Aug 10 11:23 docs
```

The file size attribute isn't something you typically set out to purposely modify. It's primarily there for reference. If someone is storing incredibly large files on your server, you can see who it is. If you do want to modify the size of a file, open the file, make some changes to it, and save it.

The modification date can be updated in the same way. Open the file, make changes, and save the file. However, the touch command can also be used to update the modification date and time without actually opening the file. If you use touch with a filename that does not exist, touch will create the file specified:

```
$ ls -l
total 3
drwxrwxr-x  2 root       other      512 Aug 10 11:23 docs
# touch file1
# ls -l
total 4
drwxrwxr-x  2 root       other      512 Aug 10 11:23 docs
-rw-r--r--  1 root       other       80 Aug 10 11:44 file1
# touch docs
# ls -l
total 4
drwxrwxr-x  2 root       other      512 Aug 10 11:45 docs
-rw-r--r--  1 root       other       80 Aug 10 11:44 file1
```

Notice how the `touch` command updated the time on the `docs` directory and created an empty file named `file1`.

Using Default Directories

During installation, Solaris creates several default directories. These directories provide the basic organization of the Solaris file system and group similar types of files together. Remember that the file system is a hierarchical tree. The main part of the tree is the root, and the branches expand from there. Table 5.3 lists the major default directories and their intended purposes.

TABLE 5.3   Solaris 9 Default Directories

Directory	Purpose
/ (root)	The top of the hierarchical file system tree. Contains directories and files critical to system operation.
/dev and /devices	Device files that represent configured devices in the system. The /dev and /devices directories are discussed in more detail in Chapter 6, "Disk and Device Management."
/etc	Machine-local configuration files. Some of the more notable files include /etc/passwd and /etc/shadow.
/export	Exported files. Typically, user home directories are located in /export/home/*username*.
/opt	Optional mount point, generally used for third-party applications.
/tmp	Temporary files and oftentimes swap space.
/usr	System files and directories that can be shared among users. The /usr/bin directory contains user commands, /usr/sbin holds system administration commands, and /usr/share contains man pages.
/var	Variable data, which includes files that change dynamically as the system runs. Log files, printer spool files, and backup files are often located here.

To run a system, the root and /usr directories are required, at a minimum. Your system will likely have all the directories listed in Table 5.3 and more.

Working with Links

As you know by now, files are stored on hard disks in computers. You also know that files have names, which is how humans reference files. On the computer, the filename is linked to the data.

In other words, the filename points to the specific location on the hard drive where the data is stored. In Solaris, it's possible to create multiple links that point to the same file.

Hard Links

A *hard link* is a pointer to a file. Bear in mind that a hard link is not a *copy* of a file, but rather a pointer to the original file. In other words, if you have seven hard links to one file and change the data in the file, all links will reflect the changed data as well.

All hard links to a file are of equal value to Solaris. If a particular file has three hard links, no one link has priority over the others. You could delete any two of the links and still access the data in the file through the third (and now only) link. If all hard links to a file are deleted, then the data is inaccessible, and the disk space is made available for other files.

So why would someone want to create hard links? Imagine that on your computer, you have five files that you commonly access. Each file is in a different directory. To open each file, you need to remember the specific directory path to each one. Granted, five isn't a terribly large number of paths to remember, but it's inconvenient nonetheless. Because of a controlling manager, all files must remain in their original directories.

To get around this, you could create a directory specifically for links or use an existing directory. Then create links in your chosen directory that point to all five files. Now, all five access points (to the data you need) are located in the same directory. Even better, the original links to the files are still intact and in their original directories, pleasing the controlling manager.

Another reason to create a link is to give another user access to a file that's in your home directory. The other user can create a link in her home directory pointing to the file in your home directory, and both of you have convenient access to the file. When you create a link, the original permissions remain intact, so you might have to modify file and/or directory permissions to get the access permissions you need. However, that's a topic for later in this chapter.

Links are created with the `ln` command. The syntax is as follows:

```
$ ln file link
```

where *file* is the path to the existing file, and *link* is the name of the link that you wish to create.

Here's an example of creating a link:

```
$ ls
file1 file2
$ ln file1 link1
$ ls
link1 file1 file2
$ ln file1 seclink
$ ls
seclink link1 file1 file2
```

By looking at a basic directory listing, it's practically impossible to tell which files are links. The `ls -i` command helps shed more light on the subject:

```
$ ls -i
   5511 seclink   5511 link1   5511 file1   242176 file2
$
```

When you use `ls -i`, the inode of the file is displayed. The *inode* contains the complete listing of all information about a file: its owner, group, permissions, last access time, and so on. Another way to look at it is that the inode points out the unique location of the data on the hard disk. In the example, `seclink`, `link1`, and `file1` all have the same inode, meaning they all reference the same data. The other file, `file2`, is obviously a different file because it has a different inode.

There are two major limitations to using hard links. First, hard links must be created to files and cannot be created to directories. Second, hard links must be in the same file system as the original file. This is because inodes are file-system-dependent. The 5511 inode in one file system will contain different data than the 5511 inode in another file system.

Soft Links

To address the limitations of hard links, soft links (also known as symbolic links) were created. A *soft link* is more flexible than a hard link; it can be used to link to a directory and can span multiple file systems. Soft links are created with the `ln -s` command.

Whereas hard links are direct pointers to a file, soft links are indirect pointers to a file. All a soft link contains is the absolute pathname to the linked file. Consequently, soft links can point to nonexistent files, and hard links cannot. Of course, if you open a soft link that is pointing to an imaginary file, you're not going to get the information you're looking for. If you're using hard links, you can delete the original file and still access data through another link. The same is not true of soft links. If you delete the original file, the data is gone, and the link becomes useless.

To delete a link, you use the `rm` command; it's the same command you use to delete regular files.

Controlling and Monitoring System Access

Now that you understand file system structure, it's time to learn how to protect your files. It's difficult to overestimate the importance of security on your Solaris computer or network. Critical data has a variety of forms. If compromised, some files could leak trade secrets, giving competitors an unfair advantage. Other files could cause legal hassles if exposed. In any case, you need to control access to your computer systems.

The first step to control system access is physical. If someone can get to your machine, they can either read sensitive data or use brute force to destroy data. The second step, one that we have talked about, is making sure that users have good passwords and change them frequently. The last step is setting up proper permissions, so the users who do log in to your network have the appropriate level of file access. This section covers the final step.

File and Directory Permissions

Solaris, like most other UNIX-based operating systems, categorizes users into three classes when it comes to resource access: the owner of the file (`owner` or `user`), a member of the group the owner belongs to (group), and everyone else (other). The basic set of UNIX permissions allows for three distinct operations on a given file: Read, Write, and Execute. Each class and permission combination is considered separately. That is, the owner can have Read, Write, and Execute permissions on a file, whereas everyone else (other) can be denied access to the same file.

The owner of the file and the superuser are the only two users who can modify permissions on a file. Regardless of permissions set on a file, the superuser always has Read, Write, and Execute privileges on every file.

Before we look at displaying and changing permissions, let's clarify what is meant by Read, Write, and Execute. Table 5.4 breaks down the permissions and how they affect what designated users can do to files and directories.

TABLE 5.4 Solaris Permissions

Permission	File Consequences	Directory Consequences
Read (r)	Can open and read the contents of the file	Can list files in the directory
Write (w)	Can modify or delete the file	Can add or remove files or links in the directory
Execute (x)	Can execute the program	Can open and execute files in the directory, and can make the directory and subdirectories under it current
None (−)	Cannot read, write, or execute the file	Cannot list, add, remove, or execute files in the directory

Giving someone Write permissions gives them the ability to delete!

Displaying and Changing Permissions

Permissions are displayed when you use ls -l to show a long directory listing. Here's an example to refresh your memory:

```
$ ls -l
total 4
drwxrwxr-x  2 qdocter    author     512 Aug 10 11:23 docs
-rw-r--r--  1 qdocter    author      80 Aug 10 11:44 file1
```

Because we're discussing permissions, the only parts of the directory listing you need to be concerned with right now are the first 10 characters and the name of the file. The first character indicates that the file is either a special type of file or a regular file. The first file listed in our example is a directory, as indicated by the lowercase *d*. The second file, named `file1`, is a regular file, as indicated by the dash preceding the permissions.

The following nine characters define permissions for that file. The first grouping of three letters (*rwx*) defines permissions for the `owner`, the second cluster is for `group` permissions, and the last tier is for `other`. In our example, the `docs` directory has Read, Write, and Execute permissions set for the `owner` and `group`, and Read and Execute set for `other`. The `file1` file has Read and Write for the `owner`, and Read-only for `group` and `other`.

The `chmod` command is used to set permissions on files. This command functions in two modes: symbolic mode and absolute mode.

Symbolic Mode

When using `chmod` in *symbolic mode*, letters designate both whom the permissions will impact and the permissions to effect. The syntax for `chmod` in symbolic mode is as follows:

`$ chmod `*`options who operator permission file`*

For example, the command:

`$ chmod o+w file21`

will add Write permission to the `owner` for `file21`. To specify multiple groups, separate the *who*, *operator*, and *permission* grouping with commas, such as:

`$ chmod o+w,g+r file21`

There are four options for the *who* variable. To set user (`owner`) permissions, use u. `group` permissions are set with g, other permissions with o, and all permissions (`owner`, `group`, and `other`) are set with a.

> When using symbolic mode to change permissions, remember that o means other, not owner. For owner permissions, use u. Failure to use the proper codes could result in serious security holes.

The *operator* variable tells `chmod` what to do with the permissions specified. There are three options for the *operator*: a + tells `chmod` to add the permission to existing permissions, a – removes permissions, and an = sets the permissions to exactly what is specified. If the = is used and no permissions are specified, then all permissions for the specified *who* are cleared.

There are 10 options for the *permission* variable. They are described in Table 5.5.

TABLE 5.5   Symbolic Mode Permissions

Letter	Description
r	Sets Read permission
w	Sets Write permission
x	Sets Execute permission

TABLE 5.5 Symbolic Mode Permissions *(continued)*

Letter	Description
l	Enables mandatory locking
s	SetUID/SetGID, depending on who is specified by the *who* variable
t	Enables the sticky bit
X	Execute permission if the file is a directory or if there is execute permission for one of the other user classes.
u	Sets the permissions to those already present for the owner
g	Sets the permissions to those already present for the group
o	Sets the permissions to those already present for others

This can be a lot to absorb; some examples might help.

```
$ ls -l
total 3
-rwxrwxr-x  2 qdocter   author    874 Aug 10 11:23 textfile
```

For the preceding file, you want to remove the Write permissions for the **group**. Here's how to do that:

```
$ chmod g-w textfile
$ ls -l
total 3
-rwxr-xr-x  2 qdocter   author    874 Aug 10 11:23 textfile
```

If you read the chmod command literally, it says, "For **group** permissions, remove Write on textfile." This next example removes execute permissions for both **group** and **other**:

```
$ chmod go-x textfile
$ ls -l
total 3
-rwxr--r--  2 qdocter   author    874 Aug 10 11:23 textfile
```

Now, members of the **author** group and everyone else have only Read permission to textfile. To quickly clear all permissions from the file, you could use the following:

```
$ chmod a= textfile
$ ls -l
total 3
----------  2 qdocter   author    874 Aug 10 11:23 textfile
```

One final example:

```
$ ls -l
total 3
-rwx------  2 qdocter   author     874 Aug 10 11:23 textfile
$ chmod go=u textfile
$ ls -l
total 3
-rwxrwxrwx  2 qdocter   author     874 Aug 10 11:23 textfile
```

As with everything else in the computer world, playing around with permissions (on a test system, please) is the best way to learn what you can and cannot do. For example, the s permission works only with a *who* of u or g, and t works only with u.

Absolute Mode

Instead of using letter designations to assign permissions, some administrators prefer to use chmod in absolute mode. *Absolute mode* enables you to assign permissions by using an octal representation instead of a user, operator, and permission code. The numerical values for all permissions are listed in Table 5.6.

TABLE 5.6   Absolute Mode Permission Codes

Number	Description
4000	Enables SetUID
20n0	Enables SetGID when the value of n is odd, or else enables mandatory locking
1000	Sets the sticky bit
0400	Sets owner permissions to Read
0200	Sets owner permissions to Write
0100	Sets owner permissions to Execute
0040	Sets group permissions to Read
0020	Sets group permissions to Write
0010	Sets group permissions to Execute
0004	Sets other permissions to Read
0002	Sets other permissions to Write
0001	Sets other permissions to Execute

To use absolute mode, you add the numbers together to achieve your desired result. (Some die-hard administrators call this ORing the numbers.) For example, if you want to grant the owner Read, Write, and Execute permissions, and the group Read-only, you would use **chmod 740 filename** (the value 740 was obtained by adding 400 + 200 + 100 + 40). Perhaps the biggest philosophical difference between symbolic and absolute modes is that with symbolic mode, you often think in terms of adding or subtracting permissions. In absolute mode, you need to think in terms of net result: what do you want the final permissions to be?

Unless you are specifying SetUID or SetGID, or enabling the sticky bit, you can use a three-digit number to specify permissions.

As with symbolic mode, let's use some examples to clarify:

```
$ ls -l
total 3
-rwxrwxr-x  2 qdocter   author      874 Aug 10 11:23 textfile
```

For the preceding file, you want to remove the Write permissions for the group. Here's how to do that in absolute mode:

```
$ chmod 755 textfile
$ ls -l
total 3
-rwxr-xr-x  2 qdocter   author      874 Aug 10 11:23 textfile
```

Again, when you use absolute mode, you need to think in terms of end result. Removing Write permissions for the group means that your second number (group) is going to be 5 (read—4, and execute—1). In the following example, you remove Execute permissions for both group and other:

```
$ chmod 744 textfile
$ ls -l
total 3
-rwxr--r--  2 qdocter   author      874 Aug 10 11:23 textfile
```

Now, members of the author group and everyone else have only Read permission to textfile. If you want to clear all permissions for the file, you can use the following:

```
$ chmod 000 textfile
$ ls -l
total 3
----------  2 qdocter   author      874 Aug 10 11:23 textfile
```

You might have noticed that I used the same examples in absolute mode as I did in symbolic mode. No, it isn't because cutting and pasting is less work than thinking of new examples. It is to show that you can perform the exact same permissions modifications with either method. Although it's an excellent idea to be familiar with both methods (especially for the test), it's likely that you'll prefer one to the other and you'll use that method almost exclusively.

Real World Scenario

Easing the Security Administration Burden

You have been the systems administrator at your company for just over a year. In that time, you have convinced management to upgrade all servers to Solaris 9, and most of your workstations have been upgraded as well. Since you started working at the company, the number of client machines has grown from about 50 to well over 300. The company is growing quickly, and you are the only network administrator!

One of your biggest problems has been keeping track of security. You have set up good security measures and have educated users on secure operational procedures. However, you find that every once in a while, something slips by you, and you worry that your network security might someday be compromised. You need something or someone to help you out, but the IT budget does not provide for another network administrator.

You might want to consider using the Automated Security Enhancement Tool (aset). This tool is a set of security utilities shipped standard with Solaris 9. It can automate security settings, including checking permissions and ownership on system files, verifying system file contents, checking the integrity of the /etc/passwd and /etc/group files, and examining environment initialization files. Not only that, but aset can be set to run periodically and to e-mail a report to any user specified. The aset tool is capable of detecting possible security holes and fixing security problems as well.

Another useful feature of aset is that it has three security levels: low, medium, and high. You can use the level that most closely matches your network's security needs. Start using aset and you will find your security burden eased significantly. For more information, type *man aset*.

SetUID and SetGID

When an application with SetUID (Set User ID) is opened, the executing process assumes the privileges of the owner of that application. Similarly, if the SetGID bit is enabled, the executing process will assume the identity of the group owner for execution of the process. This can be both a good and a bad thing.

Say there is a program that you need to run to perform your weekly job duties. This program deletes all temporary files from the system and cleans up any outdated log files and print spool files. Unfortunately, deleting these files requires that you have superuser privileges, which you don't have. By enabling SetUID, when you (or anyone else for that matter) execute this cleanup program, you will assume the identity of the superuser (we're assuming that root is the owner of the application) in order to carry out the program. When the program is completed, you will no longer have any superuser rights.

This functionality can be extremely handy. Essentially, you, the administrator, can give users the ability to run applications that might require more access to resources than they would normally have. And this can be done without giving them the root password or adding them to the sysadmin group.

Of course, any time you give regular users superuser privileges, you run the risk of a security breach. Consequently, you should be very, very careful about the use of SetUID and SetGID. Most applications don't require their use, and you should closely monitor those that do. In fact, many companies won't run software that requires enabling SetUID or SetGID.

SetUID and SetGID are enabled through the chmod command. The following example shows two files. The first one (app1) has SetUID enabled, and the second one (app2) has SetGID enabled (look for the s):

```
$ ls -l
-rwsr-xr-x  2 qdocter    author      38604 Aug 10 11:23 app1
-rwxr-sr-x  1 qdocter    author      19124 Aug 10 11:44 app2
```

SetUID and SetGID can be very useful but also pose an incredibly dangerous inherent security risk.

You cannot set or clear the SetGID bit for directories in absolute mode. It must be set or cleared in symbolic mode by using g+s or g-s. You can set and clear the SetGID bit for files in absolute mode.

Sticky Bit

A *sticky bit* is used to prevent the deletion of files in public directories. After the sticky bit is set on a directory, the only people who can delete or rename files in the directory are the owner of the file, the owner of the directory, or the superuser. Sticky bits are particularly useful in public directories, where users might have the opportunity to maliciously (or accidentally) delete common files.

When the sticky bit is set, a *T* or *t* will appear in the directory's other Execute permission slot. If the execution bit for others is off, a capital *T* will appear. If the execution bit for others is on, it will be a lowercase *t*. Here's an example:

```
$ chmod 1745 bookdir
$ ls -l
total 3
drwxr--r-t  2 qdocter    author      874 Aug 11 14:20 bookdir
$ chmod 1744 bookdir
$ ls -l
total 3
drwxr--r-T  2 qdocter    author      874 Aug 11 14:20 bookdir
```

The sticky bit can be set through absolute mode or symbolic mode.

umask

When a new file is created in Solaris, the default permissions are 666 (Read and Write for all), and when a directory is created, the default permissions are 777 (Read, Write, and Execute for all). These default permissions are modified by the *umask* specified in either the user's initialization file or a global initialization file.

The default umask is 022. When new files are created, the umask value is subtracted from the default (full access) values, thereby restricting (masking) permissions. Therefore, with a default umask, new directories will have effective permissions of 755 (777 - 022), giving the owner Read, Write, and Execute, and giving the group and other Read and Execute. Newly created files will have permissions of 644.

To display your current umask or to change your current umask value, use the umask command:

```
$ umask
022
$ umask 077
$ umask
077
```

If you change your umask with the umask command, it will default back to the mask specified in your initialization file after you log out and back in. To permanently change your umask, you must modify your initialization file.

To increase security on your network, you can make the umask more restrictive. Many companies prefer a umask setting of 077 or 027.

The Korn shell supports symbolic mode arguments with the umask -S command, but the Bourne and C shells do not.

Access Control Lists and Role Based Access Control

During the initial development stages of UNIX, the basic permission structure was sufficient for most users' needs. However, with increased networking capabilities and more extensive computer use, the existing permission structure became a bit limited. For example, you could set permissions for the owner of the file, but how would you set permissions for another user who might or might not be part of the owner's group? Security issues such as this became difficult to deal with. Access Control Lists (ACLs) were developed to enhance security flexibility.

Another security issue is the assignment of administrative duties. Suppose that you want one of your users to be able to reset user passwords or to back up files they might otherwise not be able to access. One option is to give the user the root password, but this solution screams, "Security hole!" Role Based Access Control (RBAC) enables you to create a role, which is like a user account, and assign the role certain administrative tasks. Then, a logged-in user can assume a role for temporary administrative purposes and still not have more access than they need.

ACLs and RBAC are vital big-picture security concepts in Solaris. But because ACLs and RBAC are not tested until the second Solaris Certified System Administrator exam, they don't need to be covered in depth at this time. They are covered extensively in Chapter 13, "Advanced Security Concepts."

Summary

You started this chapter by looking at the hierarchical file system structure of Solaris. Solaris considers nearly everything on your computer a file, and all files must have an owner and a group.

Then, you looked at navigating the file system and file modification commands. It's also important to know the default directories and their intended purposes, as well as how to manage links within the Solaris file system.

Finally, you examined the base security system of Solaris 9: file permissions. You should be comfortable with reading permissions, as well as setting them in both absolute and symbolic modes. You also examined SetUID and SetGID permissions, sticky bits, and the umask.

Exam Essentials

Understand the hierarchical file system structure.   The base of the file system is the root directory (/). Every directory other than root has a parent directory. Each parent can have one or more child directories, called subdirectories, or files within them.

Know the difference between an absolute pathname and a relative pathname.   A file's absolute pathname describes its place in the hierarchical file system. A relative pathname describes the path to the file in relation to the current working directory.

Understand the limitations of hard links.   Hard links cannot point to a directory, must point to an existing file, and must be located in the same file system as the linked file.

Understand the basic Solaris security structure.   Users are classified as being the owner, being a member of the owner's group, or belonging to the other group. Permissions are Read, Write, and Execute.

Know how to set file permissions by using symbolic mode.   Permissions can be set by using the chmod command with symbolic arguments. For example, to add group Execute permission on file1, you would use **chmod g+x file1**.

Know how to set file permissions by using absolute mode.   Permissions can be set by using the chmod command with an octal argument. To enable Read, Write, and Execute for the owner, Read and Execute for group, and no access for other on dir1, you would use **chmod 750 dir1**.

Understand what SetUID and SetGID do.   When either SetUID or SetGID are enabled, the application assumes the identity of the owner or group owner, respectively, of the file in order to run the application properly.

Understand what a sticky bit does.   A sticky bit prevents the file from being deleted by anyone other than the owner of the file, a member of the group owner of the file, or the superuser.

Know what the umask does.   The umask restricts the default permissions on new files and directories, increasing security.

Key Terms

Before you take the exam, be certain you are familiar with the following terms:

absolute mode	soft link
absolute pathname	sticky bit
hard link	symbolic mode
inode	umask
relative pathname	working directory

Commands Used in This Chapter

The following list contains a summary of all the commands introduced in this chapter:

Command	Description
cat	Concatenates and displays files
cd	Changes directories
chgrp	Changes the ownership group for a file
chmod	Modifies access permissions for a file
chown	Changes the owner of a file
cp	Copies files
file	Determines file type
find	Finds files
ln	Creates a link to a file

Command	Description
ls	Lists files in a directory
mkdir	Creates directories
more	Enables you to display one screen of information at a time
mv	Moves or renames files
pwd	Displays the present working directory
rm	Removes (deletes) a file
rmdir	Removes empty directories
touch	Creates a file or updates the file's last modification time
umask	Displays or changes the umask value

Review Questions

1. You are the Solaris administrator for your network. One of your servers has a public directory named `forsale`, containing classified ads posted by employees. You want to ensure that employees can post files to the directory but cannot delete files unless they are the owner. A user named `jsmith` is the owner of the directory, and the `employee` group, which contains all employees, is the group owner. Which commands can you execute to accomplish your goal? (Choose all that apply.)

   A. `chmod 1666 forsale`

   B. `chmod 4666 forsale`

   C. `chmod u+t forsale`

   D. `chmod u+s forsale`

2. You are the senior Solaris administrator for your company. One of your junior administrators was instructed by a support agent to look for a named pipe file in one of his directories. The junior administrator is confused and wants to know how to identify a named pipe. What do you tell him?

   A. Type `ls -l` in the directory and look for an *n* as the first character.

   B. Type `ls -l` in the directory and look for a *p* as the first character.

   C. Type `ls -l` in the directory and look for a file named `pipe`.

   D. Solaris does not support named pipes.

   E. Solaris does support named pipes, but they are not considered files.

3. You are the Solaris administrator for your company. Two of your administrative reports, `report1` and `report2`, contain similar information. You want to combine the two reports into a file named `finalreport`. What is the easiest way to accomplish this?

   A. `cat report1 report2 >finalreport`

   B. `cat report1 report2 =finalreport`

   C. `cat finalreport >report1 report2`

   D. `cat finalreport`

   E. `touch finalreport`

4. Consider the following directory listing:

   ```
   $ ls -l
   drwxrwxr-x  2 userx      finance      512 Aug 10 11:23 personal
   -rw-r--r--  1 userx      finance       80 Aug 10 11:44 file1
   ```

   You want to ensure that you are the only one who has access to the `personal` directory. Which commands could you use to accomplish this? (Choose all that apply.)

   A. `chmod g= o= personal`

   B. `chmod go= personal`

   C. `chmod g-rwx,o-rx personal`

   D. `chmod g-rwx o-rx personal`

5. On your Solaris workstation, you need to rename a file from `finreport` to `reportaug02`. How do you accomplish this?

   A. `cp reportaug02 finreport`

   B. `cp finreport reportaug02`

   C. `mv reportaug02 finreport`

   D. `mv finreport reportaug02`

   E. `ren reportaug02 finreport`

   F. `ren finreport reportaug02`

6. You are the Solaris administrator for your company. One of your project managers recently left the company, and a replacement has been hired. You need to give ownership of the old project manager's files to the new manager. What command do you use to accomplish this?

   A. `giveown`

   B. `chown`

   C. `chgrp`

   D. `ownfiles`

7. Consider the following directory listing:

```
$ ls -l
drwxrwxr-x  2 userx     finance     512 Aug 10 11:23 personal
-rw-r--r--  1 userx     finance      80 Aug 10 11:44 file1
```

You want to ensure that you are the only one who has access to the `personal` folder. Which command should you execute to accomplish this?

   A. `chmod 777 personal`

   B. `chmod 770 personal`

   C. `chmod 700 personal`

   D. `chmod 000 personal`

8. You are the Solaris administrator for your network. You have just installed a new Solaris workstation with default settings. Which directory on the computer will contain machine-local configuration files?

   A. root (/)

   B. /etc

   C. /local

   D. /opt

   E. /usr

9. You are the Solaris administrator for your company. You execute the following command:

`chmod 2744 dir1`

Which of the following effects are enacted by your command? (Choose all that apply.)

A. The group owner of `dir1` has read permissions.

B. Mandatory locking is enabled.

C. The SetGID bit for `dir1` is enabled.

D. The SetUID bit for `dir1` is enabled.

E. The owner of `dir1` has read, write, and execute permissions.

10. In Solaris 9, which of the following are valid special file types, displayed with a symbol other than -? (Choose all that apply.)

A. Boot

B. Directory

C. Door

D. Hard link

E. Named pipe

F. Symbolic link

G. Socket

11. Consider the following directory listing:

```
$ ls -l
drwxrwxrwt  2 userx     employee     512 Aug 10 11:23 stuff
-rw-r--r--  1 userx     employee      80 Aug 10 11:44 file1
```

Which of the following statements are true regarding the files listed? (Choose all that apply.)

A. The other execute bit is on for the `stuff` directory.

B. The other execute bit is off for the `stuff` directory.

C. Employees can delete their own files from the `stuff` directory.

D. Employees can delete any files from the `stuff` directory.

12. In Solaris 9, who has the ability to change the ownership of a file? (Choose all that apply.)

A. The owner of the file

B. A user with write permissions to the file

C. The superuser

D. A member of the group that owns the file

13. You are the Solaris administrator for your company. You are installing a new server. One of the server's responsibilities will be to host user home directories. In which directory does Sun recommend placing user home directories?

A. /usr/export

B. /export/home

C. /export/usr

D. /usr/home

14. You are the Solaris administrator for your company. You are training new users on the use of hard links. Which of the following are requirements for hard links? (Choose all that apply.)

A. Hard links must be on the same file system as the linked-to file.

B. Hard links must be linked to a directory.

C. There cannot be more than five hard links to any file.

D. When creating hard links, the inode of the linked-to file must be specified.

15. Consider the following directory listing:

```
$ ls -l
drwxrwxr-x  2 userx     finance      512 Aug 10 11:23 personal
-rw-r--r--  1 userx     finance       80 Aug 10 11:44 file1
-rwxr--r--  1 userx     finance      818 Aug 13 12:01 program1
```

You want members of the finance group to have the same permissions as the owner has to program1. Which command could be executed to accomplish this? (Choose all that apply.)

A. chmod g=userx program1

B. chmod g=u program1

C. chmod g=o program1

D. chmod g+wx program1

E. chmod g=wx program1

16. You are the Solaris administrator for your network. You create a new directory and you have this directory listing:

```
# ls -l
drwxr-xr-x  2 root      other       512 Aug 15 15:51 newdir
```

What is the umask currently in use on your computer?

A. 000

B. 022

C. 044

D. 555

E. 755

17. You are the Solaris administrator for your network. You have a file named `file1`. You want to create a hard link to `file1` named `access`. Which command should you execute to create this link?

A. `ln file1 access`

B. `ln access file1`

C. `ln -s file1 access`

D. `ln -s access file1`

E. `ln -h file1 access`

F. `ln -h access file1`

18. You are the security administrator for your company. There is a public file named `phonelist`. The owner of this file needs read and write permissions, as do members of the owner's group. No one else is to access the file. The only person who should be able to delete the file is the owner. What absolute mode command would you would need to execute in order to affect these security settings?

A. `chmod 666 phonelist`

B. `chmod 660 phonelist`

C. `chmod 600 phonelist`

D. `chmod 1666 phonelist`

E. `chmod 1660 phonelist`

F. `chmod 1600 phonelist`

19. Consider the following directory listing:

```
$ ls -i
  5150 filex      9906  file3      122800 filea
  5150 file2      5150  file4       53102 file1
```

You execute the command `rm filex`. Based on the information provided, which of the following statements are true? (Choose all that apply.)

A. `filex` will be deleted.

B. `file2` and `file4` will be deleted.

C. `file2` and `file4` will not be deleted, but they will be inaccessible.

D. `file2` and `file4` will not be deleted, and they can be used to access the data that `filex` previously accessed.

20. You are the Solaris administrator for your company. The `docs` directory on your server is currently owned by the `staff` group. You want to give the `admin` group ownership of the directory. How do you accomplish this?

A. `chown admin docs`

B. `chown docs admin`

C. `chgrp admin docs`

D. `chgrp docs admin`

Answers to Review Questions

1. **A, C.** The question describes a situation in which the sticky bit comes in handy. You have a public directory and are worried about people deleting files that aren't theirs. The sticky bit is enabled with `chmod 1000` in absolute mode, and with `chmod u+t` in symbolic mode.

2. **B.** Named pipes are one of the special types of files supported in Solaris. Named pipe files are indicated by a *p* in the first character space before the file's permissions.

3. **A.** The `cat` command can be used to display files or, alternately, combine two or more files into a new file. The correct usage of `cat` to combine files is `cat file1 file2 >newfile`.

4. **B, C.** To ensure that you are the only one with access, you must remove permissions for all other users. Essentially, you want your permission structure for the directory to look something like `drwx------`. You can use the = with no permissions listed to clear permissions for `group` and `other`, as in the second answer. You could also remove the assigned permissions, as in the third answer. The first and last answers do not work because they both call for multiple groups, and multiple groups need to be separated with a comma, not a space. If you were to execute these answers as listed, they would modify the `group` permissions but not the `other` permissions.

5. **D.** To move or rename files, use the `mv` command. The correct syntax for renaming files is `mv oldfile newfile`.

6. **B.** The `chown` command is used to change ownership of files and directories. The `giveown` and `ownfiles` commands do not exist. The `chgrp` command is used to change group ownership, not individual ownership.

7. **C.** By executing **chmod 700 personal**, you set up permissions for the directory as `drwx------`. The owner of the file will be the only one able to access it (other than the superuser, of course).

8. **B.** The `/etc` directory contains machine-local configuration files. The root is the base of the directory structure. The `/opt` directory holds optional files, typically third-party applications. The `/usr` directory contains many things, including user-based commands, administrative commands, and `man` pages.

9. **A, B, E.** The 7 in the second position gives the owner of `dir1` read, write, and execute permissions, and the 4 in the third position gives the group owner read permissions to `dir1`. Because the third number is even, the 2000 value enables mandatory locking on the directory. If the third number were odd, then the SetGID bit would, in theory, be set. However, the SetGID bit cannot be set on a *directory* when using absolute mode. It must be set through symbolic mode.

10. **B, C, E, F, G.** The special file types, which are displayed with an alternate character, are door, directory, block, character, named pipe, symbolic link, and socket. Boot files and hard links are considered regular files.

11. **A, C.** The sticky bit is set for the `stuff` directory, as evidenced by the *t* at the end of the permissions list. Because the sticky bit is set, employees can delete only files that they own. The *t* is lowercase, indicating that the other execute bit for the `stuff` directory is on.

12. A, C.   To change the ownership of a file, you must be either the owner of the file or the superuser.

13. B.   User home directories should be placed in the /export/home directory. The other directories do not exist by default. The /usr directory holds information such as commands and man pages.

14. A.   Hard links must be on the same file system as the file they are linking to. Also, hard links must be linked to files and cannot be linked to directories. There is no limit to the number of hard links. Looking at inode numbers can help determine whether a file is a hard link, but inodes are not required to create hard links.

15. B, D.   There are two ways you can accomplish your goal. One is to set permissions for the group equal to those of the owner. To do that, use chmod g=u (group = owner). Remember, o means other, not owner, when it comes to setting permissions in symbolic mode! The second way is to modify the permissions to match those of the user. In this case, that would mean adding Write and Execute to the group's existing permissions, as in the fourth answer.

16. B.   The default permissions for a new directory are drwxrwxrwx, which corresponds to 777 in octal code. The umask is subtracted from the default permissions. The effective permissions are 755 for the directory listed, meaning the umask is 022.

17. A.   Hard links are created with the ln command. If used with no arguments, the ln command creates a hard link. The -s option creates symbolic (or soft) links. The filename is specified first, then the link name.

18. E.   The chmod command is used to set security permissions. Because you don't want anyone except the owner deleting the file, you need to set the sticky bit, which has a value of 1000. Read and write for the owner has a value of 600, and read and write for the group has a value of 60. All together, that adds up to 1660.

19. A, D.   Based on their inode numbers, filex, file2, and file3 are all hard links to the same file. It's impossible to tell which one existed first, nor does it matter. If you delete filex, which the rm filex command does, it does not affect the other links to the data. Therefore, file2 and file4 still exist and can be used to access the data that filex was used to access.

20. C.   To change group ownership of a file or directory, use the chgrp command. The proper syntax for this command is chgrp *newgroup file*.

Chapter 6

Device and Disk Management

SOLARIS 9 EXAM OBJECTIVES COVERED IN THIS CHAPTER:

- ✓ Describe the basic architecture of a local disk and the naming conventions for disk devices as used in the Solaris operating environment.

- ✓ Explain when and how to list devices, reconfigure devices, perform disk partitioning, and relabel a disk in a Solaris operating environment using the appropriate files, commands, options, menus, and/or tables.

A computer system is basically a group of hardware devices teamed together. Each device has its own narrowly defined function, and some devices are understandably more important than others. The motherboard, for example, serves as a central connectivity point for all other devices. If it were to fail, your system would be rendered useless. In contrast, a keyboard, which is an incredibly useful input device, is not system-critical. A keyboard failure might be inconvenient but isn't guaranteed to cause a complete system failure.

Hard disks are another common system device. Even though some client systems are capable of functioning without one, hard disks are one of the more critical components of most computers. Of all configurable devices, hard disks have the greatest array of configuration options and therefore are given their own section in this chapter.

Although it would be possible to describe every device type you could possibly put into your computer, it would be impractical. Before discussing hard disks, this chapter shows how to install and configure some commonly used devices. The advice presented will give you a conceptual framework for device installation, which will be helpful for any device you wish to install.

Device Management

As a systems administrator, you should be able to add devices to your system. Depending on your computer's role, either as a stand-alone system or on a network, various peripherals are needed. They could include a tape drive for system backups, additional network cards, video adapters, modems, or disk drives.

Regardless of the type of device you wish to install, you need to install another component that enables the device to work with Solaris. This vital piece of software is called a *device driver*. Device drivers are small programs with one function: to enable Solaris and hardware to communicate. They are translators, if you will. Drivers are either built into Solaris or installed from floppy disk or CD-ROM. No device will function without the appropriate driver, and the driver must be written specifically for Solaris.

When Solaris boots, the system core, or *kernel*, is configured. Device drivers are called *loadable kernel modules*, because as a device is accessed, the appropriate driver is loaded into the kernel for usage. This automatic loading and unloading of device drivers is called *autoconfiguration*. Put another way, the kernel dynamically autoconfigures itself based on the drivers needed.

Autoconfiguration makes memory usage more efficient, because drivers are loaded only when they are needed. This eliminates "memory hogging" that happens in other operating systems requiring the driver to load and stay permanently loaded in memory. These types of programs are called Terminate and Stay Residents (TSRs). Also, because the kernel is configured dynamically, it's reconfigured automatically—there is no need to reboot the system to rebuild the kernel when loading and unloading device drivers for testing purposes.

Multiple files compose the kernel. The platform-generic portion of the kernel is a file called /kernel/genunix. The platform-specific kernel portion is /platform/`uname -m`/kernel /unix. By modifying the /etc/system file, you can tailor the way in which you want kernel modules to load.

Solaris comes bundled with many device drivers and natively supports a wide array of hardware products. The pre-installed drivers are located in the /kernel/drv and /platform /`uname -m`/kernel/drv directories.

The `uname -m` variable used in this chapter refers to the output that your machine produces when you use the uname -m command. For example, the Sun Blade 100 (part of the sun4u family) would have a platform-specific kernel module of /platform/sun4u/kernel/unix.

If you purchase a device that does not have a driver built into Solaris, you will need to obtain a driver from the device manufacturer. Solaris drivers come in two parts: the driver itself and its associated .conf (configuration) file. Drivers and configuration files should be placed in the /drv directories mentioned previously.

Listing Devices

Solaris has three commands to display system and device configuration information: prtconf, sysdef, and dmesg.

prtconf displays system configuration information. This includes the hardware platform, memory, and device configuration. The output of prtconf will vary widely, based on the devices installed in your computer. Here is a sample portion of a prtconf output:

```
# prtconf
System Configuration:  Sun Microsystems  sun4u
Memory size: 256 Megabytes
System Peripherals (Software Nodes):

SUNW,Sun-Blade-100
    packages (driver not attached)
        SUNW,builtin-drivers (driver not attached)
        deblocker (driver not attached)
        disk-label (driver not attached)
        terminal-emulator (driver not attached)
        obp-tftp (driver not attached)
        dropins (driver not attached)
        kbd-translator (driver not attached)
        ufs-file-system (driver not attached)
```

```
    openprom (driver not attached)
        client-services (driver not attached)
    pci, instance #0
        ebus, instance #1
            flashprom (driver not attached)
            eeprom (driver not attached)
            idprom (driver not attached)
        isa, instance #0
            dma, instance #0
                floppy, instance #0
                parallel, instance #0
            power, instance #0
            serial, instance #0
            serial, instance #1
        network, instance #0
        usb, instance #0
            mouse, instance #0
            keyboard, instance #1
        ide, instance #0
            disk (driver not attached)
            cdrom (driver not attached)
            dad, instance #0
            sd, instance #0
        SUNW,m64B, instance #0
        pci, instance #0
    SUNW,UltraSPARC-IIe, instance #0
#
```

Devices are listed in a hierarchical structure, just as the system sees them. All devices that have drivers installed are listed with their instance number. The first instance of each device type will be instance #0. If there are multiple types of the same device, such as serial ports, the second device will be instance #1.

One message you see a lot of in this output is (driver not attached). This could mean a few things. One possibility is that the device does not have a driver installed. More likely, though, is that the device is simply not being used at the moment. The computer producing this output has a CD-ROM, but the output says the driver is not attached. The CD-ROM does work, and if accessed, the driver will be automatically loaded.

sysdef lists device configuration information, including recognized system hardware, pseudo devices, loadable modules, and some kernel tunable parameters. Here is a portion from a sysdef output:

```
# sysdef
*
* Hostid
```

```
  83150d18
* sun4u Configuration
* Devices
*
pci, instance #0
        network, instance #0
        ide, instance #0
                disk (driver not attached)
                cdrom (driver not attached)
                dad, instance #0
                sd, instance #0
pseudo, instance #0
        clone, instance #0
*
* Loadable Objects
*
* Loadable Object Path = /platform/sun4u/kernel
*
genunix
unix
drv/dma
drv/power
drv/cpc
        hard link:  sys/cpc
drv/sparcv9/su
*
* System Configuration
*
  swap files
swapfile               dev  swaplo blocks   free
/dev/dsk/c0t0d0s1     136,1      16 1049312 926880
*
* Tunable Parameters
*
 2449408         maximum memory allowed in buffer cache (bufhwm)
    1866         maximum number of processes (v.v_proc)
      99         maximum global priority in sys class (MAXCLSYSPRI)
    1861         maximum processes per user id (v.v_maxup)
      30         auto update time limit in seconds (NAUTOUP)
*
* IPC Shared Memory
*
```

```
  8388608      max shared memory segment size (SHMMAX)
  100  shared memory identifiers (SHMMNI)
*
* Time Sharing Scheduler Tunables
*
60       maximum time sharing user priority (TSMAXUPRI)
SYS      system class name (SYS_NAME)
#
```

In all, sysdef can easily produce more than 20 pages of output. To make the information useful, you might want to consider using sysdef | more.

The last display command is dmesg, which presents system diagnostic messages and a list of devices attached to the system since the last boot. Here is a small sample from a dmesg output:

`# dmesg`

```
Tue Aug 20 18:16:42 MDT 2002
Aug 20 17:15:36 Q-Sol genunix: [ID 172905 kern.notice] Copyright \ 1983-2002
    Sun Microsystems, Inc.  All rights reserved.
Aug 20 17:15:36 Q-Sol Use is subject to license terms.
Aug 20 17:15:36 Q-Sol genunix: [ID 678236 kern.info] \ Ethernet address =
    0:3:ba:15:d:18
Aug 20 17:15:47 Q-Sol genunix: [ID 936769 kern.info] uata0 is /pci@1f,0/ide@d
Aug 20 17:15:48 Q-Sol swapgeneric: [ID 308332 kern.info] root on \ /pci@1f,
    0/ide@d/disk@0,0:a fstype ufs
Aug 20 17:15:49 Q-Sol usba: [ID 855233 kern.info] USB-device: keyboard@4,
    \ hid1 at bus address 3
Aug 20 17:15:50 Q-Sol unix: [ID 882636 kern.warning] WARNING:
    \ interrupt level 15 not serviced
Aug 20 17:17:06 Q-Sol pseudo: [ID 129642 kern.info] pseudo-device: lockstat0
Aug 20 17:17:07 Q-Sol pcipsy: [ID 370704 kern.info] PCI-device: pci@5, pci_pci0
#
```

dmesg shows the date and time of the message, the computer and module generating the message, and then the message or warning itself. Like sysdef, dmesg can produce dozens of pages of output.

Adding Devices

Most standard PC devices are compatible with Solaris. Generally speaking, if the device is SCSI, IDE, PCI, or USB, it will work with Solaris. The biggest question is, does the device come with a Solaris device driver? Adding a device to Solaris is accomplished with the following steps:

1. Log in as root, or assume the superuser or equivalent role.

2. Prepare Solaris for a reconfiguration boot by creating a /reconfigure file.

    `# touch /reconfigure`

3. Shut down the computer.

4. Install the new device into the computer. If the device requires parameter configuration, ensure that the device will not conflict with previously installed components. For example, if you are adding a SCSI device, make sure that the SCSI ID of this device is different from the ID of other devices.

5. Power on the computer.

6. After logging in, attempt to access the new device.

If you are unable to access the device, you might need to install the device driver. To install the driver, place the installation media (usually a floppy disk or CD-ROM) into the appropriate drive and use the pkgadd command. For more information on pkgadd, see Chapter 2, "Installation."

If after installing the driver, the device still does not work, it's time to troubleshoot. Check and double-check all your physical connections. It might even help to reseat the device (unplug it and plug it back in). Reinstall the driver. If none of these steps help, try the device in another computer if possible. If it still does not work, you might have a defective product.

Reconfiguring Devices

Solaris 9 supports the dynamic reconfiguration of devices. If the device and device adapter support hot plugging, you can add or remove devices without rebooting Solaris. If the peripherals that you are configuring do not support hot plugging, you will need to reboot Solaris in order to reconfigure the devices.

Hot plugging is the ability to add or remove components while the system is running. When hot-plugged components are added or removed, Solaris reconfigures the system in a process known as *dynamic reconfiguration*. With the cfgadm command, you can hot plug and dynamically reconfigure USB and SCSI devices on all Solaris 9 platforms, and PCI devices on Intel platforms.

The cfgadm command not only enables you to add or remove devices while the system is running, but it walks you through the steps required to properly add or remove the device. This command enables you to display and change system component configurations, test devices, and display configuration help messages.

Whereas nearly all USB devices support hot plugging, some SCSI and PCI controllers do not. To see whether your SCSI or PCI adapter supports hot plugging under Solaris 9, check with your hardware vendor or look up your device in the *Solaris 9 Hardware Compatibility List*.

Running the cfgadm command displays information about attachment points. *Attachment points* are locations within the system where dynamic reconfiguration can occur. All attachment points have two parts. The first is the *receptacle*, which is the location in the system that can accept the device. The second is the *occupant*, which is the device that can be configured. Although it might go without saying, the occupant gets plugged into the receptacle.

With no arguments, the `cfgadm` command displays the current status of hot-pluggable devices in the system:

```
# cfgadm
Ap_Id        Type         Receptacle   Occupant       Condition
c0           scsi-bus     connected    configured     unknown
usb0/1       unknown      empty        unconfigured   ok
usb0/2       usb-mouse    connected    configured     ok
usb0/3       unknown      empty        unconfigured   ok
usb0/4       usb-kbd      connected    configured     ok
#
```

The `Ap_Id` represents the attachment point ID. Attachment point IDs can be represented by either their physical or logical name. The physical `Ap_Id` is the physical name of the attachment point, and the logical `Ap_Id` is a user-friendly name for the physical point. By default, the logical `Ap_Id` is displayed by `cfgadm`.

Receptacles can be in one of three states: connected, disconnected, or empty. Connected means the receptacle has an occupant, and the occupant is available for system access. A disconnected state means that the receptacle has an occupant but has isolated the occupant from normal system operations. This is useful for testing and configuration purposes. Empty implies that the receptacle does not have any occupants.

Occupants can be listed as either configured or unconfigured. Configured means that the device is operational. Unconfigured means that the device cannot be accessed for use but can be accessed for configuration purposes.

The `Ap_Id` can be in one of five conditions: unknown, ok, failing, failed, or unusable. The condition is calculated dynamically. If a working device experiences a critical failure, its condition might go from ok to failing or failed. Devices that are failing, failed, or unusable cannot be used by the system.

 The detailed procedures for configuring hot-pluggable USB, SCSI, and PCI adapters are beyond the scope of this book. For more information, please see the *System Administration Guide: Basic Administration*, from Sun Microsystems.

Accessing Devices

Devices in Solaris 9 can be accessed in most cases by either their physical device name or their logical device name. The physical and logical device names are represented in the system by physical and logical device files.

The `devfsadm` command manages the device files, located in the /`devices` and /`dev` directories. The device files representing the physical devices are located in /`devices`, and the logical device files are located in /`dev`. By default, `devfsadm` attempts to load every driver in the system during boot. If there are no devices for the driver, the driver is ignored.

Not only does `devfsadm` manage the /`devices` and /`dev` directories, it also maintains the /`etc/path_to_inst` file. This file keeps track of mappings of physical device names to instance numbers. The instance number helps device drivers determine which device they are to manage if they are capable of handling multiple devices. Generally, you won't need to update this file. It's read only during system boot and is updated automatically.

devfsadmd, the daemon version of devfsadm, manages the dynamic updating of the /devices and /dev directories. This daemon is started automatically during the boot process by run control (rc) scripts, so no manual intervention is needed.

Device Naming

The Solaris operating system accesses devices based on their naming structure. Programs can refer to devices by their physical device name, logical device name, or instance name.

The physical device name represents the device's full pathname in the system device hierarchy. Although this name is essentially guaranteed to identify the right device, it's cumbersome to use. Physical device names are stored in the /devices directory.

Most file system commands use logical device names. This is because multiple file systems can be on one physical device (a hard disk), and referring to the disk as a whole would not properly recognize the logical divisions. Logical device names are stored in the /dev directory and are symbolically linked to files in the /devices directory.

Instance names are essentially abbreviations for devices, as designated by the kernel. These names are stored in the /etc/path_to_inst file.

The key to using device management utilities is to understand which naming convention the application is looking for. For example, the newfs command, used to create file systems, wants to see a logical name. To find out which format the command you are using requires, view the man page for your command.

Logical Disk Naming

Whereas a physical name can refer to the specific hard disk, a logical name is required to isolate divisions, or slices, within the disk. Although different commands require different interface names, the two standards used are raw device interfaces and block device interfaces. The only real difference between the two is how information is read from the devices. Raw devices can transfer only small amounts of data at a time, whereas block devices can use a buffer and therefore transfer more information at once. Generally speaking, larger disk transfers increase the efficiency of the disk.

For commands that require the raw disk interface, device names in the /dev/rdsk directory are used. Block device names are stored in the /dev/dsk directory. Accessing disks based on raw and block device names is covered in more depth in Chapter 7, "File System Management."

Disk Management

Hard disks are in your computer for one reason: to reliably store large amounts of data. This section begins with disk concepts. You need to understand the physical nature of disk management before you learn what can and can't be done on them.

After examining physical disk structure, you'll move on to the files and utilities used to manage hard disks. The ultimate goal of disk management is to create file systems in which to store data. The goal of this disk management section is to first introduce you to disk concepts and then finish by presenting the disk configuration process step-by-step, up to file system creation. File systems are covered in depth in Chapter 7.

Understanding Disk Terminology

Hard disks are physically composed of a set of magnetically coated *disk platters* spinning on a common spindle. Data is written as 0s and 1s on the disk platters by *disk heads*, also known as read/write heads. Figure 6.1 shows what the inside of a common hard disk looks like.

FIGURE 6.1 An internal view of a hard disk

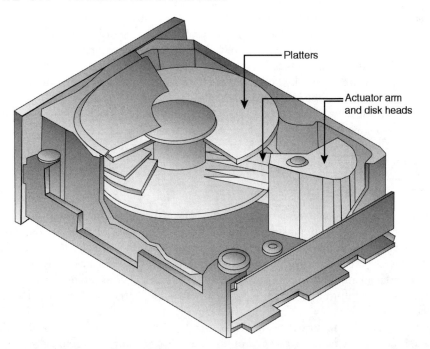

You will also hear the terms *sector*, *track*, and *cylinder* used when discussing hard disks. A *sector* is an individual storage unit, 512 bytes in length. A *track* is a group of sectors laid end to end. If the disk heads were to stay in a stationary position with the platters spinning, the area that the heads cover is a single track. A *cylinder* is all the tracks, on all platters, a specific distance from the center spindle.

The first sector of the hard disk is called the *disk label*. It contains disk geometry (the physical number of sectors, tracks, and so on) as well as partition information. The disk label is also referred to as the *Volume Table of Contents (VTOC)*. On a partitioned hard disk, the label is responsible for keeping track of where the logical divisions (called partitions or slices) start and stop. If the label becomes lost or corrupted, the data on your hard disk might become inaccessible.

Disks are managed by a *disk controller*. The disk controller is built into either the motherboard or the disk device itself. Generally, the place you plug the hard disk into is referred to as the disk controller. Although this is technically not always correct, as IDE hard disk controllers are built in to the device, it is commonly accepted jargon.

Hard disks must be partitioned and formatted before they can store data.

Partitioning and Formatting

To store data on your hard disks, you must first partition the drive. Partitioning, which is done with the `format` command, creates disk slices. A *disk slice* is a contiguous range of sectors on a hard disk. Another way to think of a slice is that it's a logical organization of data. If you were to store multiple types of items around your house, say camping gear, compact discs, and books, you would likely put all camping gear in one place, all discs in another place, and your books in a third area, apart from the others. This is what slices enable you to do.

The terms *slice* and *partition* are often used interchangeably. For the IA version of Solaris 9, the term *partition* is more widely accepted.

Conventional Solaris wisdom holds that you can create a maximum of eight slices per physical disk. However, Solaris 9 has a new feature called *soft partitioning*, which allows for more than eight slices per disk. Soft partitioning is done through the Solaris Volume Manager (SVM), which comes with Solaris 9.

Using the Solaris Volume Manager is an objective for Exam II. It is covered in detail in Chapter 12, "Managing Storage Volumes."

Here are some rules to follow when setting up slices:

- Each disk slice can contain only one file system.
- File systems cannot span multiple slices.
- Slices cannot span multiple disks.
- Multiple swap slices on separate physical disks are allowed.
- After a slice is created, it cannot be resized. To "resize" a slice, you must delete it and re-create a new one.

When you install Solaris, the installation program will automatically configure your disk slices, based on your disk size and anticipated usage. Based on the model of allowing eight slices per disk, each slice is assigned a conventional use. Table 6.1 shows the typical Solaris slices and their intended usage.

TABLE 6.1 Typical Solaris Disk Slices

Slice	File System	Intended Purpose
0	root (/)	For operating system files.
1	swap	Used for virtual memory. Also known as swap space, programs use virtual memory in place of physical memory when the physical memory on your computer runs low.
2	none	Refers to the entire disk. This slice should not be modified.
3	/export	This slice is installed on servers only and holds alternate versions of the operating environment for clients with architecture different from that of the server.
4	none	Optional slice for customization.
5	none	Optional slice for customization.
6	/usr	Contains operating system commands, documentation, and system programs.
7	/home or /export/home	For user-created files and user home directories. On clients, this slice is /home, and on servers, it is /export/home.

Generally speaking, the only differences between servers and clients in terms of default slices are slice 3 and slice 7. Client computers will not have a configured slice 3, meaning that is available for creation and usage as you see fit. Slice 7 will be /export/home on servers, and /home on clients. One other difference you might see is that some computers will not have slice 6 designated as /usr. On computers like this, the /usr directory is contained in slice 0.

Most hard disks today are large enough to hold all slices needed by Solaris. However, if you have multiple physical disks, you can separate your slices as necessary. For example, one disk could hold slices 0 and 6, while another disk holds the rest of the slices. If you are using multiple disks, the disk holding the operating system files (slice 0) is called the *system disk*, and other disks are called non-system disks or secondary disks.

Using multiple physical disks can increase disk input/output (I/O), and can increase the efficiency and speed of your system.

Before partitioning your drive, you should see its current layout. To do this, use the prtvtoc command. When you use prtvtoc, you must supply the device name of the disk you wish to examine. The device name can be either a raw device name, with the syntax /dev/rdsk/ *device_name*, or a block device name with the syntax /dev/dsk/*device_name*.

```
# prtvtoc /dev/rdsk/c0t0d0s2
* /dev/rdsk/c0t0d0s2 partition map
*
* Dimensions:
*     512 bytes/sector
*      63 sectors/track
*      16 tracks/cylinder
*    1008 sectors/cylinder
*   38792 cylinders
*   38790 accessible cylinders
*
* Flags:
*    1: unmountable
*   10: read-only
*
* Unallocated space:
*        First      Sector      Last
*       Sector       Count     Sector
*     39098304        2016   39100319
*
*                           First     Sector      Last
* Partition Tag   Flags    Sector      Count     Sector   Mount Directory
        0     2     00    1049328    4162032    5211359   /
        1     3     01          0    1049328    1049327
        2     5     00          0   39100320   39100319
        7     8     00    5211360   33886944   39098303   /export/home
#
```

As you can see, this hard disk has three slices defined: 0, 1, and 7. Slice 2 refers to the whole disk. On this particular computer, the /usr directory is on slice 0. The prtvtoc output shows you many details, including how many sectors, tracks, and cylinders are on your disk, and how the space on the disk is allocated. There are three flags for partitions: 00 means the disk is mountable read/write, 01 means the partition is not mountable, and 10 means the partition is mountable but is read-only.

There are 11 partition tags, which indicate the type of partition. Table 6.2 displays the tags.

TABLE 6.2   Partition Tags

Tag	Meaning
0	Unassigned
1	BOOT

TABLE 6.2 Partition Tags *(continued)*

Tag	Meaning
2	ROOT
3	SWAP
4	USR
5	BACKUP
6	STAND
7	VAR
8	HOME
9	ALTSCTR
a	CACHE

Even if you have no partitions defined on your hard disk, `prtvtoc` will still show slice 2. This is because slice 2 represents the whole disk.

Using the *format* Utility

The `format` utility is the most powerful and versatile utility administrators have for managing hard disks. If you need to prepare a disk for file storage, `format` will divide the disk into slices and format the slices. If the disk is operational and you need to view configuration information, `format` will display it. And if the disk is having problems, `format` can analyze the disk for surface errors and attempt to repair defective sectors.

When you purchase a new hard disk, it might come preformatted from the factory. Even so, you will still want to format the disk under Solaris, just to avoid any possible future storage or compatibility problems. Depending on the size of your disk, formatting could take a few minutes to a few hours.

 When you format a disk, all data previously on the disk will be destroyed!

You must be the superuser or have an equivalent role in order to use `format`. When you type `format` at a command prompt, you will be asked which disk you wish to work on. If you have only one disk, the choice is easy. Here's an example of the `format` command's main menu:

```
# format
Searching for disks...done
```

```
AVAILABLE DISK SELECTIONS:
       0. c0t0d0 <ST320011A cyl 38790 alt 2 hd 16 sec 63>
          /pci@1f,0/ide@d/dad@0,0
Specify disk (enter its number): 0
selecting c0t0d0
[disk formatted, no defect list found]
Warning: Current Disk has mounted partitions.

FORMAT MENU:
       disk       - select a disk
       type       - select (define) a disk type
       partition  - select (define) a partition table
       current    - describe the current disk
       format     - format and analyze the disk
       repair     - repair a defective sector
       show       - translate a disk address
       label      - write label to the disk
       analyze    - surface analysis
       defect     - defect list management
       backup     - search for backup labels
       verify     - read and display labels
       save       - save new disk/partition definitions
       volname    - set 8-character volume name
       !<cmd>     - execute <cmd>, then return
       quit
format>
```

Notice that after you select a disk, `format` tells you the name of the disk, the condition of the drive (`disk formatted` in this case), and whether there are any defects. Defects on hard disks are not good. However, as your disk ages, it might slowly develop some (or more) defects. If you start seeing a lot of defects, it might indicate that the drive is starting to fail. A certain portion of your usable disk space is reserved for storing defect and formatting information.

Most of the options in the `format` menu are commands—that is, if you type **label**, format will prompt you for a new disk label. To format your disk, type **format** from the `format>` prompt.

The `format` utility will not allow you to format the system disk from within the Solaris operating environment. This makes sense, considering that files needed to run the operating system are on the hard disk, and formatting destroys all data on the disk. If you want to format the system disk, you must do so from the Solaris installation program (boot to the CD-ROM or from the network) or use a third-party format utility.

Some of the format options display new menus. Those options are `partition`, `analyze`, and `defect`. You will know when you've invoked one of the `format` submenus, as each has its own prompt: `partition>`, `analyze>`, and `defect>`. Here is what the `partition` menu looks like:

```
format> partition
PARTITION MENU:
        0       - change '0' partition
        1       - change '1' partition
        2       - change '2' partition
        3       - change '3' partition
        4       - change '4' partition
        5       - change '5' partition
        6       - change '6' partition
        7       - change '7' partition
        select - select a predefined table
        modify - modify a predefined partition table
        name   - name the current table
        print  - display the current table
        label  - write partition map and label to the disk
        quit
partition>
```

If you wanted to change the 1 partition, you would choose 1 from the `partition` menu. It's always a good idea, though, to see your current configuration before modifying partitions. Also, remember that if you delete a partition, all data on that partition is lost. Make sure to back up your data before modifying partitions!

Before taking the test, become familiar with the `format` and `partition` menus, and know what each option does.

Earlier in this chapter, you looked at the `prtvtoc` command's output of disk information. From the `partition` menu, you can use the `print` command to view the same information:

```
partition> print
Current partition table (original):
Total disk cylinders available: 38790 + 2 (reserved cylinders)
```

Part	Tag	Flag	Cylinders	Size	Blocks	
0	root	wm	1041 - 5169	1.98GB	(4129/0/0)	4162032
1	swap	wu	0 - 1040	512.37MB	(1041/0/0)	1049328
2	backup	wm	0 - 38789	18.64GB	(38790/0/0)	39100320
3	unassigned	wm	0	0	(0/0/0)	0
4	unassigned	wm	0	0	(0/0/0)	0

5	unassigned	wm	0		0		(0/0/0)		0
6	unassigned	wm	0		0		(0/0/0)		0
7	home	wm	5170	- 38787	16.16GB		(33618/0/0)	33886944	

```
partition>
```

The flags listed are the same as the flags in `prtvtoc`, just displayed differently. In this menu, `wm` means mountable read/write, `wu` means unmountable, and `rm` means mountable read-only.

Using the *fdisk* Utility

If you are using the Solaris 9 Intel Platform Edition, you will have an additional submenu in the `format` menu, named `fdisk`. The `fdisk` utility is commonly used in the DOS and Windows world to create and delete partitions on hard disks, and it serves the same purpose in the Solaris environment.

The configuration options available with `fdisk` on IA platforms are somewhat different from the standard partitioning structure of Solaris. First of all, a single hard disk can be divided into no more than four `fdisk` partitions, and at least one of these must be a Solaris partition. Also, the Solaris partition must be made the active partition—that is, the bootable partition. You can create one `fdisk` partition to span the entire hard disk, or smaller partitions if you choose. The first `fdisk` partition must begin at cylinder 1, as cylinder 0 is reserved for the master boot record. After you have created an `fdisk` partition, the other `format` command options (such as `partition` and `label`) work just as they do on the SPARC version of Solaris.

The `fdisk` menu looks similar to the following:

```
format> fdisk

...

SELECT ONE OF THE FOLLOWING:
     1. Create a partition
     2. Change Active (Boot from) partition
     3. Delete a partition
     4. Exit (Update disk configuration and exit)
     5. Cancel (Exit without updating disk configuration)
Enter selection:
```

These menu options are fairly self-explanatory. Just remember that deleting a partition destroys all existing data on that partition. Also, if you make changes that you don't want to keep, be sure to use the Cancel option instead of the Exit option.

One other interesting thing to note about creating partitions with `fdisk` is the number of slices on that partition. On the SPARC version of Solaris, if you use the default hard disk settings, Solaris will create eight slices on the hard disk, and there can be no more than eight at any time (unless you use Solaris Volume Manager, but that's not the point here). On the IA version, Solaris will place ten slices on the hard disk, numbered 0–9.

Slices 0–7 are used for the same purposes as they are in the SPARC Solaris environment. However, slice 8 is used to hold boot information for IA computers and is known as the boot slice. It's located at the beginning of the hard disk (even though based on its number, you might not think this is the case). Slice 9 holds reserved alternate disk blocks and is called the alternate sector slice.

Modifying Partitions

From the `partition` menu, you can create, delete, and modify partitions. Based on the preceding example, assume that you want to create partition 3 and you want to make it 2GB in size. Can you do that?

The question is, where are you going to get the room? The total disk size is 18.64GB (slice 2), and the currently defined partitions 0, 1, and 7 take up all that space. You certainly don't want to modify partition 0, because it has critical operating system files. Partition 1 contains the swap space, so for now, that's best left untouched as well. That leaves partition 7, which is using 16.16GB of disk space.

To create your partition 3, you will first need to modify partition 7 to make it smaller. Be careful, though, because once you modify a partition's size, all data on that partition is lost. After you have made partition 7 smaller and freed up the required disk space, you can create partition 3.

 The `modify` command from the `partition` menu is the most user-friendly way to modify existing partitions. It enables you to specify the size of slices in megabytes and doesn't make you keep track of cylinder boundaries.

When you modify partition sizes by using the `format` command, all disk space must be accounted for by the operating system. So when you reduce the size of partition 7 by 2GB, the 2GB of free space is allocated to a temporary partition known as the *free hog*.

The term *free hog* elicits some interesting visual images. It's named this because when a new slice needs space, the temporary slice frees up the space. And when a partition is shrunk, the temporary slice hogs the space. The free hog exists only when you are installing Solaris and when you're using the `format` utility to modify your partition structure.

Using Graphical Disk Management

In Solaris 9, the Solaris Management Console (SMC) can be used to administer hard disks as well as the command line. For people who prefer icons and graphical management, the SMC is a handy interface. The Disks node of SMC is shown in Figure 6.2.

The Disks node shows all recognized hard disks in your system. Perhaps the only confusing thing about the Disks node is what is meant by Used, Free, and Percent Free space. To the unsuspecting eye, it would appear that this disk is full, when it most certainly is not. In Figure 6.2, the used space refers to the amount of disk space occupied by slices. Conversely, the free space is unoccupied space. In this case, 2.46MB of the disk does not contain any partitions. This 0.01 percent of the hard drive is reserved for partition table information and is normal.

To view more-detailed information about a particular disk, select it from the menu on the left or by double-clicking it in the right pane. Specific disk information is shown in Figure 6.3.

FIGURE 6.2   Solaris Management Console Disks node

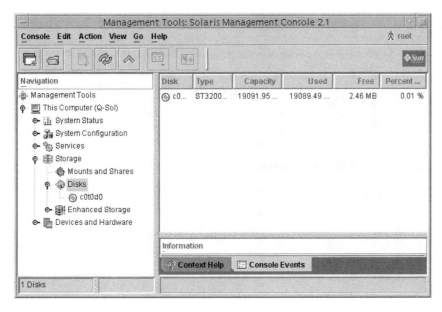

FIGURE 6.3   Disk partitions

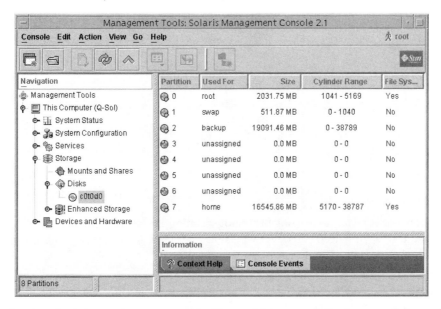

Notice that the information presented in Figure 6.3 is essentially the same information you can find by using the prtvtoc command and the format ➢ partition ➢ print command.

From the Action menu in SMC, you can create Solaris partitions and create file systems. The command line still offers the most flexibility when managing hard disks.

 You will find occasional discrepancies between how SMC and the print command in the format utility display partition sizes. For example, the swap space usually appears larger when displayed from format, whereas /home usually looks larger when displayed with SMC. These discrepancies result from the different ways that the utilities gather disk information and are no cause for alarm.

Analyzing and Repairing a Disk

One of the troubleshooting features of the format command is the ability to perform a surface analysis of a hard disk. A surface analysis can detect errors in file systems and defects on the hard disk. Here is what the analyze menu looks like:

```
format> analyze

ANALYZE MENU:
        read     - read only test    (doesn't harm SunOS)
        refresh  - read then write   (doesn't harm data)
        test     - pattern testing   (doesn't harm data)
        write    - write then read      (corrupts data)
        compare  - write, read, compare (corrupts data)
        purge    - write, read, write   (corrupts data)
        verify   - write entire disk, then verify (corrupts data)
        print    - display data buffer
        setup    - set analysis parameters
        config   - show analysis parameters
        !<cmd>   - execute <cmd> , then return
        quit
analyze>
```

Some of the analyses corrupt data and should be used only sparingly. These tests are for when you suspect the disk is damaged and you want to be very thorough in examining the disk. Of course, be sure to back up existing files before running any test that corrupts data. All seven tests attempt to repair defective blocks by default. The simplest (and quickest) test is read. When you perform a read analysis, Solaris warns you:

```
analyze> read
Ready to analyze (won't harm SunOS). This takes a long time, but is
    interruptable with CTRL-C. Continue?
```

The read analysis performs two passes on the disk. For an 18GB disk, read took a total of 19 minutes. The read analysis is the only analysis that you can perform on a mounted partition.

If you have a defective sector on your hard disk, the analysis program you ran will tell you. It will also tell you whether it was able to fix the problem. Other times, though, you might be using your system and receive an error message similar to the following:

```
Error for command 'read' Error level: Retryable
Requested Block 199, Error Block: 214
Sense Key: Media Error
```

This message indicates that block 214 might be damaged. You can try to repair the block with either the `repair` command from the `format` menu or by performing a surface analysis.

 If you know the number of the potentially defective block, you can configure `analyze` through the `setup` command to scan only a certain portion of blocks. This can save you a great deal of time as opposed to running an entire surface scan.

Adding a Disk

This section on hard disk management is a step-by-step guide to installing a new hard disk into your Solaris computer. In practice, the exact steps you need to take might differ slightly from this list.

Here's what to do to add a secondary disk to your computer:

1. If your machine is running, create a `/reconfigure` file. This will cause Solaris to check for new hardware the next time it is booted. If your system is already powered off, don't worry about this step, because a reconfiguration check can be initiated another way.

    `# touch /reconfigure`

2. Turn off your computer and all attached peripherals. Leave the computer plugged in, because this provides a natural ground. (Frying hard disks isn't as easy as frying RAM, but you still don't want to be careless with electronic equipment.)

    `# init 5` (or whichever shutdown command you prefer)

3. Connect the new hard disk to your computer. If you are unsure how to do this, consult your hard disk manufacturer's instructions. If you have SCSI disks, make sure the new disk you are connecting has a different SCSI ID than other SCSI devices in your system. If this is an IDE disk, make sure to configure the appropriate master/slave relationship.

4. Turn on all peripherals and your computer. If you have created the `/reconfigure` file, your system should detect the new disk. If you have not created the `/reconfigure` file, execute the following command to perform a reconfiguration boot:

    `ok boot -r`

5. Log in as `root`, or log in as yourself and assume the superuser identity or equivalent role.

6. At the command line, invoke the **format** command. Select the disk you wish to modify. If this is the second disk in the system, it will be displayed as disk 1. The third disk will be disk 2, and so on.

    `# format`

7. In the format command, go to the partition menu. Display the current partition table and then modify it as necessary.

   format> **partition**

   partition> **print**

   partition> **modify**

   When presented with the Select partitioning base: prompt, choose 1. All Free Hog to start from scratch. Set up the new slices as needed.

8. Name the partition table and label the disk. You will be prompted for each entry.

9. Quit the partition menu and verify the format of the disk.

   partition> **quit**

   format> **verify**

10. Create file systems for each slice and mount your new file systems. Creating and mounting file systems is covered in Chapter 7.

11. Copy data to the new file systems or restore data from backup to the new file systems.

Restoring data from backups is covered in Chapter 9, "System Backups and Restores."

If you are replacing the system disk in a computer, the installation process is slightly different. For one, with no system disk, Solaris cannot boot from a local disk. You must boot either to a CD-ROM or from the network. In many cases, if the system disk needs to be replaced, the easiest solution is to boot from CD-ROM (or the network) and perform a new installation of Solaris. Alternately, you can install the disk, create slices, and restore data from backup.

1. Here are steps to install a new system disk:

2. Turn off your computer and all attached peripherals. Leave the computer plugged in, because this provides a natural ground.

3. Remove the defective hard disk. Connect the new hard disk to your computer. If you are unsure how to do this, consult your hard disk manufacturer's instructions. If you have SCSI disks, make sure the new disk you are connecting has a different SCSI ID than other SCSI devices in your system. If this is an IDE disk, make sure to configure the appropriate master/slave relationship.

4. Turn on all peripherals and your computer. You can boot from either the CD-ROM or the network, if you have a network boot server configured:

   ok **boot cdrom**   – or–

   ok **boot net**

5. When the login prompt appears, log in as root, or log in as yourself and assume the superuser identity or equivalent role.

6. If you are not going to perform a new installation, use the installboot command to install a boot block on the new disk. This will make the disk bootable.

After completing these steps, you can either perform a new installation or create and format slices and restore from backup.

Unsupported Hard Disks

Occasionally, you will encounter a third-party disk drive that is not supported by Solaris. If the `format` utility does not recognize your hard disk, this might be the problem. In these cases, you will need to either supply a device driver from the disk manufacturer or add an entry in the `/etc/format.dat` file. If the hard disk itself is not recognized, it's more likely that you'll need a driver. If the hard disk you are installing has a geometry that's not known to Solaris, an entry in the `/etc/format.dat` file will likely do the trick.

SCSI-2-compatible disk drives are automatically configured by the `format` utility and do not require an entry in the `format.dat` file.

🌐 Real World Scenario

Adding a Secondary SCSI Hard Disk

You have just purchased a new large SCSI hard disk to increase the storage capacity on your Solaris 9 server. The current system has only three other SCSI devices: two hard disks and a CD-ROM. From previous training, you know that your Ultra 320 SCSI chain can handle up to 15 devices without a problem. After business hours, you warn all remaining users to log out of the server and you shut down the server to add the new disk.

However, when you attempt to reboot the server, it does not boot into Solaris. You get to the OpenBoot PROM and receive a message about not being able to find the boot device. After disconnecting the new disk, the server boots properly. Suspecting a bad SCSI disk, you take your new disk and plug it into your workstation. The workstation boots properly. What could be the problem?

When troubleshooting failed hardware, the first thing to check is connections. When working with SCSI, make sure that the SCSI chain has proper termination and that the cables are securely fastened. Loose cables are never good for computers. Also make sure that the drive has power. Sometimes people remember the data cables but forget to plug in the power.

One last thing to check with SCSI is the SCSI target ID. If the SCSI target ID of the new hard disk were set to the same ID as the original boot disk, it could cause your computer to not boot. In this case, that's the most likely problem. All it takes to fix it is reconfiguring jumpers on the back of the drive.

When adding new devices to your computer, make sure to double-check your connections and to ensure that the new device's settings won't conflict with existing hardware.

Summary

This chapter examined device and disk management. You started by looking at managing system devices. Listing system devices can be done with the `prtconf`, `sysdef`, and `dmesg` commands.

If you want to add a device, it's important to ensure that the device will work with Solaris. A big part of this is making sure there's a Solaris driver for that particular device. Also, Solaris supports dynamic reconfiguration and hot plugging. If you intend to use hot-plug devices, make sure the devices you purchase support it as well.

Devices can be accessed by one of three types of names: the physical name, the logical name, or the instance name. Most Solaris utilities require one of the three forms in order to function properly. There are two types of logical disk names: raw and block.

The disk management section started by defining some critical hard disk terms, such as cylinder, track, and section. You also looked at the physical structure of a hard disk.

Before you can store data on a disk, you must partition and format the disk. This is done with the `format` command. The `format` command has many options, including the ability to analyze and repair some physical disk problems.

After reviewing the physical and logical components of hard disks, you finished the chapter by walking through the steps necessary to add a new disk to your system.

Exam Essentials

Know what device drivers are.   Device drivers enable Solaris to communicate with hardware devices. To work with Solaris, the driver must be specifically written for Solaris.

Know how to display system configuration information.   The three commands used to display system hardware configuration are `prtconf`, `sysdef`, and `dmesg`.

Understand what `cfgadm` is used for.   The `cfgadm` command is used to manage hot-swapping and hot-plugging devices in Solaris 9.

Know what `devfsadm` manages.   `devfsadm` manages the /devices and /dev directories, and the /etc/path_to_inst file.

Know where raw and block disk device names are stored.   Raw disk names are located in the /dev/rdsk directory, and block names are in the /dev/dsk directory.

Know how to display the disk's Volume Table of Contents.   The VTOC is displayed with the `prtvtoc` command. The same information can also be gathered from the `format` ➢ `partition` ➢ `print` command.

Know what can be done from the `format` command.   The `format` command is very versatile. It's options are `disk`, `type`, `partition`, `current`, `format`, `repair`, `show`, `label`, `analyze`, `defect`, `backup`, `verify`, `save`, and `volname`. Be sure to recognize the menu when you see it.

Key Terms

Before you take the exam, be certain you are familiar with the following terms:

attachment points	free hog
autoconfiguration	hot plugging
cylinder	kernel
device driver	loadable kernel modules
disk controller	occupant
disk heads	receptacle
disk label	sector
disk platters	system disk
disk slice	track
dynamic reconfiguration	Volume Table of Contents (VTOC)

Commands Used in This Chapter

The following list contains a summary of all the commands introduced in this chapter:

Command	Description
cfgadm	Used for managing hot-plugging hardware
devfsadm	Manages device configuration and the /devices and /dev directories
dmesg	Displays diagnostic messages and device lists
format	Used for formatting, partitioning, and analyzing hard disks
prtconf	Prints the system's hardware configuration
prtvtoc	Displays the Volume Table of Contents
sysdef	Lists hardware device configuration information

Review Questions

1. You are the Solaris administrator for your network. You have just configured a new server. One of your other administrators asks why slice 2 is larger than the other slices on the server's system disk. What do you tell him?

   A. Slice 2 represents the whole hard disk.

   B. Slice 2 holds the root file system and therefore needs the most space.

   C. Slice 2 is empty space, and you have not created a file system on it yet.

   D. Slice 2 holds user-created files, and because this is a file server, it needed to be the largest slice.

2. You are the Solaris administrator for your network. Recently, you installed a new network adapter in one of your Solaris servers. The system is not recognizing the card. What is the best course of action to take?

   A. Run the `cfgadm` command to detect the network adapter.

   B. Run the `devfsadm` command to detect the network adapter.

   C. Contact Sun for a device driver for the network adapter.

   D. Contact the manufacturer of the network adapter for a device driver.

3. You are the Solaris administrator for your company. You are presented with the following output:

```
* /dev/rdsk/c0t0d0s2 partition map
*
* Dimensions:
*       512 bytes/sector
*        63 sectors/track
*        16 tracks/cylinder
*      1008 sectors/cylinder
*     38792 cylinders
*     38790 accessible cylinders
*
* Flags:
*       1: unmountable
*      10: read-only
*
* Unallocated space:
*       First     Sector      Last
*      Sector     Count       Sector
*     39098304     2016     39100319
*
*                          First    Sector     Last
```

* Partition	Tag	Flags	Sector	Count	Sector	Mount Directory
0	2	00	1049328	4162032	5211359	/
1	3	01	0	1049328	1049327	
2	5	00	0	39100320	39100319	
7	8	00	5211360	33886944	39098303	/export/home

What is the exact command you typed to retrieve this information?

A. `label /dev/rdsk/c0t0d0s2`

B. `prtvtoc /dev/rdsk/c0t0d0s2`

C. `partition /dev/rdsk/c0t0d0s2`

D. `format /dev/rdsk/c0t0d0s2`

4. You have just installed and configured a new Solaris workstation on your network. After rebooting, you suspect that the system kernel is not being configured properly. Which two files make up the system kernel? (Choose two.)

A. `/platform/`uname -m`/kernel/unix`

B. `/kernel/genunix`

C. `/etc/system`

D. `/etc/kernel`

5. You are the Solaris administrator for your company. You are at the `format` command menu on one of your servers. You want to see whether the disk has any sector damage. Which command should you type at the `format` menu?

A. `format`

B. `analyze`

C. `defect`

D. `show`

E. `verify`

6. You are the Solaris administrator for your network. You need to see whether a specific hardware device is being recognized by one of your Solaris workstations. Which of the following commands can you use to list the hardware devices? (Choose all that apply.)

A. `dmesg`

B. `disphw`

C. `prtconf`

D. `prtvtoc`

E. `sysdef`

F. `sysconf`

7. You are working on one of your Solaris servers. You are at the following menu:

```
0       - change '0' partition
1       - change '1' partition
2       - change '2' partition
3       - change '3' partition
4       - change '4' partition
5       - change '5' partition
6       - change '6' partition
7       - change '7' partition
select - select a predefined table
modify - modify a predefined partition table
name   - name the current table
print  - display the current table
label  - write partition map and label to the disk
quit
```

What is the last command you typed to get to this menu?

A. format

B. partition

C. slice

D. fdisk

8. Which of the following statements best describes the purpose of the /dev/dsk and /dev/rdsk directories?

A. /dev/dsk contains physical disk names, and /dev/rdsk contains logical disk names.

B. /dev/dsk contains logical disk names, and /dev/rdsk contains physical disk names.

C. /dev/dsk contains logical block disk names, and /dev/rdsk contains logical raw disk names.

D. /dev/dsk contains logical raw disk names, and /dev/rdsk contains logical block disk names.

9. You are the Solaris administrator for your company. You are installing a new workstation and will be customizing your hard disk slice configuration. When creating slices, which of the following are true? (Choose all that apply.)

A. Each disk slice can contain only one file system.

B. File systems cannot span multiple slices.

C. Slices cannot span multiple disks.

D. Multiple swap slices on separate physical disks are allowed.

E. Created slices can be dynamically resized with the format command.

10. You are the Solaris administrator for your company. You have purchased a new SCSI adapter that supports hot swapping of hard disks. Which Solaris command enables you to manage hot-swappable disks?

A. dmesg

B. cfgadm

C. devfsadm

D. hswap

11. You are the Solaris server administrator for your company. On one of your server's hard disks, you want to make a slice used to store user-created files larger. What is the best way to accomplish this?

A. Use the format command to expand the size of the slice.

B. Back up the existing data. Use the format command to delete the slice and then re-create a larger slice. Restore the data from backup.

C. Back up the existing data. Use the format command to expand the slice. Restore the data from backup.

D. Slices cannot be resized in Solaris.

12. You are at the partition menu of the format command. You just caused the following information to be displayed:

```
partition> XXXXXXXXX
Current partition table (original):
Total disk cylinders available: 38790 + 2 (reserved cylinders)
```

Part	Tag	Flag	Cylinders	Size	Blocks	
0	root	wm	1041 - 5169	1.98GB	(4129/0/0)	4162032
1	swap	wu	0 - 1040	512.37MB	(1041/0/0)	1049328
2	backup	wm	0 - 38789	18.64GB	(38790/0/0)	39100320
3	unassigned	wm	0	0	(0/0/0)	0
4	unassigned	wm	0	0	(0/0/0)	0
5	unassigned	wm	0	0	(0/0/0)	0
6	unassigned	wm	0	0	(0/0/0)	0
7	home	wm	5170 - 38787	16.16GB	(33618/0/0)	33886944

```
partition>
```

What command did you type to retrieve the displayed information?

A. print

B. label

C. display

D. select

E. name

F. modify

13. Which slice, by default, holds the root file system in Solaris 9?

A. 0

B. 2

C. 4

D. 7

14. You are the Solaris server administrator for your company. You are configuring hot-swappable hard disks on your Solaris server. Which two terms accurately describe the components you are configuring?

A. Device and port

B. Drive and bay

C. Occupant and receptacle

D. Disk and tray

15. You are the Solaris server administrator for your company. One of your servers has two hard disks. The first disk, disk 0, contains slices 0, 2, and 6. The second disk, disk 1, contains slices 2, 4, and 7. What is another name for disk 0?

A. The boot disk

B. The main disk

C. The system disk

D. The non-system disk

16. You are the Solaris administrator for your company. You just received a new workstation and have powered it on. You want to see the parameters of the computer's single hard disk, including the dimensions and allocated partitions. Which command should you type to see this information?

A. prtvtoc /dev/rdsk/c0t0d0s2

B. prtconf /dev/rdsk/c0t0d0s2

C. dispdsk /dev/rdsk/c0t0d0s2

D. dmesg /dev/rdsk/c0t0d0s2

17. Which of the following commands displays system diagnostic messages, as well as devices that have been added since the last system boot?

A. cfgadm

B. dmesg

C. prtconf

D. sysdef

18. You are the Solaris administrator for your company. You are presented with the following menu:

```
disk        - select a disk
type        - select (define) a disk type
```

```
partition  - select (define) a partition table
current    - describe the current disk
format     - format and analyze the disk
repair     - repair a defective sector
show       - translate a disk address
label      - write label to the disk
analyze    - surface analysis
defect     - defect list management
backup     - search for backup labels
verify     - read and display labels
save       - save new disk/partition definitions
volname    - set 8-character volume name
!<cmd>     - execute <cmd>, then return
```

What command (with no arguments) did you type to get to this menu?

A. fdisk

B. prtconf

C. partition

D. format

E. disk

F. hdisk

19. You are the Solaris administrator for your company. You are creating new slices on a hard disk. One of your senior administrators has advised you to choose an option she calls "All Free Hog" when beginning to slice the hard disk. What is the purpose of the free hog?

A. The free hog is another name for the slice that contains the root file system and is used as a base for the partitioning process.

B. The free hog is a temporary slice used by the format command to keep track of free space on the disk during the partitioning process.

C. The free hog refers to the entire hard drive and is used as a base for the partitioning process.

D. The free hog refers to a newly created slice that does not yet have a file system defined on it. When a file system is created on the slice, the slice is a full hog.

20. You are a Solaris administrator. You need to find a list of device instance names for your system. In which file will you find instance names of configured devices in Solaris 9?

A. /etc/path_to_inst

B. /etc/instance

C. /etc/inst

D. /path_to_inst

E. /instance

F. /inst

Answers to Review Questions

1. **A.** By convention, slice 2 represents the whole hard disk.

2. **D.** If hardware is not being recognized by Solaris, it's likely that the proper device driver is not installed. Drivers should be obtained from the hardware manufacturer. The cfgadm command manages hot-swappable parts, and devfsadm manages the /devices and /dev directories, but neither one detects hardware.

3. **B.** This is output from the prtvtoc command. The device listed in the first line is /dev/rdsk/c0t0d0s2, so the correct answer is prtvtoc /dev/rdsk/c0t0d0s2.

4. **A, B.** The two files that compose the kernel are /platform/`uname -m`/kernel/unix and /kernel/genunix. The /etc/system file can be used to modify the loading of kernel modules. The /etc/kernel file does not exist.

5. **B.** To scan the disk for sector damage, you need to analyze the disk for errors. In contrast, format formats a disk, defect shows the manufacturer's defect list, show translates disk addresses, and verify reads and displays disk labels.

6. **A, C, E.** The dmesg, prtconf, and sysdef commands can be used to display system hardware. The prtvtoc command shows a hard disk's label, or Volume Table of Contents. The sysconf command gets a list of configurable system variables. The disphw command does not exist.

7. **B.** This is the partition submenu from the format command. Before taking the test, you should recognize this menu.

8. **C.** The /dev/dsk directory contains logical block disk names, and /dev/rdsk contains logical raw disk names. One way to remember this is that the *r* in rdsk stands for *raw*.

9. **A, B, C, D.** Each disk slice can contain only one file system, file systems cannot span multiple slices, and slices cannot span multiple disks. Multiple swap slices are allowed. Slices cannot be resized dynamically. To resize a slice, you must delete it and re-create it.

10. **B.** The cfgadm command is used to manage hot-swappable parts in Solaris. The dmesg command displays hardware configuration. The devfsadm command manages the /devices and /dev directories. The hswap command does not exist.

11. **B.** To make a slice larger, you must delete the slice and re-create a larger one. If there is no more disk space, then you must delete another slice to free space for your new, larger slice.

12. **A.** At the partition menu, the print command displays current partition table information.

13. **A.** Slice 0 is for the root file system. Slice 2 represents the whole disk. Slice 4 is an optional slice. Slice 7 typically contains user home directories.

14. **C.** The cfgadm command, which configures hot-swappable devices, refers to the individual parts as the occupant and the receptacle. The receptacle is the bay on the computer, and the occupant is the device that plugs into the receptacle.

15. C. If your computer has multiple hard disks, the disk with slice 0 and the /usr file system (which is generally located on slice 0 or 6) is known as the system disk. The disk is bootable and can be considered the main disk, but its technical term is system disk. Disk 1 in this example would be a non-system disk, because it does not contain slice 0 and the /usr file system.

16. A. The prtvtoc command displays the disk's label, also known as the disk's Volume Table of Contents (VTOC). The label shows disk dimensions and partitions. The prtconf and dmesg commands show system device configuration information. The dispdsk command does not exist.

17. B. dmesg displays system diagnostic messages. Although prtconf and sysdef do display hardware devices, they do not display diagnostic messages. The cfgadm command is used to manage hot-swappable hardware.

1º D   This is the format menu. Before taking the test, make sure you recognize this menu and know what each selection does.

19. B. When using the format utility, the free disk space is occupied by the free hog. If you delete additional slices, the free hog will "hog" the new free space. If you create additional slices, the free hog will "free" space to use for the new slice. Choosing "All Free Hog" essentially wipes out all existing slices, enabling you to start over and completely customize your hard disk partitioning structure.

20. A. The /etc/path_to_inst file maintains mappings of all devices to instance names in Solaris 9. None of the other files exist.

Chapter 7

File System Management

SOLARIS 9 EXAM OBJECTIVES COVERED IN THIS CHAPTER:

- ✓ Describe the purpose, features, and functions of disk-based, distributed, and pseudo file systems in a Solaris operating environment and explain the differences among these file system types.

- ✓ Explain when and how to create a new ufs file system using the newfs command, check the file system using fsck, resolve file system inconsistencies, and monitor file system usage using associated commands.

- ✓ Explain the purpose and function of the vfstab file in mounting ufs file systems, and the function of the mnttab file in tracking current mounts.

- ✓ Explain how to perform mounts and unmounts, and either access or restrict access to mounted diskettes and CD-ROMs.

Before you can store files on a Solaris-based hard disk, you must create file systems in which to store the files. In Chapter 6, "Device and Disk Management," you looked at managing hard disks from a higher level. That is, you looked at adding, slicing, and formatting the disks. Creating file systems is the last step in the hard disk preparation process. After the disk is sliced and formatted, and a file system is created, files can be stored.

Solaris doesn't only support file systems on local hard disks. File systems located on remote disks can be used, as well as pseudo or virtual file systems. In this chapter, you'll take a detailed look at each of these file system types, including how to create and manage them.

You will also examine how to mount and unmount file systems, and look at two critical files used in file system management: `/etc/mnttab` and `/etc/vfstab`. Finally, you will explore removable media, namely floppy disks, CD-ROMs, DVD-ROMs, and removable memory cards.

This chapter is the final chapter that discusses hard disk management for Part I of the Solaris Certified Systems Administrator exam. Ideally, by the end of this chapter, you will have a solid understanding of disk management, from installing the disk to being able to store files on it.

Understanding File Systems

File systems are not new concepts at this point in the book. From the preceding two chapters, you should remember that file systems can be looked at in a few different ways. One way is that a *file system* is a logical unit of storage, such as the entire file tree, beginning with the root directory. Another way is that a file system defines the specific methods used to store and retrieve data from hard disks. Both are perfectly acceptable ways to think of file systems. Just understand that when someone mentions a file system, they might be thinking of it in a different light than you.

Solaris 9 supports several types of file systems. Again, how you define the multiple types depends on which way you look at file systems. For ease of categorization, though, this chapter classifies file systems into three categories: disk based (or local), network based (or distributed), and pseudo (or virtual). Three categories with two names each can understandably be a bit confusing. And to add to the potential confusion, a few file systems, such as Universal Disk Format (UDF), can be classified as either a local file system or a virtual file system.

There are some new file system features in Solaris 9. They include:

The use of extended file system attributes These enable developers and administrators to create certain types of attributes and associate them to a file. For example, if a developer wanted a certain type of file to be represented with a particular icon within the Common Desktop Environment (CDE), she could include the icon type as an extended file attribute.

The ability to create UNIX File System (UFS) snapshots   Traditionally, to back up a file system, you have to unmount the file system, making it temporarily inaccessible. In Solaris 9, you can take a UFS snapshot of a mounted file system for backup purposes. Snapshots are discussed in more detail in Chapter 9, "System Backups and Restores."

UFS I/O concurrency   In previous versions of Solaris, if a file was being written to, it was temporarily locked from read operations. Solaris 9 allows for concurrent read and write access to UFS files because of an improved data buffering method. This is especially helpful for database files.

Improved performance from mkfs   The mkfs (make file system) command is used to create file systems. The version of mkfs included with Solaris 9 can be up to 10 times faster than previous versions.

New labelit options   For UDF file systems, labelit now enables you to create labels to identify the person creating the file system, the organization responsible for file system creation, and contact information for the responsible parties.

As discussed in Chapter 5, "Files, Directories, and Security," the file system structure of Solaris is hierarchical. The base of the file system tree is the root, represented by a slash (/). Other directories and file systems can be represented by their absolute path from the root, such as /export/home/userx. There are nine default Solaris file systems to consider, as shown in Table 7.1.

TABLE 7.1   Default Solaris 9 File Systems

File System	Type	Purpose
root (/)	UFS	The top of the hierarchical file system. Also contains files and directories critical for system operation.
/etc/mnttab	MNTFS	A file system dedicated to maintaining the table of mounted file systems. This file system is read-only.
/export/home or /home	NFS, UFS	For user home directories.
/opt	UFS	Optional file system for third-party software. If local, it's UFS. If remote, it's NFS.
/proc	PROCFS	The active processes on the system.
/tmp	TMPFS	Temporary files. The files in this file system are removed when the system is rebooted or when /tmp is unmounted.
/usr	UFS	Files and directories that are to be shared with other users. User commands and man pages are stored in /usr.

TABLE 7.1   Default Solaris 9 File Systems *(continued)*

File System	Type	Purpose
/var	UFS	Variable data that changes over time. Examples are log files and some backup files.
/var/run	TMPFS	A file system storing temporary files that are not needed after the system is booted.

When you look at this table, you might think, "Wait a minute! This looks a lot like Table 5.3, which listed the default directories. What's the deal?" Good question.

This is when the differentiations between file systems and directories can become confusing. For example, is /usr a file system or is it a directory? The answer can be an ambiguous "yes."

Perhaps a better question to ponder is, "Does it really matter whether it's a file system or a directory?" It depends on what you're doing. If you're simply navigating the directory structure and want to get to your home directory in /export/home, it really doesn't matter. You can simply use the cd command to get to your desired working directory. However, if you're trying to create a hard link, now it does matter. As you might recall, hard links can be created only in the same file system as the original file.

Suppose that you create a new slice, slice 4, create a file system called /docs on it, and mount it. What would your users see? They would see a directory called /docs. The vast majority of your users won't know whether it's a directory or file system, and they likely won't care. All they care about is that they can access the files they need in /docs. As the administrator, you might need to differentiate because of disk space allocation and file system management (such as backups).

One last point to consider is how the file system or directory was created. If you used mkdir, it's obviously a directory. However, if you used mkfs or newfs, it's a file system. Generally speaking, though, file systems *look* like directories, and for navigational purposes, they act like directories. A directory, however, isn't necessarily its own file system.

File System Structure

Creating a file system on a hard disk divides the disk slice into cylinder groups. The cylinder groups are then subdivided into blocks to provide an organizational structure within the slice. Each block has a unique address within the slice. The four types of blocks are boot block, super-block, inode, and data (or storage) block.

The *boot block* is present only in slice 0, as this is the boot slice. In all other slices, the area normally reserved for the boot block is left blank. The boot block is very small, only 8KB, and contains enough information to begin the system's boot process.

The *superblock* contains critical file system information. The information stored by the superblock includes the size of the file system, the disk label (Volume Table of Contents), cylinder group size, number of data blocks present, the summary data block, file system state (state flag), and the pathname of the last mount point. There's no sense in memorizing this list; just know that the superblock is critical. In fact, if the superblock were lost, the file system would be inaccessible.

The superblock is located at the beginning of each slice, and is replicated within each cylinder group for redundancy. If the slice spans multiple hard disk platters, the spacing of superblock replicas is calculated to provide at least one superblock on each disk platter. Replicas can be used to replace the original superblock if the original becomes corrupt or lost.

An *inode* is a 128-byte block that contains all the information about a file except for the file's name. Filenames are stored in directories. The information stored in an inode includes the file's type (directory, regular, socket, and so on), the file's mode (basic permission set), the number of hard links to the file, the User ID and Group ID of the file's owners, the size of the file, the last modification date and time, and the date and time that the file was created. The inode also points to the blocks that contain the actual data within the file. Each file needs one inode.

By restricting the number of inodes within a slice, you can effectively restrict the number of possible files stored in the slice.

Data blocks contain the data of the file. By default, the blocks are allocated in 8KB chunks, with a certain portion reserved as 1KB fragment blocks. Fragment blocks are used to increase disk efficiency when a file does not need a full 8KB block.

Disk-Based File Systems

As their name implies, disk-based file systems are created on some sort of physical media. Generally speaking, disk-based file systems are accessed locally. Examples include hard disks, CD-ROMs, and floppy disks. Solaris supports four types of disk-based file systems:

- *UNIX File System (UFS)* for hard disks
- *High Sierra File System (HSFS)* for CD-ROMs
- *Personal Computer File System (PCFS)* for floppy disks
- *Universal Disk Format (UDF)* for DVD-ROMs

UFS is the default file system for hard disks in Solaris. Also, know that the preceding pairings are not always absolute. For example, although UFS is typically associated with hard disks, it can also be used on CD-ROMs and floppy disks. Be assured, however, that if someone mentions HSFS, they are discussing CD-ROMs, and likewise with UDF and DVD-ROMs.

If you plan on creating UFS file systems on CD-ROMs or floppy disks, you might run into compatibility problems. Generally speaking, it's best to use HSFS for CD-ROMs, because this format is industry-standard. In other words, an HSFS-based CD-ROM will work as well in a Solaris computer as it will in a Windows-based PC. The same holds true for floppy disks. Although you can use UFS, it's best to stick with PCFS.

Distributed File Systems

A *distributed file system* is also known as a network-based file system. This is because, as you might expect, they are accessed across a network. The network-based file system supported in Solaris 9 is the Network File System (NFS). NFS volumes typically reside on a server and are accessed by clients across the network.

Sharing resources is perhaps the most important reason people create networks in the first place. Understandably then, NFS is a critical topic. Because of its importance, and because it's tested on the second exam, NFS is covered extensively in Chapter 11, "Virtual File Systems and NFS."

For now, though, here's a brief introduction to NFS. The idea is that an administrator can share resources from one centralized location: the server. This saves the hassle of locating commonly used files on every client machine. Clients then attach to the server to access resources. To do this, the client computer needs to create a mount point, which points to the location of the resources on the server. A mount point looks just like any other directory on the local machine. Therefore, the mounted resources and local resources appear identical to users. Of course, as administrators, we know differently. But anything we can do to keep our users' computing lives as easy as possible is a good thing.

Remote NFS resources can be mapped automatically when the client computer boots through a process known as automounting, or AutoFS. AutoFS will automatically mount the remote resource whenever the resource is accessed and keep the connection to the resource alive while the user is in the directory or using files. After a certain period of inactivity, AutoFS will unmount the remote resource. AutoFS is covered in more detail along with NFS in Chapter 11.

Pseudo File Systems

Pseudo file systems, also known as *virtual file systems*, are named this because most of them do not use disk space. Rather, a *pseudo file system* uses system memory to complete their tasks. The notable exceptions are CacheFS and TMPFS, which do use hard disk space. There are ten common virtual file systems, six of which require no administrative attention. Some of the more important virtual file systems are as follows:

Cache File System (CacheFS)   CacheFS is designed to improve performance of remote file systems and of slow disk devices. When CacheFS is activated, it caches information located on remote drives or CD-ROMs into local memory, speeding up access to this data. CacheFS is most useful when used with NFS or with CD-ROM drives.

Loopback File System (LOFS)   You can use LOFS to create a virtual file system within your current file system. For example, you could use LOFS to create a replica of the root in a directory called `/docs/roothd`. Because it's a replica, the `/docs/roothd` directory would look just like the real root (/), including all files and subdirectories.

Mount File System (MNTFS)   The MNTFS file system is a read-only file system that tracks currently mounted file systems within the computer. MNTFS requires no administrative overhead.

Process File System (PROCFS)   PROCFS keeps a list of all active processes running on the system. This list is stored in memory and is referenced by the `/proc` directory.

Swap File System (SWAPFS)   If your computer runs low on physical memory, the kernel can use swap space (located in a SWAPFS file system) as virtual memory. The positive side to this is that when you run low on memory, your system can compensate. The negative is that disk access is significantly slower than physical memory access. If you are using swapping too much, you need to increase the amount of physical memory in your computer. Disk swapping is handled automatically and requires no administrative intervention. SWAPFS is covered extensively in Chapter 11.

Temporary File System (TMPFS)   TMPFS improves system performance by using local memory to store disk reads and writes. Memory access is significantly faster than hard disk access. Although files in TMPFS are lost when the system is powered down or TMPFS is unmounted, you can manipulate those files (located in the /tmp directory) just as you would other system files.

The other virtual file systems include First-In First-Out (FIFOFS), File Descriptors (FDFS), Name (NAMEFS), and Special (SPECFS). None of these file systems require interaction from the administrator to function properly. Also, none of these file systems are currently listed as test objectives.

Managing Disk-Based File Systems

Disk-based file systems are the most commonly used type of file systems in Solaris. So although the other types are important, especially distributed file systems in a networked environment, this section concentrates on creating and managing disk-based file systems.

Earlier in this chapter, four local file system types were introduced: UFS, HSFS, PCFS, and UDF. Of the four, UFS is the most critical and widely used. Accordingly, it gets the most coverage in this chapter.

The UNIX File System (UFS)

The *UNIX File System (UFS)* is the default file system for hard disks in a Solaris environment. In fact, if you are working on a hard disk, it's a safe assumption that the disk is using UFS to store files. UFS has quite a few features that enable it to be a flexible file system.

One of the most important features of UFS is the state flag. Each UFS entity has its own flag to show the status of the file system. The state flags can be clean, stable, active, logging, bad, or unknown. If clean, stable, or logging, then no file system checks are needed. However, if the file system is in another state, system checks can be performed, and the file system repaired if needed.

Other UFS features include support of large file systems (up to 1 terabyte), support for large files (more than 2 gigabytes), and support for 32-bit User ID (UID), Group ID (GID), and device numbers.

UFS reads and writes are stable because UFS can be configured to log transactions before applying them. If the file system were to unexpectedly crash during a disk read or write, the saved log file could be accessed to complete the operation upon reboot. Logging improves file system consistency, and during peak read/write times, can also improve disk I/O performance.

UFS logging is not enabled by default. To enable logging, use the -o logging argument with the mount command. More on the mount command later in this chapter.

UFS Planning

Before creating file systems, plan their usage according to your anticipated needs. If you expect the file system to grow, allocate enough space to accommodate that growth. Planning ahead will save you from deleting and re-creating file systems after the computer is operational, which saves you downtime.

Here are some general guidelines to follow when planning UFS file systems:

- Use as few file systems per disk as possible. Larger file systems tend to reduce file fragmentation, which speeds up disk I/O.

- Distribute the workload among as many physical disks as possible.

- Configure swap space to be evenly distributed among physical disks.

- Consider creating separate file systems for users with specific needs. An example is users who need to store large files. If they have their own file system, they won't crowd out other users.

When creating UFS file systems, the maximum size is 1TB. Files can be as large as 800GB by default. Also, in case you've ever wondered, the maximum number of subdirectories allowed in one directory is limited to 32,767. Although it's an interesting statistic, you won't likely see it on the test or probably ever have to deal with it in real life.

Creating UFS File Systems

Your hard disk must be sliced and formatted before you create a file system. Typically, file systems are created after the hard disks are sliced and formatted during the Solaris installation process. However, if you are adding an additional hard disk, changing your existing partition structure, or performing a system restoration, you might need to manually create file systems. File systems are created with the `newfs` command.

 NOTE   The newfs command is used to create disk-based file systems. Creating virtual file systems is not performed with newfs.

The `newfs` command is actually a front-end to the `mkfs` command. The `newfs` command is easier to use than `mkfs` and is therefore recommended. The syntax for using `newfs` is as follows:

```
# newfs arguments raw_device_name
```

where *arguments* enables you to customize the file system, and *raw_device_name* is the name of the device (slice) on which you wish to create this file system. When specifying the slice on which to create this file system, be sure to specify the right one. Creating a new file system destroys any existing data on the slice.

To create a file system on a hard disk, you must have superuser rights or be able to assume an equivalent role. Here are the steps to create a new file system:

1. Slice and format the hard disk. For information on these procedures, see Chapter 6.

2. Determine the disk and slice that will contain this file system.

   Example: `/dev/rdsk/c0t0d0s4`

3. Create the file system by using `newfs`.

   # **newfs /dev/rdsk/c0t0d0s4**

4. Verify the creation of file system with the `fsck` command.

   # **fsck /dev/rdsk/c0t0d0s4**

After creating the file system, you will need to mount it to make it available for file storage.

> To create a local file system other than a UFS file system, you will need to use the `mkfs -F` *FSType* command, where *FSType* is the file system type (such as HSFS or PCFS) that you wish to create.

Custom UFS File System Parameters

The `newfs` command uses default values for creating file systems. Among the default values are 8KB block size, 1KB fragment size, zero rotational delay, time as the optimization type, and one inode for each 2KB of data space. When creating a file system with `newfs`, you can customize these parameters to fit your needs:

Logical block size   This is the block size that the Solaris kernel uses to read or write data. It differs from the physical block size, which is hardware dependent (and usually 512 bytes). Logical block sizes are typically 4KB or 8KB, with 8KB as the default. For file systems with large files, 8KB is more efficient. Likewise, file systems that typically store smaller files are more efficient with a 4KB block size. You cannot change block size within a file system without deleting and re-creating the file system. One physical hard disk can have multiple file systems with differing logical block sizes.

Fragment size   For files that don't fit exactly into one logical block—and most don't—fragments are used to optimize space. Logical blocks are divided into one, two, four, or eight fragments. As an example, imagine a 9KB file. If you didn't use fragmentation, you would need two logical blocks (16KB total) to store the file, wasting 7KB in space. By using fragments, you can use one whole logical block, plus a 1KB fragment, and not waste any space.

The downside is that the more fragments you allocate and use, the slower your file system will become. Always remember to balance speed with space when optimizing file systems.

Minimum free space   When you create a file system, a certain amount of space is held in reserve. This is because as file systems become full, they become less efficient. If the file system were to totally run out of space, disk reads and writes would become painfully slow.

By default, the reserved free space is between 1 and 10 percent of the total file system space, as determined by the following formula: [(64MB/partition size) × 100] rounded down to the nearest integer. After the file system fills up, only the superuser can write additional data into the reserved minimum free space.

Rotational delay   Also known as gap, rotational delay is the expected minimum time in milliseconds that it takes the processor to complete a data transfer and initiate a new data transfer on the same hard disk. The default rotational delay is zero, because most current hard disks use caching, which essentially renders this option useless.

Optimization type   You can set your file system to optimize for either space or time. If optimized for space, block fragments are utilized heavily. Time optimization results in slightly lower space efficiency but makes the file system as quick as possible.

Some people obsess over space versus time optimization. Realistically, though, you won't likely notice a great deal of difference either way on your computers. The `tunefs` command can be used to change your optimization type.

Number of bytes per inode   Each file on your file system requires one inode. As you might remember from earlier in this chapter, inodes contain information about a file. By default, the file system uses 2048 bytes of storage space per inode for file systems 1GB or smaller, 4096 bytes per inode for file systems 2GB or smaller, 6144 bytes per node for file systems 3GB or smaller, and 8192 bytes per inode for file systems larger than 3GB.

Inodes take up space that would otherwise be reserved for file storage. Consequently, a large number of inodes can decrease storage space.

An abundance of small files and symbolic links can use up inodes quickly. If you run out of inodes, you will not be able to create additional files in that file system, even if space is available. Therefore, it's better to have too many inodes than not enough.

Note that because `newfs` generally does a good job on its own of setting up file systems, these customizations are not usually needed. The most commonly modified parameters are fragment size and number of blocks per inode. Table 7.2 lists some of the arguments for the `newfs` command.

TABLE 7.2   *newfs* Options

Argument	Description
-N	Prints the file system parameters that would be used to create the file system but does not actually create the file system
-b *bsize*	The logical block size, specified in bytes
-f *fragsize*	The fragment size, specified in bytes
-m *free*	The minimum percentage of reserved free disk space to allow
-i *nbpi*	The number of bits per inode to use when calculating how many inodes to create
-o *opt*	The optimization method to use: either space or time
-d *gap*	The expected rotational delay (not usually needed)

Managing UFS File Systems

To effectively manage UFS file systems, you need to be familiar with the commands at your disposal. Some of the more useful commands are listed in Table 7.3.

TABLE 7.3   File System Administration Commands

Command	Description
clri	Clears inodes. Useful for removing files that appear to have no directory home.
df	Displays the number of free disk blocks and files.
du	Shows disk usage.
ff	Lists filenames and statistics for file systems.
fsck	Checks file system integrity and repairs file system damage if possible.
fsdb	Debugs the file system.
fstyp	Displays the file system type for unmounted file systems.
labelit	Provides labels for file systems when they are copied to tape, or for unmounted disk file systems.
mkfs	Creates a new file system.
mount	Mounts local or remote file systems.
mountall	Mounts all file systems listed in the /etc/vfstab file.
umount	Unmounts local and remote file systems.
umountall	Unmounts all file systems listed in the /etc/vfstab file.
volcopy	Creates an image copy of a file system.

Checking File System Consistency

One of UFS' responsibilities is to keep track of used and free data blocks as well as any inodes being used. If the computer's power is unexpectedly terminated or a fatal software error occurs, the UFS database can become misaligned with what's actually stored on the hard disk. In cases like this, it's said that the file system is *inconsistent*.

It's easy to imagine why this could be a serious problem. If the file system doesn't know where to properly locate your files, it could be a long, horrible day. The good news is that file system inconsistencies don't happen very often. Even if inconsistencies do happen, you might not realize it. By default, if the file system has problems, the fsck utility will check the file system during boot and repair all problems it finds.

If your file system is inconsistent, fsck will place all data blocks that don't appear to have a home (the proper directory) into a directory called lost+found. If your computer does not have a lost+found directory, fsck will create one automatically.

How does fsck know whether it needs to check a file system for inconsistencies? The super-block of the file system contains a state flag that displays the status of the file system. Possible values for state flags are FSACTIVE, FSBAD, FSCLEAN, FSSTABLE, and FSLOG. If the file system is FSACTIVE or FSBAD, fsck knows to check the file system. If no problems are found, or fsck can repair the problems, the file system status is changed to either FSCLEAN or FSSTABLE. The FSLOG status indicates that the file system was mounted with UFS logging enabled and is subsequently ignored by fsck.

Of course, if at any time you wish to run fsck manually, you can do so. Just be aware that it will slow down your computer considerably until it's done. Here's what a sample fsck output looks like, complete with an error message:

```
# fsck
** /dev/rdsk/c0t0d0s0
** Currently Mounted on /
** Phase 1 - Check Blocks and Sizes
** Phase 2 - Check Pathnames
** Phase 3 - Check Connectivity
** Phase 4 - Check Reference Counts
** Phase 5 - Check Cyl groups

FILE SYSTEM STATE IN SUPERBLOCK IS WRONG; FIX? y

68781 files, 1683252 used, 332225 free (4441 frags, 40973 blocks, 0.2%
  fragmentation)

FILE SYSTEM IS CURRENTLY MOUNTED.  CONTINUE? y

** /dev/rdsk/c0t0d0s7
** Currently Mounted on /export/home
** Phase 1 - Check Blocks and Sizes
** Phase 2 - Check Pathnames
** Phase 3 - Check Connectivity
** Phase 4 - Check Reference Counts
** Phase 5 - Check Cyl groups
188 files, 274 used, 16673240 free (400 frags, 2084105 blocks, 0.0%
  fragmentation)
#
```

By fixing one problem, fsck might reveal a new problem. But because fsck does not rerun itself until all problems are fixed, you will need to run fsck again manually. Occasionally, you will encounter a problem that fsck cannot resolve. Other commands, including fsdb, ff, and clri, might help you determine the issue or resolve the problem. In the worst-case scenario, you will need to restore the file system from a tape backup.

Restoring a Bad Superblock

If the superblock becomes inaccessible, the file system is rendered useless. However, the super-block can be restored from backup copies located within the file system. The fsck -o b command will attempt to replace the superblock with one of the backups. If this fails, you will need to restore the file system from backup or create a new file system.

Monitoring File System Usage

The df, du, quot, and ls commands can be used to monitor file system usage. If you have one user or a few users abusing their disk space allocation, you can set up disk quotas.

To see how many 1024-byte blocks each user on the local file system is using, issue the **quot -a** command. Unfortunately, the quot command works only on local UFS file systems.

 **Real World Scenario**

Running Out of Disk Space

A group of engineers at your company has been assigned to a critical research project. Because of the sensitivity and importance of the project, management has instructed you to create a slice on your Solaris server exclusively for the engineers' use. The engineers estimate that they will need approximately 1GB of storage space. You have some free space on a 40GB non-system disk, so you decide to create the slice there.

You execute the following command to create the file system on the 1GB partition:

```
# newfs -b 8192 -f 1024 -i 8192 -o space /dev/rdsk/c0t2d0s4
```

You mount the partition and verify that the engineers have access to the volume.

A few weeks later, one of the engineers calls, saying that they have run out of disk space and need you to increase the size of the partition. When you investigate, you discover that the file system still has nearly 40 percent of its total space available. What happened?

The file system has run out of inodes, meaning that no new files can be created in the file system. Perhaps this happened because of how you created the file system. Instead of allowing the default of 2KB per inode on a 1GB or smaller file system, you created a file system that allocated one inode per 8KB of disk space (with the -i 8192 option). Now the question becomes, what's the easiest way to fix this problem?

Make a backup of the data. You're going to need to delete this file system, re-create a new one, and then restore the original data to the new file system. This time, allow the default setting for bits per inode. Also, because you're re-creating this file system in the middle of the project, reconfirm disk space with the engineers. They might have discovered that they will need more disk space, and because you're re-creating anyway, asking now might save you extra work in the long run.

Mounting and Unmounting

To access files in a file system, you must *mount* the file system. The process of mounting a file system connects the file system with a directory in the hierarchical directory structure, known as a *mount point*. The root file system is always mounted by default and must be mounted in order to access any files on the computer.

Four commands that you will use for mounting and unmounting file systems are mount, mountall, umount, and umountall.

Generally speaking, mount point directories do not contain files. As an example, imagine that you are going to mount a custom file system called /workfile into the mount point /docs. After you mount /workfile, any files that were in the /docs directory will be obscured. No permanent damage is done to them. In fact, if you were to unmount /workfile, all the original files in /docs would be available again. It's just that when /workfile is mounted, you can't get to the original /docs files or subdirectories.

The /etc/mnttab (mount table) file keeps a record of all mounted file systems within your computer. You cannot edit this file because it's read-only, but you can display its contents:

```
# cat /etc/mnttab
/dev/dsk/c0t0d0s0   /  ufs rw,intr,largefiles, ...
/proc   /proc   proc    dev=3b40000     1031950360
mnttab  /etc/mnttab     mntfs   dev=3c00000     1031950360
fd      /dev/fd fd      rw,suid,dev=3c40000     1031950362
swap    /var/run        tmpfs   xattr,dev=1     1031950363
swap    /tmp    tmpfs   xattr,dev=2     1031950367
/dev/dsk/c0t0d0s7 /export/home  ufs      rw,intr,largefiles ...
-hosts  /net    autofs  indirect,nosuid,ignore,nobrowse,...
auto_home       /home   autofs  indirect,ignore,nobrowse,...
-xfn    /xfn    autofs  indirect,ignore,dev=3dc0003     1031950370
Q-Sol:vold(pid247)  /vol nfs ignore,dev=3d80001       1031950379
/vol/dev/diskette0/unnamed_floppy       /floppy/unnamed_floppy  pcfs⤶
    rw,nohidden,nofoldcase,dev=16c0002      1031953542
#
```

Another critical file exists to assist in mounting file systems, and that's the /etc/vfstab (virtual file system table) file. This file controls the automatic mounting of file systems when Solaris is booted or when the mountall command is manually issued. This saves the hassle of manually mounting each file system every time you reboot Solaris.

Unlike /etc/mnttab, the /etc/vfstab file can be manually edited. In fact, if you want a file system to be mounted automatically, it's suggested that you do add an entry to the /etc/ vfstab file. To add an entry, you will need to know where the file system is physically located, the name of the mount point, the type of file system, whether you want the file system to mount automatically, and any mount options. Here is a sample /etc/vfstab file:

```
# cat /etc/vfstab
#device         device          mount   FS   fsck mount   mount
#to mount       to fsck         point   type pass at boot options
#
```

```
fd                      -               /dev/fd  fd    -   no    -
/proc                   -               /proc    proc  -   no    -
/dev/dsk/c0t0d0s1 -                     -        swap  -   no    -
/dev/dsk/c0t0d0s0 /dev/rdsk/c0t0d0s0    /        ufs   1   no    -
/dev/dsk/c0t0d0s7 /dev/rdsk/c0t0d0s7    /files   ufs   2   yes   -
swap                    -               /tmp     tmpfs -   yes   -
#
```

One thing that many new administrators find odd is that the root (/) and /usr file systems have the mount at boot field set to no. These file systems are obviously critical, so why are they set this way? It's because the Solaris kernel mounts these file systems during the boot sequence, before the mountall command is issued. Table 7.4 describes the fields in /etc/vfstab.

TABLE 7.4   /etc/vfstab Field

Field	Description
Device to mount	Provides the block device name for local UFS file systems or swap slices, the resource name for a remote file system, or a directory for a virtual file system.
Device to fsck	The raw device name that corresponds to the UFS file system defined in the device to mount field. For read-only, remote, and virtual file systems, this field will contain a dash (–).
mount point	The directory in which to mount the file system.
FS type	Names the type of file system.
fsck pass	Used by the fsck command to determine whether to check the file system. A dash (–) means that the file system is not checked. If the value is 0, UFS file systems are ignored, but others are checked. A value greater than 0 means that the file system is always checked.
mount at boot	A yes or no value, indicating whether the file system should be automatically mounted at boot.
mount options	A list of options, separated by commas. A dash (–) indicates no options.

Mounting File Systems

Before moving on to mounting a file system, take a moment to reflect on what a file system really is. Yes, it's a method in which to store files, but more importantly in this context, a file system is a collection of files and directories.

You have already learned that file systems need to be mounted in order to be accessed, and that file systems are mounted to a directory called a mount point. So when you mount a file system, you are inserting a directory tree, however large, into a certain place in your existing file system.

There are three ways to mount file systems. One is to use the mount command, another is to use the mountall command, and the last is to add an entry into the /etc/vfstab file. If you need to mount the file system frequently, it's much easier to use the /etc/vfstab file, or perhaps AutoFS for remote file systems. For file systems that are mounted infrequently, the mount command should be sufficient.

The mount and mountall commands will not mount a read/write file system that contains known inconsistencies. Run fsck to fix the file system before mounting.

To use mount, you must be the superuser or be able to assume an equivalent role. The mount command has quite a number of options, which will be covered shortly. Here's the syntax for mount:

mount -F *FSType* **[***generic_options***] [-o** *specific_options***]** *device_name*
  mount_point

You have to love a command that has both generic options and specific options. Specific options are invoked by using the -o switch and are separated by commas (with no spaces). If there's a conflict between a generic and a specific option, the specific option overrides the generic one. This can all be a bit confusing, so after describing the options, we'll go over a few examples. Table 7.5 displays some generic mount options.

TABLE 7.5 Generic *mount* Arguments

Argument	Description
-F *FSType*	Specifies the file system type to mount.
-m	Mounts the file system but does not create an entry in /etc/mnttab.
-O	Overlay mount. This enables you to mount a file system over an existing mount. The overwritten file system will not be accessible while the new file system is mounted.
-p	Prints a list of mounted file systems in /etc/vfstab format. Must be used alone.
-r	Mounts the file system as read-only.
-v	Prints the list of mounted file systems in verbose format. Must be used alone.

Specific mount options, as invoked with -o, are listed in Table 7.6. These mount options are available only if they correspond to the file system type specified by the -F *FSType* variable.

TABLE 7.6   *mount -o* Options

Option	File System	Description
bg | fg	NFS	Specifies whether to retry the mount operation in the background or foreground if mounting fails the first time. Foreground is the default.
hard | soft	NFS	Specifies how to proceed if the server does not respond. The soft option returns an error, and hard retires the request until the server responds. The default is hard.
retry=*n*	NFS	Retries the mount operation if it fails. The variable *n* determines the number of times to retry.
largefiles | nolargefiles	UFS	The default is largefiles, which means the file system can contain files larger than 2GB. The nolargefiles option means that the file system cannot contain files larger than 2GB.
logging | nologging	UFS	Enables or disables UFS logging on the file system. The default is nologging. Enabling logging does take up a small amount of additional disk space but helps keep the file system consistent.
remount	All	This option changes features of an already mounted file system. It can be used with any options except ro.
ro | rw	CacheFS, NFS, PCFS, UFS, HSFS	Read-only versus read/write. The default is read/write, except for HSFS, which is read-only.
suid | nosuid	CacheFS, HSFS, NFS, UFS	Enables or disables the use of SetUID. The default is suid.

As promised, here are some examples of using the mount command. Perhaps the easiest one is to check the currently mounted file systems. To do that, just type **mount** and press Enter. If you wish to mount a file system that's listed in the /etc/vfstab file, all you need is the mount command and the name of the mount point. For example, to mount the file system /files (as shown in the earlier /etc/vfstab example), you would type:

```
# mount /files
```

You could also use the name in the device to mount field (/dev/dsk/c0t0d0s7 in this case), but generally speaking, using the mount point name is easier.

Also, don't forget that you're mounting a file system into a directory. If the mount point directory does not exist, you must create that directory before attempting to mount the file system. Here's an example of mounting the device /dev/dsk/c0t0d0s4 in a directory named /finance (and the /finance directory does not yet exist):

```
# mkdir /finance
# mount /dev/dsk/c0t0d0s4 /finance
```

If you wanted to mount the same file system but make it read-only, you could use:

```
# mount -o ro /dev/dsk/c0t0d0s4 /finance
```

Or, you could mount the file system as read/write (which is the default, but the argument is listed for illustrative purposes anyway), enable logging, and disable large files:

```
# mount -o rw,logging,nolargefiles /dev/dsk/c0t0d0s4 /finance
```

Here's one more example. It's for mounting an NFS file system from a directory named docs on the gandalf server, into your local /finance directory.

```
# mount -F nfs gandalf:/docs /finance
```

I realize that we haven't covered NFS in any detail yet, but I also wanted to provide a quick example in case it pops up on the Part I test. It shouldn't, but you never know.

Unmounting File Systems

Because mounting a file system makes its resources available, it logically follows that unmounting a file system makes its resources unavailable. When you *unmount*, the file system is removed from the mount point and removes the entry from the /etc/mnttab file.

You might want to unmount a file system for a variety of reasons. One example is that the files are outdated and need to be replaced with newer files (such as an updated software package). Another example is system administration, such as backups. Backups cannot be performed on mounted file systems. When you shut down Solaris, all file systems are automatically unmounted.

To unmount file systems, you can use the umount and umountall commands. The umount command requires you to specify the file system to unmount, whereas umountall unmounts all file systems listed in the /etc/vfstab file.

To unmount a file system, you must be the superuser or assume an equivalent role. Also, the file system must not be busy. File systems are considered busy if a user is accessing a directory in the file system, a program has an open file in the file system, or the file system is being shared. You might need to use the fuser command to list and/or stop all processes that are accessing the file system.

Although umount and umountall will not unmount busy file systems, you can force a busy file system to unmount by using umount -f.

Managing Removable Media

Accessing removable media, such as CD-ROMs and floppy disks, is handled differently than accessing fixed media, such as hard disks or even networked resources. Traditionally, the management of removable media has fallen under the umbrella title of *volume management*.

In Solaris 9, volume management has been improved to recognize more media types, including DVD-ROMs and USB Zip and Jaz drives. These are in addition to the already-supported floppy disks and CD-ROMs. Another major improvement for Solaris 9 is the inclusion of the rmformat command. The `rmformat` command replaces the old `fdformat` command and has improved features over its predecessor.

Volume Management

The question, then, is: why is volume management of removable media such a big deal? There are a couple of reasons. First, you must have superuser rights to mount and unmount volumes. You certainly don't want to have to give regular users superuser rights just to use a floppy disk or CD-ROM. Second, removing mounted media causes Solaris to panic. If you were to remove a hard disk that was mounted, Solaris would give you error messages. The same applies to removing a mounted floppy disk or CD-ROM.

There was an obvious need for a mechanism to control removable media, including mounting, unmounting, and proper security access, without causing problems for the operating environment. The mechanism was developed and it was called volume manager. Volume manager works through its own daemon, `vold`. To summarize, Volume Manager provides three major benefits:

- Users can access removable media without needing superuser privileges.

- Removable media is automatically mounted, simplifying use.

- Administrators can grant other computers on the network automatic access to removable media located in your computer.

`vold` automatically mounts CD-ROM and DVD-ROM disks when they are inserted into your computer. If you wish to access files on a floppy disk or removable hard disk (Zip or Jaz drive), you will need to insert the disk and type **volcheck** at a command prompt.

If you don't want your computer to automatically mount removable media devices, you can stop the `vold` service. To do this, log on as the superuser or assume an equivalent role, and execute the following command:

```
# /etc/init.d/volmgt stop
```

To restart the volume manager, execute:

```
# /etc/init.d/volmgt start
```

Accessing Removable Media

To access files on removable media, you must insert the media and mount it. If `vold` is enabled, mounting is easy. For floppy disks and Zip and Jaz drives, insert the disk and type **volcheck** at a command prompt. For CD-ROMs, DVD-ROMs, and PCMCIA cards, just insert the media and wait a few seconds for `vold` to mount the media. If you have disabled `vold`, you will need to mount the media manually by using the **mount** command.

PCMCIA (Personal Computer Memory Card International Association) cards, also known as PC Cards, are removable expansion cards for laptops. Typically, PCMCIA devices are hot swappable.

After your removable media is inserted and mounted, accessing files on it is just like accessing any other files in your directory tree. You just need to know where to find them. Solaris makes finding files easy, by providing the following base directories:

- Files on the first floppy disk drive will be located in /floppy.

- Removable hard disk files will be in either /rmdisk/zip0 or /rmdisk/jaz0.

- Files on the first CD-ROM will be in /cdrom.

- Files on the first DVD-ROM will be in /dvd.

- PCMCIA files will be located in /pcmem.

 These directories will not exist by default unless you have the required device. For example, if you don't have a Zip or Jaz drive, you will not have an /rmdisk directory.

If you have a floppy disk named labdocs, the full pathname to the disk would be /floppy/labdocs, or alternately, /floppy/floppy0 if it's in the first floppy disk drive (/floppy/floppy1 for the second disk drive, and so on). Knowing the general location /floppy/floppy0 is handy if you don't know the name of your disk, or the disk has no volume label.

The naming convention indicated for floppy drives holds true for multiple instances of other removable device drives as well. For example, the first CD-ROM is /cdrom/cdrom0, the second CD-ROM device is /cdrom/cdrom1, the third CD-ROM device is /cdrom/cdrom2, and so on.

File management for removable devices is just like file management in other directories on a hard disk. The management commands you are used to, such as ls, cp, rm, and cat, work just as they would on files on a hard disk. You can even run fsck on floppy disks.

After you have finished accessing the removable media, you can eject it. Although for CD-ROMs, DVD-ROMs, and floppy disks, you can just press the eject button on the device, it's highly recommended you first alert vold that you are going to eject the device. Execute the eject command, followed by the device you wish to eject:

```
# eject cdrom
```

Formatting Removable Media

Formatting removable media is done with the rmformat command. The rmformat command replaces the old fdformat command, although fdformat is still available in Solaris 9.

One of the new features of rmformat is the ability to provide read/write protection on selective rewritable media such as Zip and Jaz drives. The read/write protection can also include a password. The rmformat command has three options:

quick This command formats the media without certifying the tracks on the media.

long This formats the removable media completely and certifies all tracks.

force This formats completely without any user confirmation. If the media is password protected, the password is cleared and the media is formatted. If there is no password protection, a long format is performed.

NOTE Floppy disks formatted as UFS on a SPARC computer cannot be used on an IA computer, and floppy disks formatted as UFS on an IA computer cannot be used on a SPARC computer. The same holds true for formatted PCMCIA memory cards.

The `rmformat` options are initiated by the `-F` switch, as in `rmformat -F force /floppy/ floppy0`. The `-b volname` option enables you to provide a volume name.

Floppy disks and PCMCIA memory cards can be formatted with the UFS or PCFS file systems. CD-ROMs can be formatted in either UFS or HSFS, but HSFS is recommended for compatibility reasons.

Summary

This chapter covered critical details about file systems in Solaris 9. First, you looked at what file systems are, new file system features in Solaris 9, default file systems, and file system structure.

Then, you examined the three major classifications of file systems: disk based, distributed, and pseudo. Disk-based file systems are located on the local computer and reside on the local hard disk or removable media. Distributed file systems are located over the network. Solaris uses NFS as its distributed file system. Pseudo or virtual file systems are typically local in nature but generally don't use disk space. Instead, they exist in physical memory.

From there, you moved on to managing local UFS file systems. This chapter covered planning and creating UFS file systems, as well as custom UFS file system parameters. You then looked at a critical management tool, `fsck`, before learning about mounting and unmounting file systems.

Finally, the chapter concluded with coverage of removable media and volume management. It discussed how to access, format, and manage removable media, such as floppy disks, CD-ROMs, and PCMCIA memory devices.

Exam Essentials

Know the four types of blocks in a file system and what each type is used for.   The boot block is used for booting off of a file system. The superblock contains information about the file system, including size parameters. Inodes contain information about files. Data blocks hold files.

Know the four disk-based file systems.   They are the UNIX File System (UFS), Personal Computer File System (PCFS), High Sierra File System (HSFS), and Universal Disk Format (UDF).

Understand the differences between local, distributed, and pseudo file systems.   Local file systems are on local media, such as hard disks, floppy disks, and CD-ROMs. Distributed file systems (namely NFS) are accessed over the network. Pseudo file systems generally reside in memory, not on hard disk space.

Know how to create new UFS file systems. UFS file systems can be created with the `newfs` and `mkfs` commands.

Understand what a shortage of inodes could mean. If your file system does not have enough inodes, you might not be able to create files even though space is still available in the file system. It's better to have too many inodes, even if it is inefficient, than to have not enough inodes.

Know how to check file system consistency and repair problems. File system consistency is checked with the `fsck` command. This command will also repair problems that it encounters.

Understand the purpose of the `/etc/mnttab` file. The mount table keeps track of all mounted file systems on your computer.

Understand the purpose of the `/etc/vfstab` file. The virtual file system table tells Solaris which file systems to mount automatically at boot.

Know how to mount and unmount file systems. Mounting is done with the `mount` and `mountall` commands. Unmounting is performed with `umount` or `umountall`.

Know how to make Solaris check for a floppy disk when you insert it. To have volume manager scan the floppy disk drive, execute the `volcheck` command.

Key Terms

Before you take the exam, be certain you are familiar with the following terms:

boot block	Personal Computer File System (PCFS)
distributed file system	pseudo file system
file system	superblock
High Sierra File System (HSFS)	Universal Disk Format (UDF)
inconsistent	UNIX File System (UFS)
inode	unmount
mount	virtual file systems
mount point	volume management

Commands Used in This Chapter

The following list contains a summary of all the commands introduced in this chapter:

Command	Description
clri	Clears inodes.
df	Displays the number of free disk blocks and files.
du	Shows disk usage.
eject	Ejects removable media.
fdformat	Formats removable media. Replaced by rmformat in Solaris 9.
ff	Lists filenames and statistics for file systems.
fsck	Checks file system integrity and repairs file system damage if possible.
fsdb	Debugs the file system.
fstyp	Displays the file system type for unmounted file systems.
fuser	Checks to see which users, if any, are accessing a resource.
labelit	Provides labels for file systems when they are copied to tape, or for unmounted disk file systems.
mkfs	Creates a new file system.
mount	Mounts local or remote file systems.
mountall	Mounts all file systems listed in the /etc/vfstab file.
newfs	Creates new file systems. Is a friendly front-end to the mkfs command.
quot	Displays user's file system usage.
rmformat	Formats removable media. To be used instead of fdformat.
umount	Unmounts local and remote file systems.
umountall	Unmounts all file systems listed in the /etc/vfstab file.
volcheck	Forces volume manager to check the floppy drive for newly inserted floppy disks.
volcopy	Creates an image copy of a file system.

Review Questions

1. You are the Solaris administrator for your company. You are planning on creating a PCFS file system on a local device named c0t0d0s4. Which of the following commands should you execute?

   A. `newfs -F pcfs /dev/dsk/c0t0d0s4`

   B. `newfs -F pcfs /dev/rdsk/c0t0d0s4`

   C. `mkfs -F pcfs /dev/dsk/c0t0d0s4`

   D. `mkfs -F pcfs /dev/rdsk/c0t0d0s4`

2. You are the Solaris administrator for your network. One of your servers is not mounting a file system automatically at boot, even though it should. Which file do you check to see whether this is configured properly?

   A. /etc/mnttab

   B. /etc/inittab

   C. /etc/ufstab

   D. /etc/vfstab

   E. /etc/fstab

3. You are the Solaris administrator for your company. You will be formatting a new hard disk and creating a file system on it. If you use the default options when creating the file system, which file system will be used?

   A. UDF

   B. UFS

   C. PCFS

   D. HSFS

   E. NFS

4. You are the Solaris instructor for your company. When describing file structure to a group of students, which of the following items do you tell them stores a file's name?

   A. Superblock

   B. Inode

   C. Data block

   D. Directory

5. You are the Solaris server administrator for your company. You want to create a UFS file system on a device named c0t0d0s5. Which of the following commands should you use?

    A. newfs /dev/rdsk/c0t0d0s5

    B. newfs /dev/dsk/c0t0d0s5

    C. newfs /dev/c0t0d0s5

    D. newfs /c0t0d0s5

6. Which of the following are valid types of file systems supported in Solaris 9? (Choose all that apply.)

    A. UFS

    B. VFS

    C. NFS

    D. DFS

    E. UDF

    F. FAT

7. You are the Solaris administrator for your company. One of your users has inserted a floppy disk into his machine, but he cannot seem to access the files on the disk. What do you tell the user to do in order to mount the floppy disk?

    A. Wait a few more seconds, and volume manager will mount it automatically.

    B. The disk is already mounted. The user needs to look in the /floppy directory for his files.

    C. Type **vold** at the command prompt to make volume manager mount the floppy disk.

    D. Type **volcheck** at the command prompt to make volume manager mount the floppy disk.

8. You are the Solaris server administrator on your network. You have just created a new file system on a local hard disk. Which of the following commands can you use to verify the creation of the local file system?

    A. newfs

    B. mkfs

    C. fsck

    D. fsdb

9. You are the Solaris administrator for your network. You are going to mount a new local file system on one of your servers. The file system is a UFS file system, will have logging enabled, and will be able to store files larger than 2GB in size. The mount point for the /dev/dsk/c0t3d0s2 device will be /trainers. Which of the following commands should you execute to mount this file system?

    A. mount -F ufs -o logging,largefiles /dev/dsk/c0t3d0s2 /trainers

    B. mount -F ufs -r -o logging,largefiles /dev/dsk/c0t3d0s2 /trainers

    C. mount -F ufs -o logging,largefiles /trainers /dev/dsk/c0t3d0s2

    D. mount -F ufs -r -o logging,largefiles /trainers /dev/dsk/c0t3d0s2

10. You are the Solaris administrator for your network. On all your servers, you have specified a logical block size of 8KB and the default block fragment size. You are going to store a file that is 9KB in length. Which of the following accurately describes how the file is stored?

    A. The file uses one 8KB block, and the remaining 1KB is stored in block fragments.

    B. The file uses two 8KB blocks, but the remainder of the second block is usable by another file.

    C. The file uses two 8KB blocks, and the remainder of the second block is unusable by other files.

    D. The file uses one 8KB block and 1KB of a second block. After the 1KB is allocated, the remainder of the block (7KB) is divided into logical block fragments usable by other files.

11. You are the Solaris administrator for your company. Because one of your workstations is constantly running low on physical memory, it's required to use virtual memory. Which file system is being used when the computer accesses virtual memory?

    A. SWAPFS

    B. TMPFS

    C. VMFS

    D. Virtual memory is not associated with one specific file system.

12. You are the Solaris administrator for your network. You are presented with the following information from an /etc/vfstab file, taken from one of your workstations:

    ```
    # cat /etc/vfstab
    #device            device           mount     FS    fsck  mount   mount
    #to mount          to fsck          point     type  pass  at boot options
    #
    fd                 -                /dev/fd   fd    -     no      -
    /proc              -                /proc     proc  -     no      -
    /dev/dsk/c0t0d0s1  -                -         swap  -     no      -
    /dev/dsk/c0t0d0s0  /dev/rdsk/c0t0d0s0  /      ufs   1     no      -
    /dev/dsk/c0t0d0s7  /dev/rdsk/c0t0d0s7  /files ufs   2     yes     -
    swap               -                /tmp      tmpfs -     yes     -
    ```

    Based on the information presented, which of the following statements are true? (Choose all that apply.)

    A. The device /dev/dsk/c0t0d0s0 will not be mounted automatically at boot.

    B. The device /dev/dsk/c0t0d0s7 will be mounted automatically at boot into the /files mount point.

    C. The /dev/rdsk/c0t0d0s0 and /dev/rdsk/c0t0d0s7 file systems will be checked by fsck automatically at boot.

    D. The /dev/rdsk/c0t0d0s0 file system will be checked by fsck automatically at boot, and the /dev/rdsk/c0t0d0s7 file system will be checked by fsck only if a previous problem with the file system is reported.

13. You are the Solaris administrator for your network. You need to find a list of all currently mounted file systems on one of your servers. Which file holds this information?

   A. `/etc/inittab`

   B. `/etc/mnttab`

   C. `/etc/vfstab`

   D. `/etc/mount`

14. You are the Solaris administrator for your company. Your root file system has a directory named `/acctdocs`, which contains three files and one subdirectory. You execute the following command:

   `# mount /dev/rdsk/c0t0d0s4 /acctdocs`

   Which of the following statements is true?

   A. The three files and one subdirectory located in `/acctdocs` are destroyed.

   B. The three files located in `/acctdocs` will be available, but the subdirectory will be not be available until `/dev/rdsk/c0t0d0s4` is unmounted.

   C. The three files located in `/acctdocs` will not be available until `/dev/rdsk/c0t0d0s4` is unmounted, but the subdirectory will be available.

   D. The three files and one subdirectory located in `/acctdocs` will not be available until `/dev/rdsk/c0t0d0s4` is unmounted.

15. You are the Solaris administrator for your company. For security reasons, your company wants to disable the use of SetUID on the `/app02` directory, which is the mount point for the `/dev/dsk/c0t1d0s5`. The file system is currently unmounted. Which command should you execute to mount the device with the required option?

   A. `mount –F ufs –o suid /dev/dsk/c0t1d0s5 /app02`

   B. `mount –F ufs –o suid /app02 /dev/dsk/c0t1d0s5`

   C. `mount –F ufs –o nosuid /dev/dsk/c0t1d0s5 /app02`

   D. `mount –F ufs –o nosuid /app02 /dev/dsk/c0t1d0s5`

16. You are the Solaris network manager for your company. One of your developers has just had a second CD-ROM drive installed into her workstation. She is attempting to access files located on a CD-ROM in the second drive but cannot seem to locate them. Where should you tell her to look?

   A. `/cdrom/cdrom0`

   B. `/cdrom/cdrom1`

   C. `/cdrom/cdrom2`

   D. If there is a CD-ROM in the first CD-ROM drive, its being mounted will override the mounting of the second CD-ROM drive, making files on the second CD-ROM drive inaccessible.

17. You are the network administrator for your company. You are going to create a file system on a CD-ROM and you want that CD-ROM to work in Windows-based PCs. Which file system should you create on that CD-ROM?

    A. UFS

    B. PCFS

    C. HSFS

    D. UDF

18. You are a Solaris administrator for your company. You recently unmounted two file systems to perform complete backups. Now you want to mount them as easily as possible. Another administrator suggests using the `mountall` command. Which of the following statements accurately describes the function of the `mountall` command?

    A. `mountall` mounts all file systems known to the Solaris computer.

    B. `mountall` mounts all local file systems on the Solaris computer.

    C. `mountall` mounts all file systems listed in the `/etc/inittab` file.

    D. `mountall` mounts all file systems listed in the `/etc/mnttab` file.

    E. `mountall` mounts all file systems listed in the `/etc/vfstab` file.

19. Which of the following types of blocks contains the size of the file system, the disk's VTOC, and the file system state flag?

    A. Boot block

    B. Superblock

    C. Inode

    D. Data block

20. You are the Solaris administrator for your company. One of your network users has recently had an Iomega Zip drive installed in her machine so she can back up critical project files personally. She has inserted the Zip disk, copied the necessary files to the disk, and now needs to remove the disk from the drive. She knows that Zip drives do not have a manual eject button. Based on a default device configuration, what command do you tell her to type to eject the Zip disk?

    A. `eject /rmdisk/zip0`

    B. `eject /rmdisk/zip1`

    C. `eject /rdisk/zip0`

    D. `eject /rdisk/zip1`

    E. `eject /rmdisk/iomega0`

    F. `eject /rmdisk/iomega1`

Answers to Review Questions

1. D. If you wish to create a file system that's anything other than UFS, you must use the mkfs -F command. Also, when using mkfs, like newfs, you must supply the raw disk name. Raw device names are located in the /dev/rdsk directory.

2. D. The /etc/vfstab (virtual file system table) file maintains a list of known file systems that are to be mounted during the boot process, or if the mountall command is issued.

3. B. The default file system for hard disks in Solaris 9 is the UNIX File System (UFS). UDF is used for DVD-ROMs, PCFS for floppy disks, HSFS for CD-ROMs, and NFS for distributed file systems.

4. D. The directory stores filenames. Inodes store critical information about files but do not store filenames. The superblock contains critical file system information, not data about individual files. Data blocks store data belonging to files, but not filenames.

5. A. The newfs command is used to create file systems. When using the newfs command, you need to supply the raw device name. Raw device names are located in the /dev/rdsk directory.

6. A, C, E. The UFS, NFS, and UDF file systems are all supported in Solaris 9. VFS and DFS are not valid file systems. FAT is technically supported in Solaris, but it's implemented as PCFS.

7. D. The volcheck command makes volume manager scan removable disk drives (floppy disk drives and/or Jaz and Zip drives) for new disks. After volcheck is run, the user's files should be in the /floppy directory.

8. C. The fsck command can be used to verify file system creation, as well as check the file system's consistency. The newfs and mkfs commands are for creating file systems. The fsdb command will debug an existing file system.

9. A. The -o option allows you to specify UFS-specific options such as logging and enabling large file storage. The -r option is not called for, because this would make the file system read-only. When mounting a file system, the device is listed before the mount point. Therefore, the first answer is the correct choice.

10. A. The file system will attempt to optimize space as much as possible. Therefore, one entire block will be used, and the rest of the file will be stored in a logical block fragment. As nice as it would be, block fragments are not allocated dynamically by the file system. They are created when the file system is created. Therefore, the last answer is incorrect.

11. A. When a computer uses virtual memory, the process of moving information into and out of virtual memory is called swapping. In Solaris, the swap space is part of the SWAPFS file system. TMPFS is another valid file system, but it's used for temporary file storage, not as additional memory. VMFS does not exist.

12. B, C. The root file system is always automatically mounted during the boot process. It has a no value for mount at boot only because the kernel mounts the file system before mountall is run to mount all other file systems. The device /dev/dsk/c0t0d0s7 has the mount point of /files. Because the fsck pass value is higher than 0 for /dev/rdsk/c0t0d0s0 and /dev/dsk/rc0t0d0s7, they will both be automatically checked by fsck at boot.

13. B.   The /etc/mnttab file contains information on all mounted file systems. The /etc/inittab file defines the initial boot state for the system. The /etc/vfstab file lists file systems that are to be mounted at boot. The /etc/mount file does not exist by default.

14. D.   If you mount a file system into a directory that contains files and/or subdirectories, those files and subdirectories will not be available until the file system is unmounted. There is no permanent damage done to the existing files or subdirectories.

15. C.   The -o option enables you to specify UFS-specific options such as disabling the use of SetUID. When mounting a file system, the device is listed before the mount point. Therefore, the third answer is the correct choice.

16. B.   The second CD-ROM drive has the device name /cdrom/cdrom1. She could also access the second CD-ROM as /cdrom/*volname* if she knew the volume name of the disc in the second CD-ROM.

17. C.   The High Sierra File System (HSFS) is an industry-standard file system for CD-ROM disks. CD-ROMs can also have UFS file systems, but UFS is not recognizable to Windows-based PCs. PCFS is for floppy disks, and UDF is for DVD-ROMs.

18. E.   The mountall command mounts all file systems located in the /etc/vfstab file. Although it's true that mountall might happen to mount all local file systems, or even all known file systems, that doesn't have to be the case. The /etc/inittab file contains information on booting Solaris, including the default run level. The /etc/mnttab file contains a list of all currently mounted file systems. After running mountall, you could check /etc/mnttab to see whether all appropriate file systems are mounted.

19. B.   The superblock contains the size of the file system, the disk label (Volume Table of Contents), cylinder group size, number of data blocks present, the summary data block, file system state (state flag), and the pathname of the last mount point.

20. A.   The eject command is used to eject media from devices that do not have a manual eject button. The default device name for the first Zip drive in a computer is /rmdisk/zip0.

Chapter

8

Managing Printers and Controlling Processes

SOLARIS 9 EXAM OBJECTIVES COVERED IN THIS CHAPTER:

✓ Describe the purpose, features, and functionality of printer fundamentals, including print management tools, printer configuration types, Solaris LP print service, LP print service directory structure, and the Solaris OE printing process.

✓ Explain how to configure printer classes, set the default printer, change the default printer class, remove a printer's configuration, start the LP print service, and stop the LP print service using the appropriate commands.

✓ Given a scenario, identify the appropriate commands to specify a destination printer, accept and reject print jobs, enable and disable printers, and move print jobs.

✓ Explain how to view system processes, clear hung processes, schedule an automatic one-time execution of a command and the automatic recurring execution of a command.

Printing is something most people do on a daily basis. Whether it's printing a report at work or e-mails at home, using a printer is probably a significant part of your computing experience. When it comes to networking computers, printing takes on even more importance. Networking is all about sharing resources, and printers are the most commonly shared hardware resource.

This chapter starts by discussing printing terminology and printing fundamentals. Even though you probably print regularly, you might not know what goes on behind the scenes or the proper terms for printing components. After you examine the essentials, you will move on to installing and managing printers in a Solaris environment. Our printing discussion will conclude with troubleshooting tips.

Printing is one of the most common processes regularly started and stopped on computers, and this chapter also covers processes in detail. Many people think of processes as just applications, but there's much more to processes than what you see running on your computer. You will learn what a process is, how to manage processes, and how to deal with misbehaving processes. Processes can be conveniently scheduled to run automatically, and this chapter discusses that as well.

Managing Printing

The basics of printing are pretty straightforward. You click a button or enter a command, and you receive output on a physical print device. At least that's what you hope happens. (Just in case it doesn't, printer troubleshooting is covered at the end of this "Managing Printing" section.) This chapter quickly moves beyond the basics and into detailed descriptions of the Solaris printing process.

Before getting into printing fundamentals, though, take a look at a few advantages to printing in Solaris 9:

- The print scheduler, lpsched, no longer starts automatically on computers that do not have a local printer installed. This doesn't affect clients printing on a network; it just makes Solaris a bit more efficient by not running a service unless it's necessary (which lpsched isn't, unless a local printer is installed).

- Solaris 9 supports the use of USB printers and comes equipped with a USB printer driver.

- Printers can be managed by a name service, such as LDAP, NIS, or NIS+. This makes it easier to locate network printers if you are using one of these naming services.

Printing in Solaris is based around the *Line Printer (LP) print service*. The LP print service provides a standard set of UNIX-based print commands and enables you to manage printers both locally and through a name service. Solaris 9 also comes with the graphical Solaris Print

Manager. Even though Solaris Print Manager enables you to manage both local and networked printers as well, the commands offered by the LP print service give you the best flexibility when managing printers.

Solaris 9 does not provide support for print servers defined as s5 (the System V print protocol), as previous releases of Solaris did.

Understanding Printing Fundamentals

To successfully print, a variety of items must be configured correctly. Of course, you need a printer, which is a physical hardware device. The printer must also be attached to some sort of printing manager, which is called the *print server*. Print servers can be a computer, such as a Solaris or other UNIX-based machine. A print server can also be integrated as a service into a printer's network card or can be a small hardware device that's attached to printers or the network. Typically, the print server is the device to which the printer is physically connected. Regardless of its physical location, the print server manages the printer. For the sake of ease, this chapter assumes that print servers are Solaris-based unless otherwise specified. Solaris print servers use the BSD protocol, which includes support for SVR4 (LP) print standards as well as BSD lpd-based print standards.

In a networked environment, you will have one or more print servers and many print clients. A *print client* is any machine that prints to the print server. In a stand-alone environment, the print client is the same computer as the print server.

Print clients do not have a local printer installed (unless they are the print server as well). When a print request is submitted on a print client, the `print` command checks print configuration sources to locate a print server. After a print server is located, the print client sends the print request. It's then the job of the print server to direct the request to the appropriate printer.

Here are some resources that print clients can check for printer locations:

- A user's LPDEST or PRINTER variables
- A user's $HOME/.printers file
- The local /etc/printers.conf file for the NIS name service
- An LDAP or NIS/NIS+ name service database

Print clients do not have their own local print queue. Locating the print queue only on the server reduces the client's print overhead and reduces the chances of having printing problems.

One software component required to print is the *print driver*. Print drivers vary based on make and model of the printer, and they tell the operating system how to communicate with the printer. To function properly, the print driver must be specifically written for Solaris.

The last component is also software based, and it's the *print spooler*. Print spoolers reside on the print server. Their job is to accept print jobs, format them as necessary for the printer, and direct them to the printer. You will often hear people refer to the print spooler as a print queue. Although most of the time the terms are interchangeable, the print spooler does much more than hold (queue) print jobs. In Solaris, the print spooler is represented as the LP print service. Figure 8.1 shows the relationship of the printing components.

FIGURE 8.1 Print components on a network

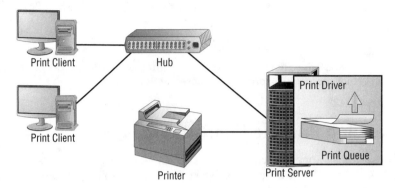

You will also hear the terms *local printer* and *network printer*. A *local printer* is one physically attached to your machine. A *network printer* is a printer that you can access but that is not located on your machine. Although Sun likes to define a network printer as one attached directly to the network (via its own network interface), we will assume that a networked printer is simply available "somewhere" on your network.

Using the LP Print Service

Originally known as the LP spooler, the *LP print service* is a set of files and utilities that provides print functionality in Solaris. The LP print service encompasses print software as well as print hardware.

The core files of the LP print service are located in the directories shown in Table 8.1.

TABLE 8.1 LP Print Service Directories

Directory	Contents
/etc/lp	More directories containing LP server configuration files.
/usr/bin	LP print service user commands.
/usr/lib/lp	LP print daemons, directories for binary files and PostScript filters, and the model directory, which contains the standard printer interface program.
/usr/lib/print	The in.lpd daemon and the printd daemon. The printd daemon transfers all waiting print jobs to the /var/spool/print directory once per minute. If there are no jobs, printd will not be running.
/usr/sbin	LP print service administrative commands.
/usr/share/lib	The terminfo database directory.

TABLE 8.1   LP Print Service Directories *(continued)*

Directory	Contents
/var/lp/logs	Logs for LP activities.
/var/spool/lp	Spool files. This is the print spooling directory.
/var/spool/print	LP print service client-side request staging area.

The /etc/lp directory contains most of the subdirectories that hold the printer's configuration information. This includes printer classes, filters and forms, directories for each local printer, and links to the log files as well as the /usr/lip/lp/model directory. Although you can directly open and examine the files in /etc/lp, you should not edit them to make printer configuration changes. Instead, use the lpadmin command.

Each of the directories listed in Table 8.1 is important to the printing process. However, if you were to pick two directories that were the most important, they would be /etc/lp (discussed in the preceding paragraph) and /var/spool/lp. The /var/spool/lp directory is the print spool directory, which holds print jobs until they are printed. If this directory runs out of disk space, printing will either become incredibly slow or cease altogether.

Another important print-related area is the terminfo database, located in /usr/share/lib. The terminfo database is a series of directories that contain definitions for many types of printers. LP uses terminfo to initialize and communicate with printers. If your printer is not supported by Solaris, you can add your own terminfo entry.

> Adding custom terminfo entries is beyond the scope of this Study Guide. For more information, please see *System Administration Guide: Advanced Administration*, by Sun Microsystems. You can access it at http://docs.sun.com/db/doc/806-4074.

Printing Commands

Although Solaris provides the graphical Solaris Print Manager, you need to be familiar with the commands used by the LP print service in order to pass the exam. Table 8.2 lists the commands you should know.

TABLE 8.2   Solaris Print Commands

Command	Description
accept	Enables the printer to receive print requests
cancel	Cancels a print request

TABLE 8.2 Solaris Print Commands *(continued)*

Command	Description
disable	Deactivates one or more printers
enable	Activates a printer
lp	Sends print jobs to a printer
lpadmin	Printer administration command, used for configuration changes
lpfilter	Sets up or changes filter parameters
lpmove	Moves print requests from one location to another
lpsched	Starts the LP print service scheduler
lpstat	Shows the status of the LP print service
lpshut	Stops the LP print service scheduler
lpusers	Sets or changes the printing queue priorities
reject	Prevents the printer from receiving print requests

To use the print commands (other than lp), you must have **root** permissions, be logged in as the lp user, or be able to assume an equivalent role. As this chapter progresses, each command will be discussed in greater detail.

Print Service Log Files

The LP print service keeps two logs. One is a list of current print requests that are in the print queue, and the other is a historical register of print requests. To enable print logging, add the lpr.debug variable to the /etc/syslog.conf file. In Solaris, there are two types of print logs: queue logs and history logs.

Queue Logs

When you submit a print job to the printer, the print scheduler keeps two copies of your print request in queue log files. One is in /var/spool/lp/tmp/*system_name* and is accessible to the user who submitted the print job. The other copy is in /var/spool/lp/requests/*system_name* and is accessible only by the **root** or the lp user.

The information in the queue logs will be present only as long as the job is in the print queue. When the print job is finished, its information is combined and appended to the /var/lp/logs/requests file. Because jobs are in the print queue for only a short time, you have only a brief amount of time to look at the logs. Consequently, they're usually not too much help in troubleshooting unless a job is stuck in the print queue.

History Logs

There are two print history logs in Solaris: `/var/lp/logs/lpsched` and `/var/lp/logs/requests`. The `lpsched` log contains information about current local printing requests, and `requests` holds information about completed print jobs that are no longer in the queue.

For troubleshooting purposes, the `requests` log is the more helpful of the two. It keeps track of a host of information, including the name of the printer, the name and the number of copies of the printed file, the type of content in the file, the name of the user who printed the file, and the outcome of the print request. Although analyzing the `requests` log is beyond the scope of this book (and the test), it can be useful for identifying abusers of print privileges. For more information on reading the `/var/lp/logs/requests` file, see the *System Administration Guide: Advanced Administration*.

As you might imagine, log files can get quite large. Consequently, the LP print service uses a `cron` job, `/var/spool/cron/crontabs/lp`, to periodically clean out old `lpsched` and `requests` log files. Three log files are kept for each: one current file and the two most recent histories. The current log file is renamed `log.1`, and `log.1` is renamed to `log.2`. The information contained in `log.2` is overwritten.

The Printer Interface Program

To interface with other parts of the operating system, the LP print service uses the standard *printer interface program*, located in `/usr/lib/lp/model`. The standard interface program is responsible for initializing the printer port with the `stty` (standard terminal) command, if necessary, and initializing the printer, printing banner pages, and printing the correct number of copies.

If the standard printer interface program does not sufficiently meet your printing needs, you can create a custom program.

Scheduling Print Requests

The scheduler for the LP print service is a daemon named `lpsched`. This daemon not only schedules print jobs, but it also updates LP system files with any printer setup or configuration changes. The `lpsched` daemon is located in the `/usr/lib/lp` directory.

Print servers might have only one LP scheduler running. If multiple LP schedulers were to be started, the LP service would become confused and printing would be problematic.

For local print requests, the scheduling process is relatively straightforward. The scheduler looks in the print queue for a print request, applies any filters for proper formatting of the document, and sends the request to the printer. The process is repeated until no more documents are in the print queue.

Printing on the network requires a bit more interaction. Now instead of having only one computer handling print requests, one computer makes the request, and another, the print server, receives the request. Print servers listen for print requests on the network with the Internet services daemon (`inetd`). After `inetd` receives a request, it starts the protocol adapter daemon, `in.lpd`. This daemon accepts the print request, translates it, and sends it to the print spooler. After the job is handed to the spooler, the print process is identical to local printing.

Each print request, whether local or remote, is logged and tracked by `lpsched`. The log file used is `/var/lp/logs/lpsched`. As mentioned previously in the "Print Service Log Files" section, log files can be helpful for tracking down printing problems.

Setting Up Printers

If you have only one Solaris computer and one printer, deciding where to place the printer is merely a matter of finding enough desk space. In a networked environment, though, you need to decide where to place printers so as to provide the required print access. Your decisions will be based on the number of printers you have, the number of users you have, and the printing needs of those users. Does the boss get her own printer, while 100 employees share another? Or does everyone share two printers? It would be impossible to provide the answer to every printer location solution. It's best to do what makes the most sense based on your company's printing needs.

In some cases, it makes sense to have all printers in one central location. That way, when users print, they can walk to the printer area and find their print jobs. In other companies, it makes more sense to give each department its own printer or two. In this case, printing is decentralized.

Whether you choose centralized or decentralized printing, you need to pick at least one computer that will function as the print server. You can choose to have more than one print server on the network, and there are advantages and disadvantages to multiple print servers. One disadvantage is potential confusion. You will need to educate users on where the printers are located. Many users won't understand why some printers are connected to one computer and others to another computer. An advantage is fault tolerance. If one print server crashes for some reason, you will still have printers installed on another server, and printing can continue.

Configuring Print Servers

Solaris is flexible enough that print servers and print clients can be running different versions of the Solaris operating environment and still function properly. Moreover, Solaris can operate as a print client or server with other operating systems, provided the other operating system supports lpd-based print standards.

Any networked computer can be a print server for the network. It doesn't necessarily need to be a machine that's otherwise designated as a server. Whichever machine you choose to be the print server just needs to have enough resources to handle the printing load.

Here are some of the requirements for print servers:

Disk space   Acting as a print server isn't terribly resource intensive, but disk space is the most critical resource. The printer spool file will be located on the hard disk, and the file system containing the print spool must never run out of space. On small networks with low printing requirements, only 25MB–50MB of disk space is needed. However, if the print server serves a large number of users, or printing requirements are high (for example, printing graphics or other large PostScript files), the print server might need close to 1GB of disk space.

The print spooler resides in the /var file system by default. The hard disk containing the mounted /var file system should be on the local computer in all cases. Never place the print server's /var on a remote machine, or printing will be unacceptably slow.

Spooling space   Spooling space runs hand in hand with disk space. The spooling location is /var/spool/lp. As mentioned previously, the /var file system must never run out of hard disk space. If it does, printing will either become incredibly slow or fail altogether. If the /var file system is part of the root file system (/), you need to find adequate disk space to give /var its own partition.

Memory   Printing in Solaris is not very memory intensive. If you have enough memory to run Solaris, you have enough memory to print in Solaris. In some cases, such as using print filters, more memory can streamline the printing process.

Swap space   Because swap space is used only when physical memory runs short, swap space should not be a major requirement for Solaris printing. However, if you are short on physical memory, make sure that your swap space is large enough to handle printing. It really shouldn't be an issue, though.

Also ensure that all users who need to print to the print server can access the server on the network.

If you are using a network naming service such as LDAP, NIS, or NIS+, you can configure the naming service switch file, /etc/nsswitch.conf, to point your print clients to the naming servers. They can provide a centralized printer configuration information repository for all network clients. Using the naming service switch file along with the proper printer configurations stored on the naming servers enables print clients to automatically have print configuration information without having to add it to their individual systems.

Setting Printer Definitions

When you install a printer in Solaris, you need to define parameters describing the printer itself, as well as how the printer will handle certain types of print jobs. The printer's collective settings are known as *printer definitions*.

Printer definitions are set through either the lpadmin command or Solaris Print Manager. Although Solaris Print Manager is easier to use because of its graphical nature, it does have some limitations. For example, limiting user access to a printer can be configured through either method, but lpadmin provides greater flexibility. Also, printer classes and fault recovery cannot be configured through Solaris Print Manager.

Here are some of the available printer definitions:

Printer name   When you install the printer, you must give it a name no longer than 14 characters. The name should be descriptive of the printer's function or location, can contain alphanumeric characters including dashes and underscores, and must be unique on the network.

Most networks establish a naming convention for their printers. Examples are prnacct and prneng, or acctprn1 and engprn1.

Printer description   This information should be used to help identify the printer. This could be a physical or departmental location, the brand of printer, or any other information that might be relevant.

Printer port   The printer port is the device to which the printer is attached. Solaris has default printer port names, based on the type of port that the printer uses:

- Serial ports will be /dev/term/a or /dev/term/b.
- Parallel ports will be /dev/printers/0 or /dev/ecpp0.
- USB ports will be /dev/printers/[1-9].

The LP print service uses the standard printer interface program to initialize the printer ports.

Printer type   This is the generic name for the printer. It will correspond to the `terminfo` database entry containing the printer's control sequences.

On IA-based systems, only the first port is enabled by default. To use more than one port, you must manually edit the device driver port configuration file for each additional port you want to use. The file path for serial port printers is `/platform/i86pc/kernel/drv/asy.conf`, and for parallel printers it's `/platform/i86pc/kernel/drv/lp.conf`.

Using Solaris Print Manager

The Solaris Print Manager can be used to set up print servers and print clients, and to manage installed printers. Solaris Print Manager is compatible with the LDAP, NIS, NIS+, and files naming services. Solaris Print Manager is started in one of three ways: from the Workspace Menu ➢ Tools ➢ Printer Administrator (right-click on your CDE desktop to get the Workspace menu), from the CDE desktop Applications Menu ➢ Applications ➢ System_Admin ➢ Printer Administrator, or by executing the `/usr/sadm/admin/bin/printmgr` command. The Solaris Print Manager's default window is shown in Figure 8.2.

FIGURE 8.2   Solaris Print Manager

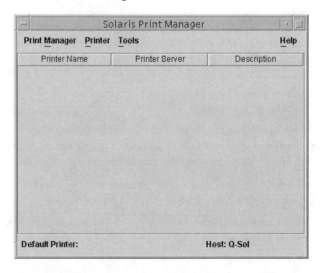

After you have chosen a computer to be the print server, attached the printer, and turned the printer on, you need to add the printer to Solaris. Open Solaris Print Manager and follow these steps:

1. From the Printer menu, choose New Attached Printer. The New Attached Printer window appears.

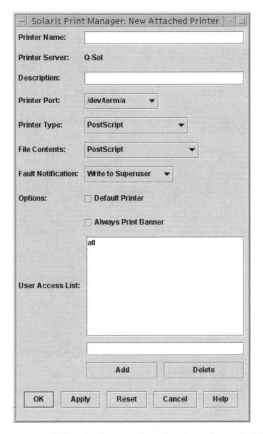

2. Add the printer's name and description, make selections from the drop-down menus, select options, and click OK when you are finished.

3. Confirm that the printer exists in the Solaris Print Manager window.

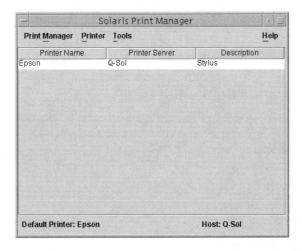

4. Complete the printer installation by verifying that it can print. Either print from the Print menu of the application of your choice (such as a text editor or StarOffice) or execute the following command.

    `# lp -d *printer_name filename*`

To set up a print client, you can also use Solaris Print Manager. You would perform this from the print client, not the print server. Here are the steps:

1. Open the Solaris Print Manager.

2. From the Printer menu, choose Add Access to Printer. The Add Access to Printer window appears

3. Add the name of the printer, the server name, and an optional description. If you want to make this printer your default printer, click the Default Printer check box to select it. Click OK to finish.

4. Complete the printer installation by verifying that it can print. Either print from the Print menu of the application of your choice (such as a text editor or StarOffice) or execute the following command.

    `# lp -d *printer_name filename*`

---

admintool can also be used to graphically add printers, but the Solaris Print Manager is the recommended interface.

Adding Printers from a Command Line

Solaris Print Manager provides an easy interface to add printers to Solaris and manage printers. There might be a time, though, when you don't have access to Solaris Print Manager and you need to add a printer to the computer. The following steps are for adding a parallel PostScript printer named `tamago`:

1. Give the root ownership of the port.

    `# chown root /dev/printers/0`

2. Make sure that the root is the only one with administrative access.

    `# chmod 600 /dev/printers/0`

These first two steps give root ownership to and exclusive access of the printer port. Although they're not necessary steps in order to configure a printer, if you fail to perform them, other users will have administrative access to the printer.

3. Configure the printer name and port.

   `# lpadmin -p tamago -v /dev/printers/0`

4. Configure printer options, such as printer type, input type, and description.

   `# lpadmin -p tamago -T PS -I postscript -D "Second Floor Water Cooler"`

5. Configure the printer to accept print requests. Failure to perform this step will prevent printing.

   `# accept tamago`

6. Enable the printer. Failure to perform this step will prevent printing.

   `# enable tamago`

The accept command enables the print queue to accept jobs. However, the jobs will sit in the queue unless the `enable` command is issued, allowing the queue to pass the print jobs to the printer.

7. Check the status to ensure that the printer is available.

   `# lpstat -p tamago`

   You want to see a message similar to the following:

   `printer tamago is idle. enabled since Sat Sep 21 11:14:15 MDT 2002.`
   `   available.`

8. Test printing to ensure that it works.

   `# lp -d tamago filename`

Adding a print client from the command line is a shorter process. These steps are performed from the print client, and the print server must be configured and available.

1. Add the printer, using the printer's name and the server name.

   `# lpadmin -p tamago -s Q-Sol`

2. Add a description, if desired, and set the printer as the default, if desired.

   `# lpadmin -p tamago -D "My Printer" -d tamago`

3. Check to verify that the printer is ready.

   `# lpstat -p tamago`

4. Test printing to ensure that it works.

   `# lp -d tamago filename`

Command-line options for `lpadmin` and `lpstat` are covered in the following section, "Performing Printer Administration."

Performing Printer Administration

Performing daily management of printers in Solaris is all about knowing which commands are available, what each command does, and when to use the commands. If all goes well, you will simply set up printers and never have to worry about them. Inevitably, though, you'll have a problem that you need to resolve. The graphical Solaris Print Manager is handy for many administrative tasks, but for complete printer management, you will need to use the command line.

This section is about management tasks that you might need to perform and the commands that you will use to perform them. Where applicable, command-line options are included as well.

Checking Printer Status

If you want to determine which printers are available or to determine characteristics of installed printers, you can do so with the `lpstat` command. The syntax of `lpstat` is as follows:

```
# lpstat -d [-p printer_name -D -l] -t
```

For example, to show the status of a printer named `kani`, along with the printer's description, you would use:

```
# lpstat -p kani -D
```

The arguments for `lpstat` are listed in Table 8.3.

TABLE 8.3 *lpstat* Arguments

Option	Description
-d	Displays the system's default printer.
-p *printer_name*	Displays the status of the specified printer. Multiple printers can be specified, separated by commas.
-D	Displays the description of the specified *printer_name*.
-l	Displays the characteristics of the specified *printer_name*.
-t	Displays the status of the LP printing service and all installed printers.

Stopping and Restarting the Print Scheduler

If the print scheduler is stopped for some reason, you will need to restart it to get printing to work. Also, occasional printing glitches might occur when print jobs are sent but nothing prints. If investigating shows that the jobs are in the queue, but nothing is printing, then stopping and restarting the print scheduler can sometimes rectify this situation.

To stop the print scheduler, use:

```
# /etc/init.d/lp stop or
# /usr/lib/lp/lpshut
```

To restart the scheduler, use:

`# /etc/init.d/lp start` or

`# /usr/lib/lp/lpsched`

 Technically speaking, the /etc/init.d/lp stop and /etc/init.d/lp start commands affect the entire LP print service, whereas lpshut and lpsched affect only the lpsched daemon. However, both sets are effective at stopping and restarting the print scheduler.

Configuring Printer Definitions

Printer definitions are essentially the variables that complete the printer's configuration. Many definitions can be set through the Solaris Print Manager, but not all. From the command line, most definitions are set with the lpadmin command. Here is the basic syntax for lpadmin:

`# lpadmin -p printer_name options`

lpadmin offers a large number of options. Some of the common ones are listed in Table 8.4.

TABLE 8.4   *lpadmin* Arguments

Option	Description
-p *printer_name*	Specifies the name of the printer to be modified.
-A *alert_type*	Defines an alert sent to the administrator when a printer fault is detected. Alert types include mail (e-mail the administrator), write (send a message to the administrator's terminal), quiet (do not send an alert about the current problem), and none (do not send messages at all).
-W *minutes*	Used with -A. Defines the number of minutes to wait between sending alerts to the administrator.
-c *class*	Adds the printer indicated by *printer_name* to the specified printer class.
-d *printer_name*	Specifies the default printer for the system.
-D *comment*	Adds a comment for the printer. For comments that have spaces, place the comment in quotes.
-f *allow:form_list*	Allows forms in the *form_list* to be printed on this printer. By default, forms are not allowed on new printers.
-f *deny:form_list*	Denies forms in the *form_list* to be printed on this printer.

TABLE 8.4 *lpadmin* Arguments *(continued)*

Option	Description
-F *fault_recovery*	Specifies the recovery method to be used if a print request fails due to a printer fault. Options are continue, beginning, and wait.
-I *content_list*	Allows the printer to print requests with the content types listed in *content_list*. Separate multiple content types with commas.
-o *option*	Specifies default printer configuration values. Options include length, width, cpi (characters per inch), lpi (lines per inch), stty (port settings), protocol (for network printers), and banner and nobanner (for print banners). Examples follow this table.
-r *class*	Removes the printer from the printer *class*. If the printer is the last one in the class, the class is removed.
-s *system_name* !*printer_name*	Makes a remote printer (one that would typically have to be accessed through another system) accessible to users on your system. The *system_name* option is the name of the remote computer, and !*printer_name* is the name of the printer on that system. An example follows this table.
-t *trays*	Specifies the number of trays available in the printer.
-T *printer_type*	Identifies the printer as being of a specific printer type, as defined by the terminfo database.
-u allow:*login_ID*	Allows the user or users listed by *login_ID* access to the printer. By default, all users are allowed access to the printer. Options for *login_ID* include *system_name*!*login_ID*, which enables a user from a remote system to access the printer, *system_name*!all, which enables all users from the named system to access the printer, and all, which gives access to all users on all systems.
-u deny:*login_ID*	Denies the user or users listed by *login_ID* access to the printer. The options for *login_ID* are the same as those for -u allow.
-v	Associates a device with a printer.
-x *printer_name*	Removes the printer.

As you can see in Table 8.4, lpadmin offers quite a range of functionality. Although in practice this is a good thing, understanding and memorizing all the options can be difficult. To help you understand lpadmin's usage, some examples follow.

To specify a description for the printer named mirugai, use the following command:

```
# lpadmin -p mirugai -D "Near the stairs on the first floor"
```

To make mirugai your default printer, you could use:

```
# lpadmin -d mirugai
```

Also, default printers can be specified by LPDEST and PRINTER environment variables (depending on the user's shell), and the _default variable in the user's $HOME/.printers file. To verify a system's default printer, use:

```
# lpstat -d
```

Banner pages are useful on networks with a large amount of print traffic. If multiple users share a printer, print jobs are generally processed in the order they are received, except for priority jobs. Because of this, waiting for a print job on a busy printer could take a while, and print jobs build up in the printer's output tray. Banner pages print the user's name, making it easy to identify where a user's print job starts and stops (the next job will have a new banner page).

The negative aspect to banner pages is that they waste paper. If they're not necessary on your network, it's best to disable them because they're enabled by default. To disable print banners on your printer, use:

```
# lpadmin -p printer_name -o banner=never
```

To enable banners, but give your users the option of disabling them, use:

```
# lpadmin -p printer_name -o banner=optional or
# lpadmin -p printer_name -o nobanner
```

Finally, to require users to use print banners, use:

```
# lpadmin -p printer_name -o banner=always or
# lpadmin -p printer_name -o banner
```

The last printer definition to discuss is invoked with the -s option. It enables users on your computer to print to a printer that is defined on another computer. This command can be helpful if your computer is a print server, but for some reason you are having problems printing. You can then tell users to print to the new printer you defined. Consider this example: Your computer is named locoduck. An associate's computer is named sushiyum, and his printer is named maguro. You want to define his maguro printer on your computer as daffy. Here's how you would do it:

```
# lpadmin -p daffy -s sushiyum!maguro
```

Users will now be able to print to your daffy printer, after you have configured it to accept print jobs and enabled it. The print output will be physically on the maguro printer.

Using Printer Classes

By using the lpadmin -c command, you can group multiple locally attached printers into a *printer class*. When users print, they specify the name of the class instead of the name of the individual printer. Printer class names must meet the required specifications for printer names (no more than 14 alphanumeric characters).

Using printer classes increases the efficiency of your printers. For example, say that your company has three laser printers. One of the laser printers is constantly busy, and users are waiting for print jobs. Another laser printer is moderately busy, and the third is rarely used. With a printer class, print jobs would be distributed evenly among the three laser printers. This is because a print job entering the queue is sent to the first available printer, the second job to the second printer, and so forth.

If you do enable printer classes, be sure to place all printers in the class in the same physical location. Otherwise, users will have to adventure throughout the office looking for their print jobs.

Solaris does not place a limit on the number of printers in a class, nor is there a limit to the number of printer classes that you can create. To add the printer named ika to the officeprinters class, you would use:

```
# lpadmin -p ika -c officeprinters
```

Printer class information is stored in the /etc/lp/classes/*printer_class* file. If the file does not exist when you add a printer to the class, the file is created automatically.

Enabling Fault Alerts and Fault Recovery

You can choose to have the printer notify you, via fault alert, if printer errors are encountered. Fault alerts are enabled through the lpadmin -A command or Solaris Print Manager. The three most popular options for fault alert notifications are sending a message to the computer where the **root** user (or other specified user) is logged in, sending an e-mail to the **root** user (or other specified user), or running a command if an alert state is encountered. The command would likely be a small program designed to rectify the situation, such as shutting down the printer and redirecting print jobs, or stopping and restarting the LP print service.

Fault recovery is a slightly different thread and is enabled with the lpadmin -F command. Fault recovery specifies what to do with the current print job if a printer fault is detected.

The three options for fault recovery are to restart printing of the job from the beginning, to continue printing from the top of the page when the fault was detected, or to wait for you to re-enable the printer and then continue to print from the top of the page where the printing stopped. Table 8.5 summarizes the fault alert and fault recovery options.

TABLE 8.5 Fault Alert and Fault Recovery Options

Option	Description
lpadmin -A "mail *username*"	E-mails the specified user, or root if no user is specified.
lpadmin -A "write *username*"	Writes a message to the console where the root is logged in, or to the console where the specified user is logged in.
lpadmin -A quiet	Does not notify for that specific printer fault.

TABLE 8.5   Fault Alert and Fault Recovery Options *(continued)*

Option	Description
lpadmin -A *command*	Executes the command when a printer fault is detected.
lpadmin -A none	Does not send any alerts for any print faults.
lpadmin -W *minutes*	Waits a specified number of *minutes* between sending fault alerts. Used in conjunction with the -A switch.
lpadmin -F beginning	Starts printing from the beginning of the file after a printer fault recovery.
lpadmin -F continue	Starts printing from the top of the page where the printing stopped after recovering from a printer fault.
lpadmin -F wait	After a fault recovery, waits to print until the printer is enabled by the administrator. Then, starts printing from the top of the page where the printing stopped.

Fault alert settings are maintained in the /etc/lp/printers/*printer_name*/alert .sh file. Fault recovery settings are noted in the /etc/lp/printers/*printer_name*/ configuration file.

Limiting User Access

By default, all users have printing rights on newly created printers. As a printer administrator, you can control user access to printers with the lpadmin -u command on the print server.

 Solaris Print Manager lets you create Allow lists only. To create Deny lists, you must use lpadmin -u.

As the names of the lists imply, an *Allow list* lets specified users access the printer, whereas a *Deny list* prohibits users from printing to the printer. Allow and Deny lists are created on the print server. When you have created one or both types of lists, sorting out who has what printing rights can be a bit confusing. Here are the rules for Allow and Deny lists:

- If you leave both lists empty or have not created lists, all users have access to the printer.
- If you specify all in the Allow list, everyone can access the printer.
- If you specify all in the Deny list, everyone is denied access to the printer, except for root and lp.
- If you add an entry to the Allow list, the Deny list is ignored. Only users specified in the Allow list (along with root and lp) have access to the printer.

- If you create an entry in the Deny list, but you do not create an Allow list or you leave the Allow list empty, users in the Deny list do not have access to the printer.

Here is the syntax for creating an Allow list:

```
# lpadmin -p printer_name -u allow: user_list
```

If you are specifying multiple users, separate usernames with a comma. To create a Deny list, simply replace allow with deny in the preceding example. The Allow list is maintained in /etc/lp/printers/printer_name/users.allow, and the Deny list is in /etc/lp/printers/printer_name/users.deny.

Managing Print Requests

After a user has submitted a print job, the print job is held in the print queue until the printer is ready for it. While the job is in the queue, the print administrator can place the job on hold or change its priority so that it's the next one to print. These actions are performed from the print server with the lpadmin -H command. Options for lpadmin -H are hold, resume, and immediate. The hold option prevents a print job from printing, resume enables a held print job to print, and immediate moves the print job to the top of the print queue.

Enabling and Disabling Printers

The enable and disable commands are used to allow a printer to print or to prevent it from printing, respectively. When a printer is disabled, it will not print. However, print jobs submitted by users will still be added to the print queue.

When a printer fault occurs, the printer might be disabled automatically. To allow the printer to continue printing, you must enable it.

To disable a printer named amaebi, you can use the following command:

```
# disable -c -r "The printer is broken!" amaebi
```

The disable command has three commonly used switches: -c, -W, and -r "reason". The -c switch cancels the current print job and then disables the printer. The -W switch waits until the current print job is finished and then disables the printer. For obvious reasons, -c and -W cannot be used at the same time. The -r "reason" switch gives the users a reason why the printer is disabled. Users will see the reason if they check the printer's status with lpstat -p.

To enable the amaebi printer, you would use:

```
# enable amaebi
```

You can enable or disable only specific printers. You cannot enable or disable printer classes.

Accepting and Rejecting Print Requests

The enable and disable commands affect the printer, whereas the accept and reject commands affect the print queue. As mentioned in the preceding section, if you disable a printer, the print queue can still receive print requests. To prevent the print queue from accepting requests, use the reject command. Even if the reject command is issued, print jobs already in the print queue will be allowed to print.

Only one argument is used with `reject`, and that is `-r "reason"`. Its usage is exactly identical to the `-r "reason"` switch used with `disable`.

To reject print jobs for the printer `unagi`, you would use:

`# reject -r "Time for maintenance." unagi`

After the maintenance is complete, you could accept new print jobs by using this command:

`# accept unagi`

Canceling Print Requests

Print jobs can be cancelled by the user who submitted the print request or by the `root` or `lp` users. The `cancel` command is used to cancel print jobs. The current print job can be cancelled, and jobs can be cancelled by request identification number (request ID) or by user who submitted the job.

A print job's request ID is displayed when the job is submitted. However, if you've forgotten the request ID, you can see it by using the `lpstat -o printer_name` command. Request IDs consist of the printer's name, a dash, and the number of the print request. An example is `unagi-19`.

Here are some examples of canceling print requests. To cancel a print request for the user `adocter`, use:

`# cancel -u adocter`

Canceling the current print job on the printer requires only the printer's name, such as:

`# cancel unagi`

whereas canceling specific print jobs requires the request ID, as in:

`# cancel unagi-19`

Multiple print jobs or printers can be specified. Separate multiple identities with commas.

Moving Print Requests

Say that one of your printers, `printer1`, crashes unexpectedly. You have another printer defined on the same print server named `printer2`. Upon further investigation, you notice that the queue for `printer1` has jobs in it, and users are submitting more jobs. What do you do?

Use the `reject` command to reject new print jobs for `printer1`, and take the jobs that are in the queue for `printer1` and move them to `printer2`. To move print jobs, you don't need to know the request IDs; you just need to know the names of the printers involved. Print jobs are moved with the `lpmove` command. Here's the syntax:

`# lpmove from_printer to_printer`

When you use `lpmove` to move all print jobs from one printer, that printer automatically stops accepting print requests. However, it's still recommended that you use the `reject` command before moving print jobs. Here's an example of moving all print jobs from the `unagi` printer to the `maguro` printer:

`# lpmove unagi maguro`

Also, you can use `lpmove` to move specific jobs based on request ID.

Changing Print Request Priorities

Priorities affect the order in which print jobs are printed and, consequently, can be changed only by the root and lp user accounts. You can change the priority of submitted print requests in one of two ways.

The first method is one described earlier in this section, but it has limited flexibility regarding priorities. You can use lpadmin -H hold to hold print jobs, or lpadmin -H immediate to raise the print job to the top of the print queue. For more flexibility, use the lp command, as follows:

```
# lp -i request_ID -H priority
```

or

```
# lp -i request_ID -q priority
```

Because -H and -q both affect priorities directly, only one can be used at a time. If you're going to use lp -H, the same options apply as for lpadmin -H. However, lp -q enables you to specify a numerical priority, from 0 to 39. 0 is the highest priority, and 39 is the lowest. If you wanted to change the priority of the print job unagi-19 to 4, you would use:

```
# lp -i unagi-19 -q 4
```

Again, because of the potential for problems (print queue "battles"), only the root and lp users can change the priority of print jobs.

Using Print Filters and Forms

Print filters convert a raw print job into a format that's acceptable to the printer. Filters also can be used to detect print faults and are necessary to handle special printing modes such as landscape printing and double-sided printing.

Solaris provides some PostScript print filters in the /usr/lib/lp/postscript directory. If you are using PostScript printers, the provided filters are enabled automatically. For other types of printers, you will have to modify an existing filter or create your own.

Creating filters is beyond the scope of this book, and it often requires experimentation to work properly. For more information, you can start with the man page for the lpfilter command.

Print forms are for print jobs that will be printed on preprinted paper. Although the form refers to the physical paper that the job will be printed on, Solaris also defines the print form as the definition of the form (what to print and where) within the LP print service.

No print forms are supplied with Solaris. To create a print form, use the lpforms command. Print forms are stored in the /etc/lp/forms directory.

Deleting Printers

Finally, if a printer needs to be removed from service or moved to another print server, it should be deleted from the existing print server and all print clients. Once deleted, the printer can be added to the new print server (if necessary) and configured on the print clients.

1. Before deleting a printer, ensure that all print jobs that have been sent to the printer are complete and that the printer cannot accept any new jobs. Printers should be deleted from print clients first. On the print client system, delete the printer.

   ```
   # lpadmin -x printer_name
   ```

2. On the print server, prevent any new requests form entering the print queue.

   # **reject** *printer_name*

3. On the print server, disable the printer when the queue is empty.

   # **disable** *printer_name*

4. Delete the printer from the print server.

   # **lpadmin -x** *printer_name*

5. Verify that the printer does not exist.

   # **lpstat -p** *printer_name*

   You should receive a message that the printer does not exist.

 Real World Scenario

Printing Errors

Your network has been running relatively trouble-free for the last few years. Recently, you purchased a new Solaris 9 server to replace one of your older Solaris servers. This new server will be a file and print server.

In an effort to consolidate printing resources, management has decided that everyone should print to the same print server. This includes the engineering department, which frequently prints blueprints on a plotter. You have the proper instructions for installing and configuring the plotter, and the plotter manufacturer has provided a Solaris driver for the device.

After a few days of using your new print server and printing configuration, you start getting occasional calls from users complaining that printing is unacceptably slow. Every once in a while, a user gets an error message about being out of memory when attempting to print. Sometimes they can try again and get it to work, but other times it takes multiple retries to print. Even when it does work, again, it's slow.

It's your job to find a solution to this printing problem.

Whenever printing is slow or users get memory errors while printing, it's a good sign that the print spooler is low on space. If the file system that contains the spool file (/var) is low on space, it will attempt to use virtual memory, which is on the hard disk. Although this works, it will slow down printing dramatically.

The first thing to check is the availability of space on the /var file system. In many cases, /var is placed on the same file system as the root (/), which is a definite problem for a print server. It's best to install a separate hard disk simply for /var, if possible. This is especially true if you have users who regularly print large files, such as blueprints or lengthy reports.

This is one problem that shouldn't be too hard to fix; it's just a matter of getting the right configuration, and enough room, for the print spooler.

Troubleshooting Printing

In an ideal computing world, you will never have printing problems. As of yet, though, no one has discovered or created the ideal computing world.

Printing problems can vary. Perhaps you sent a print job to the printer, but nothing prints. Maybe something does print, but it's unintelligible garbage. Or possibly you've entered a command and received absolutely no response. Fixing these problems is just like troubleshooting anything else on a computer. You need to find out what works, what doesn't, and narrow down the possible problem points to isolate the issue.

Nothing Is Printing

You send a print job, and nothing happens. You don't get an error message, yet you don't get your print job either. One of three things is usually the culprit: the printer, the LP print service, or the network (if applicable).

One of the first axioms in troubleshooting is, "Check the hardware." Everyone rolls their eyes at this statement, but checking the hardware is a critical first step. People often feel silly for checking things such as the power switch, but if the power is off, well, you might have found the problem. Also double-check the printer cables. Make sure that the data cable is securely fastened at both ends and that it doesn't appear to have any damage.

Check the LP print service next, because if it is not running, it needs to be. Also, the printer must be accepting print requests and be enabled to print. For other LP print service problems, you might want to enable the `lpr.debug` variable in the `syslog.conf` file or examine the `lpsched` log.

If the LP print service appears to be running and configured properly, you might want to stop the service and restart it. This "rebooting" of the service might fix your problem.

To stop the print scheduler, use:

`# /usr/lib/lp/lpshut`

And to restart the scheduler:

`# /usr/lib/lp/lpsched`

Or to stop and restart the LP print service, use:

`# /etc/init.d/lp stop`

`# /etc/init.d/lp start`

For network printing problems, finding the solution gets more complex. Again, the first thing to check is hardware. Are all cables plugged in (including network cables), and is everything powered on? If so, can you access the print server from the print client? Can someone sitting locally at the print server print? These are all good questions to ask.

Also check for printer faults or unresponsive print filters if the printer is on but seems stuck. Find out what works and what doesn't, and narrow down the problem from there.

Output Is Incorrect

If you are getting output from the printer, yet it's not the output you expected, you can be assured that the hardware is configured correctly. All cables are attached, and the power is indeed on.

Incorrect print output is more often than not a function of an incorrect configuration. If you chose the wrong printer type, the incorrect file content type, or incorrect port settings when you installed the printer, it's possible that your output will not be correct.

> If your banner page prints, but nothing else is correct, it's a good sign that you have an incorrectly configured file content type.

LP Commands Are Unresponsive

You just entered an `lpadmin` command to change a printer definition but you received no reply. Finding the lack of response odd, you use `lpstat` to check the status of your printer. Again, you get no response. Chances are good that your LP print service is hung. Stop and restart the service, and the problem should go away. If it doesn't, you might need to uninstall all printers (thereby removing the LP print service) and reinstall them.

Controlling Processes

Sending a print request starts processes on both the print client and the print server. Once the print job is complete, the processes end. When people think of processes, they generally think of applications running on a system. Although it's true that applications are processes, many other things are processes as well. Any running program in Solaris, whether it's an application, a script, a daemon, or any other "running" component, even the user shell, is considered a process. Simply defined, a *process* is a single program running in its own memory space. Various applications run multiple processes concurrently to achieve full functionality.

This section explains process management, including viewing system processes, clearing hung processes, and automatically scheduling processes.

Managing Processes

In Solaris, the system kernel manages processes. Programs are free to start or stop processes as necessary, and when a process opens another process, the procedure is called *spawning* or *forking*. Parent processes fork child processes, and if necessary, the child process can fork another process and thereby become a parent as well. To manage processes in Solaris, you need to understand the commands used. Table 8.6 lists some commonly used process management commands.

TABLE 8.6   Process Management Commands

Command	Description
dispadmin	Displays and changes process scheduler parameters.
nice	Changes the priority of a running process.

TABLE 8.6 Process Management Commands *(continued)*

Command	Description
kill	Terminates or sends a signal to a process.
ps	Reports the status of active processes, including process ID, terminal name, execution time, and command name.
pgrep	Finds active processes based on name or other attribute.
pkill	Sends a signal to a process.
priocntl	Manages process priorities, configures process classes, and displays information on the system's process scheduler.
prstat	Reports statistics of active processes. Sorts processes by CPU usage by default.
psrset	Creates and manages processor sets. Processor sets allow for the binding of specific processes to groups of processes, rather than a single processor.
ptree	Displays the process tree.

The most popular command used to list processes is ps. If you need information on running processes, ps can provide the status of the process, process ID, parent process ID, user ID, scheduling class, priority, memory used, and processor time used. By default, ps provides the process ID, terminal from which it was executed, processor time taken, and the command that generated the process.

```
# ps
PID   TTY   TIME  CMD
923   pts/4 0:10  ksh
518   pts/4 0:00  ps
```

By looking at this output from ps, you might think that only two processes are currently running on the system: the shell (ksh) and ps. However, that's not the case. With no arguments, the ps command displays only those processes that have the same effective user ID and the same controlling terminal as the person who ran the command. To see a full listing of all processes, you could use:

```
# ps -ef
    UID   PID  PPID  C   STIME TTY      TIME CMD
   root     0     0  0 10:28:54 ?       0:13 sched
   root     1     0  0 10:28:56 ?       0:00 /etc/init -
   root     2     0  0 10:28:56 ?       0:00 pageout
   root     3     0  0 10:28:56 ?       1:16 fsflush
   root   309     1  0 10:29:20 ?       0:00 /usr/lib/saf/sac -t 300
```

```
    root    243     1   0 10:29:10 ?          0:00 /usr/lib/utmpd
    root    141     1   0 10:29:06 ?          0:00 /usr/sbin/rpcbind
    root    124     1   0 10:29:06 ?          0:00 /usr/sbin/in.routed -q
    root    196     1   0 10:29:08 ?          0:00 /usr/sbin/syslogd
  daemon    177     1   0 10:29:07 ?          0:00 /usr/lib/nfs/statd
    root    219     1   0 10:29:09 ?          0:00 /usr/lib/lpsched
    root    426   331   0 19:45:13 ?          0:00 /bin/ksh
...
#
```

This listing was truncated to conserve space; otherwise, it would take about three pages to list the 63 processes currently running on this computer. Some of the options used with ps are listed in Table 8.7.

TABLE 8.7   *ps* Options

Option	Description
-a	Lists information about processes most frequently requested.
-A	Lists information about all processes. Identical to -e.
-c	Displays the class that the process belongs to.
-e	Lists information about all currently running processes.
-f	Displays a full listing.
-l	Displays a long listing.
-P	Lists the number of the processor to which the process is bound, if any.
-u *uidlist*	Displays processes whose effective user ID or login name is the same as the user ID or login name supplied in *uidlist*.

The pgrep utility is also used a lot. It's a great search tool for processes; all you need to know is what you want to look for. Here is the syntax for pgrep:

pgrep *options pattern*

Therefore, if you wanted to find the process ID of syslog, use:

pgrep syslog

and you will see the process ID returned. The pgrep utility has quite a number of switches because it's designed to give you a wide variety of options to search for processes. Some useful switches for pgrep are listed in Table 8.8.

TABLE 8.8 *pgrep* Options

Option	Description
-f	The regular expression pattern should be matched against the full process argument string, instead of against only the name of the executable file.
-g *pgrplist*	Displays processes whose process group ID is in the provided list.
-G *gidlist*	Shows processes whose real group ID is in the provided list. Group names or Group IDs can be provided.
-l	Long output format.
-n	Displays only the newest (most recently spawned) processes that match the provided pattern.
-P *ppidlist*	Shows the processes whose parent process ID is in the provided list.
-s *sidlist*	Displays processes whose session ID is in the provided list.
-t *termlist*	Displays processes that are associated with the terminal identifier supplied in the *termlist*.
-u *euidlist*	Shows processes whose effective user ID is in the provided list.
-U *uidlist*	Displays processes whose real user ID is in the provided list.
-v	Reverses matching. Displays all processes except for those that meet the specified criteria.
-x	Requires the process to exactly match the provided pattern in order to be displayed.

The best way to become familiar with the process management commands is to use them and see which ones meet your needs.

Managing Processes Graphically

By using the Solaris Management Console, you can manage processes through a graphical interface. Using the process management commands gives you greater control, but the graphical interface makes it easier to see the running processes.

The Solaris Management Console's Processes node is shown in Figure 8.3.

To view the properties of a process, double-click the process, or right-click the process and choose Properties, or select the process and choose Action ➤ Properties. The Properties window for the rpcbind process, PID 141, is shown in Figure 8.4.

FIGURE 8.3   Processes in Solaris Management Console

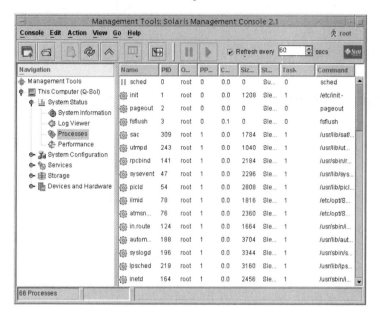

FIGURE 8.4   rpcbind Properties

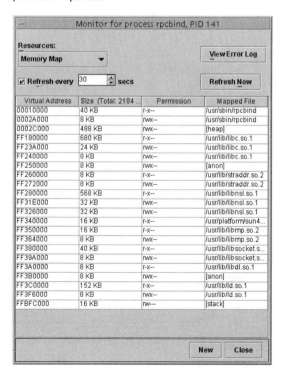

In a process' Properties page, you can choose a variety of resources to examine under the Resources menu. Choices are Memory Map, Signal Statistics, Environment, Process Limits, Credentials, Dynamic Link Libraries, Ancestry Tree, Stack Trace, and File Descriptors. Basically, anything you could want to know about the process can be found here. The Ancestry Tree for the inetd process is shown in Figure 8.5. It shows that inetd, PID 164, is the parent process of PID 401 and PID 432.

FIGURE 8.5   inetd Ancestry Tree

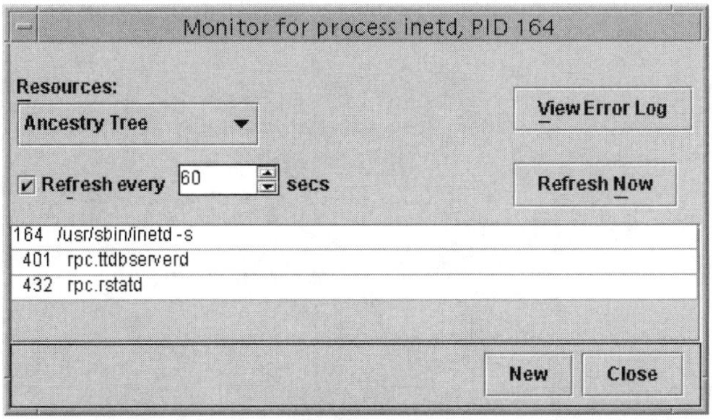

To suspend a process, select the process and choose Action ➢ Suspend, or select the process and click the Suspend button on the toolbar. It looks like a pause key (two vertical lines) on a CD player.

Processes can also be managed through Process Manager, which is shown in Figure 8.6.

FIGURE 8.6   Process Manager

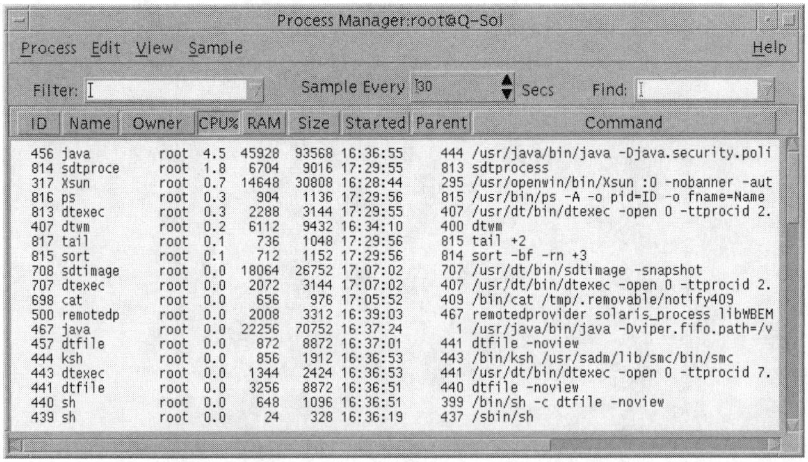

Process Manager is invoked by choosing Find Processes from the Tools menu in the CDE manager. Process Manager gives you more options for managing processes than does Solaris Management Console, including the ability to signal processes and kill the process outright.

Using the Process File System

Processes are tracked in Solaris by the Process File System (PROCFS). The /proc directory is also known as the process file system. Although this file system is read-only, it does display images of running processes on your computer. For managing processes, however, use one of the tools already discussed in this chapter.

Terminating Processes

Solaris uses signals to communicate with processes. Signals enable processes to interact with each other without needing extraneous hardware input or control. Signals are sent with the kill and pkill commands. Although the names of these commands imply that they're used exclusively to terminate processes, that's not the case. There are nearly 40 signals used by Solaris. Some of the more important ones to know are listed in Table 8.9.

TABLE 8.9   Signals

Number	Signal	Description
1	SIGHUP	Hangup. Often used in remote connections to indicate that the remote terminal has disconnected. Can also be used to attempt to reset a modem.
2	SIGINT	Interrupt. Signal 2 can also be sent by pressing Control+C or the Delete key.
3	SIGQUIT	Quits the process and creates a core dump.
6	SIGABRT	Abort.
9	SIGKILL	Forces the process to terminate unconditionally. This is the "sure kill" signal.
15	SIGTERM	Termination signal. Shuts down the process but gives the process a chance to terminate properly by cleaning up.

You can kill any process that you own, and the superuser can kill all processes except those with a PID of 0 through 4.

Used with no arguments, the kill command sends a signal 15 to the PID specified. Note that when you use the kill command, you must specify the process' PID, not its name.

If the process is still around after issuing a kill command, you can send it a kill -9, which should clean up the process without any questions. If you wanted to kill a process with PID 1814, you would use:

```
# kill -9 1814
```

The other command used to send signals to processes, pkill, functions nearly identically to pgrep. The difference is, pgrep finds and displays process information, whereas pkill sends signals to processes. Their command-line arguments, however, are very similar. When using pkill, you can specify the PID or the name of the process you wish to signal.

```
# pkill -9 lpsched
```

If no signal is specified, signal 15 (SIGTERM) is sent by default.

WARNING When killing processes, be careful what you kill because you could crash the system. Also, killing a process kills any child processes associated with it. To use the example shown in Figure 8.5, if you kill PID 164, PIDs 401 and 432 will stop as well.

Setting Process Priorities

At any given time, hundreds of processes might be running on your computer. And if you open multiple applications, all appear to be running all the time. The problem is, processors can do only one thing at a time, and most computers have only one processor. So what's really going on?

Although all processes appear to run simultaneously, only one process can actually be running at a time. Fortunately for humans, processors can perform hundreds of millions of tasks per second. Therefore, it appears that all processes and applications run together without a problem.

Processes in Solaris are given *priorities* to determine which process gets more CPU time than another. An application sitting idly in the background probably doesn't require much attention— and deserves a lower priority—than the application you are actively working on.

Process Classes

Each process in Solaris belongs to a distinct *process class* that has a unique scheduling policy. Solaris supports six process classes: real-time (RT), time-sharing (TS), interactive (IA), fair share (FSS), fixed priority (FX), and system (SYS).

With a default configuration, real-time processes run before any other process. Because real-time processes can monopolize processor time, the class should be used sparingly. The SYS class is a special class reserved for system processes. Processes that are not designated as SYS cannot be changed to this class. Table 8.10 provides a brief summary of the usable class characteristics.

TABLE 8.10 Process Classes

Class	Description
RT	Designed for processes that need extensive processor time, at the expense of other processes.
TS	Provides fair and effective allocation of processor time among running processes. Enables the user to supply a priority range for running processes within the class, affording users some control over process scheduling.

TABLE 8.10   Process Classes *(continued)*

Class	Description
IA	Provides fair and effective allocation of processor time among running processes. Enables the user to supply a priority range for running processes within the class, but individual process priorities will still be balanced by the kernel.
FSS	Provides fair allocation of processor time among projects, regardless of the number of processes associated with the project.
FX	Configures fixed priorities for processes, preventing the kernel from adjusting the process priority as necessary.

When processes are spawned, they are assigned a priority based on the process scheduler's policies. To see these policies, use the dispadmin command. The priocntl command displays process class information, assigns processes to configured classes, and manages process class priorities. Here's a sample output from priocntl:

```
# priocntl -l
CONFIGURED CLASSES
==================

SYS (System Class)

TS (Time Sharing)
      Configured TS User Priority Range: -60 through 60

FX (Fixed Priority)
      Configured FX User Priority Range: 0 through 60

IA (Interactive)
      Configured IA User Priority Range: -60 through 60

RT (Real Time)
      Maximum Configured RT Priority Range: 59
#
```

To see which class your processes belong to, use the ps -c command.

Using the *nice* Command

When a process is started, its process class determines its priority. This priority can be modified by a *nice number*. Nice numbers have a range of 0 to 39, and the default is 20. Raising the nice number of a process lowers its priority. In a sense, you are making the process "nicer" to other processes, meaning it's more willing to relinquish processor time. It's like when one of your parents told you to play nice with other kids. The nicer you got, the more accommodating you became.

 The C shell (csh) has a built-in command named nice. This section refers to the /usr/bin/nice utility, not the csh built-in.

By running the nice command with no arguments, you increase a process' nice number by 4 units. You can raise the nice number more by specifying the value, as in:

/usr/bin/nice +10 command1

This would raise the nice number for command1 to 30. You can also increase the priority of a process by lowering the nice number, as in:

/usr/bin/nice -10 command1

Users can raise the nice number of any process they own. Only the superuser can lower a nice number, thereby raising the priority of the process.

Troubleshooting Processes

Most of the time, processes run without a problem in Solaris. However, there are some issues to watch out for:

Processes that monopolize CPU time   If one process is controlling the CPU, other processes will never be able to run. Use the ps command to see which processes are taking CPU time. It's possible that the process is stuck in a loop and needs to be killed.

Runaway processes   These are processes that progressively use more and more CPU time until they monopolize the CPU. The process could be part of a poorly written program or it could be failing.

Process priorities   If your computer seems to be running slowly, check to see how many (if any) processes are running in real-time (RT). The use of real-time processes should be minimized. Also check for processes in the time-sharing class that have modified nice numbers.

Identical jobs owned by the same person   If a user has started many identical processes, perhaps as a batch program, CPU time can be unfairly constrained. The multiple instances of the identical processes need to be killed.

If a process is misbehaving, and it's not a critical system process, it might be best to attempt to kill it with the kill or pkill commands. If it's a critical system process, you might want to reboot Solaris to reset the process and clear up the problem.

Scheduling Processes

Tasks in Solaris can be scheduled to run automatically. This is useful for batch programs used to clean up systems, maintenance programs, and file backups occurring during non-peak hours.

You can schedule two types of tasks: those that need to run at regular intervals and those that need to be run only once.

For scheduling repetitive jobs, you will use *crontab*. For a job that needs to be run only once, you will use *at*.

crontab

The crontab command is for repetitive tasks that need to be run on a daily, weekly, or monthly cycle. Items such as security monitoring, backups, maintenance, and the production of reports can be automated with crontab. Tasks located in crontab files are executed by the cron daemon.

Here's a sample crontab file. It's one of the default crontab files, /var/spool/cron/crontabs/adm.

```
# cat adm
10 3 * * * /usr/sbin/logadm
15 3 * * 0 /usr/lib/fs/nfs/nfsfind
1 2 * * * [ -x /usr/sbin/rtc ] && /usr/sbin/rtc -c > /dev/null 2>&1
30 3 * * * [ -x /usr/lib/gss/gsscred_clean ] && /usr/lib/gss/gsscred_clean
```

The first line runs the /usr/sbin/logadm command at 3:10 every morning. The second line runs nfsfind at 3:15 in the morning every Sunday. The third line runs a script that checks for daylight savings time and makes changes if necessary, every morning at 2:01. The last entry checks for and removes duplicate entries in the Generic Security Service table every morning at 3:30. If this seems arcane, don't worry. You'll look at how to read a crontab file in just a bit.

crontab commands are managed and scheduled by the cron daemon. The cron daemon checks the /var/spool/cron/crontabs directory every 15 minutes for new crontab files or changes to existing crontab files. If changes are found, cron reads the execution times and starts the scheduled process at the appropriate time.

Reading *crontab* Files

Every crontab file has the same format. Basically stated, there are six fields. The first five tell cron when to run the job (the time fields), and the sixth is the job to run, with any arguments. In order, the time fields are as follows :

- Minute, from 0–59.

- Hour, from 0–23.

- Day of the month, from 1–31.

- Month, from 1–12.

- Day of the week, from 0–6. (0 is Sunday.)

crontab files support the use of special characters and wildcards for time values. Each field should be separated with a space. Commas can be used to provide multiple values, hyphens designate a range of values, and an asterisk is used to include all possible values. A pound sign (#)

at the beginning of the line is used to indicate a comment or blank line. Each command within a crontab file must reside on one line, even if the command is very long.

If you wanted to display a message saying "Happy Birthday!" to a user whose birthday was February 25th, and the message should appear at 4:15 P.M., you would create the following entry:

```
15 16 25 2 * echo Happy Birthday! > /dev/console
```

To display a message telling workers to log off and go home at 5:00 P.M., Monday through Thursday, you would create this entry:

```
0 17 * * 1,2,3,4 echo Log off and go home > /dev/console
```

It takes a bit of practice, but if you remember the time sequence used, reading a crontab file isn't too terribly painful.

Managing *crontab* Files

crontab files are created with the crontab -e command. This creates a crontab file with the name of the logged-in user. The superuser can create crontab files for the root or any user he chooses.

To display the contents of a crontab file, use crontab -l. You do not need to have /var/spool/cron/crontabs as your working directory to use this command or to see all crontab files.

To delete a crontab file, use crontab -r.

Controlling Access to *crontab* Files

Access to crontab files is controlled through two files: /etc/cron.d/cron.allow and /etc/cron.d/cron.deny. These files are accessible only to the superuser. Each file contains a list of usernames, one per line.

Here's how the access files work together:

- If cron.allow does not exist, all users can create crontab files, except for users listed in cron.deny.
- If cron.allow does exist, only users listed in this file can create, edit, display, and remove crontab files.
- If neither cron.allow nor cron.deny exists, superuser privileges are required to use the crontab command.

By default, a cron.deny file exists with the following entries: daemon, bin, smtp, nuucp, listen, nobody, noaccess. There is no cron.allow file created by default.

Using Solaris Management Console

The Solaris Management Console can be used to view and create crontab jobs. The Scheduled Jobs node of the Solaris Management Console is shown in Figure 8.7.

New crontab files can be created from the Action ➤ Add Scheduled Job menu.

FIGURE 8.7   Scheduled Jobs node

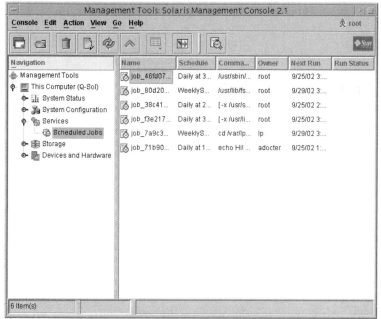

at

Whereas `crontab` files have quite a number of options, `at` files are for the simple one-time execution of a command. Users have the ability to create and manage their own `at` jobs by default. However, to access another user's `at` job, you must have superuser privileges.

When `at` jobs are created, they are given a job identification number and the `.a` extension. This becomes the file's name. The `at` jobs are read and scheduled by the `cron` daemon.

Managing *at* Jobs

Creating `at` jobs is easier than creating `crontab` jobs. For `at` jobs, all you need to know is the time, date, and command you wish to run. Here's an example of creating an `at` job:

```
# at 4:15pm Feb 25
at> echo Happy Birthday! > /dev/console
at> ^D
commands will be exectuted using /sbin/sh
job 1046215800.a Tue Feb 25 16:15:00 2003
#
```

To exit the `at` editor, press Control+D at the `at>` prompt. This was done at the second `at>` prompt in the example, and it created the rest of the output.

Time can be specified by using either A.M. or P.M. or by using a 24-hour clock. Acceptable time words are *midnight*, *noon*, and *now*. For the date, you can supply the first three letters of the month and a date, a day of the week, or the words *today* or *tomorrow*.

If you want to view jobs waiting in the at queue, use the atq command. To display information about an at job, use at -l *job_ID*. at jobs are deleted by using the at -r *job_ID* command.

Controlling *at* Access

By default, all regular users are allowed to create their own at jobs. The file that controls access to the at command is /etc/cron/at.deny. Like /etc/cron/cron.deny, the at.deny file contains a list of users, one user per line. Users listed in this file will not have access to the at command.

Summary

As an administrator, you hope that printing and processes will present no problems but, unfortunately, they sometimes do. This chapter focused on the fundamentals needed to understand printers and processes and the skills needed to manage them.

The printing section started by discussing print terms that you need to be familiar with and the core print service in Solaris, the LP print service. It covered commands used to manage printers, as well as log information for troubleshooting help.

Then, the discussion turned to setting up printers, both through Solaris Print Manager and from a command line. Next, a great deal of this chapter covered printer administration. Tasks covered include stopping and restarting the print service, enabling and disabling printing, configuring printer definitions, moving and canceling print jobs, and creating printer classes. The printing section ended with troubleshooting advice.

It's impossible to run Solaris without dealing with processes. Every running software component is related to at least one process in Solaris. Two common commands to view process information are ps and pgrep.

If a process is misbehaving, you will want to terminate the process. This is done with the kill and pkill commands. All processes run with a priority, which helps determine which processes get CPU time.

Finally, this chapter concluded with a discussion of scheduling processes. Processes can be scheduled to run once with the at command, or configured to run on a regular schedule with crontab files.

Exam Essentials

Understand the importance of the LP print service.   The LP print service controls all aspects of printing in Solaris, from the software components, such as drivers and the print spooler, to hardware, such as the printer.

Know how to stop and restart the LP print service.   The LP print service is stopped with the /etc/init.d/lp stop command and restarted with the /etc/init.d/lp start command.

Know how to add a printer.   Printers are commonly added through the graphical Solaris Print Manager. However, printers can also be added with the lpadmin command.

Know how to check a printer's status.   Printer status is examined with the lpstat command.

Know the commands used to perform printer administration.   There are really too many commands to list here, but it's a good idea to know the commands associated with printer management tasks, such as creating printer classes, disabling and enabling printers, accepting and rejecting print jobs, and moving and canceling print jobs.

Know the commands used to display process information.   Process information is typically displayed with the ps and pgrep commands.

Know how to terminate a process.   Processes are terminated with the kill and pkill commands.

Know the differences between at and crontab files.   If you wish to schedule a process to run once, you would use the at command to create an at job. For processes that need to run on a regular schedule, the crontab command can create batch files to suit your needs.

Key Terms

Before you take the exam, be certain you are familiar with the following terms:

Allow list	print driver
at	print server
crontab	print service
Deny list	print spooler
forking	printer class
Line Printer (LP)	printer definitions
local printer	printer interface program
LP print service	priorities
network printer	process
nice number	process class
print client	spawning

Commands Used in This Chapter

The following list contains a summary of all the commands introduced in this chapter:

Command	Description
accept	Enables the printer to receive print requests.
at	Creates and manages at jobs.
cancel	Cancels a print request.
crontab	Creates and manages crontab jobs.
disable	Deactivates one or more printers.
dispadmin	Displays and changes process scheduler parameters.
enable	Activates a printer.
kill	Terminates or sends a signal to a process.
lp	Sends print jobs to a printer.
lpadmin	Printer administration command, used for configuration changes.
lpfilter	Sets up or changes filter parameters.
lpmove	Moves print requests from one location to another.
lpsched	Starts the LP print service scheduler.
lpstat	Shows the status of the LP print service.
lpshut	Stops the LP print service scheduler.
lpusers	Sets or changes the printing queue priorities.
nice	Changes the priority of a running process.
ps	Reports the status of active processes, including process ID, terminal name, execution time, and the command name.
pgrep	Finds active processes based on name or other attribute.
pkill	Sends a signal to a process.
priocntl	Manages process priorities, configures process classes, and displays information on the system's process scheduler.

Command	Description
prstat	Reports statistics of active processes. Sorts processes by CPU usage by default.
psrset	Creates and manages processor sets. Processor sets allow for the binding of specific processes to groups of processes, rather than a single processor.
ptree	Displays the process tree.
reject	Prevents the printer from receiving print requests.

Review Questions

1. You are the Solaris print administrator for your company. You have one print server named `print01`. It has two printers installed, `saba` and `masu`. The `saba` printer is having problems printing, so you prevent it from accepting new print jobs and disable it from printing. Now you want to move all print jobs sitting in the `saba` print queue to the `masu` printer. Which command will you need to use to accomplish this?

   A. `lpdest saba misu`

   B. `lpdest misu saba`

   C. `lpmove saba misu`

   D. `lpmove misu saba`

2. You are the Solaris administrator for your company. Instead of using the `root` account, you log in using a regular user account to check the viability of the `crontab` feature. When you execute the `crontab` command, you get the following message:

   `crontab: you are not authorized to use cron. Sorry.`

   Which of the following could this message indicate? (Choose all that apply.)

   A. Neither a `cron.allow` nor a `cron.deny` file exists.

   B. Both the `cron.allow` and `cron.deny` files exist; the user account that you are using is not listed in `cron.allow`.

   C. The user account that you are using is listed in the `cron.allow` file, but a `cron.deny` file does not exist.

   D. The user account that you are using is listed in the `cron.deny` file.

3. You are the Solaris systems administrator for your company. You are creating user initialization files and want to specify default printers for all users. Which two variables are valid for indicating a default printer for users using the Korn shell (`ksh`)? (Choose two.)

   A. PRN

   B. LPDEST

   C. PRINTER

   D. LPR

   E. LP

4. You are the Solaris administrator for your company. One of the junior administrators notices slow printing on one print server. She wants to move the print spooler onto a slice with more space for the file system. Which file in Solaris represents the print spooler?

   A. `/etc/lp/spool`

   B. `/var/lp/spool`

   C. `/var/spool/lp`

   D. `/var/spool/print`

5. You are working on a Solaris network. Before you print your 100-page report, you want to make sure that you're printing to the correct printer. Which of the following commands can you use to see which printer is set as your default printer?

A. `lpadmin -D`

B. `lpadmin -d`

C. `lpstat -D`

D. `lpstat -d`

6. You are the Solaris printer administrator. One of your print servers is having problems, and you want to locate the server's print history logs. Which two of the following files are you looking for? (Choose two.)

A. `/var/lp/logs/requests`

B. `/var/lp/logs/lpsched`

C. `/var/lp/logs/history`

D. `/var/lp/logs/print`

7. You are the Solaris administrator for your company. You need to add a new parallel printer to the print server and will be doing it from a command line. The print server's name is `server1`, and the printer's name is `tako`. Which of the following commands can you use to add the new printer?

A. `lpadmin -p tako -v /dev/ecpp0`

B. `lpadmin -p tako -S server1 -v /dev/ecpp0`

C. `lpadmin -p tako -v /dev/term/a`

D. `lpadmin -p tako -S server 1 -v /dev/term/a`

8. You have just installed a printer named `hokkigai` onto your Solaris print server from the command line. You have configured the printer correctly and told the printer to accept print requests. Users are submitting requests, but nothing is printing. You investigate and find all the print jobs sitting in the print queue. The users are receiving no error messages when submitting print jobs. Which of the following should you do first to rectify the situation?

A. Run the **accept hokkigai** command from the print server.

B. Run the **enable hokkigai** command from the print server.

C. Stop and restart the print spooler with the **lpshut** and **lpsched** commands.

D. Delete and reinstall the `hokkigai` printer from the print server.

9. You are the Solaris administrator for your company. A process named abc1, with a PID of 555, is consuming a considerable amount of processor time and appears to be hung. Which of the following commands would unconditionally stop the abc1 process? (Choose all that apply.)

    A. kill -9 abc1

    B. kill -9 555

    C. pkill -9 abc1

    D. pkill -9 555

    E. pkill abc1

    F. pkill 555

10. You are the network administrator for your company. The company has three laser printers, one of which is badly overworked and two of which are mostly idle. What should you do to help remedy this situation?

    A. Install all three printers on one print server. Instruct users to print by using the print server's name instead of the individual printer names.

    B. Install one print spooler for all three printers. Inform users that when they print, they can print to the printer they are used to using, but the print output might appear on any of the three printers.

    C. Install all three printers into one printer class. Instruct users to print to the printer class instead of printing to the individual printer names.

    D. Install all three printers into one printer group. Instruct users to print to the printer group instead of printing to the individual printer names.

11. You are the Solaris administrator for your company. One of your printers is being replaced. The printer's name is hamachi and will be replaced by a printer named buri. Which of the following commands should you use to delete the old printer from the print server?

    A. lpadmin -d hamachi

    B. lpadmin -x hamachi

    C. lpadmin -d hamachi -p buri

    D. lpadmin -x hamachi -p buri

12. You are a Solaris administrator for your company. One of the other network administrators has output from a crontab file and needs help deciphering it. Here is the output:

```
30 5 * * * /usr/sbin/logadm
10 1 * * 4 /usr/lib/fs/nfs/nfsfind
1 2 * * * [ -x /usr/sbin/rtc ] && /usr/sbin/rtc -c > /dev/null 2>&1
```

Which of the following statements are true about this crontab output? (Choose all that apply.)

A. The logadm command is executed at 5:30 P.M. daily.

B. The nfsfind command is executed on October 1st each year.

C. The rtc command is executed at 2:01 A.M. daily.

D. The rtc command has a priority of 1, the nfsfind command has a priority of 10, and the logadm command has a priority of 30.

E. Each of the programs is executed once, except for nfsfind, which is executed four times.

13. You are the Solaris printer administrator for your network. One of your print servers, named print01, has a printer named hirame installed on it. Users printing to hirame complain that nothing is printing. You determine that the printer is powered on and online, and by running the lpstat command, you determine that the printer is enabled and ready to print. However, jobs are sitting in the print queue and not printing. Which course of action should you take to solve this problem?

A. Stop the print spooler with the **lpshut** command and restart it with the **lpsched** command.

B. Enable the printer to print by using the **enable hirame** command.

C. Enable the printer to print by using the **accept hirame** command.

D. Delete the hirame printer and reinstall it by using the **lpadmin** command.

14. You are the Solaris administrator for your company. You are configuring an in-house Solaris 9 print server. All users on your network will use this print server. Which of the following directories contains information on the print server's printer configurations?

A. /etc/lp

B. /usr/lib/lp

C. /usr/lib/print

D. /var/spool/lp

15. To help distribute the printing load on your network, you are going to create a printer class. The first printer that you are adding to the `sushi` printer class is named `toro`. Which command do you need to use to add this printer to the printer class?

- **A.** `lpadd -p toro -c sushi`
- **B.** `lpclass -p toro -c sushi`
- **C.** `lpadmin -p toro -c sushi`
- **D.** `lp -p toro -c sushi`

16. You are the Solaris administrator for your company. Instead of using the `root` account, you log in using a regular user account to check the viability of creating `at` jobs. When you execute the `at` command, you get the following message:

`at: you are not authorized to use at. Sorry.`

Which of the following could this message indicate? (Choose all that apply.)

- **A.** Neither an `at.allow` nor an `at.deny` file exists.
- **B.** Both the `at.allow` and `at.deny` files exist; the user account that you are using is not listed in `at.allow`.
- **C.** The user account that you are using is listed in the `at.allow` file, but an `at.deny` file does not exist.
- **D.** The user account that you are using is listed in the `at.deny` file.

17. You are the Solaris printer administrator for your network. You are configuring fault recovery for the printer named `tako`. When a fault is detected, you want the printer to restart the printing of the document from the first page. Which of the following commands should you use to configure this properly?

- **A.** `lpadmin -p tako -F restart`
- **B.** `lpadmin -p tako -F start`
- **C.** `lpadmin -p tako -F front`
- **D.** `lpadmin -p tako -F beginning`

18. Which of the following statements best describes the relationship between `crontab` and `at` jobs?

- **A.** Both `crontab` and `at` are designed to run multiple jobs on a regular schedule.
- **B.** Both `crontab` and `at` are designed to run one job one time.
- **C.** `crontab` is designed to run multiple jobs on a regular schedule, and `at` is designed to run one job one time.
- **D.** `crontab` is designed to run one job one time, and `at` is designed to run multiple jobs on a regular schedule.

19. You are the Solaris administrator for your network. You are educating other administrators about processes and priorities. As an example, you use the following command:

`# /usr/bin/nice process1`

What does executing the command accomplish?

A. The command raises the nice number of `process1` by four, thereby increasing the priority of `process1` by four.

B. The command raises the nice number of `process1` by four, thereby decreasing the priority of `process1` by four.

C. The command lowers the nice number of `process1` by four, thereby increasing the priority of `process1` by four.

D. The command lowers the nice number of `process1` by four, thereby decreasing the priority of `process1` by four.

20. You are the Solaris printer administrator for your network. A printer named `tobiko` will be moved from one print server to another. You want to prevent users from submitting jobs to the printer, but you also want submitted jobs to print before you turn off the printer. Which of the following commands should you use to accomplish this goal?

A. `disable tobiko`

B. `reject tobiko`

C. `stop tobiko`

D. `/etc/init.d/lp stop`

Answers to Review Questions

1. C. To move print jobs, use the lpmove command. The syntax is lpmove *from_printer to_ printer*. In this case, because you are moving jobs from saba to masu, the answer is lpmove saba masu.

2. A, B, D. If cron.allow and cron.deny do not exist, only the superuser is allowed to create crontab files. If a cron.allow exists, only users listed in that file are allowed to use crontab. If there is no cron.allow, but there is a cron.deny, users in cron.deny are prevented from using crontab.

3. B, C. LPDEST and PRINTER are two acceptable environment variables for setting a user's default printer.

4. C. The print spooler is located in the /var/spool/lp directory.

5. D. The lpstat -d command will return the name of your default printer. The lpstat -D command returns the printer's description (the -p *printer_name* switch would be required also). The lpadmin command is for administering printers.

6. A, B. The two print history logs are /var/lp/logs/requests and /var/lp/logs/lpsched. The requests log holds historical print requests, and the lpsched log contains information about print jobs currently in the print queue.

7. B. The lpadmin command is used to add and manage currently installed printers. To add the new printer, you must specify the printer's name and the port to which the printer will be attached. The designation for the first parallel port is /dev/ecpp0 or /dev/printers/0.

8. B. When you install a printer from the command line, you must configure the printer to accept print jobs and then enable the printer to print those jobs. This is done with the accept and enable commands, respectively. Stopping the print spooler and restarting it will do no good. Deleting and reinstalling the printer is unnecessary and too much work at this point.

9. B, C, D. The kill and pkill commands are used to kill running processes. With the kill command, you can specify only the PID number, not the process name. The pkill command understands PIDs and process names. However, without an argument, the pkill command sends signal 15 (SIGTERM), which attempts a graceful, not an unconditional, termination of the process.

10. C. This is the perfect situation for a printer class. All three printers can be placed in the same class. When users print to the class, their output will be equally shared among the individual print devices. For the class to work, all three printers must be defined on the same print server, but users will not specify the name of the print server in order to print. Printer groups do not exist.

11. B. The lpadmin -x command is used to delete printers from a print server. There is no need to specify the name of the printer that you are going to install.

12. C. Only the third statement is true: the rtc command is run at 2:01 A.M. daily. The first five fields of a crontab file are time and date fields. In order, they are minute, hour, day of the month, month, day of the week.

13. A.   In a case such as this, it might be best to reset the print spooler by stopping and restarting it. The printer is enabled, so there is no need to rerun the `enable` command. Because the printer is accepting print jobs, there is no need to run the `accept` command. Deleting and reinstalling the printer is overkill, and all pending print jobs would be lost.

14. A.   The `/etc/lp` directory contains information about print server configuration. Both `/usr` directories contain print daemons, and `/usr/lib/lp` contains print filters and the standard printer interface program. The `/var/spool/lp` directory is the print spool directory.

15. C.   The `lpadmin` command is used to create printer classes and add printers to printer classes. To add the printer to the printer class, you need to know the name of the printer you're adding (specified with the `-p` switch) and the name of the class (specified with the `-c` switch). Therefore, the correct command would be `lpadmin -p toro -c sushi`.

16. D.   To deny users access to the `at` command, place their usernames in the `at.deny` file. There is no `at.allow` file.

17. D.   The correct option to supply with the `-F` switch for starting over at the beginning of a job is `beginning`. Other options for `-F` are `continue` and `wait`.

18. C.   `crontab` is for running jobs on a periodic schedule, whether it is daily, weekly, monthly, or on a specific day once per year. The `at` command is much simpler and will run a job or a series of jobs only once.

19. B.   The `nice` command is used to modify a process' nice number. By default, the `nice` command with no arguments raises the nice number by four. Raising the nice number means that the process will be "nicer" to other processes (by yielding more processor time) and therefore have a lower priority.

20. B.   To prevent a printer from accepting print requests, use the `reject` command. The `disable` command would stop the printer from printing, and the `stop` command does not exist. The last answer, `/etc/init.d/lp stop`, would stop the entire LP print service, causing `tobiko` to stop printing, as well as affecting other printers that might be attached to the print server.

Chapter

9

System Backups and Restores

SOLARIS 9 EXAM OBJECTIVES COVERED IN THIS CHAPTER:

✓ Given backup requirements, develop a backup strategy that includes scheduled backups, number of tapes required, naming conventions, command protocols, and backup frequency/levels.

✓ Explain how to perform incremental, full, and remote backups to tape for an unmounted file system using the ufsdump command or explain how to back up a mounted file system using ufs snapshot.

✓ Explain how to perform ufs file system restores and special case recoveries.

Backing up critical data is one of the most important aspects of computer and network administration. Not having a backup of irreplaceable data is just asking for trouble. Imagine that your banking institution didn't back up its data, and the server containing all your information crashed. Would you be a very understanding customer if they lost your financial records? Not likely. As another example, imagine a small service business that keeps all its customer information in a database. What happens if the database is lost or corrupted? The outlook for the company is bleak—unless it has a reliable data backup.

Your backups do you no good unless you know how to restore them. Logically then, after discussing backing up data, this chapter covers restorations. It introduces various aspects of backing up and restoring data on your Solaris computer. Included are options to back up and restore the entire file system (as well as individual files), backup scheduling, and backup strategies.

Backing Up File Systems

People back up files for a variety of reasons. Perhaps the obvious reason is safety. If a system with critical data crashes, you need to have a copy of that data available, or business could be severely affected. Files are also backed up in case of accidental deletion, hardware failure, natural disasters, hackers, and a variety of other reasons. The point is: if you can't afford to lose it, you had better back it up.

A *backup* is an exact replica of a set of data, stored on an alternate media. Most of the time, you will be backing up hard disks. Hard disks can be backed up to other hard disks, tape drives, CD-ROMs, or even floppy disks. In recent years, compact disc backups have become increasingly popular as prices have dropped. Backing up to floppy disk is a ridiculous notion in many cases, unless you want a portable copy of only a few files. The most popular choice is magnetic tape backups. Of course, to back up to a magnetic tape, you need a tape drive.

The mention of natural disasters brings up another good point. It's advisable to store copies of your backups off-site. That way, if a disaster such as a tornado, hurricane, earthquake, or fire hits and your building is destroyed, your data is safe (hopefully) in an alternate location. A variety of companies provide secure off-site backup storage.

Solaris 9 has a new feature called UFS snapshots. Previously, file systems needed to be unmounted in order to be backed up. This was because backups have problems backing up files that could be modified, and unmounting the file system guarantees that the files wouldn't be touched. Now, the `fssnap` command can take a snapshot of a mounted file system, and that snapshot can be used to perform a backup.

The primary utilities used to back up and restore file systems are `ufsdump` and `ufsrestore`. The main focus of this chapter is on these two utilities. However, other backup and copy utilities such as `tar`, `cpio`, `pax`, and `dd` are covered as well. More advanced backup situations, such as backing up all systems across a network, call for the Solstice Backup software, which is beyond the scope of the Solaris Certified System Administrator exams.

Planning a Backup Strategy

Haphazardly backing up files and directories with no plan in mind would be as futile as trying to herd cats. Running backups takes time, and the tapes you will be backing up to cost money. In the long run, your company will be better served and you'll make better use of your resources if you plan a comprehensive backup strategy.

Deciding What to Back Up

The first question you need to ask is, "What needs to be backed up?" Critical files, such as customer service databases and financial records, are obvious choices. What about user files? It's generally a good idea to back up user home directories. Users trust you, the administrator, to protect their files, and that includes backing them up in case the server crashes. How about operating system files? Generally, most of these can be replaced easily enough from installation CDs. However, your custom operating system configuration files (such as `/etc/passwd`, `/etc/shadow`, `/etc/system`, and a host of others) can't be easily replaced, so you might want those backed up in one location. The last major category of software is applications. These can usually be recovered from their installation media, so they're not necessary to back up. However, data files should be. As an example, you probably don't need to back up the StarOffice application, but any data created with StarOffice is a candidate for backup.

 When backing up sensitive information, such as the `/etc/passwd` and `/etc/shadow`
WARNING files (or other sensitive material), be sure to save the backup tapes in a secure
location. You don't want the material to end up in the wrong person's hands.

One of the convenient backup features of Solaris is that file systems are automatically configured for backup ease. As an example, you can be assured that all critical operating system files are located on the root file system, located on slice 0. User files should be in `/export/home`, or slice 7. This grouping is convenient; if you want to back up all user files, for example, you can back up slice 7 and be assured you got them all.

Choosing a Backup Method

After you have decided what you need to back up, you need to decide what type of backup you will be performing. The three major choices you have are a full backup, incremental backup, or snapshot backup.

Full backup   A *full backup* backs up all the data in the specified location (all files in a particular file system, for example). This kind of backup stores all data in one place, which makes all of your backed up files easy to locate. However, full backups can take a large number of tapes, depending on how much data you have. Also, you need to unmount all file systems to perform a full backup, and full backups take the longest amount of time of any of the backup types to complete.

Incremental backup   An *incremental backup* backs up only the data that has changed recently. There are a variety of strategies for incremental backups. The strategies are important enough to warrant their own section a little later. Incremental backups are faster (they back up only those files that have changed) and require less space than the other backup types. However, if you have a lot of incremental backups, it can be difficult to locate the exact data you require.

Snapshot backup   A *snapshot backup* is created with the `fssnap` command. The single biggest advantage of a snapshot is that it can be taken while the file system is mounted. If you have a large file system, users will notice a performance decrease while the snapshot is being generated, but it's much more convenient than having to unmount the file system, perform a backup, and then mount the file system for user access.

The type of backup that you want to perform often goes hand in hand with your proposed backup schedule. A *backup schedule* is the schedule you establish to ensure timely and complete backups of your data. The backup schedule you devise will depend on the amount of time needed to perform a backup, time available to perform backups, and time required to restore critical file systems. You should also attempt to create a schedule that minimizes the number of required backup tapes, to save costs.

The frequency of your backups determines the number of backup tapes you will use. Typically, administrators like to rotate backup tapes and use one tape per backup volume. So if you perform a full backup every Sunday and an incremental backup every night, you will need seven tapes to rotate (plus at least one spare). If you were to do a full backup every night, you would need only two tapes (provided that one tape can store all your data): one for the current night and one for the previous night.

In terms of how often you should back up, a good general rule is that if it's critical or it changes frequently, back it up often. In other words, files that might change once a week probably don't need to be backed up every night. Similarly, if a file changes daily, backing it up once a week might increase the chances of data loss.

If you do not have a lot of time to perform backups, then an incremental backup is a good choice. Both full and incremental backups are initiated with the `ufsdump` *dump_level* command. A dump level of 0 indicates a full backup. Levels 1 through 9 are various levels of incremental backups. The numbers themselves have no built-in meanings. They're just used in relation to other incremental backups. A few examples should clarify the numbering issue.

Example 1   You perform a full backup (level 0) on Sunday night. Monday night, you perform an incremental level 3 backup. The level 3 backup will back up files that have changed since the last lower-level backup. In other words, it will archive all files that changed Monday.

Example 2   Sunday night, you perform a full (level 0) backup. Monday night, you perform a level 3 backup, which backs up all files changed on Monday. Tuesday, you run a level 3 backup again. It will back up all files that have changed on Monday and/or Tuesday. The key is, it will back up all files modified *since the last lower-level backup*, which was on Sunday (level 0).

Example 3 Sunday night, you perform a level 0 backup. Monday night, you perform a level 3 backup, which backs up all files changed on Monday. Tuesday night, you run a level 5 backup. This backup will back up all files that have changed since Monday's backup.

Example 4 Sunday night, you perform a level 0 backup. Monday through Thursday nights, you run level 5 backups. Each night will back up progressively more material. On Friday night, you perform a level 3 backup. The level 3 backup will back up all files changed since the last lower-level backup, which was Sunday.

Example 5 Sunday night, you perform a level 0 backup. Here's the rest of your schedule: Monday level 4, Tuesday level 5, Wednesday level 6, Thursday level 7, and Friday level 3. The levels 4, 5, 6, and 7 backups will just back up their respective days' changes. The level 3 on Friday will back up all files changed during the week, back to the level 0 performed on Sunday.

The key thing to remember about the incremental backups is that the numbers 1–9 themselves have no importance. In other words, you could do a whole week of level 3 backups, or a whole week of level 7 backups (just think of extending Example 2 into a whole week), and there would be no difference. The numbers become important only when used in relation to other incremental backups.

Most facilities use a combination of full and incremental backups. Some prefer to run a full backup every weekend, when there's the most time to run backups, and incremental backups every night. Others prefer a monthly full backup. The right answer for your network depends on the importance of your data and how much time you want to spend restoring a server if it does crash.

Finally, here are some points to remember about performing backups:

- Unmount the file system before running `ufsdump` unless you are using `fssnap` to create a snapshot.

- If you choose to back up a file system that is mounted, directory changes or file-level changes might not be backed up properly.

- The `ufsdump` command can be used to back up remote machines onto a local machine with a tape drive.

- If you are performing backups across the network, the system containing the tape drive must have an entry in its `/.rhosts` file for each client machine that will be using the tape drive.

- To back up an NIS+ server database, use the `nisbackup` command.

Choosing Backup Media

When backing up hard disks, you have a limited number of choices for backup media. The most common destinations for backups are another hard disk, tape drive, floppy disk, or CD-ROM. Backing up to CD-ROM is becoming increasingly popular, but has yet to become as well practiced as backing up to tape drive.

If you are backing up only a few files, you can back them up to a floppy disk. However, for most networks, this is not an option for repeated backups. Backing up to another hard disk is possible, but if done in large volumes, this backup option is not very cost-effective. For most networks, backing up to a tape volume is the best choice.

Choosing a Tape Device and Understanding Tape Device Naming

Depending on your company's budget, you can choose from a variety of tape drives to purchase and install. Some of the older tape technologies, such as the 1/2-inch reel tape, hold approximately 140MB each. Other options include 8mm 14GB cartridge tapes, and DLT 7000 tapes, which hold up to 70GB of data. If budget is not an issue to you, you can spend tens of thousands of dollars on auto-loading tape drives that hold multiple tapes, store thousands of gigabytes, and transfer nearly 2GB per minute.

Regardless of the tape device you choose, if it's going to be managed by Solaris, you need to understand the naming conventions used. The first tape device in Solaris is referenced by its raw logical name of /dev/rmt/0. The /dev directory, as you know by now, holds logical device names, not physical device names. The /dev/rmt directory stands for raw magnetic tape. A tape device number can also be followed by a density rating of 1 for low, m for medium, h for high, u for ultra, or c for compressed. If no density is specified, the tape drive will write at its preferred density (the highest density it supports). The last option that follows a tape device name is n, for no rewind. As an example, the second tape drive in a machine, using medium density and no rewind, would be represented as /dev/rmt/1mn.

Managing Tape Devices

The mt (magnetic tape control) command can be used to check the status of a tape drive, such as the parameters the tape drive is configured with. Tape devices described in the /kernel/drv/st.conf file can be queried by using mt. To check the status of your first tape drive, you would use:

```
# mt -f /dev/rmt/0 status
```

The mt command can also be used to rewind, forward, re-tension, and erase magnetic tapes. See man mt for more information.

Taking proper care of your tapes and tape drives is critical to your backup planning. Poor-quality tapes might not be able to be read, and if the backup data can't be read, it's useless.

When you first install a tape device, perform a trial backup and ensure that you can read files off of the tape. Always store tapes in a dry, dust-free place, away from magnetic devices. Label your tapes with the date, backup type, and general contents, and maintain a separate log of tape backups and locations. If a tape starts to show wear, replace it immediately.

Using *ufsdump* to Perform Backups

After you've acquired your backup hardware and completed your backup planning, you are ready to use the ufsdump command to back up files.

Because of the name of the backup program, ufsdump, you will hear a lot of people refer to backups as *dumps*.

One of the negatives about using ufsdump is that it doesn't automatically detect the number of tapes you'll need. Then again, considering the different technologies and tape sizes available, one could hardly expect ufsdump to know every possibility. Therefore, to find out how many tapes you'll need, you will need to run a test:

```
# ufsdump S /
177897280
```

The S displays an estimate of the number of bytes needed to perform a backup of this file system, in this case, the root (/). If you can convert the number to megabytes in your head, great. If not, feel free to use a calculator. The number of bytes listed in this example is 177,897,280, which is roughly 170MB. Now, based on the capacity of the tapes you are using, you can determine how many tapes you'll need to back up the root.

How *ufsdump* Works

Executing the ufsdump command initiates a two-phase process. In the first phase, ufsdump scans the raw device for the file system, builds a table (in memory) of directories and files found, and then writes the table of contents to the backup media. In the second phase, ufsdump parses the inodes in numerical order, reading file contents and writing the data to the backup media.

When ufsdump writes data to the backup media, it does so in a default block size. (Although the block size can be specified, the default is generally adequate.) When ufsdump receives a message from the tape device that a partial block of data was written, ufsdump assumes that the physical end of the media has been reached. If more backup data needs to be written, and you don't have an automatic tape loader, ufsdump will instruct you to insert an additional tape to continue.

Because ufsdump copies data from the raw disk slice, any files that are being modified (meaning the new information is stored in memory buffers) will not be backed up properly. This is why it's recommended that you unmount file systems before backing them up. Additionally, ufsdump does not back up free blocks or make an exact image of a disk slice. If your slice contains symbolic links, the link will be backed up, not the file that the link points to.

The */etc/dumpdates* File

When used with the -u option, ufsdump updates the /etc/dumpdates file. Each line in /etc/dumpdates is a separate entry and shows the file system backed up, the level of the backup, and the day, date, and time of the backup. Here is a sample /etc/dumpdates file:

```
# more /etc/dumpdates
/dev/rdsk/c0t0d0s0          0 Sun Sep 29 20:30:05 2002
/dev/rdsk/c0t0d0s7          0 Sun Sep 29 22:09:32 2002
/dev/rdsk/c0t0d0s0          5 Mon Sep 30 20:04:18 2002
/dev/rdsk/c0t0d0s7          9 Mon Sep 30 22:02:58 2002
#
```

There's absolutely no reason *not* to update the /etc/dumpdates file. Updating it doesn't slow down your backups, or inconvenience users. However, not updating it can cause problems for your proposed backup schedule.

Problems can be caused because when you perform an incremental backup, ufsdump checks the /etc/dumpdates file to see when the last backup of that file system occurred. Then, based on the level of that backup, ufsdump knows which files it needs to back up and which files it can ignore. Not only does ufsdump use the /etc/dumpdates file as a log, you as an administrator can verify that backups are being completed by periodically inspecting /etc/dumpdates.

Using *ufsdump*

The basic syntax for ufsdump is as follows:

ufsdump *options arguments filenames*

By default, ufsdump is executed with the following options and arguments:

ufsdump 9uf /dev/rmt/0 *filenames*

 Notice that unlike most other commands in Solaris, arguments for ufsdump are not preceded with a dash (−).

Table 9.1 lists valid ufsdump options.

TABLE 9.1   *ufsdump* Options

Option	Description
0–9	Defines a dump level. 0 is a full dump, and 1–9 are incremental dumps.
a *archive_file*	Writes a backup copy of the table of contents to the specified *archive_file*, readable only by ufsrestore.
b *factor*	Specifies a blocking factor (the number of 512-byte blocks to write) for tape writes.
c	Sets the tape drive type to cartridge and block size to 126 instead of 1/2-inch reel tape.
d *bpi*	Defines tape density in bytes per inch.
D	Backs up files to floppy disk.
f *dump_file*	Uses the *dump_file* as the backup media, instead of the default /dev/rmt/0. The *dump_file* can be another hard disk on a local or remote machine. If on a remote machine, the format for *dump_file* must be *machine_name: device_name*.
l	Auto-loads tape devices. The ufsdump command waits two minutes for the tape device to be ready and then continues. If the device is not ready, ufsdump prompts the administrator to continue.
n	Notifies all members in the sys group that ufsdump requires immediate attention, by sending messages to their terminal.

TABLE 9.1   *ufsdump* Options *(continued)*

Option	Description
N *device_name*	Uses the *device_name* specified when recording information in /etc/dumpdates, and when comparing against information in /etc/dumpdates for incremental backups.
o	Takes the tape device offline when the dump is completed, or rewinds and ejects the media if end-of-media is detected.
s *size*	Defines the size of the media being backed up to. Specified in feet for reel media, or 1024-byte blocks for floppy disks.
S	Estimates the space needed for the backup, in bytes.
t *tracks*	Defines the number of tracks for cartridge tapes.
u	Adds an entry into the /etc/dumpdates file.
v	Verifies the backup by comparing written backup data against the source file(s).
w	Warning mode. Lists the file systems present in /etc/dumpdates that have not been backed up within a day. This option must be used alone.
W	Warning mode with highlights. Similar to w, except that W displays all file systems in /etc/dumpdates and highlights the file systems that haven't been backed up within a day.

Because ufsdump can detect end-of-media for most tape devices, the c, d, s, and t options are rarely needed.

Even though the default output for dump files is /dev/rmt/0, many administrators prefer to specify the device name by using the f option anyway. The f option can also be used to designate another hard disk, or even a remote hard disk, as the backup media to use. For instance, if you wanted to back up your local slice 7 to a hard disk slice on a remote computer named igor, you could use the following command:

ufsdump 0uf igor:/dev/rdsk/c0t0d0s4 /dev/rdsk/c0t0d0s7

Remember, though, in order to back up to a remote system, the computer you are on must have an entry in the remote computer's /.rhosts file.

Another common scenario would be to perform an incremental backup and to not rewind the tape. This might be because you want to add additional backup information to the tape because it's not yet filled up. Here's how you could do that:

ufsdump 9uf /dev/rmt/0n /dev/rdsk/c0t0d0s7

Notice the *n* at the end of the device name. That tells the tape drive to not rewind after the dump is completed. You will also notice that the file system to back up is always at the end of the command. You can specify either the raw device name (as the examples in this chapter have so far) or the mount point directory for the device, as long as the device has an entry in the /etc/vfstab file.

When using ufsdump, you don't need to back up entire file systems. Individual files and/or directories can be specified instead of file systems. When you back up files or directories, though, a level 0 backup is always performed. You cannot incrementally back up individual files or directories. Multiple files or directories can be specified for the *filenames* variable; separate multiple entries with spaces.

Here are a few more examples. To back up the root file system (remember, you have to unmount the file system, so to back up root, you need to take the computer into the S run level) to a cartridge tape device and verify the backup:

```
# ufsdump 0uvcf /dev/rmt/0 /
```

To back up an individual directory, such as a home directory, and not rewind the cartridge tape, you could use:

```
# ufsdump 0ucf /dev/rmt/0n /export/home/ldocter
```

In summary, although the ufsdump utility is a solid performer, it does have a few limitations. The first is that it can't calculate the number of tapes needed to perform a given backup. That's why you need to use ufsdump S to get an idea of how many tapes you need. Second, ufsdump cannot accurately perform backups of mounted file systems. Third, ufsdump cannot back up files mounted from a remote server. The files must be backed up from the server they are located on.

Finally, to increase security on your network, make sure that root is the only user that has access to the ufsdump command. And if you're doing centralized backups on your network, remove all root access entries from the /.rhosts files on clients and servers. This will prevent any unauthorized over-the-network backups.

Using UFS Snapshots

Traditionally, to back up a UFS file system, you were instructed to unmount the file system, making it inaccessible to users. This typically meant performing your backups late at night and on the weekends. For networks that required 24-hour access, there was no choice but to inconvenience users. Now another method is available: a UFS snapshot. A snapshot can be taken of a mounted UFS file system and then used to create a backup archive, while leaving the file system mounted and accessible the entire time.

UFS snapshots were originally introduced with the Solaris 8 1/01 release and are an integrated part of Solaris 9. A *UFS snapshot* is a backing-store image (a fancy name for an image used as a backup) of a file system at a given point in time and is created with the fssnap command.

UFS snapshots are based on the Sun StorEdge Instant Image tool. There are, however, some differences. Whereas an image taken with Instant Image remains on the system after reboots, images taken with fssnap do not. This means that if you want to use an fssnap backing-store file for backup purposes, you must make the backup before rebooting. The fssnap command works on all UFS file systems, but Instant Image does not work on the root (/) or /usr file systems. Finally, while Instant Image backing-store files are the same size as the file system they are copies of, UFS snapshots are designed to take as little space as possible, and maximum size limits can be placed on UFS snapshot backing-store files.

Creating, Displaying, and Deleting Snapshots

Because creating a UFS snapshot is memory intensive, users will notice a performance drain when fssnap is used. Creating snapshots of larger file systems will increase the delay in performance.

When you execute the fssnap command, the backing-store file will initially consume no disk space and then grow rapidly as the snapshot is created. Make sure the snapshot has plenty of room to grow; if it runs out of space, it might delete itself, causing the backup operation to fail. Check the /var/adm/messages log for possible errors. You can limit the size of a backing-store file by using the -o maxsize=*n* [k,m,g] option, where *n* is the size in kilobytes, megabytes, gigabytes, or a combination of the three.

To create a snapshot, use the following syntax:

fssnap -F ufs -o bs=/*backing_store_file* **/***file_system*

The *backing_store_file* option is the name of the snapshot you are creating, and *file_system* is the file system you are making the snapshot of. Snapshots must reside in an alternate file system; they can't be part of the file system that's having its snapshot taken.

Here's an example of creating a snapshot, named /snapshot1, of the /export/home file system:

```
# fssnap -F ufs -o bs=/snapshot1 /export/home
/dev/fssnap/0
#
```

Running the fssnap command created the snapshot, as the /snapshot1 file exists, and it also created a virtual device representing the snapshot. The virtual device is named /dev/fssnap/0. Later in this chapter, you'll see how the virtual device name can be used to create a backup of the snapshot.

To display existing snapshots or to get detailed information about snapshots, use the fssnap -i command. For detailed information on a snapshot, you can either specify the snapshot name or use the UFS file system–specific version of fssnap:

```
# fssnap -i
   0    /export/home
# /usr/lib/fs/ufs/fssnap -i
Snapshot number            : 0
Block Device               : /dev/fssnap/0
Raw Device                 : /dev/rfssnap/0
Mount point                : /export/home
Device state               : idle
Backing store path         : /snapshot1
Backing store size         : 0 KB
Maximum backing store size : Unlimited
Snapshot create time       : Fri Oct 04 09:06:50 2002
Copy-on-write granularity  : 32 KB
```

Snapshots can be deleted in one of two ways. Either reboot the system or execute the fssnap -d /*file_system* command.

Backing Up and Restoring Snapshots

Backing up a snapshot is just like backing up an unmounted file system. You can use the ufsdump command to either fully or incrementally back up snapshots. Here's an example of performing a full backup of the UFS snapshot, snapshot1, used previously in this chapter:

```
# ufsdump 0ucf /dev/rmt/0 /dev/rfssnap/0
```

 The ufsdump command wants to see raw device names, so you need to know the raw device name of your snapshot. To get this information, use /usr/lib/fs /ufs/fssnap -i.

Creating incremental backups of snapshots is a bit more involved. When performing an incremental backup of a snapshot, only the files modified since the last snapshot was taken will be backed up. The tricky part is, you have a snapshot that has a raw device name, yet it doesn't necessarily correspond to the raw device name of the file system you took the snapshot of. For example, looking at the previous output from /usr/lib/fs/ufs/fssnap -i, all you know of the original snapshot file system is that it's /export/home. So, to perform an incremental backup, you need to specify the original raw device as well (this is done with the -o raw option). Here's an example:

```
# ufsdump 9ufN /dev/rmt/0 /dev/rdsk/c0t0d0s7 `fssnap -F ufs -o raw,bs=/
  snapshot1,unlink /dev/rdsk/c0t0d0s7`
```

Backups created with UFS snapshots are restored just as any other backup is restored. If you used ufsdump to perform the backup, you will use ufsrestore to restore.

Restoring File Systems

The whole idea of backing up files is to have a copy of critical data in case something happens to the server. Ideally, you will never have to restore from backup in your administrative career. Achieving that ideal, though, is unlikely. You need to know how to restore backups after you've created them.

The ufsrestore command is used to restore files backed up with ufsdump. When you *restore*, you copy files from a backup media back to an active hard disk. Files can be restored from full or incremental dumps, with no major differences in ufsrestore syntax. If the superuser runs ufsrestore, files are restored with their original owner, last modification time, and permissions.

Before you begin a restore, you should have the tapes you need to perform the restore, the raw device name of the device you want to restore to, and a list of files or file systems you want to restore.

One of the features of ufsrestore is that it restores files in relation to their original directory location. For example, files in /export/home/qdocter are saved in relation to the file system, in this case /export/home. Therefore, the file /export/home/qdocter/solbook is written to tape as ./qdocter/solbook, and when restored to the /var/tmp directory, it would be restored to /var/tmp/qdocter/solbook.

This restoration procedure can become quite confusing if you are restoring a large number of files. If you want, you can create subdirectories in /var/tmp to restore to and then move the files to their needed locations after the restorations are complete.

Never restore files to the /tmp directory. The /tmp directory uses the TMPFS file system, which does not support UFS security features such as Access Control Lists (ACLs).

Using the *ufsrestore* Command

The syntax for ufsrestore is as follows:

```
# ufsrestore options arguments filename(s)
```

There are only five options for ufsrestore. They are shown in Table 9.2.

TABLE 9.2   *ufsrestore* Options

Option	Description
i	Interactive; gives you some control over the restoration.
r	Recursive; re-creates the entire file system relative to the current working directory.
R	Resume; resumes an interrupted r-mode ufsrestore.
t	Table of contents; lists each filename that appears on the media.
x	Extract; enables you to remove only the requested files from the media.

Quite a number of arguments are available for ufsrestore. Some of the more common ones are listed in Table 9.3.

TABLE 9.3   *ufsrestore* Command-Line Arguments

Argument	Description
a archive_file	Reads the table of contents from the specified *archive_file* instead of the tape backup media. It's used with t, i, and x modes to check whether the needed files are on the media without actually having to mount the media.
b factor	Specifies a blocking factor (the number of 512-byte blocks to read in one pass) to use. By default, ufsrestore attempts to detect the blocking factor used in the ufsdump.
d	Turns on debugging output.

TABLE 9.3 *ufsrestore* Command-Line Arguments *(continued)*

Argument	Description
f *dump_file*	Uses the *dump_file* instead of /dev/rmt/0 as the file to restore from. If the *dump_file* is specified as –, ufsrestore reads from the standard input.
m	Extracts files by inode number instead of by filename and restores them into the current working directory, regardless of where they were previously located within the file system.
o	Takes the tape drive offline and ejects the media, if possible, after the restoration is complete.
s *n*	Skips to the *n*th file, if multiple dump files are on the same tape. For example, ufsrestore xfs /dev/rmt/0n 3 skips to the third dump file on the tape.
v	Enables verbose mode.

As an example, if you wanted to begin a recursive restore from the first tape device, you could use the following command:

ufsrestore rf /dev/rmt/0

Or, to begin an interactive restore from the same device, you could use:

ufsrestore if /dev/rmt/0

Interactive restorations enable you to use some shell-like commands to browse and interact with the restore media. The interactive commands supported are listed in Table 9.4.

TABLE 9.4 Interactive Restoration Commands

Command	Description
add *filename*	Adds the named file or directory to the list of files to extract. If a directory is specified, the directory and all files within the directory are added to the extraction list.
cd *directory*	Changes directories within the dump file.
delete *filename*	Deletes the file or directory from the list of files to be extracted. If a directory name is specified, that directory and all its files and subdirectories will be removed from the extraction list.
extract	Extracts all files on the extraction list and restores them into the current working directory on the hard disk. If you are asked to specify a volume number, enter 1 for the first volume (recommended).

TABLE 9.4   Interactive Restoration Commands *(continued)*

Command	Description
help	Displays a list of available commands.
ls	Lists files within the present directory or the directory specified. Directories and files marked for extraction are prefixed with an asterisk (*).
marked	Functions like ls, except only files that are marked for extraction are listed.
pwd	Prints the present working directory within the backup hierarchy.
quit	Exits the interactive restore.
setmodes	Prompts the administrator with set owner/mode for '.' [yn]. Choose "yes" to set the mode (permissions, owner, and access times) of the current directory (into which files are being restored) equal to the mode of the root directory of the file system from which they were dumped. If restoring an entire file system, or files into their original directory, this is a good choice. Choose "no" to leave the mode of the current directory (into which files are being restored) unchanged. If you are restoring files into a directory other than the one they originally came from, this is the best choice.
verbose	Enables verbose mode. In verbose mode, ls lists the inode numbers of all files and directories, and ufsrestore displays information about each file as it's extracted.

As you can see by the commands available, interactive mode gives you a considerable amount of control over the restoration process.

If you do not specify a setmodes option, you will be prompted with set owner /mode for '.' [yn] after the restoration is complete. Understanding the differences between saying "yes" and saying "no" is critical because your answer will greatly affect the security of restored files.

You can also restore from remote locations, such as remote tape drives or remote hard disks. To restore remotely, you need to specify the location of the media you want to restore from. Here's an example of restoring from the first tape device on a server named fido:

```
# ufsrestore xf fido:/dev/rmt/0
```

Interactive and recursive restorations can also be performed when the restoration media is located on a remote system.

🌐 Real World Scenario

Are You Missing Something in the Restore?

The hard disk containing the user home directories on your Solaris file server crashed. As recommended, you have created regular backups. You have replaced the hardware and now are going to perform a restore by using ufsrestore.

Your backup schedule is to perform a level 0 dump on Sunday, followed by a level 2 on Monday, 3 on Tuesday, 4 on Wednesday, 5 on Thursday, and 6 on Friday. You follow this routine every week. The hard disk crashed on Wednesday.

When you perform the restore, you restore from the tape marked "Sunday" and then from the tape marked "Tuesday." You verify that the new hard disk is operational and run a quick check to make sure files are there. Everything seems okay.

Later that day, you receive calls from users saying that their restored data doesn't quite look right. Some files are missing, and others contain incorrect data, while others seem to be fine. The users are concerned and not sure how this could have happened. They quickly dismiss the idea that the files they are talking about were modified on Wednesday and therefore lost when the hard disk crashed. What could be the problem?

It appears as though you missed a tape during the restoration process. Incremental backups back up only the files that have changed since the last lower-level backup. The dump you ran Tuesday backed up files that had changed since the last lower-level backup, which was done Monday. The Tuesday tape didn't have Monday's changes. That explains why some files might be okay (because they weren't modified Monday), and others weren't.

There are two solutions to your problem, one of which you can use now. To get the users' files back, you need to restore the full backup (Sunday), followed by Monday's tape and then Tuesday's tape. The second solution requires a bit of planning. If you were to run a level 0 dump on Sunday, followed by the same level dump (level 5 for example) each weeknight, you could restore as you had originally, and all files should be as up-to-date as possible.

Special Case Restorations

So far, this chapter has discussed only restoring files from a tape backup, not necessarily restoring entire file systems. Restoring full file systems is an involved process and can take quite a bit of time if the file system is large. But if the file system is irreparably damaged or corrupted, or the hard disk has failed, you might not have any other choice. Restoring the root (/) and /usr file systems requires its own special process, which will be covered later in this section.

Restoring Entire File Systems

Before you can restore an entire file system, you must have superuser or equivalent rights. These steps also require you to have unmounted the old file system, replaced hardware as necessary, and created a new file system at least large enough to hold the file system you want to restore.

 For information on creating file systems, see Chapter 7, "File System Management."

After you have created the new file system, you can follow these steps to restore the old file system from backup:

1. Mount the file system you just created on a temporary mount point. The temporary mount point can be called anything you would like, but for brevity, you can use /new.

   # **mount /dev/dsk/***device_name* **/new**

2. Change directories to your new mount point.

   # **cd /new**

3. Insert the tape containing your last full backup into the tape drive and restore the files.

   # **ufsrestore rvf /dev/rmt/0**

4. If you have incremental dumps more current than your last full dump, continue restoring, from lowest-level dump to highest, until all your dumps are restored.

5. Check to ensure that the file system is restored properly. How you do this is up to you, but an easy way is to use the ls command to verify that the right files are in the right places.

6. Remove the restoresymtable file. This file is used by ufsrestore as a check point in the restore process and is no longer needed.

   # **rm restoresymtable**

7. Change to another directory (such as the root) and unmount the new file system.

   # **cd /**

   # **umount /new**

8. Insert a new, blank tape and make a full backup of the new file system. After all the work you have performed to restore this file system, you had better make a fresh dump.

   # **ufsdump 0uf /dev/rmt/0 /dev/rdsk/***device_name*

9. Mount the new file system.

   # **mount /dev/dsk/***device_name mount_point*

10. Verify access to the newly restored and mounted file system.

    # **ls** *mount_point*

Your file system should be restored and operational.

The root (/) and /usr file systems are the two most critical file systems to Solaris operation. In fact, they are the only two required file systems to operate Solaris. Because of their critical nature, and because the root file system is used to boot, restoring these two file systems requires special steps.

As with restoring any other file system, you need to have superuser or equivalent rights. You also must have added a new system disk to the computer and created a new file system on it.

You will have to boot to the CD-ROM or to the network to restore the file system. After those tasks are completed, follow this procedure:

1. Mount the file system you just created on a temporary mount point. The temporary mount point can be called anything you would like, but for brevity, you can use /new.

   # **mount /dev/dsk/*device_name* /new**

2. Change directories to your new mount point.

   # **cd /new**

3. Insert the tape containing your last full backup into the tape drive and restore the files.

   # **ufsrestore rvf /dev/rmt/0**

4. If you have incremental dumps more current than your last full dump, continue restoring, from lowest-level dump to highest, until all your dumps are restored.

5. Check to ensure that the file system is restored properly. How you do this is up to you, but an easy way is to use the ls command to verify that the right files are in the right places.

6. Remove the restoresymtable file. This file is used by ufsrestore as a check point in the restore process and is no longer needed.

   # **rm restoresymtable**

7. Change to another directory (such as the root) and unmount the new file system.

   # **cd /**
   # **umount /new**

8. Check the new file system for consistency.

   # **fsck /dev/rdsk/*device_name***

9. Create boot blocks on the new root partition.

   # **installboot /usr/platform/`uname -i`/lib/fs/ufs/bootblk**
   ↳**/dev/rdsk/*device_name***

10. Insert a new, blank tape and make a full backup of the new file system. After all the work you have performed to restore this file system, you had better make a fresh dump.

    # **ufsdump 0uf /dev/rmt/0 /dev/rdsk/*device_name***

11. Repeat steps 1 through 10 for the /usr file system, if necessary.

12. Reboot the system.

    # **init 6**

Your root (/) and /usr file systems should be restored and operational.

Using Other Copy and Backup Utilities

The tar, cpio, and pax commands can also be used to perform backups of files and file systems. Generally speaking, these three utilities are intended for smaller file systems and are not often used to back up entire servers. If you want to copy or move individual files or portions of file systems, these three commands, along with dd, provide an alternative to using ufsdump and ufsrestore.

Making File System Copies With *dd*

If you want to copy individual files or file systems, the dd command can be used to make a block-level, physical copy of a file system to another file system or tape device. The dd command copies standard input to standard output by default, but the standard input and standard output can be replaced by keyword pairs if desired. The following is an example of using dd with standard input and standard output, followed by keyword pairs. Both commands accomplish the same task, copying the contents of a floppy disk into a file in the temporary directory:

```
# dd < /floppy/floppy0 > /tmp/file1
# dd if=/floppy/floppy0 of=/tmp/file1
```

If you are going to use keyword pairs with dd, the syntax is *keyword=value*. This differs from most other Solaris commands. In the example, if means input file (input path), and of means output file (output path). You can also specify input block sizes with ibs=*n* (*n* is in bytes), output block sizes with obs=*n*, and block sizes for both input and output with bs=*n*. Larger block sizes increase copying efficiency. The default block size is 512 bytes.

The dd command can also convert data with different formats, such as differing record lengths or block sizes.

Using *cpio*

The cpio (copy in and out) command is used to copy data from one place to another. Typically, this means copying data from a hard disk to a tape backup, or restoring data from a backup onto a hard disk. The cpio command provides flexible syntax and acts as a filter program, taking data from standard input and delivering it to standard output. This command can back up and restore individual files, is more efficient than tar in terms of disk space, and is capable of spanning multiple tapes. The syntax for cpio is as follows:

```
# cpio mode options
```

There are three modes for cpio: copy in (-i) for restoring from tape, copy out (-o) for archiving to tape, and pass mode (-p), which is used to copy files from one location to another on a hard disk.

Table 9.5 lists some of the common options for cpio.

TABLE 9.5   *cpio* Command-Line Options

Option	Description
-A	Appends files to a cpio archive. Requires the -0 option to work.
-B	Uses blocks of 5120 bytes instead of the default 512 bytes, increasing transfer speed.

TABLE 9.5   *cpio* Command-Line Options *(continued)*

Option	Description
-c	Reads or writes header information in ASCII character form for portability between UNIX-based operating systems.
-d	Creates directories as needed.
-E *file*	Specifies an input file that contains a list of filenames to be extracted from the archive. Filenames should be listed one per line in the input file.
-I *file*	Specifies the contents of the file as the input archive, instead of standard input.
-k	Attempts to skip corrupted file headers and I/O errors.
-m	Retains previous file modification time, instead of updating it.
-O *file*	Directs the output of cpio to a file, instead of standard output.
-P	Preserves Access Control Lists.
-t	Prints a table of contents of the input.
-u	Unconditionally copies, regardless of file modification dates. Normally, older files will not replace newer files with the same name.
-v	Verbose mode; prints a list of files and their extended attributes.
-@	Includes extended attributes in the archive.

The most common way to use cpio is to use file commands such as ls or find to locate files and then pipe the output to cpio for archiving. For example, if you wanted to copy all files and subdirectories from a user's home directory to tape backup, you could use the following command from the user's home directory:

```
# ls -R | cpio -oc > /dev/rmt/0
```

WARNING   Executing this command from the root directory (/) will cause cpio to attempt to back up your entire directory structure.

Or, you could find the entire list of files created by a user (adocter in this case) and back them up to tape:

```
# find . -user adocter | cpio -o > /dev/rmt/o
```

And, after copying files to the tape device, you will want to make sure that the files were copied properly:

cpio -civt < /dev/rmt/0

To import files from a cpio archive, you could use the following:

cpio -icvd < /dev/rmt/0

For most backup jobs that don't require you to back up the entire file system, you will generally find cpio to be the most flexible command to use.

Using *tar* and *pax*

The tar (tape archiver) command is primarily used to copy file systems from hard disk to tape, or from tape to hard disk. The tar command is popular because it's widely available across UNIX platforms. However, it's limited to a single tape or floppy disk. Here is the syntax for tar:

tar *options* tarfile file_list

When using tar to make a backup, the file you are creating is called a tarfile. The file_list is the list of files you want to back up. Table 9.6 lists some common tar options.

TABLE 9.6   *tar* Command-Line Options

Option	Description
c	Creates a tarfile.
f	Uses the tarfile argument as the name of the tarfile. If omitted, tar will use the name of the device indicated in the TAPE environment variable, if set, or else it will use the default values listed in /etc/default/tar.
r	Replaces existing files in the tarfile. The files named in file_list are added to the end of the tarfile.
t	Table of contents. Lists the names of the files located within the tarfile.
u	Updates the files named in file_list.
v	Enables verbose mode.
x	Extracts files from the tarfile.

To create a new tarfile on tape, backing up all files in the /export/home/ldocter directory, you could use:

tar cvf /dev/rmt/0 /export/home/ldocter

To show the table of contents in the archive you just created, you would use:

tar tvf /dev/rmt/0

And to restore the tape archive, you could use:

tar xvf /dev/rmt/0 /export/home/ldocter

If you use absolute paths to create tar backups, the original files will be overwritten during a restoration, regardless of the directory you restore to. Accordingly, most administrators use relative pathnames when backing up using tar.

Copying files to a floppy disk is nearly identical to copying files to a tape drive. In the previous example, the tape drive device name was used as the name for the tarfile. For a floppy disk, using the tape device name doesn't make sense:

tar cvf /vol/dev/aliases/floppy0/floppy.bkp /export/home/ldocter

Floppy disks containing tarfiles are not mountable.

Because tar is limited to a single tape or single floppy disk, it's not usually used to make backups to a floppy disk.

Like the tar command, pax is used to create archives on tape or floppy disk. The pax command has the same disadvantages as tar, in that it's not aware of system boundaries, does not support full pathnames longer than 255 characters, and does not copy empty directories or special files (such as device files). However, unlike tar, pax can be used to create volumes that span multiple tapes or disks.

pax has four operational modes: read (-r), write (-w), copy (-rw), and list (neither -r nor -w). The -a command line argument can be used to append an existing pax archive, -v displays information in verbose mode, and -f *archive* is used to specify the archive name.

The syntax to create a pax archive is as follows:

pax -w -f /dev/rmt/0 *file_list*

The pax command can also read and write tar and cpio archives.

Summary

This chapter covered principles and concepts needed to effectively design and implement a backup strategy for your local computer or your network. First, you learned about backing up file systems, including backup planning, details about incremental backups, and the ufsdump command. Then, you read about a new standard feature of Solaris 9, UFS snapshots, taken with the fssnap command. UFS snapshots enable you to back up a file system without unmounting it first.

Next, you learned how to restore backups with the `ufsrestore` command. A variety of restoration types were covered, including special case restorations of an entire file system, as well as the root (/) and /usr file systems.

Finally, this chapter concluded with an examination of other helpful copy and backup utilities. Commands covered were `dd`, `cpio`, `tar`, and `pax`.

Exam Essentials

Know how to determine the number of tapes required to perform your backup.   The number of tapes depends on the amount of data you have to back up. Run the `ufsdump S /file_system` command, where `file_system` is the file system you want to back up, and convert the number you get back (it's in bytes) to megabytes. Then, depending on the capacity of the tape you are using, you know how many tapes you need.

Understand the difference between full and incremental backups.   Full backups back up all data within a file system. Incremental backups back up only the data that has been modified since the last lower-level backup.

Know how to perform full and incremental backups.   Both types of backups are executed with the `ufsdump` command. The level of backup specified determines backup type. Level 0 is a full dump, and levels 1–9 are incremental backups.

Understand how to back up a file system by using a UFS snapshot.   First, you take a snapshot of a mounted file system with the `fssnap` command. Then, using the snapshot as a virtual device, you use the `ufsdump` command to make a backup archive based on the snapshot.

Know how to restore backed up file systems.   File systems backed up with the `ufsdump` command are restored with the `ufsrestore` command.

Know which situations call for a special case restoration.   If you are restoring an entire file system, it will be a special case restoration. If you are restoring the root (/) or /usr file systems, there are even more steps involved.

Key Terms

Before you take the exam, be certain you are familiar with the following terms:

backup	incremental backup
backup schedule	restore
full backup	UFS snapshot

Commands Used in This Chapter

The following list contains a summary of all the commands introduced in this chapter:

Command	Description
cpio	Makes backups of individual files and partial file systems
dd	Directly copies data from one location to another
fssnap	Creates UFS snapshots of mounted file systems
mt	Controls magnetic tape devices
pax	Copies data from one location to another and perform backups
tar	Copies data from one location to another and perform backups
ufsdump	Makes backup archives of UFS file systems
ufsrestore	Restores backed-up UFS file system archives

Review Questions

1. Your Solaris 9 server's hard disk failed on Thursday afternoon, and you need to restore the file system on the disk. Fortunately, you have current backups available. You replace the failed hard disk and prepare it for restoration. Here are the backup tapes you have available:

Tape 1: Level 0 backup, Sunday night

Tape 2: Level 7 backup, Monday night

Tape 3: Level 7 backup, Tuesday night

Tape 4: Level 7 backup, Wednesday night

Which tapes do you need to restore, in the exact order, to achieve a complete restoration of the file system?

A. Tape 1, Tape 2, Tape 3, Tape 4

B. Tape 1, Tape 4

C. Tape 1 only

D. Tape 2, Tape 3, Tape 4

2. You are a Solaris administrator for your network. You have encountered a `pax` backup file created by another systems administrator. You want to see which files are included in the `pax` file. Which command should you issue to find out?

A. `pax -r -f /dev/rmt/0`

B. `pax -w -f /dev/rmt/0`

C. `pax -rw -f /dev/rmt/0`

D. `pax -f /dev/rmt/0`

3. Before performing a backup of the `/export/home` file system on your Solaris 9 computer by using `ufsdump`, which of the following should you do? (Choose all that apply.)

A. Log in as root or assume an equivalent role.

B. Mount the `/export/home` file system.

C. Unmount the `/export/home` file system.

D. Run the `fsck` command to lock the file system.

4. You are the Solaris administrator for your company. You are performing an interactive restoration on one of your servers. Which command should you enter to display a list of files that are marked for extraction?

A. `extract`

B. `marked`

C. `ls`

D. `dispmrk`

5. Which of the following statements best describes an incremental backup?

   A. Incremental backups back up all files on the file system.

   B. Incremental backups back up all files on the file system that have changed since the last full backup.

   C. Incremental backups back up all files on the file system that have changed since the last incremental backup.

   D. Incremental backups back up all files on the file system that have changed since the last lower-level backup.

6. You are the Solaris administrator for your network. The hard disk containing the root file system (/) on your server crashed. You have purchased a new hard disk and installed it into the failed server. Here are the procedures you need to perform:

   1. Change directories and unmount the file system.

   2. Perform a system restoration with the `ufsrestore` command.

   3. Create a new file system on the new hard disk.

   4. Create a new full backup.

   5. Install boot files with `installboot`.

   6. Mount the new file system on a temporary mount point.

   7. Remove the `restoresymtable` file.

   8. Reboot the system.

   9. Run `fsck` to check the file system for consistency.

   10. Change directories to the temporary mount point.

   Which of the following is the correct order in which you must perform these procedures?

   A. 3, 6, 2, 7, 10, 9, 1, 5, 4, 8

   B. 3, 6, 10, 9, 5, 2, 7, 1, 4, 8

   C. 3, 6, 10, 2, 7, 1, 9, 5, 4, 8

   D. 3, 6, 10, 2, 5, 9, 7, 1, 4, 8

7. Which two of the following statements accurately describe the device /dev/rmt/0? (Choose two.)

   A. It is the default tape device as described in the `/dev/rmt/default` file.

   B. It is the default tape device as described in the `/kernel/drv/st.conf` file.

   C. It is the default tape device as described in the `/kernel/rmt/mt.conf` file.

   D. It is the first tape device in the computer.

   E. It is the second tape device in the computer.

8. You are the Solaris administrator for your network. You want to create a full backup of the /export/home/adocter directory. The backup should be verified, copied to the default tape device, and an entry created in /etc/dumpdates. Which of the following commands should you issue?

A. ufsdump 0uvd /export/home/adocter

B. ufsdump 0uf /dev/rmt/0 /export/home/adocter

C. ufsdump 9uvf /dev/rmt/0 /export/home/adocter

D. ufsdump 0uvf /dev/rmt/0 /export/home/adocter

9. You are the Solaris administrator for your company. You are performing a full backup of the root (/) file system on one of your Solaris 9 servers with the ufsdump utility. Which of the following statements is correct in describing the location of the table of contents on the backup media?

A. The table of contents for directories and files is located at the beginning of the backup media.

B. The table of contents for directories and files is located at the end of the backup media.

C. The table of contents for directories is located at the beginning of the backup media, and the table of contents for files is located at the end of the backup media.

D. The table of contents for directories is located at the end of the backup media, and the table of contents for files is located at the beginning of the backup media.

10. You are the Solaris administrator for your network. You want to back up files from one of your client machines, but the tape backup device is located on a remote server. Which of the following files do you need to edit to enable you to perform this remote backup?

A. The /.rhosts file on the client

B. The /.rhosts file on the server

C. The /etc/hosts.equiv file on the client

D. The /etc/hosts.equiv file on the server

11. Which of the following statements accurately describe dd? (Choose all that apply.)

A. It can convert and copy files with different data formats.

B. It can copy information from one hard disk to another hard disk.

C. It is more efficient at backing up data than ufsdump.

D. It is capable of transferring an entire file system from a hard disk to a backup tape.

12. You are the Solaris administrator for your company. You are in the middle of performing an interactive restoration and you execute the following command:

ufsrestore> **delete file1**

What does this command accomplish?

A. file1 is deleted from the tape archive.

B. file1 is deleted from the hard disk.

C. file1 is removed from the list of files to be extracted.

D. file1 is moved into a temporary cache and will be deleted when you exit the interactive restore.

13. You are performing the restoration of a user's home directory to the server. The files are being restored to the /var/tmp directory. At the end of the restoration, you choose "yes" when prompted with set owner/mode for '.' [yn]. What does your answer accomplish?

   A. The mode of /var/tmp will be set to match that of the user's home directory located on the backup media.

   B. The mode of /var/tmp will remain as it currently is.

   C. The owner of /var/tmp will be set to root, and the permissions for /var/tmp will match those of the user's home directory located on the backup media.

   D. The owner of /var/tmp will not change, and the permissions for /var/tmp will be set to read-only for the user.

14. Your Solaris 9 server's hard disk failed on Wednesday morning, and you need to restore the file system on the disk. Fortunately, you have current backups available. You replace the failed hard disk and prepare it for restoration. Here are the backup tapes you have available:

Tape 1: Level 0 backup, Sunday night

Tape 2: Level 2 backup, Monday night

Tape 3: Level 3 backup, Tuesday night

Which tapes do you need to restore, in the exact order, to achieve a complete restoration of the file system?

   A. Tape 1, Tape 2, Tape 3

   B. Tape 1, Tape 3

   C. Tape 1 only

   D. Tape 2, Tape 3

15. You are the network administrator for your company. You have configured your server, which contains a tape backup device, to allow remote tape backups. From one of your client machines, you want to perform a full backup of the /docs file system on the server's tape device. The client computer name is electra, and the server's name is freud. Which of the following commands accomplishes this task?

   A. ufsdump 0uf freud:/dev/rmt/0 /docs

   B. ufsdump 0uf /dev/rmt/0 electra:/docs

   C. ufsdump 0uf electra:/dev/rmt/0 freud:/docs

   D. ufsdump 0uf /dev/rmt/0 /docs

   E. ufsdump 9uf freud:/dev/rmt/0 /docs

16. You are devising a backup strategy for your Solaris server. On the first of the month, you will perform a full backup of the /docs file system. Each weeknight, you will perform an incremental backup, and you want each backup to back up only files that have changed that day. On Saturday nights, you want to perform a backup of all files that have changed that week only. This schedule is to be repeated throughout the course of the month. Which of the following shows appropriate backup levels for you to use, beginning with Monday and ending with Saturday?

A. 3, 4, 5, 6, 7, 2

B. 2, 3, 4, 5, 6, 7

C. 5, 5, 5, 5, 5, 2

D. 5, 5, 5, 5, 5, 9

17. You are the Solaris administrator for your company. You have created a backup file by using the tar command. You want to see a list of files located within the backup archive. Which of the following commands could you use?

A. tar xvf

B. tar cvf

C. tar tvf

D. tar uvf

18. You are the Solaris administrator for your network. You want to create a snapshot of the /usr file system for backup purposes. The snapshot should be named snap01. Which of the following commands should you execute?

A. fssnap -F ufs -o bs=/snap01 fs=/usr

B. fssnap -F ufs -o /usr bs=/snap01

C. fssnap -F ufs -o fs=/usr bs=/snap01

D. fssnap -F ufs -o bs=/snap01 /usr

19. You are the Solaris administrator for your company. On Sunday, you performed a level 0 backup of the /opt file system on your server. Monday, you performed a level 5 backup of the same file system. Tuesday, you want to back up all files that have changed since Sunday. Which of the following commands enable you to do this? (Choose all that apply.)

A. ufsdump 1uf /dev/rmt/0 /opt

B. ufsdump 5uf /dev/rmt/0 /opt

C. ufsdump 7uf /dev/rmt/0 /opt

D. ufsdump <0uf /dev/rmt/0 /opt

20. Later this afternoon, you will be performing a backup of your root file system (/) by using the ufsdump command. Before performing the backup, which of the following tasks should you perform? (Choose all that apply.)

A. Log in as root or assume an equivalent role.

B. Mount the root (/) file system.

C. Unmount the root (/) file system.

D. Run the fsck command to lock the file system.

E. Issue the init S command.

Answers to Review Questions

1. **B.** To restore the file system in the best possible way, you need to begin with the full backup, created on Tape 1 on Sunday. Because each weekday you made the same level backups, the Wednesday night tape (Tape 4) has all changes made since Sunday. Therefore, all you need is Tape 1, followed by Tape 4.

2. **D.** The pax command operates in four modes: read (-r), write (-w), copy (-rw), and list (neither -r nor -w). To list files in the pax archive, you want to omit the -r and -w options. Therefore, the last answer is correct.

3. **A, C.** To run a backup of a file system, you need to have root permissions or an equivalent role. Also, it's strongly recommended that you unmount the file system before backing it up. The fsck command does not lock file systems; it checks them for consistency.

4. **B.** The marked command lists the files marked for extraction. The extract command begins the extraction process, and ls functions just as it would in the shell; it lists files. The dispmrk command does not exist.

5. **D.** By definition, incremental backups back up all files on the file system that have changed since the last lower-level backup. The last lower-level backup might have been a full backup or a lower-level incremental backup.

6. **C.** This procedure is complex and must be followed in the exact order. To restore a root file system (/), you must create a new file system on the new hard disk, mount the new file system on a temporary mount point, change directories to the temporary mount point, perform a system restoration with the ufsrestore command, remove the restoresymtable file, change directories and unmount the file system, run fsck to check the file system for consistency, install boot files with installboot, create a new full backup, and reboot the system.

7. **B, D.** The device /dev/rmt/0 describes the first tape device in the computer. It's also the default tape device as described in the /kernel/drv/st.conf file.

8. **D.** The ufsdump command is used to create the full backup. The appropriate switches for this question are 0 for a full backup, u to update /etc/dumpdates, v to verify, and f to indicate the backup device.

9. **A.** When you run ufsdump, a two-step process is performed. In the first step, the table of contents, including directories and files, is written to the backup media. Then, all the data is written to the media, based on inode sequence number.

10. **B.** To perform this remote backup, you need to add the client machine name, and username if desired, to the /.rhosts file on the server machine.

11. **A, B, D.** The dd command is good at copying data, and it can copy and convert data with different data formats. However, it is not more efficient at backing up data than ufsdump.

12. **C.** The delete command, when issued within ufsrestore, removes the file from the list of files to be extracted.

13. **A.**   The prompt `set owner/mode for '.' [yn]` is perhaps the most critical question asked during the restoration process, because it directly affects file permissions. Saying "yes" will set the mode (owner, permissions, and file access time) of the restore directory to match those of the original directory located on the backup media. Choosing "no" will leave the mode of the restore directory as it currently is.

14. **A.**   To restore the file system in the best possible way, you need to begin with the full backup, created on Tape 1 on Sunday. Because each weekday you increased the level of the backups, each tape has only changes made that day. Therefore, to get all appropriate changes, you need to restore Tape 1, followed by Tape 2 and Tape 3.

15. **A.**   To perform the remote backup, you must specify the device to which you are backing up. In this case, it's the default tape device on the `freud` machine, or `freud:/dev/rmt/0`. The client machine name is not needed, as `ufsdump` assumes the directory that is to be backed up is local. Full backups are level 0 backups.

16. **A.**   Incremental backups back up the files that have changed since the last lower-level backup. So, to back up files that have changed daily, you need to increase the backup levels by at least one each day. On Saturday, you will need to use a lower level than any of the backups used during the week. Therefore, the first answer is correct.

17. **C.**   The `t` option is used with `tar` to list a table of contents.

18. **D.**   The correct syntax for `fssnap` is `fssnap -F ufs -o bs=`*backing_store_file file_system*.

19. **A, B.**   To back up all files changed since Sunday, you need to perform an incremental backup. Incremental backups use levels 1–9. Incremental backups also back up all files changed since the last lower-level backup. Therefore, if on Tuesday you want to back up all files changed since Sunday, you need to use a level less than or equal to the one used Monday. This eliminates the third answer. The last answer uses invalid syntax (the < is invalid).

20. **A, E.**   To run a backup of a file system, you need to have root permissions or an equivalent role. The `fsck` command does not lock file systems; it checks them for consistency. You cannot unmount the root file system if Solaris is in multiuser mode. Therefore, you will need to bring Solaris into single-user mode with the `init S` command.

Solaris 9 Sun Certified System Administrator

PART

II

Chapter

10

The Solaris Networking Environment

SOLARIS 9 EXAM OBJECTIVES COVERED IN THIS CHAPTER:

✓ Explain how to use network files to configure and test the IPv4 interfaces.

✓ Explain how to start server processes within a client-server model.

Welcome to Part II of this Study Guide. The first half of this book and the Solaris Certified System Administrator Part I test concentrate on Solaris administration basics. The second half of this book, starting with this chapter, and the SCSA Part II test focus on more difficult topics such as advanced security, Network File System (NFS) server configuration, advanced disk management, and networking issues.

This chapter covers networking information needed to pass the Part II test. First, the chapter starts with networking concepts. These concepts are not unique to Solaris, but you need to understand them before moving on to more advanced topics. After reading about networking concepts, you'll learn about how Solaris needs to be configured to participate on the network.

Understanding Network Concepts

One chapter could not possibly cover everything you need to know about networking. Entire certifications built around networking and encyclopedias of information on the subject exist. This section of the chapter aims to introduce or re-familiarize you with some general networking knowledge. After understanding these concepts, you can think about how Solaris specifically needs to be configured to participate on a network.

Having said that, a network is more than one computer linked to another to share information or resources. Although the number of possibilities for configuring a network is nearly limitless, there are some common configuration themes.

Network Topologies

The term *network topology* generally refers to the way that the network is physically connected. Are all your computers in the same room? If so, you have a *local area network (LAN)*. What if your computers are located in three states? That would be called a *wide area network (WAN)*.

The two preceding examples are pretty straightforward. There is no debating that a multiple-state network is a WAN. However, in some cases, the lines between a LAN and a WAN become confusing. For example, say you have computers located in two buildings. Is that a LAN or a WAN? Well, it depends. Generally speaking, a LAN is defined as a network of computers that share a high-speed connection. Historically, a "high-speed" connection has been defined as 10 megabits per second (Mbps). However, some new long-distance networking technologies, ones that would typically be considered WAN technologies, are approaching or exceeding 10Mbps.

To answer the question of the two-building network, you need to know how the buildings are connected. Is there a network cable connecting the buildings, and is that connection running at the same speed as the rest of the network? If so, it would be considered a LAN. If the connection between the two buildings is a dial-up connection or an equally slow network connection, it could be classified as a WAN.

Network topology can also refer to the layout of your network within your building. This refers to a much smaller scale than even a LAN designation. The four major classifications of intra-network topologies are star, bus, ring, and hybrid.

On a star network, all computers are connected to a central device known as a *hub*. If you think about the hub being the center of the network, with all computers radiating out as arms of the star, you get the picture. Multiple hubs can be connected to one another to extend the star (which technically becomes a star-star network, but few people care to designate that deeply). Twisted-pair cabling is common on star networks, and the star is the most popular network configuration.

Bus networks do not require a central hub. All computers are connected in a serial fashion. The main cable connecting the computers is called the backbone and is often coaxial cable. Bus networks can be difficult to troubleshoot because one break in the backbone will cause the entire bus to fail. For this reason, bus networks are not very popular.

A ring network physically looks like it sounds: a ring of computers. Like a bus, a ring does not require a central hub. Generally speaking, ring networks consist of two rings. The first is the primary ring, and the second is a redundant ring, in case the primary ring fails. Ring networks use either fiber-optic or coaxial cable.

Hybrid networks are typically combinations of stars, with multiple redundant paths. That way, if one link between networks fails, another link is available for use. You'll see hybrids only on large networks. A good example of a hybrid network is the Internet.

Network Hardware

Obviously, to get on a network, you need a computer. This computer might function as a client or a server, but regardless, it's known as a host. A *host* is any device on the network that has an Internet Protocol (IP) address (more on TCP/IP in a bit).

On networks, clients are the most common type of computer. A *client* is the computer where the user sits to do their daily work. Clients request information from servers, and in comparison to servers, they don't require hardware that is as powerful.

Servers are typically locked away in a server closet or network room. Users should not have direct access to servers. A network might have hundreds of clients but only a few servers. Servers come in a variety of forms, including everything from "regular" computer cases to rack-mounted devices. The hardware in a server needs to be powerful enough to serve its clients, which in many cases means multiple processors, terabytes of disk storage space, gigabytes of memory, and multiple network cards.

Network Cards

Every computer that wants to participate on the network needs to have a *network interface card (NIC)* installed. NICs are also called network adapters. Network cards are built to work with one specific networking technology. In other words, if you are running an Ethernet network, you need an Ethernet NIC. Similarly, if your network is running IBM's Token Ring technology, you need a Token Ring NIC.

Some network cards have interfaces (called transceivers, because they transmit and receive) for multiple types of cable, or multiple connectors. Unless otherwise specified, a network card can use only one of its connectors at once. If the network card has connectors for twisted-pair and coaxial cabling, you can use one or the other, but not both.

As long as expansion slots are available, most computers can handle more than one network card. In fact, to speed up network access to servers, most heavily utilized servers have multiple NICs.

Connectivity Devices

If you are running a star network, which is likely, you will need a central point to plug your computers' network cables into. As stated earlier, this central device is called a hub. A variety of hubs are available. Some common classifications of hubs include passive hubs, which do not amplify the signal, and active hubs, which do amplify the signal.

Another common connectivity device is a *switch*. Switches look like hubs and connect multiple computers just as hubs do. However, switches are more "intelligent" than hubs, sending the network packets to the intended recipient instead of broadcasting the information out on all its ports. Because of this, switches provide for greater bandwidth than do standard hubs. Common speeds for switches and hubs are 10Mbps, 100Mbps, and 1Gbps.

Other Network Devices

If your network has multiple IP subnets, or you have another reason to logically divide your network, you will need a *router*. Whereas hubs and switches connect computers on a LAN, routers connect LANs to each other.

Routers are "intelligent" devices that selectively pass or block network traffic as directed. One of the major bandwidth drainers on networks is broadcast traffic. Broadcast traffic is sent from one computer and addressed to everyone else on the network. It's like getting the junk mail addressed to "Recipient" in your mailbox. The problem is, on a network with limited bandwidth, excessive broadcasts can severely hamper productivity. Routers do not pass broadcasts, making them an important tool for segmenting networks.

There are other, but less common, devices you will encounter. *Bridges* are like routers, but bridges direct traffic based on physical address, not logical address. This makes them a bit less flexible, and bridges do pass along broadcasts.

Gateways translate one protocol into another. If your network is running a single protocol, you will not need to worry about using a gateway.

The Logical Network

So far, this chapter has covered physical components critical to networking. There are also a number of logical components you need to understand. Logical networking components include the language that the computers will speak, as well as the rules that computers use to communicate, much like syntax in human languages. They're called logical components because they're things you cannot touch, unlike a network card or a network cable which you can physically hold.

After your computers are physically connected, rules need to be established to govern communications. To this end, various communication methods have been developed. Among them are Token Ring, Fiber Distributed Data Interface (FDDI), Asynchronous Transfer Mode (ATM), and Ethernet. Because Ethernet is the most popular LAN communications method and is supported by Solaris, it will receive all of the attention here.

Ethernet is a contention-based network access method, based on a protocol called Carrier Sense Multiple Access with Collision Detection (CSMA/CD). On an Ethernet network, a computer wishing to communicate listens to see whether there's any traffic on the network. This is called carrier sense (it's like picking up the phone and listening for a dial tone before you begin to dial). If there is no traffic on the network, the computer sends its message, in the form of packets and addressed to its intended destination, out onto the network. Ideally, the destination computer receives the packets, and there are no problems.

But now consider an example of hundreds of computers on a network. Ethernet provides for multiple access, meaning that more than one computer can be physically attached to the network at one time. With hundreds of computers, though, more than one computer might be listening for carrier sense at one given time and might send packets out at the same time. In such cases, a packet collision happens, and neither destination receives their information. CSMA/CD provides for built-in packet collision detection, meaning that the colliding packets get bounced back to the sender, who realizes that there was a collision. After waiting a random number of milliseconds, each sender will retry to send their message.

Ethernet sounds a bit barbaric in terms of access, and in reality it can be quite inefficient. But it works, and it's one of the least expensive technologies to implement. Ethernet has standards for 10Mbps and 100Mbps (fast Ethernet) communication, as well as newer standards for 1Gbps (gigabit Ethernet) and 10Gbps. In order for your network to run Ethernet, all connectivity devices (network adapters, hubs, switches, routers, and so on) must support Ethernet. Ethernet is so common that finding compatible equipment is usually not a problem.

The OSI Model

In the early 1980s, the International Organization for Standardization (ISO) developed a seven-layer networking model called *Open Systems Interconnect (OSI)*. OSI grew out of the increasing need for standardization in networking protocols. The OSI model is a theoretical model of how networking should happen.

OSI's seven layers describe the functions that need to be taken care of by networking protocols. How the functions are taken care of is up to the designer of the protocol. For the most part, the OSI model is used as a frame of reference only. It's not a hard and fast model that everyone copies when designing network protocols. Table 10.1 shows the seven layers of OSI.

TABLE 10.1 The OSI Model

Layer	Number	Description
Physical	1	Describes the network hardware, as well as signaling mechanisms on network cabling.
Data Link	2	Fragments data into frames when sending it to the Physical layer. Receives and acknowledges the receipt of frames from the sender. Provides error correction of the data within the frames. Responsible for physical Media Access Control (MAC) addresses.

TABLE 10.1 The OSI Model *(continued)*

Layer	Number	Description
Network	3	Responsible for addressing and routing packets. Logical network addresses are identified at this level. Routers work at this level.
Transport	4	Provides error correction if packets needed to complete a message are missing or corrupt.
Session	5	Establishes, maintains, and disconnects communication sessions between hosts, including security measures.
Presentation	6	Responsible for data translation, compression, and format conversions.
Application	7	The applications that users use to access the network, such as Internet browser, e-mail client, or network access client (such as Telnet or FTP).

As you can see in Table 10.1, each layer is responsible for a distinct portion of the networking process. When developers program a communications protocol, however, they don't necessarily program one piece of their protocol to match one layer of OSI. For example, TCP/IP follows a five-layer model, which corresponds to the seven-layer OSI model. The top layer in the TCP/IP model covers the functionality of layers 5, 6, and 7 of OSI.

Transmission Control Protocol/Internet Protocol (TCP/IP)

The *Transmission Control Protocol/Internet Protocol (TCP/IP)* suite was originally developed in the late 1960s and today is the most popular networking protocol available. TCP/IP was developed in the UNIX networking world, so it should come as no surprise that it's the default protocol for Solaris.

TCP/IP is referred to as a protocol suite because a number of protocols combine to give you full network communications. If you had only the TCP and IP protocols, you'd be missing most of the picture.

The TCP/IP networking model corresponds to the OSI model, except that it's a five-layer model instead of seven layers. Here's a description of the five layers:

Hardware layer The first layer in the TCP/IP model is the Hardware layer, which corresponds to the OSI model's Physical layer. There are no protocols at this layer. However, there are standards, including Ethernet (IEEE 802.3) and Token Ring (IEEE 802.5). In many cases, you will see networking reference materials ignore this layer because there are no protocols functioning at this layer.

The Institute of Electrical and Electronics Engineers (IEEE) designed communications standards for Ethernet, Token Ring, and most other network transmission methods.

Network Interface layer   The second layer takes the place of the OSI Data Link layer. Similar to the Hardware layer, it's responsible for Ethernet communications as well as the network card driver.

Internet layer   The Internet layer is where the core protocol of TCP/IP, Internet Protocol (IP), works. IP is responsible for addressing and routing network packets. Included with IP at this layer are the Internet Control Message Protocol (ICMP), which is responsible for generating IP error messages, Address Resolution Protocol (ARP), which resolves logical IP addresses to physical MAC addresses for communication, and Reverse Address Resolution Protocol (RARP), which maps MAC addresses to IP addresses.

Transport layer   The fourth has two protocols: the Transmission Control Protocol (TCP) and the User Datagram Protocol (UDP). TCP is responsible for providing a reliable, connection-oriented communications channel. If an error happens in communications, TCP is the one to send an error message and attempt to fix the problem. TCP guarantees delivery of packets. UDP is a connectionless protocol, meaning that it does not guarantee delivery. Because it doesn't have the overhead of guaranteeing delivery, it's faster than TCP. However, guaranteed data delivery must then be handled by the application.

Application layer   The top layer of the TCP/IP model covers the functionality of layers 5, 6, and 7 of the OSI model. The vast majority of protocols in the TCP/IP protocol suite reside at this layer. They include Network File System (NFS), Telnet, File Transfer Protocol (FTP), Hypertext Transfer Protocol (HTTP), Routing Information Protocol (RIP), Simple Mail Transport Protocol (SMTP), Remote Procedure Call (RPC), and Simple Network Management Protocol (SNMP).

When most people think about TCP/IP, they think of the Internet, and that's certainly a valid link. The Internet would not exist without TCP/IP, and TCP/IP would not be nearly as popular as it is without the Internet.

All devices on a network using TCP/IP need to have an IP address. Going into great detail about how to use IP addresses could take an entire book in its own right; instead, here are a few pointers:

- IP addresses are 32 bits long and are written as four octets in dotted decimal notation. An example is 199.104.125.33.

- Each node (client, server, printer, and so on) on the network needs a unique IP address.

- Each port on a router needs a separate IP address.

- If your network is directly connected to the Internet, you must purchase unique addresses to use.

The last pointer brings up an important topic about IP addresses. If your network is not connected to the Internet or uses some sort of translator (for example, a router using Network Address Translation), you can use nearly any IP addresses you want for your network, as specified by RFC 1918. However, if your computers are going to be out on the Internet, the addresses you use must be unique on the Internet.

Understanding Solaris Networking

The Solaris operating environment is built for networking. Although some operating systems function well as clients, and others are designed to be servers, Solaris has the flexibility to be a client or a server, and the power to be a client and a server at the same time. To get Solaris to work on a network, however, you need to properly configure the network support files. If you installed network support during initial installation of Solaris, these files will already be configured for you. If not, you will have to set them up manually.

Understanding networking isn't just about configuring local files, however. You also need to know how computers communicate over the network, and how to access remote machines. Included in this is the understanding of Remote Procedure Calls (RPCs) and the commands used for network access and troubleshooting.

This section covers the files you need to configure on your local computer in order to participate on a network, as well as some network procedures and commands used in networking.

Network Configuration Files

When configuring Solaris computers on a network, you have a choice between two modes: local files mode or network client mode.

In *local files mode*, all configuration information is stored in files on the computer. Network configuration servers, name servers, mail servers, Network File System (NFS) servers, and routers should always run in local files mode. Depending on the size of your network, all other machines, including workstations, can run in local files mode as well. If you have a large network, though, using local files can increase administrative overhead.

In *network client mode*, client computers retrieve network configuration information (such as an IP address, host name, and router configuration) from a *network configuration server*. There needs to be only one network configuration server per network. If your network is subnetted though, you will need to have one network configuration server per subnet. Although any computer (workstation, server, and so on) can be a network client, and running a network configuration server saves administrative overhead, it's recommended that you run servers in local files mode if at all possible.

Many network administrators will physically and logically break up their existing network into smaller networks called subnets. Subnetting has a few distinct advantages. The biggest is that network traffic is reduced between computers (think of having 20 computers trying to talk at once on the same line versus having 10 on their own private line and the other 10 on another private line). Also, as subnets are physically separated by routers (which don't pass broadcast traffic), network traffic is further reduced. Subnets can also provide greater network security for groups of computers. Each subnet on a network has its own unique network address that fits into the scheme of the overall network address.

Networks do not have to be entirely in local files mode or in network client mode. Mixed networks that include computers running in local files mode and network client mode are common. On such a network, client workstations will be running in network client mode, and servers (including file and print servers), routers, and printers will be running in local files mode. The workstations can run in network client mode because they don't always need to have the same IP address. Computers generally don't contact other client computers for files or other information. However, servers, routers, and printers need to remain in the same location (always have the same IP address) so that they can easily be located by clients. If clients can't find a server or a printer because its address has changed, you could experience network problems. Here are some of the parameters you will need to specify to get networking support to function on your Solaris computer:

- IP address for every network interface
- Subnet mask (if your network has multiple subnets or connects to the Internet)
- Default router address, if applicable
- Host names for every computer on the network
- DNS, NIS, or NIS+ domain name, if you have a configured domain

How you specifically configure your computer depends on whether you're running in local files mode or network client mode.

When Solaris boots, the /etc/rc2.d/S30sysid.net run control script is responsible for configuring basic network parameters on all network interfaces.

Local Files Mode

The first file you need to configure when running in local files mode is /etc/nodename. This file needs to have your computer's host name (also called a node name) in it. Your computer's name should be the only entry in this file. When typing in your computer's name, remember that Solaris is case sensitive.

Next, you will need to create a host name interface file. The name of this file will be /etc/hostname.*interface*. In the filename, the *interface* variable is replaced by the interface name of your primary network connection. For example, if your primary network interface is le0, the filename would be /etc/hostname.le0. If you have multiple network connections, you will have multiple /etc/hostname.*interface* files, one for each network connection. The only entry inside the file will be your host name, just as in /etc/nodename. You can also substitute the interface IP address instead of a host name in this file.

After creating or configuring /etc/hostname.*interface*, you will need to set up the /etc/inet/hosts file. This file is also known as the hosts database. This file needs to contain the IP address and corresponding host name for every computer on your network. When you attempt to access another computer on your network by host name, your computer will check the hosts database for the computer's name and then attempt to contact the computer by its IP address.

The /etc/hosts file is a symbolic link to the /etc/inet/hosts file.

For large networks, using hosts files can be impractical and cumbersome. Using a Domain Name Server (DNS), Network Information Server (NIS), or NIS+ server is recommended for large networks. Naming services are covered in detail in Chapter 15, "Naming Services."

Inside the hosts file, one line represents one entry. Information is always in the following order: IP address, host name, nicknames (if any), and an optional comment. Here's a sample hosts file:

```
#
# Internet host table
#
127.0.0.1     localhost     loghost     Q-Sol     #admin computer
10.0.0.1      Q-Sol
10.0.0.2      rob           punnyboy
10.0.0.3      mike          macaholic
10.0.0.4      scott         #user on probationary period
```

The IP address of each machine is on the left, followed by one or more names that identify the computer. A hosts file will always have the entry 127.0.0.1, which is known as the loopback address and always refers to the local machine. The computer with the address of 10.0.0.2 can be referenced by one of two names, rob or punnyboy. Any information preceded by a pound sign (#) is a comment, meaning that the computer ignores any information after the pound sign. If your computer has multiple network interfaces, each interface requires an entry in the hosts database.

The /etc/defaultdomain file needs to contain one entry, and that is the fully qualified domain name of the domain that your computer belongs to. Obviously, if you don't have a domain, you don't need to configure this file. For example, if your domain name is www.flyingsushi.com, you would type **www.flyingsushi.com** into the /etc/defaultdomain file.

If the domain that you are creating is not going to participate in the Internet, you can create any naming convention you want. Examples are network.solaris, local.net.solaris, or whatever you choose. However, if the computers you are setting up will participate in the Internet directly, the naming structure of your domain must conform to Internet standards, having a primary domain name such as .com, .edu, .net, or other accepted standard names.

If your network has routers, you will need to create an entry for each one in the /etc/defaultrouter file. Although you can use the name of the router if you wish, it's recommended that you use the router's IP address.

One more file you might need to configure is the /etc/inet/netmasks file. You'll need this file only if you've configured subnetting on your network. Entries in this file consist of a list of networks (network IDs) and subnet masks for the networks. If your network is running NIS or NIS+, you will not need to configure the /etc/inet/netmasks file.

Finally, the name service switch file, /etc/nsswitch.conf, needs to be configured properly. This file tells your computer where to look to request naming service information. In other words, if you want your computer to use the hosts file for name resolution, this file needs to reflect that choice. The nsswitch.conf file is discussed in more detail in Chapter 15.

Network Client Mode

To set up your network to run in network client mode, you need to configure a network configuration server in addition to the network clients. You will need superuser permissions or an equivalent role to set up the network configuration server.

Instead of each client having its own local configuration files, you will be configuring a server to provide the same information. The server will use the bootstrap protocol (BOOTP) to relay information to clients. As you might imagine, this can save you a lot of administrative overhead. From the server, follow these steps:

1. Create the `/tftpboot` directory. This will enable the `in.tftpd` daemon and configure the server as a Trivial File Transfer Protocol (TFTP), bootparams, and RARP server. TFTP and RARP are used to boot client computers.

    `# mkdir /tftpboot`

2. Create a symbolic link to the `/tftpboot` directory.

    `# ln -s /tftpboot/. /tftpboot/tftpboot`

3. In the `inetd.conf` file, enable the `tftp` line. The line should read as follows:

    `tftp dgram udp wait root /usr/sbin/in.tftpd in.tftpd -s /tftpboot`

4. Add the IP addresses and host names for each client on the network to the `/etc/inet/hosts` file.

5. Add an entry for every network client into the ethers database (`/etc/ethers`). The ethers database contains the client's Ethernet address (with separating colons), host name, and optional comments. Here is an example:

    `0:3:ba:15:d:18    Q-Sol    :this computer`

6. Create an entry for all client computers that will be running in network client mode in the bootparams database (`/etc/bootparams`). The bootparams file lists a client name, followed by a keyword value pair. Here is an example:

    `client1    root=server1:/export/client/root`

7. Run the following command to hang up (reset) the `inetd` daemon.

    `# pkill -HUP inetd`

This server is now configured to provide network information to client computers. Now instead of configuring clients to have their own local network files, you need to configure clients to look to the network configuration server for information. Here's how to configure network clients to use a network configuration server:

1. Delete the `/etc/nodename` file, if it exists. This will force the client computer to use the `hostconfig` program to obtain its host name, domain name, and router information from the network configuration server.

2. Create the `/etc/hostname.`*`interface`* file, if it doesn't exist. Ensure that this file is empty. The client will then contact the network configuration server for IP configuration information.

3. Make sure that the local hosts database contains only an entry for the loopback address.

4. Delete the `/etc/defaultdomain` file if it exists.

5. Configure the `/etc/nsswitch.conf` file to reflect your network's name service configuration.

If you have local copies of these files, along with configured files on a network configuration server, the local copies will override information provided from the server, if there is a conflict.

Real World Scenario

Bigger Network, Less Administration

You have been the network administrator for your company for two years. When you started, the company had fifteen Solaris workstations and two Solaris servers. Now, there are nearly one hundred client machines and five servers.

You have always used local files mode for network configuration. It was easy to set up, and you didn't need to dedicate a server to be a network configuration server. Now, however, you are running into some network problems: improper name resolution, duplicate IP addresses, and intermittent connectivity problems. You also need to attach your network to the Internet so that users can have Internet access. How do you solve your problems?

The first thing you want to do is to set up a network configuration server and have all clients use the server to obtain network configuration information. This will result in a uniform configuration for all clients. The good news is, you don't need a dedicated server for this function; you can use one of your three existing servers. Also, you can easily specify DNS servers for the clients to use after you are attached to the Internet. Using a network configuration server and network client mode for your client computers will greatly ease your administrative burden while streamlining your configurations.

Remote Procedure Calls

A *Remote Procedure Call (RPC)* is a protocol used to start processes on remote computers. Think of it as the language that client computers use to start a process on a server. Virtually every UNIX service, including NIS, NIS+, and NFS use RPCs to function properly. If a host is to use RPCs, the RPC server service (rpcbind) must be started. Services that use RPCs are located in /etc/inetd.conf. A list of network services is also maintained in the /etc/rpc file.

The critical component of RPC is the rpcbind service. It's responsible for mapping incoming RPC requests to TCP or UDP port numbers on the local machine, ultimately resulting in correct RPC operation. Also, rpcbind registers all RPC daemons as they start up. This service must be started before your computer can use RPCs.

The rpcbind service allows a network-aware application to use whichever port number it chooses, as long as that port number is not already in use. When a client application attempts to connect to the server, the rpcbind service intercepts the bind request and tells the client which port the application is using. After the client has the server's IP address and the port number of the application, the client-server application can communicate. Without rpcbind, all applications would have to use a predefined port number, which makes for difficult possible port number conflicts (if two applications are programmed to use the same port).

Accessing Remote Systems

In most client-server networks, if you want to access a hard disk on a server from a client, you must mount the remote file system on the client. This book already covered mounting hard disks in Chapter 7, "File System Management." Printing on a network simply means being a client on the network and having appropriate access to the print server. In other cases, however, you might need to access a remote machine but you might not need to mount hard disks or print. Some examples are remotely logging in to a machine or copying files from a remote computer. This section describes methods for accessing remote systems through TCP/IP commands.

rlogin

The `rlogin` command enables you to log in to a remote system. After you are logged in, you can navigate the computer's file system, based on your user's assigned permissions. You can also copy files and execute remote commands when logged in with `rlogin`. To remotely log in to the `server1` computer, you would type **rlogin server1**.

Users attempting to use `rlogin` must be validated. Validation can be performed by the remote computer (the one you are logging into) or by the network environment. If the remote computer is to validate you, one of three conditions must exist. First, the user account you are using must be located on the remote machine, and you must provide a correct password when prompted. Second, the remote machine must have an `/etc/hosts.equiv` file set up. Third, the remote machine must have an `.rhosts` file configured. If you're being validated by the network, you won't be prompted for a password when trying to access the remote machine, because the network already knows who you are (based on your login to your local machine).

WARNING   Using the `/etc/hosts.equiv` and/or `.rhosts` files can pose a significant security risk. Use them with caution, and never give root access using these files.

Here are the details on `/etc/hosts.equiv` and `.rhosts`:

/etc/hosts.equiv   This file contains a list of computers that are trusted for remote login. Computer names are listed, one per line. Any user attempting to remotely log in from a computer listed in `/etc/hosts.equiv` is considered trusted. You can, however, specify a username after the computer's host name. In that case, only that user from the specified computer will be allowed to remotely log in. This is a more secure method when you know who the remote users will be.

Maintaining an `/etc/hosts.equiv` file can pose a security problem. If you are using one, make sure that only trusted hosts are listed in the file. Misconfiguration can cause serious security problems. For example, a single entry of a plus sign (+) in the `/etc/hosts.equiv` file means that the computer trusts all hosts on the network.

.rhosts   The `.rhosts` file is similar to `/etc/hosts.equiv` but is meant for users instead of computer names. This file must be located in the user's home directory and contains a computer-user pairing list. The specified user must be using the specified computer to log in remotely.

The biggest security problem with `.rhosts` is that users can configure their own `.rhosts` file, instead of the administrator being in control (as is the case with `/etc/hosts.equiv`).

Both `/etc/hosts.equiv` and `.rhosts` share the same syntax. The first entry is the host name, and the second entry is the username (if applicable). Acceptable wildcards are the plus sign (+) to allow access to all, and the minus sign (–) to deny access to all. Table 10.2 discusses some sample /etc/hosts.equiv entries. Many of the so-called *r* utilities (such as rlogin, rcp, rsh, and rexec) use the /etc/hosts.equiv and/or .rhosts files for authentication.

TABLE 10.2   */etc/hosts.equiv and .rhosts Syntax*

Entry	Effect
+	Allows all users from all remote computers to access this computer as the local user
+ *username*	Allows the named user to access this computer from any remote host
hostname +	Allows any user from the specified host to access this computer
- *username*	Denies access to the named user from any host
hostname -	Denies access to any user from the named host
-@*netgroup*	Explicitly denies access from all hosts in the named netgroup
+ -@*netgroup*	Denies access by all users in the named netgroup from all hosts

To use rlogin, the in.rlogind daemon must be started on the server. By default, it is launched by the inetd daemon, which starts automatically at boot. The rlogin command enables you to attempt both direct and indirect remote logins. In a direct login, you attempt to log in by using your current username. An indirect login means that you supply a username during the remote login attempt.

By default, rlogin attempts to log you in directly. To log in indirectly, use the rlogin -1 command.

After you log in to the remote system, rlogin attempts to find your home directory. If it finds your home directory, it parses your .cshrc and .login files, and configures your remote session appropriately. Your prompt would be the same as if you were logged in locally, as will your current working directory. If your home directory cannot be located, you are temporarily assigned the remote system's root directory (/) as your working directory.

To log out of a remote system that you are logged into, use the **exit** command, ~, or Control+D.

telnet

The telnet (terminal emulation) utility is an alternative to logging in remotely with rlogin. The biggest difference between the two is that telnet always asks you to provide a username for login, whereas rlogin does not. The telnet command also works with non-UNIX computers, making it the most popular choice for remote logins. Perhaps the only negative to using telnet is that it doesn't natively encrypt passwords or data. This could cause security problems. When you are successfully logged in by using telnet, you will receive a telnet> prompt. For help, type the question mark (?).

The in.telnetd daemon manages telnet servers. This daemon is started automatically by inetd. To exit a telnet session, type **close** or **quit**.

ftp

FTP stands for File Transfer Protocol. It's also a utility you can use to transfer files from one computer to another. By using the ftp command, you are logging into a remote computer but you don't have the full functionality of a user shell as you do with rlogin. Instead, ftp is streamlined for file downloads. In addition, the computer that you ftp to does not have to be running UNIX, whereas the rlogin host does need to be UNIX-based. The ftp command is controlled by the in.ftpd daemon, which is started automatically by inetd.

You can configure user authentication for FTP by including your password entry in the remote system's /etc/passwd file or by using a network authentication service. However, most ftp connections are made anonymously. You might have used FTP and not known it. Chances are if you have downloaded anything from the Internet, you've used this protocol. It's designed for optimizing downloads, whereas the Internet protocol HTTP is not.

To ftp to a remote system, type **ftp *host_name***, where *host_name* is the system you want to log into. When the system asks for a username, type **anonymous** (or use your username if the FTP server is secure). For a password, enter your password. If you ftp anonymously, most sites prefer that you use your e-mail address for your password, but there's no specific standard for providing anonymous ftp passwords. When you are successfully logged in by using ftp, you will receive an ftp> prompt.

Many standard file system navigation commands, such as ls, pwd, and cd, work just as you would expect them to. In addition, ftp provides the get and mget commands to download files, and the put and mput commands for uploading files to the remote machine. The close, bye, and quit commands can be used to end an ftp session. And as always, if you're stuck and don't know what to type, type **help**.

TCP/IP Commands

The TCP/IP protocol suite is considered public domain. No one company owns it, and no one organization has absolute authority over new TCP/IP developments—although, technically, the Internet Engineering Task Force (ITEF) is responsible for implementing changes. Therefore, literally anyone can suggest an improvement or addition to TCP/IP and have it considered. Each suggestion for TCP/IP improvements and TCP/IP standards is published as a paper called a Request for Comments (RFC). Each RFC has a number to identify it. You might hear someone comment, "Yeah, it meets RFC 2065 standards."

RFC 2065 is a DNS security standard (you don't need to memorize this—it's just for illustrative purposes). If you hear people quoting RFC numbers, odds are they have way too much time on their hands. Many Internet sites list RFCs. One such site is http://www.ietf.org/rfc.html.

Because of the open access to TCP/IP, a large number of improvements and utilities have been implemented over the years. This section describes some of the more common and useful utilities.

r Utilities

A whole series of utilities begin with the letter *r*. The *r* always stands for *remote*. Examples are rlogin (discussed previously), rcp, rsh, rwho, rusers, and rup.

The rcp utility is for copying files to or from a remote computer. It's like ftp, but with fewer options. After logging in to a remote machine with rlogin, you could use rcp to copy files.

If you wanted to start a shell on a remote computer (to remotely execute a program, for instance), you could use the rsh (remote shell) command. To use the rsh command, you must be authenticated by the remote computer.

To display the names of users on computers attached to the network, use the rwho command. You can also use rwho to see when the users logged in and the amount of time that their computer has been idle. In order for rwho to work, the rwhod daemon must be started. Although rwhod can provide helpful information about who is on the network, rwhod broadcasts its information, causing excessive network traffic. The rusers command provides the same information as rwho, but a computer name must be specified. The rusers command has more options than rwho.

The rup (remote up) command is used to see whether computers are online, and if so, gives uptime status on the machine.

finger

The finger utility is used to display login names of users, along with their full names, home directory location, login shell, device numbers, the number of times they have logged in, and other information. If you want to find out something about someone, finger is the command to use. The finger command can be used both locally and remotely.

In order for finger to run, the fingerd daemon must be running. Because searching for and finding detailed information about users can pose a security risk, a lot of network administrators disable the fingerd daemon.

ping

The ping (packet internet groper) utility is one of the most useful utilities for determining whether a remote computer is accessible. To ping a computer, you can type **ping IPAddress** or **ping hostname**. If your network is not using name resolution, you will not get a response from pinging a host name. The ping command sends ICMP packets to the remote computer.

The ping command uses the ICMP protocol. Some website administrators have configured their sites to not respond to ICMP packets, as hackers have been known to try to use this protocol. Besides, responding to hollow ICMP requests takes server time, and slows down legitimate website requests. Also, if you are behind a security firewall, the ping command may not work.

When you ping a computer, you will get one of three responses:

- *hostname* is alive tells you that the remote computer is operational.

- `ping: no answer from` *hostname* tells you that the computer is not functioning or is unable to respond to ICMP requests.

- `ping: unknown host` *hostname* means that you typed in an invalid name or address and were unable to contact the machine. This message could result from an incorrect DNS setting or bad information in a hosts file.

You can also use `ping` to run a quick test to see whether your system's IP stack is working properly. To do this, ping your loopback IP address: **`ping 127.0.0.1`**. You should receive a response. If you get an error message, TCP/IP is not configured correctly on your computer.

Pinging the loopback address (127.0.0.1) tests the validity of the TCP/IP installation on your computer, but does not test the physical hardware (network card).

spray

The `spray` command is used to spray a one-way stream of packets to a remote host. This command reports the number of packets that were received and the transfer rate between the two hosts. Although `spray` can give you an idea as to how well your network is performing, it should not be used as a network benchmark. The `spray` command is unreliable because it uses the UDP protocol.

traceroute

The `traceroute` utility is another helpful network troubleshooting tool. It traces the route of a packet from your computer to the destination host, listing all routers in the path, as well as how long the trip from one router to the next (called a hop) took. On small networks, `traceroute` has little value. However, on large networks, and even the Internet, `traceroute` can tell you how far a packet gets before running into network problems.

ifconfig

To configure network interface parameters, use the `ifconfig` command. It's used to assign addresses to network interfaces, configure other network interface parameters, and display network interface configuration information. The `ifconfig -a` command will print out the addressing information (including the Ethernet address) for each network interface.

netstat

The `netstat` command is a versatile command that shows network status and protocol statistics. Common uses for `netstat` are to show routing tables, protocol statistics, and the state of interfaces being used for IP traffic.

snoop

The `snoop` command is used to capture and inspect network packets. Because of the obvious security concerns, only the superuser can use `snoop`. If you were to capture unencrypted packets on a network, you could literally see all data (including unencrypted passwords) being transmitted on your network. Although this sounds powerful and it is, busy networks can generate tens of thousands of packets per minute.

Logging Incoming IP Connections

If your computer is part of a public domain, it is smart to keep a log of all incoming IP connections made to your computer. If you use logging, you will know the IP address of every computer that connects to your machine, which could be useful if trying to track down someone who tried to hack your computer. Without logging, you will have no idea who has accessed your machine through IP.

To turn on logging, edit the /etc/default/inetd file and add this line:

ENABLE_CONNECTION_LOGGING=YES

After adding this line, stop and restart the inetd daemon, and your computer will log all incoming IP connections.

Finding Network Configuration Information in OpenBoot

Although commands such as netstat and ifconfig can be used to gather network configuration information, some information is stored in the OpenBoot PROM (OBP). You need to know the commands to find network information in OBP.

When a Solaris computer boots, it displays a boot banner, similar to the following:

Sun Blade 100 (UltraSPARC-IIe), Keyboard Present
Copyright 1998-2002 Sun Microsystems, Inc. All rights reserved.
OpenBoot 4.5, 256 MB memory installed, Serial #8675309.
Ethernet address 0:3:ba:15:d:18, Host ID: 84107d19.

You will notice that the banner displays the host's Ethernet address.

 Ethernet addresses are also called MAC addresses or hardware addresses.

If the banner appeared and disappeared too quickly for you to read, you can type the **banner** command at the ok prompt to display it again. If you just want the Ethernet address without the bother of the rest of the banner, type **.enet-addr** at the ok prompt.

OpenBoot also comes with a few network diagnostics. One is the test net command, which tests the network adapter. Another is watch-net, which scans the network for broadcast packets.

Summary

This chapter started by reviewing essential network knowledge. Topics included network topologies, networking hardware, Ethernet, the OSI model, and TCP/IP basics. This chapter is not designed to teach you everything you need to know about networking; no single chapter could accomplish that. The items presented are ones you must be familiar with for the test.

You then learned about network configuration files. Two options are available for providing clients with network configuration information. The first is to use local files, and the second is to create a network configuration server. If you have a large network, using network configuration servers can greatly reduce your administrative overhead.

Then, the chapter covered Remote Procedure Calls (RPCs). RPCs are used to start processes on remote computers. In a client-server network, RPCs are used to establish most client-to-server communications.

After reading about RPCs, you learned about remote access using TCP/IP commands. The three main commands you will use for remote access are `rlogin`, `telnet`, and `ftp`. Next, you learned about various other TCP/IP commands.

Finally, the chapter ended by discussing where to find networking information within the OpenBoot PROM.

Exam Essentials

Know what an Ethernet address is.   The Ethernet address, also known as a MAC address or hardware address, is the physical address of the network adapter.

Know how to find the Ethernet address in OpenBoot.   You can use the `banner` or `.enet-addr` commands within OpenBoot to find the Ethernet address.

Understand the difference between local files mode and network client mode.   In local files mode, the computer retrieves all network configuration information from files stored locally on the machine. Computers using network client mode access network configuration information from a network configuration server.

Know what RPCs are.   Remote Procedure Calls are used to start processes on remote computers.

Key Terms

Before you take the exam, be certain you are familiar with the following terms:

bridge	network configuration server
client	network interface card (NIC)
Ethernet	Open Systems Interconnect (OSI)
gateway	Remote Procedure Call (RPC)
host	router
hub	server
local area network (LAN)	switch
local files mode	Transmission Control Protocol/Internet Protocol (TCP/IP)
network client mode	wide area network (WAN)

Commands Used in This Chapter

The following list contains a summary of all the commands introduced in this chapter:

Command	Description
finger	Retrieves information about a user
ftp	Logs into a remote system for the purpose of downloading files
ifconfig	Displays and configures network interfaces
netstat	Displays network information
ping	Checks whether a remote computer can reply to ICMP packets.
rcp	Remotely copies files
rlogin	Logs you into a remote computer
rsh	Launches a shell on a remote computer
rup	Checks whether a remote computer is operational
rusers	Displays users logged into remote computers on the network
rwho	Displays users logged into remote computers on the network
snoop	Captures and analyzes network packets
spray	Sprays a remote computer with network packets
telnet	Terminal emulation—used to remotely log into computers
traceroute	Traces the route a packet takes from your computer to the destination computer

Review Questions

1. You are working on your network but are not able to mount a remote hard disk. To see whether the remote resource is available, you are going to try to log into the remote computer. Which of the following utilities can be used to log into a remote computer? (Choose all that apply.)

   A. `rcp`

   B. `telnet`

   C. `rlogin`

   D. `login`

2. You are attempting to log into a remote computer on your network. Which of the following files are used to provide authentication if you want to log in remotely? (Choose two.)

   A. `/etc/hosts.equiv`

   B. `/etc/.rlogin`

   C. `.rlogin`

   D. `/hosts.equiv`

3. Which of the following statements accurately describe the function of the TCP protocol? (Choose all that apply.)

   A. It provides guaranteed delivery of packets.

   B. It is faster than the UDP protocol.

   C. It addresses and routes packets.

   D. It provides error correction if a packet is missing.

4. Which of the following statements accurately describes the function of the IP protocol?

   A. It provides guaranteed delivery of packets.

   B. It is faster than the UDP protocol.

   C. It addresses and routes packets.

   D. It provides error correction if a packet is missing.

5. Which of the following protocols is responsible for starting processes on remote computers on a network?

   A. RCP

   B. RPC

   C. TCP

   D. UDP

   E. IP

6.   You are attempting to access one of your servers, named `server1`. However, the server seems to be unavailable. You type the command **ping server1** and get the response `ping: no answer from server1`. What does this indicate?

   A. `server1` is functioning properly.

   B. `ping server1` is not a valid command.

   C. The name `server1` is not recognized by the `ping` command.

   D. `server1` is down or unable to respond to ICMP requests

7.   You are attempting to access one of your servers, named `server1`. However, the server seems to be unavailable. You type the command **ping server1** and get the response `ping: unknown host server1`. What does this indicate?

   A. `server1` is functioning properly.

   B. `ping server1` is not a valid command.

   C. The name `server1` is not recognized by the `ping` command.

   D. `server1` is down or unable to respond to ICMP requests.

8.   You are configuring your workstations to operate in local files mode. Your network consists of several subnets. Which of the following are required pieces of configuration information for your client computers? (Choose all that apply.)

   A. IP address

   B. Subnet mask

   C. Default router address

   D. Name of every host on the network

   E. Address of a DNS server

   F. Name of the network configuration server

9.   You are the Solaris administrator for your company. You are trying to log in to a server by using the `ftp` command. However, you are receiving no response. You suspect that the problem might be an improperly functioning daemon. Which of the following daemons controls the FTP service?

   A. `in.ftpd`

   B. `ftpd`

   C. `inetd`

   D. `rpc.ftpd`

10. During boot, your Solaris 9 computer displays the following information:

```
Sun Blade 100 (UltraSPARC-IIe), Keyboard Present
Copyright 1998-2002 Sun Microsystems, Inc. All rights reserved.
OpenBoot 4.5, 256 MB memory installed, ████████████████.
█████████████████████████████, ████████████████.
```

Which of the following is the computer's Ethernet address?

A. #8675309

B. 0:3:ba:15:d:18

C. 84107d19

D. The Ethernet address is not listed.

11. You are booting your Sun-manufactured Solaris server. The server boots to an ok prompt, and you want to identify the server's MAC address. Which commands can you use to find it? (Choose all that apply.)

A. enet-addr

B. mac-addr

C. banner

D. .enet-addr

E. show-net

F. test net

12. The computers on your network are configured in local files mode. Your computer is missing the /etc/nodename file. Which of the following best describes what will happen?

A. Your computer will obtain its node name from the OpenBoot program.

B. Your computer will prompt you for its node name during boot.

C. Your computer will not be able to participate on the network.

D. Your computer will run the hostconfig program to attempt to obtain a host name from a network configuration server.

E. Your computer will automatically re-create a blank /etc/nodename file.

13. Your Solaris workstation is named comp1. The primary network interface is named smc0. What is the name of the host name interface file?

A. /etc/hostname.smc0

B. /etc/hostname.comp1

C. /etc/comp1.smc0

D. /etc/comp1.interface

14. Which of the following statements accurately describe the /etc/inet/hosts file? (Choose all that apply.)

    A. It contains mappings of IP addresses to host names on the network.

    B. Comments in the file are preceded with a pound sign.

    C. Only one host name can be listed per line.

    D. The file is known as the hosts database.

15. You are the Solaris administrator for your company. You are configuring client computers to run in local files mode. Your network has one domain, one subnet, and is not connected to the Internet. Which of the following files are not needed on your client computers? (Choose all that apply.)

    A. /etc/nodename

    B. /etc/defaultdomain

    C. /etc/defaultrouter

    D. /etc/inet/netmasks

16. Which of the following correctly describes the information present in an /etc/defaultdomain file?

    A. The computer's node name.

    B. The fully qualified domain name of the domain that the computer belongs to.

    C. The fully qualified domain name of the domain that the computer's login server belongs to.

    D. The computer's node name and the fully qualified domain name of the domain that the computer belongs to.

17. In Solaris, which of the following utilities can be used to copy files from one computer to another? (Choose all that apply.)

    A. rpc

    B. rcp

    C. rsh

    D. rup

    E. ftp

18. Which of the following statements accurately describe IP addresses? (Choose all that apply.)

    A. They are 32-bit addresses.

    B. They are 48-bit addresses.

    C. IP addresses must be unique on the network.

    D. IP addresses identify computers on the network.

    E. Only servers and printers need IP addresses on the network.

19. Which of the following TCP/IP commands can be used to display usernames of users logged into remote computers on the network? (Choose all that apply.)

A. who

B. rwho

C. rusers

D. spray

E. ping

20. You are the Solaris administrator on your network. You are logged in under a regular user account without superuser privileges. You want to remotely log into one of your servers to perform an administrative task and you want to supply a different username than the one you are currently using when you log in remotely. Which of the following commands will enable you to do this? (Choose all that apply.)

A. telnet

B. rlogin

C. telnet -l

D. rlogin -l

Answers to Review Questions

1. **B, C.** The `telnet` and `rlogin` commands can be used to log into a remote computer. Additionally, the `ftp` command can be used, but it's for downloading files. The `rcp` command copies files, and the `login` command is not valid.

2. **A, C.** The `/etc/hosts.equiv` and `.rlogin` files are used to provide remote authentication for users logging in over the network.

3. **A, D.** TCP provides guaranteed delivery of packets and also provides error correction. However, because of its additional responsibilities, it is not faster than UDP. Addressing and routing is the responsibility of the IP protocol.

4. **C.** Addressing and routing is the responsibility of the IP protocol. TCP provides guaranteed delivery of packets and also provides error correction. IP must be used in conjunction with either TCP or UDP to provide network service. IP is not faster than the UDP protocol.

5. **B.** Processes are started remotely with the Remote Procedure Call (RPC) protocol. RCP is not a protocol; `rcp` is the remote copy command. TCP, UDP, and IP are core protocols in the TCP/IP protocol suite.

6. **D.** The "no answer" message indicates that ping was able to resolve the name `server1`, but that `server1` was unable to respond to the ICMP request. This could indicate that the server is down or malfunctioning, or it could also indicate that a firewall between the client and server is preventing the ICMP packets from passing through.

7. **C.** The "unknown host" message indicates that ping was not able to resolve the name `server1`. This could indicate a name resolution problem or that the name of the server was typed in wrong.

8. **A, B, C.** For your client computers, an IP address, subnet mask, and default router are required. Knowing the names of every host on the network or having a DNS server would be very useful for resolving names on the network, but they are not required. Because you are running in local files mode, you do not need a network configuration server.

9. **A.** The `in.ftpd` daemon is responsible for running the FTP service. The `inetd` daemon starts `in.ftpd` but is not directly responsible for `ftp`. The other two are not valid daemons.

10. **B.** The display is from the system banner. The Ethernet address will always have colons and be the left entry on the bottom line. In this example, the Ethernet address is 0:3:ba:15:d:18.

11. **C, D.** The two valid commands to display the Ethernet address are `banner` and `.enet-addr`. The only other valid command listed is `test net`, which tests the network adapter.

12. **D.** If your computer is missing the `/etc/nodename` file, it will run `hostconfig` to obtain a host name from a network configuration server. If no server is available, your host will not have a name.

13. **A.** The format for the host name interface file is `/etc/hostname.`*`interface`*, where *`interface`* is the name of the network adapter. Your system's host name or IP address is entered into the file itself.

14. A, B, D. The /etc/inet/hosts file (and the /etc/hosts file, because /etc/hosts is symbolically linked to /etc/inet/hosts) is used by your computer to resolve host names to IP addresses on your network. Comments in the file are preceded with a pound sign, multiple host names can appear on one line, and the file is also called the hosts database.

15. B, C, D. The /etc/nodename file is required on all computers on the network. The other files are not needed unless you have multiple domains (in the case of /etc/defaultdomain) or multiple subnets (for /etc/defaultrouter and /etc/inet/netmasks).

16. B. The only piece of information in the /etc/defaultdomain file is the fully qualified domain name (such as www.sun.com) of the domain that the computer belongs to.

17. B, E. The rcp and ftp utilities are used to copy files from remote computers in Solaris. RPC is a protocol, not a utility. The rsh command invokes a remote shell, and rup checks whether a remote computer is operational.

18. A, C, D. IP addresses are 32-bit addresses that identify computers on the network. On any given network, each IP address must be unique. All computers that need to communicate on the network need an IP address, not just servers and printers.

19. B, C. The rwho and rusers commands can display usernames of users logged into the network. The who command can display users, but only on the local machine. The spray and ping commands are both network testers.

20. A, D. The telnet and rlogin commands enable you to log into a remote system. The telnet command automatically asks you for your username. The rlogin command assumes that you are logging in as your current identity. To specify otherwise, use the rlogin -l command.

Chapter

11

Virtual File Systems and NFS

SOLARIS 9 EXAM OBJECTIVES COVERED IN THIS CHAPTER:

- ✓ Explain when and how to add and remove swap space.
- ✓ Given a crash dump scenario, change the crash dump and core file configuration.
- ✓ Identify the appropriate commands and procedures to manage files; list, start, and stop daemons; and manage utilities on NFS servers and clients.
- ✓ Explain how to enable NFS server logging and how to configure nfslogd behavior.
- ✓ Given a problem scenario and resulting NFS error message, infer causes and select an appropriate course of action to resolve the problem.
- ✓ Explain how to configure AutoFS using automount maps.

Chapter 7, "File System Management," introduced the three classifications of file systems in Solaris: disk-based, pseudo (or virtual), and distributed. Chapter 7 also went on to explain in detail how disk-based file systems work. This chapter covers the other two types of file systems: virtual file systems and distributed (or network) file systems.

Virtual file systems are different from disk-based file systems in that most virtual file systems are created in memory, not on disk space. And while disk-based file systems are primarily used to store files, virtual file systems provide some sort of auxiliary service, such as improving the speed of system performance.

When talking about a distributed file system in Solaris, the topic of the conversation must be the Network File System (NFS). NFS enables disk-based file systems to be easily shared across a network. Although managing NFS can be complex, NFS is not too difficult to manage if you think of it as a network extension to disk-based file systems such as UFS.

Managing Virtual File Systems

Virtual file systems (or pseudo file systems) are so named because they reside in memory instead of consuming physical hard disk space. The name *virtual* is a bit misleading, considering that two of the more important virtual file systems, the Cache File System (CacheFS) and the Temporary File System (TMPFS), both use disk space. A better way to think about virtual file systems is that they aren't used for permanent storage, as are disk-based file systems. Instead, virtual file systems exist to improve system performance or provide a specific function, such as maintaining a list of mounted file systems or managing virtual memory.

Table 11.1 lists 10 Solaris virtual file systems and their functions.

TABLE 11.1 Virtual File Systems

File System Name	Type	Description
Cache	CacheFS	Improves performance of slow file systems and devices, such as remote file systems or CD-ROM drives.
Temporary	TMPFS	Manages temporary files and the /tmp directory (by default). Speeds up system performance.
Loopback	LOFS	Creates a new virtual file system, enabling you to access files by an alternate pathname.

TABLE 11.1   Virtual File Systems *(continued)*

File System Name	Type	Description
Process	PROCFS	Contains a list of active processes and process numbers. Manages the /proc directory.
First-In First-Out	FIFOFS	Named pipe that gives processes common access to data.
File Descriptors	FDFS	Maintains a list of explicit names for opened files by using file descriptors.
Mount	MNTFS	Maintains a list of mounted file systems, as displayed by the /etc/mnttab file.
Name	NAMEFS	Used by STREAMS for dynamic mounts of file descriptors on top of files.
Special	SPECFS	Enables access to character special devices and block devices.
Swap	SWAPFS	Used by the kernel for swapping. Manages virtual memory.

Most virtual file systems do not require any administration. The file systems you will likely never administer are FIFOFS, FDFS, MNTFS, NAMEFS, and SPECFS. On the other hand, because of their importance and because they are the virtual file systems that you'll most likely need to configure at some point, this chapter covers PROCFS, LOFS, CacheFS, TMPFS, and SWAPFS.

Core files and crash dumps, which often use virtual file systems, are also covered in this section.

Process File System

The *Process File System (PROCFS)* contains detailed information about running processes on your computer. When you execute the ps command (or other process management commands), the /proc file system is accessed for information.

/proc is mounted automatically at boot. Generally speaking, you won't need to perform any administrative tasks on /proc because it's self-administering. In fact, it's recommended that you not delete any files in the /proc directory, or processes could crash. Entries are automatically created in /proc when you start a process, and the same entries are automatically removed when the process is finished.

Each entry in the /proc directory is a decimal number that corresponds to a process ID. The directories in /proc contain additional files that contain more detailed information about those processes. Ownership of each file in /proc and its subdirectories is determined by the User ID of the process.

Here is a sample directory listing of /proc:

```
# ls /proc
0    164  196  219  254  294  309  318  335  386  402  411  422  54
```

1	177	2	232	256	295	310	319	342	387	403	412	434	76
124	179	201	243	257	298	316	320	352	389	409	414	438	78
141	188	214	253	285	3	317	333	356	401	410	421	47	

Further analysis of the /proc directory listing will show that every one of these entries is in fact a directory. Here's a sample of the files you might find in a process's directory:

```
# ls -l /proc/319
total 13812
-rw-------   1 root     root      7004160 Oct 26 15:33 as
-r--------   1 root     root          152 Oct 26 15:33 auxv
-r--------   1 root     root           72 Oct 26 15:33 cred
--w-------   1 root     root            0 Oct 26 15:33 ctl
lr-x------   1 root     root            0 Oct 26 15:33 cwd ->
dr-x------   2 root     root          528 Oct 26 15:33 fd
-r--r--r--   1 root     root          120 Oct 26 15:33 lpsinfo
-r--------   1 root     root          912 Oct 26 15:33 lstatus
-r--r--r--   1 root     root          536 Oct 26 15:33 lusage
dr-xr-xr-x   3 root     root           48 Oct 26 15:33 lwp
-r--------   1 root     root        11424 Oct 26 15:33 map
dr-x------   2 root     root         2080 Oct 26 15:33 object
-r--------   1 root     root        12976 Oct 26 15:33 pagedata
-r--r--r--   1 root     root          336 Oct 26 15:33 psinfo
-r--------   1 root     root        11808 Oct 26 15:33 rmap
lr-x------   1 root     root            0 Oct 26 15:33 root ->
-r--------   1 root     root         1472 Oct 26 15:33 sigact
-r--------   1 root     root         1232 Oct 26 15:33 status
-r--r--r--   1 root     root          256 Oct 26 15:33 usage
-r--------   1 root     root            0 Oct 26 15:33 watch
-r--------   1 root     root        18088 Oct 26 15:33 xmap
#
```

From the directory listing, it's apparent that the root owns process 319. Although the information presented by this directory listing isn't likely to help you a great deal as displayed, Solaris uses it when you run utilities such as pgrep or ptree to look for process information.

For more information on process management and commands, see Chapter 8, "Managing Printers and Controlling Processes."

Loopback File System

The *Loopback File System (LOFS)* enables you to create a new virtual file system within your existing file system. Files and directories that are in this new virtual file system can be accessed by their original path or by their new virtual path.

For example, imagine that you have created a UFS file system named /docs. Located in this /docs directory are critical project files that users in your engineering and production departments need to access. The users in your production department are accustomed to accessing project files in the /prod/projects directory, which is currently empty. With LOFS, you can create a copy of /docs located in /prod/projects.

To enable LOFS, you need superuser or equivalent rights. Here's how to set up LOFS:

1. Create the directory that you want to mount as a loopback, if necessary.

> # mkdir *loopback_directory*

2. Create the new mount point, if necessary.

> # mkdir */mount_point*

3. Mount the LOFS file system.

> # mount -F lofs *loopback_directory* */mount_point*

4. Configure the appropriate permissions on the new mount point.

For the preceding example of the /docs directory, you wouldn't need to create the loopback directory or mount point directory. All you would need to do is mount the loopback:

mount -F lofs /docs /prod/projects

To verify that the file system is mounted properly, use:

mount -v

If you want the Loopback File System to mount at boot, you can add an entry for the file system in the /etc/vfstab file. It's best to add the entry for the Loopback File System to the end of the /etc/vfstab file, though. That way, you're assured that the file system you're shadowing is mounted and ready before you mount the loopback.

One question a lot of people wonder about is, when creating a Loopback File System, can you create an endless loop? Take an example of creating a loopback of the root on a mount point named /tmp/newroot. By doing so, the entire root directory is shadowed in the /tmp/newroot directory. So, if you navigate to /tmp/newroot/tmp/newroot, will you see another copy of the root? The answer is no. The /tmp/newroot/tmp/newroot directory will appear as it did before the loopback was performed. If /tmp/newroot was blank, then /tmp/newroot/tmp/newroot will be blank as well.

Creating loopback file systems can potentially cause confusion for users and programs. Use Loopback File Systems sparingly to avoid confusion.

Using LOFS also can cause a few potential problems. To understand the problems, though, you need to know exactly how LOFS works. LOFS works by shadowing directories of the underlying file system. No other file types are shadowed. This can cause two problems:

- Files located on a mounted read-only Loopback File System can be modified.
- Loopback File Systems can be unmounted even if there is an open regular file on the file system.

Both of these things can happen because, again, the Loopback File System shadows only directories, not regular files. Therefore, file permissions (such as Read-only) are not shadowed, nor can the Loopback File System detect that a file is open. To alleviate the security problem, you need to set proper security on the Loopback File System. There is no work-around for detecting open files; LOFS simply cannot do it.

Cache File System

A cache can be defined as a temporary storage area. The *Cache File System (CacheFS)* is designed to be a temporary holding area, used to increase access times when users attempt to access data. Caching has little effect when accessing files on a local UFS file system. However, caching can provide a dramatic increase in speed for a user accessing networked file systems or slow devices such as CD-ROM drives.

When using CacheFS, you create a local, cached copy (called a *front file system*) of data located on a remote file system or CD-ROM (known as the *back file system*). Attempts to access data on the cached file system will result in the computer trying to access the data from the local cache first, and then the back file system if the data is not available in the cache. Table 11.2 lists some terms you need to be familiar with to understand CacheFS.

TABLE 11.2 CacheFS Terms

Term	Description
Back file system	The file system located on the remote host or CD-ROM. This is the file system being cached and must be NFS or HSFS. Files located here are called back files.
Front file system	The local file system containing the cached data. Files located here are called front files. Front file systems must be UFS.
Cache directory	The local directory where the cached data is stored.
Cache hit	An attempt to access data that is currently in cache.
Cache miss	An attempt to access data that is not in the cache.
Cold cache	A front file system that does not contain any files. A front file system must be populated with files from the back file system before it is useful.
Warm cache	A front file system that contains the desired data, meaning that no action is needed from the back file system.

Ideally, a cached file system not only speeds up user access to files but also reduces the amount of network traffic. If users are getting a lot of cache hits, then there's no need for the computer containing the front file system to request data from the computer with the back file system. CacheFS can greatly improve network performance over slow network links.

When a user initially attempts to access a file in a file system set up for caching, the access might appear slow because the file might not be populated into the cache yet. However, the user accessing the file causes the file to be placed in the front file system. Subsequent attempts to access the file will be much quicker.

Creating and Mounting CacheFS

To enable disk caching, you must first create a cache directory within a local file system. After the cache directory is created, you specify a file system to mount within the cache directory. This will be the back file system. No files are copied to the front file system when you mount the back file system. By default, files are copied to the cache only when a user attempts to access them.

CacheFS cannot be used to cache the root (/) or /usr file systems.

The `cfsadmin` command is used to create and manage a file system cache. To create a file system cache, use the following command:

```
# cfsadmin -c /cache_directory
```

The `cache_directory` variable is the name of the directory in which you will mount the cache. The only restriction as to where this directory can be created is that it must be on a local UFS file system. You have the option of creating a file system specifically for the cache or creating the cache as a subdirectory of an existing file system. For example, if you want to create a cache directory named `cache01`, you would use the following command:

```
# cfsadmin -c /cache01
```

After creating the cache directory, do not perform any operations on the cache directory itself. Doing so will cause problems with the CacheFS software.

After the cache directory has been created, you need to mount a file system in the cache. You have three options for mounting a file system into cache:

- Manually mount the file system by using the `mount` command.
- Create an entry in the local computer's `/etc/vfstab` file for the mount point.
- Use the automounter (AutoFS).

If you choose to use the `mount` command, you will have to manually mount the file system every time you want it to be cached. Editing the `/etc/vfstab` file or using AutoFS is a one-time configuration, and both provide automatic mounting.

The automounter (AutoFS) will be covered in detail in the "Managing Network File System (NFS)" section of this chapter.

If you want to use the `mount` command to mount the file system manually, here is the syntax:

```
# mount -F cachefs -o backfstype=fstype,cachedir=/cache_directory,options↵
  /back_file_system /mount_point
```

Table 11.3 explains the variables used in mounting a cached file system.

TABLE 11.3 Variables for Mounting a File System in Cache

Variable	Description
fstype	The file system type of the back file system. Can be either NFS or HSFS.
/cache_directory	The name of the local UFS directory where the cache resides.
options	Mount options. Examples are noconst to disable cache consistency checking, suid to allow SetUID execution, and non-shared to specify the non-shared write mode.
/back_file_system	The mount point of the file system to cache. If the file system is remote, you must use the following format: host:/mount_point.
/mount_point	The directory where the file system is mounted.

Here is an example: you want to mount into cache a file system named /docs on the server1 computer. The cache directory that you have created is called cache01. Here is the syntax:

```
# mount -F cachefs -o backfstype=nfs,cachedir=/cache01 server1:/docs /docs
```

To mount a remote file system, the remote file system must be shared.

After you have created and mounted your cache file system, you might want to verify that the cache is mounted properly:

```
# cachefsstat /mount_point
```

This command should return statistics about your cache file system, such as the cache hit rate. If the file system was not mounted properly in cache, you will receive an error message.

Each cache you create has a set of parameters that determine how it behaves. These parameters are listed in Table 11.4.

TABLE 11.4 CacheFS Parameters

Parameter	Default	Description
maxblocks	90%	Defines the maximum number of blocks that the front file system is allowed to claim.
minblocks	0%	Determines the minimum number of blocks that a front file system is allowed to claim.

TABLE 11.4   CacheFS Parameters *(continued)*

Parameter	Default	Description
threshblocks	85%	Specifies the number of blocks that must be available in the front file system before CacheFS can claim more blocks than specified by minblocks.
maxfiles	90%	Defines the maximum number of inodes that CacheFS is allowed to claim within the front file system.
minfiles	0%	Determines the minimum number of inodes that CacheFS is allowed to claim within the front file system.
threshfiles	85%	Specifies the number of inodes that must be available in the front file system before CacheFS can claim more inodes than specified by minfiles.

These values are set to achieve optimal cache behavior and generally do not need to be modified. However, you can modify the maxblocks and maxfiles values if your front file system has room that's not being used by the cache, and you want to use the space for some other file system. These parameters are modified by using the cfsadmin -o command.

Managing CacheFS

For the most part, CacheFS is very good at managing itself. Consequently, it doesn't often require a lot of interactive management or maintenance.

If you modify the file system being cached, you will need to delete, re-create, and remount the cache. Modifications include moving the mount point of the cached file system or changing the size of the cached file system.

Displaying Cache Parameters

The cfsadmin -l command displays your cache parameters. Here is an example, using the cache of cache01 created earlier:

```
# cfsadmin -l /cache01
cfsadmin: list cache FS information
  maxblocks    90%
  minblocks     0%
  threshblocks 85%
  maxfiles     90%
  minfiles      0%
  threshfiles  85%
  maxfilesize  5MB
server1:_docs
```

The parameters listed can be modified by using the cfsadmin -o command.

Checking Cache Consistency

CacheFS periodically checks its own consistency by comparing the file modification times of files in the cache with file modification times in the back file system. If CacheFS determines that data in the cache is not current, the cached data is purged and new data is retrieved from the back file system.

By default, consistency checks are performed when a user tries to open or perform another operation on a file in cache. If you want to be able to perform consistency checks on demand, you must first mount the cache file system with the `-o demandconst` option. You can then use the `cfsadmin -s /mount_point` command to request a consistency check.

Checking Cache File System Integrity

In Chapter 7, you learned that the `fsck` command is used to check file system integrity. Because CacheFS is a file system, you use `fsck` to check its integrity as well. To check the integrity of the `cache01` cache created earlier, you would use the following:

```
# fsck -F cachefs /cache01
```

Consistency and *integrity* are terms that can cause confusion. *Consistency* refers to making sure that the data within the file system is current. *Integrity* refers to the well-being of the file system as a whole and not to whether the data within the file system is current.

Deleting a Cache

If the cache file system is no longer needed, you can delete it. First, you must unmount the cache file system by using the `umount` command. Then, run the `cfsadmin -d` command:

```
# cfsadmin -d cache_ID /cache_directory
```

The cache directory is the directory in which you mounted the cache file system. The cache ID is the last line of the `cfsadmin -l` output as shown previously.

After you have deleted a cache, run the `cfsadmin -l` command again. If it was deleted properly, the cache ID should not be present.

Packing CacheFS

CacheFS runs automatically after being set up. When users request files from a cached file system, the front file system is checked first. If the file is not found or is not consistent with the cached file in the back file system, the file is retrieved from the back file system. Because the whole reason for using CacheFS is to increase speed, especially over slow network connections, waiting for first-time file retrieval can be frustrating.

By using the *CacheFS packing* feature, you can actively manage which files are included in the cache, as opposed to passively waiting for the first access. Files are specified for packing into cache with the `cachefspack` command.

To pack a file in cache, use `cachefspack -p filename`, as in the following example:

```
# cachefspack -p file1 file2 file3 /dir1
```

The files `file1`, `file2`, and `file3` and the directory `/dir1` will be packed into cache.

The `cachefspack` command can also be used to create a packing list, a list of specific files and directories to automatically be packed. This saves you the hassle of manually packing files every time you boot. Packing lists can also contain other packing lists. If you specify a directory to be packed, all of its contents, including subdirectories, are packed as well. For more information on packing, use the `man cachefspack` command.

Monitoring CacheFS Performance

As mentioned before, CacheFS runs automatically after being set up and is configured for optimal performance. However, there are commands you can use to collect statistics about CacheFS, which will enable you to determine an appropriate cache size as well as observe cache performance. The three commands are listed in Table 11.5.

TABLE 11.5 CacheFS Statistics Commands

Command	Description
cachefslog	Displays where cache statistics are currently being logged, enables you to stop logging, and specifies the location of the log file.
cachefsstat	Provides statistical information about a specific cache or all cached file systems.
cachefswssize	Reads the log file and gives you a recommended cache size. You must be the superuser to execute this command.

To get the most out of these cache statistics commands, you must first enable your cache, determine how long you want to gather statistical information (typically a workday, week, or month), and select a location for your log file. Keep in mind that the longer you log data, the larger the log file will be. Make sure that the log file is located on a file system where it has plenty of room to grow.

After your cache is enabled and you have collected data, you can review the data. By using `cachefsstat` to display statistics, you can determine how effective your caching is and perhaps decide whether you want to pack certain files or directories into cache. If you want to see what the recommended cache file size is for your computer, use the `cachefswssize` command. For more information on cache statistics, see the `man` page for the appropriate command.

Temporary File System

The *Temporary File System (TMPFS)* is the default file system for the `/tmp` directory. TMPFS uses local memory instead of disk space to perform file system reads and writes and, consequently, is much faster than disk-based file systems. Files can be moved in and out of the `/tmp` directory (or other TMPFS file systems) just as they can with any other directory in the directory structure. However, files located in a TMPFS file system do not survive across reboots. If you unmount the file system or reboot the computer, all files in a TMPFS file system are lost.

Creating a temporary file system is done by creating a directory and then mounting the TMPFS file system in it. You must have superuser privileges to create a TMPFS file system. Here's how:

1. Create a directory for the temporary file system.

    ```
    # mkdir /mount_point
    ```

2. Mount the TMPFS file system by using the mount command.

    ```
    # mount -F tmpfs -o size=number swap /mount_point
    ```

3. Verify the creation of the file system.

    ```
    # mount -v
    ```

The */mount_point* variable can be any directory on a local file system. When using the mount command to mount the file system, the -o size=*number* argument is optional. It is useful for limiting the size of the temporary file system, however. And because TMPFS uses swap space (physical memory, and virtual memory, if needed), you might want to limit TMPFS size if your computer is low on memory.

If you want to use a temporary file system that is created automatically during each boot, you can add an entry into the /etc/vfstab file.

Swap File System

Each process or application that runs on your Solaris computer uses memory. There are two types of memory available: *physical memory* and *virtual memory*. Physical memory is the amount of random access memory (RAM) in your computer. However, not all physical memory is available for use by processes or applications. A certain portion of physical memory is reserved for the operating system. The portion that is left over is called *available memory*.

After your computer's available memory is exhausted, virtual memory is used. Virtual memory is hard disk space reserved to emulate physical memory. Even though hard disk access is considerably slower than physical memory access, disk space is less expensive than RAM. Therefore, using virtual memory is a cost-effective alternative to adding gigabytes of RAM to your computer. Virtual memory is also called *swap space*. Swap space can take the form of its own partition (a swap partition) or a file in an existing slice (a swap file).

Applications and processes using memory are allocated memory in units called pages. When an application or process needs more memory than is physically available, certain pages are written to virtual memory. This process is known as paging or swapping.

The *Swap File System (SWAPFS)* is responsible for managing virtual and physical memory, as well as the paging process. Understand that applications cannot read information from virtual memory; the information must be in physical memory to be "used." Therefore, SWAPFS plays a critical role in transferring data between physical and virtual memory as needed.

 If your computer is performing slowly, and you suspect that it's because of excessive paging, the only proven way to increase system speed is to add RAM.

By default, the system's swap space is also configured to be the computer's dump device. This will be covered further in the "Core Files and Crash Dumps" section later in this chapter.

 The TMPFS file system uses memory instead of hard disk space. Consequently, TMPFS and SWAPFS work closely together. If you are using a lot of temporary space, or TMPFS is using a large amount of space, it will adversely affect your swap performance. One way to avoid this problem is to limit the size of your TMPFS files, as explained in the earlier "Temporary File System" section.

Allocating Swap Space

Swap space is configured initially during Solaris installation. In many cases, you will not need to reallocate or add additional swap space. However, if you want to create additional swap space, you can do so with the mkfile and swap commands.

You will want to create additional swap space if your system requires it. Running out of swap space will generate "out of memory" errors and temporarily cause Solaris to appear locked up. Even if you become very low on virtual memory, Solaris performance will be seriously degraded. You might need additional swap space for one or more of the following reasons:

- If applications that you are using require significant amounts of virtual memory. This can usually be determined by the application's documentation. Examples of "memory-hogging" applications are computer aided design programs and some database management tools.

- If applications will be using the /tmp directory a lot. These additional used temporary resources will cut into the amount of available swap space.

- If you want to save crash dumps. In the case of a fatal system crash, the contents of physical memory are "dumped" to swap space for future analysis. If you want to use this feature, your swap space needs to be at least as large as the amount of physical memory in your computer.

Monitoring Swap Usage

Another way to determine that you need additional swap space is to regularly monitor swap usage. Obviously, if you consistently get errors about applications being out of memory, you don't need to monitor your swap space to know you need more of it. Most of the time, though, you won't get errors but might notice that the computer seems to be running slower than it should be.

Two common commands to monitor swap usage are swap -l and swap -s. Here is sample output from each command:

```
# swap -l
swapfile              dev   swaplo blocks   free
/dev/dsk/c0t0d0s1    136,1      16 1049312 1049312
# swap -s
total: 32496k bytes allocated + 5424k reserved = 37920k used, 573864k available
```

Both of these commands show that plenty of swap space is available on this computer. No additional swap space configuration is necessary.

The swap -1 command displays swap space in 512-byte blocks, and swap -s displays swap space in 1024-byte blocks. The swap -1 command also does not include physical memory in its calculation of swap space.

When you issue the swap -1 and swap -s commands, you are taking a snapshot of a dynamic memory allocation process. Because memory allocation can change dramatically, you should periodically monitor swap usage if you're concerned that it could be a problem.

Adding More Swap Space

As mentioned previously, swap space is created during the initial installation of Solaris. The swap partition is created, and an entry for the slice is added to the /etc/vfstab file. If you want to add additional swap space, you have two choices. The first choice is to create an additional swap partition. The second choice is to create a swap file in an existing partition.

There is a lot of healthy debate in the computer industry about which is better: swap files or swap partitions. Sun recommends that you use swap files only as a temporary or short-term solution, and if you need a long-term solution, to use a swap slice. Here are a few notes about swap files and swap partitions:

- Swap files are considered a file within the file system. Therefore, when backing up the file system, you will back up a large blank swap file unless you specifically exclude it.

- You will not be able to unmount a file system containing a swap file that's in use. And you can assume that after the swap file is created, it's considered "being used" by Solaris.

- Swap files work through their existing file system for disk reads and writes, whereas swap partitions use the SWAPFS file system directly, making them slightly faster because they can bypass the secondary file system.

- Systems running 32-bit versions of Solaris cannot have swap areas that exceed 2GB. The 64-bit versions of Solaris can support swap areas of any size.

- Spreading the swap area out among multiple physical disks provides a large performance boost. This is because you have multiple sets of disk read/write heads working at once to read and/or write swap information.

In an emergency, you can also create swap space on an NFS file system. However, because this would greatly increase network traffic, it's not a recommended solution.

Note that in order to create a swap file, you do not need superuser privileges. However, to prevent accidental overwriting of your swap file, it's recommended that the root create it. Here is how to create a swap file:

1. Create a directory specifically for the swap file, if needed. It's a good idea to do this, even though it's not necessary. That way, your swap file is easily identifiable.

2. Create the swap file with the mkfile command. The *nnn* variable represents the size of the file that you want to create, in bytes (b), kilobytes (k), or megabytes (m).

   # mkfile *nnn*[b|k|m] *filename*

3. Activate the swap file with the `swap` command. You must supply the absolute pathname to the swap file.

   `# swap -a /path/filename`

4. If you want the swap file to be permanently available, even after reboots, add an entry for the new swap file in the `/etc/vfstab` file.

   To verify that the new swap space is available, use the `swap -l` command.

   Creating a new swap partition is nearly identical to creating a swap file. However, you must first create the new partition and format it before creating the swap file on it. For information on creating and formatting partitions, see Chapter 6, "Device and Disk Management."

Removing Swap Files

If you no longer need the swap space that you created, you can remove the swap file and free up disk space for other uses. Here's how:

1. Remove the swap file. This step does not actually delete the swap file, but it makes the file unavailable for swapping purposes.

   `# swap -d /path/filename`

2. If you added an entry for the swap file in the `/etc/vfstab` file, remove the entry.

3. Recover the disk space if needed.

   `# rm /path/filename`

   If the swap space is a separate slice, not a file within a partition, you can delete the slice and re-create it as necessary.

Core Files and Crash Dumps

Two of the automated system processes that makes extensive use of virtual file systems are the generation of core files and crash dumps. Core files and crash dumps are generated when an unexpected fatal error happens to an application or the operating system. Both can be used to troubleshoot problems in Solaris. Solaris can be configured to generate core files and crash dumps in different ways.

Managing Core Files

A *core file* is generated when an application or process terminates abnormally. Core files are used to troubleshoot problematic applications, although it helps to have programming experience to read them. Core files are managed with the `coreadm` command.

Solaris 9 provides two configurable core paths, which operate independently of each other. The first is a per-process core file path, which is enabled by default. If a process terminates abnormally, a `core` file is generated in the current working directory. The owner of the process has Read/Write permissions to the `core` file. No one else can read the file.

The second path is called a global core file path, and it's disabled by default. If it's enabled, an abnormally terminated process will generate an additional `core` file, with the same contents as the per-process `core` file, in a global core file directory.

By default, SetUID processes do not generate core files.

If you have enabled global core files, you can establish a core file naming convention to distinguish one core file from another. Variables for distinguishing core file names are explained in Table 11.6.

TABLE 11.6   Global Core File Variables

Variable	Description
%p	Process ID
%u	Effective User ID of the process
%g	Effective Group ID of the process
%f	Executable filename of the process generating the core file
%n	System node name
%m	Machine name

To set global core file naming standards, use the `coreadm` command, as in:

```
# coreadm -i /corepath/core.%p.%u
```

Based on the example, a `core` file generated by the Process ID 5150, with an effective User ID of 1100, will have the name `core.5150.1100` and be located in the */corepath* directory. Global `core` values are stored in the /etc/coreadm.conf file.

The per-process core file naming pattern is configured with `coreadm -p`. After establishing a global or per-process naming pattern, you must enable the pattern with the `coreadm -e` command. The core file naming patterns can also be set in the user's .profile or .login files.

To display your current core file configuration, use the `coreadm` command with no arguments:

```
#coreadm
        global core file pattern:
          init core file pattern: core
                global core dumps: disabled
           per-process core dumps: enabled
          global setid core dumps: disabled
     per-process setid core dumps: disabled
          global core dump logging: disabled
```

Core files can be examined with the `proc` tools available for the /proc file system. Instead of supplying a process ID, supply the name of the `core` file you want to examine. Tools available include pcred, pflags, pldd, pstack, and pmap.

Managing System Crashes

While core dumps are the result of application crashes, *crash dump* files are the result of an operating system crash. If the system crashes, you will get a message displayed on the console, followed by a dump of the contents of physical memory to the dump device and a system reboot. When Solaris reboots, the savecore command automatically retrieves the dumped memory from the dump device and writes a crash dump to your savecore directory. The crash dump file can be helpful in troubleshooting the reason for the system crash.

The savecore command generates two files that compose the crash dump: unix.*X* and vmcore.*X*. The *X* identifies the dump sequence number. Also unlike core dumps, crash dump files are saved to a predetermined directory: /var/crash/*hostname*. Saving of crash dump files is enabled by default. Crash dump files and configuration are managed with the dumpadm command.

Crash dump configuration information is saved in the /etc/dumpadm.conf file. Don't edit this file directly; instead, use the dumpadm command to modify crash dump behavior.

Here are some features of dumpadm and crash dumps in Solaris:

- The dumpadm command enables you to configure dump content, the dump device, and the dump directory.

- Dumped data is stored in compressed format on the dump device, saving disk space and increasing dump speed.

- If you have established a dedicated dump device, instead of the default swap area, the crash dump is performed in the background. The system will not wait for savecore to finish before rebooting, and the system might be available for use before savecore finishes. This is particularly true on systems with a large amount of physical memory.

- The savecore -L command enables you to generate a crash dump of a live system. On the surface, this might not seem useful. But if the system is running in an error state but has not crashed, generating this dump can provide useful troubleshooting information. You can use savecore -L only if you have configured a dedicated dump device.

You must have superuser privileges to manage crash dump information. Running the dumpadm command displays your current crash dump configuration:

```
# dumpadm
      Dump content: kernel pages
       Dump device: /dev/dsk/c0t0d0s1 (swap)
Savecore directory: /var/crash/Q-Sol
  Savecore enabled: yes
```

To disable the automatic saving of crash dump information, use dumpadm -n. Re-enabling crash dumps is done with dumpadm -y.

```
# dumpadm -n
      Dump content: kernel pages
       Dump device: /dev/dsk/c0t0d0s1 (swap)
Savecore directory: /var/crash/Q-Sol
  Savecore enabled: no
# dumpadm -y
```

```
    Dump content: kernel pages
     Dump device: /dev/dsk/c0t0d0s1 (swap)
Savecore directory: /var/crash/Q-Sol
  Savecore enabled: yes
#
```

Because of the troubleshooting benefits of saving crash dump files, it's recommended that you leave crash dumps enabled and designate a specific device, such as a lesser-used hard disk, as the dedicated crash dump device.

Managing the Network File System (NFS)

The *Network File System (NFS)* is a distributed file system that enables you to share files and directories on one computer and to access those resources from any other computer on the network. Users accessing the resources on an NFS server might or might not know that they're accessing files across the network. The actual location is made irrelevant, because resources accessed through NFS appear nearly identical to local files and directories.

One of the best features of NFS is that it enables Solaris to interface with a variety of network operating systems. Resources shared by NFS can be accessed by a Linux-based or Windows-based client, with relatively few configuration difficulties.

Files must be shared to be accessed across the network. You can share data manually with the `share` and `shareall` commands, or by adding an entry to the `/etc/dfs/dfstab` (distributed file system table) file. For a server that will be sharing numerous resources, using the `dfstab` file is the recommended option.

Shared NFS resources are known as file systems. Because NFS is supported across computer platforms, and because the term *file system* differs across platforms, an NFS file system simply refers to the portion of data being shared, even though this "file system" might be a single directory or a single file.

Here are some of the benefits of using NFS:

- Multiple computers can use the same files, meaning that everyone on the network has access to the same data.

- Data will be consistently reliable, because each user has access to the same data.

- Computers can share applications as well as data, reducing the amount of storage needed on each computer.

- The mounting and accessing of remote file systems is transparent to users.

- Multiple network operating systems are supported as NFS clients.

A computer can become an NFS server simply by sharing files or directories on the network. Computers that access the NFS server are NFS clients. A computer can be both an NFS server and an NFS client to another machine. When a client machine mounts an NFS file system, the files on the NFS server are not actually copied to the client. Instead, NFS enables the client system to access files on the server's hard disk through a series of Remote Procedure Calls (RPCs).

The History and Evolution of NFS

NFS was originally developed by Sun Microsystems and has since been developed for many other popular network operating systems. The implementations of NFS vary across operating systems, but you can get a sense of the evolution of NFS by looking at the history and features of Sun's version.

The first version of NFS in wide use was NFS 2. Although NFS 2 continues to be popular, it lacks a lot of the features of current NFS implementations. Solaris versions older than Solaris 2.5 support NFS 2 only. Some limitations of NFS 2 are that it doesn't support 64-bit data transfers and it's restricted to 8KB data packet sizes.

With the release of Solaris 2.5, NFS 3 was introduced. As you might expect, a lot of enhancements were made to NFS 3. However, to enjoy the full functionality of NFS 3, both the client and server must support the version. Here are some of the more notable features of NFS 3 as released with Solaris 2.5:

- The NFS server can batch requests, improving the server's response time.

- NFS operations return file attributes, which are stored in local cache. Because the attributes don't need a separate operation to be updated, the number of RPCs being sent to the server is reduced, improving efficiency.

- The default protocol for NFS 3 is the reliable Transmission Control Protocol (TCP) instead of the connectionless User Datagram Protocol (UDP).

- The 8KB transfer size limit was eliminated. The client and server can negotiate a transfer size, with the default size being 32KB. Larger file transfers increase efficiency.

- Improvements were made in verifying file access permissions. In version 2, if a user did not have permissions to read or write a file, they would get a generic "read error" or "write error." In version 3, users trying to access a file to which they don't have permissions receive an "open error."

- Support for Access Control Lists (ACLs) was added. This increases the flexibility of security administration.

- Improvements were made to the network lock manager. The more reliable lock manager reduces hanging from commands that use file locking, such as `ksh` and `mail`.

Solaris 2.6 also released improvements to NFS, although the version number remained unchanged. Here are some NFS 3 enhancements released with Solaris 2.6:

- Files larger than 2GB could be transferred.

- Dynamic failover of read-only file systems was introduced. This increases availability, as multiple replicas of read-only data can be created. If one NFS server is not available, another one can take its place.

- The authentication protocol for commands such as `mount` and `share` was updated from Kerberos v4 to Kerberos v5.

- WebFS was introduced, making file systems shared on the Internet available through network firewalls.

Solaris 8 introduced NFS logging. NFS logging enables an administrator to track all file operations that have been performed on the NFS server's shared file systems. With NFS logging, you can see which resources were accessed, when they were accessed, and by whom. The implications for security are tremendous, especially for sites that allow Internet-based or anonymous access.

NFS Files and Daemons

NFS provides a critical network resource-sharing service, and in terms of the number of files and daemons needed to support NFS, it's a complex service. There are 13 configuration files used, and six daemons needed to support full NFS functionality.

The files used for NFS configuration are listed in Table 11.7.

TABLE 11.7 NFS Files

File	Contents
/etc/default/fs	The default file system type for local file systems (usually UFS).
/etc/default/nfs	Configuration information for the nfsd and lockd daemons.
/etc/default/nfslogd	Configuration information for nfslogd, the NFS logging daemon.
/etc/dfs/dfstab	A list of local resources to be shared.
/etc/dfs/fstypes	Default file system types for remote file systems (usually NFS).
/etc/dfs/sharetab	Local and remote resources that are currently shared. Do not edit this file.
/etc/mnttab	A list of file systems that are currently mounted. Do not edit this file.
/etc/netconfig	Transport protocols. Do not edit this file.
/etc/nfs/nfslog.conf	General configuration information about NFS logging.
/etc/nfs/nfslogtab	Information for NFS log processing by nfslogd. Do not edit this file.
/etc/nfssec.conf	NFS security services. Do not edit this file.
/etc/rmtab	A table of file systems remotely mounted by NFS clients. Do not edit this file.
/etc/vfstab	File systems that are to be mounted locally.

Questions about the functionality of and differences between /etc/default/fs and /etc/dfs/fstypes are commonly found on the exam. The /etc/default/fs file contains one entry, and that's the default local file system type. Of course, local file systems on hard disks usually use UFS. The /etc/dfs/fstypes file contains a list of remote file systems; the first entry is the default, which is usually NFS.

Some files listed in Table 11.7 include the warning "Do not edit." These files are updated and maintained by Solaris, and require no configuration from the administrator. In fact, editing these files directly could cause NFS to malfunction.

When Solaris is booted into run level 3, the NFS daemons are started. Six daemons are used to support NFS. Two of them, mountd and nfsd, are run exclusively on the NFS server. Two others, lockd and statd, are run on both clients and servers to facilitate NFS file locking. The NFS daemons are listed in Table 11.8.

TABLE 11.8   NFS Daemons

Daemon	Function
automountd	Handles the mounting and unmounting of file systems based on requests from the AutoFS service. AutoFS will be discussed in the "Using AutoFS" section later in this chapter.
lockd	Manages record locking for NFS files.
mountd	Handles file system mount requests from remote computers. When a remote user attempts to mount a resource, mountd checks the /etc/dfs/sharetab file to determine which file systems can be mounted and by whom.
nfsd	After a remote file system is mounted, nfsd handles file system requests, such as file access permissions and opening and copying files. Older versions of Solaris required one instance of nfsd per remote file request. In Solaris 9, only one instance of nfsd is required to run.
nfslogd	Manages NFS logging.
statd	Interacts with the lockd daemon to provide crash and recovery functions for file locking services. If an NFS server crashes, upon reboot, statd will allow the client computers to reclaim locks they had on NFS-shared resources.

The daemons that function over the network, such as mountd, nfsd, and statd, use the RPC protocol. The logging daemon, nfslogd, keeps records of all RPC operations. If your computer is having problems using the RPC protocol (or its corresponding rpcbind daemon, which helps establish RPC connections), NFS will not be able to work either.

Setting Up NFS

Don't let the number of files and daemons required to support NFS scare you away from using it. The number of files to manage can make the service seem overly complex, but the principles behind setting up NFS are straightforward.

The first step is to install and configure an NFS server. This computer or computers will host resources for clients on the network. After a server is configured, resources need to be shared, so that clients can access them. To finish, you need to configure clients to access the shared resources.

Of course, there are many optional items you can configure, which adds to the complexity of setup. For example, you can configure shared resources to be shared automatically upon boot. Although this is optional, it's highly recommended you choose to do this, or else you'll be manually sharing resources every time you need to reboot the server.

Another optional feature is NFS logging. As with any other type of logging, NFS logging adds overhead and will slightly slow the response time of the server. It's up to you to decide whether logging is important for your NFS servers. However, logging is strongly recommended if you have high security requirements or are allowing anonymous or Internet-based access.

Sharing Network File Systems

File systems on an NFS server can be shared in one of two ways. The first is to use the share (or shareall) command to manually share resources. The second is to configure the /etc /dfs/dfstab file to automatically share directories every time the server is entered into init state 3.

As you might imagine, if your NFS server has a large number of resources to share, it's both impractical and cumbersome to use the share command. However, the share command is useful for testing or troubleshooting purposes. For normal NFS use, it's recommended that you make entries in the /etc/dfs/dfstab file to automatically share directories with clients.

Here is a sample /etc/dfs/dfstab file:

```
# more /etc/dfs/dfstab

#   Place share(1M) commands here for automatic execution
#   on entering init state 3.
#
#   Issue the command '/etc/init.d/nfs.server start' to run the NFS
#   daemon processes and the share commands, after adding the very
#   first entry to this file.
#       '
#   share [-F fstype] [ -o options] [-d "<text>"] <pathname> [resource]
#   .e.g,
#   share  -F nfs  -o rw=engineering  -d "home dirs"  /export/home2
share -F nfs /export
share -F nfs -o ro -d "phone lists" /data/phlist

#
```

As you can see, the /etc/dfs/dfstab file contains a list of resources to share, as specified by the share command. The file also instructs you, in the commented out section, that to start the NFS server daemon processes, you should run the **/etc/init.d/nfs.server start** command after adding the first entry into the file. If you do not do this, NFS will not start properly. You need to run this command only after you make the first entry, though, because the next time Solaris enters run level 3, the nfsd and mountd daemons will start automatically. They won't start, however, if the /etc/dfs/dfstab file is empty.

To successfully use the /etc/dfs/dfstab file, you need to understand the share command syntax. Understanding the syntax is also helpful if you are going to use the share command manually. Here is the syntax for share:

share -F *fstype* **-o** *options* **-d** *"text"* *pathname*

If you omit the -F *fstype* option, the first file system type listed in /etc/dfs/fstypes will be used. Although this is generally NFS, it's a good idea to specify a file system type just to be certain. The options you can use when mounting an NFS file system are explained in Table 11.9. You can add optional text with the -d argument; this might be useful for clients searching for a certain shared data point. The *pathname* is the path of the local resource (directory) to be shared.

The share command with no arguments displays the shared resources on your computer.

TABLE 11.9   NFS Share Options

Option	Explanation
aclok	Enables the NFS server to perform access control for NFS clients running NFS version 2. If set, aclok gives maximum access to all clients—meaning, with aclok set, if anyone has Read permission, then everyone has Read permission. If aclok is not set, then everyone is given minimal access.
anon=*uid*	Sets the *uid* to be the effective UID of unknown users. By default, unknown users are given the User ID of nobody. If this option is set to −1, access by unknown users is denied.
log=*tag*	Enables NFS server logging. The optional *tag* specifies the location of the related log files. If no *tag* is specified, the default global log file, as defined in /etc/nfs/nfslog.conf, is used.
nosub	Prohibits clients from mounting subdirectories of shared directories.
nosuid	Disallows the use of SetUID and SetGID permissions on shared resources.
root=*access_list*	Indicates that only root users from hosts specified in the *access_list* will have root access. By default, no host has root access.
ro	Indicates that the shared resource will be Read-only to all clients.

TABLE 11.9   NFS Share Options *(continued)*

Option	Explanation
ro=*access_list*	Those specified in the access list have Read-only access; all others are denied access.
rw	Indicates that shared resource will be Read and Write to all clients. This is the default.
rw=*access_list*	Indicates that those specified in the access list have Read and Write access; all others are denied access.
sec=*mode*	Specifies one or more security modes to authenticate clients. Options are sys, for AUTH_SYS authentication (clear-text authentication), which is the default, dh for Diffie-Hellman public key authentication, krb5 for Kerberos v5 (or krb5i or krb5p for variations), or none, which uses AUTH_NONE authentication, meaning that users have no identity and are mapped to the anonymous user nobody.

If you are using an option that requires an *access_list*, multiple entries in the *access_list* are separated by colons. For example, if you want to share a file system named /files1 and you want three clients, named larry, curly, and moe, to have Read-only access, you would use:

```
# share -F nfs -o ro=larry:curly:moe /files1
```

Alternately, if you want to give fred and wilma Read and Write access, while limiting barney and betty to read-only, you could use:

```
# share -F nfs -o ro=barney:betty rw=fred:wilma /files1
```

You also have the option of using a minus sign (−) to exclude a computer from being able to mount a remote resource. For example, if you want everyone in the finance netgroup except the client1 computer to be able to access /files1, you could use:

```
# share -F nfs -o rw=-client1:finance /files1
```

If multiple share commands are issued for the same file system, the last instance will invalidate previous commands. The share options specified by the last instance will override any other share options.

WARNING   root permissions should not be enabled on NFS file system shares. Enabling root permissions could open a serious security hole in your network by allowing users to have root access to files on a server.

After all your shares are entered into the /etc/dfs/dfstab file, you can begin automatically sharing the file systems by rebooting or running the shareall command.

To stop the sharing of a shared file system, use the unshare command. For example, to stop the sharing of /files1, you could use:

```
# unshare /files1
```

Enabling NFS Logging

Logging NFS enables you to track who accessed what resources and when on your NFS server. Although enabling logging slows the NFS server response time, the slowdown is not significant except on the most heavily utilized servers. In any case, the security and tracking benefits of using NFS logging outweigh any possible inconveniences.

To enable NFS logging, add the log argument to the appropriate share command in /etc /dfs/dfstab. Each share point can be logged separately, but you must specify each share point you want to log. One of the questions you need to ask is: what do you want to log? If you wanted to log the /files1 file system, you could use the following command in your dfstab file:

```
# share -F nfs -o log /files1
```

You can configure two files to affect the behavior of NFS logging: /etc/nfs/nfslog.conf and /etc/default/nfslogd. The nfslog.conf file contains information on the location of log files. The locations are referenced by what is called a tag. By default, nfslog.conf contains one tag, named global. If you do not specify and create an alternate tag, the global tag will be used. Here's a sample nfslog.conf file:

```
# more /etc/nfs/nfslog.conf
#
# NFS server log configuration file.
#
# <tag> [ defaultdir=<dir_path> ] \
#       [ log=<logfile_path> ] [ fhtable=<table_path> ] \
#       [ buffer=<bufferfile_path> ] [ logformat=basic|extended ]
#

global  defaultdir=/var/nfs \
        log=nfslog fhtable=fhtable buffer=nfslog_workbuffer
```

As you can see, the global tag uses the /var/nfs directory by default, and the log file name is nfslog.

After you have decided what you want to log, you can configure the nfslog.conf file with multiple tags and log file locations if you choose. If you are doing a lot of logging and want to be able to quickly access log file information for a specific share point, you will want to create a separate log for each share. If you do not use extensive logging or want all your logging to be in one location, you can use the default global tag.

The other file you can use to configure NFS logging behavior is /etc/default/nfslogd. Whereas the nfslog.conf file specifies specific logs to use, the nfslogd file contains more general NFS server logging configuration information, such as the maximum number of old logs to preserve and default permissions for log files.

The nfslogd daemon needs to be started for NFS logging to work. Restarting the NFS daemons with the **nfs.server start** command will also start nfslogd, if an nfslog.conf file exists. If the nfslog.conf file does not exist, you must first run the **/usr/lib/nfs/ nfslogd** command to create it. Then, subsequent restarts of NFS will automatically start NFS logging as well.

Accessing NFS Resources from Clients

Sharing NFS resources is a convenient way to make sure that network clients each have access to the same data located on a server. After you have configured your NFS server, you need to configure clients to access the server.

If you are unsure of which resources are shared and available to the client, you can use the `dfshares` command, which displays the available shared resources on a given computer. For example, if you wanted to see the shares available on the `bedrock` server, you could use:

dfshares bedrock

To access remotely shared resources from your local computer, you need to mount the shared file system locally. One of three ways to do this is manually with the `mount` command. You originally learned of the `mount` command in Chapter 7, and the usage of `mount` does not change from the explanations in that chapter. For review, Table 11.10 lists the generic `mount` arguments, and Table 11.11 lists `mount`-specific options for NFS file systems.

TABLE 11.10   Generic *mount* Arguments

Argument	Description
-F *FSType*	Specifies the file system type to mount.
-m	Mounts the file system but does not create an entry in /etc/mnttab.
-O	Overlay mount. This enables you to mount a file system over an existing mount. The overwritten file system will not be accessible while the new file system is mounted.
-p	Prints a list of mounted file systems in /etc/vfstab format. Must be used alone.
-r	Mounts the file system as Read-only.
-v	Prints the list of mounted file systems in verbose format. Must be used alone.

Specific `mount` options, as invoked with -o, are listed in Table 11.11. These `mount` options are available for NFS mounts.

TABLE 11.11   NFS *mount -o* Options

Option	Description
bg | fg	Specifies whether to retry the mount operation in the background or foreground if mounting fails the first time. Foreground is the default.
hard | soft	Specifies how to proceed if the server does not respond. The soft option returns an error, and hard retires the request until the server responds. The default is hard.

TABLE 11.11   NFS *mount -o* Options *(continued)*

Option	Description
intr | nointr	Enables or disables keyboard interrupts to kill a process that hangs while waiting for a response from a hard-mounted file system on the NFS server. The default is intr, which enables clients to interrupt hung applications.
port=*n*	Indicates the server IP port number. The default is NFS_PORT.
quota | noquota	Checks whether the user is over the quota limits on the NFS server, if quotas are enabled, or prevents quota checking.
retry=*n*	Retries the mount operation if it fails. The variable *n* determines the number of times to retry.
remount	Changes features of an already mounted file system. It can be used with any options except ro.
ro | rw	Indicates Read-only versus Read/Write. The default is Read/Write.
rsize=*n*	Sets the read buffer size to *n* bytes. The default for NFS version 3 is 32,768 bytes.
suid | nosuid	Enables or disables the use of SetUID. The default is suid.
timeo=*n*	Sets the NFS time-out to *n* tenths of a second. For connectionless transports, the default is 11 tenths of a second, and for connection-oriented transports, the default is 600 tenths of a second.
wsize=*n*	Sets the write buffer size to *n* bytes. The default for NFS version 3 is 32,768 bytes.

Here is the syntax for mount:

```
# mount -F FSType generic_options -o specific_options ⏎
  device_name mount_point
```

For example, say you want to mount a shared file system named /files1 from the pebbles server. The mounted file system should be located at /localfiles. You could use:

```
# mount -F nfs pebbles:/files1 /localfiles
```

If you have remote resources to mount on a consistent basis, manual mounting is not very efficient. You have two other choices: use the /etc/vfstab file or use the automounter. The vfstab file is covered in Chapter 7, and the automounter is covered in detail later in this chapter, in the "Using AutoFS" section.

Here's a quick introduction to the automounter. By default, clients can automatically mount remote resources through the /net mount point. So, to mount the /export/files/data file system located on the pebbles server, you would use the following command:

```
$ cd /net/pebbles/export/files/data
```

Automounter enables users to mount file systems, so superuser access is not required. The automounter will also automatically unmount the file system after the user is finished using it.

File systems mounted as Read/Write or those containing executable files should always be mounted as hard. Soft mounting such file systems can cause unexpected I/O errors. Read/Write file systems should also be mounted with the intr option, so as to allow users to kill processes that appear to be hung if necessary.

If a file system is mounted as hard, and intr is not specified, a process can hang until the remote file system responds. This can cause annoying delays for terminal processes. If you use intr, then an interrupt signal can be sent to the server to terminate the process. For foreground processes, Control+C usually works. For background processes, you can send an INT or QUIT signal, such as:

```
# kill -QUIT 11234
```

   KILL signals (–9) do not kill hung NFS processes.

To unmount NFS file systems, use the umount command.

Starting and Stopping NFS Services

In some cases, you will need to stop the NFS services. You might have an emergency on the NFS server, or you might want to perform system maintenance. To enable or disable NFS services, you must have superuser privileges.

To stop NFS services, use:

```
# /etc/init.d/nfs.server stop
```

And to restart NFS services, use:

```
# /etc/init.d/nfs.server start
```

You can also stop the automounter with the following:

```
# /etc/init.d/autofs stop
```

Or you can restart the automounter with:

```
# /etc/init.d/autofs start
```

Troubleshooting NFS

Good troubleshooters will tell you that solving problems is all about isolating the problem before you try to fix it. As logical as this sounds, many people will think they know what's wrong and try to fix it before gathering all the information they need to make a proper decision. With NFS, there could be one of three problem areas: the client, the server, or the network connection.

To help isolate the problem, find out what works and what doesn't. For example, if one client machine cannot attach to the NFS server, it's possibly a problem on the client side. However, if no one can get to the NFS server, it's more likely a network problem or an NFS server problem.

Before beginning any NFS troubleshooting, ensure that the `nfsd` and `mountd` daemons are running on the NFS server. They should start automatically at boot, provided that there is at least one entry in the `/etc/dfs/dfstab` file.

 By default, all mounts are made with the `intr` option. If your remote program hangs, and you get a `server not responding` error message, pressing Control+C on your keyboard should kill the remote application.

Hard-mounted remote file systems will behave differently than soft-mounted remote file systems. Accordingly, you will receive different error messages if the server stops responding, depending on whether you have used a hard or soft mount. If your remote file system is hard mounted, and the server (named `filesrv` in this example) fails to respond, you will see the following error message:

`NFS server filesrv not responding still trying`

Because of the hard mount, though, your client computer will continue to try the mount. If you have used soft mounts, you will see the following error when the server fails to respond:

`NFS operation failed for server filesrv: error # (error message)`

Soft mounts increase the chance of corrupted data on Read/Write file systems or file systems that contain executable programs. Therefore, only hard-mount file systems such as these.

One useful troubleshooting command is `nfsstat`. If NFS response seems slow, the `nfsstat` command can return statistics about the NFS server and clients. To display client statistics, use `nfsstat -c`. Server statistics are displayed with `nfsstat -s`, and `nfsstat -m` shows statistics for each file system.

Using AutoFS

If your network has a large number of NFS resources, managing the mapping of these resources can become cumbersome. *AutoFS*, also called the *automounter*, is a client-side service that provides automatic mounting of remote file systems. If you use AutoFS, remote directories are mounted only when they are being accessed by a client and are automatically unmounted after the client is finished.

Using AutoFS eliminates the need for mounting file systems at boot, which both reduces network traffic and speeds up the boot process. Also, users do not need to use the `mount` and `umount` commands, meaning that they do not need superuser access to mount file systems.

Here is how AutoFS works: when a user attempts to access a remote file system, a mount is established by the automounter. When the file system has not been accessed for a certain period of time, the mount is automatically broken. AutoFS is managed by the `automountd` daemon, which runs continuously on the client machine and handles mounts and unmounts, and by the `automount` service, which sets up mount points and manages automount maps.

When the system boots up, the `automount` command reads the master map file, named `auto_master`, and creates the initial set of AutoFS mounts. These mounts are not automatically mounted at startup; instead, they are mount points under which file systems will be mounted in the future. These are called *trigger nodes*.

After the initial AutoFS mounts are configured, they can trigger file systems to be mounted under them. So when a user tries to mount a file system by using AutoFS, `automountd` mounts the requested file system under the trigger node.

The `automount` command is used to invoke the AutoFS service. The syntax of `automount` is as follows:

```
# automount -t time -v
```

The `-t` variable sets the time, in seconds, that a file system should remain mounted if not in use. The default is five minutes. However, on systems with a lot of automounted resources, you might want to increase this value to reduce the overhead caused by checking file systems to see whether they're active. The `-v` option reports automounting information in verbose mode, which can be useful in troubleshooting AutoFS problems.

The automount service does not read the `/etc/vfstab` file for a list of file systems to mount. Instead, it's configured through its own set of files, known as *AutoFS maps*.

AutoFS Maps

AutoFS uses three types of maps: master, direct, and indirect. Maps can be located on each local system or centrally located on a name server such as NIS or NIS+. If you have a network with a large number of clients, using a name service is preferred over maintaining local files.

Master Map

The *master map* associates a directory with a map point, and also lists direct and indirect maps used. In a sense, the master map (`/etc/auto_master`) configures AutoFS. Here is the default master map:

```
# more /etc/auto_master
# Master map for automounter
#
+auto_master
/net            -hosts          -nosuid,nobrowse
/home           auto_home       -nobrowse
/xfn            -xfn
/-              auto_direct     -ro
```

This map file contains one entry, which begins with the `+auto_master` statement. Each line in the entry contains the following information: mount point, map name, and mount options. For example, the line beginning with `/net` (the mount point) has `-hosts` as the map name and the `nosuid` and `nobrowse` mount options. Table 11.12 describes the master map fields.

TABLE 11.12 `/etc/auto_master` Fields

Field	Description
mount_point	The full absolute pathname of a directory to be used as the mount point. AutoFS will create the directory if it does not already exist. The notation /- as a mount point indicates that the map is a direct map; no particular mount point is associated with the map.

TABLE 11.12   /etc/auto_master Fields *(continued)*

Field	Description
map_name	The map that AutoFS uses to find directories or mount information. A preceding slash (/) indicates that a local file is to be used; otherwise, AutoFS uses the name service specified in the name service switch file (/etc/nsswitch.conf) to locate mount information. The /net and /xfn mount points use special maps.
mount_options	Optional, comma-separated list of options that pertain to the mount point.

Without making any changes to the auto_master map, users can access remote file systems through the /net mount point. This is because of the /net entry, which uses a built-in special map named -hosts that uses only the hosts database.

For example, imagine that your network has an NFS server named gumby, which has a shared file system named /files. Clients using only the default map could access the resource by using the following command:

```
$ cd /net/gumby/files
```

The path used is dependent on the network name, though. For example, if you then wanted to access the /docs file system on the remote system pokey, you would need to use:

```
$ cd /net/pokey/docs
```

The /home mount point references the /etc/auto_home map, which is an indirect map that supports the mounting of home directories from anywhere on the network.

Again, keep in mind that although the master map sets up the map points for /net and /home automatically, its other primary responsibility is to point clients to direct and indirect maps for the automatic mounting of remote resources.

Anytime you modify a master map, you will need to stop and restart the automounter for the changes to take effect.

Direct Map

A *direct map* is an automount point that contains a direct association between a mount point on a client and a directory on a server. Direct maps require a full pathname to explicitly indicate the relationship. Here is a sample auto_direct map:

```
# more /etc/auto_direct
/usr/local    -ro
  /bin    server1:/export/local/sun4
  /share server1:/export/local/share
/usr/man      -ro server1:/usr/man server2:/usr/man server3:/usr/man
/docfiles         filesrv:/docs
#
```

A direct map has three fields: key, mount options, and location. The key is the pathname of the local mount point—for example, the local /docfiles directory. The mount options are standard options that you want to apply to the mount. Finally, the location is the absolute path of the remote file system that you want to mount. Locations should not contain mount point names, but full, absolute pathnames. For example, a home directory should be listed as server:/export/home/*username*, not as server:/home/*username*.

You will notice that for the /usr/man mount point, three servers are listed. Multiple locations can be used for failover. If the client attempts to access /usr/man, it has three servers it can access the information from. If the first server is busy or unavailable, the client can attempt to use the next server. By default, the client will attempt to connect to the closest server in the list, based on network distance and response time. However, if you want, you can indicate priorities for the listed servers, as in this example:

```
/usr/man -ro serverx,servery(1),serverz(2):/usr/man
```

The first server, serverx, does not have a priority and therefore defaults to the highest priority available (0). The servery server will be tried second, and the serverz server last.

Any time you modify a direct map, you will need to stop and restart the automounter for the changes to take effect.

Indirect Map

Whereas a direct map uses mount points that are specified in the named direct map file, an *indirect map* uses mount points that are defined in the auto_master file. Indirect maps establish associations between mount points and directories by using a substitution key value. Home directories are easily accessed through indirect maps, and the auto_home map is an example of an indirect map for this purpose. Here is a sample auto_home map:

```
# more /etc/auto_home
# Home directory map for automounter
#
+auto_home
qdocter Q-Sol:/export/home/qdocter
kdocter Q-Sol:/export/home/kdocter
mgantz Q-Sol:/export/home/mgantz
sjohnson Q-Sol:/export/home/sjohnson
fredee Q-Sol:/export/home/fredee
ramini Q-Sol:/export/home/ramini
```

As with direct maps, there are three fields: key, mount options, and location. In an indirect map, though, the key is a simple reference name in the indirect map. The location should always be an absolute path.

As mentioned in the introduction to this section, indirect maps use mount points as specified in the auto_master file. Here is an example:

```
# more /etc/auto_master
# Master map for automounter
#
+auto_master
/net        -hosts      -nosuid,nobrowse
/home       auto_home   -nobrowse
/xfn        -xfn
/files      auto_files
```

This `auto_master` file contains the `/files` mount point, which references the `auto_files` indirect map. Here is the `auto_files` map:

```
# more /etc/auto_files
#
+auto_files
docs        server1:/projects/data/files
```

When the `/files` directory is accessed (as indicated in the `auto_master` file), then the automounter will trigger a node for the `/files/docs` directory. After the `/files/docs` directory is accessed, AutoFS will complete the mounting of the `server1:/projects/data/files` file system. The user can trigger this whole process by using directory navigation or management commands, such as `cd` or `ls`, and does not need to use the `mount` command at all.

Automount Summary

Although using the automounter is convenient, its best usage is for infrequently used file systems. This is because as the file system is mounted, network traffic is generated. Also, the automounter must continually check whether the automounted resources are still being used, and unmount the unused file systems. This adds some overhead to the NFS server.

For NFS resources that are frequently accessed, standard NFS mounting might be more efficient for your network.

 Real World Scenario

Efficient File System Usage

You work for a natural gas management company, and your network has two physical locations: Denver and Cheyenne. The Denver office is the main corporate office and contains four of the five network's servers. Although the Cheyenne office has only about 30 employees, it has a dedicated connection to the Denver office.

One of your Denver servers is configured as an NFS server and contains user home directories, project files, and the company's database. Home directories for Cheyenne users are stored on the Cheyenne server. However, users in Cheyenne need to access the company database as well as critical project files located on the Denver NFS server. These users complain that access to files stored in Denver is very slow, as the dedicated connection is only 128Kbps. What can you do to speed up file access?

You're already using NFS, which is a good thing. The problem is speed, though. This is a good time to use the CacheFS file system to improve performance for Cheyenne users. CacheFS can be set up on computers in the Cheyenne office to cache the files that users need to perform their jobs. In fact, it would probably even be a good idea to pack the cache, if you know which files will be used on a consistent basis.

The CacheFS file system is designed to improve response time over slow network connections, and this seems like an ideal case in which to implement it.

Summary

This chapter covered a plethora of file systems used in Solaris. The first half of this chapter was dedicated to virtual, or pseudo, file systems. Most virtual file systems reside in memory and do not consume physical disk space. Virtual file systems exist to improve the performance of Solaris.

The Process File System (PROCFS) manages a list of running system processes, as well as the /proc directory. The Loopback File System (LOFS) creates a virtual copy of a file system in a new mount point. The Cache File System (CacheFS) speeds up system performance by caching information located on slow network links or slow data devices such as CD-ROMs. The /tmp directory is managed by the Temporary File System (TMPFS), which again speeds up Solaris. The Swap File System (SWAPFS) manages virtual memory in Solaris; without virtual memory, you would need to purchase excessive amounts of RAM for your computer.

After discussing virtual file systems, core files and crash dump configuration was examined. A core file is generated when an application has a fatal error. Crash dumps are generated by Solaris when a critical system error occurs.

The Network File System (NFS) is one of the most important network services in Solaris. NFS enables you to place files on a server and make those files readily available to all clients on the network. You learned a bit of NFS history, which files and daemons are important, how to set up NFS, how to set up NFS logging, and NFS troubleshooting.

Finally, this chapter concluded with a discussion of the automounter, AutoFS. AutoFS provides for automatic mounting and unmounting of file systems, eliminating the need for clients to use the mount and umount commands. AutoFS uses three types of maps for configuration: master, direct, and indirect.

Exam Essentials

Know what the /proc directory contains and what manages it.   The /proc directory contains decimal numbers corresponding to process IDs of running processes. The Process File System (PROCFS) manages the /proc directory.

Understand what CacheFS is used for.   The Cache File System is used to improve the performance of slow network connections or slow data devices (such as CD-ROMs) by caching files that users have used. Subsequent accesses of these files will be quicker because the files are cached on the local hard disk.

Know the difference between a front file system and a back file system.   In CacheFS, the front file system is located on the local machine and contains copies of cached files. The back file system is located on the remote machine (or is the CD-ROM) and contains the original files.

Understand what virtual memory is used for.   Virtual memory is hard disk space used to emulate physical memory, and virtual memory increases the amount of memory available to Solaris. Even though hard disk access is slower than memory access, virtual memory is good for computers because it reduces cost. It's much less expensive to purchase 2GB worth of disk space to use as virtual memory than to purchase 2GB of RAM.

Know how to create an additional swap file.   First, you must create a file of the desired size with the `mkfile` command. Then, you use the `swap -a` command to make the new file a swap file.

Know the difference between a core file and a crash dump.   A core file is generated when an application experiences a critical failure. Crash dumps are generated when Solaris experiences a critical failure.

Know which two files make up the crash dump.   The two files are `unix.X` and `vmcore.X`. The *X* in each file will be the crash dump sequence number.

Know the difference between `coreadm` and `dumpadm`.   The `coreadm` command is used to manage core files, and the `dumpadm` command is used to manage crash dump files.

Know the name and location of the two files that are used to configure NFS logging.   The two files used are `/etc/default/nfslogd` and `/etc/nfs/nfslog.conf`. The `nfslog.conf` file contains tags and specifics regarding individual logging options, whereas `nfslogd` contains information that can be used to manage logging computer-wide.

Know which two daemons must be running on an NFS server for NFS services to function.   The two critical server-side daemons are `nfsd` and `mountd`.

Know what the `/etc/dfs/dfstab` file is used for.   The `/etc/dfs/dfstab` file is used to automatically mount shared file systems for use in NFS. The `dfstab` file contains one or more `share` commands used to share file systems.

Know how to stop and start NFS services.   The NFS server is stopped with the `/etc/init.d/nfs.server stop` command and restarted with the `/etc/init.d/nfs.server start` command.

Know how to access shared NFS resources from clients.   Clients wanting to access NFS resources must mount the volume locally by using the `mount` command, or by another mounting method, such as AutoFS.

Know which daemon manages AutoFS.   AutoFS is managed by the `automountd` daemon.

Know the three types of maps used by the automounter.   The maps are master, direct, and indirect.

Key Terms

Before you take the exam, be certain you are familiar with the following terms:

AutoFS	CacheFS packing
AutoFS maps	core file
automounter	crash dump
available memory	direct map
back file system	front file system
Cache File System (CacheFS)	indirect map

Loopback File System (LOFS)

master map

Network File System (NFS)

physical memory

Process File System (PROCFS)

Swap File System (SWAPFS)

swap space

Temporary File System (TMPFS)

trigger nodes

virtual file systems

virtual memory

Commands Used in This Chapter

The following list contains a summary of all the commands introduced in this chapter:

Command	Description
automount	Manages the automounter, AutoFS
cachefslog	Manages CacheFS logging
cachefspack	Enables you to pack the system cache with files before they are used
cachefsstat	Displays statistics on the Cache File System
cachefswssize	Reads the CacheFS log file and recommends an optimal log size
cfsadmin	Manages the Cache File System
coreadm	Manages core file behavior
dumpadm	Manages crash dump behavior
share	Shares a file system, making it available to other computers on the network
swap	Manages swap file creation, administration, and deletion
unshared	Stops the sharing of a shared file system

Review Questions

1. Which of the following file systems is managed by the Process File System? (Choose all that apply).

   A. `/tmp`

   B. `/var`

   C. `/proc`

   D. `/process`

2. You are mounting a remote file system to which you will have Read and Write access. Which of the following options are recommended when you mount this file system locally? (Choose all that apply.)

   A. `soft`

   B. `hard`

   C. `intr`

   D. `nointr`

3. You are configuring an NFS server for your network. When you share the `/docs` file system, you use the following command:

   `# share -F nfs -o anon=-1 sec=none /docs`

   When users attempt to mount the file system, they are unable to. What is the cause of the problem?

   A. Users attempting to mount the file system need to use the ID of −1 when mounting the shared file system.

   B. Users attempting to mount the file system need to ensure that their computers are configured to use no security authentication.

   C. When you shared the file system, you failed to include the computers that are allowed to mount the file system.

   D. When you shared the file system and set `sec=none`, you forced users to use no authentication. Because you set `anon=-1`, anonymous access is disabled.

4. You have just added additional swap space to your Solaris server. Which of the following can you do to ensure that the swap space is automatically available upon subsequent reboots?

   A. Use the `swapadd -a` command to ensure that the swap space is available upon reboot.

   B. Use the `swap -a` command to ensure that the swap space is available upon reboot.

   C. Add an entry for the new swap space into the `/etc/vfstab` file.

   D. Swap space must be added to the original swap file. Therefore, no additional action is necessary to make the new swap space available upon subsequent reboots.

5. Which of the following statements best describe front and back file systems? (Choose all that apply.)

    A. A front file system is located on the local computer, and a back file system is located on a remote computer.

    B. A front file system is located on a remote computer, and a back file system is located on the local computer.

    C. A front file system contains cached copies of files, and a back file system contains the original files.

    D. A front file system contains the original files, and a back file system contains cached copies of files.

6. You are the Solaris administrator for your company. Your Solaris server crashed during the evening and has rebooted automatically. Which of the following commands can you use to manage the file created (the output of system memory) when the server crashed?

    A. crashadm

    B. dumpadm

    C. coreadm

    D. dumpmem

7. What is the full path and filename of the NFS server's logging daemon?

    A. /etc/nfs/nfslog.conf

    B. /etc/default/nfslogd

    C. /usr/lib/nfs/nfslogd

    D. /etc/nfs/nfslogtab

8. You are using AutoFS on your client computers. Which of the following files no longer needs to be checked to mount file systems, because its functionality is replaced by the automounter?

    A. /etc/mnttab

    B. /etc/vfstab

    C. /etc/inittab

    D. /etc/autotab

9. You are configuring the automounter on your client computer. Which of the following types of maps provides mapping of a mount point to a specific directory?

    A. AutoFS

    B. Direct

    C. Indirect

    D. Master

10. You have just created an additional Cache File System on your Solaris workstation named `/fastcache`. When you run the `cachefsstat` command, you receive the following message:

`cachefsstat: /fastcache: not a cachefs mountpoint`

What is the most likely cause of the problem?

A. The file system was not mounted in the cache.

B. The file system was mounted in the cache but was not activated. Run the `cache` command to activate it.

C. The file system was mounted in the cache but was not activated. Reboot your computer to activate it.

D. The `cachefsstat` command recognizes only the default cache created during system installation and will not recognize additional Cache File Systems.

11. You are configuring the automounter for your Solaris computer. Which of the following is the name of the default direct automount map?

A. `/etc/auto_direct`

B. `/etc/auto_master`

C. `/etc/master_auto`

D. `/etc/direct_auto`

E. `/etc/direct`

12. Which of the following commands do you use to create a new file to be used as swap space?

A. `swap`

B. `swapadd`

C. `mkfs`

D. `newfs`

E. `touch`

F. `mkfile`

13. One of your applications has been crashing intermittently, and you want to examine the per-process core files generated. The application is installed in the `/app1` directory. Which of the following directories should you go to examine the per-process core files?

A. `/app1`

B. `/var/tmp`

C. `/corepath`

D. The current working directory

14. You have shared your /docs file system manually by using the share command. Now you want to stop sharing the file system. Which of the following commands is explicitly used to stop the sharing of file systems?

A. share –d /docs

B. ushare /docs

C. unshare /docs

D. umount /docs

15. You are configuring the automounter on your Solaris workstation. Which of the following commands would you use to adjust to 10 minutes the amount of time an idle file system remains mounted?

A. automount –t 600

B. automount –t 10

C. automountd –t 600

D. automountd –t 10

E. You cannot adjust the time that an idle file system will remain mounted.

16. You are the Solaris administrator for your company. You are presented with the following information from an /etc/dfstab file:

share –F nfs /export

share –F nfs –o ro log –d "phone lists" /data/phlist

Provided you are using NFS logging with default settings, which of the following directories will contain the log file for the /data/phlist file system? (Choose all that apply.)

A. The default local log file as specified in the /etc/nfs/nfslog.conf file.

B. The default global log file as specified in the /etc/nfs/nfslog.conf file.

C. The default global log file as specified in the /etc/default/nfslogd file.

D. /var/log

E. /var/nfs

F. It's impossible to determine the log file location based on the provided information.

17. You are planning on adding additional swap space to your Solaris workstation. Which of the following is a valid reason for logging in as the superuser to create the swap space?

A. Only the superuser can create additional swap space.

B. Creating additional swap space as the superuser prevents accidental overwrite and deletion of the swap file.

C. Swap space must be created in the swap partition, and only the superuser has access to the swap partition.

D. There is no valid reason to log in as superuser to create additional swap space.

18. You are the Solaris administrator for your network. On a client machine, you have just made changes to the master automount map. What do you need to do to effect the changes you just made?

A. autofs

B. automount

C. automountd

D. /etc/init.d/autofs stop
   /etc/init.d/autofs start

19. You are the Solaris server administrator for your company. On your server, you notice multiple unix.*X* and vmcore.*X* files. Which of the following events cause the creation of these two types of files?

A. Crash dumps

B. Core file generation

C. Creating additional virtual memory

D. Failed attempts to mount shared file systems

20. You are configuring the automounter for your Solaris computer. Where is the mount point for an indirect automount map located?

A. In the indirect map.

B. In the direct map.

C. In the master map.

D. Indirect automount maps do not specify mount points.

Answers to Review Questions

1. C. The Process File System (PROCFS) manages the /proc file system. It does not manage the /tmp or /var file systems. The /process file system does not exist by default.

2. B, C. When mounting a file system to which you'll have Read and Write access, you should always mount the file system hard and intr. This allows you more control over the mounting process, reduces the chance of file corruption on the NFS server, and enables you to kill hung processes with keyboard interrupts.

3. D. This is an example of using options that cause problems when used together. The anon=-1 option sets the User ID for anonymous users to –1, which is an invalid UID. Therefore, anonymous access is prohibited. At the same time, you set sec=none, which means that no security is enforced, and the system classifies the user as an anonymous user.

4. C. To make additional swap space available, you can add an entry in the /etc/vfstab file. The swap -a command is used to activate a file as swap space. The swapadd command does not exist.

5. A, C. *Front file systems* and *back file systems* are terms used with the CacheFS file system. The front file system is on the local computer and contains cached copies of files. The back file system is located on a remote computer (or it can be a slow local device, such as a CD-ROM) and contains the original files.

6. B. The dumpadm command is used to manage crash dump files. The coreadm command is used to manage core files, but core files are generated when an application crashes, not when the system experiences a critical error and Solaris crashes. The crashadm and dumpmem commands do not exist.

7. C. The /usr/lib/nfs/nfslogd file is the NFS logging daemon. The nfslog.conf and /etc/default/nfslogd files are for configuring NFS logging behavior. The /etc/nfs/nfslogtab file is a table containing information for analyzing NFS logs by the nfslogd daemon.

8. B. If you are using the automounter, the computer does not need to read the /etc/vfstab file to mount virtual file systems. The /etc/inittab file is still needed for system initialization, and the /etc/mnttab file is still required to mount local file systems. The /etc/autotab file does not exist.

9. B. A direct map configures a specific map point to a directory on a server.

10. A. The cachefsstat command displays statistics about Cache File Systems. If the command tells you that the mount point you entered is not a cache mount point, it's likely that the file system was not properly mounted as a Cache File System. If this file system is supposed to be cache, unmount it, and remount it by using the mount command.

11. A. The default direct automount map is named /etc/auto_direct. The master map is named /etc/auto_master.

12. F. The mkfile command is used to create the file you want to use as swap space. After the file is created, you use the swap -a command to activate the file as swap space.

13. D. Per-process core files are created in the current working directory.

14. C. The `unshare` command is used to stop the sharing of shared file systems. The `share` command shares file systems, `umount` unmounts file systems, and the `ushare` command does not exist.

15. A. The `automount` command is used to adjust this time. The `-t` option is used, and the time must be specified in seconds.

16. B, E. In the `share` command for the `/data/phlist` command, the log option does not have a tag; therefore, it uses the default global log file as specified in the `/etc/nfs/nfslog.conf` file. By default, this file is located in `/var/nfs` and is named `nfslog`.

17. B. Regular "non-superuser" users can create swap space. However, to prevent accidental overwriting of the new swap space, Sun recommends that you create the new swap space while logged in as the superuser.

18. D. After you make changes to a master or direct automount map, you must stop and restart the AutoFS service for the changes to take effect. This is done with the **autofs stop** and **autofs start** commands from the `/etc/init.d` directory.

19. A. The `unix.X` and `vmcore.X` files are the two files that make up a crash dump and therefore are generated during crash dumps. Core file generation creates core files. Creating additional virtual memory and failed mount attempts do not create additional error or log files.

20. C. The mount point for an indirect automount map is referenced by the master map.

Chapter 12

Managing Storage Volumes

SOLARIS 9 EXAM OBJECTIVES COVERED IN THIS CHAPTER:

- ✓ Explain the purpose, features, and functionalities of RAID, and identify the guidelines to follow when using RAID 0, RAID 1, and RAID 5, including hardware considerations.

- ✓ Define key SVM concepts, including volumes and state databases.

In Chapter 7, "File System Management," you learned how to create disk-based file systems for permanent file storage. You also learned that Solaris defines eight slices by default, numbered 0 through 7. Although basic hard disk management tools discussed in Chapter 7 are sufficient for most computers and networks, they do have some shortcomings.

For example, the default disk management tools do not provide for fault tolerance. In other words, if one disk fails, all information on all slices on that disk is lost. Of course, you can make regular backups of data onto a tape device or other backup media (known as fault recovery), but this method requires you to make time-consuming restorations of lost data while the computer is down.

The Solaris Volume Manager enables you to create a variety of volume types to both increase your computer's speed and provide fault tolerance. Several of these advanced storage configurations are categorized into RAID levels, such as RAID 0, RAID 1, and RAID 5.

This chapter begins with a discussion of RAID. After that, you will spend some time learning about the Solaris Volume Manager and how you can use the Solaris Volume Manager to ease your hard disk administration, speed up your computer's disk I/O, and provide automatic fault tolerance for your system's data.

Understanding RAID

RAID—Redundant Array of Inexpensive (or Independent) Disks—is a set of industry standards that defines storage solutions involving more than one hard disk. RAID is not unique to the Solaris environment, or even UNIX for that matter.

There are two common ways to implement RAID: hardware-based and software-based. Hardware-based RAID requires you to purchase storage units (or storage devices) that have RAID-aware controllers built directly into them. For example, you might see a hardware RAID storage cabinet of 20 hard disks. This cabinet will likely have its own processor and memory, in addition to hot-swappable hard disks. Fault tolerance is built in, and hardware RAID solutions are usually very fast in terms of disk I/O. The downside to hardware RAID is that it's usually prohibitively expensive. You can easily spend tens of thousands of dollars just for storage. For some administrators this isn't a big deal, but for most people, spending the money just isn't justifiable.

Software RAID is controlled by an operating system. Many popular network operating systems, including Solaris, other UNIX versions, Linux, and Windows NT and 2000 support software RAID. Instead of purchasing independent hardware devices, you can use your existing hard disks and implement RAID through the operating system. Software RAID is a bit slower and not quite as efficient as hardware RAID, but a very cost-effective solution. After all, you already own the operating system!

A number of RAID levels are defined, including RAID 0 through RAID 7, RAID 10 (also called RAID 1+0), and RAID 0+1. Many RAID vendors will combine RAID levels in their products, so you might see something like RAID 53, which means RAID 5 plus RAID 3. All of these implementations can make learning about and implementing RAID confusing. The three most common levels, and the levels supported by Solaris Volume Manager, are RAID 0, RAID 1, and RAID 5.

RAID 0

RAID 0 is known as *disk striping*. Solaris also implements a concatenation version of RAID 0. In RAID 0, data is written evenly across all disks that are part of the set, making the data appear as a "stripe" across all involved disks. To implement RAID 0, you need at least two hard disks.

The advantages of RAID 0 are that it provides fast disk I/O (the fastest of any RAID level), it has a simple design, and it's easy to implement. The negative to RAID 0 is that it does *not* provide fault tolerance. *Fault tolerance* means that if one disk fails, the computer can still operate properly. Without fault tolerance, if one of the disks in the volume fails, the entire RAID 0 volume will cease to operate. RAID 0 is the only one of the RAID levels that does not provide fault tolerance. Figure 12.1 illustrates what a RAID 0 striped volume logically looks like.

FIGURE 12.1   RAID 0

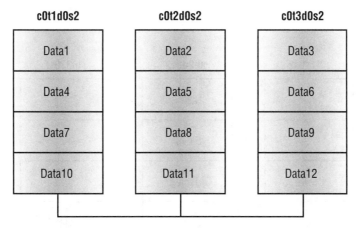

To summarize RAID 0, it's fast, but it doesn't provide fault tolerance.

RAID 1

RAID 1 is known as *disk mirroring*. In a RAID 1 volume, file systems (or entire hard disks) are mirrored onto one or more additional hard disks. Consequently, in order to use RAID 1, you need at least two hard disks. If one of the disks fails, another disk containing the same information is available for use. Of course, if a disk fails and its mirror fails at the same time, you then have a serious problem. For this reason, even if you use a mirrored volume, always maintain current data backups (just as if you had no fault tolerance).

 You will sometimes hear people refer to RAID 1 as disk duplexing. The difference between disk mirroring and disk duplexing is which disk controllers the hard disks are located on. If both disks in your set are on the same controller, it's a mirror. If they're on different controllers, it's a duplex. The difference is really only a technicality, as setting up a mirror is no different from setting up a duplex in Solaris.

Most RAID 1 implementations are slow when it comes to writing data to the disk (because the data has to be written to two or more disks), but comparatively fast when reading (because data can be read from one or more disks at the same time). It's still not as fast as RAID 0 for disk reads, though.

One of the advantages of RAID 1 is that it can be used to mirror system partitions (such as the root or /usr), whereas other RAID versions cannot contain these file systems.

The biggest downside to RAID 1 is that it's very inefficient. For example, to provide a complete mirror of 10GB of disk storage, you need to purchase 20GB of hard disk space. It's a trade-off: you get complete fault tolerance but you waste disk space. Figure 12.2 shows a RAID 1 volume.

FIGURE 12.2   RAID 1

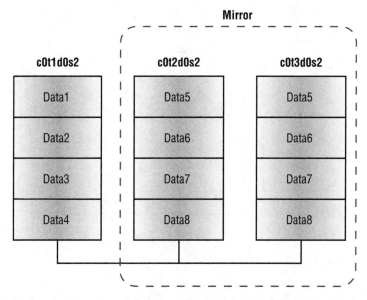

Solaris 9 supports combinations of RAID 0 and RAID 1, known as RAID 0+1 and RAID 1+0. How to implement these is covered later in this chapter ("Combining RAID 0 and RAID 1").

RAID 5

RAID 5 is called *disk striping with parity*. In a RAID 5 volume, data is written across the disks in stripes, just as it is in RAID 0. But unlike RAID 0, RAID 5 provides fault tolerance. Each stripe contains *parity information*, which provides data redundancy. A RAID 5 volume requires at least three components to implement, and parity is equally distributed among the three components. Although it's possible to create a RAID 5 volume with two or more components on the same hard disk, it's recommended that you use at least three separate hard disks. If one of the components fails, the computer can continue to operate normally, albeit slowly. If more than one component fails in a RAID 5 volume, the entire volume fails.

The term *component* is used in this chapter to refer to any individual slice, soft partition, or hard disk used to create a volume.

RAID 5 is slower than RAID 0 when writing to disk, because RAID 5 needs to calculate and write the parity information. Reading from a RAID 5 volume is as fast as RAID 0; however, if anyone asks you which is the fastest, because of the write speed differences, always answer RAID 0.

In a RAID 5 volume, you lose storage space equivalent to one component, for parity purposes. If you have three 10GB hard disks in a RAID 5 volume, you will have a 30GB volume capable of storing 20GB of data. If you have fifteen 10GB hard disks, you will have a 150GB volume capable of holding 140GB of data. Figure 12.3 shows a simple RAID 5 volume.

FIGURE 12.3   RAID 5

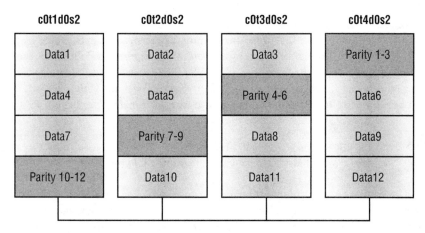

In terms of storage space, RAID 5 is more efficient than its fault-tolerant counterpart, RAID 1. In fact, the more disks you use in a RAID 5 volume, the more efficient your storage usage becomes. However, when you use more disks, you assume a greater risk of a single disk failure.

RAID levels are not mutually exclusive on one computer. In other words, you can have a RAID 1 and a RAID 5 volume on the same computer, depending on your storage needs.

Using Solaris Volume Manager

The *Solaris Volume Manager (SVM)* is packaged with Solaris 9 and provides advanced hard disk management capabilities, including creating RAID volumes, soft partitions, hot spare pools, and transactional volumes. Using SVM can help increase your storage capacity, ensure data availability, improve disk I/O, and lower administrative overhead. SVM was formerly known as the Solstice DiskSuite.

One new enhancement of Solaris Volume Manager is the inclusion of soft partitions. A *soft partition* enables you to create more than the standard eight slices available per hard disk.

Overview of Solaris Volume Manager

Solaris Volume Manager enables you to manage large numbers of hard disks and data volumes. SVM works by using virtual disks to manage physical disks and the data on those disks. A virtual disk is also called a *volume* or a *metadevice*. Sun currently prefers the term *volume*, although some documentation and command-line utilities still refer to metadevices.

Volumes are built from disk slices or other volumes. In terms of functionality, applications and utilities see volumes just as they see physical disks or file systems. In a sense, the virtual disk sits transparently on top of the physical disk. So when a request to read or write data is passed from an application to the operating system, Solaris Volume Manager intercepts the request on behalf of the virtual disk and passes it to the appropriate physical disk.

Do not confuse Solaris Volume Manager with the volume manager daemon (vold), which automatically mounts removable media such as CD-ROMs.

You can access the Solaris Volume Manager through one of two ways: a graphical interface or the command line. The graphical interface provided by the Solaris Management Console is easy to use and affords you complete flexibility when managing storage volumes. The Enhanced Storage node of the Solaris Management Console is shown in Figure 12.4.

If you prefer using a command line, most of the SVM commands begin with *meta*, such as metainit, metadb, and metastat. The available SVM commands are listed in Table 12.1, and their usage is covered in depth throughout the rest of the chapter.

FIGURE 12.4   Solaris Volume Manager's graphical interface

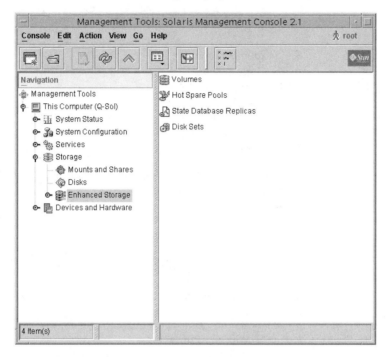

TABLE 12.1   Solaris Volume Manager Commands

Command	Function
growfs	Increases the size of a UFS file system without destroying data
metaclear	Removes active volumes and hot spare pools
metadb	Creates and deletes state database replicas
metadetach	Detaches a volume from a RAID 1 volume, or a logging device from a transactional volume
metadevadm	Checks the configuration of device IDs
metahs	Manages hot spare devices and hot spare pools
metainit	Configures volumes
metaoffline	Takes submirrors offline

TABLE 12.1 Solaris Volume Manager Commands *(continued)*

Command	Function
metaonline	Brings submirrors online
metaparam	Modifies volume parameters
metarecover	Recovers configuration information for soft partitions
metarename	Renames volumes
metareplace	Replaces components in submirrors and RAID 5 volumes
metaroot	Creates mirroring of the root file system (/)
metaset	Manages disk sets
metastat	Displays volume status or hot spare pool status
metasync	Synchronizes volumes
metattach	Attaches a component to a RAID 0 or RAID 1 volume, or a log device to a transactional volume

Regardless of whether you choose to use the graphical or command-line interface, you need root privileges to use Solaris Volume Manager.

Solaris Volume Manager and Crash Dumps

Although the Solaris Volume Manager is capable of managing all hard disks and storage devices in your system, it's best to keep your dump device for crash dumps out of the control of SVM.

Think about it this way: SVM is a software application that manages your hard disks. If the system crashes (and produces a crash dump), by definition, SVM is not running. So, if your dump device is controlled by SVM, you now have an inaccessible device to which a crash dump is supposed to be written. It won't work.

By default, your swap space is the crash dump device. It's okay to have Solaris Volume Manager control your swap space, but if you do, designate a dedicated dump device that's *not* controlled by SVM. For more information on crash dumps, see Chapter 11, "Virtual File Systems and NFS."

Key Files

Like any other Solaris service, Solaris Volume Manager requires several files to operate properly. The Solaris Volume Manager is started by the **/etc/rcS.d/S35svm.init** script during boot and synchronized (if necessary) by the /etc/rc2.d/S95svm.sync script, which also starts the active monitoring daemon.

The /etc/lvm/mddb.cf file contains the locations of your state database replicas and is considered the "metadevice database." The /etc/lvm/md.cf file holds information automatically generated for the default (unspecified or local) disk set. Never edit either of these files directly or you will corrupt your Solaris Volume Manager configuration.

The /kernel/drv/md.conf file is read by SVM at system startup. It contains configuration information, and there are two fields within this file you can edit. The first field is nmd, which sets the number of metadevices that your computer can support, and the second is md_nsets, which is the number of disk sets that your computer can support. The nmd field has a default of 128, but can be increased to a maximum of 8192. The md_nsets field defaults to 4 and can be increased up to 32.

Do not increase the nmd and md_nsets values unless you need to support additional volumes or disk sets. Increasing these values causes more memory to be reserved for volume and disk set management, even if the volumes or disk sets do not exist. Using unnecessarily high values could degrade system performance.

One last file important to Solaris Volume Manager configuration is /etc/lvm/md.tab. It contains configuration information that an administrator can use to reconstruct an SVM configuration. SVM can use this file for input with utilities such as metadb, metahs, and metainit.

Solaris Volume Manager does not input information into the md.tab file. It exists to enable the administrator to create a configuration and input the configuration for use by SVM.

Volume Details

Logical storage devices created by Solaris Volume Manager are called volumes. A volume can reside on one physical disk or be a combination of slices from multiple physical disks.

There are five classes of volumes you can create in Solaris 9: RAID 0, RAID 1, RAID 5, transactional, and soft partitions. You have already had an introduction to RAID levels. Details about transactional volumes and soft partitions are covered in their sections later in this chapter.

After volumes are created, you can use most file system management commands to manipulate them. Commands such as mount, umount, mkfs, and ufsdump work normally, as do all file system navigation commands, such as ls and cd. The one command that does not work on volumes is format.

Expanding Volumes

Existing volumes can be enlarged by adding additional slices. After you grow your volume, you will probably want to grow the file system that uses that volume by using the growfs command. Although growing file systems does not result in data loss, it's still a good idea to back up your file system before attempting configuration changes. Volumes can be expanded but cannot be shrunk without destroying the volume and creating a new one.

Volume Names

Each volume is assigned a name, just as each disk slice is assigned a name by Solaris. Here are volume naming requirements and guidelines:

- Volume names must have the format of d followed by a number—for example, d19 or d74.

- By default, Solaris supports 128 volume names, from d0–d127. If you need more volumes, you must edit the /kernel/drv/md.conf file.

- Each volume has a logical name that appears in the file system. For example, block device names are in the /dev/md/dsk directory, and raw device names are in the /dev/md/rdsk directory.

- When using meta* commands, instead of supplying the full volume name, such as /dev/md/dsk/d0, you can use abbreviated names, such as d0.

- You can rename a volume if it is not currently in use. However, each volume must have a unique name.

Before you can create volumes with Solaris Volume Manager, you must first create a state database.

Understanding State Databases

A *state database* is a database on the hard disk that stores information about your Solaris Volume Manager configuration. Changes made to your configuration are automatically updated within the state database.

The state database is a collection of multiple replicated database copies. Each copy is known as a *state database replica*. You should create at least three replicas for the state database and place the replicas on different controllers and/or different hard disks for maximum reliability. Obviously, if you have only one hard disk, this is not possible, so place all three replicas on the same slice. Replicas can be placed on dedicated slices, but it's not necessary. Placing replicas on slices that will become part of a volume is acceptable.

 Replicas cannot be placed on existing file systems or on the root (/), /usr, or swap file systems.

State database replicas are only 4MB each, so they don't take up a lot of room. You can add additional state database replicas to your system at any time.

If your state database becomes lost or corrupted, Solaris will poll the various replicas to see which ones still contain valid data. It determines this by using a majority consensus algorithm. Basically, Solaris reads the replicas and decides which information is valid by requiring a majority of the replicas to be available and in agreement. After valid data is determined, the state database can be restored, and the configuration corrected, if necessary.

You can create state database replicas from a command line by using the metadb command or from the Solaris Management Console.

Managing State Database Replicas from the Command Line

State database replicas are managed with the metadb command. To create the first state database replica, use **metadb -a -f** *slice*, where *slice* is the partition that will hold the replica. For example, you could use:

```
# metadb -a -f c0t2d0s0
```

After you have added the first replica, you can add additional ones; additional replicas do not need the -f switch. If you wanted to add two replicas to one slice, you could use:

```
# metadb -a -c 2 c0t0d0s7
```

Table 12.2 lists the switches available for metadb.

TABLE 12.2   *metadb* Arguments

Argument	Function
-a	Adds a new device to the database.
-c *number*	Specifies the number of replicas to add to the device. The default is 1.
-d	Deletes all replicas on the device.
-f	Creates the initial state database. Also forces the deletion of the last state database replica.
-h	Displays a usage message.
-i	Inquires about replica status.
-k *file*	Specifies the name of the kernel file to which the replica information should be written. It can be used only with the local disk set. The default file is /kernel/drv/md.conf.
-l *blocks*	Specifies the length of the replica. The default is 8192 blocks.
-p	Updates the system file (/kernel/drv/md.conf) with entries from the /etc/lvm/mddb.cf file. Normally used to update a newly built system before it is rebooted for the first time.
-s	Specifies the name of the disk set to use.

Using metadb, you can also specify multiple devices at the same time. For example, if you wanted to create an initial state database on four devices, you could use:

```
# metadb -a -f c0t0d0s7 c0t2d0s1 c0t2d0s5 c0t2d0s7
```

To check the status of your state database replicas, use **metadb -i**, as shown here:

```
# metadb -i
    flags       first blk      block count
    a    u      16             8192              /dev/dsk/c0t0d0s7
    a    u      16             8192              /dev/dsk/c0t2d0s0
 r - replica does not have device relocation information
 o - replica active prior to last mddb configuration change
 u - replica is up to date
 l - locator for this replica was read successfully
 c - replica's location was in /etc/lvm/mddb.cf
 p - replica's location was patched in kernel
 m - replica is master, this is replica selected as input
 W - replica has device write errors
 a - replica is active, commits are occurring to this replica
 M - replica had problem with master blocks
 D - replica had problem with data blocks
 F - replica had format problems
 S - replica is too small to hold current data base
 R - replica had device read errors
#
```

You don't need to memorize all the state flags. However, do notice that lowercase flags indicate proper operation, whereas uppercase flags indicate some sort of problem.

To delete a state replica database, use **metadb -d**. If it's the last replica, you will need to use -f as well. Here's an example:

```
# metadb -d -f c0t2d0s7
```

> **WARNING** If your computer has metadevices defined, do not delete all of your state database replicas. Doing so will cause the defined metadevices to fail.

Graphically Managing State Database Replicas

Here is how to create state database replicas by using the Solaris Management Console:

1. Select the State Database Replicas node to highlight it and then choose Action ➤ Create Replicas.

2. The first screen that appears will ask whether you want to use a disk set. If you haven't defined any disk sets or don't want to use an existing disk set for replicas, choose <none> and click Next.

3. You will then be asked to select the components on which you want to create the replicas.

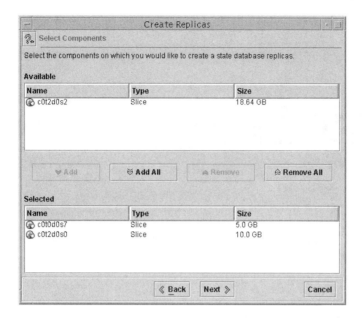

4. Next, you will be asked to specify a replica length (the default is 8192 blocks, or 4MB) and number of replicas per device. After you have entered values (the defaults are usually okay), click Next.

5. The last screen enables you to review your selections and shows you the commands that will be executed by the Solaris Volume Manager. To make any changes, use the Back button. If you are satisfied with your selections, click Finish.

When the replicas are created, you will see them appear on the right side of the Solaris Management Console, as shown in Figure 12.5.

FIGURE 12.5 State Database Replicas

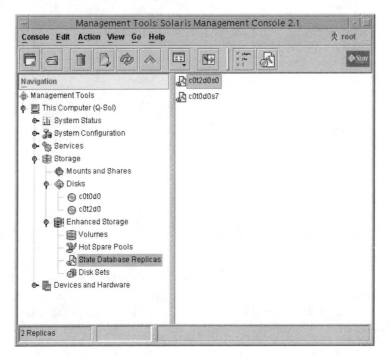

Double-clicking a replica will provide status information.

To delete a replica, right-click it in the right pane and choose Delete. Or, you can select it to highlight it and then choose Edit ➢ Delete.

Managing RAID with Solaris Volume Manager

Because of the diversity they afford, RAID volumes are the most common type of volumes you will create with Solaris Volume Manager. Depending on your needs, you can create a RAID 0 volume for speed or a RAID 5 volume for fault tolerance. In all, there are three types of RAID supported in Solaris 9, as stated earlier. They are RAID 0, RAID 1, and RAID 5.

Managing RAID 0

Solaris 9 supports two types of RAID 0 volumes: striped volumes and concatenated volumes. A striped volume, as you learned earlier in this chapter, writes data evenly across all member disks, making the written data appear to create a "stripe" among the disks.

A *concatenated volume* also uses multiple disks, but unlike a stripe (where data is evenly distributed), a concatenation uses all available space on one component (slice, soft partition, or disk) before moving on to fill the next component. These types of volumes are not as fast as striped volumes but enable you to combine small areas of hard disk space into a larger logical volume.

A hybrid of the two RAID 0 levels is called a concatenated stripe. A *concatenated stripe* is a striped volume that has been expanded beyond its original size. Data in the original stripe will be written as a stripe; data in the expanded section will be written as a concatenation. None of the RAID 0 levels provide fault tolerance. If one device that's part of a RAID 0 volume fails, the entire volume fails.

RAID 0 volumes can be composed of slices, soft partitions, or entire hard disks. However, a RAID 0 volume cannot contain the following file systems: root (/), /usr, swap, /var, /opt, or any other file system used during an operating system installation or upgrade.

Striped Volumes

Striped volumes use equal amounts of space from two or more components. In fact, if you were to attempt to create a stripe out of two hard disks, one 10GB and the other 20GB, you would get a stripe 20GB in size (10GB from each disk). The remaining 10GB on the second disk would be free to use for another volume.

For striped volumes, use components located on different controllers for optimal performance. This enables multiple sets of disk heads to be reading and/or writing at the same time.

A block of data written to a stripe is called an *interlace*. If you were to create a stripe from three disks, interlace 1 would be on disk 1, interlace 2 on disk 2, and interlace 3 on disk 3. Interlace 4 would be on disk 1 again, and the sequence would repeat itself. The default interlace value is 16KB, and the valid interlace range is 8KB to 100MB. You can adjust the interlace value when creating the striped volume, but after the volume is created, you cannot change the interlace value without re-creating the stripe.

Set your interlace value to optimize disk I/O. Generally speaking, you want your disk I/O size to be larger than your interlace size. If your computer performs a lot of large file transfers, a larger interlace will be more efficient. For computers that utilize many smaller file transfers, you will want a smaller interlace.

Existing file systems cannot be converted into a stripe. You must back up the data, create the stripe, and then restore the data from backup.

You must have a state database before you can create volumes.

Striped volumes are created with the metainit command. Here is the syntax:

```
# metainit volume_name #_stripes components_per_stripe component_name1↵
    component_name2 component_nameN -i interlace
```

The syntax for `metainit` might look complex, but it doesn't need to be difficult in practice. For example, if you wanted to create a stripe named d7, made of four slices with an interlace of 64KB, you could use:

```
# metainit d7 1 4 c0t2d0s2 c0t3d0s2 c0t4d0s2 c0t5d0s2 -i 64k
```

The 1 in the `metainit` command means that you are creating one stripe, and the 4 indicates four components, which are listed individually after the 4. If you don't specify an interlace value, the default of 16KB will be used.

Concatenation Volumes

Concatenated volumes enable you to combine space from multiple physical disks into a larger logical volume. Concatenations also enable you to expand active UFS volumes without needing to bring the server down. During the expansion, no write operations can be performed on the file system, but the inconvenience is much less than if you had to reboot the computer.

Data is written sequentially among the member components. Interlaces 1, 2, and 3 (and so forth) will be on the first component until it fills up. Then, data will be written to the second component, and so on.

 Because of the way disk reads and writes are handled, concatenated volumes use less CPU time than striped volumes.

Concatenated volumes are created by using the `metainit` command. The syntax is very similar to the syntax used for creating a stripe:

```
# metainit volume_name #_stripes [components_per_stripe component_names]
```

Here is an example. If you want to create a concatenation made of three slices, you could use:

```
# metainit d12 3 1 c0t2d0s7 1 c0t3d0s5 1 c0t4d0s2
```

The newly created d12 volume consists of three components (stripes), each made of a single slice per disk (the 1 in front of each component).

 The syntax for `metainit` differs only slightly for each type of volume you want to create. When using `metainit`, you must be careful because the syntax itself determines the type of volume you create. This will become evident again when you look at how to create RAID 1 and RAID 5 volumes, as well as soft partitions and transactional volumes.

Concatenations are also used as building blocks for mirrored volumes or volumes that you might want to easily expand later. To begin the process of mirroring a volume, you typically start by creating a concatenation of one volume. To do this, you would use a command such as:

```
# metainit d55 1 1 c0t0d0s7
```

This creates a concatenation of one volume. Creating a mirror by using this concatenation is covered later in this chapter in the "Managing RAID 1 Volumes" section.

EXPANDING EXISTING FILE SYSTEMS

You can use concatenated volumes to expand existing file systems without needing to reboot your computer. In the following example, you will expand the /files1 file system, which is located on the /dev/dsk/c0t0d0s5 slice:

1. Unmount the existing file system.

   `# umount /files1`

2. Expand the file system by using metainit. The first slice indicated in the command must be the slice that contains the existing data, or else the data will be corrupted.

   `# metainit d44 2 1 c0t0d0s5 1 c0t1d0s2`

3. Edit the /etc/vfstab file to reference the new d44 volume instead of the c0t0d0s5 slice.

4. Remount the file system.

   `# mount /files1`

EXPANDING STRIPED VOLUMES

By expanding a striped volume, you have created a concatenated stripe. This is done with the metattach command. Use the following syntax for metattach:

`# metattach volume_name component_names`

If you have a striped volume named d53, you could attach an additional slice with the following command:

`# metattach d53 c0t4d0s2`

To add additional slices to the volume, simply specify each component you want to add.

If the volume you are expanding contains a UFS file system, after you have expanded the volume, you need to run the growfs command to grow the UFS file system to utilize the full space of the volume. Although the growfs command works on mounted file systems, the file system will be unavailable for write operations during the growing period.

Removing Volumes

Volumes are deleted with the metaclear command. Before removing any volume, you must unmount it if it's currently mounted. After it's unmounted, use **metaclear volume_name**. For example, to remove the d92 volume, use:

`# metaclear d92`

If the volume you removed has an entry in the /etc/vfstab file, be sure to remove the entry so Solaris does not try to mount the nonexistent volume during the next reboot or mountall command usage.

Creating RAID 0 with Solaris Volume Manager

To create RAID volumes in Solaris Volume Manager, you need to select the Volumes node to highlight it, as shown in Figure 12.6.

FIGURE 12.6 Volumes node of Enhanced Storage

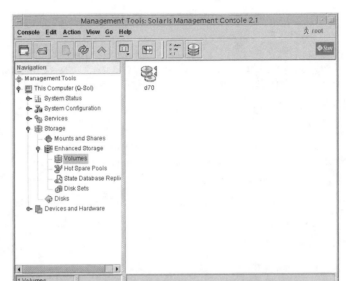

After you are in the Volumes node, click Action ➢ Create Volume and follow these steps:

1. Choose whether to use an existing state database or to create a new state database. If you already have one, there is no need to create another. Click Next.

2. Choose a disk set if you want to. If not, leave the disk set choice at <none>. Click Next.

3. Select the type of volume you want to create. After you have made your choice (Stripe for this example), click Next.

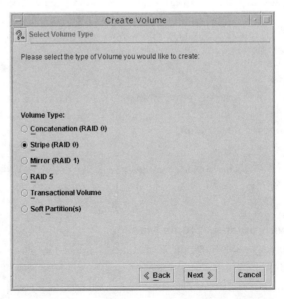

4. Specify a volume name for your volume. Make sure that the name you choose isn't already being used.

5. Choose the components you want to create the volume on. After you have made your selection, click Next.

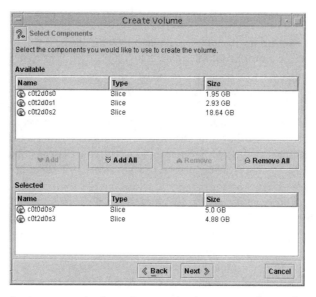

6. Set the order of components in the volume and select an interlace value. Click Next.

7. Choose a hot spare pool, if you want to use one. Click Next.

8. Confirm your choices in the Review screen. If you need to make any changes, use the Back button. Otherwise, click Finish.

The computer will take a moment to create the volume. After it's finished, the volume will appear in the right pane of the Solaris Management Console.

Volumes cannot be expanded through the Solaris Management Console. To delete a volume, right-click it and choose Delete, or choose Edit ➢ Delete.

Managing RAID 1

Mirrored volumes contain multiple identical copies of data in RAID 0 volumes. Mirrors provide data redundancy but cost more to implement than standard volumes or RAID 1 volumes because mirrors require double the hard disk space.

Mirroring requires writing data to two or three hard disks instead of one, so it slows down your disk write speed. Data can be read from any of the mirrored components, meaning that disk reads are faster than from standard volumes. After the mirror is created, applications and users see it as a single volume; they don't have to worry about writing the data twice or where they're reading it from because SVM handles all of that in the background.

Solaris implements mirrors by using a series of *submirrors*. Mirrors must have between one and three submirrors. A one-way mirror would contain one submirror, but does not provide any data redundancy (however, you typically start the creation of a mirrored volume by creating one submirror—the volume that has the data—and then adding a second submirror for redundancy). For practical purposes, a two-way mirror (one that contains two submirrors) is sufficient for fault tolerance. By creating a three-way mirror, you can bring one submirror offline for backup purposes while retaining your online fault tolerance.

If you are using multiple submirrors, one or more can be detached from the mirror at any time, as long as one submirror is always attached. When submirrors are detached, Solaris Volume Manager keeps track of the data written to the active mirrored volume. After the detached submirrors are brought back online, the portion of data written during the downtime is written to the out-of-date submirrors. This portion of data that needs to be updated across all mirrors is called a *resynchronization region*.

Combining RAID 0 and RAID 1

Solaris supports both RAID 1+0 and RAID 0+1. RAID 1+0 is a mirrored volume that is then striped, and is not always possible to create because of software limitations. However, if the submirrors are identical and made up of disk slices (not soft partitions), implementing RAID 1+0 should not be a problem.

RAID 0+1 is having striped sets that are mirrored. Technically, all RAID 1 in Solaris is RAID 0+1, because you create either a stripe or a concatenated volume first and then mirror it. Although at first this sounds overly complex for creating a mirror, it has a distinct advantage.

Imagine that you have a two-way mirror of a striped volume. For the sake of ease, assume that slices A, B, and C are part of submirror 1, and slices D, E, and F are part of submirror 2. Slices D, E, and F mirror A, B, and C, respectively. In Solaris, if slice A were to fail, the system could operate normally with the data from slice D. In fact, three slices could fail, and as long as one good copy of each set of data was present, data reads would proceed normally. If both parts of a mirror were to fail, such as slices A and D, the mirrored volume would function like a hard disk that has bad blocks. The data on slices B and C would still be accessible.

If Solaris used strict RAID 1 instead of RAID 0+1, then the previous scenario would not be possible. If one slice were to fail, then one entire side of the mirror would fail. A second slice failure on the second submirror would cripple the storage unit.

RAID 1 Read and Write Policies

Solaris Volume Manager enables you to configure three mirror read policies and two mirror write policies. Using the right policy for your mirrored volumes can increase your overall disk access speed. These policies are configured when the mirror is set up but can be changed while the mirror is operational.

Here are the three read policies:

Round robin   This is the default read policy, which attempts to balance reads across all submirrors. Disk reads are made in a round-robin fashion from all submirrors in the mirrored volume.

Geometric   This policy divides reads among submirrors based on logical disk block addresses. When you configure a hard disk, each block on the disk is assigned a logical address. Because the data is mirrored, the logical block addresses will be identical across submirrors.

For example, with a two-way submirror, each disk is "assigned" half of the logical block addresses from which to read. Data recalled from the range assigned to the first submirror will be read exclusively from the first submirror.

The geometric policy can reduce disk read time, because the seek time for data is effectively reduced. The amount of speed increase depends on your computer, configuration, and volume of disk access.

First   With the first policy, all reads are directed to the first submirror. Only use this policy if the first submirror is significantly faster than other submirrors, or if one of the submirrors is offline.

You can use any of the three read policies with either of the two write policies. Different combinations of policies can be used on different mirrored volumes. There are two write policies, parallel and serial:

Parallel   The default write policy, parallel writes data to all submirrors simultaneously.

Serial   Serial writes to one submirror at a time. The write operation must be completed on the first submirror before it can be started on the second submirror. If one submirror is unavailable, this option might increase disk efficiency.

Resynchronization

If a submirror fails for any reason, or is taken offline for backup or maintenance purposes, the data between the submirrors can become out of synch. When the failed or offline submirror is brought back online, Solaris Volume Manager automatically resynchronizes the submirrors to ensure that users are able to access the proper data. Not only is resynchronization automatic—it's mandatory. You do not need to do anything to make it happen.

During the resynchronization process, all involved submirrors are available for reading and writing data. Solaris Volume Manager can perform three types of synchronization: full, optimized, and partial. Synchronization order is determined by a pass number.

Full resynchronization   A *full resynchronization* happens when a new submirror is attached to a mirror. All data is copied to the new submirror. After the data is written to the new submirror, the data is available for reading.

Optimized resynchronization   If you experience a system failure or if you bring a submirror offline, an *optimized resynchronization* occurs when the system or submirror is brought back online. Solaris Volume Manager tracks which regions of the mirror might be out of synch (known as *dirty regions*) and synchronizes those regions only.

Partial resynchronization   If you've replaced part of a mirror, say a slice that failed, Solaris will perform a *partial resynchronization* after the replacement is complete. Data will be copied from working slices to the new slice.

Pass numbers   When performing a resynchronization, Solaris Volume Manager uses a *pass number* to determine the order in which mirrors are resynchronized. The default pass number is 1, and smaller pass numbers are resynchronized first. A pass number of 0 indicates that mirror resynchronization should be skipped. Pass numbers should be set to 0 only on read-only mirrors.

If a computer with a mirror on the root (/), /usr, or swap partitions is booted into single-user mode (run level S), the mirror will display the Needing Maintenance state when viewed with metastat. This situation, although apparently problematic, is normal. It happens because the metasync -r command, which is normally run during boot, is interrupted when Solaris is booted into single-user mode. After the system is rebooted into multiuser mode, the error will disappear.

Creating and Managing RAID 1 Volumes

Mirrors are created by using the metainit command or through the Solaris Management Console. You will start by creating a one-way mirror, called the *primary submirror*. Then you will attach additional submirrors.

It is not always necessary to create a one-way mirror first and then attach additional submirrors. However, following this procedure ensures that your data is properly replicated across all submirrors.

Here are some guidelines for creating and using mirrors:

- Create a RAID 0 stripe or concatenation to serve as components for your mirror.
- When creating a mirror of an existing file system, be sure to create the primary submirror on the existing file system, or data will be destroyed.
- You can mirror unmountable file systems, such as root (/) and /usr, for fault tolerance.
- To increase storage efficiency, use same-sized components for creating mirrors.
- If possible, keep mirrored hard disks on different disk controllers, and mirrored volumes on different hard disks. This reduces the chance of a catastrophic failure.
- Do not mount submirrors directly; mount only the mirror. Mounting submirrors could cause data corruption or crash the system.
- Just because you have a mirrored volume doesn't mean you can avoid making system backups. You still need to do this regularly.

The method you will use to create a mirror depends on the disk configuration you have before you mirror, as well as the volumes you want to mirror. Here is the first example, creating a mirror from two unused slices:

1. Create two RAID 0 volumes (stripes or concatenations) to use as submirrors.

2. Create a one-way mirror by using `metainit` *volume_name* `-m` *submirror_name*. Using this example, you will create a mirror named d40, with a submirror of d41.

   ```
   # metainit d40 -m d41
   ```

3. Add a second submirror by using `metattach` *mirror_name* *submirror_name*. In this example, you are adding the d42 submirror to the d40 mirror created in step 2.

   ```
   # metattach d40 d42
   ```

After creating the d40 mirror, you should be able to use `metastat` or the Solaris Management Console to see the d41 and d42 submirrors as part of the d40 mirror. You can also create a mirror without creating a primary submirror first, but it's not recommended because proper synchronization cannot be guaranteed. (However, if you know that the d41 volume is empty, it's not a major problem.) If you wanted to perform the preceding example in one step, without guaranteeing synchronization, you could use the following command:

```
# metainit d40 -m d41 d42
```

Solaris will set up the mirror d40, but it will also give you a warning about using `metainit` in that way.

Setting up a mirror of an existing file system is similar to the previous procedure. If you are going to mirror an existing file system, though, you want to be sure to create a one-way mirror first and then attach the second submirror. Mirroring an umountable file system, such as the root (/) or /usr, requires a few extra steps, including rebooting. Here is how to create a mirror for an existing file system:

1. Identify the slice that contains the file system you want to create a mirror of. Create a new RAID 0 volume on that slice. For example, if the slice is c0t1d0s0, you could use:

   ```
   # metainit d101 -f 1 1 c0t1d0s0
   ```

2. Create a second RAID 0 volume on the slice you want to make the second submirror. For example, if the slice is c0t2d0s0, you could use:

   ```
   # metainit d102 1 1 c0t2d0s0
   ```

3. Create a one-way mirror using the `metainit` command. In this example, you are creating a mirror named d100.

   ```
   # metainit d100 -m d101
   ```

4. Unmount the file system (if possible) by using the **umount** command.

5. If you are mirroring a file system other than the root (/), edit the /etc/vfstab file to mount the mirror instead of the old device. For example, you would change all instances of c0t1d0s0 to d100. Failure to edit the /etc/vfstab file to mount the mirror instead of the submirror could cause data corruption.

6. Remount your newly mirrored file system. How you do this depends on the type of file system you are mirroring.

a. If you are mirroring a file system that can be unmounted, then unmount and remount the file system with the umount and mount commands.

b. If you are mirroring an unmountable file system other than the root (/), reboot your system.

c. If you are mirroring the root file system (/), run the **metaroot d100** command. (Replace d100 with the name of your mirror if you used a different volume number.) Then run the **lockfs -fa** command and reboot.

7. Attach the second submirror.

    # metattach d100 d102

8. Verify the creation of the mirrored volume.

    # metastat d100

If you are mirroring the root file system (/), it's a good idea to record the path to the alternate boot device. That way, if your original root fails, you can modify the boot device in OpenBoot to boot to the mirrored root.

If you're mirroring the root file system (/) on an IA system, be sure to install the boot information on the alternate boot disk before creating the RAID 0 or RAID 1 device.

SUBMIRROR MANAGEMENT

In addition to creating mirrors, you have a variety of commands to attach and detach submirrors, as well as bring submirrors online and offline. Submirrors are attached with the metattach command and detached with the metadetach command. You can have up to three submirrors per mirror.

To attach a submirror, use the metattach *mirror submirror* command. For example, to add the d33 submirror to the d30 mirror, you would use:

metattach d30 d33

To detach a submirror, the metadetach command is used. It has the same syntax as metattach. To detach the d33 submirror, you would use:

metadetach d30 d33

The metaoffline and metaonline commands are used to bring submirrors offline and online, respectively. Both commands follow the syntax of metattach. To bring the d33 submirror offline, use:

metaoffline d30 d33

And to bring it back online, use:

metaonline d30 d33

RAID 1 VOLUME STATUS

The metastat command is used to check the status of volumes. Submirrors can be in one of three states: okay, resynching, or needs maintenance. The okay and resynching statuses indicate that the submirror is operational, although resynching does indicate that a resynchronization is in progress. If your submirror is in the needs maintenance state, then all reads and writes from this submirror have been suspended, and you need to investigate further.

Slice states give you more detail than do submirror states. Submirror slices can be in one of four states: okay, resynching, maintenance, and last erred. As with submirror states, okay and resynching are acceptable states.

If you encounter the maintenance state, the component has failed, and no reads or writes are being performed. You must enable or replace the failed component. The metareplace -e command will give you further information as to how to proceed.

The last erred state means that the slice has failed to replicate information because of another slice failure. If you see a maintenance state, you will usually encounter a last erred state on another slice as well. Fix the slice needing maintenance, and the error should clear itself up after resynching.

Here is a sample metastat output for the d10 mirrored volume:

```
# metastat d10
d10: Mirror
    Submirror 0: d12
      State: Okay
    Submirror 1: d13
      State: Resyncing
    Resync in progress: 12 % done
    Pass: 1
    Read option: roundrobin (default)
    Write option: parallel (default)
    Size: 10240272 blocks
d12: Submirror of d10
    State: Okay
    Size: 10240272 blocks
    Stripe 0:
        Device       Start Block  Dbase        State Reloc Hot Spare
        c0t2d0s3           0       No          Okay   Yes
d13: Submirror of d10
    State: Resyncing
    Size: 10477152 blocks
    Stripe 0:
        Device       Start Block  Dbase        State Reloc Hot Spare
        c0t0d0s7         9072      Yes          Okay   Yes
```

```
Device Relocation Information:
Device   Reloc  Device ID
c0t2d0   Yes    id1,dad@AWDC_WD200BB-00DGA0=WD-WMADL1128126
c0t0d0   Yes    id1,dad@AST320011A=3HT3DP98
#
```

As you can see, the d13 submirror is resynching and is currently 12 percent complete. This is because the mirror was just created and is in the process of initially synchronizing all submirrors.

CHANGING RAID 1 VOLUME OPTIONS

The metaparam command is used to change volume options, such as read policies, write policies, and pass number. The -r switch is used to change read policy, the -w switch changes write policy, and the -p switch changes pass number. For example, to change the read policy of mirror d10 to geometric, you would use:

 # metaparam -r geometric d10

You can also use metaparam to check the volume's parameters. After you have changed the read policy, verify that your setting took effect:

```
# metaparam -r geometric d10
# metaparam d10
d10: Mirror current parameters are:
    Pass: 1
    Read option: geometric (-g)
    Write option: parallel (default)
#
```

UNMIRRORING

There might be a time when you want to delete a mirrored volume. To do this, you must first unmount the volume, detach the mirror, and then clear the mirror.

At least one of the submirrors must be in the okay state before you can detach the mirror. Here is an example of detaching a mirror. The mirror is d10, composed of the d12 and d13 submirrors. The mirror is mounted as /docs. Here are the steps:

1. Verify that at least one submirror is in the okay state.

   # metastat d10

2. Unmount the file system.

   # umount /docs

3. Use metadetach to detach the first submirror. This submirror will be used for the remaining file system after the mirror is destroyed.

   # metadetach d10 d12

4. Delete the mirror and the second submirror with the metaclear command.

   # metaclear -r d10

5. If necessary, edit the /etc/vfstab file to point to the underlying volume instead of the mirror. In this case, you would change all references to d10 to d12.

For a file system that cannot be unmounted, such as the root (/), you need to follow a slightly different procedure:

1. Verify that at least one submirror is in the okay state.

   # **metastat d10**

2. Use metadetach on the mirror that contains the root file system (/).

   # **metadetach d10 d13**

3. Run the metaroot command on the slice that will be the boot slice.

   # **metaroot /dev/dsk/c0t0d0s0**

4. Reboot.

5. Clear the mirror and clear the remaining submirror.

   # **metaclear -r d10**

   # **metaclear d13**

   The mirrored root should be cleared.

Managing RAID 1 with the Solaris Management Console

The Solaris Management Console enables you to create mirrors through a graphical interface that is much easier to use than the command line. First, open the Solaris Management Console and navigate to the Volumes node. From there, choose Action ➢ Create Volume and follow these steps:

1. Choose to create an additional state database replica or use an existing one. Click Next.

2. Choose a disk set. If you do not want to use a disk set, choose <none> and click Next.

3. Select the Mirror (RAID 1) radio button and click Next.

4. Specify a volume name and click Next.

5. Select a volume to be a primary submirror. After you have made your selection, click Next.

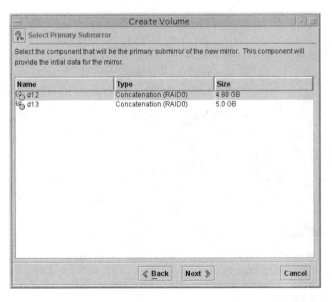

6. Select your secondary submirrors. Click Next.

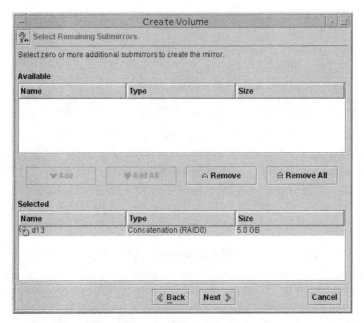

7. Configure your mirror read, write, and pass number parameters. Click Next.

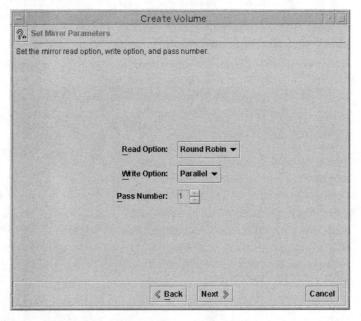

8. The final screen displays your choices. If you need to change any parameters, use the Back button. Otherwise, click Finish.

You can change the mirror policies by selecting the mirror to highlight it in the right pane of the Solaris Management Console and choosing Action ➢ Properties. Select the Parameters tab and click the Set Parameters button. You will see a screen like the one following step 7.

To delete the mirror, right-click it in the Solaris Management Console and choose Delete, or choose Edit ➢ Delete.

Managing RAID 5

RAID 5 volumes combine speed with data redundancy. Like a RAID 0 volume, RAID 5 volumes write data in stripes, and like RAID 1, RAID 5 provides fault tolerance. RAID 5 isn't as fast as a striped volume but is more efficient in terms of disk usage than a mirrored volume.

The Solaris Volume Manager will automatically resynchronize a RAID 5 volume if a component fails (and is replaced) or if it detects that data is out of synch. RAID 5 volumes cannot be used for the root (/), /usr, or swap file systems. Creating a RAID 5 volume on an existing volume will destroy all data on that volume.

After you have created a RAID 5 volume, you can concatenate the volume by adding additional components. However, the new components will not have parity contained on them. The parity blocks assigned during the original creation of the volume will hold parity for the new interlaces. Concatenated RAID 5 volumes are not designed for long-term use; rather, they are a temporary solution if your RAID 5 volume needs more space and you do not have enough time to back the volume up, re-create it, and restore data.

Here are some guidelines for creating and using RAID 5 volumes:

- You must use at least three components. Using three or more physical hard disks is recommended.

- RAID 5 volumes cannot be part of a mirror or other striped volume, nor can RAID 5 volumes be concatenated with each other.

- Creating a RAID 5 volume from a component containing existing data will destroy the existing data.

- RAID 5 volumes have a configurable interlace value, just like RAID 0 volumes.

- A RAID 5 volume can operate with a single component failure. Multiple component failures will cause the volume to fail.

- When creating a RAID 5 volume, use components of the same size.

- If your volume writes more than 20 percent of the time, RAID 5 volumes are inefficient because of parity calculation. Using a mirrored volume would be a better solution.

As with creating RAID 0 and RAID 1 volumes, you need to be the superuser or have an equivalent role to create RAID 5 volumes. RAID 5 volumes are created by using the metainit command with the -r switch. Here is an example of creating a RAID 5 volume consisting of three slices:

```
# metainit d70 -r c0t1d0s2 c1t1d0s2 c1t2d0s2
```

This command creates a RAID 5 volume named d70. If you wanted to specify an interlace value, you could do so with the -i switch, just as you did when you created a striped volume.

You will not be able to use the RAID 5 volume immediately. Solaris Volume Manager needs to initialize the volume, which might take several minutes, depending on how large the components are as well as how busy the computer is.

RAID 5 Maintenance, Repair, and Expansion

To check the status of your RAID 5 device, use the `metastat` command. For example, to check the status of the device you just created, you could use:

```
# metastat d70
```

The `metastat` command will show the status of the RAID 5 volume, as well as the status of each member component in the volume. After you create a RAID 5 volume, the state of the volume will be `initializing`. After it's done initializing, the status will change to okay. If there are any problems, the `needs maintenance` state will be displayed. If you see a `needs maintenance` status, look to see which component is causing the problem.

Here is an example of a `metastat` output indicating that a RAID 5 component needs to be replaced:

```
# metastat d70
d70: RAID
State: Needs Maintenance
     Invoke: metareplace d70 c0t5d0s2 <new device>
     Interlace: 32 blocks
     Size: 16305020 blocks
Original device:
     Size: 16305520 blocks
     Device          Start Block     Dbase    State           Hot Spare
     c0t3d0s2          330           No       Okay
     c0t4d0s2          330           No       Okay
     c0t5d0s2          330           No       Maintenance
     c0t6d0s2          330           No       Okay
```

This output shows that the d70 RAID 5 volume needs maintenance. The line beginning with `Invoke:` even shows you which command you should use to fix the problem. To fix the problem, you need another slice as large or larger than the slice you are replacing, `c0t5d0s2` in this case. If you had another suitable device available, say `c0t7d0s2`, you could issue the following command:

```
# metareplace d70 c0t5d0s2 c0t7d0s2
```

You will receive a message that `c0t5d0s2` was replaced with `c0t7d0s2`. Running `metastat d70` again should show that the volume is resynching.

There is one other way in which you can use `metareplace`. It's for cases when you are replacing a failed component with another component using the same identifier. Of course, two slices cannot have the same logical ID. However, perhaps the original slice had a soft failure, or you replaced the failed hard disk and labeled the new disk the same as the disk it replaced. In that case, you could use the following command (assuming the same problem component as in the last example):

```
# metareplace -e d70 c0t5d0s2
```

This command will reactivate the `c0t5d0s2` component and begin resynchronizing the RAID 5 volume.

RAID 5 volumes can also be expanded by using the `metattach` command. For example, if you wanted to add the `c0t8d0s2` component to the existing `d70` volume, you could use:

```
# metattach d70 c0t8d0s2
```

But because parity will not be stored on this new component, it's recommended that you not use concatenated RAID 5 volumes as a long-term storage solution. If you do expand your RAID 5 volume, be sure to use the `growfs` command to expand the UFS file system residing on the volume as well.

RAID 5 volumes are removed with the `metaclear` command.

Managing RAID 5 with the Solaris Management Console

If you prefer a graphical interface, the Solaris Management Console provides complete RAID 5 administration. First, open the Solaris Management Console and navigate to the Volumes node. From there, choose Action ➢ Create Volume and follow these steps:

1. Choose to create an additional state database replica or use an existing one. Click Next.

2. Choose a disk set. If you do not want to use a disk set, choose `<none>` and click Next.

3. Select the RAID 5 radio button and click Next.

4. Specify a volume name and click Next.

5. Select the components you want to make part of the volume, as shown in the following graphic. After you have made your selection, click Next.

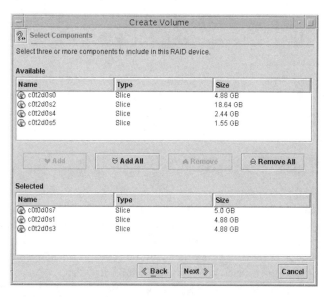

6. Choose an interlace value in KB, MB, or blocks. Click Next.

7. Choose whether you want to use a hot spare pool. You can create a new hot spare pool now if you want. Make your selection and click Next.

8. The final screen displays your choices. If you need to change any parameters, use the Back button. Otherwise, click Finish.

The Solaris Volume Manager will create the RAID 5 volume. During initialization of the volume, system performance will be degraded. The RAID 5 volume will appear in the right pane of the Solaris Management Console, as shown in Figure 12.7, before initialization of the volume is complete.

FIGURE 12.7   RAID 5 volume

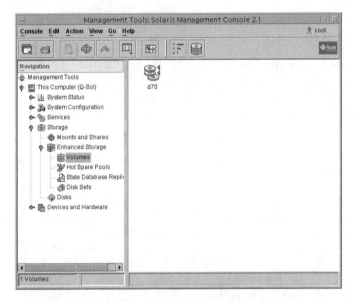

By highlighting the RAID 5 volume in the right pane of the Solaris Management Console and choosing Action ➤ Properties, you can add additional components (on the Components tab) or view volume performance statistics (on the Performance tab).

To delete the volume, right-click it in the Solaris Management Console and choose Delete, or choose Edit ➤ Delete.

Managing Soft Partitions

A soft partition enables you to overcome the traditional Solaris limit of eight slices per hard disk. When you create a soft partition, you can create as many logical volumes as you want to within the soft partition. You are, however, still limited to 8192 logical volumes because that's the maximum number of volumes that Solaris Volume Manager supports.

Each soft partition is named, just as other volume types (stripes, mirrors, and RAID 5) are named. Soft partitions can be created on top of hard disk slices, or on stripes, mirrors, or RAID 5 volumes. However, nesting of soft partitions is not allowed. For example, you cannot create a soft partition on a striped volume and then create a mirror on the soft partition.

Here are some guidelines for creating and using soft partitions:

- To allow soft partitions on an entire hard disk, create a single slice that occupies the entire hard disk and then create the soft partition on that slice.

- The maximum size of a soft partition is dependent upon the size of the slice on which it is created.

- For speed or data redundancy, create a RAID 0, 1, or 5 volume and then create soft partitions within that RAID volume.

The management of soft partitions is done with the same Solaris Volume Manager commands that you are already familiar with: `metainit`, `metastat`, `metattach`, and `metaclear`.

Using the Command Line to Manage Soft Partitions

Soft partitions are created with the `metainit -p` command. The syntax for `metainit` is similar to what you've seen before, but with soft partitions, you need to specify a partition size as well. For example, to create a 12GB soft partition named d33 on the `c0t2d0s0` slice, you would use:

`# metainit d33 -p c0t2d0s0 12g`

One of the interesting `metainit` switches you can use with soft partitioning is -e. The -e switch tells `metainit` to reformat the entire disk as slice 0, except for a 4MB slice 7 reserved for a state database replica. This switch is useful if you know that you want your entire hard disk to be used for soft partitions.

 WARNING   Using `metainit -e` will destroy any existing data on the hard disk.

After your soft partition is created, you can use the `metastat` command to view the volume's status. To view the status of the soft partition just created (d33), you would use:

`# metastat d33`

To increase the size of a soft partition, use the `metattach` command. With `metattach`, you must specify the soft partition you are growing, as well as the amount you want to add to the soft partition. For example, to grow d33 by 5GB, you would use:

`# metattach d33 5g`

You might think this `metattach` command looks wrong; after all, it doesn't specify where to take the additional disk space from. When expanding a soft partition, the space is taken from the available free space designated for soft partitions. If you do not have enough space available, you will get an error message.

Soft partitions are removed with the `metaclear` command. You do have a few options as to what to delete, though, because soft partitioning on a volume can get complex. When using `metaclear`, you can specify a soft partition to delete or you can instruct `metaclear` to delete all soft partitions on a particular component. For example, `metaclear -p c0t2d0s0` clears all soft partitions on the `c0t2d0s0` slice, whereas `metaclear -p d33` deletes only the d33 soft partition.

Using the Solaris Management Console to Manage Soft Partitions

Once again, it's time to look at your favorite graphical management interface: the Solaris Management Console. In the Solaris Management Console, navigate to the Volumes node. To create a soft partition, choose Action ➤ Create Volume and follow these steps:

1. Choose to create an additional state database replica or use an existing one. Click Next.
2. Choose a disk set. If you do not want to use a disk set, choose <none> and click Next.

3. Select the Soft Partition(s) radio button and click Next.

4. Select the components on which you want to create the soft partition. You will notice that if you have RAID volumes, they will appear here as valid choices. After you have made your selection, click Next.

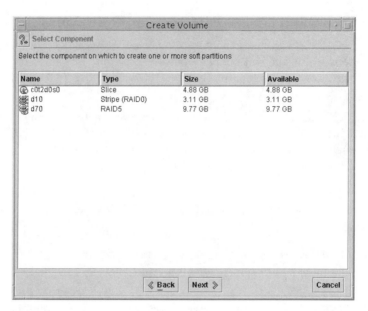

5. Choose how you want to allocate the space selected for soft partitions. Click Next.

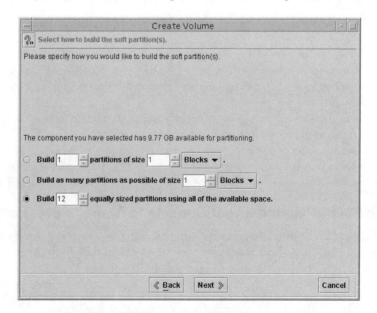

6. Provide a name for the soft partition you just created and click Next.

7. The final screen displays your choices. If you need to change any parameters, use the Back button. Otherwise, click Finish.

The Solaris Volume Manager will create your soft partitions; this might take some time. Figure 12.8 shows the finished product. Volumes d33 through d44 are soft partitions. Volume d10 is a striped volume, and volume d70 is a RAID 5 volume.

FIGURE 12.8   Solaris Management Console Volumes node

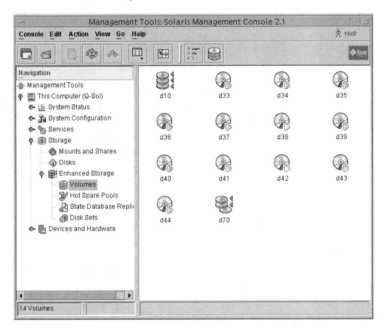

If you have space left in your soft partition, you can grow any of your existing soft partitions by selecting Action ➤ Properties and clicking the Grow button on the General tab. Soft partitions can be deleted individually, by right-clicking each one in the Solaris Management Console and choosing Delete, or choosing Edit ➤ Delete.

Overview of Transactional Volumes

There are two types of file system logging available in Solaris 9: transactional volumes and UFS logging. A *transactional volume* is a logical volume on a hard disk slice used specifically to log UFS transactions.

When you use file system logging, all disk reads or writes are first written to a log file and then applied to the file system later. If the hard disk is incredibly busy, file system logging can help alleviate poor performance by saving the information and writing it to the disk when the disk is less busy.

With the release of Solaris 8, UFS logging was introduced. UFS logging provides the same capabilities of transactional volumes, but provides superior performance and lower system administration overhead. Another advantage of UFS logging is that it enables administrators to log the root file system (/), which transactional volumes do not.

Because of the obvious superiority of UFS logging over transactional volumes, Sun is quick to promote the use of UFS logging. In fact, transactional volumes are scheduled to be removed in an upcoming Solaris release. If you want to log your UFS file systems, use UFS logging.

 For information on how to enable UFS logging, see Chapter 7.

A transactional volume consists of two devices: the master device and the log device. The master device is the device that's being logged, and the log device is the slice or volume that contains the log file. Master and log devices can be a physical slice or a logical volume, but should always be separate devices. Multiple master devices can share one log device. For speed and data redundancy, you can place log files on RAID volumes.

Transactional volumes are managed with the `meta*` commands used to manage other volume types.

Managing Hot Spare Pools

RAID 1 and RAID 5 volumes provide data redundancy and fault tolerance. If one component in your RAID 1 or RAID 5 volume fails, the volume can still perform disk reads and writes. Granted, system performance will be slower, but at least Solaris will still be operational.

Multiple component failures can cause the operating system to crash, however. That's where hot spare pools become critical. A *hot spare pool* is a collection of slices used to provide additional fault tolerance for RAID 1 or RAID 5 volumes in the event of a component failure. Individually, the slices that are part of the pool are called *hot spares*.

If you are using a hot spare pool and a RAID 1 or RAID 5 component fails, Solaris Volume Manager automatically replaces the failed component with a hot spare. The hot spare is then synchronized with the rest of the volume. For hot spares to work, redundant data must be available. Because of this, hot spare pools do not work with RAID 0 volumes or one-way mirrors.

The only disadvantage to using hot spare pools is cost. The slices in the hot spare pool cannot be used to hold data while they are in the pool. They must remain idle and are used only in the event of a component failure. Consequently, you must spend more on hard disks than you would if you didn't use hot spares. However, if computer uptime is critical to you, the benefits far outweigh the costs.

Understanding How Hot Spare Pools Work

When you create a hot spare pool in Solaris Volume Manager, you specify one or more slices that will be part of the pool. You then associate the pool with one or more active RAID 1 or RAID 5 volumes. You can create multiple pools if you choose, and individual hot spares can be part of more than one pool. Although a hot spare pool can be associated with several RAID volumes, each RAID volume can use only one hot spare pool.

In the event of a component failure, Solaris Volume Manager searches the hot spare pool in the order in which the hot spares were added to the pool. After Solaris Volume Manager finds a hot spare as large or larger than the component that needs to be replaced, that hot spare is taken, marked "In-use," and synchronized with the impaired volume. The used hot spare cannot be used by any other volume, unless the original volume is repaired and the hot spare returned to "Available" status in the pool.

Because Solaris Volume Manager searches the pool based on the order that the slices were added, it's a good idea to add slices in order of size; add the smallest ones first. If you do this, then you reduce the chance of Solaris Volume Manager using a slice that's far bigger than the one it's replacing and wasting space. For example, if you have a 1GB slice fail and you can replace it with a 1GB or a 10GB hot spare, which would you choose? Obviously, all you need is the 1GB hot spare. If Solaris Volume Manager sees the 10GB hot spare first, though, it will use that slice.

As with RAID volumes, hot spare pools can be managed from the command line or through the Solaris Management Console.

Managing Hot Spare Pools from the Command Line

You must give a hot spare pool a name, just as you did RAID volumes. However, hot spare pools are named with an hsp prefix. Some administrators like to name their hot spare pools similarly to the RAID volume that they serve. For example, if your RAID 5 volume is d10, then your hot spare pool for that volume could be hsp010.

Hot spare pools will have a three-digit number in their name. If you tell Solaris Volume Manager to create the hot spare pool hsp10, it will be created as hsp010.

Hot spare pools are created with the `metainit` command. If you wanted to create a hot spare pool named hsp010 containing two disk slices, you could use:

```
# metainit hsp010 c0t2d0s2 c0t3d0s2
```

When you create a hot spare pool, be sure that the slices you pick as hot spares are large enough to replace the components that they are designed to replace. Solaris Volume Manager doesn't check this for you, nor will it give you an error if your hot spare slices are too small.

Adding an additional slice to the hot spare pool is done with the metahs command. The metahs command has several important switches. The -a switch adds the slice to one hot spare pool. Here's how you would add a slice to the hot spare pool created earlier:

```
# metahs -a hsp010 c0t3d0s2
```

Or, if you had several hot spare pools and wanted the same slice added as a hot spare to all pools, you would use:

```
# metahs -a all c0t3d0s2
```

The metahs command is also used to manage several details of hot spare pools. Table 12.3 shows some of the options for the metahs command.

TABLE 12.3   *metahs* Usage Options

Syntax	Example	Description
metahs -a *pool slice*	metahs -a hsp010 c0t2d0s2	Adds the slice to the specified hot spare pool. You can also use all instead of a pool number to add the slice to all pools.
metahs -d *pool slice*	metahs -d hsp011 c0t2d0s2	Removes the slice from the hot spare pool.
metahs -e *slice*	metahs -e c0t2d0s2	Enables the hot spare slice. This is used after a slice is repaired or if the slice needs to be placed back in "Available" status.
metahs -i *pool*	metahs -i hsp013	Displays the status of the hot spare pool.
metahs -r *pool* \ *old_slice new_slice*	metahs -r hsp014 c0t2d0s2 \ c0t3d0s2	Replaces the old hot spare slice with a new hot spare slice in the pool.

The all argument can be used in place of slice designations with the -a, -d, and -r switches. Although specifying all slices at once can be useful, it can also be dangerous. Use it carefully, or you might end up re-creating your hot spare pool configuration.

After your hot spare pool is created, you can attach it to a RAID 1 or RAID 5 volume. This is done with the metaparam command; here's the syntax:

```
# metaparam -h hot_spare_pool component
```

So, to add your hot spare pool hsp010 as the pool for the d10 RAID 5 volume, you would use:

```
# metaparam -h hsp010 d10
```

If you want to remove the hot spare pool association, use none instead of hsp010 in the previous command example.

To check the status of your hot spare pool, use the `metastat` command. Here is an example:

```
# metastat hsp010
hsp010: 2 hot spares
        c0t2d0s2          Available          44000 blocks
        c0t3d0s2          Available          56000 blocks
#
```

Hot spares can be in one of three states: `Available`, `In-use`, or `Broken`. `Available` means that the hot spare is ready for use; `In-use` means that it's being used. The `Broken` state indicates that there is a problem with the hot spare or that all hot spares are being used.

Managing Hot Spare Pools from the Solaris Management Console

The Solaris Management Console enables you to manage hot spare pools through a convenient graphical interface. In the Solaris Management Console, navigate to the Hot Spare Pools node as shown in Figure 12.9.

FIGURE 12.9   Hot Spare Pools

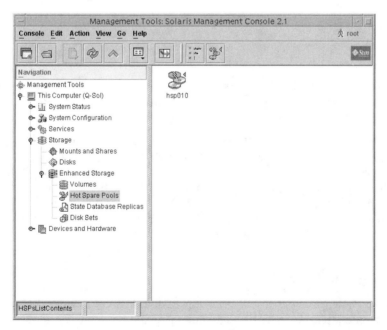

To create a hot spare pool, click Action ➢ Create Hot Spare Pool and follow these steps:

1. Choose whether to use an existing state database replica or to create a new state database replica. Click Next.

2. Choose a disk set. If you do not want to use a disk set, choose `<none>` and click Next.

3. Select a name for the hot spare pool you are creating and click Next.

4. Select the components you want to place in the hot spare pool. After you have made your selection, click Next.

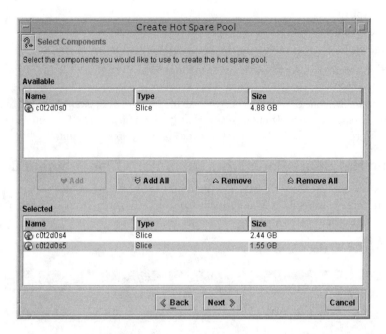

5. The Review screen displays a summary of your selections and the commands that will be executed to configure the system. If you want to make any changes now, use the Back button. Otherwise, click Finish.

Solaris Volume Manager will configure your hot spare pool. By right-clicking the hot spare pool (as shown in Figure 12.9) and choosing Properties, or by highlighting the hot spare pool and choosing Action ➤ Properties, you can configure additional information about the pool. For example, adding, deleting, replacing, and enabling hot spares is done from the Hot Spares tab, and attaching hot spares to a RAID 1 or RAID 5 volume is done from the Used By tab.

Hot spare pools can be deleted by right-clicking them in the Solaris Management Console and choosing Delete, or choosing Edit ➤ Delete.

Managing Disk Sets

A *disk set* (also known as a *shared disk set*) is a set of disk drives that can be shared by multiple hosts. A disk set contains its own volumes and hot spares, and in a sense, is like its own separate, independent drive configuration within your Solaris computer. Disk sets can be shared between hosts, but only one host can control the disk set at once.

If a host with a shared disk set fails, then another host can take over the failed host's disk set. This is called a failover configuration. The version of Solaris Volume Manager supplied with Solaris 9 does not provide all the necessary components needed to fully implement failover configurations. To provide this, you need Sun Cluster, Solstice HA (High Availability), or another third-party HA package.

Each host has one disk set by default, known as the *local disk set*. The devices configured within the local disk set are not shared and cannot be taken over by another host in the event of a system failure. By default, all storage devices and volumes are considered to be part of the local disk set.

Because Solaris 9 does not support the full management of disk sets, this chapter doesn't cover them in great detail. However, here are some basic facts for you:

- Volumes and hot spare pools built within a shared disk set must be built upon hard disks contained in that shared disk set.

- Volumes created in shared disk sets cannot be mounted by the /etc/vfstab file.

- State database replicas are created automatically by the Solaris Volume Manager.

- When you add disks to a shared disk set, Solaris Volume Manager will repartition the disk automatically, placing the state database replica on slice 7.

- Shared disk sets are given a name, and that name becomes part of the full path of the volume. For example, if your disk set is named set01 and you have a RAID volume named d0, the full path to the block device would be /dev/md/set01/dsk/d0.

The default maximum number of disk sets per computer is four, as specified by the md_nsets parameter in the /kernel/drv/md.conf file. You can edit this parameter to support a maximum of 32 disk sets. The number of disk sets you create is actually one less than whatever this parameter is set to, because the default local disk set counts as one.

Disk sets are created and managed with the metaset command or from the Solaris Management Console. For more information, see **man metaset**.

 Real World Scenario

Optimizing RAID on Your Server

You just got permission from management to upgrade your Solaris 8 server to Solaris 9. It took a lot of bargaining, but you also appropriated funds to purchase an additional SCSI controller and new hard disks to place in the upgraded server. When your new hardware arrives, you will have two SCSI controllers in the server, along with two 20GB hard disks and ten 40GB hard disks (even though you could have gotten bigger drives, you got a great deal on the 40GB ones and you decided to impress management with your economic savvy).

Because your office runs on a Monday–Friday schedule, you are planning to come in on the weekend to perform a complete upgrade of the server. You are going to back up the existing data on the server, redesign the volume structure as necessary, and reinstall the data. You are also going to place a large amount of data on this server from an older server that desperately needs to be retired.

Here is what you will need to accommodate: a bootable system disk (of course), user storage for approximately 150 users (users are given, on average, 200MB of storage each on the server), two mission-critical databases (one customer service and one development), and various applications and miscellaneous data. The two databases are perhaps the most important. The customer service database is about 25GB, and the engineering one is nearly 40GB. Both databases must be accessible at all times.

There are a variety of ways you could tackle this problem with your newly available hardware. Here is one solution (feel free to design your own, and if possible, debate the merits of each design with your peers). Use one of the 20GB hard disks for the root (/) and /usr partitions (slices 0 and 6). This, of course, will be your system disk. Mirror the system disk with your other 20GB hard disk. Create a RAID 0 volume from two of the 40GB hard disks for user file storage. (Currently, you need about 30GB for user storage, and this gives you room to grow.) Create two RAID 5 volumes (three 40GB disks each), one for each database. This will provide a speed increase, as well as fault tolerance for the databases. Use one 40GB hard disk for applications and miscellaneous storage. You could perhaps create one slice and use soft partitions if you would like. Make the remaining 40GB hard disk a hot spare. Assign it to both of the RAID 5 volumes.

Again, this is only one possible solution that could be used. However, the volume types presented in this chapter are there to make your storage situation easier to deal with. Use them and combine them as you see fit, to optimize your storage and meet your storage needs.

Summary

This chapter started by covering the essentials of RAID volumes. RAID 0 volumes are commonly implemented as striped volumes and are used to increase disk I/O. Solaris also supports RAID 0 concatenated volumes. RAID 1 volumes are mirrored volumes. They provide data redundancy, but at the cost of using double the disk space. RAID 5 volumes provide both striping and data redundancy.

The Solaris Volume Manager enables you to create and manage storage volumes in Solaris 9. Through the command line, SVM is accessed through a series of `meta*` commands, such as `metainit`, `metastat`, and `metadb`. The Solaris Management Console also provides an interface for Solaris Volume Manager.

Through SVM, you can create RAID 0, RAID 1, and RAID 5 volumes. You can also create soft partitions, which enable you to exceed the rigid limit of eight slices per hard disk. You can also create transactional volumes, although these are being phased out in favor of UFS logging.

SVM also enables you to create hot spare pools, which are a series of backup slices provided in case of a RAID 1 or RAID 5 component failure. For computers that require high availability, hot spares are essential. Disk sets can also be created with SVM, but to get the full functionality out of using disk sets (such as failover), you will need an additional high availability management product.

Exam Essentials

Know the features of a RAID 0 striped volume. RAID 0 volumes are created on two or more hard disks, and are used to increase disk read and write speed. RAID 0 volumes do not provide any fault tolerance.

Know the features of a RAID 1 mirrored volume. Mirrored volumes provide data redundancy. If a mirrored device fails, the "copy" of the data is still available online for use. Implementing RAID 1 requires an investment in hard disk space.

Know the three RAID 1 read policies. The three read policies are round robin, geometric, and first. Round robin, the default, means that each submirror is read in a serial fashion. On the first read, the first submirror is read. On the second read, the second submirror is read, and so on. The geometric read policy attempts to optimize disk access time by assigning each submirror a set of logical disk addresses to read from. The first policy means that the first submirror is always consulted first.

Know the two RAID 1 write policies. The two write policies are parallel and serial. Parallel is the default write policy, and it means that all submirrors are written to at the same time. With the serial policy, the first submirror's write must be completed before the second submirror's write is started.

Know the features of a RAID 5 volume. RAID 5 volumes write the data in stripes, just as a RAID 0 striped volume does. However, RAID 5 also provides fault tolerance by calculating and writing parity information on the hard disks. Although you lose storage capacity (for the parity information), RAID 5 volumes are more ergonomically correct than RAID 1 volumes.

Understand what a volume is. A volume (also known as a metadevice) is a logical unit of slices, acting as one, and managed by the Solaris Volume Manager.

Know what the metadevice database is. The /etc/lvm/mddb.cf file, which contains the list of state database replicas, is the metadevice database.

Know how to grow a file system. Volumes are increased by adding slices. After the volume size is increased, you can grow your file system (to use all of the new space) with the growfs command.

Know what state database replicas are. State database replicas contain the configuration information for volumes created on your computer. For optimal results, you should have at least three state database replicas, located on different hard disks and controllers if possible.

Know how to create volumes from the command line. Volumes are created by using the metainit command.

Know what resynchronization is. When a RAID 1 or RAID 5 component fails and is replaced by a new component, the new component needs to have current data copied to it. This process is called resynchronization.

Know the advantages of using soft partitions. Soft partitions enable you to create more than eight logical volumes per disk. Also, soft partitions can have their size increased (growing the partition) dynamically, without requiring a reboot of the system.

Know what transactional volumes are used for.   Transactional volumes are used to log UFS reads and writes. They are being phased out in favor of UFS logging.

Know what hot spare pools are for.   A hot spare pool is a collection of unused slices that are standing by in case of a RAID 1 or RAID 5 component failure. When a RAID 1 or RAID 5 component fails, a hot spare is automatically pulled from the pool and used to replace the failed component.

Know what a disk set is.   A disk set is a logical collection of volumes and hot spares. Shared disk sets can be controlled by more than one computer, but never more than one computer at any given time.

Key Terms

Before you take the exam, be certain you are familiar with the following terms:

concatenated stripe	partial resynchronization
concatenated volume	pass number
dirty regions	primary submirror
disk mirroring	RAID 0
disk set	RAID 1
disk striping	RAID 5
disk striping with parity	RAID (Redundant Array of Inexpensive (or Independent) Disks)
fault tolerance	resynchronization region
full resynchronization	shared disk set
hot spare pool	soft partition
hot spares	Solaris Volume Manager (SVM)
interlace	state database
local disk set	state database replica
metadevice	submirrors
optimized resynchronization	transactional volume
parity information	volume

Commands Used in This Chapter

The following list contains a summary of all the commands introduced in this chapter:

Command	Function
growfs	Increases the size of a UFS file system without destroying data
metaclear	Removes active volumes and hot spare pools
metadb	Creates and deletes state database replicas
metadetach	Detaches a volume from a RAID 1 volume, or a logging device from a transactional volume
metadevadm	Checks the configuration of device IDs
metahs	Manages hot spare devices and hot spare pools
metainit	Configures volumes
metaoffline	Takes submirrors offline
metaonline	Brings submirrors online
metaparam	Modifies volume parameters
metarecover	Recovers configuration information for soft partitions
metarename	Renames volumes
metareplace	Replaces components in submirrors and RAID 5 volumes
metaroot	Creates mirroring of the root file system (/)
metaset	Manages disk sets
metastat	Displays volume status or hot spare pool status
metasync	Synchronizes volumes
metattach	Attaches a component to a RAID 0 or RAID 1 volume, or a log device to a transactional volume

Review Questions

1. You are the Solaris administrator for your company. You want to create a fault-tolerant solution for your server named filesrv1. Your objectives are to provide data redundancy for all critical data, including the root (/) and /usr file systems, and to keep costs to a minimum. Which of the following is the best solution for your situation?

    A. Create a mirrored volume with two submirrors for the root (/) and /usr file systems. Create a RAID 5 volume for application and user data.

    B. Create two-way mirrored volumes for all file systems on filesrv1.

    C. Create one RAID 5 volume, encompassing all hard disks in filesrv1.

    D. Create one RAID 5 volume for the root (/) and /usr file systems. Create a second RAID 5 volume for application and user data.

    E. Create a mirrored volume with two submirrors for the root (/) and /usr file systems. Create a RAID 0 volume for application and user data.

2. On your Solaris server, you have several RAID 0, RAID 1, and RAID 5 volumes. For extra fault tolerance, you have created a hot spare pool named hsp001. You believe that one of your hard disks in a RAID 5 volume failed and want to see whether any of your hot spares are being used. Which of the following commands can you use to check the status of your hot spare pool? (Choose all that apply.)

    A. metastat hsp001

    B. metadb hsp001

    C. metahs -s hsp001

    D. metahs -i hsp001

3. You are configuring Solaris Volume Manager for your Solaris server. Which of the following files keeps track of the locations of state database replicas?

    A. /etc/lvm/md.cf

    B. /etc/rc2.d/S95svm.sync

    C. /kernel/drv/md.conf

    D. /etc/lvm/mddb.cf

4. You are the Solaris administrator for your company. You have just had a hard disk crash. The disk that crashed contained one of your five state database replicas. Solaris Volume Manager needs to know that the replica is no longer available, because you are replacing the device. Which of the following commands can you use to delete the state database replica?

    A. metadel

    B. metainit

    C. metadb

    D. metadetach

    E. metareplace

5. You are the Solaris administrator for your network. You are configuring Solaris Volume Manager for first-time use on your Solaris server. When you try to create a RAID 5 volume, Solaris tells you that you must first create state database replicas. Your server has six hard disks. At a minimum, what is the recommended number of state database replicas you should create?

   A. One

   B. Three

   C. Six

   D. Seven

   E. It depends on the number of slices you have.

6. You are the Solaris administrator for your company. Your file server SolData1 has a mirrored volume named d10, composed of the submirrors d11 and d12. You bring d12 offline to perform a backup. You know that when you bring d12 back online, it will need to be resynchronized. Which of the following statements accurately describe what will be resynchronized when d12 is brought back online?

   A. The entire d12 volume.

   B. Only the regions on d12 that fail a parity check test.

   C. Only the dirty regions on d12.

   D. Only the regions on d12 that are not controlled by the local state database replica.

7. You are creating a fault-tolerant solution for your Solaris server. You want to ensure that if a single disk or slice fails, your data will still be available online. Which of the following volume types protect your data if one device fails? (Choose all that apply.)

   A. RAID 0

   B. RAID 1

   C. RAID 5

   D. Soft partitions

   E. Transactional volumes

   F. Hot spare pools

8. You are the Solaris administrator for your network. One of your file servers has three hard disks. You want to create a total of 25 volumes on this file server. How can this be accomplished?

   A. You cannot create that many volumes on this computer with its current configuration.

   B. Create eight slices on all three hard disks, for a total of 24 volumes, and leave extra space on the last hard disk. Concatenate the last volume on the hard disk into two volumes, giving you a total of 25 volumes.

   C. Use disk sets to create 25 virtual slices across the hard disks.

   D. Use soft partitions to create 25 virtual slices across the hard disks.

9. You have recently implemented a RAID 1 volume on one of your file servers. Which of the following are Solaris read policies for RAID 1 volumes that you can choose from? (Choose all that apply.)

   A. First

   B. Random

   C. Geometric

   D. Round robin

   E. Default

10. You are the Solaris administrator for your network. You want to create a RAID 0 striped volume containing disk slices `c0t2d0s6` and `c0t3d0s6`. Which of the following commands should you use to accomplish this?

    A. `metainit d0 1 2 c0t2d0s6 c0t3d0s6`

    B. `metainit d0 -r 1 2 c0t2d0s6 c0t3d0s6`

    C. `metainit d0 2 1 c0t2d0s6 c0t3d0s6`

    D. `metainit d0 -r 2 1 c0t2d0s6 c0t3d0s6`

11. You are the Solaris administrator for your network. You have just increased the size of your RAID 5 volume by adding additional slices. How do you get the file system that resides on that RAID 5 volume to recognize the additional space without losing the existing data?

    A. Back up existing data. Delete the existing file system and re-create it. Restore data from backup.

    B. Back up existing data. Use the `growfs` command to expand the existing file system.

    C. Back up existing data. Use the `growfs` command to expand the existing file system. Restore data from backup.

    D. Back up existing data. Use the Solaris Volume Manager to expand the existing file system.

12. You are the Solaris administrator for your company. You have implemented a RAID 5 volume on your server. One of the hard disks in the RAID 5 volume recently crashed. You replaced the hard disk and rebooted Solaris. What do you need to do to resynchronize the RAID 5 volume?

    A. From a command line, run the `metasync` command.

    B. From a command line, run the `metasynch` command.

    C. Do nothing; Solaris Volume Manager will resynchronize the volume automatically.

    D. RAID 5 volumes cannot be resynchronized. You will need to delete the volume and then re-create it with the new component.

13. You are the Solaris server administrator for your company. You have created a mirrored volume named d30, which uses a three-way submirror consisting of volumes d31, d32, and d33. You want to make a tape backup from the d33 volume. Which command should you use first so you can make the backup?

A. metadetach d30 d33

B. metaoffline d30 d33

C. metabackup d30 d33

D. metaremove d30 d33

14. You are the Solaris administrator for your company. In Solaris Volume Manager, you have a RAID volume named d0. You have been instructed to increase the size of d0. Which of the following commands can you use to accomplish this?

A. growfs d0 c0t2d0s2

B. metadd d0 c0t2d0s2

C. metaonline d0 c0t2d0s2

D. metattach d0 c0t2d0s2

E. metainit d0 c0t2d0s2

15. You are configuring RAID on your Solaris server. Which of the following statements accurately describes the differences between RAID 0+1 and RAID 1+0?

A. RAID 0+1 is a striped volume that is then mirrored. RAID 1+0 is a mirrored volume that is striped.

B. RAID 0+1 is a mirrored volume that is then striped. RAID 1+0 is a striped volume that is mirrored.

C. RAID 0+1 is a striped volume that is expanded to include a concatenated volume. RAID 1+0 is a mirrored volume that expanded to include a concatenated volume.

D. Both RAID 0+1 and RAID 1+0 refer to volumes that are striped and consequently mirrored.

16. You are creating a RAID 5 volume from three existing slices: c1t0d0s2, c2t0d0s2, and c1t1d0s2. Each of the slices is currently in use and has existing data. You run the command **metainit d40 -r c1t0d0s2 c2t0d0s2 c1t1d0s2**. Solaris Volume Manager confirms that the d40 volume exists and reports the status as initializing. After the volume changes to okay status, you notice that there is no data on d40. What is the most likely cause of the problem?

A. The volume name you chose, d40, was already in use by another volume.

B. When you created the d40 volume, you should have used the metattach command instead of the metainit command to preserve the existing data.

C. When creating a RAID 5 volume, all existing data on the disks is erased.

D. When you created the d40 volume by using metainit, you should have used volume numbers representing the slices instead of the slice designations. This would have preserved the existing data.

17. You are the Solaris administrator for your network. You have recently expanded the size of one of your file systems. Now, however, you need to make the file system smaller, so you have room to create another file system on that hard disk. Which of the following should you do to accomplish this?

A. Back up existing data. Use the `growfs` command to shrink the file system. Create the new file system as needed.

B. Back up existing data. Use the `growfs -r` command to recursively claim the expanded file system's space. Create the new file system as needed.

C. Back up existing data. Use the `shrinkfs` command to shrink the file system. Create the new file system as needed.

D. Back up existing data. Delete the existing file system and re-create two smaller ones. Restore data from backup. Create the new file system as needed.

18. You are the Solaris administrator for your company. One of your file servers has been serving more users recently, and users are complaining that file access times on the server are decreasing. Which of the following can you implement to provide the greatest speed increase to users accessing this file server?

A. RAID 0 striped volume

B. RAID 0 concatenated volume

C. RAID 1

D. RAID 5

E. Soft partitions

F. Transactional volumes

19. You have recently implemented a RAID 1 volume on one of your file servers. Which of the following are Solaris write policies for RAID 1 volumes that you can choose from? (Choose all that apply.)

A. Parity checking

B. Write through

C. Write back

D. Parallel

E. Serial

20. One of your Solaris servers contains a large number of hard disks. Because of RAID volumes and soft partitions, you need to increase the default number of volumes you can create on that server. Which file do you edit to perform this task?

A. `/kernel/drv/md.conf`

B. `/etc/lvm/md.cf`

C. `/etc/rc2.d/S95svm.sync`

D. `/etc/lvm/mddb.cf`

Answers to Review Questions

1. A. The only two fault-tolerant volume types available (by default) in Solaris 9 are RAID 1 (mirrored volumes) and RAID 5 (disk striping with parity). RAID 5 volumes are more cost-effective than mirrored volumes. However, you cannot place the root (/) and /usr file systems on a RAID 5 volume. If you want to protect data on those two volumes, you must use a mirror.

2. A, D. The two commands you can use are metastat and metahs -i. The metadb command is used to manage state database replicas. The metahs -s switch is used to specify disk sets when creating hot spare pools.

3. D. The /etc/lvm/mddb.cf file, also known as the metadevice database, keeps track of the locations of state database replicas.

4. C. The metadb command is used to create, manage, and delete state database replicas. metadel does not exist. metainit creates volumes, metadetach detaches components from a RAID 1 or transactional volume, and metareplace is used to replace devices in a RAID 1 or RAID 5 volume.

5. B. The recommended minimum number of state database replicas is three. Because your computer has more than three hard disks, it wouldn't be a bad idea to create more (and an odd number is better than an even number). However, three is still the minimum.

6. C. When a submirror is brought offline, the other submirror still reads and writes data. The new data written is tracked by Solaris Volume Manager, and regions that are not updated (on the offline volume) are called dirty regions. When the d12 submirror is brought back online, the dirty regions need to be synchronized.

7. B, C. The only two types of volumes that provide fault tolerance (data redundancy) are RAID 1 and RAID 5. RAID 0, soft partitions, and transactional volumes do not provide fault tolerance. Hot spare pools can be used by RAID 1 and RAID 5 volumes for added redundancy; however, hot spare pools in and of themselves provide no fault tolerance, nor are they a volume type.

8. D. The only way to increase the number of volumes on a hard disk beyond the limit of eight is to use soft partitions. Even with soft partitions, you will never get more than eight slices on one hard disk. However, you will be able to get more than eight logical volumes, which, for all practical purposes, act like slices when it comes to file and application access.

9. A, C, D. There are three RAID 1 (mirrored volume) read policies in Solaris 9. They are round robin (the default), which reads disks in order, geometric, which assigns logical disk address ranges to components, and first, which always reads the first disk if it's available.

10. A. The correct syntax for creating a striped RAID 0 volume is # **metainit *volume_name* #_ *stripes components_per_stripe component_names* -i *interlace***. The -r switch is used to create RAID 5 volumes.

11. B. After a volume is expanded, the growfs command can be used to expand the underlying file system. The growfs command does not destroy data, so there is no need to restore data from backup after using growfs.

12. C.   Upon replacement of a failed component, Solaris Volume Manager will automatically resynchronize a RAID 5 volume. It is possible to manually synchronize volumes with the `metasync` command (`metasynch` does not exist), but it's not necessary to run the command in this case.

13. B.   The `metaoffline` command is used to bring submirrors offline. After they are offline, you can use the d33 volume to make a tape backup. After you bring d33 back online (with the `metaonline` command), it will resynchronize with the rest of the d30 volume immediately.

14. D.   The `metattach` command is used to expand existing RAID volumes. The `growfs` command grows file systems, not volumes (although after running `metattach`, it might be a good idea to expand the file system with `growfs`). The `metadd` command does not exist; `metaonline` brings submirrors online in a RAID 1 volume, and `metainit` creates new volumes.

15. A.   A RAID 0+1 volume starts off as a RAID 0 volume (typically a striped volume) and then is mirrored. RAID 1 volumes are mirrors, which can then be striped to enhance performance. These types of volumes are called RAID 1+0.

16. C.   When you create a RAID 5 volume, all data that is on the slices used to create the volume will be destroyed. This is because when the RAID 5 volume is created, Solaris Volume Manager needs to calculate parity bits. These parity bits will be used to provide an online backup of data. RAID 5 volumes are created with the `metainit` command, and you must specify slice names, not volume names, as components.

17. D.   After a file system is grown, it cannot be shrunk. To free up space for another file system, you will have to delete the existing file system and re-create a smaller one.

18. A.   Of the RAID volumes, RAID 0 striped volumes provide the fastest read and write access times. Soft partitions and transactional volumes do not provide a disk speed increase.

19. D, E.   There are two RAID 1 write policies: parallel (the default) and serial. In parallel, all disks are written to at the same time. In serial, the first write must complete before the second write begins.

20. A.   The `/kernel/drv/md.conf` file is what you're looking for. Inside this file, the field you need to edit is called nmd. Increase the number from 128 to whatever you need it to be. Remember, though, that increasing this value unnecessarily high can slow your system, and the maximum value is 8192.

Chapter 13

Advanced Security Concepts

SOLARIS 9 EXAM OBJECTIVES COVERED IN THIS CHAPTER:

- ✓ Explain how to display and set Access Control Lists (ACLs) using the command line and create default ACLs.
- ✓ Explain fundamental concepts of role-based access control (RBAC), including rights, roles, profiles, authorizations, administrator profile shells, and RBAC databases.
- ✓ Explain how to build user accounts, rights profiles, and the role when managing RBAC.

Security is one of the most critical factors of any network operating system. It should come as no surprise to you that Solaris provides a very secure computing environment.

All Solaris security is based upon file access. If you want to open a document, you must have the proper permissions. To manage a slice on a hard disk, you need sufficient access to the file that represents that slice within Solaris.

As you learned in Chapter 5, "Files, Directories, and Security," Solaris provides three levels of access: Read, Write, and Execute. Those three permissions can be assigned in any combination to three different groups: the user who owns the file (owner), the group owner of the file (group), and everyone else (other). Although for the most part these basic permission structures are sufficient to manage security, in some cases this basic structure is limiting.

To address more complex security needs, Access Control Lists (ACLs) and role-based access control (RBAC) were developed. The extended security attributes used in ACLs still rely on the underlying Read, Write, and Execute permission structure, but afford the administrator additional flexibility in assigning permissions, such as to multiple groups. RBAC provides the administrator a tool to grant other users some administrative powers while maintaining overall system integrity.

Using Access Control Lists

The basic UNIX permission structure enables administrators to assign Read, Write, and/or Execute permissions to three classes of users: the owner (user), group, and everyone else (other). In many cases, these permissions will be sufficient to manage Solaris.

However, what happens when a user other than the owner needs to access the file? There are several ways, using standard permissions, that you could accomplish this. One would be to change the owner of the file to the new user. But then what about the previous owner's access? A second way would be to put the user in the group that owns the file and to make sure that the group has proper access. But then other users who might be part of the group have access, which might be undesirable. A third way would be to create a group specifically for the user, make the new group the owner, and give the new group permissions. This can cause a lot of problems, the least of which is an excessive number of groups. Finally, you could grant permissions to everyone (other), but this could cause a serious security problem. None of these solutions seems very good, so what can you do?

Access Control Lists (ACLs) enable you to not only assign permissions via the traditional security structure, but to define permissions for additional specific users and groups. Using the previous example, all you would need to do is set up an ACL and give the user's account proper permissions to the file. The problem is solved.

Understanding ACL Entries

To understand the syntax used in creating and managing ACLs, it helps to know what the structure of an access control entry looks like for both files and directories. When ACLs are created on a file, each entry will have the following fields:

`entry_type:UID(orGID):permissions`

One file can have several entries. For example, you can define the owner's permissions, as well as permissions for several groups and individual users. Each ACL entry will have its own line. Table 13.1 lists the different ACL entry types for files.

TABLE 13.1   File-Based ACL Entries

Entry	Description
user::*permissions*	Permissions for the file's owner.
group::*permissions*	Permissions for the file's group owner.
other:*permissions*	Permissions for the other group.
mask:*permissions*	Defines the ACL mask. This entry defines the maximum allowable permissions for users (other than the owner) and groups. For example, if you were to set mask::r--, users (other than the owner) and groups could have no more than Read access.
user:*UID*:*permissions*	Permissions for a specific user. You can specify a username or UID in the *UID* field.
group:*GID*:*permissions*	Permissions for a specific group. You can specify a group name or GID in the *GID* field.

So when looking at an ACL for a file, you might see an entry such as user::rwx, which would mean that the owner has Read, Write, and Execute permissions. Another possible entry would be group:1850:r--, meaning that users in the group with GID 1850 have Read access to the file.

When creating access control entries, you can abbreviate user with u, group with g, other with o, and mask with m.

A quick way to change permissions for all users is to modify the mask. Changing the mask value to mask:--- will disable access for all users except for the file's owner.

Access Control Lists can also be set on directories. If you have a large number of files that you want to enable ACLs on, then putting them into a directory might ease your file management burden. If you create a file or directory in a directory that has an ACL, the new file or directory will have the same permission structure as its parent directory.

When you create an ACL on a directory for the first time, you must specify default permissions for the directory's user `owner`, `group` owner, and `other`, and a mask, in addition to any permissions you want to assign to specific users or groups.

ACLs created on directories have the same entries as ACLs created on files, except that directories also have default entries with the following fields:

`default:entry_type:UID(orGID):permissions`

As you can see, the only difference between file and directory ACLs is the inclusion of the *default* entries for directories. The *default* field can be abbreviated with d, which makes it easy to remember that it's for directories only. (The entries are called *default* because any new files or directories will have those permissions automatically.) Otherwise, the fields for directories are identical to the fields for files, as shown in Table 13.1.

Managing ACLs

Now that you know what an ACL entry looks like, it's time to learn about creating them. ACLs are managed by two commands. The `setfacl` command is used to set, modify, and delete access control entries, and the `getfacl` command is for viewing current ACL entries.

For a review of access permissions, see Chapter 5.

Creating ACLs on Files

Setting up and modifying ACLs is done with the `setfacl` (set file access control list) command. Here is the syntax for `setfacl`:

`# setfacl -s entry_type::permissions,acl_entries filename`

For example, imagine that you are setting an ACL on a file named `doc1`. The `owner` needs full permissions, the `group` needs read, and a user named `ldocter` needs read access as well. When setting ACLs for the first time on a file, it's recommended that you specify permissions for all three standard classes (`owner`, `group`, `other`), as well as the mask. Here's the syntax you could use:

`# setfacl -s user::rwx,group::r--,other:---,mask:r--,user:ldocter:r-- doc1`

As noted earlier, you can also use first-letter abbreviations for user, group, other, and mask. In this example, if you had used `user:ldocter:rwx`, what permissions would `ldocter` have? The answer is Read-only. At first you might wonder why, but remember that the mask value determines the maximum permissions that users (other than the `owner`) and groups can have to the file. Because the mask is set to `r--`, all `ldocter` would have is Read access.

NOTE   You can use either absolute or symbolic mode to set permissions when using setfacl.

The setfacl command has five arguments, which are shown in Table 13.2.

TABLE 13.2   *setfacl* Arguments

Argument	Description
-d *acl_entry*	Deletes the specified ACL entry. Note that deleting an entry doesn't necessarily guarantee that access to the file has been removed.
-f *file*	Sets the ACL for a new file based on the ACL for an existing file. Useful for copying ACLs between files.
-m *acl_entry*	Modifies an existing ACL entry.
-r	Recalculates the mask value. The permissions in the ACL mask are ignored and replaced by the maximum permissions necessary to allow access to all additional user, group, and other entries in the ACL. The permissions on additional users, groups, and other are not directly modified.
-s *acl_entry*	Sets a new ACL entry. Deletes any existing entries and replaces them with the specified *acl_entry*.

After you have created your ACL, you can check to ensure that your changes have taken effect. The first thing you can do is use the ls -l command to provide a directory listing. All files with ACLs have a + after the permissions. For example, in this directory listing, the doc1 file has an ACL, whereas doc2 does not:

```
# ls -l
-rwxr-----+  1 qdocter    author         554 Nov 29 13:46 doc1
-rwxr--r--   1 qdocter    author         554 Nov 29 13:47 doc2
```

To see your Access Control List, use the getfacl (get file access control list) command. Here's an example showing the results of the setfacl command used earlier:

```
# getfacl doc1

# file: doc1
# owner: qdocter
# group: author
user::rwx
user:1docter:r--        #effective:r--
group::r--              #effective:r--
mask:r--
other:---
```

In the previous directory listing, the doc2 file did not have an ACL. If you wanted to give doc2 an ACL identical to the ACL for doc1, you could use the setfacl -s command to create a new ACL. However, this is far too much work. An easier solution is to use getfacl and setfacl together to copy the ACL from doc1 to doc2. Here's how you would do it:

```
# getfacl doc1 | setfacl -f - doc2
```

This command takes the output of getfacl for doc1 and pipes it to the setfacl command for doc2. It's quick and it's easy.

Creating ACLs on Directories

Creating ACLs on directories is very similar to creating ACLs on files. The only major difference is that directories have default permissions. When you create an ACL on a directory for the first time, you must specify defaults for the directory owner, group, other, and mask. These defaults are in addition to the normal permissions you must create for the owner, group, other, and mask.

The list of setfacl entries can get quite cumbersome. Here's an example of setting an ACL on a directory named dir1:

```
# setfacl -s d:u::7,d:g::4,d:o:0,d:m:6,u::4,g::4,o:0,m:6,u:501:7,u:502:6 dir1
# ls -l
total 2
dr--r-----+  2 qdocter  author      512 Nov 30 11:25 dir1
-rwxr-----+  1 qdocter  author       80 Nov 29 13:46 doc1
-rwxr-----+  1 qdocter  author       80 Nov 29 14:04 doc2
-rw-r--r--   1 qdocter  author       80 Nov 29 14:05 doc3
# getfacl dir1

# file: dir1
# owner: qdocter
# group: author
user::r--
user:501:rwx        #effective:rw-
user:502:rw-        #effective:rw-
group::r--          #effective:r--
mask:rw-
other:---
default:user::rwx
default:group::r--
default:mask:rw-
default:other:---
```

Because of the sheer length of the setfacl command, absolute mode was used instead of symbolic mode to shorten things up. As you can see in the getfacl output, the permissions are set, as are the defaults. The getfacl -d command shows only the default settings for directories:

```
# getfacl -d dir1
```

```
# file: dir1
# owner: qdocter
# group: author
default:user::rwx
default:group::r--
default:mask:rw-
default:other:---
```

Now that the `dir1` directory has an ACL, any new files created within `dir1` will have their permissions defined by the default settings. New subdirectories in `dir1` will have an ACL identical to `dir1`.

After you have created an ACL on a directory, you can use `getfacl` and `setfacl` to copy the ACL to another directory, just as you would for ACLs on files. You cannot, however, copy ACLs between files and directories.

Modifying ACLs

If you want to add an entry to an existing ACL, do so with the `setfacl -m` command. For example, to give the `adocter` user Read and Write access to `doc1`, you could use:

setfacl -m u:adocter:rw- doc1

However, because of the restrictive mask, `adocter` would still have only Read access. To remedy this, change the mask with:

setfacl -m m:rw- doc1

or

setfacl -r doc1

To ensure that your changes have taken effect, use the `getfacl` command.

Removing ACLs

Entries are deleted from ACLs with the `setfacl -d` command. For example, to remove the `adocter` user from the ACL, you could use:

setfacl -d u:adocter doc1

Once again, to ensure that your changes have taken effect, use `getfacl`.

Other ACL Information

You might wonder about potential conflicts between already-configured standard permissions and new permissions established in Access Control Lists. Is there a conflict? Does one override the other?

When you create an ACL, the permissions you set for the `owner`, `group`, and `other` will change the existing permissions (if applicable) set on the file or directory. Subsequently, when you modify permissions within the ACL, the standard permissions are modified as well. So when you use `ls -l` (and the file has an ACL), the permissions you see for user, group, and other are the same as defined in the ACL. The only way to see permissions for additional users and groups is to use `getfacl`.

Along the same lines, if you are using ACLs, don't use chmod to change file permissions. There's no rule prohibiting you from doing so, but it could cause unexpected problems. For example, if you use chmod to change the permissions for the group owner, chmod might modify the mask in the ACL to enable your specified permissions for the group to take effect. This could cause a security breach by opening up access to other groups specified in the ACL.

Finally, know that ACLs are a UFS file system attribute and are not currently available on any other type of file system. So, if you copy files to a floppy disk formatted with PCFS or restore files to the /tmp file system (which is typically TMPFS), all ACL entries will be lost. Normally, this isn't an issue, but if you accidentally restore files into /tmp instead of /var/tmp, it could cause problems.

Managing Role-Based Access Control

In the traditional UNIX security model, the root user was the all-powerful administrator account. There were no other users with administrative privileges. To allow a user to perform administrative tasks, even common ones such as changing user passwords, mounting file systems, or shutting down the system, you had to give them the root password. This of course posed a major security threat. You were giving the user way too much power to perform their task. Also, although you might trust the user, security always becomes easier to compromise when several people know the administrative password.

Some third-party utilities, such as sudo, were developed to alleviate this problem. These security programs created roles, enabling users to assume some administrative responsibilities without knowing the root password.

Finally, a UNIX standard was developed to combat the all-or-nothing security approach of using the superuser account for administration. The standard is *role-based access control (RBAC)*. RBAC enables the administrator to assign certain administrative tasks to specific users or to special user accounts called roles. This assignment process limits security vulnerability and grants the users only the minimum access they need to perform administrative tasks.

Understanding RBAC Concepts

Role-based access control is a complex service based upon four critical concepts: privileged applications, roles, authorizations, and rights profiles.

A *privileged application* is an application that can override standard security and check for specific UIDs, GIDs, or authorizations. A user might or might not have administrative access. However, if the user attempts to open a privileged application, the application can allow the user to run it as if the user had root privileges (the application would assume the UID of 0, for example). For all other applications, however, the user has their normal access.

Privileged applications can check for a real or an effective UID or GID. Using effective IDs is the recommended method and is equivalent to using the SetUID or SetGID features. Some applications, however, require a real ID instead of an effective ID. For this reason, you can set either. Other applications, such as the Solaris Management Console, at, atq, crontab, allocate, list_devices, and cdrw are capable of checking authorizations to determine access.

Privileged application information is stored in the `exec_attr` database.

A *role* is a special user account that is allowed to run privileged applications. Users log into Solaris with their normal user account and use the `su` command to log in as a role. Users cannot log into Solaris as a role directly; you must use `su` to access the role. Users must be authorized to `su` to a role. If the user is not authorized, they will receive an error message telling them that only authorized users can use `su`.

When a user assumes a role, they are allowed to perform any tasks that the role is authorized to perform. For example, you could create a role that allows users to manage printers as well as reset user passwords. Multiple users can access the same role, as long as they know the role's name and the password. There are no predefined roles in Solaris. Role information is stored in the `passwd`, `shadow`, `user_attr`, and `audit_user` databases.

An *authorization* is a right that is granted to a role or a user. When a user attempts to access an application that is RBAC-aware, the application can check whether the user has the appropriate authorization. If not, the user is denied access. Solaris contains a list of predefined authorizations in the `auth_attr` database.

Finally, there are rights profiles. A *rights profile* is a collection of authorizations and privileged applications. Rights profiles can contain other rights profiles as well, and information on rights profiles is stored in the `prof_attr` and `exec_attr` databases.

Here's how everything fits together: A user is assigned to a role. Roles get their abilities from rights profiles and/or authorizations. Authorizations are generally assigned to rights profiles to make management easier, but they can be assigned directly to roles. Privileged applications are assigned to rights profiles.

You can assign rights profiles and authorizations directly to users, but this practice is not recommended. It's best to assign the user to a role that has the rights profiles and authorizations. This forces the user to su to the role, perform their administrative tasks, and reassume their regular user account.

To say that everything in RBAC revolves around roles is a safe assumption. Although there are no predefined roles, Sun recommends that you set up levels of administrative hierarchy. For example, you could create a primary administrator role that is basically an equivalent to the `root` user, a secondary administrator that handles all administration except for security, and an operator level that handles small administrative tasks such as printer management, and backups and restores.

To maximize your security based on Sun's recommendation, you would make `root` a role instead of a user. This forces the user to log in (and be audited) and use `su` (again, to be audited) to perform `root` functions.

Whether or not you choose to follow Sun's recommendations, RBAC is flexible enough to accommodate any organization's administrative needs.

Using the RBAC Databases

All RBAC information is stored in four databases:

- `/etc/user_attr`
- `/etc/security/auth_attr`

- `/etc/security/prof_attr`
- `/etc/security/exec_attr`

These databases work together to provide RBAC functionality. They can be located on each local host or managed by a name service such as NIS, NIS+, or LDAP. If the default entries in the four databases are not sufficient to meet your security needs, you can always add additional entries.

The `/etc/security` directory is the primary directory for RBAC-related files. However, the `user_attr` database is located in `/etc`.

There is also one additional configuration file used, and that is the `/etc/security/policy.conf` file. The `policy.conf` file contains rights profiles and authorizations granted to all users. Here are the default entries in `policy.conf`:

```
AUTHS_GRANTED=solaris.device.cdrw
PROFS_GRANTED=Basic Solaris User
```

You can see that the first line grants authorizations, and the second line grants rights profiles. Because you haven't learned specifics about authorizations or profiles yet, don't worry if you don't know what `solaris.device.cdrw` or Basic Solaris User do for you. You'll learn about those in a bit. Just remember that authorizations and profiles granted in `policy.conf` affect all Solaris users.

user_attr

The `user_attr` database contains a list of users and roles, along with assigned authorizations, profiles, and roles. Each entry in `user_attr` has five fields, separated by colons. Three of the fields are reserved for future use, so the only ones you need to worry about are the first and last fields. Here are the fields:

    user:qualifier:res1:res2:attributes

The *user* field refers to the user or role, as defined in the `/etc/passwd` database (when you create a role, it's added to `/etc/password` just as a user account is). The middle three fields are not currently used. The *attributes* field is a list of semicolon-delimited key-value pairs that describe the security traits of the user or role. Each key pair uses the syntax of *key=value* to provide flexibility for adding profiles and authorizations and enables Solaris to ignore a key-value pair if it doesn't recognize what it means.

There are four valid keys for the `user_attr` database: `type`, `auths`, `profiles`, and `roles`. Here is a description of each one:

- The `type` key defines whether the entry refers to a user or a role. For a user, the value is `normal`; for a role, it is `role`.
- Authorizations are specified with the `auths` key. Any authorizations specified must be listed in the `auths_attr` database, and multiple authorizations can be specified, separated by commas. Authorizations can include an asterisk (*) as a wildcard. For example, `solaris.admin.*` signifies all of the Solaris `admin` authorizations.

- Profiles are assigned with the `profiles` key. Multiple profiles can be assigned, just as multiple authorizations can be assigned. Profiles are defined in the `prof_attr` database. If multiple profiles are provided, the first profile that allows access to the command will be used.

- Roles are assigned to users through the `roles` key. Roles cannot be assigned to other roles. Several roles can be assigned to one user, and one role can be assigned to several users. Roles are defined in the `user_attr` database.

The default `user_attr` file contains three entries:

```
root:::::auths=solaris.*,solaris.grant;profiles=All
lp:::::profiles=Printer Management
adm:::::profiles=Log Management
```

You can identify these three entries as entries for three of the default Solaris users. The `lp` and `adm` users are granted only a profile. However, the `root` user is granted two authorizations and a profile. The first authorization, `solaris.*`, gives the root user access to all authorizations. The second authorization, `solaris.grant`, allows `root` to assign authorizations to other users. Both are very handy for the all-powerful user account.

If you were to add some custom entries to `user_attr`, they might look like this:

```
jradmin:::::type=role;auths=solaris.admin.*,solaris.profmgr.*;profiles=All
sjohnson:::::type=normal;roles=jradmin
```

The first entry defines a role named `jradmin`. The second line associates your junior administrator, `sjohnson`, with the `jradmin` role. Therefore, the `sjohnson` user has some administrative abilities.

auth_attr

The `auth_attr` database stores RBAC authorizations. Authorizations can be assigned to users or roles in the `user_attr` database, or to rights profiles in the `prof_attr` database. Each entry in the `auth_attr` database has six fields:

```
authname:res1:res2:short_desc:long_desc:attributes
```

Authorizations are named with the *authname* field. Each authorization must have a unique name. Names take the form of *prefix.suffix*, and each Solaris authorization begins with the `solaris` prefix (for example, `solaris.system.date`). The suffix describes the area to be authorized. When the authorization ends in a period, the *authname* serves as a header for similarly grouped authorizations. When you use graphical interfaces to manage RBAC, the GUI uses the headings to organize authorizations. Authorizations that end with the word `grant` enable authorized individuals to assign other authorizations with the same prefix and functional area to other users or roles. For example, anyone with the `solaris.grant` authorization can assign any `solaris.*` authorization to other users or roles. Obviously, this is a very powerful authorization to have.

The second and third fields are reserved for future use. The *short_desc* field is a short description of the authorization and is displayed by the graphical RBAC management interface. The *long_desc* is a long description, which can include the purpose of the authorization and the users who might be interested in using it.

The *attributes* field is a list of semicolon-separated key-value pairs that describe the authorization. The `help` key identifies an HTML Help file (located in the `/usr/lib/help/auths/locale/C` directory).

Here is a sample from the `auth_attr` database

```
solaris.admin.volmgr.:::Logical Volume Manager::
solaris.admin.volmgr.write:::Manage Logical Volumes::help=AuthVolmgrWrite.html
solaris.admin.volmgr.read:::View Logical Volumes::help=AuthVolmgrRead.html
solaris.admin.printer.modify:::Update Printer↵
    Information::help=AuthPrinterModify.html
solaris.profmgr.:::Rights::help=ProfmgrHeader.html
solaris.device.cdrw:::CD-R/RW Recording Authorizations::help=DevCDRW.html
solaris.profmgr.write:::Manage Rights::help=AuthProfmgrWrite.html
solaris.system.shutdown:::Shutdown the System::help=SysShutdown.html
solaris.:::All Solaris Authorizations::help=AllSolAuthsHeader.html
solaris.jobs.grant:::Delegate Cron & At Administration::help=JobsGrant.html
...
```

The reason that only a sampling is given is simple: by default there are more than 80 separate authorizations. Remember that when granting authorizations, an asterisk can be used as a wildcard. For example, granting a user `solaris.*` gives him superuser powers, and `solaris.admin.*` gives him quite a number of authorizations as well.

prof_attr

Rights profiles are a collection of authorizations. Instead of assigning roles a long list of authorizations, you can group authorizations into profiles and then assign the profile to the role. Names, descriptions, Help file locations, and authorizations assigned to rights profiles are stored in the `prof_attr` database. The `prof_attr` database has five fields:

profile_name:res1:res2:description:attributes

The *profile_name* field names the profile, and profile names are case sensitive. Fields *res1* and *res2* are reserved for future use. The description is intended to be a detailed description of the profile. Authorizations and Help files are specified by the `auths` and `help` keywords in the *attributes* field. Profiles can also contain other profiles, indicated by the `profiles` keyword.

Here is a sampling of the `prof_attr` database (the entries are broken to improve readability, although each entry in `prof_attr` should be one line):

```
# /etc/security/prof_attr
File System Management:::Manage, mount, share file systems:help= \
    RtFileSysMngmnt.html;auths=solaris.admin.fsmgr.*, \
    solaris.admin.diskmgr.*,solaris.admin.volmgr.*
File System Security:::Manage file system security attributes:help= \
    RtFileSysSecurity.html;auths=solaris.admin.fsmgr.*, \
    solaris.admin.diskmgr.*,solaris.admin.volmgr.*
```

```
Basic Solaris User:::Automatically assigned rights: \
   auths=solaris.profmgr.read,solaris.jobs.users, \
   solaris.mail.mailq,solaris.admin.usermgr.read, \
   solaris.admin.logsvc.read,solaris.admin.fsmgr.read, \
   solaris.admin.serialmgr.read,solaris.admin.diskmgr.read, \
   solaris.admin.procmgr.user,solaris.compsys.read, \
   solaris.admin.printer.read,solaris.admin.prodreg.read, \
   solaris.admin.dcmgr.read,solaris.snmp.read,solaris.project.read, \
   solaris.admin.patchmgr.read,,solaris.network.hosts.read, \
   solaris.admin.volmgr.read;profiles=All;help=RtDefault.html
Media Restore:::Restore files and file systems from backups: \
   help=RtMediaRestore.html
User Management:::Manage users, groups, home directory: \
   auths=solaris.profmgr.read,solaris.admin.usermgr.write, \
   solaris.admin.usermgr.read;help=RtUserMngmnt.html
Printer Management:::Manage printers, daemons, spooling: \
   help=RtPrntAdmin.html;auths=solaris.admin.printer.read, \
   solaris.admin.printer.modify,solaris.admin.printer.delete
Primary Administrator:::Can perform all administrative tasks: \
   auths=solaris.*,solaris.grant;help=RtPriAdmin.html
All:::Execute any command as the user or role:help=RtAll.html
System Administrator:::Can perform most non-security administrative \
   tasks:profiles=Audit Review,Printer Management,Cron Management, \
   Device Management,File System Management,Mail Management,Maintenance \
   and Repair,Media Backup,Media Restore,Name Service Management, \
   Network Management,Object Access Management,Process Management, \
   Software Installation,User Management,All;help=RtSysAdmin.html
...
```

Looking at the nine profiles listed here (there are almost 40 provided by Solaris), you can see that each one has a list of authorizations as well as an HTML Help file. Based on the sheer volume of profiles listed, you might assume that the Basic Solaris User profile is quite powerful. In fact, it's not. Rather, the Basic Solaris User has the ability to do a lot of reading of files, but very little administrative power. Also interesting to note is that some profiles overlap functionality with other profiles. For example, look at the first two profiles listed, File System Management and File System Security. They are two separate profiles, but they are granted the exact same authorizations.

exec_attr

An execution attribute is a command associated with a specific UID or GID, and then assigned to a specific rights profile. The command can then be run by users or roles who have been assigned the appropriate rights profile. The exec_attr database holds the execution attributes. There are seven fields in exec_attr:

name:policy:type:res1:res2:id:attributes

The *name* field, which is case sensitive, refers to the name of a rights profile in the prof_attr database. For example, anything in exec_attr beginning with Media Restore refers to the same

Media Restore that was in the prof_attr file. The *policy* field contains the security policy associated with the entry. Currently, the only valid policy is suser (the superuser policy model). The *type* field defines the type of entry; cmd (command) is currently the only valid option.

Two fields, *res1* and *res2*, are reserved for future use. The *id* identifies the entry. This is an executable command and can be the full absolute path to the command, or you can use wildcards such as an asterisk (*). Finally, the *attributes* field defines the security attributes that the command(s) can be run under. Attributes are listed as key-value pairs, and valid keywords are euid, uid, egid, and gid. These enable the application to run with an effective or real UID or GID. Basically, if you set the UID to 0 for an application, anyone with association to the rights profile that contains the execution attribute can run the command as if they were the superuser.

Here is a sampling from the exec_attr database:

```
Software Installation:suser:cmd:::/usr/bin/pkgparam:uid=0
Media Backup:suser:cmd:::/usr/bin/mt:euid=0
Printer Management:suser:cmd:::/usr/sbin/accept:euid=lp
File System Management:suser:cmd:::/usr/sbin/format:uid=0
User Security:suser:cmd:::/usr/bin/passwd:uid=0
File System Management:suser:cmd:::/usr/sbin/unshareall:uid=0;gid=root
Software Installation:suser:cmd:::/usr/bin/pkginfo:uid=0
File System Management:suser:cmd:::/usr/lib/fs/autofs/automount:euid=0
Object Access Management:suser:cmd:::/usr/bin/getfacl:euid=0
File System Management:suser:cmd:::/usr/sbin/fsck:euid=0
Printer Management:suser:cmd:::/usr/bin/lpstat:euid=0
File System Management:suser:cmd:::/usr/sbin/mountall:uid=0
All:suser:cmd:::*:
Printer Management:suser:cmd:::/usr/bin/disable:euid=lp
Cron Management:suser:cmd:::/usr/bin/crontab:euid=0
Object Access Management:suser:cmd:::/usr/bin/chown:euid=0
Name Service Security:suser:cmd:::/usr/sbin/rpc.nisd:uid=0;gid=0
Network Management:suser:cmd:::/usr/bin/setuname:euid=0
...
```

There are several hundred entries in the default exec_attr database. As you can see, some of the profiles listed in prof_attr are represented in this sampling (in fact, all profiles are represented in the full exec_attr file).

One interesting entry to note is All:suser:cmd:::*:. This grants everyone with the All profile (basically, everybody) the ability to run every command. This is necessary so that users can run both privileged and normal commands, such as ls and cd. If you worry that this might be a security hole, it's not. Notice that no attributes are listed. Because there are no attributes, users will run the commands with their own GID and UID, meaning that normal security measures are followed. However, if you were to append the All: line with an attribute of uid=0, then all users could run all commands as if they were the superuser. For most networks, this probably isn't a very good idea.

Managing RBAC

The developers at Sun did an excellent job of setting up RBAC. There are a large number of rights profiles, execution policies, and authorizations built into Solaris. The one thing that's missing is roles. Sun didn't include a lot of roles with Solaris because each network is different and, consequently, each network will make use of roles in different ways. Although Sun has their recommended way of setting up roles, they realize that network administrators need the flexibility to configure them as they see fit.

Most of the management of RBAC involves creating and maintaining roles. You will need to create roles, assign users to the roles, and decide which abilities will be granted to the roles. You can manage roles through the command-line interface, or graphically with the Solaris Management Console.

Creating and Managing Roles from the Command Line

When you create a role, you are creating what amounts to a user in Solaris, down to the additions of the role in the /etc/passwd and /etc/shadow files. (The role account is also added to the /etc/user_attr file.) The big difference between roles and users is that you cannot log directly into Solaris by using a role. You must log in with a valid user account and then use the su command to assume the role's identity. The three primary commands you will use to create and manage roles are roleadd, rolemod, and roledel. Not surprisingly, these three commands behave a lot like the useradd, usermod, and userdel commands that you learned about in Chapter 4, "User and Group Administration."

Before creating a role, carefully plan what you want the role to be able to do. For example, will the role be able to reset user passwords? Or will the role be able to back up and restore file systems from tape backup? There is no limit to the number of roles you can create or to the combination of profiles and authorizations you can assign to one role. However, it's a good idea to carefully plan your security structure before haphazardly creating roles. To create a role, you use the roleadd command. Here's the syntax for roleadd:

roleadd *arguments role_username*

Most of the command-line arguments are the same as for useradd. Table 13.3 lists some of the more important arguments for roleadd.

TABLE 13.3   *roleadd* Command-Line Arguments

Argument	Description
-A *authorization*	Adds one or more authorizations (separated by commas) to the role.
-c *comment*	Provides an optional description of the role.
-d *dir*	Specifies a home directory for the role account.
-e *date*	Sets an expiration date for the role.

TABLE 13.3   *roleadd* Command-Line Arguments *(continued)*

Argument	Description
-g *group*	Defines a primary group for the role.
-G *group*	Defines one or more secondary groups for the role.
-m	Creates the new role's home directory if it does not already exist.
-P *profile*	Adds one or more rights profiles to the role. Multiple rights profiles are separated by commas. Also remember that because profiles often have spaces in their names, you need to enclose them in quotes—for example, roleadd -P "Media Restore".
-s *shell*	Specifies a shell for the role account. The default is /bin/sh.
-u *UID*	Specifies a UID for the role. Roles take UIDs just as user accounts do.

Creating a role does you no good unless you grant the role specific authorizations and/or rights profiles. Therefore, the –A and –P arguments are of critical importance. After the role is created, you can add additional authorizations and rights profiles by using the rolemod command.

If you wanted to add a role named passmgr to be able to reset user passwords, here's how you could do it:

roleadd -P "User Security" passmgr

Now, the passmgr role exists. As you might imagine, if you have a long list of profiles or authorizations to add for a role, the roleadd command can get quite long.

Even though the passmgr role exists, there are no users that can use the role. Not only that, but just as if you created a user from the command line, the role is disabled until you provide a password for the role. First, provide a password:

passwd passmgr

Then, associate a user with the role. For example, if you wanted your junior administrator sjohnson to be able to change user passwords, you could associate his account with the role by using the following command:

usermod -R passmgr sjohnson

Now, the sjohnson user will be able to use the su passmgr command to access the passmgr role.

The usermod –P command can be used to assign profiles directly to user accounts. However, to maintain tighter security, it's best to create roles, assign the profiles to roles, and then associate a user account to the role.

If you have an existing role and want to make changes to it, you can use the rolemod command. The rolemod command uses most of the same arguments as the usermod command. Using rolemod -A or rolemod -P will replace the existing authorizations or profiles, not add to the existing ones.

To delete a role, use roledel. If you want to delete the role's home directory as well, use roledel -r.

Viewing Roles, Authorizations, and Profiles

If you are logged in as a user, how can you tell which roles, authorizations, or profiles you can use? There are three commands to help you with this: roles, auths, and profiles. Consider the following sequence:

```
$ whoami
sjohnson
$ roles sjohnson
passmgr
$ profiles sjohnson
All
Basic Solaris User
$
```

Similarly, if you used the auths sjohnson command, you would see a long list of authorizations assigned to the sjohnson account. Notice that when you looked at the profiles, only the profiles for the current user account were listed, not the profiles available for the roles that sjohnson can assume.

Using Other RBAC Management Commands

Additional commands are available to manage roles, as well as create rights profiles and execution attributes. Keep in mind that if you want to directly manage profiles, authorizations, and rights profiles, you can manually edit the prof_attr, auth_attr, and exec_attr databases.

The additional commands you can use are smexec (for managing exec_attr), smuser (for managing user entries), smmultiuser (for managing multiple user entries), smprofile (for managing the prof_attr and exec_attr files), and smrole (for managing roles). Each of the sm* commands require authentication to use. For more information on each of these commands, please see the man pages associated with each command.

Creating and Managing Roles by Using the Solaris Management Console

Using the Solaris Management Console to manage RBAC is a lot easier than using the command line. For one, you will be presented with a readable list of rights that you can assign to the role. Adding a role is done from the Administrative Roles node of the Solaris Management Console, as shown in Figure 13.1. No administrative roles are included here by default; however, Figure 13.1 shows the passmgr role created earlier in this chapter.

FIGURE 13.1 Administrative roles

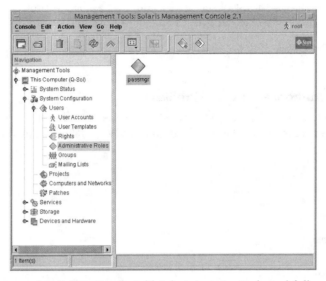

To create a new role, click Action ➢ Add Administrative Role and follow these steps:

1. Provide a role name, full name, description, and role ID number, and choose a shell for the role. Click Next.

2. Type the password for the role. The password must contain at least six characters, with at least two alphabetic and one numeric or special character. Click Next.

3. Select rights for the role. As you can see in the following graphic, some of the rights listed are categories (Operator and System Administrator are examples). Clicking the lever to the left of these categories displays more available rights. (These categories are the authorizations that ended in a period in the auth_attr database.) After you have chosen rights for this role, click Next.

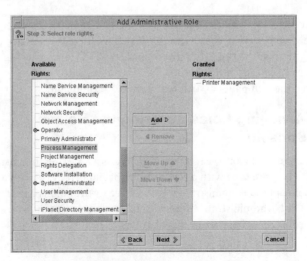

4. Select a home directory for the role. Click Next.

5. Assign users to the role. After you have assigned users, click Next.

6. On the Add Administrative Role screen, confirm that your choices are correct, and click Finish to create the role. If you want to make any changes, click Back.

After the role is created, you can manage the role by selecting the role in the right pane of the Solaris Management Console and viewing its properties. To do so, either right-click the role and choose Properties, or highlight the role and choose Action ➢ Properties. You will see a screen similar to the one shown in Figure 13.2.

FIGURE 13.2   Role properties

The two most useful tabs in Properties are the Users tab and the Rights tab. On the Users tab, you can assign additional users to the role. The Rights tab enables you to assign additional rights.

To delete a role from within the Solaris Management Console, right-click the role and choose Delete, or highlight the role and choose Edit ➢ Delete.

 Real World Scenario

Easing Your Administrative Burden

You are the only network administrator for a small engineering firm, which has approximately 40 employees. Recently, the company has grown, and so has the network. Because of your increasing responsibilities within the organization, you are finding it difficult to perform your daily network management tasks. However, there is neither enough work nor the budget to hire another administrator.

Fortunately, you've been allowed to procure some junior administrators from the ranks of the current employees. These employees will be trained by you and given some administrative duties but will also retain their current position. You will be allowed to select three people. You will need to decide which tasks they will perform, train them, and make sure they can do their new jobs.

The first thing you should do is to decide which types of tasks you want these new administrators to perform. You will probably not want to give them full administrative powers, but you do want them to be able to do things like manage printers, manage user accounts (reset passwords, perhaps change group assignments), and load and unload devices.

After you have decided what you want the administrators to do, create roles that can perform the tasks you need. Create the roles and assume their identities to make sure they can do what you want them to do. You have some flexibility in creating roles. One way would be to create a role for each user that can perform all tasks. Another way would be to create a role for each task (such as one for printer management, one for user management, and so on), but that can get confusing because each user would have to remember three (or more) role names and passwords. Finally, you could create one role that can perform all tasks, and let each user know their role name and password. This is probably the easiest solution because you can log su activity as well as the functions the role performs. However, the final decision on how to create your roles is up to you.

By creating roles and using RBAC, you can allow others to perform administrative tasks, while maintaining overall control of the security on your network.

Summary

This chapter covered two important advanced security components of Solaris 9: Access Control Lists and role-based access control.

ACLs are used to supplement the standard UNIX security structure. You learned what an ACL entry looks like, how to create and manage ACLs with the setfacl command, and how to view ACLs with the getfacl command.

Role-based access control enables you to create roles and to assign specialized rights and authorizations to users or roles. Proper use of RBAC will enable you to delegate administrative tasks within your company while maintaining tight security. Roles are managed with the roleadd, rolemod, and roledel commands.

Exam Essentials

Know how to set up and manage ACLs. ACLs are managed with the setfacl command.

Know how to view ACLs. ACLs are viewed with the getfacl command.

Understand what RBAC is used for. RBAC provides a mechanism for administrators to delegate certain administrative duties to junior administrators or users. Administrators can assign roles, rights, or profiles to users, which enables the administrator to also maintain strict security standards.

Know the commands used to manage roles. The commands are `roleadd`, `rolemod`, and `roledel`.

Key Terms

Before you take the exam, be certain you are familiar with the following terms:

Access Control Lists (ACLs)	rights profile
authorization	role
privileged application	role-based access control

Commands Used in This Chapter

The following list contains a summary of all the commands introduced in this chapter:

Command	Description
`getfacl`	Displays Access Control Lists
`roleadd`	Creates roles
`roledel`	Deletes roles
`rolemod`	Modifies roles
`setfacl`	Creates and manages Access Control Lists

Review Questions

1. Examine the following sequence of executed commands and system responses:

   ```
   $ whoami
   user1
   $ su passmgr
   Password:
   Roles can only be assumed by authorized users
   su: Sorry
   $
   ```

   Which of the following statements best describes the results of the command sequence?

   A. The `passmgr` role has not been configured by the administrator or does not exist.

   B. The `user1` has not been authorized to use the `passmgr` role.

   C. The wrong password was supplied for the `passmgr` role.

   D. Someone else is already logged in as the `passmgr` role.

   E. You cannot `su` to a role; you must log in as a role from the login screen.

2. You are the Solaris administrator for a small group of workstations. Because of your current workload, you decide to allow all users to have administrative rights on their workstations. However, you still want them logging in under their own user account. Which of the following solutions meets your needs, without directly granting users access to the superuser account? (Choose all that apply.)

   A. Instruct all users to log in as `root` and give them the `root` password.

   B. Add a line to the `policy.conf` file that reads AUTHS_GRANTED=`solaris.*`.

   C. Add a line to the `user_attr` database that reads AUTHS_GRANTED=`solaris.*`.

   D. Add a line to the `prof_attr` database that reads PROFS_GRANTED=System Administrator.

   E. Add a line to the `policy.conf` file that reads PROFS_GRANTED=Primary Administrator.

3. You have just created a junior administrator role on your Solaris computer. You are going to assign the role, named `jradmin`, to a user named `abradley`. Which of the following commands do you use to perform this task?

   A. `usermod -R jradmin abradley`

   B. `usermod -R abradley jradmin`

   C. `rolemod -R jradmin abradley`

   D. `rolemod -R abradley jradmin`

4. Here is an excerpt from the `user_attr` database:

```
root::::auths=solaris.*,solaris.grant;profiles=All
lp::::profiles=Printer Management
adm::::profiles=Log Management
jradmin::::type=role;auths=solaris.admin.*,solaris.profmgr.*;profiles=All
cmalcolm::::type=normal;roles=jradmin
```

Based on this information, which of the following statements are true? (Choose all that apply.)

A. `jradmin` has full administrative powers on this Solaris computer.

B. Anyone logging in as `cmalcolm` can use same authorizations and profiles as `jradmin`.

C. `jradmin` is a user account on this Solaris computer.

D. `cmalcolm` is a user account on this Solaris computer.

5. Which of the following RBAC-related files contain information about both authorizations and profiles? (Choose all that apply.)

A. `user_attr`

B. `auth_attr`

C. `prof_attr`

D. `exec_attr`

E. `policy.conf`

6. Examine the following command sequence:

```
# ls -l
-rw-rw-r--  1 qdocter  author       880 Nov 29 13:46 doc1
-rwxr-----  1 qdocter  author       880 Nov 29 14:04 file1
# setfacl -s u::rwx,g::r--,o:---,m:r--,u:3486:rw- doc1
```

Which of the following statements are true regarding the results of the command sequence? (Choose all that apply.)

A. The `qdocter` user will still have only read and write permissions on `doc1`.

B. The `author` group will still have only read and write permissions on `doc1`.

C. Anyone not belonging to the `author` group will not have any access to `doc1`.

D. The 3486 user will have read and write permissions to `doc1`.

E. The `qdocter` user will have read, write, and execute permissions on `doc1`.

7. You are configuring RBAC for your Solaris server. Instead of using the command line, you want to manually edit the RBAC database files. Which of the following files is not located in the /etc/security directory?

   A. `user_attr`

   B. `auth_attr`

   C. `prof_attr`

   D. `exec_attr`

   E. `policy.conf`

8. You are the Solaris security administrator for your network. You are going to configure an Access Control List on a file that several users need access to. Which of the following statements are true regarding setting the ACL? (Choose all that apply.)

   A. Setting an ACL will override any existing permissions on the file.

   B. To display any of the permissions set by the `setfacl` command, you must use the `getfacl` command.

   C. The ACL will enable you to assign individual permissions to each user needing access to the file.

   D. To create the ACL on a file that does not have one, you must use the `setfacl -s` command.

9. Examine the following information:

   `# getfacl doc1`

   ```
   # file: doc1
   # owner: qdocter
   # group: author
   user::rwx
   user:3856:rw-        #effective:rw-
   group::r--           #effective:r--
   mask:r--
   other:---
   ```

   One of these lines has been modified from the real `getfacl` output. Which piece of information from this simulated `getfacl` output must be incorrect, based on the rules for ACLs?

   A. `user::rwx`

   B. `user:3856:rw-  #effective:rw-`

   C. `group::r--  #effective:r--`

   D. `mask:r--`

   E. `other:---`

10. You have created an Access Control List on a file named `abcfile`. Now, you want to delete the Access Control List. Which command do you execute to perform this task?

A. `setfacl -s abcfile`

B. `setfacl -r abcfile`

C. `setfacl -d abcfile`

D. `setfacl -m none abcfile`

11. You are the Solaris administrator for your network. You want to grant one rights policy to all users on the network. Which file can you edit to accomplish this in one step?

A. `user_attr`

B. `prof_attr`

C. `auth_attr`

D. `policy.conf`

12. Here is an excerpt from the `user_attr` database:

```
root::::auths=solaris.*,solaris.grant;profiles=All
lp::::profiles=Printer Management
adm::::profiles=Log Management
jradmin::::type=role;auths=solaris.admin.*,solaris.profmgr.*;profiles=All
jgebelt::::type=normal;roles=admin2,jradmin;auths=solaris.jobs.*
admin2::::type=role;auths=solaris.*
```

Based on this information, which of the following statements are true? (Choose all that apply.)

A. `admin2` has full administrative powers on this Solaris computer.

B. `jradmin` has full administrative powers on this Solaris computer.

C. The `admin2` account has more power than the `jradmin` account.

D. The `jgebelt` user can use `su` to assume the role of `admin2`, and then while logged in as `admin2`, use `su` to assume `jradmin`.

13. You are the security administrator for your network. A file named `app1` has an existing Access Control List. You want to change the ACL to include additional users, while keeping the existing settings. Which of the following commands would you execute to perform this task?

A. `setfacl -s app1`

B. `setfacl -m app1`

C. `setfacl -d app1`

D. `setfacl -r app1`

14. Here is an excerpt from one of the RBAC databases:

```
Software Installation:suser:cmd:::/usr/bin/pkginfo:uid=0
File System Management:suser:cmd:::/usr/lib/fs/autofs/automount:euid=0
Object Access Management:suser:cmd:::/usr/bin/getfacl:euid=0
```

Which one of the databases is this data from?

A. user_attr

B. auth_attr

C. prof_attr

D. exec_attr

E. policy.conf

15. Examine the following information, which is the complete output from an executed command (which is blacked out for obvious reasons):

```
# ███████████

# file:  ███████
# owner: abradley
# group: mdte
default:user::rwx
default:group::r--
default:mask:rw-
default:other:---
```

Based on this information, which of the following statements must be true? (Choose all that apply.)

A. The command executed was getfacl -d.

B. The output displayed is for a directory.

C. Because the mask value is set to rw-, the group permissions should be at least rw-.

D. Because this output displays only default settings, the ACL is not enabled on this file.

16. Examine the following information:

```
# getfacl doc1

# file: doc1
# owner: jgebelt
# group: cpuguru
user::rwx
user:3856:rw-        #effective:rw-
group::r--           #effective:r--
mask:rw-
other:---
```

Which of the following commands did you execute to configure this ACL?

A. `setfacl -s u:7,g:4,o:0,m:6,u:3856:6 doc1`

B. `setfacl -s u:3856:6,g::4,o:0,m:6 doc1`

C. `setfacl -s u::7,g::4,o:0,m:6,u:3856:6 doc1`

D. `setfacl -s u::7,g::6,o:0,m:4,u:3856:6 doc1`

17. You are the senior Solaris administrator for your company. One of the junior administrators has been assigned the task of granting 10 users access to a project file. Each of the users will need read and write access to the file. The users are from several departments, and for logistical reasons (potential security difficulties), you have instructed the junior administrator not to create a group for the individuals involved in the project. Now he is confused as to how to best apply security on the file. What do you instruct him to do?

A. Create an Access Control List for each user that needs access to the file. Within each ACL, set the appropriate permissions for an individual user.

B. Create one Access Control List for the file and add each user to the ACL. In the ACL, grant each user the appropriate permissions to the file.

C. Create a role and give the role ownership of the file, including read and write permissions. Give each user the role's username and password, and instruct them to use the role to access the file.

D. Create 10 copies of the file, each in the same directory. Make each user the owner of one copy. Grant the users the appropriate permissions to their file. Instruct the users to use their file only. Create a batch job to concatenate the files into one master project file at midnight each night.

18. You are the Solaris security administrator for your company. You have just set up an ACL on a file named `phonelist`, and you want to configure the exact same ACL on a file named `addresses`. What is the easiest way you can accomplish this task using the Bourne shell (sh)?

    A. Use the `setfacl` command to create a new ACL for the `addresses` file, using the same parameters you used for `phonelist`.

    B. Create a copy of the `phonelist` file. Rename the new file to `addresses`.

    C. Use the `getfacl phonelist | setfacl -f - addresses` command to copy the ACL from `phonelist` to `addresses`.

    D. Use the `getfacl phonelist | setfacl addresses` command to copy the ACL from `phonelist` to `addresses`.

19. Examine the following command sequence:

    ```
    # ls -l
    -rw-rw-r-- 1 qdocter  author      880 Nov 29 13:46 doc1
    -rwxr----- 1 qdocter  author      880 Nov 29 14:04 file1
    # setfacl -s u::rwx,g::rw-,o:---,m:rw-,u:3486:rw- doc1
    ```

    Which of the following statements are true regarding the results of the command sequence? (Choose all that apply.)

    A. When you run `ls -l`, the permission structure for `doc1` will appear unchanged, except for a + at the end indicating that an ACL is present.

    B. The `author` group will still have only read and write permissions on `doc1`.

    C. Anyone not belonging to the `author` group will have read and write access to `doc1`.

    D. The 3486 user will have read and write permissions to `doc1`.

    E. The `qdocter` user will have read, write, and execute permissions on `doc1`.

20. Here is an excerpt from one of the RBAC databases:

    ```
    Media Restore:::Restore files and file systems from backups: \
        help=RtMediaRestore.html
    User Management:::Manage users, groups, home directory: \
        auths=solaris.profmgr.read,solaris.admin.usermgr.write, \
        solaris.admin.usermgr.read;help=RtUserMngmnt.html
    ```

    Which one of the databases is this data from?

    A. `user_attr`

    B. `auth_attr`

    C. `prof_attr`

    D. `exec_attr`

    E. `policy.conf`

Answers to Review Questions

1.   B.   If you try to use a role that you do not have access to, you will receive this error message. If the role did not exist, you would receive a message that the ID was unknown. Supplying an incorrect password will result in only su: Sorry. You must use su to assume a role.

2.   B, E.   By giving all users the root username and password, you are giving them direct access to the root user account. Instead, either add an authorization for all users in policy.conf for solaris.*, or grant a profile of Primary Administrator. Neither the user_attr nor the prof_attr databases use the *keyword=value* pairing used in the answers.

3.   A.   Users are associated with roles through the usermod command, not the rolemod command. The proper syntax is usermod -R *rolename username*.

4.   B, D.   The jradmin account is a role, not a user account. This is identified by the type=role key pair. The cmalcolm account is a user account (type=normal), and has been authorized to use the jradmin role. Therefore, anyone logging in as cmalcolm (and has the password for jradmin) can assume jradmin's role.

5.   A, E.   The user_attr file contains user and role accounts, and can contain associations for both authorizations and profiles. The auth_attr file contains only authorizations, the prof_attr file contains only profiles, and exec_attr contains execution attributes. Authorizations and profiles can be assigned to all users in the policy.conf file.

6.   C, E.   The setfacl command set an Access Control List on the file doc1. When you use setfacl, the existing permissions on the file are replaced by the new permissions set by the ACL. Therefore, the user (owner) will have rwx, as specified by u::rwx. The author group will be granted Read-only access (g::r--), and everyone else will have no access (o::---). The 3486 user will have only Read permission, as the mask is set to r--, limiting the user to Read-only, even though they were explicitly granted Read and Write.

7.   A.   The full path for the user database is /etc/user_attr. All of the other files listed are in /etc/security.

8.   A, C, D.   When you enable an ACL, it will override any existing permissions on the file. ACLs are set with the setfacl -s command and enable you to set separate permissions for each user or group that needs access to the file. Using the ls -l command will still display permissions set for the owner and group (which are set in the ACL); you don't need to run getfacl. However, to see the permissions for the additional users, you will need to use getfacl.

9.   B.   Because the mask is set to r--, other users can have no more than read access. Therefore, the effective rights for user 3856 cannot be rw-.

10.   C.   ACLs are deleted with the setfacl -d command. The -s switch sets a new ACL (and requires parameters to configure the ACL), the -r switch recalculates the mask, and -m modifies the ACL, although none is not a valid option.

11.   D.   Authorizations or profiles assigned in the policy.conf file affect all users who use the computer.

12. A, B, C. The admin2 account has been granted the solaris.* authorization, meaning that the role has access to all administrative functions of Solaris. It's also more powerful than the jradmin role, which has many, but not all, administrative powers. The jgebelt user can assume the role of either admin account, but the admin2 account does not have authorization to assume jradmin. When someone uses su to assume the role of another user or role, all of their security settings become those of the new user or role.

13. B. The setfacl -m command is used to modify an existing ACL. The -s switch replaces any current settings. The -r switch recalculates the mask, and -d deletes the ACL.

14. D. The information presented is a list of three execution attributes. They are the only database entries to contain uid or euid entries. These are stored in the /etc/security/exec_attr database.

15. A, B. This output is from a getfacl -d command run on a directory. Directories have default settings, but files do not. Also, the mask limits the maximum permissions for users other than the owner (and the owner's group), not the minimum permissions. After an ACL is created, it is enabled by default.

16. C. To set an ACL, you must use the setfacl -s command. The third answer uses the correct syntax for setting the ACL for the doc1 file.

17. B. You can create only one ACL per file, but you can list as many individual users in an ACL as you want to. This is by far the best (and only plausible) solution presented.

18. C. You can copy an ACL by piping the output from getfacl to the setfacl command for the new file. However, you must use setfacl -f - filename for the piped destination. Using setfacl again to create another ACL would be more work than is necessary. Creating a copy of the phonelist file will copy the ACL. However, it's unlikely that you want to overwrite your address list with a phone list.

19. B, D, E. The setfacl command set an Access Control List on the file doc1. When you use setfacl, the existing permissions on the file are replaced by the new permissions set by the ACL, and the new permissions are reflected by the ls -l command. Based on the command, the user (owner) will have rwx, as specified by u::rwx. The author group will be granted read and write access (g::rw-), and everyone else will have no access (o:---). The 3486 user will have read and write permission, as they were granted rw-, and the mask enables other users to have read and write access.

20. C. The information presented is two profiles: the Media Restore profile and the User Management profile. Profiles are stored in the /etc/security/prof_attr database.

Chapter
14

Auditing and System Messaging

SOLARIS 9 EXAM OBJECTIVES COVERED IN THIS CHAPTER:

✓ Describe the fundamentals of the syslog function including the /etc/syslog.conf file and the relationship between syslogd and m4 macro processor.

✓ Explain how to configure system messaging, including configuring the /etc/syslog.conf, modifying the inetd process and using the logger command.

Ideally, when you install Solaris on your computer, everything will run perfectly. And when you configure a large number of computers on a network, everything will be fine as well. Realistically, though, this ideal computing world does not exist. The major problems that can happen, such as getting hacked or having a server crash, will always get your attention. However, the smaller problems, such as failed services, problematic daemons, and minor security breaches, can go unnoticed.

If you set up your computer to perform system logging (also called auditing), a notice for all problems—both major and minor—can be recorded and then viewed at a later time, as well as sent to the console you are logged into. By enabling system logging and messaging, you can have a record of major system events, and you can also note smaller problems and do something about them before they turn into bigger ones.

Managing System Logging

If one of your mail services crashes, you will want to be notified. If a daemon fails, or if someone is trying to hack into the network, you will want to know as well. Solaris provides a centralized logging service, called *syslog*, to keep track of these types of events through *system logging*. The *syslogd* daemon manages system logging. It is responsible for retrieving and logging messages, as well as forwarding alerts to the proper users and consoles.

Thus far in this chapter, the scope of system logging has been limited to critical events. However, syslog messages can range from emergency-type alerts to notices that don't require immediate attention to informational postings. One of the benefits of syslog is that it's very flexible.

The syslogd daemon depends on the presence of the m4 macro processor to operate properly. The m4 macro processor is a UNIX-standard front-end processor intended for use with the C, assembler, and other programming languages. m4 helps syslogd process messages and is also capable of performing integer arithmetic, file inclusions, conditional macro expansions, and string and substring manipulations. Macros, in general, enable you to create short programs to automate repetitive tasks, thus saving you work. Because the logging and sending of messages generated from auditing is a repetitive task, the m4 macro processor fits in perfectly with system auditing. The support files for m4 are located in /usr/ccs/bin/m4. For more information, type **man m4** at the command prompt.

During boot, syslogd is started by the /etc/rc2.d/S74syslog script. The syslogd daemon reads the STREAMS log driver (/dev/log), the /etc/netconfig file, and the /etc/syslog.conf file for configuration information, and then creates the /etc/syslog.pid file, which contains its process ID. Rebooting the system or sending a HUP (hangup) signal to `syslogd` will cause it to restart and reconfigure itself. Information on the behavior of `syslogd` is stored in /etc/default/syslogd. For example, in /etc/default/syslogd, you can configure `syslogd` to log remote messages in addition to local messages with the line LOG_FROM_REMOTE=YES. A value of NO disables remote logging. By default, this line is commented out.

Most error messages collected by `syslogd` are logged in the /var/adm directory and written to the local console. However, logging behavior is configurable through the /etc/syslog.conf file.

Configuring *syslog.conf*

The single most critical configuration file for system auditing and messaging is the /etc/syslog.conf file. Entries in the `syslog.conf` file have two fields: a `selector` and an `action`. These fields are separated by tabs. The `selector` field consists of a pair of keywords, a `facility` and a `level`, and classifies both the source of the message and the level of severity of the problem. The `action` field can take one of four forms and defines the action to take based on the message type received.

Table 14.1 lists the valid `facility` keywords.

TABLE 14.1   facility Keywords

Value	Description
user	Messages generated by user processes. Also used for applications, programs, or other facilities not explicitly listed in this file.
kern	Messages generated by the system kernel.
mail	sendmail messages.
daemon	Messages generated by recognized system daemons.
auth	The Solaris authorization system, such as login, su, and getty.
lpr	Printing messages and errors.
news	The USENET network news system.
uucp	Reserved for future UUCP logging, as UUCP currently does not use syslog.
cron	cron/at messages. Includes crontab, atq, and associated commands.
local0-7	Reserved for local system use.
mark	Timestamp messages produced by syslogd.
*	Indicates all facilities except for mark.

Facilities are paired with levels to complete the `selector` field. The valid `level` values are listed in Table 14.2, in decreasing order of severity.

T A B L E   1 4 . 2   `level` Keywords

Value	Description
emerg	Panic conditions, normally broadcast to all logged-in users.
alert	Situations that should be corrected immediately, such as a corrupted system database.
crit	Critical conditions, such as unrecoverable device errors.
err	Other errors.
warning	Warning messages.
notice	Conditions that are not error messages but might require special handling.
info	Informational messages.
debug	Messages used for the debugging of programs.
none	Does not send a message from the facility to the log file. Using the none keyword effectively turns off auditing for that facility.

 The severity level priorities are defined in the sys/syslog.h file (the actual physical location will depend on your computer's platform).

After the `selector` field is the `action` field. There are four possibilities for actions:

- A filename indicating where to write messages generated by the `selector` field. New messages will be appended to the existing message file. If the file specified does not exist, logging will silently fail.

- The name of a remote host, in the form of *@computer*. The message will be forwarded to `syslogd` on the remote host and processed accordingly.

- A list of usernames, separated by commas. If the specified users are logged in, a message will be written to the console they are logged into.

- An asterisk, which means that the message generated will be written to all logged-in users.

Here is a sample /etc/syslog.conf file:

```
#ident     "@(#)syslog.conf   1.5    98/12/14 SMI"     /* SunOS 5.0 */
#
# Copyright (c) 1991-1998 by Sun Microsystems, Inc.
# All rights reserved.
#
# syslog configuration file.
#
# This file is processed by m4 so be careful to quote (`') names
# that match m4 reserved words.  Also, within ifdef's, arguments
# containing commas must be quoted.
#
*.err;kern.notice;auth.notice          /dev/sysmsg
*.err;kern.debug;daemon.notice;mail.crit /var/adm/messages

*.alert;kern.err;daemon.err            operator
*.alert                                root

*.emerg                                    *

# if a non-loghost machine chooses to have authentication messages
# sent to the loghost machine, un-comment out the following line:
#auth.notice              ifdef(`LOGHOST', /var/log/authlog, @loghost)

mail.debug               ifdef(`LOGHOST', /var/log/syslog, @loghost)

#
# non-loghost machines will use the following lines to cause "user"
# log messages to be logged locally.
#
ifdef(`LOGHOST', ,
user.err                      /dev/sysmsg
user.err                      /var/adm/messages
user.alert                    `root, operator'
user.emerg                        *
)
```

Blank lines are ignored, and lines beginning with a pound sign (#) are comments (they're not processed—they're there only for our information). The syslog.conf file can use ifdef statements to explain actions to the m4 processor. In other words, "If A exists, do B." In the syslog.conf file, ifdef statements allow for three arguments (enclosed in parentheses and separated by commas). The first is the `if` condition, the second is the `def` condition for when the `if` exists, and the third is the `def` condition for when the `if` does not exist. For more information, type **man m4** at the command prompt.

Now that you know what the `ifdef` statement means, take a look at the selector and actions pairs, separate from the rest of the file:

```
*.err;kern.notice;auth.notice             /dev/sysmsg
*.err;kern.debug;daemon.notice;mail.crit  /var/adm/messages
*.alert;kern.err;daemon.err               operator
*.alert                                   root
*.emerg                                   *
```

The first line logs all errors, kernel notices, and authorization notices to the `/dev/sysmsg` file. The second line sends all errors, kernel debugs, daemon notices, and critical mail problems to the `/var/adm/messages` file. The third line sends all alerts, kernel errors, and daemon errors to the `operator` user. The fourth line sends all alerts to the `root`, if they are logged in, and the last line will, in the event of an emergency, write a message to the console of every logged-in user.

To illustrate some of the other options, here are a few more lines:

```
mail.debug          /var/spool/mqueue/logfile
auth.*              @server1
```

The first line will send any mail debug messages to the `/var/spool/mqueue/logfile` file, and the second line will send any messages involving Solaris authorization to the `server1` computer. You can also disable messaging for a service, such as with this option:

```
*.debug;mail.none   /var/adm/messages
```

This will log all debug messages but disable mail messages. Because the mail system, `sendmail`, logs a lot of messages, this might not be a bad idea. Just keep in mind, though, that if you're troubleshooting an e-mail problem, the messages generated by `sendmail` can be extremely helpful.

Managing Log Files

Solaris has a number of built-in log files that it uses to store information. Most of the log files are located in the `/var/adm` directory, although you can place log files in any file system you want (but it's best to avoid `/tmp` for obvious reasons).

Here is a list of some of the more important log files:

- `/var/adm/messages` lists information that prints to the local console. This file will usually include all root logins and can grow very large very fast.

- `/var/adm/lastlog` contains the most recent login time for each user in the system.

- `/var/adm/utmpx` stores user access and accounting information. Running the `who` command will display information from this file.

- /var/adm/wtmpx holds a history of user access to the system. Running the last command will pull information on the last logged-in user, from this file.

- /var/adm/sulog shows all su attempts, both successful and failed.

- /var/log/syslog displays logged system information.

- /var/cron/log tracks all cron and at activity.

Because most logs are located in /var/adm anyway, most administrators will create their own specific logs there as well. But as was mentioned earlier in this chapter, if you attempt to log to a file that does not exist, the logging will silently fail. Therefore, if you intend to use your own unique log file, you need to ensure that it's created and ready for use. For example, if you wanted to create a log file named /var/adm/adminlog, you could follow these steps:

```
# touch /var/adm/adminlog
# chmod 600 adminlog
```

You'll also want to verify the ownership of the log file because you don't want the log falling into the wrong hands.

Log files can get very large, so you will want to periodically clean out old log files to save hard disk space. Also, log files are rotated by Solaris through the logadm command listed in the root crontab file. (The old method of using the /usr/lib/newsyslog script is no longer used.) To define the system log rotation, edit the /etc/logadm.conf file. Old log files are renamed with a numeric extension. For example, when a new syslog file is created, the old file becomes syslog.0, and the next recent file becomes syslog.1, and so on.

Using the *logger* Command

System logging is an automatic process. You configure it, and then logging happens automatically based on system events occurring. Although automatic logging is convenient, at times you might want to manually add an entry into the system log. For example, you might want to add a line to the system log as a bookmark (perhaps you've reviewed the log up to that point), or you might want to log a note describing why you manually rebooted the server. You can do this from the command line with the logger command.

Here is the syntax for logger:

```
# logger arguments message
```

The logger command supports four arguments. They are listed in Table 14.3.

TABLE 14.3   *logger* Command-Line Arguments

Argument	Description
-f *file*	Logs the contents of the specified *file*.
-i	Includes the process ID of the logger command with each line logged.

TABLE 14.3 *logger* Command-Line Arguments *(continued)*

Argument	Description
-p *priority*	Enters the message with the specified priority, in the form of *facility.level*. The default priority is user.notice.
-t *tag*	Marks each line added to the log with the specified *tag*.

You can supply one message to log at a time, unless you use a file to log. In that case, each line of the file is logged separately. You'll notice that the default priority is user.notice. If you look at the default /etc/syslog.conf file provided earlier in this chapter, you will see no default destinations for user.notice. So, if you want logger to actually log something, you will either need to reconfigure your syslog.conf file (and restart syslogd), or use another priority, such as user.err (or another *facility.level* pair that's already set up for logging).

WARNING   If you use *.emerg with the default syslog.conf, the message you log will be written to all users logged into your Solaris computer, so be careful what you say!

Configuring the *inetd* Process

The Internet services daemon (inetd) is a critical process for logging connections over networks. Started during the Solaris boot process, inetd actively listens for remote service requests on the TCP or UDP ports associated with the services listed in its configuration file. When a request is received, inetd starts the local process associated with the request.

inetd is responsible for allowing remote connections and is capable of logging all remote TCP or UDP connections. Both IPv4 and IPv6 are supported by inetd. The configuration file for inetd is /etc/inetd.conf. Another important file for the inetd daemon is /etc/default/inetd, which contains the parameter to enable connection logging.

The /etc/default/inetd file has two parameters: ENABLE_CONNECTION_LOGGING and ENABLE_TCPWRAPPERS. Both settings are commented out (as well as set to NO) by default. If you want to log all incoming connections, you need to change ENABLE_CONNECTION_LOGGING to YES and uncomment the line.

TIP   Disabling unneeded connection types in the inetd.conf file is a good way to increase your network security. If the services are disabled, no one can connect to your computer by using them nor use the ports that those services use as a back door to hack your computer.

For security purposes, it's a good idea to log all incoming requests on important machines such as servers. This is especially true for servers that can be directly accessed from the Internet, such as e-mail, web, or FTP servers.

Real World Scenario

Making Your Troubleshooting Easier

You have been the Solaris administrator at your company for just over a year. Most of the time, the network operates with few problems. Occasionally, however, "mysterious" problems develop, and it seems to take you a long time to figure out why the problem is happening. After you track down the problem, you can usually fix it quickly. The more common problems involve the e-mail server and printing, but you're also concerned about potential security breaches.

You're constantly looking for tools to help you in your troubleshooting. One of the things you can do is use system messaging to your advantage. Create separate log files for the e-mail and print servers, and set up the syslog.conf file (with the mail and lpr facilities) to log e-mail and printer messages to their respective files. You can also set up an additional log file to track all user logins, using the auth facility in the syslog.conf file.

The log files themselves won't fix your problems, but at least the messages contained within can help you track down the problem in less time than it would take you otherwise.

Summary

This chapter covered the auditing of system events and the logs that hold the messages generated from audited events.

The syslog facility is the logging mechanism for Solaris 9 and is managed by the syslogd daemon. The primary configuration file for syslogd is /etc/syslog.conf, and the other file controlling syslog behavior is /etc/default/syslogd.

If you want to manually create entries in log files, you can use the logger command. The logger command enables you to enter your own comments or import data from existing files to be logged.

Finally, this chapter covered the Internet services daemon, inetd. The inetd daemon is responsible for listening for and responding to remote service requests. Although the /etc/inetd.conf file is considered the primary configuration file, the /etc/default/inetd file enables you to choose whether you want to log all incoming network requests.

Exam Essentials

Know which daemon controls system auditing.   Auditing is controlled by the syslogd daemon.

Know which configuration file contains the option to enable remote logging.   The option LOG_FROM_REMOTE=YES is contained in the /etc/default/syslogd file.

Know how to read the /etc/syslog.conf file. All entries start with a keyword pair of *facility.level*. Then, after a tab, an action is specified, such as writing to a file or sending a message to a logged-in user's console.

Know the facilities in syslog.conf. The possible facilities are user, kern, mail, daemon, auth, lpr, news, uucp, cron, local0-7, mark, and * (meaning all).

Know the levels of severity of events in syslog.conf. From most severe to least, the levels are emerg, alert, crit, err, warning, notice, info, debug, and none.

Know how to manually add entries to the system log. Logs are manually updated with the logger command.

Know what inetd is responsible for. The Internet services daemon is responsible for listening for and responding to all incoming TCP and UDP connections.

Key Terms

Before you take the exam, be certain you are familiar with the following terms:

syslog

syslogd

system logging

Commands Used in This Chapter

The following list contains a summary of all the commands introduced in this chapter:

Command	Description
logger	Manually adds entries to the system log file

Review Questions

1. You are the Solaris security administrator for your network. Aware of the possibility of hackers trying to use brute force to log into your network, you want to enable the logging of all failed login attempts. Which facility do you want to enable for tracking in the `syslog.conf` file?

   A. user

   B. kern

   C. auth

   D. sec

   E. login

   F. security

2. You are configuring auditing for your Solaris 9 server. You want to find out information on the severity levels of entries located in your `syslog.conf` file. Which file can you look in to see how the severity levels are defined to the `syslogd` daemon?

   A. /etc/default/syslogd

   B. /etc/syslogd.conf

   C. /etc/syslog.conf

   D. sys/syslog.h

3. You have recently configured role-based access control (RBAC) on your Solaris server. Three employees within your company have been assigned roles. You want to ensure that only these three employees have used their role accounts. What is the easiest way to check this, without seeing extraneous information?

   A. Examine the /var/adm/sulog file periodically.

   B. Examine the /var/log/syslog file periodically.

   C. Create a line in the /etc/syslog.conf file that reads su.* /var/su/log. Examine the /var/su/log file periodically.

   D. Create a line in the /etc/syslog.conf file that reads auth.* /var/su/log. Examine the /var/su/log file periodically.

4. You are the Solaris server administrator for your company. Your custom-designed accounting database recently crashed and will not open. The `syslog.conf` file on the server that hosts the database is configured with all facilities. Which of the following facilities will generate messages regarding your failed accounting database?

   A. user

   B. kern

   C. daemon

   D. app

   E. alert

   F. err

   G. debug

5. Examine the following excerpt from a `syslog.conf` file:

   ```
   *.err;kern.notice;auth.notice              /dev/sysmsg
   *.err;kern.debug;daemon.notice;mail.crit   /var/adm/messages
   *.alert;kern.err;daemon.err                operator
   *.alert                                    root
   *.emerg                                    *
   mail.debug                                 /var/spool/mqueue/logfile
   auth.*                                     @server1
   ```

   Based on the information provided, which of the following are possible destinations for daemon-generated messages? (Choose all that apply.)

   A. /dev/sysmsg

   B. /var/adm/messages

   C. operator

   D. root

   E. All logged-in users

   F. /var/spool/mqueue/logfile

   G. server1

6. You are configuring logging for all computers on your Solaris 9 network. You want one of your servers to collect logged messages for all computers on the network. Which file do you edit to find the LOG_FROM_REMOTE option to set it to YES?

   A. /etc/syslog.conf

   B. /etc/default/syslogd

   C. /etc/inetd.conf

   D. /etc/default/inetd

7.   You are the primary Solaris administrator for your company. You have recently hired two new network administrators and you need to explain the severity levels of system logging. Which of the following is the correct order of severity, from most severe to least severe?

A. `emerg, crit, alert, err, warning, notice`

B. `emerg, crit, err, alert, warning, notice`

C. `emerg, alert, crit, err, warning, notice`

D. `emerg, alert, err, crit, warning, notice`

8.   Examine the following excerpt from a `syslog.conf` file:

```
*.err;kern.notice;auth.notice              /dev/sysmsg
*.err;kern.debug;daemon.notice;mail.crit   /var/adm/messages
*.alert;kern.err;daemon.err                operator
*.alert                                    root
*.emerg                                    *
auth.*                                     @server1
*.debug;mail.none                          /var/adm/messages
sendmail.*                                 /var/spool/mqueue/log
```

Based on the information provided, where will messages from the `sendmail` service be logged?

A. `/dev/sysmsg`

B. `/var/adm/messages`

C. `server1`

D. `/var/spool/mqueue/log`

E. `sendmail` messages will not be logged.

9.   You are the Solaris administrator for your company. You want to use system logging and you currently have a default `syslog.conf` file on your computer. You've heard that the `logger` command can be used to manually enter comments into the system log file. You execute the following command:

`# logger Testing to see if this logger thing works`

Where should you look to see your logged message?

A. `/dev/sysmsg`

B. `/var/adm/messages`

C. `/var/log/syslog`

D. The console from which you issued the command.

E. The message will not be logged.

10. You are configuring system logging on your Solaris server. Which of the following pairs are valid selectors? (Choose all that apply.)

    A. `news.info`

    B. `auth.warning`

    C. `daemon.err`

    D. `lpr.alert`

11. You are the Solaris server administrator for your company. You are configuring your external e-mail server, and you want it to record a log of all incoming TCP and UDP connections. Which file and option do you need to configure? (Choose two.)

    A. `/etc/default/syslogd`

    B. `/etc/default/inetd`

    C. `/etc/syslog.conf`

    D. `/etc/inetd.conf`

    E. `LOG_FROM_REMOTE=YES`

    F. `ENABLE_CONNECTION_LOGGING=YES`

12. You are the Solaris administrator for your network. You are concerned that your log files generated by `syslog` are getting too large and unmanageable, and you want to rotate the logs more frequently. Which file is responsible for holding the configuration for log file rotation?

    A. `/usr/lib/newsyslog`

    B. `/etc/logadm.conf`

    C. `/etc/syslog.conf`

    D. `/etc/inetd.conf`

13. Examine the following excerpt from a `syslog.conf` file:

    ```
    *.err;kern.notice;auth.notice              /dev/sysmsg
    *.err;kern.debug;daemon.notice;mail.crit   /var/adm/messages
    *.alert;kern.err;daemon.err                operator
    *.alert                                    root
    *.emerg                                    *
    lpr.*                                      /var/adm/log1
    cron.warning                               /var/adm/log2
    info.alert                                 /var/adm/log3
    auth.*                                     /var/adm/log4
    ```

    Based on this information, which log file or files will never receive any messages? (Choose all that apply.)

    A. `/var/adm/log1`

    B. `/var/adm/log2`

    C. `/var/adm/log3`

    D. `/var/adm/log4`

14. You are configuring the `syslog` service for your Solaris 9 server. Which of the following are valid destinations for logged messages? (Choose all that apply.)

   A. A filename on the local computer

   B. A remote computer, in the form of `@computer`

   C. The console of all logged-in users

   D. The console of a specific user or list of users

15. Examine the following excerpt from a `syslog.conf` file:

```
*.emerg                                 *
```

Based on the provided information, where will emergency messages be written?

   A. To all known log files on the computer

   B. To the default system log file on the computer

   C. To the console of the operator logged into the computer

   D. To all logged-in users on the computer

16. You are configuring your Solaris server to support logging. When you boot your Solaris server, which run level starts the `syslog` service?

   A. 1

   B. 2

   C. 3

   D. S

17. You are the Solaris administrator for your network. You are running a routine security audit and want to see who was the last user logged into the computer that you are on. You run the `last` command. From which database does the `last` command pull its data?

   A. /var/adm/wtmpx

   B. /var/adm/utmpx

   C. /var/log/syslog

   D. /var/adm/messages

18. Examine the following excerpt from a `syslog.conf` file:

```
*.err;kern.notice;auth.notice              /dev/sysmsg
*.err;kern.debug;daemon.notice;mail.crit   /var/adm/messages
*.alert;kern.err;daemon.err                operator
*.alert                                    root
*.emerg                                    *
mail.debug                                 /var/spool/mqueue/logfile
auth.*                                     /var/adm/authlog
user.*                                     /var/adm/userlog
```

You want to start tracking user logins as part of your normal security procedures. Which of the following files will contain information about user logins?

A. /dev/sysmsg

B. /var/adm/messages

C. /var/adm/authlog

D. /var/adm/userlog

19. The purpose of this daemon is to collect system messages. It also interfaces with the m4 macro processor and writes system messages to the console if necessary. Which daemon is it?

A. sysd

B. msgd

C. syslogd

D. inetd

20. Examine the following excerpt from a syslog.conf file:

```
*.err;kern.notice;auth.notice              /dev/sysmsg
*.err;kern.debug;daemon.notice;mail.crit   /var/adm/messages
*.alert;kern.err;daemon.err                operator
*.alert                                    root
*.emerg                                    *
mail.*                                     /var/spool/mqueue/logfile
auth.*                                     @server1
```

You have recently implemented the sendmail service on the server by using this syslog.conf file. You have included an option to log all mail messages to the /var/spool/mqueue/logfile file. However, this file does not exist. Which of the following will happen when a sendmail message is generated?

A. The syslog service will attempt to write the message and silently fail.

B. The syslog service will attempt to write the message and will create the file as necessary.

C. The syslog service will attempt to write the message and write an error to the console when the file is not found.

D. The syslog service will write the message to the /var/adm/messages file instead of /var/spool/mqueue/logfile.

E. The syslog service will write the message to the /var/log/syslog file instead of /var/spool/mqueue/logfile.

Answers to Review Questions

1. C. The correct facility for logging security-related events is `auth`. Although `sec`, `login`, and `security` are tempting choices, none of them are legitimate facilities.

2. D. The file containing severity level information is `sys/syslog.h`. The `/etc/default/syslogd` and `/etc/syslog.conf` files contain configuration information for the `syslog` service. The `/etc/syslogd.conf` file does not exist.

3. A. The `/var/adm/sulog` file is built in and it logs all `su` activity. Users must use `su` to assume a role. The `/var/log/syslog` file collects system messages, not security information. In the `syslog.conf` file, `su` is not a valid facility; `auth` is, but it will log all information about security authorizations, which is far more than you want to log in this case.

4. A. The `user` facility logs all user-generated messages, as well as messages from applications not expressly defined in the `syslog.conf` file. Databases are not defined by their own facility in `syslog.conf`; therefore, the `user` facility is correct. The `kern` facility is for kernel errors, and `daemon` is for daemon errors. There is no `app` facility. `alert`, `err`, and `debug` are warning levels, not facilities.

5. A, B, C, D, E. Messages generated by daemons will use the `daemon` facility. The `/var/adm/messages` file and `operator` user are expressly mentioned as `daemon` message recipients in the file. However, a `daemon.alert` could go to the `root` user, a `daemon.emerg` message could be written to all logged-in users, and a `daemon.err` could be written to `/dev/sysmsg`.

6. B. The `LOG_FROM_REMOTE=YES` option is set within the `/etc/default/syslogd` file.

7. C. From most severe to least, the levels are `emerg`, `alert`, `crit`, `err`, `warning`, `notice`, `info`, `debug`, and `none`.

8. E. Because of the `mail.none` setting in the seventh line of the excerpt, `sendmail` messages will not be logged. The word `sendmail` is not a valid facility.

9. E. The correct answer is that the message will not be logged. But why? The default priority for the `logger` command is `user.notice`, which is not defined in the default `syslog.conf` file. Therefore, the message will be written nowhere, and the attempted message write will silently fail. You need to either write the message with an already defined `selector` (with the -p option) or change the `syslog.conf` file to recognize `user.notice` messages.

10. A, B, C, D. All of the provided answers are legitimate selector pairs. The possible facilities are `user`, `kern`, `mail`, `daemon`, `auth`, `lpr`, `news`, `uucp`, `cron`, `local0-7`, `mark`, and * (meaning all). The levels, from most severe to least, are `emerg`, `alert`, `crit`, `err`, `warning`, `notice`, `info`, `debug`, and `none`.

11. B, F. The option you need to configure is `ENABLE_CONNECTION_LOGGING`, which is located in the `/etc/default/inetd` file.

12. B. The `/etc/logadm.conf` file contains configuration information for log file rotation. The old mechanism for rotating log files was the `/usr/lib/newsyslog` script, but that method is no longer used.

13. C.   The /var/adm/log3 file will never receive any messages. This is because the keyword info is a level, not a facility. Therefore, the word info will always appear after the period in the selector.

14. A, B, C, D.   The answers represent all four valid options for the destination of logged messages. These are defined in the action field of the syslog.conf file.

15. D.   The asterisk (*) in the action field tells syslog to write the message to the console of all logged-in users. Most of the time, emergency situations will be the result of the computer (or at least a critical component) failing, and all logged-in users will need to be warned.

16. B.   The syslog service is started by the /etc/rc2.d/S74syslog script, which means that it's started by run level 2.

17. A.   The last command gets its information from the /var/adm/wtmpx file. The who command gets its information from the /var/adm/utpmx file.

18. C.   Anything involving security processes will be logged under the auth facility. So, in this case, logins will be logged to /var/adm/authlog.

19. C.   The explanation describes the syslogd daemon. The inetd daemon is responsible for listening for incoming network connections. The sysd and msgd daemons do not exist.

20. A.   If the log file specified in /etc/syslog.conf does not exist, the syslog service will silently fail when attempting to write the message. The file will not be automatically created, nor will an alternate log file be used.

Chapter

15

Naming Services

SOLARIS 9 EXAM OBJECTIVES COVERED IN THIS CHAPTER:

- ✓ Describe naming service concepts, and explain how to use the naming service switch file, the Name Service Cache Daemon (NSCD), and the getent command to get naming service information.

- ✓ Given a description of a naming service client, identify the steps and commands to configure the DNS client and set up the LDAP client.

- ✓ Explain the purpose, features, and functions of NIS namespace information, domains, and daemons.

- ✓ Explain how to configure the name service switch for different lookups, and configure a NIS domain using the required maps, files, commands, and scripts.

- ✓ Explain how to build custom NIS maps.

Throughout the course of this book, you've learned about a variety of configuration options and services needed to support the Solaris environment. After you transition from using only a local computer to running on a network, more configuration options and services come into play. You will need a network address and a netmask. You'll also need to know how to contact other computers on the network. These examples certainly aren't a complete list of configurable options, but you get the idea. To provide the variables for these configurations, you can either edit local files (called the /etc files), or use a naming or directory service over the network.

This chapter focuses on the naming and directory services used by Solaris to provide network-wide configuration for client computers. Using these services can reduce the chance of configuration mistakes, as well as ease network configuration administration by providing a centralized administration point.

Introducing Naming Service Concepts

When you installed your Solaris computer, you provided information such as the computer's name and network address (if networked). After you logged in as root, you probably also created user accounts and groups, and associated users with those groups. Perhaps you added a printer and configured the appropriate permissions to use the printer, as well as the permissions needed for users to access certain files and folders. Where is all of this configuration information stored?

If yours is the only Solaris computer around, this information is stored in local files, most of which are located in the /etc directory (/etc/passwd, /etc/group, /etc/printers.conf, and /etc/netmasks to name a few). However, the more computers you have (in a network setting, for example), the more local configuration files you will need to update. On small networks this is a tedious job, and on large networks it's impossible to keep up with all of the required changes.

For example, imagine that you are using the hosts file to locate other computers on the network and that you have 50 computers total. Changing the IP address of one computer will require you to manually edit the hosts file on each of the other computers. That doesn't sound like a fun task. Now imagine the task with 500 computers.

Directory and naming services are used to ease this administrative burden by providing a centralized location that stores configuration information. So, in the earlier hosts example, instead of editing 50 or 500 local hosts files, you could use the Domain Name Service (DNS) installed on a server and edit one file on the DNS server to make the change known to all clients.

In general, naming services can provide a centralized location to store computer names and addresses, usernames and passwords, security permissions, group memberships, printer information, and so forth. Properly used, they can ease your daily network administration work-load, and they are flexible enough to accommodate growth and change within your organization.

Overview of Naming and Directory Services

Currently, the Solaris environment supports six naming and directory services: *local files, Domain Name Service (DNS), Network Information Service (NIS), Network Information Service Plus (NIS+), Federated Naming Service (FNS),* and *Lightweight Directory Access Protocol (LDAP).* You can choose to use any combination of one or more of these services. It's common practice to use two or more services concurrently, such as local files, DNS, and NIS together.

 NIS+ and FNS are not test objectives for the Sun Certified Systems Administrator exams and therefore are not covered in detail in this book.

 Technically, *naming services* are those that simply resolve names, whereas *directory services* have much broader object definition and location responsibilities. However, the two are lumped together (due to their similar function) as naming and directory services.

The original UNIX naming system was the /etc files. For stand-alone computers, local files are entirely sufficient. When you start moving into larger networks, though, using local files is difficult—if not impossible—to manage.

DNS is the naming service designed to work with the TCP/IP protocol suite and is the name resolution method used on the Internet. So, although you might not have realized it, you've probably used DNS a lot more than you have any other naming service.

DNS is designed to resolve computer (host) names to IP addresses. People like to use names for ease (such as www.sun.com, which is easy to remember), whereas computers need to use IP addresses (such as 64.124.140.181, which is harder to remember) to initialize communications. Although DNS is most noted for providing this valuable resolution service on the Internet, it can also function well on local networks.

 Throughout this chapter (and in the real world), the terms *computer name* and *host name* are often used synonymously.

NIS makes local network administration easier by centrally storing network information, such as computer names and addresses, usernames and passwords, printers, and other network services. NIS is very commonly used in Solaris environments.

Most people think that NIS+ is merely an extension or upgrade of the NIS service, but it's not. NIS+ is a completely separate service. It's true, though, that NIS and NIS+ provide the same types of services. NIS+ is a more advanced service: it can store more information, is more efficient, and is generally faster than NIS.

FNS does not replace any of the other naming services. Rather, it sits on top of the existing naming services and provides a common interface between them. This enables you to use one common naming schema to identify all objects in your network. FNS is defined by the X/Open Federated Naming (XFN) standard.

LDAP is a newer industry-standard directory and naming service. It provides many of the same features as NIS+ and can be used as a replacement for NIS+. More detail on LDAP is provided in the "Understanding LDAP" section later in this chapter.

One of the similarities you will find among all of these services is that each one (with the exception of local files) is a client-server service. This means that you need to configure at least one computer as a server (a DNS or NIS+ server, for example), and then all other computers will function as clients to that server. The clients that use that server will be part of the server's *namespace*. For example, all clients using DNS are part of the DNS namespace.

In a client-server environment, you have two ways of getting the clients and servers to recognize each other in their appropriate roles. The first way is to configure the server with each client's information. This type of configuration has traditionally been shunned because it's difficult to maintain. Instead, most clients are configured to locate the servers. Using this configuration method, the client knows how to contact the server (or multiple servers, if necessary), and each server simply responds to each client request.

In Solaris, the client configuration is controlled by the *name service switch file*, /etc/nsswitch.conf. Each client has its own name service switch file, which tells it the naming service to use, based on the type of information the client is seeking.

Using the *nsswitch.conf* File

The nsswitch.conf file controls how a client computer or an application on the client computer responds when it needs network information. Every computer on the network must have its own nsswitch.conf file. Each entry in the nsswitch.conf file identifies a type of information, such as a host, netmask, group, or service, as well as one or more sources from which the client can obtain the information, such as local files or a NIS server.

Client computers can use practically any combination of sources for information. For example, a client could use its local /etc files for user and password information, but use a DNS server to locate host names. Alternatively, a client could be configured to use NIS for all information first, and then use the local /etc files only when or if the NIS server doesn't have the requested information.

When you install Solaris, a default nsswitch.conf file is selected from one of five default template files, depending on your installation choices. The five template files are nsswitch.dns, nsswitch.ldap, nsswitch.nis, nsswitch.nisplus, and nsswitch.files. If, for example, you have chosen to use NIS+, the nsswitch.nisplus file will be copied to nsswitch.conf automatically. If you're not on a network, the nsswitch.files file will be copied to nsswitch.conf.

Reading the *nsswitch.conf* File

The nsswitch.conf file is a list of approximately 20 types of information that clients can request. Listed alphabetically here (but not necessarily in the file itself), these keywords include aliases, automount, bootparams, ethers, group, hosts, ipnodes, netgroup, netmasks, networks, passwd (which also refers to shadow information), protocols, publickey, rpc, services, and sendmailvars.

Each of the searches for different types of information is configured independently and can be supplied with any of the six information sources listed in Table 15.1.

TABLE 15.1   *nsswitch.conf* Information Sources

Source	Description
compat	Password or group information. Used to support the old-style (Sun OE 4.*x*) + or – syntax in the /etc/passwd, /etc/shadow, and /etc/group files.
dns	DNS server.
files	Local /etc files.
ldap	LDAP server.
nis	NIS server (NIS servers use maps).
nisplus	NIS+ server (NIS+ servers use tables).

If a single source is supplied, then the client computer will consult only that source when seeking the requested information. If the source can supply the information, a success message is returned. If the source does not have the information, then a failure message is returned.

Consider the following nsswitch.conf file, which is the default file from a non-networked Solaris computer (the nsswitch.files template):

```
# /etc/nsswitch.files:
#
# An example file that could be copied over to /etc/nsswitch.conf; it
# does not use any naming service.
#
# "hosts:" and "services:" in this file are used only if the
# /etc/netconfig file has a "-" for nametoaddr_libs of "inet" transports.
passwd:      files
group:       files
hosts:       files
ipnodes:     files
networks:    files
protocols:   files
rpc:         files
```

```
ethers:     files
netmasks:   files
bootparams: files
publickey:  files
# At present there isn't a 'files' backend for netgroup;  the system will
#  figure it out pretty quickly, and won't use netgroups at all.
netgroup:   files
automount:  files
aliases:    files
services:   files
sendmailvars:   files
printers:   user files

auth_attr:  files
prof_attr:  files
project:    files
```

As is the case in all other Solaris files, lines that begin with a pound sign (#) are comments and are not processed. Looking at the file, you can see that each of these lines has one source: files. (The printers keyword is an exception, as it points to the user's configuration files.)

Multiple sources can also be supplied. If multiple sources are supplied, the sources will be checked in consecutive order. The number of sources checked depends on the result of the prior source search. Here's an example, taken from the nsswitch.nis file, of configuring the system to use multiple sources:

```
# /etc/nsswitch.nis:
#
# An example file that could be copied over to /etc/nsswitch.conf; it
# uses NIS (YP) in conjunction with files.
#
# "hosts:" and "services:" in this file are used only if the
# /etc/netconfig file has a "-" for nametoaddr_libs of "inet" transports.

# the following two lines obviate the "+" entry in /etc/passwd and /etc/group.
passwd:     files nis
group:      files nis

# consult /etc "files" only if nis is down.
hosts:      nis [NOTFOUND=return] files
ipnodes:    files
# Uncomment the following line and comment out the above to resolve
# both IPv4 and IPv6 addresses from the ipnodes databases. Note that
# IPv4 addresses are searched in all of the ipnodes databases before
```

```
# searching the hosts databases. Before turning this option on, consult
# the Network Administration Guide for more details on using IPv6.
#ipnodes:    nis [NOTFOUND=return] files

networks:    nis [NOTFOUND=return] files
protocols:   nis [NOTFOUND=return] files
rpc:         nis [NOTFOUND=return] files
ethers:      nis [NOTFOUND=return] files
netmasks:    nis [NOTFOUND=return] files
bootparams:  nis [NOTFOUND=return] files
publickey:   nis [NOTFOUND=return] files

netgroup:    nis

automount:   files nis
aliases:     files nis

# for efficient getservbyname() avoid nis
services:    files nis
sendmailvars:   files
printers:    user files nis

auth_attr:   files nis
prof_attr:   files nis
project:     files nis
```

In this file, many of the network-specific options, such as networks, rpc, and netmasks, refer the client to the NIS server first, and then local files. However, other information, such as role-based access control (RBAC) information (auth_attr and prof_attr), is pulled from local files first.

When searching for information, the requesting client (or application on the client) can return one of four status messages. There is one message for a successful information retrieval, and three messages for failures. Each of the four status messages is shown in Table 15.2.

TABLE 15.2   Status Messages

Message	Description
SUCCESS	The requested information was returned by the specified source.
NOTFOUND	The source responded with No such entry. The file, map, or table was accessed but did not contain the requested information.

TABLE 15.2 Status Messages *(continued)*

Message	Description
TRYAGAIN	The source was busy. Try again later.
UNAVAIL	The source did not respond or was not available. The file, map, or table could not be accessed.

Based on the status message returned, your computer can continue in one of two ways. It can either stop looking for the requested information, or try the next source, if available. These actions are defined by the keywords return (stop looking) and continue (keep looking).

Each status message has a default action. They are:

SUCCESS=return   Stop looking for the information, because you already found it.

NOTFOUND=continue   Use the next source to attempt to locate the requested information. If this is the last or only source, return with a NOTFOUND status.

TRYAGAIN=continue   Use the next source to attempt to locate the requested information. If this is the last or only source, return with a NOTFOUND status.

UNAVAIL=continue   Use the next source to attempt to locate the requested information. If this is the last or only source, return with a NOTFOUND status.

In other words, if you've found what you're looking for, stop looking. There's no sense in continuing (humans have to explain these obvious concepts to computers). If you haven't located the information, keep trying if you have another place to look.

Because these actions are default criteria, they do not need to be explicitly defined in the nsswitch.conf file. However, if you want to use a different search criteria, such as NOTFOUND=return, you can do so by editing the nsswitch.conf file. In the sample nsswitch.nis file shown previously, several lines used this syntax. For example:

```
hosts:     nis [NOTFOUND=return] files
```

This line tells the computer that if the hosts information is found in the NIS map, return a SUCCESS message and stop searching. If either an UNAVAIL or a TRYAGAIN message is returned, then consult the local /etc files for hosts information. If the NOTFOUND message is returned from the NIS server, then the search will cease, even though the correct information was not located.

Modifying the *nsswitch.conf* File

Assume for a moment that when you originally installed your Solaris computer, you were not a member of a network. However, now you are joining a network that uses the NIS service. Your nsswitch.conf file is configured to look at local files only. What should you do?

There are two ways you could make your computer look for the NIS server. One is to manually edit your existing nsswitch.conf file. Doing so might take a while, but you have another choice. The other way is to use the existing template files to your advantage. Copy the nsswitch.nis file to nsswitch.conf, and other than any custom modifications you might need to make, you're pretty much done. All you need to do is reboot your computer to make the changes take effect. Whenever you're making modifications to files, and in this case you're changing the nsswitch.conf file, it's a good idea to save the original file as an alternate filename or in a different location. That way, if something gets messed up in the configuration, you can just restore the original file.

If you are installing NIS+ by using the NIS+ installation scripts, the scripts will automatically copy the nsswitch.nisplus file to nsswitch.conf for you.

LDAP clients require additional configuration beyond copying the template file. These configuration requirements will be described later in this chapter, in the "Configuring DNS and LDAP Clients" section.

For security reasons, files should be the first search option for password information (passwd), even if your network is using NIS, NIS+, or LDAP.

Understanding the Name Service Cache Daemon

When you need to use one of the name resolution services, the *Name Service Cache Daemon (NSCD)* automatically caches information it finds in the nsswitch.conf file. Because some programs do not recheck the nsswitch.conf file directly (they rely on the NSCD), you need to restart the NSCD service after changes are made to nsswitch.conf to ensure that all applications will have current information. To do this, you can use the /etc/init.d/nscd stop and /etc/init.d/nscd start commands, or reboot the computer.

Deploying NIS

NIS was developed to make computer network administration easier. An alternative to using local /etc files, NIS provides a centralized repository for storing important configuration information.

    If you are running a Solaris network, using NIS can save you a lot of time. For example, if users on your network needed access to several different computers, you would have to update the local /etc/passwd (not to mention shadow and group) files on each computer that each user needed to log into. This could be not only cumbersome, but potentially confusing and a possible security risk. Each time a user changed her password on one computer, she would either have to change it on all other computers as well, or notify the administrator to make the change.

    What if you were to add another computer to the network? You would have to manually edit the hosts file on each computer to recognize the new machine. Even if you simply changed an IP address on one computer, you would have to update all `hosts` files. These types of situations cause unneeded stress for users and administrators alike.

By using NIS, though, all of these changes can be maintained in a centralized location. The administrator needs to make the changes on only one computer, and they will affect the entire network. It sounds a lot easier than using `/etc` files, and it is.

 NIS was originally called the Sun Yellow Pages (YP). However, the term *Yellow Pages* is a registered trademark, so Sun had to change the name. You'll notice that most of the commands and directories associated with NIS still have YP somewhere in their names (such as `/var/yp`, `ypcat`, and `yppush`).

The Logical NIS Structure

The logical grouping of computers supported by NIS is called a *NIS domain*. Each NIS domain must have one and only one *master server*. The master server is the primary source of information for the domain. Information is held in a series of databases known as *NIS maps*. These maps are stored in the `/var/yp/domainname` directory on the master server. If, for example, your domain name is `abc.com`, the directory is `/var/yp/abc.com`. Each map is stored as two files: `mapname.dir` and `mapname.pag`. The master server should be a fast, reliable server with high uptime.

 Although NIS domains support Internet naming standards (`abc.com`), a NIS domain cannot be directly connected to the Internet with just a NIS server. You can, however, use NIS and DNS together to provide an Internet solution.

You can also install one or more NIS *slave servers*. Slave servers function as backups to the master server and help spread the workload among NIS servers. Slave servers, like master servers, provide information to client computers. The master server will propagate its NIS information to the slave server(s), which is how all NIS servers stay synchronized. Each slave server has a map directory identical to the map directory on the master server.

Typically, all computers on the network, including the NIS master and slave servers, will be NIS clients. When client computers boot up, they will broadcast a request looking for the nearest NIS server. The client will bind to the first NIS server that responds and will subsequently request information from that server for the duration of the client's session (until it's rebooted).

A master server can be a master for only one domain. It can, however, be a slave for another domain. Slave servers can be slaves for multiple domains. Client computers can belong to only one domain at a time.

The conventional wisdom for NIS servers says that you need one NIS server for every 30 clients. If the client computers are faster than the server (which shouldn't be the case), then you will need more NIS servers. If the server is faster than the clients, it can generally handle about 50 clients before showing signs of performance degradation. If your network has multiple IP subnets, you should place one NIS server on each subnet. NIS clients older than Solaris 8 will require this, but Solaris 8 and Solaris 9 clients do not require their NIS servers to be on the same subnet as they are.

 Even if your network is made up of all Solaris 9 NIS clients, place a NIS server on each subnet. It will speed up NIS performance.

Overview of NIS Maps

NIS stores its information in a set of files called maps. As mentioned earlier, these maps are stored in a central location (on the master server) and can be replicated to backup servers (called slave servers).

NIS maps are two-column tables. The first column is the key, which is used by NIS as a search criteria when NIS information is requested. The second column is the information related to the key. Some information is stored in multiple maps. For example, Ethernet addresses are stored in two maps: `ethers.byadr` and `ethers.byname`. The first one sorts Ethernet addresses by address (the address is the key, and the name is the value), and the second map stores the addresses by name (the name is the key, and the address is the value). Both maps contain the same information, just sorted differently.

Maps are stored in the NIS server's `/var/yp/domainname` directory. If your domain name is `abc.com`, the directory containing the maps will be `/var/yp/abc.com`.

Maps are created from source files that contain the information to be included in the maps. By default, these source files are located in the `/etc` directory (`/etc/passwd`, `/etc/hosts`, and so forth), but you can change the default directory if you want to. Running the `make` command in the directory containing the source files causes the `makedbm` program to create or modify the default NIS maps based on the input files.

 Always run the make command on the master server. Never run it on slave servers. Running make on the master server will ensure that maps are properly pushed to slave servers, whereas maps "made" on slave servers will not be pushed to the master server or other slaves, and will be subsequently overwritten the next time the master pushes changes to slaves.

Table 15.3 lists the default NIS maps.

TABLE 15.3   Default NIS Maps

Name	Source File	Contents
bootparams	bootparams	The pathnames of files that clients need to boot.
ethers.byaddr	ethers	Machine names (host names) and Ethernet addresses, with the address as the key.

TABLE 15.3 Default NIS Maps *(continued)*

Name	Source File	Contents
ethers.byname	ethers	Machine names (host names) and Ethernet addresses, with the host name as the key.
group.bygid	group	Group security information, with the GID as the key.
group.byname	group	Group security information, with the group name as the key.
hosts.byaddr	hosts	Host names and IP addresses, with the address as the key.
hosts.byname	hosts	Host names and IP addresses, with the host name as the key.
mail.aliases	aliases	Mail aliases and mail addresses, with the alias as the key.
mail.byaddr	aliases	Mail aliases and mail addresses, with the mail address as the key.
netgroup.byhost	netgroup	Netgroup names, usernames, and computer names, with the host name as the key.
netgroup.byuser	netgroup	Netgroup names, usernames, and computer names, with the username as the key.
netgroup	netgroup	Netgroup names, user names, and computer names, with netgroup name as the key.
netid.byname	passwd, hosts, and group	Host names, mail addresses, and domain names. Used for UNIX-style authentication. If the netid file is available, it's consulted in addition to other files containing the same data.
netmasks.byaddr	netmasks	Network masks to be used with IP subnetting.
networks.byaddr	networks	Names of networks known to this computer, with the network address as the key.
networks.byname	networks	Names of networks known to this computer, with the network name as the key.
passwd.adjunct.byname	passwd and shadow	Auditing information and hidden password information for C2 network clients.

TABLE 15.3   Default NIS Maps *(continued)*

Name	Source File	Contents
passwd.byname	passwd and shadow	Password information, with the username as the key.
passwd.byuid	passwd and shadow	Password information, with the UID as the key.
protocols.byname	protocols	Network protocols known to your network, with the protocol name as the key.
protocols.bynumber	protocols	Network protocols known to your network, with the protocol number as the key.
rpc.bynumber	rpc	Program numbers and names of RPCs known to the computer.
services.byname	services	Internet services known to your network, with the key port or protocol as the key.
services.byservice	services	Internet services known to your network, with the service name as the key.
ypservers	N/A	NIS servers known to your network.

Keep in mind that these are only the default databases. Applications can install their own NIS maps, and you can also create custom NIS maps as necessary. For the most part, though, the default maps are sufficient to serve most networks.

Two useful commands related to maps are ypcat and ypwhich. The ypcat command performs similarly to the cat command, except that it shows the contents of a map file. For example, to see the data in the passwd.byname map, you would use ypcat passwd.byname. If a map contains only keys (such as the ypservers map), use ypcat -k *mapname*. To see which server is the master server for a particular map, use ypwhich -m *mapname*.

Some maps can also be referenced by nicknames instead of their full names. For example, the passwd.byname map can also be referenced simply as passwd. Nicknames can be used with any of the yp* management commands. The /var/yp/nicknames file contains a list of nicknames associated with map names. You can add or modify nicknames for any map file.

NIS Daemons and Utilities

The two software packages composing the NIS service, SUNWypu and SUNWypr, should have been installed by default when you installed Solaris. You can check to see whether these packages are installed by using the pkginfo command. The NIS service is supported by five daemons. They are listed in Table 15.4.

TABLE 15.4 NIS Daemons

Daemon	Description
ypserv	The NIS server daemon looks up information in the NIS server's maps. It is also responsible for logging error conditions in the NIS service to the /var/yp/ypserv.log file, if the file exists.
ypbind	The NIS binding daemon is responsible for connecting the client to a server (called binding), and initiating future communications between the client and server.
ypxfr	Provides high-speed map transfers between NIS servers.
rpc.yppasswdd	Responsible for handling password changes, as requested with the yppasswd command. It updates the passwd and shadow files.
rpc.ypupdated	Updates NIS information, such as which maps need to be updated after changes are made to the source files.

Table 15.5 lists the commands you will use to manage NIS.

TABLE 15.5 NIS Commands

Command	Description
make	Creates or updates NIS maps by reading the makefile (/var/yp/makefile) and the NIS source files.
makedbm	Creates a dbm file for a NIS map. Running the make command initiates the makedbm command, creating or updating maps.
ypcat	Displays the data in a map.
ypinit	Automatically creates NIS maps from the source files. Used to set up NIS servers for the first time, and on clients to initialize the NIS service and update the client's ypservers list.
ypmatch	Displays the value for one or more keys in a specified map.
yppoll	Gets a map version number from a NIS server.
yppush	Manually initiates a push of the NIS maps from the master server to the slave server(s).
ypset	Configures NIS client binding to a specific server.

TABLE 15.5   NIS Commands *(continued)*

Command	Description
ypstart	Starts the NIS service.
ypstop	Stops the NIS service.
ypwhich	Lists the name of the NIS server that supplies NIS information to that client, or displays the name of the master for a given map.
ypxfr	Copies a NIS map from the NIS master server to the local host. Similar to the yppush command.

You will get a feel for when and how to use these commands as you continue to read through this chapter.

Installing a NIS Master Server

If you are going to use NIS, the first NIS computer that you must install is the NIS master server. As mentioned before, this server will contain the master copies of map files and will provide service to clients as well as slave servers. You should pick a server that is both fast and highly reliable. Interruptions in the NIS service due to poor server performance can cripple your network if you rely on NIS as your only naming service.

Before configuring your NIS master server, decide on a domain name for your NIS domain. The domain name must have 256 characters or fewer (preferably fewer) and is case sensitive. If you already have an Internet domain name, you can use the same name for your NIS domain. Each computer that will use NIS must have the correct domain name in their /etc/defaultdomain file, as well as a unique computer name defined in their /etc/nodename file.

Preparing Source Files

The first thing you need to do when setting up a NIS master server is to prepare the source file for the master passwd map. *Source files* contain the information from which you will build maps. All source files (which are listed in Table 15.3) are located in the /etc directory by default. For most files, this is not a problem. But for the passwd and shadow files, this presents a security risk, because the /etc/passwd and /etc/shadow files include all user account information, including that of the root user. If you were to create the NIS maps from these files, all users on the network would have access to the root password, because all users need access to the master maps. Yes, the password is encrypted. But given enough time, users can easily hack it by using brute force.

So, for security reasons, it is best to place the source passwd and shadow files in a directory other than /etc. Many administrators like to put these source files in the /var/yp directory because that makes them easy to locate. Others like to create a subdirectory in /var/yp, such as

/var/yp/source, to locate the files. In either case, ensure that the security on the source directory allows only root access to the files.

After you have created your source directory and copied the passwd and shadow files into it, you can prepare them for use as source files. The whole reason you moved them to an alternate location in the first place was because of security concerns: you don't want everyone having access to the root password. And, of course, if you were to delete the root entry from /etc/passwd and /etc/shadow, you wouldn't be able to log in as the root user. So, in your copied passwd and shadow files, remove the entries for root, as well as for other accounts you don't want users trying to log in as.

There's one more step you need to complete before creating your passwd map. By default, the NIS service looks to the /etc directory for its source files. The /var/yp/makefile file contains the parameters used by NIS to create maps. You need to edit makefile to point to your new source directory; otherwise, NIS will just pull data from the /etc files.

/var/yp/makefile is quite large, but here's a sampling of it showing the lines that you will need to modify:

```
# /var/yp/makefile
#
B=
DIR =/etc
#
INETDIR=/etc/inet
#
RBACDIR=/etc/security
#
PWDIR =/etc
DOM = `domainname`
NOPUSH = ""
ALIASES = /etc/mail/aliases
YPDIR=/usr/lib/netsvc/yp
SBINDIR=/usr/sbin
YPDBDIR=/var/yp
YPPUSH=$(YPDIR)/yppush
MAKEDBM=$(SBINDIR)/makedbm
MULTI=$(YPDIR)/multi
REVNETGROUP=$(SBINDIR)/revnetgroup
STDETHERS=$(YPDIR)/stdethers
STDHOSTS=$(YPDIR)/stdhosts
MKNETID=$(SBINDIR)/mknetid
MKALIAS=$(YPDIR)/mkalias
...
#
```

You need to change DIR =/etc and PWDIR =/etc to point to your new source file location. If, for example, you copied the passwd file to /var/yp, then you need to change each of these lines to read =/var/yp. You can also see that other Solaris services, such as RBAC (RBACDIR=) and e-mail (ALIASES=), have their own lines in makefile as well.

Creating Source Files

After you have created your new source directory (such as /var/yp) and made the necessary modifications to makefile, you need to verify that all of your source files contain the correct information. Remember, the point of using NIS is to ensure that all users and computers have access to current network information, located in a centralized place. It's imperative to ensure that the source files you are working with are correct.

There are several ways you could approach this process. One would be to copy the /etc/passwd files from each host to the server and then use the cat command to concatenate each file into a master passwd file. After removing duplicate entries (usernames and/or UIDs), you could use the new master passwd file for the source file. You could do the same with the shadow and group files as well. There are utilities that will help you sort these files, as well as ensure that each entry is unique, such as sort and uniq.

Another way you could create master source files is to manually edit each source file, ensuring that the information contained within is correct. For files such as hosts, bootparams, and netmasks, this is often the preferred method. You can also do the same for the passwd, shadow, and group files. If you have a large network, creating source files this way might take a long time, but the time you invest in the beginning will save you a lot of work in the long run.

The purpose of this section isn't to teach you the best way to create source files for your NIS server, as that can be a matter of opinion. But, there are some general guidelines to follow when setting up source files on your master server:

- Create an alternate directory, other than /etc, for your source files.

- Copy all source files that you want to make maps for into your new source directory.

- Ensure that the makefile file points to your new source directory.

- And most importantly, make sure your source files have information that reflects the current status of your network.

The one source file that cannot be moved is the /etc/mail/aliases file. It must remain in the /etc/mail directory. If you want your e-mail aliases to be available through the NIS server, ensure that this file is current as well.

After your source files are ready, you are ready to use the ypinit command to initialize your master server.

Setting Up the Master Server

The ypinit command is a versatile command that is used to install and configure NIS servers and clients. On the computer that will be your master server, ypinit creates the master maps. It does this by calling the make program, which in turn reads makefile, which contains scripts to create all appropriate databases (by using makedbm) from the source files. After the source data is passed through makedbm, it is collected in two files, *mapname*.dir and *mapname*.pag, both of which are located in the /var/yp/*domainname* directory on the master server.

The passwd maps are built from the /PWDIR/passwd, /PWDIR/shadow, and /PWDIR/security/passwd.adjunct files, as appropriate.

To install a NIS master server, you must have **root** permissions on the computer. Here are the steps to set up your master server by using ypinit:

1. Ensure that the local computer receives its name service information from local /etc files, not from NIS. This might seem counterintuitive, but it's a necessary step, and you will fix this "problem" later.

   # **cp /etc/nsswitch.files /etc/nsswitch.conf**

2. Make sure that the /etc/hosts file contains the names and IP addresses of each computer that will become a NIS slave server. (If your network has a properly configured DNS server, this step is optional.)

3. Build the master maps with the ypinit command.

   # **ypinit -m**

   The ypinit program will ask you for a list of other computers that will become NIS servers. You will enter the name of the server you are working on, as well as the names of all planned NIS slave servers. Type each server name separately and then press the Enter key. When you are done entering slave servers, press Control+D.

4. ypinit will ask whether you want to terminate the procedure at the first nonfatal error or to continue despite nonfatal errors. Type **y**. This will cause ypinit to terminate if it encounters an error, enabling you to fix the problem and restart ypinit. This option is recommended if this is the first time you have run ypinit on this computer. (Nonfatal errors can occur when some of the map files aren't present. This doesn't necessarily affect NIS functionality, but it might be a situation you want to rectify.)

5. If you have previously installed NIS, ypinit will ask whether the existing files in /var/yp/*domainname* can be destroyed. To continue with a new installation of NIS, answer **yes**.

6. ypinit will construct a list of NIS servers and invoke the **make** command. This will create the appropriate maps and set the name of the master server for each map.

7. After this is complete, you will want the local computer to use NIS as the name service. You can edit your current nsswitch.conf file, but the preferred method is to copy the switch file template for NIS.

   # **cp /etc/nsswitch.nis /etc/nsswitch.conf**

8. Edit your new nsswitch.conf file, if needed, to reflect any custom name service settings.

After these steps are completed, you need to start the NIS service. The two services that need to be running are ypserv and ypbind. Both of these daemons are started by the /usr/lib/netsvc/yp/ypstart command. After NIS is installed, the ypstart command will run automatically at boot, starting the NIS service for you. If you want to stop the NIS service for any reason, issue the /usr/lib/netsvc/yp/ypstop command.

Configuring NIS Clients

NIS clients will use the NIS server to obtain network information. Although some networks use a combination of NIS and local /etc files for name service information, this section is going to assume that all network clients will be NIS clients and will use the NIS service exclusively.

To set up a NIS client, you must have root permissions on the client computer. You then need to complete these three tasks:

- Remove user account information from the /etc/passwd, /etc/shadow, and /etc/group files on the local computer. You will be requesting login validation from the NIS server.

> For security purposes, some networks require user account information to be obtained from local /etc files, whereas all other information is obtained from the NIS server. This prevents usernames and passwords from being transmitted across the network.

- Ensure that the domain name is configured in the client computer's /etc/defaultdomain file. Remember that domain names are case sensitive.
- Configure the client with the appropriate name service switch file. Copying /etc/nsswitch.nis to /etc/nsswitch.conf should work in most cases.

After these tasks are complete, you are ready to configure the client computer to use NIS. You have two choices on how to accomplish this. The recommended way is to issue the following command:

```
# ypinit -c
```

The ypinit -c command will configure the computer to be a NIS client. Running this command will prompt you for a list of NIS servers in the domain. You can list as many or as few servers as you would like. For performance reasons, you should list servers that are physically closest to the client.

The other method of configuring NIS clients is to use broadcasting. After the domain name is set for the client, you can run the **ypbind -broadcast** command to broadcast on the local subnet looking for a NIS server. If a NIS server is located, the client binds to it. If, however, there is no NIS server on the local subnet, this method will fail.

Binding is an important concept to NIS clients. When a NIS client boots up, it will attempt to locate a NIS server. It can do this by searching its /var/yp/binding/*domainname*/ypservers list for valid NIS servers or by broadcasting. After a client locates a server, it will *bind* to that server and ask only that NIS server for NIS information. If or when the client is rebooted, the binding process will start over.

If you set up the NIS client with the ypinit -c command, the ypservers list will exist. If you configured the client to broadcast, or the ypservers list does not exist, the client will broadcast for a NIS server during boot. It's preferable to have clients search a list instead of creating excessive network broadcast traffic.

> The yppasswd command is used to change user passwords for clients using the NIS service.

Installing NIS Slave Servers

It's good practice to have at least one NIS slave server on your network. Slave servers can help offset the load from the master server, and can keep name service resolution up and running if the master server fails for any reason. NIS slave servers are also NIS clients and consequently must be set up as NIS clients as part of the slave server installation process.

Before you configure a slave server, ensure that the domain name is properly set in the local /etc/defaultdomain file. Also, you will need to make sure that the network is functioning properly. When you attempt to create the slave, it will try to copy the maps from the master. The copying process is similar to the one used by the rcp command. So, if rcp works between the master and slave-to-be, then the slave installation process should run smoothly.

Just as in setting up a master server or NIS client, you need superuser permissions to install a NIS slave server. Here are the steps:

1. Ensure that the local /etc/hosts file contains the names and IP addresses of all other NIS servers on the network. (If your network has a properly configured DNS server, this step is optional.)

2. Change to the /var/yp directory on the slave server.

   # **cd /var/yp**

3. Initialize the slave server as a NIS client by using the ypinit command.

   # **ypinit -c**

   The ypinit command will prompt you for a list of NIS servers. Enter the name of the slave you are working on first, followed by the master server, and then the other slave servers on the network. For performance reasons, add slave servers in order of proximity to this computer (closest first).

4. Check to see whether the ypbind service is running. If it is, then you will need to stop and restart it. If it's not, you need to start it.

   # **pgrep ypbind**

   a. If a listing is displayed from this command, then ypbind is running. Stop it with the /usr/lib/netsvc/yp/ypstop command.

   b. If no listing is displayed, or if you've stopped ypbind, then you need to restart it with the /usr/lib/netsvc/yp/ypstart command.

5. Configure the computer to be a NIS slave by using the ypinit command. The *master* variable is the name of the NIS master server.

   # **ypinit -s *master***

6. Stop and restart the NIS daemons.

   # **/usr/lib/netsvc/yp/ypstop**
   # **/usr/lib/netsvc/yp/ypstart**

7. Repeat these steps on all computers that you want to make NIS slave servers.

Be sure to plan which computers you want to be slave servers before you begin your initial NIS installation. You can always add NIS slave servers later, but that process is different and more complex than the initial installation process.

> To change a NIS computer's NIS domain name, you must first change the computer's domain name in the /etc/defaultdomain file and then rerun ypinit to set up the computer as a master, slave, or client.

Working with NIS Maps

After maps are created on your NIS master server and propagated to the slave servers, the NIS map replication process is automatic. If any changes are made to maps on the master server, the changed maps will be pushed automatically to the slave servers.

Solaris provides two commands to help propagate maps manually. The yppush command, run from the NIS master server, pushes maps to the slave servers. The ypxfr command pulls maps from the NIS master server to the local host.

Solaris also provides several utilities to view and manage the data within existing maps.

Using Map Utilities

If you want to see the data in a specific map, you can use the ypcat command to list all values within the map. Here's an example:

```
# ypcat passwd
efrederick:JYa9rCO/9zq6Y:105:10:hey der eh:/home/efrederick:/bin/sh
sjohnson:VAPzqVS9aBxL2:103:10:movie star:/home/sjohnsin:/bin/sh
abradley:*LK*:3422:1:::/export/home/abradley:/bin/sh
ldocter:uXKXU926ue29M:107:100:Lauren:/home/ldocter:/bin/sh
ramini:fWYc2uvcLUmc6:102:10:punny boy:/home/ramini:/bin/sh
lfrederick:*LK*:109:1:::/home/lfrederick:/bin/sh
qdocter:6uoVIHZIxXiVI:100:10:author:/home/qdocter:/bin/ksh
passmgr:kOiiZaj.onTg:108:14:::/home/passmgr:/bin/pfsh
kdocter:SXBMd1wKhMN2k:101:10:support staff:/home/kdocter:/bin/sh
adocter:hXVI4wCsDRVKs:106:100:Abbie:/home/adocter:/bin/sh
mgantz:5Y/YmRlbWY/3g:104:10:Mac user:/home/mgantz:/bin/sh
#
```

To display the keys along with the values in a map, use ypcat -k. In the case of the passwd database, the key will be the same as the username.

Another command, ypwhich, will show the name of the master server for a given map:

```
# ypwhich -m passwd
Q-Sol
#
```

Running the ypwhich command with no arguments will display the name of the NIS master server providing information to your local machine.

One other useful command is ypmatch, which looks for and displays specific keys within a map. In the following example, the passwd database is searched for a user:

```
# ypmatch qdocter passwd.byname
qdocter:6uoVIHZIxXiVI:100:10:author:/home/qdocter:/bin/ksh
#
```

The key in this case is qdocter, which is found within the passwd.byname map. If the key were not matched, ypmatch would inform you that there is no such key in the map.

You'll notice that with ypcat, as well as the other yp* utilities, you can use either the full name of the map or the map's nickname (if it has one) as the command-line argument. To display the list of available nicknames, use the -x option with ypcat, ypwhich, or ypmatch.

Changing a Map's Master Server

When you build a NIS map, the map's master server name is included as a key pair within the map. Therefore, you can't just copy (or move) a map to another server (by using a utility such as ypxfr) and have the new server be the master server. It would be nice if it were that easy, but it's not.

If you want to change master servers for a map, you must rebuild the map on the new master server. This is done to re-associate the key with the new master server's name. If the original map has an ASCII source file, you should copy this file to the new master.

To change a map's master server, log into the new master server as the superuser and change to the /var/yp directory. Once there, follow these steps:

1. Examine makefile to ensure that there's an entry for the new map you want to create. If not, you will need to create an entry. For example, if you were creating a custom map file named clients.byname, you would need a clients.byname entry in makefile.

2. After the entry is in makefile, you can create the new map by using the following command:

   ```
   # make clients.byname
   ```

   Of course, if your map name is different from clients.byname, substitute it here.

3. After you make the new map, log onto the old master server and comment out the line in makefile that refers to the map. This will prevent the old master server from remaking the map.

4. You now need to send a copy of the new map out to the slave servers. However, if you were to run yppush at this time, the other slaves would try to get the map from the original master, because their copy still contains the original master's key pair. The way around this is to log back onto the original master and use ypxfr to pull the map from the new master.

   ```
   # /usr/lib/netsvc/yp/ypxfr -h newmaster clients.byname
   ```

5. It's now safe to use yppush to disseminate the new map. When slave servers receive the updated map, they will know who the new master is for the map.

If for some reason the push fails, you can log onto each slave server and run the `ypxfr` command as shown in step 4 to pull the map to each slave individually.

Although it's possible to have several servers act as master servers for different maps (each map can have only one master), to avoid confusion, it's generally best to have one master server for all maps.

Customizing Maps

Most network administrators will find that the default maps provided by NIS are sufficient to serve their needs. However, in some cases, a custom map needs to be created. In addition, applications have the ability to add their own custom maps as necessary.

To add a new NIS map, you need to get the map's `ndbm` files into the master server's `/var/yp/`*domainname* directory. Normally this is done by `makefile` during the map creation process. It stands to reason then, that in order to create a custom map, the easiest way is to add an entry for the map in `makefile`. When you modify `makefile`, you need to add the name of the database to the `all` rule, write the `time` rule, and add a rule for the new database.

The specific steps required to create entries in `makefile` are beyond the scope of this book. For more information, see *System Administration Guide: Naming and Directory Services (DNS, NIS, and LDAP)* from Sun Microsystems. This document is also available online at docs.sun.com.

Creating a new map after an entry is in the `makefile` file is a relatively simple process. Use the `make` command on the master server to make the new map:

```
# make mapname
```

After the map is created, use `ypxfr` from each of the slave servers to retrieve the map. You would think that you could just use `yppush`, but `yppush` will not work properly if the new map doesn't yet exist on the slave servers. If the map does exist on the slave servers, you can use `yppush` to push the map to the slave servers. The "make and push" process works well if you've made changes to the source files for an existing NIS map. Remake the map and then push it out.

You can also create maps without modifying `makefile`. Custom maps, such as those with ASCII or text source files, are created with the makedbm command. To modify the map, edit the source file, and then rerun makedbm to re-create the dbm file.

Automating Map Transfers

Some maps rarely change, yet others, such as `passwd`, change frequently. Either way, it's important to ensure that maps on all slave servers have current information. To help facilitate this process, you can create a `crontab` file (or use the root `crontab` file) on each slave server. In the `crontab`, use the `ypxfr` command to pull the maps you want. You can specify different `ypxfr` commands for each map if you want to. When initiated, `ypxfr` will contact the master server and, if changes in the map are present, will pull the map to the slave.

Additionally, you can log all ypxfr activity with the /var/yp/ypxfr.log file. By default, this file does not exist. However, if you create one, all ypxfr activity will be automatically logged by the ypxfrd daemon.

Troubleshooting NIS

NIS is a complex network-based service. For the most part, it runs well and doesn't have any inherent problems. But because of its complexity and network-based nature, you will occasionally run into trouble.

Errors in NIS have different forms. You might receive a message saying that ypbind can't find a server, or an error stating that the server is not responding or that NIS is not available. Alternatively, commands that need name resolution might take an inordinate amount of time to complete or just completely hang with no error message at all.

As with any network-based service, always keep the possibility of network problems in the back of your troubleshooting mind. To that end, check to see whether any other network services are accessible. If not, then you know the problem probably isn't with NIS.

If the problem seems to be isolated to NIS only, the next thing to check is whether the problem is affecting one computer or several computers.

Here are some things to check if only one computer is (or a few computers are) having problems:

Make sure that ypbind is running on the client. You can check this by running the pgrep ypbind command and looking for ypbind. If it's not there, log on as the superuser and issue a /usr/lib/netsvc/yp/ypstart command.

Check the client's domain name. If the domain name is set incorrectly, the client will not be able to obtain information from a NIS server. Run the domainname command to see what the client's domain name is, or check the /etc/defaultdomain file. Remember that the domain name is case sensitive.

Ensure that the client is bound to a NIS server. Check this by running the ypwhich command. The name of a NIS server should be returned. If you just restarted ypbind, run the ypwhich command several times, because sometimes the first time will report that the client is not bound, and the second (or third) try might succeed.

Check for server availability. If the server is unavailable, it could indicate a number of possible problems. First, check whether the client has a /var/yp/binding/*domainname*/ypservers file. This file should have several servers listed, just in case one or two NIS servers are unavailable. If the file doesn't exist, run ypinit -c to create one. If no servers are listed or are available, the client will attempt to broadcast to locate one. Also, if the NIS server doesn't have the client listed in its hosts file (or the DNS service isn't working properly), NIS can fail.

Investigate other miscellaneous problems. Check to make sure that the client's /etc/nsswitch file is correct. Looking to local files instead of the NIS server can be a problem. Also remember that NIS relies on the rpc service. If that network service is having problems, NIS will likely fail as well.

If, instead of being isolated to one computer, the problem is network-wide, then the problem is most likely with the NIS server. One of the first things to consider is whether you have enough

NIS servers for your network. Having too few servers can cause the existing ones to become overloaded, and they won't respond to clients in time.

Here are a few specific things to look for if the problem seems to be widespread:

Check server availability. Are the servers up and running? Use the `ping` command to verify.

Check whether the NIS daemons are running. On the server, both the `ypserv` and `ypbind` processes need to be running. Check by using the `pgrep yp` command. If needed, stop and restart the NIS service by using the `/usr/lib/netsvc/yp/ypstop` and `/usr/lib/netsvc/yp/ypstart` commands.

Make sure that the servers all have the same map versions. Map inconsistencies can cause network problems. The `yppoll` command can tell you a map's version number. If you need to manually initiate a map transfer, use the `yppush` (from the master server) or `ypxfr` (from the slave server) command.

It would be difficult to come up with a complete list of possible NIS problems, but the ones provided in this section should give you a good jump on troubleshooting. The key to troubleshooting anything is to first narrow down the problem—where does it work and where doesn't it work—and then look for a solution.

Overview of NIS+

Although NIS provides a functional naming service structure for many networks, its flat naming structure does have some limitations. Although their names are similar, Network Information Service Plus (NIS+) was developed independently of NIS. NIS+ uses a hierarchical naming structure, much like that of a UNIX file system structure, to name and locate objects and can provide more information to clients than can NIS.

NIS+ is designed to be flexible enough to accommodate any logical network structure and to grow as the network grows. To that end, NIS+ namespaces can be divided into multiple domains, and clients can access information from several domains if necessary. NIS+ is virtually unlimited in scope.

NIS+ follows the client-server model. The main server in a domain is called a master server, and the backup servers are called replicas. Information is stored in *NIS+ tables* (as opposed to NIS maps) on the master server and all replicas.

In addition, NIS+ includes advanced security mechanisms not present in NIS, such as Data Encryption Standard (DES) authentication. Also unlike NIS, the `yp*` series of commands is not used to manage NIS+. Rather, NIS+ has its own series of `nis*` management commands, such as `niscat`, `nisinit`, and `nisgrep`. NIS+ is designed to replace NIS, and the two are not commonly found running on the same network.

Configuring DNS and LDAP Clients

Two other common naming services used in Solaris environments are DNS and LDAP. Both services are industry standards and not specific to Solaris. Even though Solaris can function as DNS and LDAP servers, the Sun Certified System Administrator exams focus on setting up only DNS and LDAP clients. Therefore, an overview of each service will be provided, as well as details on setting up the respective clients.

Understanding DNS

DNS is the name resolution service developed explicitly for the Transmission Control Protocol/ Internet Protocol (TCP/IP) networking protocol suite. Developed in the mid-1980s, DNS was designed to replace the antiquated and cumbersome method of using `hosts` files to resolve computer names to IP addresses. Whereas other naming services discussed in this chapter, such as NIS, NIS+, and LDAP, can do much more than just resolve names and addresses, that's all DNS does. DNS is the only name resolution method used on the Internet, but it can work in smaller, local area networks as well.

Solaris 9 can function as both a DNS server and a DNS client. DNS is designed in such a way that different software platforms can be clients and servers to each other. For example, a Windows-based client can use a Solaris DNS server and vice versa. There shouldn't be any problems, as long as both computers understand TCP/IP.

DNS zones of authority are logically organized into domains, much like NIS+ domains. Each domain has a hierarchical domain name, such as `sun.com` or `sybex.com`, and computers within the domain take their name from their parent, such as `docs.sun.com` or `www.sybex.com`. The master server contains a list of computers and their IP addresses within the domain. DNS domains can also have backup servers and caching-only or stub servers. All DNS servers are configured to resolve computer names to IP addresses and can ask each other for information.

To run DNS, a Solaris server uses the `in.named` daemon. Information about computers in the domain is stored in a series of files on the DNS server. These files are similar to the `/etc/hosts` file but contain more information. Most DNS implementations follow the Berkeley Internet Name Domain (BIND) standard. Solaris 9 supports BIND version 8.2.4.

Configuring DNS Clients

Before configuring your DNS clients, make sure that you have access to at least one DNS server. If you are providing Internet-based DNS services, you are required to have at least two DNS servers up and running.

Setting up Solaris to be a DNS client is a relatively simple two-step process. First, you need to have a local `/etc/resolv.conf` file configured. This file is also called the *resolver*. Second, you must configure the `/etc/nsswitch.conf` file to look for a DNS server.

If your computer does not have a `resolv.conf` file, you can create one. Use **touch /etc/resolv.conf** or whatever method of file creation you prefer. The `resolv.conf` file needs to have two types of information: the domain name and DNS servers to query. The format of the file will be like this:

```
domain domainname
nameserver IP_address
```

A computer in the `pinkeel.com` domain might have a `resolv.conf` file that looks like this:

```
# /etc/resolv.conf
domain pinkeel.com
; local name servers
nameserver  10.0.0.34
nameserver  10.0.0.35
;other name servers
nameserver  192.168.32.2
nameserver  192.168.32.3
```

The computer will try the name servers in the listed order. If the first name server cannot resolve the query, the second one will be tried, and so forth, until one of the name servers returns an IP address to match the requested host name. Lines that begin with a semicolon (;) are comments and are not parsed by the computer.

After your `resolv.conf` file is configured, you need to edit the `nsswitch.conf` file to look for the DNS server. Because DNS has a single purpose, to resolve host names to IP addresses, there is only one line in your `nsswitch.conf` file that you need to configure. It begins with `hosts:`.

You will want to modify the line to look something like this:

```
hosts:      dns [NOTFOUND=return] files
```

The computer with this line will ask the DNS server to resolve host names first, and then attempt to use a local `hosts` file. If your network is using NIS or NIS+, you can also enter those naming services on this line, such as:

```
hosts:      dns [NOTFOUND=return] nis files
```

In this case, DNS will be queried first, followed by NIS, and then the local `hosts` file. If none of the sources can resolve the name, the name resolution process will fail. If you're trying to access a website or another local computer, you will not be able to do so by the computer's host name.

Understanding LDAP

The newest naming service to be included with Solaris is the Lightweight Directory Access Protocol (LDAP). LDAP was originally developed as a directory service, meaning that it held objects and attributes. You can think of LDAP as a telephone book, but one that has not only the user's name, address, and phone number, but also that person's birth date, identification number, children's names, and a slew of other information. In this example, the person would be considered an object, and the information bits would be properties of that object.

Since its original development, LDAP has expanded to take on the role of a naming service as well as a simple resource locator. Like DNS and NIS+, LDAP uses a hierarchical naming structure to classify objects within its organization, also called a domain or a namespace. LDAP naming is based on the Internet standard X.500 naming system. The top level of the LDAP organizational tree often represents a country but can also represent a company name. The second layer in the organization can represent states within the country, or divisions within an organization, and so forth. The LDAP tree, known as the *Directory Information Tree (DIT)*, can be adapted to fit any organization.

One of the big advantages of using LDAP is its scope. LDAP gives you the ability to include and classify a large number of objects into one database, reducing the need to manage several databases. Also, LDAP allows for frequent database synchronizations between servers (the term *lightweight* implies that it doesn't produce a lot of network overhead by itself), and LDAP is supported by a variety of hardware and software platforms and vendors.

On the downside, pre-Solaris 8 clients are not supported by the current version of LDAP. Also, an LDAP server cannot be its own client. Therefore, you need at least two LDAP servers if you want all computers on your network to use LDAP. Finally, setting up LDAP is more complex than setting up NIS, NIS+, or DNS.

 Sun is planning on phasing out NIS+ in favor of LDAP. There are tools available to help in the migration of NIS+ to LDAP in Solaris 9. For more information, see www.sun.com/directory/nisplus/transition.html.

Solaris 9 can function as an LDAP server through the iPlanet Directory Server software, bundled with Solaris 9.

Configuring LDAP Clients

As is the case with any other client-server service, in order to get your LDAP clients to work properly, you need an LDAP server. Only Solaris 8 and Solaris 9 systems can be LDAP clients. To function as an LDAP client, the following are required:

- The client's domain must be serviced by an LDAP server, and at least one LDAP server must be up and running.

- The client's domain name must be set in the local /etc/defaultdomain file.

- The nsswitch.conf file needs to be configured to point to the LDAP server. (The nsswitch.ldap template is provided for this purpose.)

- The client needs to be configured with the required parameters (*LDAP client profile*).

- The ldap_cachemgr service needs to be running on the client.

Solaris 9 comes with a utility called ldapclient, which sets up all required client parameters, including modifying the nsswitch.conf file. You can run ldapclient in two modes: profile and manual. Either option configures the necessary parameters. It's recommended, though, that you set up a client profile on the LDAP server and then use this profile to configure your clients with ldapclient. This will greatly reduce the amount of time needed to set up LDAP clients on your network.

Another reason to set up clients by using a profile is that if you change profile parameters on the LDAP server, the correct parameters will be pushed to the LDAP clients. If you set up LDAP clients manually, their parameters are stored in local cache files and are not updated by the server.

Table 15.6 lists the profile attributes in a client profile. These attributes can be configured on the LDAP server by using `idsconfig`.

TABLE 15.6   LDAP Client Profile Attributes

Attribute	Description
cn	The profile name. You must provide a profile name.
preferredServerList	The IP address of one or more preferred servers to connect to. The servers in this list are tried, in order, before those in the defaultServerList. At least one server must be provided in the preferredServerList or the defaultServerList.
defaultServerList	The IP address of one or more default LDAP servers to connect to, in order of preference (separate multiple server addresses with spaces).
defaultSearchBase	The base object (DN) used to provide a relation from which to locate well-known containers.
defaultSearchScope	Defines the scope of a database search by an LDAP client.
authenticationMethod	Specifies the authentication method to be used by the client. The default is none. Other options are simple, sasl/digest-MD5, sasl/cram-MD5, tls:simple, tls:sasl/digest-MD5, and tls:sasl/cram-MD5.
credentialLevel	The type of credentials the client should use to authenticate with the LDAP server. The default is anonymous, and the other choice is proxy, if you're using a proxy server.
serviceSearchDescriptor	Defines how and where a client should search for a naming database. For example, which point(s) in the DIT the client should search in.
serviceAuthentication-Method	Authentication method used by a client for the specified service. This authentication is service specific, but if no value is present, it will default to the value in authenticationMethod.
attributeMap	Attribute mappings used by the client.
objectclassMap	Object class mappings used by the client.
searchTimeLimit	Maximum number of seconds the client should search for an object before timing out. The default is 30 seconds.

TABLE 15.6 LDAP Client Profile Attributes *(continued)*

Attribute	Description
bindTimeLimit	Maximum number of seconds a client should try binding with a server before timing out. The default is 30 seconds.
followReferrals	Indicates whether a client should follow an LDAP referral. The default is TRUE, and the other option is FALSE.
profileTTL	Number of seconds between refreshes of the client profile from the LDAP server. Refreshes are handled by ldap_cachemgr. The default is 43,200 seconds, or 12 hours. If the value is set to 0, the client profile will never be refreshed.

In addition to the profile attributes listed in Table 15.6, four local client attributes can be set locally through the ldapclient command. They are listed in Table 15.7.

TABLE 15.7 Local LDAP Client Attributes

Attribute	Description
domainName	Specifies the client's domain name. You must specify a value for the client's domain name.
proxyDN	The distinguished name of the client's proxy server. If the proxy option is specified in credentialLevel, the proxyDN must also be specified.
proxyPassword	The password for the proxy server.
certificatePath	The directory on the local computer containing the certificate databases. If the client is using Transport Layer Security (TLS) as an authentication method, then this attribute needs to be configured. The default is /var/ldap.

If you've never worked with LDAP before, the list of attributes, not to mention the LDAP terminology, can be quite confusing. Fortunately, for the test, you're not going to be required to know explicit details about each of these attributes, nor will you be asked how to set up an iPlanet Directory Server.

To set up an LDAP client by using the default profile on the LDAP server (10.0.0.44), you could use the following command:

```
# ldapclient init 10.0.0.44
```

That command will work only if either the credential level is set to anonymous or the authentication method is set to none. If your LDAP server has several profiles, or you want to specify other attributes, the -a switch is used. Look at the following example:

```
# ldapclient init -a profileName=eng -a domainName=sushi.pinkeel.com 10.0.0.44
```

This command instructs the LDAP client to use the eng profile, set the domain name to sushi.pinkeel.com, and use the 10.0.0.44 LDAP server.

Manually configuring an LDAP client requires a lot of typing because you need to manually enter all attributes that you want to set. For example, assume that you want to set up an LDAP client manually. The credential level is set to proxy, the authentication method is sasl/digest-MD5, and you do not want the client to follow LDAP referrals. The LDAP server is 10.0.0.44, and LDAP services are running on port 33888. Here is the command you would use (the command is broken across lines for readability):

```
# ldapclient manual -a credentialLevel=proxy \
-a authenticationMethod=sasl/digest-MD5 \
-a proxyPassword=abracadabra \
-a proxyDN=cn=proxy1,ou=profile,dc=sushi,dc=pinkeel,dc=com \
-a defaultSearchBase=dc=sushi,dc=pinkeel,dc=com \
-a domainName=sushi.pinkeel.com \
-a followReferrals=false \
-a preferredServerList=10.0.0.44:33888
```

That's one long command to set up an LDAP client.

> When configuring authentication, know that the TLS methods encrypt both the password and the session, whereas the non-TLS methods might encrypt the password, but not the session.

After you have configured your LDAP client, you can use the **ldapclient list** command to display your LDAP parameters. The **ldapclient mod** command enables you to modify parameters.

If you no longer want your computer to be an LDAP client, use the **ldapclient uninit** command. This will restore your client's name service to what it was before the LDAP client was initiated.

Using *getent*

Earlier in this chapter, you learned of a way to look in the NIS maps for a specific piece of information by using the ypcat and ypmatch commands. There is another command you can use, and it works with all of the naming services: getent.

The syntax for getent is simple:

```
# getent database key
```

If you wanted to search the passwd database for the user qdocter, you would use the following command:

```
# getent passwd qdocter
qdocter:6uoVIHZIxXiVI:100:10:author:/home/qdocter:/bin/ksh
```

The getent command can be used to look in local files and LDAP databases as well.

 Real World Scenario

Coming Out of the Stone Age

You have been the network administrator at your company for nearly two years. During those two years, you have used local /etc files for name resolution. Several of your users need access to multiple computers, and keeping their configuration properly maintained can be a nightmare. And when you add computers to the network, you must reconfigure the hosts file on each computer to recognize the new additions. You've developed scripts to help automate the process, but it's still not a pleasant experience. Now that your network is growing, you're not sure if you can handle all of the work. Hiring an assistant is not within the budget. Surely there has to be a solution.

Of course, there is. You need to eliminate the need for using local /etc files for your naming service. Using local /etc files is fine on very small networks but is too cumbersome and antiquated for most implementations. You need to choose a naming service. Possibilities are DNS, NIS, NIS+, and LDAP.

If your network is attached to the Internet, then DNS is a solid choice for part of your naming service solution. DNS can handle resolving Internet-based names as well as local computer names. If you're not attached to the Internet, though, then although DNS will work, it would be better to choose a single naming service that can handle all of your networking needs, such as NIS, NIS+, or LDAP.

In terms of ease, NIS is the easiest to set up and maintain. It is, however, the oldest and provides little security. NIS+ is a good choice, as it provides security and isn't much harder to set up than is NIS. The only "problem" with NIS+ is that Sun is phasing it out in favor of LDAP. So, you could choose LDAP. It has the reputation as being the most difficult to properly configure, but with a little time, you're likely to become an LDAP expert (and deserve a significant raise!).

Even if you do implement a solution by using DNS and another naming service, using two services isn't going to be a significant issue, as NIS, NIS+, and LDAP all work well in conjunction with DNS.

Whatever solution you decide to implement, do it fast. It's time to get into the modern era of computing and out of the Stone Age.

Summary

In this chapter, you learned about the available naming services in Solaris 9. The chapter started by discussing naming service concepts, such as why you would want to use naming services and when to use them.

The first major concept in Solaris naming services is the /etc/nsswitch.conf file. Residing on all clients, this file tells the client where to retrieve naming service information. Options are local files, NIS, NIS+, DNS, and LDAP. You learned how to read, configure, and modify the nsswitch.conf file to meet your networking needs. You also learned about the purpose and function of the Name Service Cache Daemon (NSCD).

After discussing nsswitch.conf, the majority of this chapter focused on the Network Information Service (NIS). NIS was one of the early fully functional naming services developed and is still widely used today. You learned about the structure of NIS, including daemons needed and commands used. You also learned that NIS information is stored in a series of maps. You learned how to create and modify maps, as well as install NIS servers and clients.

Finally, after a brief tour of NIS+, you learned how to configure DNS and LDAP clients. Solaris can function as DNS and LDAP servers as well as clients. In this chapter, you learned how to configure Solaris to function as clients of these important network services.

Exam Essentials

Know what the nsswitch.conf file does.   The nsswitch.conf file is critical for naming services. It tells the client where to look to find naming service information.

Know which daemons need to be running on NIS servers and clients.   NIS servers need to be running the ypserv and ypbind daemons. NIS clients need the ypbind daemon.

Know why you would use a directory besides /etc for NIS source files.   An alternate directory for source files, such as /var/yp, is preferable for security reasons. If you use an alternate directory, you can remove the root entries from the passwd and shadow source files. This prevents the root password from being widely available across the network.

Know how to set up a NIS master server.   After your source files are prepared, use the ypinit -m command.

Know how to make a custom map if there is an entry in makefile.   Maps can be created with the make command if there is an entry for the map in makefile.

Know how to create maps if the source file is a text file.   Maps can be created with the makedbm command.

Know which naming services use a hierarchical naming scheme.   The NIS+, DNS, LDAP, and FNS naming services use hierarchical naming.

Know what DNS does and how to set up a DNS client.   DNS resolves computer (host) names to IP addresses. The DNS client must have a local resolv.conf file properly configured, as well as the DNS service specified on the hosts: line in the nsswitch.conf file.

Know what LDAP does and how to set up an LDAP client by using profiles.   LDAP was originally designed as a directory service protocol, and now the LDAP service acts as a naming service. LDAP will eventually replace NIS+ in Solaris. To set up an LDAP client by using a profile, use the ldapclient init command.

Key Terms

Before you take the exam, be certain you are familiar with the following terms:

bind	namespace
Directory Information Tree (DIT)	Network Information Service (NIS)
Domain Name Service (DNS)	Network Information Service Plus (NIS+)
Federated Naming Service (FNS)	NIS domain
LDAP client profile	NIS maps
Lightweight Directory Access Protocol (LDAP)	NIS+ tables
local files	resolver
master server	slave servers
Name Service Cache Daemon (NSCD)	source files
name service switch file (nsswitch)	

Commands Used in This Chapter

The following list contains a summary of all the commands introduced in this chapter:

Command	Description
getent	Searches administrative databases for keys.
ldapclient	Configures an LDAP client computer.
make	Creates or updates NIS maps by reading the makefile (/var/yp/makefile) and the NIS source files.
makedbm	Creates a dbm file for a NIS map. Running the make command initiates the makedbm command, creating or updating maps.
ypcat	Displays the data in a map.
ypinit	Automatically creates NIS maps from the source files. Used to set up NIS servers for the first time, and on clients to initialize the NIS service and update the client's ypservers list.
ypmatch	Displays the value for one or more keys in a specified map.

Command	Description
yppoll	Gets a map version number from a NIS server.
yppush	Manually initiates a push of the NIS maps from the master server to the slave server(s).
ypset	Configures NIS client binding to a specific server.
ypstart	Starts the NIS service.
ypstop	Stops the NIS service.
ypwhich	Lists the name of the NIS server that supplies NIS information to that client or displays the name of the master for a given map.
ypxfr	Pulls a NIS map from the NIS master server to the local host.

Review Questions

1. You have just set up a new Solaris network and you are going to use LDAP as your naming service. On the LDAP server, you have created one profile named `client`. The name of the LDAP server is `server1`, and its IP address is 10.0.0.1. Which of the following commands do you use to set up a computer named `comp1` with an IP address of 10.0.0.22 as an LDAP client?

   A. `ldapclient init 10.0.0.1`

   B. `ldapclient init server1`

   C. `ldapclient init 10.0.0.22`

   D. `ldapclient init comp1`

   E. `ldapclient init client`

2. You are the network administrator for your company. You are going to implement a naming service to be used throughout the company. The naming service needs to be scalable to accommodate future expansion. Which of the following naming services use a hierarchical naming structure, making future expansion of your network easier to manage? (Choose all that apply.)

   A. local files

   B. FNS

   C. LDAP

   D. DNS

   E. NIS

   F. NIS+

3. You are the Solaris network administrator for your company. You have just configured a computer named `server1` to act as the NIS master server. Now, you are at `server2` and want to make it a NIS slave server. Which of the following commands do you execute first to begin the slave setup process?

   A. `ypinit -c`

   B. `ypinit -s server1`

   C. `ypinit -s server2`

   D. `ypinit -m`

4. On your Solaris network, all computers use local `hosts` files for computer name resolution. You want to replace the `hosts` files with a centralized service that can provide the same functionality. Which of the following name services was designed specifically for this function?

   A. NIS+

   B. NIS

   C. LDAP

   D. DNS

5. You are the Solaris administrator for your network. The network uses NIS as its only naming service. You have just created a new map on the NIS master server and now want to push the map to your slave server. You run the yppush command, but the process fails. You cannot find the new map on the slave server. At the command line, you ping the slave server and receive a response. What is the most likely reason the push failed?

    A. You must run the yppush command from the slave server instead of the master server.

    B. You cannot use yppush to push a map to a slave if the slave doesn't have an existing copy of the map.

    C. You need to run the ypxfr command from the master server to push the map to the slave server.

    D. The network connection between the master server and slave server is not functioning properly.

6. You have configured NIS on your Solaris network, and it is functioning properly. You are briefing other administrators on how NIS works, and one of the administrators asks a question about server communication. Which of the following daemons is responsible for initiating and maintaining communications between the NIS server and NIS client?

    A. ypserv

    B. ypbind

    C. ypinit

    D. ypxfr

7. You are configuring your Solaris network to use DNS as its naming service. Which of the following files specific to DNS must be created and configured on client machines?

    A. /etc/nsswitch.conf

    B. /etc/dns.conf

    C. /etc/resolv.conf

    D. /etc/in.named

8. You are creating a custom map file called clients.byname for your NIS domain. You want to be able to create the map and easily update the new map at the same time as other maps are updated. Which file do you modify to make an entry for the new map?

    A. /var/yp/make

    B. /var/yp/makedbm

    C. /var/yp/mapfile

    D. /var/yp/makefile

9. You are the Solaris administrator for your network. You want to ensure that the information in all NIS maps located on your four NIS slave servers is current on a daily basis. What is the easiest way to accomplish this?

   A. Edit the root `crontab` file on each slave server, and include the `ypxfr` command to pull changed maps at midnight each night.

   B. Edit the root `crontab` file on the master server, and include the `ypxfr` command to push changed maps at midnight each night.

   C. Use the `ypxfr -a -u 100` command on the server to initiate a map transfer at one o'clock each morning.

   D. Instruct the night operator to run the `ypxfr` command from each slave server each night at or around midnight as part of his nightly duties.

10. You are the Solaris administrator for your network. Until recently, all client computers on your network were using local `/etc` files for name resolution. Now, you are implementing LDAP as your name resolution method. Which file do you need to edit on your client computers to instruct them to use the LDAP server instead of local `/etc` files?

    A. `/etc/ldap.conf`

    B. `/etc/resolv.conf`

    C. `/etc/nameres.conf`

    D. `/etc/nsswitch.conf`

11. You are configuring your Solaris network to use LDAP as its naming service. Because of security concerns, you want the user's login as well as all communication with the LDAP server to be secure. Which option do you need to properly configure in the client LDAP profile?

    A. `securityMethod`

    B. `authenticationMethod`

    C. `credentialLevel`

    D. `cn`

12. You are the Solaris administrator for your network. You want to manually propagate maps from the NIS master server to NIS slave servers. Which of the following commands enable you to accomplish this? (Choose all that apply.)

    A. `ypxfr` run from the master server

    B. `ypxfr` run from the slave server

    C. `yppush` run from the master server

    D. `yppush` run from the slave server

13. Consider the following example from an `nsswitch.conf` file:

```
passwd:       files nis
group:        files nis
hosts:        dns nis [NOTFOUND=return] files
netmask:      files
```

Which of the following statements regarding the example are true? (Choose all that apply.)

A. For user login information, the local /etc files will be consulted before the NIS server.

B. To determine group membership, the NIS server will be consulted before the local /etc files.

C. When attempting to resolve a computer name to an IP address, the DNS server will be consulted first, followed by the NIS server. If the NIS server cannot find the information, local /etc files will be consulted.

D. When attempting to resolve a computer name to an IP address, the DNS server will be consulted first, followed by the NIS server. If the NIS server is not available, local /etc files will be consulted.

14. Your network uses the LDAP naming service for name resolution. All network workstations are configured with the default profile to use LDAP. One of your workstations is going to be moved to a remote office that does not use LDAP. At the remote office, they use local files for name resolution, which is what you used to use. What is the recommended way to reconfigure the workstation to use local files instead of LDAP so that it's properly configured when it's moved?

A. Delete the `nsswitch.conf` file and run **cp nsswitch.files nsswitch.conf**.

B. Delete the `nsswitch.conf` file and run **cp nsswitch.etc nsswitch.conf**.

C. Run the **ldapclient uninit** command on the workstation.

D. Reinstall Solaris 9 on the workstation.

15. You are the Solaris administrator for your network. You believe that the NIS service is misbehaving on the NIS master server, and you want to stop and restart the NIS service. Which command do you issue to stop the NIS service on the NIS master server?

A. /usr/lib/netsvc/yp/stop

B. /usr/lib/netsvc/yp/ypstop

C. /usr/lib/netsvc/yp stop

D. /usr/lib/netsvc/yp/nisstop

16. One of your network users is having trouble logging into the network. Your network uses NIS to validate user login requests. You suspect that the NIS server that the client computer is bound to does not have the most current version of the NIS passwd.byname map. Which of the following commands can you run to show you the map version number?

    A. yppoll passwd.byname

    B. ypcat passwd.byname

    C. ypmatch passwd.byname

    D. ypwhich passwd.byname

17. You are configuring NIS on your network. You have just installed a NIS master server, and stopped and restarted NIS. Which two of the following daemons must be running on the NIS server to provide functionality to client computers? (Choose two.)

    A. ypxfr

    B. ypbind

    C. ypserv

    D. rpc.ypupdated

18. You are configuring a NIS slave server in your NIS domain. Which of the following statements are true regarding the slave server creation process? (Choose all that apply.)

    A. When the NIS slave server is created, the maps are automatically propagated from the NIS master server.

    B. When the NIS slave server is created, the maps must be manually copied from the NIS master server.

    C. NIS slave servers must be set up first as NIS master servers and then as NIS slave servers.

    D. NIS slave servers must be set up first as NIS clients and then as NIS slave servers.

    E. A NIS slave server is created with the ypinit -s *master* command.

19. You are creating a custom map for your NIS domain. The source file is in ASCII format. Which command do you run to create map files from this source file?

    A. make

    B. makedbm

    C. makemap

    D. makefile

20. You are configuring the name service switch file on all computers on your network. When configuring the file, what is the limit to the number of services that you can specify per key?

    A. One

    B. Two

    C. Three

    D. You can specify all of the naming services you have available.

Answers to Review Questions

1. A. The ldapclient command is used to set up computers to be LDAP clients. If there is only one profile on the LDAP server, you do not need to specify the profile name. The init option tells ldapclient to use a profile, and then the IP address (not the name) of the server is specified.

2. B, C, D, F. Looking at all of the available naming services in Solaris, only local files and NIS use a flat naming scheme. All of the other naming services (FNS, LDAP, DNS, and NIS+) use a hierarchical naming system.

3. A. To set up a computer as a NIS slave, it first must be set up as a NIS client. Therefore, the first command you must run is ypinit -c. After that is complete, and you have restarted the ypbind service, then you can run the ypinit -s master command.

4. D. Although all of the services listed can resolve host names to IP addresses, only DNS was specifically designed for this purpose. DNS was created to replace hosts files.

5. B. The yppush command, run from the master server, pushes copies of maps to slave servers. However, the yppush command will not work for maps that do not already exist on the slave servers. The ypxfr command pulls maps and is the command you need to run in this case. It must be run from the slave server, though. Although it's possible that the network connection is not working properly, it's unlikely, considering that a ping between the two computers was successful.

6. B. The ypbind daemon is responsible for establishing communications. That process is called binding. The ypserv daemon is responsible for finding information in the NIS database, and the ypxfr daemon handles map transfers. ypinit is a command used to set up NIS servers and clients, not a daemon.

7. C. The resolver, resolv.conf, must be on each DNS client computer. Each computer also needs an nsswitch.conf file, but that file is not specific to the DNS service. The dns.conf file does not exist. in.named is the daemon that runs on the DNS server.

8. D. The makefile file contains listings of all the maps. If you create an entry in the new map for makefile, the new map will be remade every time you run the make command.

9. A. You can help ensure map consistency by using the root crontab file on each slave server. Include the ypxfr command to pull maps at specified intervals. The command ypxfr -a -u 100 might sound good, but it was made up.

10. D. The name service switch file, nsswitch.conf, is the file you need to edit to make the computers look for the LDAP server. The ldap.conf and nameres.conf files do not exist. The resolv.conf file is used only with DNS. When you set up LDAP clients with the ldapclient command, ldapclient automatically configures your nsswitch.conf file for you.

11. B. The authenticationMethod attribute is the proper answer. Because you want all communications to be secure, you should use TLS, and probably sasl/digest-MD5 or sasl/cram-MD5. The credentialLevel attribute is used if your network is using a proxy server. The cn attribute is the profile name. There is no securityMethod attribute.

12. B, C.   The `ypxfr` command initiates a map pull and therefore must be executed from the slave server. The `yppush` command pushes maps and is executed from the master server.

13. A, D.   For login information, the `passwd:` key is consulted, which says to look at the local `/etc` files first, then NIS. Group information is configured the same way. The `hosts:` key determines host name lookup. The DNS server will be consulted first, and if no resolution is made, NIS will be consulted. However, if the NIS server cannot find the information (`[NOTFOUND=return]`), the process will stop. If the NIS server is unavailable (which would return an `UNAVAIL` message, not `NOTFOUND`), then the local `/etc` files will be consulted.

14. C.   The `ldapclient uninit` command will remove the client configuration for the LDAP service and return the computer to the naming service client state it was in before the LDAP service was introduced. You could also rename the `nsswitch.files` template to `nsswitch.conf`. However, running `ldapclient uninit` is recommended. The `nsswitch.etc` file does not exist, and reinstalling Solaris is unnecessary.

15. B.   The `/usr/lib/netsvc/yp/ypstop` command is used to stop the NIS service. Running the `ypstart` command in the same directory will restart the NIS service.

16. A.   The `yppoll` command will display an order number (synonymous with a version number) of the map specified. You can compare this to the order number of the map taken from the NIS master server.

17. B, C.   All four of the provided answers are valid NIS daemons. However, the only two that are required to run NIS and provide functionality to clients are `ypbind` and `ypserv`.

18. A, D, E.   To create a NIS slave server, you must first make the computer a NIS client with the `ypinit -c` command. Then after restarting `ypbind`, you make the computer a slave server with the `ypinit -s` command. When you make a computer a NIS slave server, the maps are pulled automatically from the NIS master server.

19. B.   To create maps that have an ASCII source file, use the `makedbm` command. The `make` command is for maps that have entry in `makefile`. The `makemap` command does not exist.

20. D.   There is no hard-coded limit. Realistically, though, it's unlikely you'll have more than three options on your network (local files, DNS, and NIS or NIS+ as an example).

Chapter

16

Advanced Installation Procedures

SOLARIS 9 EXAM OBJECTIVES COVERED IN THIS CHAPTER:

✓ Explain the purpose, features, and functionality of JumpStart, including boot services, identification services, configuration services, and installation services.

✓ Given a scenario, explain the procedures, scripts, and commands to implement a JumpStart server.

✓ Given a scenario describing JumpStart configuration alternatives, explain how to establish a boot-only server, identification service alternatives, configuration service alternatives, and installation service alternatives.

✓ Given scenarios involving JumpStart problems with booting, identification, configuration, install, or begin/finish scripts, analyze and select a course of action to resolve the problem.

✓ Explain how to use the Flash installation feature, and describe requirements and limitations of this feature.

✓ Explain how to create and use a Flash archive and how to use a Flash archive for installation with Web Start, interactive install, and JumpStart.

Installing operating systems is an essential task for system administration. After all, if you don't install an operating system, what will you have to administer? Although installation is a necessary chore, you won't find many network administrators who classify it as an exciting task.

The first two or three times you install a new operating system might be informative and even somewhat interesting. The first time, the installation is new to you, so you're likely to pay attention. The second time, you will pay less attention, but you might notice something you missed the first time. The third time…well, from here the excitement probably wanes significantly. Now, imagine the thrill of installing two or three dozen computers, or perhaps even two or three hundred.

To help with the process of installing large numbers of computers, and ensuring that they all have similar configurations, Sun has developed utilities to automate installations. In Chapter 2, "Installation," you learned about the four programs you could use to install Solaris. The automated methods described in this chapter, custom JumpStart and Flash, are extensions of installation processes you learned about in Chapter 2.

Using these automated installations requires more preparation time, but will save you a significant amount of time when installing a large number of computers. And just as important, you can be assured that the computers you install will have the software configuration you want.

Using JumpStart

JumpStart is one of the four installation methods you can use to install Solaris. The others that you learned about in Chapter 2 are `suninstall`, Web Start, and Solaris Live Upgrade. Jump-Start is a flexible and comprehensive installation program that has two versions: *custom JumpStart* and *factory JumpStart*.

The factory JumpStart installation program is commonly referred to just as JumpStart, whereas the custom method is almost always clarified by its "custom" moniker. Factory JumpStart installations are automated but do not give the administrator flexibility when installing Solaris.

What factory JumpStart does is automatically install Solaris 9 on a new SPARC-based computer when you insert the Solaris 9 DVD or Solaris 9 Software 1 of 2 CD into the computer and reboot it. Detecting the system type and disk size, factory JumpStart installs Solaris according to a default profile. The profile determines slice layout as well as the software installed on the computer. Although it's a handy installation method, it's not the most accommodating.

The JumpStart that this chapter focuses on is custom JumpStart. Custom JumpStart enables you to install several systems based on profiles that you create. In the profile, you can include which software components to install, as well as specify pre- and post-installation tasks to complete.

Because this chapter concentrates on custom JumpStart, all references to JumpStart from this point forward refer to custom JumpStart.

Creating installation profiles takes time. In fact, if you're installing only a few computers, it might take more time to create profiles than to install the computers. But if you have a large number of installations to make or if you frequently reinstall client computers, the profiles can save you a significant amount of time.

In a nutshell, custom JumpStart is designed to efficiently install Solaris on a large number of computers, while ensuring that the computers have a specific software configuration. By combining a custom JumpStart profile with a `sysidcfg` file to provide system information, you can make a custom JumpStart installation totally automated.

Overview of JumpStart

JumpStart is a client-server program used to install Solaris client computers with little to no interaction required from the administrator. The larger the number of clients you need to install, the more efficient JumpStart becomes.

For JumpStart to work properly, you must configure one or more JumpStart servers. These servers will help the client computer boot, identify the client, and provide installation and configuration files to help install Solaris. These servers will be covered in depth in the "Configuring JumpStart Servers" section later in this chapter.

A scenario can best help you understand how the overall JumpStart process works. In this scenario, you are installing Solaris 9 on 100 client computers, none of which have an operating system currently installed. Fifty of the computers are for your research and development group, and the other fifty are for the administrative group, which includes accounting, human resources, and other administrative staff. The R&D group will need to have the Developers software group installed, whereas the administrative staff will need the standard End User software group.

You can see that there are two distinct configurations that you need to install. For each configuration, you must create a `rules` file as well as a profile. The `rules` file will determine which configuration is installed, based on some characteristic of the computer that the software will be installed on. The `rules` file points to the profile, which performs the installation based on parameters you've specified within the profile. So, as the administrator, you create two `rules` files and two profiles, one each for the R&D group and the administrative group. These files will be stored in a JumpStart directory on the profile server.

Because you will be installing over the network, you also need to configure a boot server. To make things easier, you are going to make one server your JumpStart server, meaning that it performs boot as well as installation services for clients.

With your server properly configured, you need to boot your clients from the network. After the client boots, it will begin installing Solaris.

Obviously, this scenario is a simplified version of what you, the administrator, need to do to get JumpStart to work properly. Hopefully, though, you now have a good idea of the basic concepts of JumpStart and of how the process works.

Planning for Installation

Before you start your installation, you need to carefully plan it out. This concept was drilled repeatedly in Chapter 2, but it's more important now. Why? Because now that you're dealing with JumpStart, it can be assumed that you are installing a large number of client computers. Each of these computers will have certain software requirements. You will want to install the systems in the shortest amount of time possible, but of course with the correct parameters. This can't be done haphazardly. Plan before you install.

Some of the questions you can ask before installing include the following:

- Who will be using the computer?

- What software will they need to access?

- Is this going to be an upgrade of Solaris or a new installation?

- Where is the computer located?

- Will the installation be local or over the network?

These questions can also bring up other questions. For example, engineering or development employees might require more virtual memory (meaning more swap space) than users who might do only light data entry or word processing. Also, based on the users' needs, you might need to install a specific Solaris software package, as well as third-party applications.

After you have answered these questions and decided what each computer needs, you need to create the two configuration files used to perform a JumpStart installation of Solaris. These files can be placed on either a floppy disk or a profile server. If your computers are not networked, or if you will be installing Solaris locally from the CD-ROM or DVD-ROM drive, you can use the disk. If you're installing over the network, then the configuration files will be on the profile server.

Knowing the JumpStart Commands

Setting up and configuring JumpStart requires several commands. There currently is no way to set up JumpStart through a graphical interface. Table 16.1 lists some of the commands used with JumpStart.

TABLE 16.1   JumpStart Commands

Command	Description
add_install_client	Adds network installation information about a client to the JumpStart server.
add_to_install_server	Copies additional Solaris packages to an existing installation server configuration.
check	Validates the rules file and creates a rules.ok file.
modify_install_server	Modifies an existing package on the install server.

TABLE 16.1   JumpStart Commands *(continued)*

Command	Description
pfinstall	Performs a trial run installation. Used to see if any potential problems exist.
rm_install_client	Removes client information from the JumpStart server.
setup_install_server	Performs the initial installation of the JumpStart server.

Most of the commands associated with JumpStart are used to set up and configure the server. Considering that the majority of work needed to get JumpStart running properly is done during setup, this makes perfect sense.

Configuring JumpStart Servers

The three servers that are required for JumpStart are the boot, install, and profile servers. For cost and convenience, one server can perform all three functions, and that's how most Jump-Start installations are configured. To learn how JumpStart works, though, it's best to think of them as three separate servers.

Installing a Boot Server

The *boot server* is the first computer that JumpStart clients will come into contact with during the installation process. Although some client computers might have an existing operating system installed, you can assume that clients using JumpStart are a blank slate. They have no operating system, meaning that they also have no boot files. The boot server provides the files that clients need to boot.

If your client does not have an operating system installed, you can boot from the network with the **boot net** command at the ok prompt.

When a client is first booted, it broadcasts on the network to look for a boot server. Specifically, the client computer is looking for boot files and an IP address. Because client computers broadcast looking for information, the boot server must be on the same subnet as the client computer for the boot process to work properly. If you have several IP subnets, you will need one boot server per subnet.

An alternative to having boot servers on each subnet is to have the routers also function as boot servers. However, this configuration can result in performance degradation, especially on heavily utilized networks. Another alternative to using boot servers on each subnet is to use the Dynamic DNS (DDNS) service along with DHCP for your network clients.

The boot server needs to be running the *Reverse Address Resolution Protocol (RARP)* daemon, named `in.rarpd`, to service the clients' requests. If this daemon is running and it receives a network boot request, it will look up the client's Ethernet address in the local `/etc/ethers` file. The daemon then passes the located address back to the client computer.

 If the `in.rarpd` daemon is not running, JumpStart will fail.

WARNING

After the IP address is passed back to the client, the boot server looks for the appropriate boot file for the client, based on the client processor architecture. The boot file is transmitted to the client via the *Trivial File Transfer Protocol (TFTP)* and its associated daemon, `in.tftpd`. The client uses the boot program to start up.

The boot program tries to mount the root file system (/) on the client. To do this, it issues a `whoami` request, asking for the client's host name. The boot server, using the `rpc.bootparamd` daemon, looks up the host name and returns it to the client. Then, the boot program uses a `getfile` request to locate the client's root file system (/) and swap space. The boot server gets this data from its local `/etc/bootparams` file and returns it to the client.

After obtaining its boot parameters, the boot program mounts the local root file system (/) from the boot server. Then, the kernel is loaded on the local system, and the `init` process is started. After `init` loads, the boot server redirects the client computer to the profile server. At this point, the client computer has a very rudimentary, skeletal version of Solaris running. It is not the whole operating system and is not yet usable by people.

Using the information obtained from `bootparams`, the client searches for the profile server. After the server is located, the client locates the directory where the Solaris installation files are located and then begins the installation with the `suninstall` program.

 This boot process seems complex, and although it is, the back-and-forth queries and loading are completed relatively quickly. It's not like you will be sitting there for hours waiting for the boot process to complete.

NOTE

The files that are important to the boot process (and therefore must be properly configured on the boot server) are `/etc/ethers`, `/etc/hosts`, `/etc/bootparams`, `/etc/dfs/dfstab`, and `/tftpboot`:

/etc/ethers This file contains a mapping of Ethernet addresses to IP addresses. When a client computer boots, it will know its Ethernet address but not its IP. Using RARP, the client can obtain the needed address from this file.

You can manually create entries in `/etc/ethers`, but this can be a painstaking process. The easier way to modify this file is to use the `add_install_client` command, which will create the entries for you.

/etc/hosts By now, you should know that the `hosts` file resolves computer names to IP addresses. When the client looks for its host name (provided that it found a valid IP address in

/etc/ethers), this file will be consulted. If you are running a name service such as DNS or NIS, then the name service will take the place of this file.

/etc/bootparams This file contains boot parameters, such as root file system and swap space location, for network-based clients. For the server to properly respond to a client requesting this information, the rpc.bootparamd daemon must be running.

/etc/dfs/dfstab This file, as you might remember, lists local file systems to be shared on the network. If the root file system (/) is not shared, then clients will not be able to access files from it.

/tftpboot This is actually a directory, not a file. When you run the add_install_client program, a boot file for the JumpStart client will be added to this directory. The boot file will be associated with the client based on the client's IP address, expressed in hexadecimal format.

The first command that you need to run to set up the boot server is setup_install_server -b. The -b option specifies that this computer will be a boot server. After this command is completed, clients can be added with the add_install_client command.

Setting Up the Install Server

Most of the time, the boot server and the install server are the same computer. However, they have different duties. The boot server provides the client with a boot configuration, and the *install server* contains the source files used to install Solaris. While the boot server must be on the same subnet as the client computer, the install server can be located virtually anywhere on the network.

The install server is configured with the setup_install_server command. When you execute this command, you will need to specify an empty directory in which you want the Solaris source files to be installed. The directory can be any directory you choose, but the directory must be shared so that JumpStart clients can access it across the network. Some administrators like to use /export/install as the source directory, whereas others like to create a /jumpstart/install directory.

The biggest requirement for the install server is disk space. You will be copying the installation files for Solaris 9 to the hard disk, so it's best to make sure that you have about 1GB of free space. Also, if you're copying Solaris for both SPARC and Intel platforms, you can count on needing double the free space.

Because most of the time your boot server and install server will be the same computer, you can set both of them up at once. After inserting the Solaris 9 Installation CD, here's what you need to do:

```
# cd /cdrom/cdrom0/s0/Solaris_9/Tools
# ./setup_install_server /jumpstart/install
```

The first command line shows you the directory you need to be in. The second command line issues the setup_install_server command, with the /jumpstart/install directory as the JumpStart source directory. If you're using the CD-ROM version of Solaris as the source files, you will also need to copy both Solaris 9 Software CDs to the install directory as well.

(If you're using the DVD-ROM version, all required files are located on the single DVD.) Here's how you can expedite that process (insert the Solaris 9 Software 1 of 2 CD first):

```
# ./add_to_install_server /jumpstart/install
```

The `add_to_install_server` program will add the Solaris Software 1 of 2 CD to the image on the server. If you don't want to add the entire CD, but only a subset of packages, use the `add_to_install_server -s` option. When the copy process is finished, repeat the process with the Solaris Software 2 of 2 CD, and the Solaris 9 Languages CD, if needed. After the software is copied, you can also use the `patchadd -c` command to patch the image, so that clients will not need to be patched after their initial installation.

Configuring the Profile Server

The *profile server* contains the `rules` files and profiles for Solaris installations. These files will be located in a JumpStart directory. This directory can be any directory you want as long as it's in the root directory (/) of the profile server. For convenience, many administrators create a `/jumpstart` directory. The profile server can be the same computer as the install and/or boot servers, or it can be a different computer.

You must have superuser or equivalent privileges to create this directory. Here's how to create the JumpStart directory that will contain the `rules` files and profiles:

1. Create the JumpStart directory. It can be called anything you want, but it must be located in the root directory of the profile server. The permissions should be set to 755.

    ```
    # mkdir -m 755 /jumpstart
    ```

2. Edit the /etc/dfs/dfstab file to share the new directory. You want to allow anonymous access.

    ```
    # share -F nfs -o ro,anon=0 /jumpstart
    ```

3. Share the new directory.

    ```
    # shareall
    ```

4. The directory is now created and shared. If you have already created your `rules` files and profiles, you can now copy them to this location. If, instead, you would like to copy some sample files from the Solaris 9 Software 1 of 2 CD, use the following command:

    ```
    # cp -r /cdrom/cdrom0/s0/Solaris_9/Misc/jumpstart_sample/* /jumpstart
    ```

Now that your JumpStart directory is created, you need to allow client computers access to the directory.

Configuring Clients to Access the Profile Server

You can grant access to clients in one of three ways:

- Use the `add_install_client -c` command
- Use the `boot` command
- Edit the /etc/bootparams file

Perhaps the most convenient way is to use the add_install_client -c command. It needs to be run once for each client.

By using the boot command, you can specify the location of the JumpStart directory when you boot the client computer. For this to work correctly, you must first compress the custom JumpStart configuration files into one file by using tar, compressed tar, zip, or bzip tar formats. Next, store the compressed file on an NFS server, an HTTP server, or local media for the client system to access. Then issue the following command:

ok **boot cdrom:net - install** *url***:ask**

This syntax might be a bit confusing if you're not familiar with the boot command. The first option specifies to boot from either the CD-ROM or the network. You use either cdrom or net as your option. The -install argument is the key, as it tells the boot program that you are attempting an installation. Finally, you can specify a URL pointing to the configuration files, or use the argument ask, which will prompt you for the location of the compressed configuration file after the client computer boots and attaches to the network.

Table 16.2 lists some examples of URL syntax to use with the boot command.

TABLE 16.2   *boot* Command URL Examples

File Location	Syntax
Local hard disk	file://*jumpstart_dir/compressed_config_file*
	file://jumpstart/config.tar
NFS server	nfs://*server_name:server_IP/jumpstart_dir/compressed_ config_file*
	nfs://Athena/jumpstart/config.tar
	nfs://192.168.0.33/jumpstart/config.tar
HTTP server	http://*server_name:server_IP/jumpstart_dir/compressed_ config_file*
	http://www.solarisbook.com/jumpstart/config.tar
	http://192.168.0.34/jumpstart/config.tar
HTTP server behind a proxy server	http://*server_name:server_IP/jumpstart_dir/compressed_ config_file&proxy_info*
	http://www.solarisbook.com/jumpstart/config.tar&proxy =192.168.0.35

If you are using a sysidcfg file and placed the file in the compressed configuration file, then you must use the server's IP address instead of the server's name. If you are putting the compressed file on an HTTP server that's behind a proxy server, then you must specify the proxy information, but you do not need to use the IP address of the server.

The final option is to use a wildcard in the /etc/bootparams file on the boot server. The wildcard entry needed in bootparams will look like * install_config=*server:jumpstart_dir*. For example, if your JumpStart server is named Athena, and the directory is called /jumpstart, your line would be * install_config=Athena:/jumpstart. This will enable all clients to access the profile server, instead of creating lines for each specific client.

Editing the bootparams file to help locate the JumpStart server can cause the following error message to appear on clients attempting to connect:

WARNING: getfile: RPC failed: error 5: (RPC Timed out).

This error message occurs for one of three reasons. The first is that there are /etc/bootparams files on more than one server with an entry for this client. Check to make sure that only one boot server has an entry for this client (or the wildcard) in /etc/bootparams. The second and closely related possibility is that one boot server on the network has a bootparams entry specifically for the client, whereas another server has the wildcard * install_config= line. Either remove the wildcard line or remove the entry for the specific client computer. The third potential cause is that multiple instances of the /tftpboot or /rplboot directories exist for this client. Make sure that only one exists for the client.

Using Profile Diskettes

So far, the profile server has been discussed, but you have another option for stand-alone client computers. You can create a *profile diskette*. If you want to install a large number of client computers, but you have no network, this is a great option.

Instead of creating a JumpStart directory on a profile server, you are going to create the same directory, including the rules, rules.ok, profile, and sysidcfg files on the disk. Then, when you install the client by using the local CD-ROM or DVD-ROM, the disk can provide all the necessary answers to complete the automated installation.

First, format a floppy disk, and create a UFS file system on the disk. Then, create a JumpStart directory. If you like using the /jumpstart convention, then by all means keep using it for the floppy. After that directory is created, make sure that the root has ownership of the directory and that the permissions are set to 755. Finally, copy the custom JumpStart configuration files to the /jumpstart directory on the floppy disk.

To use the profile diskette, boot the computer with both the disk and the Solaris 9 Installation CD-ROM inserted, and begin the installation. For example, to boot to the CD-ROM and install, you could use the following command:

ok **boot cdrom - install ask**

Provided that your configuration files were created properly, the installation should proceed unattended.

Creating *rules* Files and Profiles

Now that you've learned about the server roles critical to JumpStart, it's time to focus on the files that make JumpStart work. These files must be located in the JumpStart directory on the profile server or profile diskette.

Understanding *rules* Files

A *rules file* is a text file containing a rule for each group of systems that you are going to be installing Solaris on. Each rule identifies a group of computers based on one or more system attributes. When first learning about JumpStart in this chapter, you read an example of installing 100 client computers. Fifty of them were in the R&D group, and the other fifty were in the administrative group. Because you have two groups, you need two rules, one to identify each group. Later in this section, you will learn how you can differentiate the two groups. You can create one rules file with both rules, or separate rules files for each group. Generally, it's better to go with the single rules file as to avoid confusion during installations, but the choice is up to you.

Each rule is responsible for first distinguishing a group of computers and then linking each group to a profile. The rule determines which computers get which profile, and then the profile determines how to install Solaris.

The name of the rules file should not be changed, and for it to work, it must contain at least one rule. The rules file can also contain comments, blank lines, and rules that use multiple lines. To continue a rule on a second line, place a backslash (\) at the end of a line and press Enter. A rules file can be created from any text editor, or you can modify the sample rules file provided on the Solaris 9 Software 1 of 2 CD.

The rules file should be owned by root and have permissions of 644.

Here is part of the sample rules file from the CD-ROM:

```
# The rules file is a text file used to create the rules.ok file for
# a custom JumpStart installation. The rules file is a lookup table
# consisting of one or more rules that define matches between system
# attributes and profiles.
#
# This example rules file contains:
#    o syntax of a rule used in the rules file
#    o rule_keyword and rule_value descriptions
#    o rule examples
#
# See the installation manual for a complete description of the rules file.
#
# RULE EXAMPLES
#
# The following rule matches only one system:
#
hostname sample_host    -        host_class      set_root_pw


# The following rule matches any system that is on the 924.222.43.0 network
```

```
# and has the sun4c kernel architecture:
#    Note: The backslash (\) is used to continue the rule to a new line.
network 924.222.43.0 && \
          karch sun4c      -         net924_sun4c      -

# The following rule matches any sparc system with a c0t3d0 disk that
# is between 400 to 600 MBytes and has Solaris 2.1 installed on it:
arch sparc && \
          disksize c0t3d0 400-600 && \
          installed c0t3d0s0 solaris_2.1 - upgrade  -
#
# The following rule matches all x86 systems:
arch i386   x86-begin   x86-class   -

# The following rule matches any system:
any -   -   any_machine   -
```

The full sample `rules` file does a good job of explaining the syntax and options for creating rules. The only problem is that it's more than three pages long. Remember that if you use the sample file to make your own rules, comment out the included rule examples with a pound sign (#).

Here is the syntax for rule entries in the `rules` file:

```
[!] rule_keyword rule_value [&& [!] rule_keyword rule_value] ...⏎
    begin profile finish
```

The brackets ([and]) indicate optional fields. The exclamation point (!) is used to negate keywords, and the double *and* symbols (&&) are used to tie more than one rule keyword and value pair together. Table 16.3 describes the fields within the `rules` file.

TABLE 16.3   *rules* Fields

Field	Description
rule_keyword	A predefined term that describes a general system attribute, such as the host name, memory size, hard disk size, or processor architecture.
rule_value	A value that describes the keyword, such as the host name, size of the memory or hard disk, or processor architecture.
begin	An optional Bourne shell (sh) script to run before the installation begins. If you do not want to run a begin script, fill this field with a minus sign (-). All begin scripts must be located in the JumpStart directory.
profile	The name of the profile to be used by computers that fit this rule. All profiles must be located in the JumpStart directory.

TABLE 16.3   *rules* Fields *(continued)*

Field	Description
finish	An optional Bourne shell (sh) script to be executed after the installation is complete. If you are not using a finish script, place a minus sign (-) in this field. All finish scripts must be located in the JumpStart directory.

At the very least, each rule must contain a keyword, a value, and a profile. Here's a simple entry that you might find in a `rules` file:

```
karch sun4u - profile1 -
```

The `rule_keyword` is `karch` (kernel architecture, or platform group), and the `rule_value` is `sun4u`, indicating the sun4u platform. There is no begin or finish script specified, and the profile that all sun4u computers will use is named `profile1`.

There are 14 rule keywords available for your use. Table 16.4 lists these keywords, the possible value types, and a brief description of each.

TABLE 16.4   Rule Keywords and Values

Keyword	Value(s)	Description
any	A minus sign (-)	The any keyword matches all computers.
arch	*processor_type*	The system's processor type, as returned by the uname -p command. An example of a valid value is sparc.
disksize	*disk_name size_range*	The name and size of the computer's disk, in megabytes. The disk name is in the form of cxtydz, such as c0t3d0, or the word rootdisk. The rootdisk value will match to the disk that has the preinstalled boot image, the c0t3d0 disk, or the first available disk that is found by a kernel probe. The size range must be specified in megabytes. Example: disksize c0t3d0 750-1000.
domainname	*domain_name*	The name of the domain that the computer belongs to.
hostaddress	*IP_address*	The IP address of the computer.
hostname	*host_name*	The name of the computer.

TABLE 16.4   Rule Keywords and Values *(continued)*

Keyword	Value(s)	Description
installed	*slice version*	This keyword is looking for computers that already have Solaris installed. The slice value means a computer with Solaris installed on that slice, and the version value matches to specific versions of Solaris. The slice value is in the form c*wtxdysz*, or the special word rootdisk. The version value can have a Solaris version name, or the words any or upgrade. If any is used, all Solaris versions are matched. If upgrade is used, then any Solaris 2.1 or compatible version that can be upgraded is matched.
karch	*platform_group*	The computer's platform group. You can find this information by using the arch -k and uname -m commands.
memsize	*physical_memory*	The amount of memory in the computer, specified in megabytes. This can be a single number or a range.
model	*platform_name*	The computer's platform name. You can find this information with the uname -i command or the prtconf command, line 5.
network	*network_number*	The network address of the computer (*not* necessarily the entire IP address).
osname	Solaris_x	A version of Solaris already installed on the computer. Example: osname Solaris_8.
probe	*probe_keyword*	A probe keyword. Probe keywords are used by custom_probe files, which, in a nutshell, ask the computer for information, return a value, and then take a course of action determined by the returned value.
totaldisk	*total_disk_size*	The total disk size on the computer, specified as a megabyte range. This includes all hard disks installed in the computer.

When calculating disk size or memory size, remember that one megabyte is equal to 1,048,576 bytes. This might throw you off in your ranges. For example, an 800MB hard disk will appear to JumpStart as a 763MB hard disk (800,000,000 / 1,048,576 = 763). Therefore, a range of 775–825 will not match to this hard disk.

As you can see from Table 16.4, some keywords are designed for only one computer (such as hostname or hostaddress), while others can include the entire network (such as domainname or any). When configuring a rules file, you really have all the granularity you could possibly want.

 If you want one profile to be used to install all computers on your network, the rule should read any - - *profile_name* -, where *profile_name* is the name of the profile you want to use.

Now that you know the structure of the rules file and what the keywords are, here are five sample entries to look at:

```
hostname Sol-1 - sol_profile -
network 192.168.0.32 && karch sun4u begin1 4u_profile finish1
network 192.168.0.32 && !karch sun4u begin2 otro_profile finish2
model SUNW,Sun-Blade-100 - blade_profile backup
any - - basic_profile -
```

The first entry will match to only the Sol-1 computer. It will install by using the sol_profile profile, and not use a begin or a finish script. The second line will match to computers that are on the 192.168.0.32 network and have the sun4u architecture. The 4u_profile will be used, as will the begin1 and finish1 scripts. The third entry will match to the computers on the same network as the second entry, but only those that are *not* sun4u computers. The profile will be otro_profile, and begin2 and finish2 are the begin and finish scripts. The fourth entry matches to Sun Blade 100 computers, with no begin script, the blade_profile profile, and the backup finish script. The final entry matches to all computers and runs the basic_profile.

Keep in mind that when JumpStart installs, it searches the rules.ok file and uses the profile that it finds when it receives its first client match. So if you put the any entry first, then all computers would get the basic_profile.

 Be familiar with the rules file syntax before you take the exam.

Validating the *rules* File

Before the rules file can be used, it must be validated with the check script. The check script ensures that the rules file is set up correctly. If so, a validated rules.ok file is created.

The check script is in the Solaris_9/Misc/jumpstart_sample directory on the Solaris 9 Software 1 of 2 CD, as well as on the Solaris 9 DVD. You can also find it in the JumpStart directory on your hard disk if you copied the sample files from your source media. Here's the syntax for check:

```
# ./check -p path -r file_name
```

The -p option enables you to specify a specific path for the check script. The -r option is used if you are using a file named something besides rules. In most cases, you will run check with no command-line options.

If the check script finds no errors in the rules file, it creates a rules.ok file, which is the file used by JumpStart to match client computers. When no errors are encountered, the computer will return the message The custom JumpStart configuration is ok.

Using Begin Scripts

Begin scripts are Bourne shell (sh) scripts that run before the Solaris installation takes place. Begin scripts are called from the rules file and can be used only if you're performing a custom JumpStart installation.

A begin script is used primarily to perform one of two functions: to create a derived profile or to back up existing files before upgrading Solaris.

A derived profile is used when you cannot set up a rules file to match some of your computers to a profile. For example, you might have systems that are the same model, but have different hardware configurations. A begin script can dynamically create a derived profile to match the computers.

To use a derived profile, set the profile field to an equal sign (=) in the rules file for the computers you want to match. Then, specify a begin script that creates a derived profile depending on the system hardware of the computer on which you want to install Solaris. The derived profile will then be used instead of the standard profile.

When creating begin scripts, make sure that root owns the file and that permissions are set to 644. Also, ensure that nothing in the script will prevent the mounting of file systems onto /a during the initial install or upgrade. If JumpStart cannot mount file systems onto /a, the installation will fail. Output from the begin script will be logged in /var/sadm/begin.log.

Using Finish Scripts

Finish scripts are Bourne shell (sh) scripts that run after the Solaris installation takes place, but before the computer reboots. Finish scripts are called from the rules file and can be used only if you're performing a custom JumpStart installation.

Finish scripts enable you to add additional files to the computer, add individual software packages or patches, customize the root environment, set the computer's root password, and install additional software as needed.

Finish scripts should be located in the JumpStart directory, be owned by root, and have permissions of 644. Also know that the suninstall program mounts file systems on /a during the installation, and those file systems remain mounted on /a until the computer reboots. So if you're modifying file systems with a finish script, remember to modify the correct file system in relation to /a.

You can use custom JumpStart environment variables in finish scripts. Output from finish scripts is logged in /var/sadm/finish.log.

 Creating begin and finish scripts is beyond the scope of the Sun Certified System Administrator exams and this book. For detailed information on creating these scripts, see the *Solaris 9 Installation Guide,* available at docs.sun.com.

Understanding Profiles

After the `rules` file matches a client computer to one of its rules, the custom JumpStart installation process calls a profile to determine how to install Solaris. A *profile* is a text file that defines how to install Solaris on that particular computer. There are no restrictions on how you can define rules and profiles. Several rules might use the same profile, or you can have separate profiles for every rule.

Compared to the `rules` file, the syntax of profiles is pretty basic. All a profile contains is a list of keywords and their associated values. Each keyword controls how a specific aspect of Solaris is to be installed. Enter one keyword and value pair per line.

You can name a profile anything you would like, but it's a good idea to name it something that makes sense based on what you're using it for. For example, an accounting profile might be called `acct_profile`, or the general network profile might be called `basic_profile`. Profiles must be located in the JumpStart directory, be owned by `root`, and have permissions of 644.

 Profiles used to be called class files.

A profile must contain the `install_type` keyword as its first entry. Also, if the computer is being upgraded and contains more than one root file system (/) that can be upgraded, the `root_device` keyword is needed. Profiles can contain blank lines and can also contain comments preceded with a pound sign (#).

To create a profile, you can use any text editor, or you can use one of the sample profiles provided in the `Solaris_9/Misc/jumpstart_sample` directory on the Solaris 9 Software 1 of 2 CD, as well as on the Solaris 9 DVD.

Table 16.5 lists the 20 valid profile keywords and the situations when they can be used.

TABLE 16.5   Profile Keywords

Keyword	Description	To Be Used When...
archive_location	Location of the Web Start Flash archive (if applicable).	Installing a stand-alone non-networked or networked client, or a networked server.
backup_media	Location used to back up file systems if disk space will be reallocated during an upgrade.	Upgrading a computer and using disk space reallocation.
boot_device	Device where JumpStart will install the root file system (/) and boot device.	Installing a stand-alone non-networked or networked client, a networked server, or an OS server.
client_arch	The platform that the OS server will support, when it's a different platform than what the OS server uses.	Installing an OS server.

TABLE 16.5   Profile Keywords *(continued)*

Keyword	Description	To Be Used When...
client_root	The amount of root file system (/) space reserved for each client.	Installing an OS server.
client_swap	The amount of swap space to reserve for each diskless client.	Installing an OS server.
cluster (adding software groups)	The software group to add to the client computer.	Installing a stand-alone non-networked or networked client, a networked server, or an OS server.
cluster (adding or deleting clusters)	The cluster to add or delete from the software group.	Installing or upgrading in all situations.
dontuse	One or more hard disks that you don't want JumpStart to use.	Installing a stand-alone non-networked or networked client, a networked server, or an OS server.
filesys (mounting remote file systems)	Remote file systems that installed clients will automatically mount when they boot.	Installing a stand-alone networked client, a networked server, or an OS server.
filesys (creating local file systems)	Specific local file systems that will be created during the installation.	Installing a stand-alone non-networked or networked client, a networked server, or an OS server.
geo	The regional locale or locales you want to install.	Installing or upgrading in all situations.
install_type	The installation type, such as initial_install, upgrade, or flash_install.	Installing or upgrading in all situations.
isa_bits	The version of Solaris to be installed (32-bit or 64-bit).	Installing or upgrading in all situations.
layout_constraint	The constraints that auto-layout has on the existing file systems.	Upgrading a computer and using disk space reallocation.
locale	The locale of the packages you want to install or add.	All installation or upgrade situations.
num_clients	The number of diskless clients that the OS sever can support.	Installing an OS server.

TABLE 16.5   Profile Keywords *(continued)*

Keyword	Description	To Be Used When...
package	The software package to be added or deleted from the software group.	Installing or upgrading in all situations.
partitioning	The way that the hard disks will be divided into slices.	Installing a stand-alone non-networked or networked client, a networked server, or an OS server.
root_device	The installed computer's root disk.	Installing or upgrading in all situations.
system_type	The type of system, such as server or standalone.	Installing a stand-alone non-networked or networked client, a networked server, or an OS server.
usedisk	The hard disk that you want JumpStart to use.	Installing a stand-alone non-networked or networked client, a networked server, or an OS server.

Based on this table, you can tell that there are quite a few options you can use with a custom JumpStart installation. Some options are commonly used, whereas others are rarely employed. Following are some examples of profiles, and explanations of the keyword and value combinations used.

The package names for the software groups are: SUNWCreq for Core, SUNWCuser for User, SUNWCprog for Developer, SUNWCall for Entire, and SUNWCXall for Entire Plus OEM.

Examples of Profiles

The sample profiles provided in the Solaris_9/Misc/jumpstart_sample directory on the Solaris 9 Software 1 of 2 CD and the Solaris 9 DVD provide a good place to start if you're not sure what you want in your profile. Even experienced administrators will tell you, though, to get profiles to work exactly the way you want them to takes trial and error.

This first example is one of the easiest profiles you will see. It's designed to perform an initial installation (as opposed to an upgrade) on a stand-alone computer by using default partitioning and installing the End User software group:

```
install_type      initial_install
system_type       standalone
partitioning      default
cluster           SUNWCuser
```

Most of the value types listed in this first example should be self-explanatory. The last value, SUNWCuser, is the designation for the Solaris End User software group. You can specify only one software group in a profile. You can, however, add or remove software clusters from the group. Just make sure to list the group before using other `cluster` or `package` keywords.

This next example deletes a cluster, as well as adds a cluster:

```
install_type      initial_install
system_type       standalone
partitioning      default
cluster           SUNWCuser
cluster           SUNWCxgl delete
package           SUNWaudmo add
filesys           any 40 swap
filesys           any 50 /opt
```

After this profile installs the End User software group, it deletes the SUNWCxgl cluster and adds the SUNWaudmo package. This profile also places the swap space (40MB) on any slice, and the /opt file system (50MB) on any slice.

Here's one more example initial installation:

```
install_type      initial_install
system_type       server
partitioning      default
cluster           SUNWCall
num_clients       7
client_swap       32
client_arch       sun4c
client_arch       sun4m
filesys           c0t3d0s0 20 /
filesys           c0t3d0s1 40 swap
filesys           c0t3d0s5 80 /opt
```

This initial installation will install an OS server by using the Entire Solaris software group (SUNWCall). You can tell that this will be an OS server for diskless clients because of the num_clients and three client_* keywords. Also notice that this profile is specific about which slice the root (/), swap, and /opt file systems will be on.

If the first example in this section is one of the easiest to look at, then this next one must be the easiest:

```
install_type upgrade
```

That's it. Remember that the only required keyword is `install_type`, and in this case, it's an upgrade with no frills. Simply upgrade the computer; that's it.

But because all upgrades aren't that simple, take a look at another upgrade example. This time, the profile will reallocate disk space during the upgrade:

```
install_type      upgrade
root_device       c0t3d0s2
```

```
backup_media         remote_filesystem server1:/export/backup
layout_constraint c0t3d0s2 changeable 100
layout_constraint c0t3d0s4 changeable
layout_constraint c0t3d0s5 movable
cluster              SUNWCall
package              SUNWbcp delete
package              SUNWxwman add
locale               ja
```

This upgrade profile is the most complex example yet. You can see that it's an upgrade and that the root file system (/) will be placed on c0t3d0s2. This profile also specifies a remote file system located on the server1 server to back up files before the upgrade. You can also see that three file systems have layout constraints placed on them. For the c0t3d0s2 file system, the size can be changed, but the minimum size allowed is 100MB. The c0t3d0s4 file system can also be changed, but because no minimum size was specified, the smallest it can be is 110 percent of its original size. The c0t3d0s5 file system can be moved to a different hard disk if the auto-layout process determines that to be the best course of action. The only other new option in this profile is locale, which specifies the Japanese locale (ja).

As you can see, you can specify a large number of options by using the 20 available keywords. The best way to create a profile is to research your options, create a profile, and then test it to make sure it works. For more information on profile keywords, values, and options, see the *Solaris 9 Installation Guide*, available at docs.sun.com.

Testing Profiles

It would be annoying to have to perform a complete installation of Solaris to see whether your profile is configured correctly. Because of the obvious need, Sun has developed a tool to help you test profiles. The pfinstall command can be used to test your profile before you begin an installation.

If you're testing an installation of Solaris 9, then you must run the pfinstall program on a Solaris 9 computer. If you don't already have Solaris 9 installed, you can boot to the Solaris 9 Software 1 of 2 CD (or the Solaris 9 DVD), exit the setup program, and perform your test from the shell. If you're testing an upgrade, test it on the computer that you intend on upgrading.

Here is how to test a profile:

1. Locate a system to perform the test on, and ensure that you have superuser or equivalent privileges.

2. Create a temporary mount point for the test.

    # **mkdir /tmp/mount**

3. Mount the directory that contains the profile you want to test.

    # **mount -F nfs** *server_name:path* **/tmp/mount**

    or

    # **mount -f ufs /dev/diskette /tmp/mount**

4. If you mounted a directory in step 3, change to that directory. If not, change to the directory that contains the profile, which should be the JumpStart directory.

    # **cd /tmp/mount**

    or

    # **cd /jumpstart**

5. Test the profile.

    # **/usr/sbin/install.d/pfinstall -D** *profile*

If you do not use the -D option, then the install will take place, and your existing data will be overwritten. An alternative to -D is the -d *disk_config_file* option, if you are using a disk configuration file.

If your profile works, and your rules file has been validated, and your JumpStart servers are up and running, you should be ready to install!

 Real World Scenario

Upgrading the Network to Solaris 9

The Pinkeel company has hired you to upgrade their network to Solaris 9. They are in the planning stages of upgrading their current installation and are dedicated to using JumpStart. On their network, they have a centralized server room and 120 client computers. Of those, 90 clients are part of the development group, and 30 are administrative staff, including human resources, accounting, marketing, and general management. The network has four subnets: the server room is one, the development group is equally divided between two subnets, and the administrative staff is on its own subnet.

Most of the clients on the network have Solaris 8 installed, but a handful of computers have older Solaris versions. All computers need to be upgraded to Solaris 9.

The first thing you need to do is create the install server. The company has a server available in the server room, named BigFish, that will serve as the JumpStart server. Use the setup_ install_server command to designate BigFish as the install server and then copy the Solaris software CDs to the server's JumpStart directory. For the sake of ease, you will create and use a directory named /jumpstart. Don't forget to share it!

Because the install server is on a different subnet than the JumpStart clients, you will need a boot server on each subnet. You will need three boot servers: one for each development subnet and one for the administrative subnet. The boot servers can be any computer on the subnet; they don't spe-cifically need to be a server. Use the setup_install_server -b command to set these computers up.

Next, create profiles for the client computers. It's likely that you will need two profiles: one for the development computers and another for the administrative staff. The install_type will be upgrade. Other than that keyword, you can configure the profiles however you want. For example, you could assign the End User software group to the administrative staff, and the Developers software group to the developer staff.

Then, add rules to the `rules` file. The most logical way to identify computers on this network is based on network address. You can do that with the `network` keyword. Assign the correct profiles to the rules you create. Then, validate the `rules` file by running the `check` script and creating a `rules.ok` file.

Back on the `BigFish` server, use the `add_install_client` command to add the clients you want to install across the network. Because you have 120 clients, this might take a little while.

Finally, on each client, boot to the network by using the `boot net -install` command at the ok prompt. The installation should begin.

There isn't necessarily a specific order in which you need to complete all of these tasks. For example, you could run `add_install_client` before you even create the profiles or `rules` files. Or, you could create the `rules` file before the profiles. The order of creation doesn't matter, as long as they exist before you begin the installation.

Custom JumpStart installations are flexible and enable you to install a large number of computers in a relatively small amount of time. Using JumpStart takes some setup work, but will likely save you a lot of time in the long run.

Using Web Start Flash

Web Start Flash enables you to install several systems with the same software configuration. The configuration can include the Solaris Operating Environment and any additional software packages you choose. Web Start Flash is most useful for installing large numbers of client computers that require the same software configuration or for reinstalling client computers that are frequently reinstalled.

To use Web Start Flash, you first create a master system, which has the configuration you want to replicate. Then, you create a Flash archive from the master computer. Finally, using any of the Solaris installation methods, you install the archive on the client computers.

Using Web Start Flash for installation is much faster than performing an installation from the CD-ROM, DVD-ROM, or over the network. Combine that with the fact that you can be assured of a specific configuration, and Web Start Flash is an attractive option for installing and reinstalling client computers.

Overview of Web Start Flash

Web Start Flash makes the process of installing several identical client computers easy. With Web Start Flash, you install and configure Solaris on one computer, which is called the *master system*.

The master system needs to have the exact configuration that you want to replicate. Then, you create a Flash archive from the master system. The *Web Start Flash archive* is essentially just a copy of all the files on the master system.

After you have created your archive, you can use `suninstall`, JumpStart, Web Start, or Solaris Live Upgrade to propagate the archive image to client computers. The clients, also called clones, will have the exact same configuration as the master system.

 Web Start Flash is for initial installations only and cannot be used for upgrades.

Creating Web Start Flash Archives

The basis of Web Start Flash installations is the archive, which is created from the master system. Because you are creating the archive from a specific computer, it makes sense that you need to install and configure this computer before you can create the archive.

Your first task, then, is to install and configure the master system. You can install Solaris by using any installation method you choose. After Solaris is installed, you can add, remove, or modify software to suit your needs, including adding third-party applications. Remember, you will be making an exact copy of this computer, to be installed on other computers.

One of the keys to Web Start Flash is that the master system must have the same kernel architecture as the clones. In other words, if the master archive was created from a computer that has the sun4u architecture, then the clones must also be sun4u. Along the same lines, computers requiring different software configurations also need different archives.

There is no limit to the number of archives that you can create, other than hard disk limitations. Archives can get quite large, in the range of hundreds of megabytes to gigabytes.

Two issues that are always raised when talking about Web Start Flash are system peripherals and host-specific files:

Peripheral devices   It's possible that your master and clone systems will have different peripheral devices. If you install the master system with the Core, End User, Developer, or Entire Software groups, the master system (and therefore the clones) will support only those devices attached to the master computer at the time of archive creation.

If your clone systems have peripheral devices that your master system does not have, you can install support for those devices on the master in one of two ways. The first is to install the Entire Plus OEM Software group on the master computer. The other is to add the specific software packages needed to support the additional peripherals. Then, when the archive is installed on the clones, the devices on the clones will be supported.

Host-specific files   When the archive is copied to clone systems, some host-specific files are automatically deleted and re-created. Using the `sys-unconfig` and `sysidtool` commands, the system re-creates the necessary files, including `/etc/hosts`, `/etc/defaultrouter`, and `/etc/defaultdomain`.

After your master system is installed and configured, you can create the archive. Web Start Flash archives can be created while Solaris is in single-user or multiuser mode, and it's best to create the archive when the master system is in as static of a state as possible. You don't want a lot of system activity when trying to create the archive, so most people will recommend booting the system to single-user mode, even though it's not required. The archive will contain all the files located on the master system, as well as some identification information, such as the archive name, master system name, and author of the archive.

Archives are created with the `flarcreate` command. When you initially create the archive, you can store it on the local hard disk or a tape device. After the archive is saved, you can copy it to any file system location or media type you want. Examples are NFS, HTTP, or FTP servers, tape device, CD-ROM or DVD-ROM, or hard disk. Archives can be compressed to save disk space with the `compress` utility, or with a command-line option in `flarcreate`.

Here are the steps to create an archive:

1. Install and configure your master system. For information on Installing and configuring Solaris, see Chapter 2.

2. Boot the master system. If possible, boot into single-user mode. If not, close down all applications. Additionally, you can create an archive if you boot to the Solaris 9 DVD or the Solaris 9 Software 1 of 2 CD.

3. Create the archive.

   # **flarcreate -n** *name options path/filename*

The *name* variable is the name of the archive, which is stored in the archive under the `content_name` keyword. The options for `flarcreate` are explained in Table 16.6. Finally, *path/filename* is the path and filename of the archive. If you do not specify a path, the archive will be created in the current directory.

After the archive is created, you can move or copy the file just as you would any other file in your file system.

TABLE 16.6   *flarcreate* Options

Option	Description
-n *name*	The name of the archive, stored in the archive as the content_ name keyword.
-a *author*	For identification purposes; uses author as the value for the content_author keyword.
-b *blocksize*	Block size that flarcreate uses when creating the archive on a tape device. The default is 64KB.
-c	Compresses the archive by using the compress utility.
-d *dir*	Retrieves the user-defined section file that is specified with the -u switch.
-e *desc*	For identification purposes; uses *desc* as the value of the content_description keyword.

TABLE 16.6   *flarcreate* Options *(continued)*

Option	Description
-E *desc_file*	For identification purposes; obtains the value for the content_ description keyword from the *desc_file*. Cannot be used with –e.
-f *file_list*	Adds the files in the *file_list* to the archive. Specify one file per line.
-F	Uses only the files in the *file_list* to create the archive.
-H	Does not generate the hash identifier.
-i *date*	For identification purposes; uses *date* as the value for the creation_date keyword, in the format of *YYYYMMDDhhmmss*.
-m *master*	For identification purposes; uses *master* as the value for the creation_master keyword. The name of the master system.
-p *posn*	Used with the –t option to specify the position on the tape device on which to store the archive. If not used, the tape's current position is used.
-R *root*	Uses *root* as the root file system for archive creation. By default, the *root* is the root file system (/).
-S	Does not include sizing information in the archive.
-T *type*	For identification purposes; uses *type* as the value for the content_type keyword.
-u *section*	Includes a user-defined section in the archive.
-x *exclude*	Excludes the file or directory specified from the archive.

Installing Web Start Flash Archives

One of the endearing qualities of using Web Start Flash archives is that they can be used with any of the four Solaris installation methods.

In this section, you will learn how to install Web Start Flash archives by using the Web Start, suninstall, JumpStart, and Live Upgrade installation methods. It's assumed at this point that you understand the basic installation processes. If you need a review, see Chapter 2.

Using Web Start

If you're using Web Start to install Solaris, the archive can be located on a DVD-ROM or CD-ROM, NFS, HTTP, or FTP server, or a local tape device. Here's how to install a Web Start

Flash archive by using the Solaris Web Start program:

1. Begin the Solaris Web Start installation.

2. On the Specify Media panel, choose the location of your Web Start Flash archive.

3. Specify the path to the Web Start Flash archive, including server name if necessary.

4. If you are installing an archive from DVD, CD, or an NFS server, the Select Flash Archives screen will be displayed. Select one or more archives that you want to install.

5. Confirm your choices on the Flash Archives Summary screen.

6. Select the media on which another archive is located, if you want to install layered archives. If you do not want to install an additional archive, choose None and click Next to continue installing Solaris.

Using *suninstall*

If you want to use the `suninstall` program to install Solaris with a Flash archive, you can use archives that are located on an HTTP, FTP, or NFS server, local hard disk, local tape device, or local CD-ROM. Here's how to install a Web Start Flash archive by using `suninstall`:

1. Launch the `suninstall` installation program.

2. On the Flash Archive Retrieval Method screen, select the location of your Web Start Flash archive.

3. Specify the path to the archive, including the server name, if the archive is not on a local device.

4. On the Flash Archive Selection screen, choose New if you want to install layered archives. If not, choose Continue to finish the installation.

Using Custom JumpStart

Web Start Flash archives can be located on NFS, HTTP, and FTP servers, as well as local devices, to be used with custom JumpStart. Here are the steps needed to use a Flash archive with custom JumpStart:

1. On the JumpStart install server, create a `rules` file.

2. On the JumpStart profile server, create a profile.

   a. Make sure that the `install_type` is `flash_install`.

   b. Use the `archive_location` keyword to indicate the Web Start Flash archive path.

   c. Specify the file system configuration, as installing with Web Start Flash archives does not allow for file system auto-layout.

   d. If you want to specify layered archives, add an `archive_location` line for each archive.

3. On the JumpStart install server, add the clients you are installing by using the Web Start Flash archive.

4. Begin the custom JumpStart installation.

If you are using custom JumpStart to install a Web Start Flash archive, only four of the keywords covered earlier in this chapter are valid in the JumpStart profile. They are `install_type` (which is required), `filesys` (which cannot be set to auto), `partitioning` (which can be explicit or existing), and `archive_location`.

Here is an example of a custom JumpStart profile designed to install a Web Start Flash archive:

```
install_type       flash_install
archive_location   nfs Athena:/jumpstart/wsfarchive
partitioning       explicit
filesys            c0t3d0s0 6000 /
filesys            c0t3d0s1 1024 swap
filesys            c0t3d0s7 free /export/home
```

Using Solaris Live Upgrade

Finally, you can install Web Start Flash archives from within the Solaris Live Upgrade program. This combination might seem counterintuitive. After all, Live Upgrade is for upgrading in place, whereas Web Start Flash archives can be used only for initial installations, not upgrades. As odd as it might seem, it still works.

To use a Flash archive with Solaris Live Upgrade, the archive must be located on an HTTP, FTP, or NFS server, or a local hard disk, tape device, or CD-ROM or DVD-ROM. Installing a Web Start Flash archive overwrites all files on the new boot environment, except for shared files.

To upgrade or install a Flash archive on a new boot environment, the device containing the new boot environment must be a physical slice. If the new boot environment is contained on a Solaris Volume Manager metadevice or other logical volume, the installation of flash archive will fail.

Here is how to install a Flash archive on a boot environment from the character interface:

1. From the Solaris Live Upgrade main menu, choose Flash.

2. Type the name of the boot environment where the archive will be installed and the location of the installation media.

3. Press the F1 key to add an archive. You can add or remove archives at this point. If you have multiple archives listed, then you will layer the Flash installation.

4. Press the F3 key to install the archive or archives. After completion, the boot environment is ready to be activated.

Here is how to install a Flash archive on a boot environment from a command-line interface:

1. Log on as the superuser and type the following:

   ```
   # luupgrade -f -n BE_name -s os_image_path -j profile_path
   ```

NOTE You must use the -J, -j, or -a options. The luupgrade options are explained in Table 16.7.

The boot environment is ready to be activated.

TABLE 16.7 *luupgrade* Options

Option	Description
-f	Upgrades an operating system from a Flash archive
-n *BE_name*	The name of the boot environment to be upgraded
-s *os_image_path*	The pathname of a directory containing an operating system image
-J *'profile'*	Entry from a JumpStart profile that is configured for a Flash installation
-j *profile_path*	Path to a JumpStart profile that is configured for a Flash installation
-a *archive*	Path to the Flash archive, if the archive is on a local file system

Using Web Start Flash archives with Solaris Live Upgrade is an uncommon event. Most of the time, Flash archives are used in conjunction with suninstall or Web Start, because they are both quick and convenient installation choices.

Managing Web Start Flash Archives

Web Start Flash archives are text files, broken down into sections. Three of the sections are automatically created for you when you use the flarcreate command. The fourth section type is the user-defined section(s). User-defined sections are not processed by flarcreate. However, you can create a script to process archives, and then user-defined sections could be of benefit.

Here is a sample Flash archive:

```
FlAsH-aRcHiVe-1.1
section_begin=identification
archive_id=5d4eff1fd3221cbfd41a579f3ea2c5c2
files_archived_method=cpio
creation_date=20030122004540
creation_master=Q-Sol
content_name=optprof
```

```
creation_node=Q-Sol
creation_hardware_class=sun4u
creation_platform=SUNW,Sun-Blade-100
creation_processor=sparc
creation_release=5.9
creation_os_name=SunOS
creation_os_version=Generic
files_compressed_method=none
files_archived_size=512
content_architectures=sun4u
section_end=identification
section_begin=archive
070701000000000000000000000000000000000000000010000000000000000000000000
```

The three sections are the `cookie` section (which is not present in the example), the `identification` section, and the `file` section. Each section is defined by `section_begin` and `section_end` keywords. The keyword for the `cookie` section is `cookie`, for the `identification` section is `identification`, and for the `file` section is `archive`.

Layering Archives

In the "Installing Web Start Flash Archives" section, you probably noticed mention of layering archives. Laying archives literally means installing one archive over another. Layering archives gives you flexibility.

For example, say that you create one archive that contains the Solaris Operating Environment. Then, you create a second archive that contains the files necessary to run a web server, and a third archive that contains the files needed for an NIS+ installation. To create a backup web server, you could install archives 1 and 2, and to create another NIS+ server, you can install archives 1 and 3. Layering archives gives you flexibility. If you wanted just a "normal" Solaris server, you could just install the first archive.

 NOTE   If you layer archives, the Solaris Product Registry database will have no knowledge of the software installed by the additional archives.

To create layered archives, you first create an archive with the `flarcreate` command. Then, you use the `flar` command to split the archives. To split archives into individual sections, the `flar -s` command is used:

```
# flar -s -d dir -u section -f archive -S section filename
```

The −d option gets the archive sections from the specified directory instead of the current directory. The −u option is used to copy specified sections, instead of the default of copying all sections in the archive. The −f option copies the archive section into the specified directory instead of placing it in the current directory with the filename of `archive`. The −S option copies only the specified section from the archive.

Combining Archives

If you have split archives into individual sections, you can recombine sections into one archive with the `flar -c` command.

Also, to get information about existing archives, use the `flar -i` command.

Summary

This chapter covered advanced installation techniques using custom JumpStart and Web Start Flash.

First, you learned how custom JumpStart works, including daemons and commands used. Custom JumpStart requires three servers: the boot, install, and profile servers. For convenience, they can all physically be the same computer. The two files to make custom JumpStart work properly are the `rules` file and a profile. In addition, you can specify begin and finish scripts in the `rules` file.

The second part of this chapter covered Web Start Flash. Web Start Flash enables you to install several systems based on the profile of a configured master system. You use the master system to create a Web Start Flash profile, and then you use one of the four Solaris installation methods to install the profile on clone computers.

Exam Essentials

Know how to set up a custom JumpStart server.   The `setup_install_server` command is used to set up JumpStart servers.

Know the recommended way to add clients to the JumpStart server for installation.   The easiest way is to use the `add_install_client` command.

Know the three types of custom JumpStart servers that are needed to complete a JumpStart installation.   The three server types are boot, install, and profile.

Understand what the `rules` file does.   The `rules` file identifies a client based on a specific hardware or software characteristic, and then matches the client to a profile.

Know what profiles are for.   Profiles define how to install Solaris on a JumpStart client computer.

Know how to create a Web Start Flash archive.   Archives are created with the `flarcreate` command.

Know how to install Web Start Flash archives.   Archives are installed from within one of the four Solaris installation programs: Web Start, `suninstall`, JumpStart, or Live Upgrade.

Key Terms

Before you take the exam, be certain you are familiar with the following terms:

begin scripts	profile diskette
boot server	profile server
custom JumpStart	Reverse Address Resolution Protocol (RARP)
factory JumpStart	`rules` file
finish scripts	Trivial File Transfer Protocol (TFTP)
install server	Web Start Flash
master system	Web Start Flash archive
profile	

Commands Used in This Chapter

The following list contains a summary of all the commands introduced in this chapter:

Command	Description
`add_install_client`	Adds network installation information about a client to the JumpStart server.
`add_to_install_server`	Copies additional Solaris packages to an existing installation server configuration.
`check`	Validates the `rules` file and creates a `rules.ok` file.
`flar`	Manages Web Start Flash archives.
`flarcreate`	Creates Web Start Flash archives.
`luupgrade`	Manages features of a Solaris Live Upgrade boot environment.
`modify_install_server`	Modifies an existing package on the install server.
`pfinstall`	Performs a trial run installation. Used to see if any potential problems exist.
`rm_install_client`	Removes client information from the JumpStart server.
`setup_install_server`	Performs the initial installation of the JumpStart server.

Review Questions

1. You are configuring the custom JumpStart installation for a large network. The network has JumpStart clients on six separate IP subnets. The install server is on the second subnet. What is the total number of boot servers you will need to install to get the JumpStart installation to work properly?

    A. None

    B. One

    C. Five

    D. Six

2. Your network consists of 30 Solaris 8 client computers. You are going to use custom JumpStart to upgrade all computers to Solaris 9. Most of the computers have critical files located on them. Although the files are backed up periodically, you want to ensure that all local files are backed up before the upgrade procedure. Which of the following should you configure to initiate the backup?

    A. An install script

    B. A custom rule in the `rules` file

    C. A begin script

    D. A finish script

    E. The `backup` keyword in each computer's profile

3. You are using Web Start Flash to install Solaris 9 on the client computers on your network. The network has two hardware platforms, sun4u and i386. You also have three major software configurations to support, including one for engineering, one for accounting, and one for the development staff. Each department has a mix of hardware platforms. If you want to create Web Start Flash archives for each client computer on your network, how many archives will you need to create?

    A. One

    B. Two

    C. Three

    D. Six

    E. None of the above

4. You are planning the JumpStart implementation for your network. Which protocol is responsible for transmitting boot files from the boot server to JumpStart clients?

    A. TFTP

    B. RARP

    C. FTP

    D. RCP

    E. RPC

5. Consider the following file output:

```
install_type        flash_install
archive_location    nfs Athena:/jumpstart/wsfarchive
partitioning        explicit
filesys             c0t3d0s0 6000 /
filesys             c0t3d0s1 1024 swap
filesys             c0t3d0s7 free /export/home
```

Which of the following is the type of file that this output is taken from?

A. Web Start Flash archive

B. Custom JumpStart `rules` file

C. Custom JumpStart profile

D. Custom JumpStart begin script

6. You are configuring the JumpStart implementation for your Solaris 9 network. Which of the following, at a minimum, are required server roles for your JumpStart configuration? (Choose all that apply.)

A. Network

B. Boot

C. Install

D. Installation

E. Config

F. Profile

7. You are the Solaris administrator for your network. You are creating Web Start Flash archives to make the reinstallation of client computers easier on your staff. Which of the following commands do you use to create a new Web Start Flash archive?

A. `flarcreate -n`

B. `flarcreate -a`

C. `flar -n`

D. `flar -a`

8. You are beginning to set up custom JumpStart and have installed the one server to act as the JumpStart server. After creating the `rules` file, what is the next logical step to take to ensure that your JumpStart installation will work properly?

A. Create a JumpStart directory on your JumpStart server.

B. Run the `check` script to validate the `rules` file and create a `rules.ok` file.

C. Create profiles to define how to install Solaris on the JumpStart client computers.

D. Add clients to the JumpStart server.

9. Consider the following information:

    ```
    hostname Sol-1 - sol_profile -
    network 192.168.0.32 && karch sun4u 4u_1 4u_profile 4u_2
    network 192.168.0.32 && !karch sun4u - otro_profile -
    model SUNW,Sun-Blade-100 - blade_profile backup
    any - - basic_profile -
    ```

    Based on the information presented from this file, which of the following statements are true? (Choose all that apply.)

    A. Computers that have the network address of 192.168.0.32 will receive the 4u_profile profile.

    B. The only computers that will use a begin script are those with the sun4u architecture.

    C. If a computer does not match to any of the first four rules, it will receive the profile named basic_profile.

    D. The only computers that will use a finish script are those on the 192.168.0.32 network.

10. You are planning on creating Web Start Flash archives to use on your network. Which of the following is a limitation of using Web Start Flash archives?

    A. They cannot be used to perform initial installations.

    B. They cannot be used to perform upgrades.

    C. They cannot be used on Intel-based computers.

    D. You can create only one Web Start Flash archive for your network.

11. You are the Solaris administrator for your company. You are reconfiguring custom JumpStart and have three existing profiles. Each profile has been tested and works properly. You just modified one of the profiles and want to test it to make sure it works. Which of the following commands do you use to test the modified profile?

    A. modify_install_server

    B. check

    C. pkgcheck

    D. pfinstall

    E. luupgrade

12. Consider the following information:

    ```
    install_type     initial_install
    system_type      standalone
    partitioning     default
    cluster          SUNWCuser
    ```

Which of the following software clusters will this profile install?

A. Entire Plus OEM

B. Entire

C. End User

D. Developer

13. You are configuring custom JumpStart for your network. You have created profiles for all computers on your network. Some of the computers are on the network, and others are not connected. Which two of the following are valid profile locations, if the profiles are to be used with custom JumpStart? (Choose two.)

A. The JumpStart directory on the boot server

B. The JumpStart directory on the install server

C. The JumpStart directory on the profile server

D. The JumpStart directory on the profile diskette

14. You have configured a custom JumpStart server for your network. Now you are in the process of granting clients access to the server. Which of the following commands is used to add clients to the server?

A. add_install_client

B. add_install_server

C. add_to_install_client

D. add_to_install_server

E. modify_install_server

15. You are configuring your Solaris server to act as a JumpStart server. You want to create a finish script to change the root password after the operating system is installed. From where do you specify the use of a finish script?

A. The begin script

B. The rules file

C. The custom JumpStart profile

D. The Web Start Flash archive

16. You are the Solaris administrator for your network. You have created a Web Start Flash archive to install several client computers on your network. Which of the following methods can you use to install the archive? (Choose all that apply.)

A. suninstall

B. Solaris Live Upgrade

C. Custom JumpStart

D. Web Start

17. Which of the following server roles in JumpStart is responsible for storing and supplying the installation files for Solaris 9?

A. Boot server

B. Install server

C. Installation server

D. Profile server

E. Config server

18. You are attempting to use custom JumpStart to install Solaris on 15 client computers. When you boot the first computer, the computer seems to hang and gets this error message:

`WARNING: getfile: RPC failed: error 5: (RPC Timed out).`

Which of the following is a specific cause of this error message?

A. The network connection between the client and the server is down.

B. The `inetd.rpc` daemon on the server has failed.

C. There are entries for this client computer in the `/etc/bootparams` file of two JumpStart boot servers.

D. The client computer was not properly added to any JumpStart boot server.

19. You are the Solaris administrator for your network. You have created two Web Start Flash archives for use on your network. Now you want to start working with layered archives, and you want to break your existing archives into their individual sections. Which of the following commands enables you to do this? (Choose one command and one option.)

A. `flar`

B. `flarmod`

C. `flarcreate`

D. `-b`

E. `-i`

F. `-s`

G. `-c`

20. You are configuring custom JumpStart on your network. You want all client computers to be able to access the profile server, which is named `Athena`. To which of the following file(s), and on which server(s) do you add this line: `* install_config=Athena:/jumpstart`? (Choose all that apply.)

A. `/etc/bootparams`

B. `/jumpstart/rules.ok`

C. `/jumpstart/profile_name`

D. Boot server

E. Install server

F. Profile server

Answers to Review Questions

1. D. You need one boot server for each subnet. The second subnet contains the install server, which can also function as the boot server. Each of the other subnets will need their own boot server.

2. C. A begin script runs before the installation or upgrade takes place. One of the common uses of begin scripts is to back up existing files before installing or upgrading Solaris.

3. D. You have two separate hardware platforms and three separate software configurations. Because you need to account for all possible hardware and software combinations, you will need a total of six Web Start Flash archives.

4. A. The Trivial File Transfer Protocol (TFTP) is used to transfer the boot file from the boot server to client computers. The Reverse Address Resolution Protocol (RARP) helps boot clients locate their IP address. The File Transfer Protocol (FTP) is used for file transfers, as is the Remote Copy (RCP). However, neither is used in this case. Remote Procedure Calls (RPCs) initiate processes on remote computers and are not responsible for transferring boot files.

5. C. The information is from a custom JumpStart profile, which tells JumpStart how to install Solaris on a computer. In this case, the installation type will be a Web Start Flash installation (as indicated by the `flash_install` value).

6. B, C, F. The three required server roles for JumpStart are boot, install, and profile.

7. A. The `flarcreate -n` command is used to create Web Start Flash archives. The `flar` command is used to manage existing archives.

8. B. After creating the `rules` file, you need to validate it by running the `check` script. The `check` script validates the `rules` file and creates the `rules.ok` file, which is used by JumpStart. All of the other answers are valid tasks to complete when setting up JumpStart, but the logical step to take after creating a `rules` file is to validate it.

9. B, C. Some of the computers on the 192.168.0.32 network will receive the `4u_profile` profile, but only those that have the sun4u architecture. The next line negates the architecture, so that computers on that network without the sun4u architecture will get the `otro_profile` profile. The any profile matches to any computer. Finish scripts are supplied on the second and fourth lines of information, not just for computers on the 192.168.0.32 network.

10. B. Web Start Flash archives are for initial installations only; they cannot be used to upgrade operating system installations. You can create as many archives as you want, and archives can be used on all Solaris client computers.

11. D. The `pfinstall` command is used to test profiles. The `modify_install_server` command is used to modify the installation files on the JumpStart install server. The `check` command validates `rules` files, and `pkgcheck` was made up for this question. The `luupgrade` command is used to modify a boot environment when using Solaris Live Upgrade.

12. C. This profile will install the Solaris End User software cluster, based on the `SUNWCuser` value in the `cluster` keyword.

13. C, D. Profiles and `rules` files can be located on the profile server or on a profile diskette. In most cases, the profile server is the same computer as the boot server and the install server, but if you use separate servers for each function, the profile belongs on the profile server.

14. A. The `add_install_client` command is used to add JumpStart clients to the JumpStart server. Although all of the other commands are valid commands for modifying the install server, none of them are used to add clients.

15. B. Begin and finish scripts are fields in the `rules` file. Therefore, begin and finish scripts are called from the `rules` file.

16. A, B, C, D. All four methods are valid. You can install Web Start Flash archives from within any of the listed installation programs.

17. B. The install server contains copies of the Solaris installation files. The installation server and config servers do not exist.

18. C. This error usually indicates that there is more than one entry for the client computer in the `/etc/bootparams` file of one or more boot servers. This becomes more common if you use the wildcard to specify client computers. Although it's possible that the network is down, it's not a specific problem to this error message. There is no `inetd.rpc` daemon.

19. A, F. The `flar -s` command enables you to split archives into their component sections. There is no `flarmod` command. The `flarcreate` command is used to create Web Start Flash archives. The `flar -i` command enables you to view archive information, and the `flar -c` command is used to combine archive sections. The `-b` switch specifies block size if you're working with tape devices.

20. A, D. You add this line to the `/etc/bootparams` file on the boot server. This line functions as a wildcard and enables all client computers access to the profile server.

Glossary

A

absolute mode   A mode of the chmod command that enables you to use numbers to represent permission settings.

absolute path   The unique location of a file or a directory within a computer, represented as the file's relation to the root directory (/).

Access Control List (ACL)   A structure that enables administrators to set permissions beyond the standard UNIX permissions. An ACL enables administrators to set permissions for several individual users and/or groups.

at   A list of programs (jobs) entered into the system that need to be run only once.

attachment points   Locations within the computer that can accommodate dynamic reconfiguration of system hardware. Each attachment point consists of a receptacle and an occupant.

authorization   Used in conjunction with role-based access control, an authorization is a right that is granted to a role or a user.

autoconfiguration   The automatic loading and unloading of device drivers by the Solaris kernel.

AutoFS   Also called the *automounter*, AutoFS is a client-side service that allows for the automatic mounting of remote file systems.

AutoFS maps   The files that provide configuration information to the AutoFS service. AutoFS maps replace the functionality of the /etc/vfstab file.

auto-layout   A feature of suninstall, Web Start, and custom JumpStart that automatically reallocates disk space during an upgrade (if the space is available) to accommodate the new version of Solaris. Also called *reallocation*.

automounter   Another name for AutoFS, the automounter is a client-side service that allows for the automatic mounting of remote file systems.

available memory   The remaining, usable portion of physical memory left over after the operating system reserves the memory it needs.

B

back file system   Used with CacheFS, the back file system contains the original data to be cached and is located on a remote computer.

backup   A replica of data stored in an alternate location. Most frequently, backups are made to tape devices or CD-ROMs, but they can also be made to hard disks and floppy disks.

backup schedule   The frequency of backups made, to ensure the timeliness and completeness of your data backup.

begin script   An optional Bourne shell script that runs before a custom JumpStart installation of Solaris takes place.

Berkeley Internet Name Domain (BIND)   An industry-wide standard for the implementation of DNS.

Berkeley Software Distribution (BSD)   One of the two major UNIX architecture standards. The original versions of SunOS were based on this standard.

bind   In a client-server networking environment, a client will connect to a server and maintain that connection until the communication between those computers is done. The connection process is called a bind.

boot block   An 8KB sector present in slice 0 of a hard disk that contains information on how to begin the computer's boot process.

boot server   A computer that provides boot information, such as a boot file and IP address, to diskless clients or clients that do not have an operating system, on the network.

bridge   A networking device that can connect local area networks to each other. Bridges forward network traffic based on a physical (MAC) address.

C

Cache File System (CacheFS)   A file system that acts as a temporary holding area for data located on slow or remote file systems. CacheFS speeds up the performance of your computer if you access network resources or slow CD-ROM drives.

CacheFS packing   Actively placing files into CacheFS to speed up performance, as opposed to waiting for the files to be accessed and then placed into CacheFS.

client   Also called a *workstation*, a client is a computer on the network that users work from. Clients typically request information from servers.

command-line interface (CLI)   The Solaris software interface in which you type commands in order to execute them.

Common Desktop Environment (CDE)   The default graphical user interface provided with Solaris 9.

core file   A file generated when an application or a process terminates abnormally. Used in troubleshooting.

crash dump   The contents of physical memory, dumped into two files, when the operating system experiences a fatal crash.

crontab   A file containing programs that need to be run on a routine schedule, such as backups or system maintenance programs.

custom JumpStart   A Solaris installation and upgrade program that enables an administrator to customize a specific software configuration and to install that configuration on other computers with little to no human intervention.

cylinder   On a hard disk, all of the tracks, on all platters, a specific distance from the center spindle.

D

daemon   A program that runs automatically and in the background. Daemons often provide valuable services such as automated file transfers and establishing network connections.

device   Another term for a hardware component in a computer.

device alias   An ordinary name for a configured hardware device, used for human convenience.

device driver   A small software program that enables a hardware device to communicate with the operating system.

device tree   A hierarchical list of all configured devices in the computer.

direct map   An automount point that contains a direct association between a mount point on a client and a directory on a server.

Directory Information Tree (DIT)   The hierarchical database that stores information on a Lightweight Directory Access Protocol (LDAP) server.

dirty regions   Areas of a mirrored volume that are out of synchronization with the other submirror or submirrors.

disk controller   A hardware device built into the hard disk or motherboard that controls hard disk behavior.

disk heads   Also known as *read/write heads*, disk heads are responsible for reading and writing information on hard disks.

disk label   The first sector of the hard disk, which contains disk geometry information as well as partition information. The disk label is also called the *Volume Table of Contents (VTOC)*.

disk mirroring   The process of using two or three submirrors (different hard disks) to hold identical copies of data. Disk mirroring is used as a form of online fault tolerance.

disk platters   Magnetically coated plates located within a hard disk. Data is stored on the disk platters.

disk set   Also known as a *shared disk set*, it's a logical grouping of hard disk slices that can be shared by multiple hosts.

disk slice   A range of continuous sectors located on a hard disk, logically defined as one unit. Disk slices are also often called *partitions*.

disk striping   A process in which data is written evenly across hard disks or slices. Also called *RAID 0*, disk striping is done to improve overall disk read and write performance.

disk striping with parity   A process in which data is written evenly across hard disks or slices, and a parity (backup) block is also written. Also called *RAID 5*, disk striping with parity provides online fault tolerance as well as some overall increase in disk read and write performance.

distributed file system   Also known as a *network file system*, a distributed file system is one that is accessed across a network connection.

Domain Name Service (DNS)   A service that resolves host names to IP addresses. DNS replaces the need for local hosts files and is the name resolution method used on the Internet.

dynamic reconfiguration   The automatic configuring or disabling of a device added to or removed from the computer while the computer is running.

E

Ethernet   A contention-based network access method that uses the Carrier Sense Multiple Access with Collision Detection (CSMA/CD) protocol.

F

factory JumpStart   A Solaris installation method that installs Solaris on a computer based on a profile determined by the computer's model and hard disk size.

fault tolerance   Indicates that if one component were to fail, the computer would still operate normally. Typically used to refer to hard disks and RAID volumes. If one hard disk were to fail and fault tolerance was enabled, the computer could still operate normally.

Federated Naming Service (FNS)   An umbrella naming service that is designed to sit on top of existing naming services. If your network has several naming services, FNS will provide a common interface between them all.

file system   A logical grouping of files and directories on a hard disk, or the specific method used to store and read information from a hard disk.

finish script   An optional Bourne shell script that runs after a custom JumpStart installation finishes. A finish script can perform such tasks as backing up file systems and changing the superuser password.

forking   When one process causes another process to start. Also called *spawning*.

Forth Monitor   The user interface for the OpenBoot PROM. The Forth Monitor presents a user with an ok prompt.

free hog   A temporary slice that exists only during the partitioning process. The free hog represents the remaining free space available (the space that does not have an existing slice) on the hard disk.

front file system   Used in CacheFS, the front file system contains the cached copies of original data located on the back file system. The front file system is located on the local computer.

full backup   A backup of all the data in a specific location, such as on a file system or on an entire computer.

full resynchronization   In a mirrored volume, when a new submirror is added to the volume, it must have all of the information on the volume written to it. This process is called a full resynchronization.

G

gateway   A network device that can connect local area networks to each other and translate protocols.

Group ID (GID)   A unique number that identifies a group on a Solaris computer.

H

hard link   A pointer to another file in the same Solaris file system.

High Sierra File System (HSFS)   The file system used for CD-ROMs.

home directory   A location on a local computer or on a server in which users can store their files.

host   Any computer or device on the network that has its own IP address.

hot plugging   Adding or removing system devices while the computer is still running. Both the device and the computer must support hot plugging for it to work.

hot spare pool   A collection of unused hard disk slices that are available to automatically replace a failed disk slice.

hot spares   The individual hard disk slices in a hot spare pool.

hub   A network device that enables several computers to communicate with one another.

I

inconsistent   In the UNIX File System (UFS), this state exists when the information stored on the disk is different from what is indicated in the UFS database. This can occur from a sudden loss of power or hard disk damage.

incremental backups   A backup that backs up only data that has changed recently, as opposed to backing up an entire volume.

indirect map   An AutoFS map file that uses mount points defined in the master map, or the `auto_master` file. Indirect maps establish map points by using a substitution key value.

init state   Also known as a *run level*, an init state defines the operation of Solaris, including which resources and services are available to users. Solaris 9 has eight init states, although only seven are used.

initialization files   The individual configuration files that make up the user profile.

inode   A file system entry that contains a complete listing of a file's attributes, such as the file's owner, group, permissions, and last access time.

install server   A custom JumpStart server that contains images of the Solaris installation files to be installed on client computers.

interactive package   A software installation option that enables you to install software without human intervention, through the use of a response file.

interlace   A block of data written to a stripe in a striped volume. The interlace value (which indicates the size of the data blocks) can be configured within Solaris.

Internet Protocol (IP)   The Network layer protocol in the TCP/IP protocol suite. IP is responsible for host addressing and the routing of network packets.

J

JumpStart   One of the four Solaris installation programs. There are two varieties of JumpStart: factory JumpStart, which installs Solaris by using a profile determined by the computer's hardware, and custom JumpStart, which enables the administrator to configure automated installations.

K

kernel   The core of the Solaris operating environment.

L

LDAP client profile   The parameters needed on a client computer in order to use the LDAP naming service.

Lightweight Directory Access Protocol (LDAP)   A networking protocol originally designed as a directory service to hold objects and values for those objects. Now, LDAP is also a naming service used in Solaris. LDAP can replace the functionality of NIS and NIS+.

Line Printer (LP) print service   The Solaris service that manages all printing on the computer.

Live Upgrade   One of the four Solaris installation programs. Live Upgrade is designed to upgrade Solaris while the computer is still running. Upon a reboot, the new operating system will take over.

loadable kernel modules   Another name for device drivers, as they are loaded into the kernel when a device is accessed.

local area network (LAN)   A network in which all computers are in a small geographical area and linked by high-speed connections.

local disk set   The default disk set located on each host. These disks cannot be taken over by other computers (as opposed to a shared disk set, which can be taken over by other computers).

local files   One of the Solaris naming services, local files are files located on each computer in the /etc directory.

Loopback File System (LOFS)   A virtual file system that enables you to create a new virtual file system within an existing file system. Files and directories in this new virtual file system can be accessed either by their original pathname, or by their new virtual pathname.

LP print service   See *Line Printer (LP) print service*.

M

master map   The main AutoFS map file, a master map associates directories with mount points, and also lists direct and indirect maps used.

master server   In a NIS domain, the master server is the computer set up as the first NIS server. The master server contains the main copies of the NIS maps.

master system   The Solaris computer that you will replicate and create an archive from, in order to perform Web Start Flash installations.

metadevice   Also known as a *volume*, a metadevice is a collection of hard disk slices acting as one logical unit and managed by the Solaris Volume Manager (SVM).

mount point   A directory in a file system into which another file system is loaded.

mount   The process of making a file system available by loading it into a mount point.

N

Name Service Cache Daemon (NSCD)   The Solaris service that caches information found in the name service switch file, nsswitch.conf.

name service switch file   The local /etc/nsswitch.conf file, which contains information on which naming services the computer is to use.

namespace   The collection of computers served by a domain server, such as a NIS, NIS+, DNS, or LDAP server.

network client   A computer on the network that retrieves its networking configuration information from a network configuration server.

network configuration server   A computer on the network that provides networking configuration information, such as an IP address, to network clients.

Network File System (NFS)   A distributed (network-based) file system that enables you to share files and directories from one computer and to access those resources from any other computer on the network.

Network Information Service (NIS)   One of the early naming services developed for use with Solaris. NIS uses a flat naming structure.

Network Information Service Plus (NIS+)   A naming service, designed for use with Solaris, that uses a hierarchical naming structure.

network interface card (NIC)   Also called a *network adapter*, it's a hardware device in the computer that enables the computer to participate in a networked environment.

nice number   A number that modifies the default priority of a process. By using a nice number, you can grant certain processes more or less processor time than they would normally get. If your process concedes processor time, it's said to be a "nice process."

NIS domain   The logical grouping of computers configured to use a particular NIS server.

NIS maps   The files in which naming service information is stored on a NIS server.

NIS+ tables   The files in which naming service information is stored on a NIS+ server.

Non-Volatile Random Access Memory (NVRAM)   A portion of the OpenBoot PROM that contains built-in hardware diagnostics, device information, device aliases, the host ID, Ethernet address, and system Time of Day (TOD) clock.

Non-Volatile Random Access Memory Run Control (NVRAMRC)   A portion of NVRAM that is capable of permanently storing device alias information.

O

occupant   The hot pluggable device (hardware component) that is located in the receptacle and can be configured.

Open Systems Interconnect (OSI)   A seven-layer theoretical networking model developed in the early 1980s by the International Organization for Standardization (ISO).

OpenBoot PROM (OBP) The firmware built into the motherboard of a Sun computer that controls the boot process and enables users to configure the boot process.

operating environment (OE) The operating system combined with all bundled features and programs. In most cases, this term can be replaced by *operating system* and not cause problems.

operating system A software program designed to enable you to run other programs and to provide a functional interface between the computer hardware and software.

optimized resynchronization In a mirrored volume, when you bring a submirror back online, only the dirty regions are resynchronized. This is called an optimized resynchronization.

P

pages Units of physical and virtual memory allocation.

paging The process of writing information located in physical memory into virtual memory.

parity information Part of each RAID 5 stripe that contains information designed to provide data redundancy.

partial resynchronization The process of resynchronizing a part of a mirrored volume with the rest of the mirrored volume.

pass number A number that determines in which order the submirrors in a mirrored volume will be resynchronized.

password aging A feature that forces users to change their passwords periodically.

patch A collection of files designed to improve the performance of a program or an operating system. Put another way, patches fix bugs.

Personal Computer File System (PCFS) The file system used in Solaris on floppy disks.

physical memory The amount of RAM physically in a computer.

primary group Every Solaris user account must belong to at least one group. The first group that a user belongs to is their primary group.

primary submirror The first submirror created when creating a mirrored volume.

print client A computer on the network that does not have a printer attached locally; instead, a print client will print to printers located on a remote print server.

print driver The piece of software that tells Solaris how to talk to the printer.

print queue An area on the print server that accepts, holds, and processes print jobs, and redirects the jobs to the appropriate printer. Also called a *print spooler*.

print server   A computer (or specialized device) on the network that has printers attached to it and enables other computers to print to those printers.

print spooler   An area on the print server that accepts, holds, and processes print jobs, and redirects the jobs to the appropriate printer. Also called a *print queue*.

printer class   A logical grouping of several locally attached printers. Instead of printing to a specific printer, users will print to the printer class, and their print job can appear on any of the printers in the class.

printer definitions   The printer's configured settings, such as the printer name, description, port, and type.

printer interface program   An application located in /usr/lib/lp/model and used by the LP print service to interface with other parts of the operating system.

priorities   A ranking system used by Solaris to determine which process or processes get more CPU time than other processes.

privileged application   An application that can override standard security and check for specific User IDs, Group IDs, or authorizations.

process   A single program running in its own memory space.

process class   A grouping of processes in Solaris. Each process belongs to a process class, which defines the default priority of the process. There are six process classes: real-time (RT), time-sharing (TS), interactive (IA), fair share (FSS), fixed priority (FX), and system (SYS).

Process File System (PROCFS)   A virtual file system that tracks all active processes on the computer and manages the /proc directory.

processes   The running parts of an application or service. Each process runs individually and is managed by the Solaris kernel.

profile   A file used with custom JumpStart that contains information on how to install Solaris on the specified computer.

profile diskette   The floppy disk that contains the custom JumpStart profile. Profile diskettes are used on computers that do not have a network connection.

profile server   The custom JumpStart server that contains the custom JumpStart profile.

project   A workload component that can be used to allow system usage or to provide a basis for resource allocation charge-back. Functionally, a project is a lot like a group, but is task based and provides more features.

protocol   The set of rules that computers use to communicate with each other over a network.

pseudo file system   Also known as a *virtual file system*, a pseudo file system is one that resides in memory instead of on a hard disk.

R

RAID (Redundant Array of Inexpensive [or Independent] Disks)   A set of industry standards that defines storage solutions involving more than one hard disk.

RAID 0   Also known as *disk striping*, data in a RAID 0 volume is written evenly among hard disks (or slices), resulting in a data "stripe." Solaris also supports a disk concatenation version of RAID 0. RAID 0 does not provide any fault tolerance.

RAID 1   Also known as *disk mirroring*, RAID 1 volumes duplicate file systems (or entire hard disks) onto one or more additional hard disks. RAID 1 provides fault tolerance.

RAID 5   Also known as *disk striping with parity*, RAID 5 volumes write data across several hard disks (or slices) like a RAID 0 volume, but also write a parity block for fault tolerance.

reallocation   Also called *auto-layout*, reallocation is a feature of `suninstall`, Web Start, and custom JumpStart that automatically reallocates disk space during an upgrade (if the space is available) to accommodate the new version of Solaris.

receptacle   The location on the computer that is configured to accept a hot pluggable device.

relative pathname   The location of a file or directory, based on your current working directory.

Remote Procedure Call (RPC)   A protocol used to start processes on remote computers.

resolver   A client computer configured to use the DNS naming service. A resolver is also another name for a DNS client configuration file, `/etc/resolv.conf`.

response file   Used during an interactive installation, a response file provides answers to questions that software packages ask during the installation process. A response file allows for installations to complete without human intervention.

restore   To copy files from a tape backup (or other backup media) onto a hard disk for use.

resynchronization region   In a mirrored volume, the area of a submirror that needs to be resynchronized.

Reverse Address Resolution Protocol (RARP)   The protocol used by a boot server to pass the IP address back to the client during the boot process.

rights profile   A collection of authorizations and privileged applications.

role   A specialized user account that is often granted limited or full administrative abilities. A role can be accessed only by using the `su` command.

role-based access control   A standard that enables an administrator to assign certain administrative tasks to specific users or roles, without giving the user full administrative privileges.

router   A network connectivity device that connects local and wide area networks to each other. Routers direct network traffic based on a logical network address (an IP address) and are the backbone of the Internet.

rules file   A text file that contains one or more descriptive characteristics about a client computer, matched with a custom JumpStart profile name. A client computer that matches the listed characteristic(s) will use the specified profile.

run control (rc) scripts   Small scripts that execute other scripts in order to complete the initialization of the operating system.

run level   A designation that defines the operation of Solaris, including which resources and services are available to users. Solaris has eight run levels, although only seven are currently used. Also called an *init state*.

S

secondary group   Solaris users must belong to one group, which is their primary group. However, users can also belong to several other groups, known as secondary groups.

sector   A 512-byte individual storage unit on a hard disk.

server   A computer on the network that provides services or information to other devices on the network.

shared disk set   A logical grouping of hard disks that can be shared with other computers. If the host computer were to fail, another computer could take over the management of the hard disks.

shell   The interface that enables users to input information to be interpreted by the operating system. Examples are the Bourne shell (sh), Korn shell (ksh), and C shell (csh).

site initialization file   A file located on a server that affects all user login profiles.

slave servers   In a NIS domain, these computers contain copies of the NIS maps, resolve queries for client computers, and act as backups for the NIS master server.

snapshot backup   A file created with the fssnap command, a snapshot is a picture of the file system at a given time. The snapshot can be used to create a backup archive while the file system remains mounted.

soft link   Also known as a *symbolic link*, a soft link is an indirect pointer to a file or a directory. Soft links can span file systems.

soft partition   A logical volume created on a hard disk (from within the Solaris Volume Manager) that enables you to create more than eight volumes per hard disk.

software group   A collection of Solaris software packages. Solaris 9 has five software groups: Core, End User, Developer, Entire, and Entire plus OEM.

software package   A collection of files and directories needed to run a specific program, application, or service.

Solaris Volume Manager (SVM)   A utility packaged with Solaris that provides advanced storage management capabilities, including creating RAID volumes, soft partitions, hot spare pools, and transactional volumes.

source files   On a NIS master server, these are the files from which the maps are created or updated.

SPARC (Scalable Processor Architecture)   A RISC processor type developed and used by Sun Microsystems.

spawning   Also known as *forking*, it's when a process causes another process to start.

state database   A database on your hard disk that stores information about the computer's Solaris Volume Manager configuration. A state database is composed of several state database replicas.

state database replica   Each individual copy of a state database. There should be a minimum of three replicas per computer.

sticky bit   A security attribute that can be enabled to prevent the accidental deletion of files located in public directories.

submirrors   The individual hard disks or slices that are components in a mirrored volume.

suninstall   One of the four Solaris installation programs, it uses a rudimentary graphical and command-line interface.

superblock   An area at the beginning of each disk slice (and replicated throughout the slice) that stores critical file system information such as the size of the file system, disk label (VTOC), cylinder group size, number of data blocks present, summary data block, file system state, and pathname of the last mount point.

Swap File System (SWAPFS)   A virtual file system responsible for managing physical and virtual memory as well as the paging process.

switch   A network device, similar to a hub, that enables several computers to communicate with one another. Switches are more intelligent than hubs and can do a better job of managing network traffic.

symbolic mode   When setting permissions by using the chmod command, symbolic mode uses letters to identify whom the permissions will affect as well as the permissions that will be set.

sysidcfg   A file that provides system network identification information to a computer.

syslog   The name of the Solaris logging service.

syslogd   The daemon responsible for system logging.

system disk   The hard disk that contains the operating system files (located on slice 0).

system logging   Tracking events (such as user logins, file access, and various problems) as they happen on the computer.

System V Release 4 (SVR4)   One of the two major UNIX architecture standards and the most commonly used one today. Since 1992 (with the release of Solaris 2), Solaris has been based on SVR4.

T

Temporary File System (TMPFS)   The default virtual file system for the /tmp directory, TMPFS holds temporary files and uses local memory to make file system reads and writes. All data in TMPFS is deleted when the computer is shut off.

track   A group of hard disk sectors, laid end to end.

transactional volume   A logical hard disk volume that stores information about UNIX File System (UFS) read and write transactions.

Transmission Control Protocol/Internet Protocol (TCP/IP)   A networking protocol suite developed in the UNIX world in the late 1960s. TCP/IP is the most popular networking protocol in the world and is the protocol of the Internet.

trigger nodes   AutoFS mount points that do not have file systems mounted under them during the boot process, but will at a later point when the file system needs to be accessed.

Trivial File Transfer Protocol (TFTP)   The protocol used by the boot server to transfer a boot file to client computers.

U

UFS snapshot   A backing store image (fancy term for an image used as a backup) of a file system at a given point in time.

umask   A value that modifies the default permissions on a newly created file or directory, resulting in the file or directory's real permission structure.

Universal Disk Format (UDF)   The file system used for DVD-ROMs.

UNIX File System (UFS)   The standard hard disk–based file system used in Solaris (and most of the rest of the UNIX world).

unmount   To make a file system unavailable for use.

User ID (UID)   A number that uniquely identifies a user on the computer.

username   A character string that uniquely identifies a user on the computer. Users log in by using their username and a password.

user profile   A set of files run during the login process that configures the user's working environment.

V

virtual file system   Also called a *pseudo file system*, a virtual file system resides in memory instead of on a hard disk.

virtual memory   Hard disk space used to emulate physical memory.

volume   Also known as a *metadevice*, a volume is a collection of hard disk slices acting as one logical unit and managed by the Solaris Volume Manager (SVM).

volume management   The management of removable media, including floppy disks and CD-ROMs.

Volume Table of Contents (VTOC)   Also known as the *disk label*, the VTOC contains disk geometry information and disk partition information.

W

Web Start   One of the four Solaris installation programs, it uses a Web-style interface.

Web Start Flash   A Solaris installation method that enables you to create an archive from a master system and then use that archive to install Solaris (with an identical configuration) on several other computers.

Web Start Flash archive   The file that contains the image of the Web Start Flash master system. The archive is used to install Solaris on other systems and give them the same software configuration as the master system.

wide area network (WAN)   A network distributed over a large geographical area, with the remote sites typically linked together with relatively slow (10Mbps or slower) connections.

working directory   The directory in which the user is currently located, as displayed by the pwd command.

Index

Note to the reader: Throughout this index **boldfaced** page numbers indicate primary discussions of a topic. *Italicized* page numbers indicate illustrations.

G

N

Q

R

T

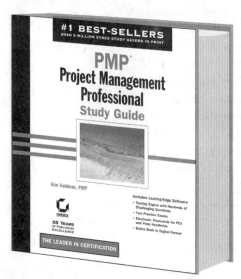

The Complete Java™ 2 Certification Solution

Java 2 Web Developer Certification Study Guide
Natalie Levi, Philip Heller · ISBN: 0-7821-4202-8 · $59.99
Completely Revised and Updated!

Here's the book you need to prepare for Exam 310-080, Sun Certified Web Component Developer for J2EE Platform. This Study Guide for experienced Java programmers covers all enterprise-level topics and exam objectives including:

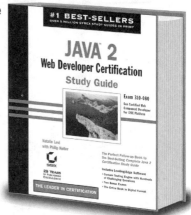

- The servlet model
- The structure and deployment of modern servlet web applications
- The servlet container model
- Designing and developing servlets
- Designing and developing secure web applications
- Designing and developing thread-safe servlets
- The JavaServer Pages (JSP) technology model
- Designing and developing reusable web components
- Designing and developing a custom tag library

The companion CD is packed with vital preparation tools and materials, including a custom testing engine for the Java web developer exam. Loaded with hundreds of practice questions, it lets you test yourself chapter by chapter. You'll also find three bonus exams that will help you prepare for the test and a fully searchable electronic version of the book.

Complete Java 2 Certification Study Guide
Philip Heller, Simon Roberts · ISBN 0-7821-4077-7 · 816pp · $59.99

- New practice programmer exam
- New Developer Exam Section
- Over 200 new test questions on CD

SYBEX®

www.sybex.com

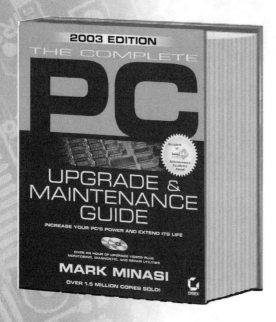